Understanding Variability in Second Language Acquisition, Bilingualism, and Cognition

This collection brings together linguistic, psychological, and sociological perspectives reflecting on the relationships and interactions of the multilayered factors impacting second language development and cognitive competence.

The book advocates a system approach as a counterpoint to existing scholarship, which has tended to focus on a small set of variables. The 13 chapters demonstrate the ways in which cognitive and linguistic development are intrinsically linked, occurring within a nested structure of multiple levels: individual neuro-cognitive systems and processes, individual engagement with the social world, and the wider social and institutional environments and cultural contexts affecting the belief systems and linguistic conventions of social groups. The volume begins by outlining the theoretical and methodological foundations before moving into a more focused look at the interplay of these different variables at the macro, meso, and micro levels. A final section features two commentary chapters from linguistics and psychology, respectively, synthesizing insights from earlier chapters and situating the collection within broader scholarship on linguistic and cognitive development, theoretical and methodological implications, and discussions of avenues for future empirical research.

This book will be of particular interest to scholars in second language acquisition, psycholinguistics, cognition, psychology, and sociology.

Kristin Kersten is professor of Language Acquisition and English Language Teaching at Hildesheim University, Germany. Her research and publications focus on psycholinguistics, bilingualism and cognition, bilingual education (CLIL, immersion), and instructed second language acquisition. She headed the interdisciplinary research projects Early Language and Intercultural Acquisition Studies (ELIAS), an EU Comenius project, and Studies on Multilingualism in Language Education (SMILE) on language acquisition in bilingual preschool and primary education.

Adam Winsler is Professor of Applied Developmental Psychology at George Mason University in Fairfax, Virginia, USA. He has published more than 100 journal articles and 2 books on topics including English-Spanish bilingualism, bilingual education, L1 language maintenance and loss, and the academic performance over time of ethnically diverse dual language learners and immigrant students in poverty in the USA. He also does research on children's private speech, self-regulation, and executive function and was the former editor of *Early Childhood Research Quarterly*.

Routledge Studies in Applied Linguistics

Learning-Oriented Language Assessment
Putting Theory into Practice
Edited by Atta Gebril

Language, Mobility and Study Abroad in the Contemporary European Context
Edited by Rosamond Mitchell and Henry Tyne

Intonation in L2 Discourse
Research Insights
María Dolores Ramirez-Verdugo

Contexts of Co-Constructed Discourse
Interaction, Pragmatics, and Second Language Applications
Edited by Lori Czerwionka, Rachel Showstack, and Judith Liskin-Gasparro

Second Language Prosody and Computer Modeling
Okim Kang, David O. Johnson, Alyssa Kermad

Reconsidering Context in Language Assessment
Transdisciplinary Perspectives, Social Theories, and Validity
Janna Fox and Natasha Artemeva

Evaluation Across Newspaper Genres
Hard News Stories, Editorials and Feature Articles
Jonathan Ngai

Understanding Variability in Second Language Acquisition, Bilingualism, and Cognition
A Multi-Layered Perspective
Edited by Kristin Kersten and Adam Winsler

For more information about this series, please visit: www.routledge.com/Routledge-Studies-in-Applied-Linguistics/book-series/RSAL

Understanding Variability in Second Language Acquisition, Bilingualism, and Cognition

A Multi-Layered Perspective

Edited by Kristin Kersten and Adam Winsler

Routledge
Taylor & Francis Group
NEW YORK AND LONDON

First published 2023
by Routledge
605 Third Avenue, New York, NY 10158

and by Routledge
4 Park Square, Milton Park, Abingdon, Oxon, OX14 4RN

Routledge is an imprint of the Taylor & Francis Group, an informa business

Library of Congress Cataloging-in-Publication Data
A catalog record for this book has been requested

ISBN: 978-0-367-72638-6 (hbk)
ISBN: 978-0-367-72641-6 (pbk)
ISBN: 978-1-003-15568-3 (ebk)

DOI: 10.4324/9781003155683

Typeset in Sabon
by Apex CoVantage, LLC

To amity, music, mirth, and merriment

Contents

List of contributors x
Preface xiv

PART I
Theoretical and methodological considerations 1

1 **Investigating cognitive-linguistic development in SLA: Theoretical and methodological challenges for empirical research** 3
KRISTIN KERSTEN AND WERNER GREVE

2 **Lost in translation? On some key features of dynamical systems theorizing invoked in SLA research** 39
ANKE LENZING, MANFRED PIENEMANN, AND HOWARD NICHOLAS

3 **How many moderators does it take till we know . . . that too many bilingual advantage effects have died?** 80
JULIA FESTMAN, SOPHIA CZAPKA, AND ADAM WINSLER

PART II
The interplay of variables on macro, meso, and micro levels 129

4 **The Proximity of Stimulation Hypothesis: Investigating the interplay of social and instructional variables with the cognitive-linguistic skills of young L2 learners** 131
KRISTIN KERSTEN

5 **Becoming bilingual in Miami, USA: Predictors and outcomes of speed of English acquisition for low-income, dual-language learners** 160
ADAM WINSLER

6 **Immigrant achievement and language use across countries: The role of family background and education systems** 185
JANNA TELTEMANN, MAXIMILIAN BRINKMANN, NORA HUTH-STÖCKLE, AND REINHARD SCHUNCK

7 **The interplay between learner-internal variables and levels of anxiety and enjoyment among Spanish EFL learners** 217
JEAN-MARC DEWAELE

8 **Early bilingualism increases the likelihood of taking (and mastering) foreign language courses later in secondary school** 240
MY VIET HA NGUYEN AND ADAM WINSLER

9 **From differential to dynamic: The role of working memory in second language (L2) learning** 268
ELLEN J. SERAFINI

10 **Can type of schooling compensate for low SES? Investigating effects of instruction and SES on cognitive skills** 292
ANN-CHRISTIN BRUHN, LISA MILLER, CLAUDIA MÄHLER, KATHARINA PONTO, AND KRISTIN KERSTEN

PART III
Synthesis 321

11 **Commentary on *Understanding Variability in Second Language Acquisition, Bilingualism, and Cognition*: A second language acquisition perspective** 323
GABRIELE PALLOTTI

12 **Commentary: Toward a developmental science of language acquisition** 337
WERNER GREVE

Index 355

Contributors

Maximilian Brinkmann is a research assistant in the project Education Systems and Ethnic Educational Inequality at the University of Hildesheim. After his studies in sociology (B.A.) and economics (B.Sc.), he gained an M.Sc. in behavioral and social sciences from the University of Groningen. His research interests include educational sociology and quantitative methods.

Ann-Christin Bruhn is a research assistant at the English Department at Hildesheim University. Her research focuses on SLA and bilingual education. She coordinated the interdisciplinary longitudinal projects FLINK – Foreign Language Learning in Inclusive Contexts and SMILE – Studies on Multilingualism in Language Education, which aim to shed light on the role of internal and external factors in the acquisition of a second language by young mono- and multilingual learners in different pre- and primary school contexts.

Sophia Czapka is a researcher at the Leibniz-Centre General Linguistics in Berlin after completing her doctoral dissertation at the University of Potsdam. Her research focuses on the language and literary development of bilingual and multilingual children. She is also interested in their cognitive abilities, specifically their executive functions and working memory.

Jean-Marc Dewaele is Professor of Applied Linguistics and Multilingualism. He has published widely on individual differences. He is former president of the International Association of Multilingualism and the European Second Language Association, and he is general editor of *Journal of Multilingual and Multicultural Development*. He won the Robert Gardner Award for Excellence in Second Language and Bilingualism Research (2016) from the International Association of Language and Social Psychology and the EUROSLA Distinguished Scholar Award (2022).

Julia Festman is professor of Multilingualism at the Pedagogical University Tyrol in Austria. She studied in Germany (Bamberg, Berlin) and Israel (Ph.D.) and worked in France, the UK, and Germany

(Magdeburg, Habilitation in Potsdam). Her research covers psycholinguistic/neuroscientific approaches to acquisition, learning, and processing of language(s). She published on multilingual language processing, the diversity of bilinguals, the bilingual advantage debate, raising multilinguals, diversity, and primary school education.

Werner Greve is Professor of Developmental Psychology. His research examines processes of development and adaptation across the life span, including (among other issues) the theoretical and empirical relationship between coping and development, evolutionary developmental psychology, and the developmental significance of critical life events. He is particularly interested both in methodological and theoretical foundations of empirical research and in the empirical investigation of developmental processes (e.g., goal regulation, adaptation). He is co-PI of several interdisciplinary projects in various fields, including multilingualism, inclusion, and criminology.

Nora Huth-Stöckle is a research assistant at the University of Wuppertal in the project Education Systems and Ethnic Educational Inequality. She studied social sciences and economics at the University of Cologne (B.Sc.) and sociology at the University of Duisburg-Essen (M.A.). In her research, she investigates attitudes towards migrants in cross-national comparison and intergroup relations. Her research interests furthermore include ethnic inequality in education and quantitative methods.

Anke Lenzing is professor of English language teaching at Innsbruck University. She has previously taught at Paderborn University and has been a visiting scholar at Flinders University. Her research engages with psycholinguistic aspects of (instructed) second language acquisition, and her publications focus on issues such as early L2 acquisition, the role of formulaic sequences in instructed SLA, L2 transfer, and the interface between comprehension and production in SLA.

Claudia Mähler is Professor of Educational Psychology and Diagnostics at the University of Hildesheim. In her research, she is interested in precursors of school achievement and learning disabilities as well as assessment and intervention of learning disabilities with a focus on the development and training of working memory. She is the head of the research and intervention center "KiM – Kind im Mittelpunkt" (Child in focus) at the Institute for Psychology at the University of Hildesheim.

Lisa Miller is a psychologist and research assistant at the University of Hildesheim. In her research, she investigates determinants of literacy as well as institutional prevention and intervention methods to facilitate early literacy acquisition for children at risk. Her research interests include inclusive education and its methodological challenges.

My Viet Ha Nguyen is a doctoral student in developmental, cognitive, and behavioral neuroscience at the University of Houston. Her research interests include the neural basis of bilingualism and second language acquisition. She investigates the relationship between the bilingual experience and cognitive control as well as the brain mechanism underlying this relationship.

Howard Nicholas is Adjunct Professor in the School of Education at La Trobe University. He has been president of the Applied Linguistics Association of Australia and editor of the *Australian Review of Applied Linguistics*. He has also taught at the University of Hawaii at Manoa; Concordia University, Montreal; the University of Western Australia, and Paderborn University. He has researched child and adult second language acquisition, literacy development in additional languages, and inclusive and bilingual education as well as his work on the multiplicity framework of the communicative repertoire.

Gabriele Pallotti is Professor of Language Teaching Methodology at the University of Modena and Reggio Emilia. His research focuses on interlanguage development, linguistic complexity, morphology, L2 interaction, methodology, and epistemology in applied linguistics. He coordinates the project Observing interlanguage and is the associate editor of the Eurosla Studies Series (Language Science Press).

Manfred Pienemann is Professor Emeritus of English Linguistics at Paderborn University and co-chair of Linguistic Engineering Co. He has held positions in linguistics and applied linguistics at the Universities of Newcastle (UK), the Australian National University, the University of Sydney, and the Universities of Hamburg and Passau (Germany). He is the co-founder of PacSLRF and co-editor of the PALART series.

Katharina Ponto is a researcher in the field of instructed second language acquisition at the University of Hildesheim. Her research interest focuses on vocabulary acquisition, bilingual education, and multilingualism. She coordinated the SMILE-project (Studies on Multilingualism in Language Education) and the FLINK-project (Foreign Language Learning in Inclusive Contexts) at Hildesheim University, which focus on investigating the roles of internal and external factors in the acquisition of a second language in different primary and preschool settings.

Reinhard Schunck is Professor of Sociology at the University of Wuppertal. His research examines how migration and family related processes shape patterns of social inequality. In addition to that, he has a focus on quantitative methods. He is a principal investigator of the project Education Systems and Ethnic Educational Inequality, which has the aim to harmonize data from several large-scale school assessments in order to build a better database for causal-oriented analyses on education systems and their effects on inequality.

Ellen J. Serafini is Associate Professor of Spanish Applied Linguistics at George Mason University. Her research takes a holistic view of language learning with a focus on exploring the dynamic interaction among individual differences and pedagogical and social factors in diverse settings and their variable impact on short- and long-term language development. In the classroom, Dr. Serafini integrates principles of task-based language teaching, critical language pedagogy, and service learning to optimize outcomes.

Janna Teltemann is Professor of Educational Sociology at the University of Hildesheim. In her research, she examines how features of education systems shape patterns of educational inequality. She is a principal investigator of the project Education Systems and Ethnic Educational Inequality, has the aim to harmonize data from several large-scale school assessments in order to build a better database for causal-oriented analyses on education systems and their effects on inequality.

Preface

> We cannot live for ourselves alone. Our lives are connected by a thousand invisible threads, and along these sympathetic fibers, our actions run as causes and return to us as results.
>
> Herman Melville

Human cognitive and linguistic development are intrinsically intertwined and take place within a nested structure of contextual levels: the level of the individual's engagement with the social world, the level of social and institutional environments, the society, and the broader cultural context that affects the normative belief systems and linguistic conventions of the social groups at large (Lerner, 2013; Douglas Fir Group, 2016; Truscott & Sharwood Smith, 2019). All of these factors are considered crucial in understanding the processes that shape human development in general. They have also been described as strong predictors for second language acquisition. They have, however, often been looked at in isolation and less from an overarching systemic view that tries to shed light on their various (and dynamic) interconnections.

This interdisciplinary volume focuses on the interplay of such factors from different perspectives with regard to theoretical and methodological aspects as well as empirical findings. The idea for this volume originated at an interdisciplinary symposium on External and Internal Variables Affecting (Language) Learning Processes at Hildesheim University, Germany. The symposium took place in January 2020 at the occasion of a research fellowship of Adam Winsler at Hildesheim University. Scholars from linguistic, psychological, and sociological backgrounds addressed the topic from the perspectives of their respective disciplines. Lively discussions after the presentations (as well as during nightly Scotch-inspired guitar sessions) showed us that there was genuine interest in this topic and a notable research gap from theoretical, methodological, and empirical angles. The idea developed from there.

Accordingly, Part I of the volume focuses on theoretical aspects and methodological reflections on researching an interconnected network of variables. In Chapter 1, Kristin Kersten and Werner Greve focus on methodological facets that need to be taken into consideration to disentangle and account for variables on different conceptual levels, differentiating between causal and conceptual interrelations of variables, and methodological analyses that remain "blind" to these theoretical problems. Chapter 2 by Anke Lenzing, Manfred Pienemann, and Howard Nicholas takes a critical look at the role of the "dynamic approach" in SLA and advocates a mathematical rather than metaphorical application to the field, scrutinizing mathematical conditions to demonstrate that deterministic dynamical systems indeed hold the potential to predict or explain learner variation in SLA. In Chapter 3, Julia Festman, Sophia Czapka, and Adam Winsler use the example of the "bilingual advantage debate" to review and give an in-depth overview of numerous potentially moderating and confounding variables when researching the relationship between two complex constructs such as multilingualism and cognition.

Part II contains seven chapters that concretely investigate the interplay of numerous variables on different conceptual levels. In Chapter 4, Kristin Kersten examines the predictions of the Proximity of Stimulation Hypothesis, which holds that mediating proximal factors explain effects of distal container variables on SLA and cognition, using structural equation modeling, with social status and L2 program as distal and parent–child interaction and teacher's L2 input as proximal factors. Adam Winsler (Chapter 5) reports on a large-scale longitudinal study focusing on the interplay of low-income, dual-language learners' linguistic cognitive, socioemotional, and behavioral skills and the impact of L1 support in bilingual education (immersion) programs on English and academic skills. Janna Teltemann, Maximilian Brinkmann, Nora Huth-Stöckle, and Reinhard Schunck (Chapter 6) introduce a framework of factors for educational success of migrant populations using large-scale, cross-sectional PISA (2018) data to investigate the differential impact of family background, linguistic resources, and education systems on immigrant learners' academic achievement. The study of Jean-Marc Dewaele (Chapter 7) focuses on the relationship between personal variables such as age, gender, and foreign language variables, with foreign language classroom anxiety and foreign language enjoyment, including a discussion of attitudes toward the teacher and the directionality of these effects. In Chapter 8, My Ngyuen and Adam Winsler discuss a large-scale 14-year longitudinal study that focuses on diverse low-income children's degree of bilingualism, cognitive skills, and academic performance as predictors of enrolment and performance in later foreign language classes, stressing the benefit of maintaining multiple language exposure, and especially the minority language at home. Ellen J. Serafini's Chapter 9 synthesizes the heterogeneous research findings on the differential effects of working memory on L2 development, as well as numerous possible moderating factors from a complex dynamic systems perspective, with a specific discussion of learners' individual differences and their role for SLA. In Chapter 10, Ann-Christin Bruhn, Lisa Miller, Claudia Mähler, Katharina

Ponto, and Kristin Kersten investigate, in a two-study design, whether two forms of cognitive-linguistic interventions, a training program and a bilingual preschool, moderate the influence of social status on different cognitive skills such as intelligence, working memory, and phonological awareness of very young learners.

In Part III, two commentaries provide a synthesis on the volume from two different disciplines. In Chapter 11, from an SLA perspective, Gabriele Pallotti makes a case for generalizable interdisciplinary research and calls for cooperative cumulative research, methodological rigor in terms of transparency in measures and data, standardization of methods and tasks, and increased replication studies, not least to inform practice concerning viable ways of L2 teaching. In Chapter 12, from a psychological point of view, Werner Greve points out as overarching common denominator within the book that all contributions investigate influencing factors at different conceptual levels that have to be identified, empirically tested, and substantiated. He interprets the goal of the volume as an approach in the frame of a "developmental science of language acquisition."

This volume would not have come into existence without the Wippermann Research Fellowship. We are especially grateful to Jutta and Professor Dr. Burkhard Wippermann and to Martin Schreiner, Vice President of Foundation Development, Transfer and Cooperations at Hildesheim University, for the research grant given to Adam Winsler; to Janna Teltemann and Werner Greve for contributing to the conceptualization of the symposium; to Tanja Bartol, Ann-Christin Bruhn, Martin Koch, Katharina Ponto, and Lia Röttger for their wonderful assistance in organizing it; to Frederike Klose for her help with final formatting and the index; and to Janna Teltemann and Christian May for providing the inspirational surroundings and liquids at their Still Spirits store[1] for companionship, music, and professional creativity. Finally, and most importantly, we would never have made the deadline for this volume without the tremendous work of Gabrielle Norvell and her impeccable and invaluable help with proofreading and layout. All remaining errors are ours.

While the contributions of this volume can only provide small pieces of a highly complex jigsaw puzzle, we hope that the general idea behind this project that inspired us all may stimulate further ideas along the dynamic paths of interdisciplinary discussion. Still Spirits remains open to lend some wings to future visions if need be. We hope to see you there along the way.

November 2021
Kristin Kersten and Adam Winsler

Note

1. https://still-spirits.de/

Part I

Theoretical and methodological considerations

1 Investigating cognitive-linguistic development in SLA

Theoretical and methodological challenges for empirical research

Kristin Kersten and Werner Greve

Introduction

It should be general consensus among researchers in the second language acquisition (SLA) field that the acquisition of a second language cannot be explained without taking a multitude of developmental conditions into account. Possible influencing factors are manifold and highly diverse in nature: individual factors (such as, e.g., brain structures, working memory, intelligence, or motivation), social factors (e.g., parent–child interactions or the family's socioeconomic background), and institutional factors (e.g. a specific school program, the intensity and duration of L2 contact, a submersive vs. immersive school context) have all been identified as influential for (S)LA by numerous studies (Dörnyei, 2009; Ellis, 2007; Larsen-Freeman & Cameron, 2008).

The contribution of these various (potential) influencing factors to predict and explain (S)LA is an empirical question. This endeavor, however, is challenging not only for methodological reasons but also because the relations and interactions between these potential factors need to be accounted for theoretically. An appropriate *explanation* (here: of SLA) does not only require the identification of potential factors but rather the identification of their causal and conceptual interrelations in the form of a model. In other words, it requires a *theory*.

The beginning of theory formation is often to look for empirical support for a factor's prognostic or explanatory power and for its relative or partial weight in relation to other factors. This also includes the question of whether a certain factor does *not* have any predictive value and could thus be neglected in the analysis or even in the explanation. We do not want to discuss the fundamental questions pertaining to this inductive proceeding of theory development. Rather, we attempt to outline some conceptual problems with analyzing the predictive value of several factors at the same time, which can be done from both an inductive (developing a theory from empirical evidence) and a deductive (testing a theory by confronting it with empirical tests) point of view.

DOI: 10.4324/9781003155683-2

Such investigations have generally been carried out with the help of multivariate analyses and lately increasingly with structural equation models and multilevel modeling. Based on the argumentation outlined in this chapter, however, we hold that these types of analysis are often not sufficient to discover and/or confirm the *causal* effects of factors on different hierarchical levels, because they remain "blind," so to say, to a number of theoretical problems outlined in what follows. In particular, it has to be taken into account that factors may be related to each other in different *conceptual* ways. If these conceptual relations are disregarded, a prediction or a causal explanation can be incomplete or, at worst, downright wrong. It is, therefore, the goal of this contribution to discuss the various difficulties that are connected to the investigation of influencing factors on different conceptual levels for developmental processes.

Line of reasoning

To this end, we will discuss six types of problems. The structure of the chapter will then follow this line of reasoning depicted here.

1. *Explanation versus prediction:* As a prerequisite of investigation, studies have to clarify whether they intend to generate a *causal explanation* or whether they just state a *statistical prediction*. While predictions or relations derived from statistical models are often called "explanations," it is crucial for the current line of argumentation to differentiate between both concepts, because the conceptual problems outlined in this chapter may impair an explanatory approach, while a predictive approach is often not affected by these problems in the same way.
2. *Conceptual layers ("vertical perspective I"):* The next section, which we call a "vertical perspective" on the issues in question, discusses the difference between conceptual layers of both internal (individual) and external factors. We use the term "vertical" to refer to interfactorial relations without reference to their development over time, because this differentiation becomes relevant even in a synchronic perspective in which factors are assessed at the same time. (The time-dependent perspective will be discussed under (4) and (5), "horizontal" levels I and II.) In both the internal and external layers, we will differentiate between macro, meso, micro, and nano levels.
3. *Qualities of relations ("vertical perspective II"):* Regarding factors on different conceptual layers, a number of different types of relationships can be distinguished. We call these different "qualities of relations." In particular, they comprise *causal* and *constitutive*, or logical, relations. In addition, we will discuss *emergent* relations, which might go beyond these two types of relations. When we describe these different types and the role they play, the individual development of a learner (of a language) is used as *explanandum*,

i.e., as the dependent variable to be explained. The careful distinction of these types of relations has consequences for both the explanatory and the predictive perspective of an investigation.

4. *Development across time ("horizontal perspective I"):* A further complication is added when the interrelation of factors is regarded "horizontally," i.e., across time. Here, we will discuss time-dependent relations in general. These include mediating and moderating effects.[1] A prediction and, even more so, an explanation will be incomplete if such effects are not taken into account. The sheer number of possible relations and interactions renders both statistical predictions and causal models (and their falsification) complex and confusing (and, in reality, always incomplete); however, this complexity is merely a practical problem, not a theoretical one.
5. *Dynamic processes across time ("horizontal perspective II"):* A further problem arises when we take into account that the nature of these interrelations between factors is, as a rule, dynamic. In SLA research, longitudinal processes have almost always been investigated with the help of linear statistical models. Over the last two decades, however, researchers have started to point out that linear models are not sufficient to depict the complexity of individual developmental processes (Lenzing et al., 2023, this volume). One strand of discussion has, therefore, started to focus on describing properties of SLA development across time with the help of *dynamic systems* (DS) theory. Since the statistical modeling of nonlinear dynamic systems is comparatively sophisticated because it requires very large data sets and sufficient accuracy of measurement, mathematical modeling of nonlinear dynamic systems has rarely been attempted (Dörnyei, 2009; for an exception, see van Geert, 1994, 2008, 2014). While a thorough discussion of these problems goes beyond the scope of this chapter, it has to be pointed out that it is necessary for an explanatory theory as well as for a predictive perspective to take a dynamic perspective into account. Even if a statistical approximation of a linear model yields a practically useful prediction, a mathematically more correct modeling of a dynamic progression would increase the accuracy of the prediction. This also means that we do not agree with those DS approaches that altogether deny the possibility of modeling (and thus predicting and explaining) a process based on its assumed "dynamicity." Complexity certainly does not necessarily entail unpredictability (Lenzing, 2015; Lenzing et al., 2023, this volume).
6. *General methodological challenges:* These "vertical" and "horizontal" layers of problems are connected to a number of methodological problems in a more technical sense, which are logically independent from conceptual problems (2) to (5). While it is not our intention in this chapter to discuss the challenges of numerous statistical approaches, we will reflect on three "practical" aspects of empirical investigation used to investigate human development resulting from

the previous discussion. First, all constructs used in a model require suitable methods of assessment: For an explanatory as well as for a predictive perspective, each construct has to be validly and reliably captured. Second, certain methodological approaches (e.g., analysis of variance) entail specific methodological assumptions (e.g., an independent, "additive" impact of each factor on the phenomenon to be explained). Third, for the test of causal hypotheses (theories), correlational approaches (in contrast to experimental approaches) are generally weak and, as a rule, insufficient, while they can be sufficient at times for predictive approaches. In other words, each approach requires an appropriate research design.

Influencing factors: It is helpful for the purpose of this text to clarify our definition of "influencing factor." To this end, Mackie's (1965) concept of *INUS conditions* has proven helpful: He conceptualizes a "cause" as an ***insufficient** but **necessary** part of an **unnecessary** but **sufficient*** constellation: That means that the aspects (variables) in question, such as the intelligence of the child, the climate of the class, the teaching approach of the teacher, the educational background of the parents, the language of the environment, etc., are part of a *constellation* that, *in its entirety*, is *sufficient* to explain a phenomenon (here: SLA). In this constellation, each of the variables that is thought to be a "cause" is *necessary* to explain the phenomenon, that is, contributes to the explanation of SLA *beyond* the contribution of all other influencing factors considered – this is exactly why it is a *necessary* condition of *this sufficient* constellation (of factors). Whether or not a particular factor is indeed a necessary part of this constellation remains an empirical question. This does not preclude, however, that other constellations of (partly or entirely) different INUS conditions might result in the very same outcome (i.e., language competence); this is why this particular constellation is called *sufficient but unnecessary*.

Explanation versus prediction

In the investigation of influencing factors in human development, two intentions need to be differentiated, which are affected by the problems outlined here in different ways. The aim of a scientific *explanation* for a developmental phenomenon (here: SLA) is to identify conditions and causes which, in specific combinations or configurations, are *sufficient* to explain the given phenomenon. In other words, the aim of the explanatory perspective is to formulate an (approximately) true (developmental) theory. The basis of this perspective is a scientific understanding of causality which holds that natural phenomena have natural causes that are, in general, accessible in empirical research.[2]

The aim of a *predictive* (prognostic) approach, on the other hand, is just to predict the phenomenon (here: language development) in question.[3]

A good prediction, or the occurrence of a predicted effect of an intervention, however, does not necessarily imply that the underlying theory is true. Predictions that are effective in practice can also follow from incorrect theories: In medieval times, for instance, pest infections were effectively reduced through isolation, although the underlying theory that infections were transmitted by contact with another person's "aura" was, in all probability, incorrect. Good predictions or successful intervention effects are therefore no "proof" for a theory. For the same reason, successful interventions (e.g., taking an aspirin often reduces headaches) do not offer a promising way to infer explanatory (causal) theories (e.g., "headaches are caused by a lack of aspirin"). On the other hand, incorrect predictions can falsify causal hypotheses (under certain conditions) (Jordan, 2004). The predictive and the explanatory approaches converge only in the sense that a correct causal explanation leads to a correct prognosis and an effective intervention. Predictions based on incorrect theories will, in the end, only be partially successful. Both approaches, however, need to be empirically tested (Shmueli, 2010).

In the following, we will first discuss a number of theoretical (conceptual) problems that present challenges especially for an explanatory perspective, followed by conceptual problems concerning interactions and dynamics across time, which present different challenges for both an explanatory and a predictive approach.

Developmental conditions on several conceptual layers ("vertical perspective I")

Variables identified in the research literature as relevant for SLA range from factors with narrowly defined functions (such as functional components of working memory) to factors that comprise or imply a number of components (such as socioeconomic status [SES], or the culture of a person's environment). We will refer to these different types as constituent versus container variables: constituent refers to elements on a lower hierarchical level, while container refers to a higher hierarchical level that is composed of several lower-level constituents; in other words: we use these concepts in a relative manner. In this sense, we will try to outline a hierarchical structure of factors that describes the different levels and their possible interrelations in the following discussion (Ushioda, 2015).

For this purpose, we will differentiate between internal (individual, or personal, and intraindividual, or subpersonal) and external levels (e.g., social structures), and we will refer to these levels as macro, meso and micro level respectively, and add a nano level for reasons that will become clear later and will be illustrated in Figure 1.5. As the same type of hierarchy can be applied to the external as well as to the internal factors, we will use the index "e" (e.g., micro_e) for the external levels and the index "i" (e.g., macro_i) for the internal hierarchy.

Personal and subpersonal conditions of SLA: Conceptual levels "within" the person

Regarding internal factors, we can differentiate between attributes of a person, as, for example, a person's motivation or intelligence, and functional or physiological factors within a person, as, e.g., functional components of working memory or neural processes in the CNS.

Personal factors

When investigating the (linguistic) development of an individual, it seems natural to first identify other aspects or characteristics of the person in question, such as his or her motivation to learn, intelligence, or language aptitude, among other factors (Dörnyei, 2009). Even though these aspects do not describe "the person" in her/his entirety, they are "personal" constructs in the sense that they are ascribed to the person, as opposed to single parts of it: it is the person who is motivated or intelligent, not his or her brain or memory. Language proficiency, which is the focus of this volume, can be understood as a "personal" variable in this sense. Lower levels are referred to as "subpersonal" (i.e., intraindividual) levels (see what follows).

The differentiation between personal and subpersonal levels combines two "kinds" of conceptual leveling. Of course, the individual is to be viewed as a complex system of interacting (sub)systems: organs and muscles, veins and neurons, bones and liquids constitute "the" individual. As these subsystems are systems themselves (cells are complex organs, chemicals in the muscles make them move, etc.), "the" individual can be seen as a nested hierarchy of subsystems. Certainly, the conceptual relations between these different hierarchical layers are therefore confronted with the very same conceptual difficulties as the differentiation between different social (interpersonal) layers (e.g., family, neighborhood, city, country, culture), which we will discuss in the following section more thoroughly. Viewed from this angle, then, this multilevel differentiation just continues "within" the person. We call it "within" just because our interest focuses on phenomena (in particular: language) that can be observed at the level of persons only (neither brains nor societies talk). As a consequence, "internal" versus "external" is used throughout this chapter in relation to a person who acquires a language. This boundary is, of course, arbitrary, as it only reflects our present focus. Certainly, the arguments discussed here could be applied to other segmentations as well (e.g., "within" a body cell vs. "outside" of it but still within the human body). A more complete theory of explanatory layers would have to take this relativity into account.

This leads to a second perspective at the individual layer. The fact that only persons (not brains) talk reminds us that certain phenomena "exist" only given a certain phenomenological perspective.

Language, intentions, consciousness, etc. are restricted to the level of persons (hence the term "personal"). If we investigate these *mental* phenomena, we have to apply what Dennett (1987) has termed the "intentional stance." With intentional stance, he means a perspective in which we perceive human beings as intentional beings with mental phenomena, and in which we describe these phenomena with the help of a language that uses mental terms (the "mental idiom"), i.e., wanting, perceiving, thinking, talking. These activities can only be carried out by mental beings, i.e., persons.[4] Conceptually, the explanation of mental phenomena entails the usage of the mental idiom. Referring only to "functional" or "physical" concepts leaves the gap between functional and physical entities on the one hand and mental phenomena on the other hand unbridged (Bieri, 1981, quoted in Fuchs, 2018). The decisive question, however, is whether this unbridged gap is more than a different linguistic way of describing the same phenomenon (i.e., more than switching between "stances," in Dennett's words). In other words, the question is: if we want to explain mental phenomena, is it necessary to presuppose that "mental entities/processes" (such as consciousness or will) actually exist, or is it possible to explain them just by referring to physical entities/processes (such as electrochemical transmission in neurons)?

We certainly cannot discuss, not even aptly describe the mind–body problem (this is exactly what we are touching upon here) in this chapter; however, one has to keep in mind that this is a theoretical problem to be treated whenever we attempt to explain mental phenomena such as thinking or talking. This conceptual gap has to be taken into account even if we attempt to subdivide a certain phenomenon into components or subsystems. For instance, intelligence does not consist of neurons, even if one component of intelligence is memory, and memory, among human beings, is realized in a brain consisting of neurons. This is why it is necessary for an explanatory approach to differentiate between various conceptual levels even within the individual.

Subpersonal factors

Intraindividual or subpersonal factors are not ascribed to the entire person but denote functional components (units) of larger factors. Processes carried out by the working memory are, for example, constitutive for the person's intelligence. For the sake of organization, we will conceptualize personal factors such as motivation, aptitude, or intelligence on the $meso_i$ level and subpersonal factors such as working memory (WM), phonological short-term memory (PSTM), phonological awareness on the $micro_i$ level.

It seems important to extend this hierarchy into an even lower level of neurons or neural complexes ($nano_i$ level, Figure 1.5). Of course, this hierarchical structure repeats itself on many different levels: The neural level itself can, again, be subdivided into different cellular or even atomic components. The inclusion of $nano_i$ levels in this hierarchy (i.e., to conceptualize neurons as a sublevel of, say, motivation or even memory), however, ignores the mind–body problem mentioned earlier and brings the functional level (Dennett, 1987: "design stance") into the physical level. While statistically harmless, this ignorance is theoretically inappropriate. We cannot delve into the theoretical problems associated with this particular difficulty in this chapter – although it actually touches upon the core of the question of what actually can appropriately be considered an adequate explanation.[5]

This distinction illustrates the complication already addressed. On the one hand, "the person" is sort of an aggregation of different (sub(sub))systems, but on the other hand, a person can "do things" the subsystems are not capable of alone. Moreover, these personal activities may have causal consequences for the subsystems of the system that performs these activities. To use an illustration, components of the language faculty ($micro_i$ level) cannot, for instance, decide to drink a bottle of red wine for dinner; only the person ($macro_i$ level) can do so – however, a relatively large amount of alcoholic intake can indeed have an influence on the functioning of the language faculty during dinner conversations.

External conditions on (S)LA: Conceptual levels "outside" of the person

As mentioned, the corresponding problem can be described on the level of "external" conditions for SLA. Enumerating these external (contextual) factors presents a complex challenge not only in the face of the sheer number of possible influences but also because of the innumerable interactions between them. In the following, we will conceptualize the (external) $micro_e$ level as the immediate interaction of the individual with its direct environment (e.g., with a communication partner, in a didactic intervention in the classroom, but also with a linguistic medium such as a book or a computer). The $meso_e$ level describes the environment for these $micro_e$-level interactions (such as the culture of a family, the rules in a school etc.), whereas the $macro_e$ level refers to the wider social context such as the laws of the given country, the cultural background of the language community, or informal social norms for behavior (rules of politeness) (Figure 1.5; see Bronfenbrenner, 2005, for a classical approach and Lerner, 2013, for a more differentiated extension).

Such a complex hierarchy of a multitude of factors prompts the question of whether and how they interrelate with each other and how this conceptual hierarchy can affect the prediction and/or explanation of a dependent variable. We will try to systematize some important aspects pertaining to this question in the following section.

Qualities of relations ("vertical perspective II")

Factors on different levels influence the dependent variable independently of one another

One option to capture the influence of several factors (statistically modeled as *independent variables*, henceforth IV) on a developmental phenomenon proceeds with the assumption that they impact the dependent variable (DV) independently of one another, that is to say, in an *additive* way. This approach does not take into account, however, on which level these factors are located. Rather, in multivariate analyses (e.g., multiple regression analysis), the factors under investigation are analyzed with respect to their respective predictive contribution, that is, their partial contribution, i.e., the contribution of each particular factor given the contribution of the other factors in this analysis (Figure 1.1).

Although in these analyses, the partial contribution takes the statistical contribution of the other variables (located on the same or on different conceptual levels) into account, their *conceptual* relation is ignored. For instance, the individual's subjective motivation to learn might contribute statistically to the prediction of his/her language development beyond the socioeconomic status of the family, but since the child is a part of the family and motivation to learn might be seen as one aspect or indicator for SES, the child's motivation can be seen as conceptually related to SES. Consequently, it would be misleading (in an explanatory approach) just to add the contribution of motivation to learn to the contribution of the SES. The finding that the "addition" of both variables in the analysis shows a unique (additional) statistical contribution might just be the consequence of an insufficient assessment of (all facets of) SES. We will return to this problem, and to the intricacies connected with the interaction of conditions in particular, in the following sections.

In some analyses, such IVs are grouped according to larger concepts and analyzed in a stepwise manner (Figure 1.2). As this kind of grouping

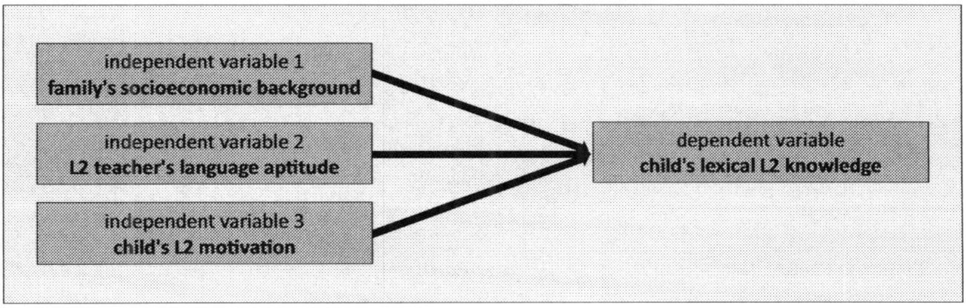

Figure 1.1 Examples of independent variables on different hierarchical levels which are conceptualized as influencing the dependent variable independently of each other (example of analysis: multiple regression)

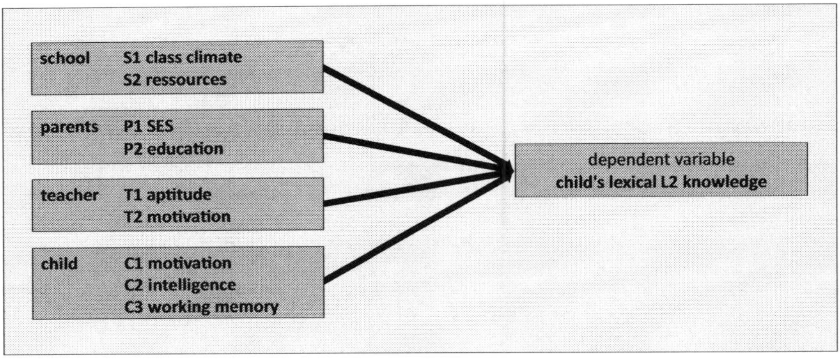

Figure 1.2 Examples of independent variables on different hierarchical levels which are grouped and analyzed in a stepwise manner and which are conceptualized as influencing the dependent variable independently of each other (example of analysis: stepwise multiple regression)

still assumes an independent influence of each IV on the DV, this does not change the disregard of possible conceptual relations between variables and levels (or the mere fact that there *is* more than one level).

Nowadays, the fact that variables are "located" on different conceptual levels is increasingly accounted for with the help of multilevel analyses (Cunnings, 2012; Windzio, 2008). Such analyses *statistically* take the hierarchy of levels into account by incorporating intra-class correlations (i.e., if one factor is similar for a number of different individuals, e.g., the teacher's language aptitude is equal for all pupils of the class). As will become clear in the following sections, however, they also remain *theoretically* insensitive to the *reasons* for intra-class correlations, that is, for the causal or conceptual quality of the interrelations between variables or levels.

To sum up, this type of conceptualization is based on the presupposition that the impact of the IVs is *independent* of other factors, that it is *direct*, and that it is *additive*. In other words, this type of analysis does not differentiate between internal and external levels or between $\text{nano}_{i/e}$, $\text{micro}_{i/e}$, $\text{meso}_{i/e}$, or $\text{macro}_{i/e}$ levels, nor does it take into account different conceptual relations between these factors and/or levels. If an analysis pursues an *explanatory* approach, we claim that simple multivariate analyses of factors on different conceptual levels (e.g., the impact of the school climate, of the pupil's L2 motivation, of the pupil's working memory capacity) on the pupil's language competence do not do justice to the complexity of relations between variables, even if the variables are *measured independently* of each other (see the following section). Predictive goals, on the other hand, can often be achieved, but as always, the interpretation of the data and the conclusions drawn from them need to be carefully limited to what is actually investigated in the analysis.

Of course, no model will ever do full justice to the complexity of reality; however, the mere empirical comparison of the predictive value of simple or more complex statistical models is not the crucial point. Even a (statistically) superior model might be a theoretically weaker one (e.g., if it does not take into account conceptual relationships between predictor and criterion that artificially boosts the statistical prediction).

Factors on different levels do not influence the dependent variable independently of one another

If the influencing factors (IVs) are to be seen as interrelated, we can think of several types of relations. First, higher-level IVs can exert their impact on a DV *via* lower-level IVs (or vice versa); "via" means that the impact under investigation is a mediator relation.[6] It is important to note that this relation (a *causal* dependence) presupposes a *conceptual independence* of the factors (levels) involved as conceptually related concepts cannot have a causal relationship. This is an important aspect of our argument; we will return to this particular condition of causal explanation in what follows.

Second, lower-level factors can (conceptually) partly or fully *constitute* a higher-level factor. In this latter case, the dependency between factors (levels) is a conceptual one and thus precludes a causal relation. It might be worth stressing that causal and constitutive relationships are sometimes confused because not only causal but also conceptual relationships imply correct *predictions*: We can, for example, predict that all bachelors we will meet tomorrow will be unmarried – because this is what bachelors are. However, being unmarried does not *cause* the status of a bachelor, it rather *entails* it and thus denotes a conceptual relationship. With respect to relationships across levels, it would be equally wrong to say that the living room, bathroom, and bedroom *cause* an apartment – they *constitute* it. This is what Ryle (1949) referred to as *category mistake*. In the same way it is incorrect to claim that the phonological loop, the visuospatial sketchpad, etc., *cause* working memory – the structure of working memory is *constituted* by its lower-level components. Assuming a causal relationship in a multivariate analysis in the sense that the "impact" of the phonological loop on working memory is measured would thus be theoretically misleading. The following sections will elaborate on these distinctions.

A factor on a higher level influences factors on a lower level, which influence the dependent variable

In Figure 1.3, examples of indirect (mediator) relations are depicted. Note that these relationships can occur both between and within levels. For the sake of illustration, in both cases, a *complete* mediator effect is shown in contrast to partial mediation, which is the more typical case.

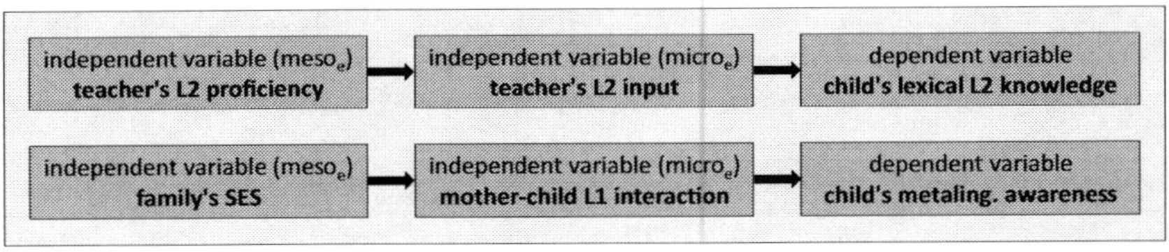

Figure 1.3 Influence of a higher-order independent variable on DV is mediated by a lower-order independent variable (two examples) (example of analysis: mediator analysis via multiple regression)

For instance, the intelligence of a person might influence both his or her L2 motivation and language aptitude. Since L2 aptitude influences language motivation as well (Dörnyei, 2010), the effect of intelligence on language motivation is partially mediated by L2 aptitude.

As mentioned, in all cases, the *conceptual* independence of the IVs involved is presupposed (if the analysis pursues an explanatory purpose). It is important, moreover, to distinguish the conceptual (in)dependence of two factors from the (in)dependence of the assessment (method) of these factors: If two factors are confounded in the assessment, e.g., by using some identical items for both factors, any correlation that was found in the analysis would be (partly) artificially created: If we find a correlation between working memory capacity and intelligence, and if the assessment of intelligence includes the assessment of working memory capacity, this correlation is not based on an actual relation but is partly created artificially through the selection of the measuring instrument.

But even if the method of assessment of two constructs is independent, e.g., by using one specific test for working memory and a completely different one that does not include a direct assessment of working memory for intelligence, a conceptual relation might still exist. For instance, it could be argued theoretically that all subtests of any given intelligence test entail an indirect assessment of working memory capacity (since WM is a component of intelligence). In other words: even if we *measure* factors independently of each other, this does not imply *conceptual independence*. Even if we check, for instance, in the official record whether Peter is unmarried (one type of measurement) and then assess his status as a bachelor by asking several of his friends to report on his relationships with others (another type of measurement), this does not alter the fact that "being unmarried" and "being a bachelor" are conceptually related even if both measures would predictably not correlate perfectly (due to measurement errors that are different for both forms of assessment) (Brandtstädter, 1987). This conceptual relation would preclude a causal relation.

Of course, the conceptual independence of the variables (concepts) included in an analysis cannot be taken for granted, in particular if the analysis comprises variables on different levels. Actually, causal relationships such as mediator relationships are easy to confuse with conceptual relationships, in particular with a "container relationship" between variables.

A factor on a higher level is constituted by factors on a lower level

While in the cases discussed so far, high-level container variables are treated as independent variables with a direct impact on the developmental phenomenon and are ranked as equally important, such contributions of independent variables on different levels are further complicated by the fact that often, these independent variables on different levels are *not conceptually independent* of each other, which precludes both independent direct effects on the DV (Figure 1.1) and an indirect (mediator) effect (Figure 1.3).

It is important to differentiate between two constellations here: often, a container variable is *constituted* by a number of constituent variables and has no independent effect of its own (Figure 1.4, relation B). We will refer to this type of variable as a *container variable*. The other option is that a container variable, even though it is constituted by a number of lower-level variables, exerts a *causal effect of its own* that surpasses the added effect of the constituent ones (see Figure 1.6). This phenomenon is referred to as *emergence* (Noordhof, 2010). Both possibilities will be discussed in the following sections.

Container variables without independent effects on the dependent variable

The problem that relations between different conceptual levels can obscure the causal explanation of the dependent variable is most obvious when elements on the higher level are *constituted by* elements of the lower level. A prototypical example for a container variable constituted by a number of lower-level variables in developmental research is age. Age can be seen as a textbook predictor for L1 competence (at the age of 2 months, it is commonly extremely restricted, while at the age of 20, it's usually very good). However, in the explanation of various developmental L1 acquisition trajectories, age functions as an "umbrella term" for more specific processes, such as the developmental state of working memory, the developing effectiveness of the individual's executive functions, the change of complexity of the neural networks of the brain, etc. (Pfenniger, 2021).

Actually, it is often the case that variables of different levels are considered in one analysis without taking their relationships into account (compare discussion in Kersten, 2023, this volume), even in cases of obvious constitution (container variables). Another example of this is the common practice of "controlling" for gender in social science. Obviously,

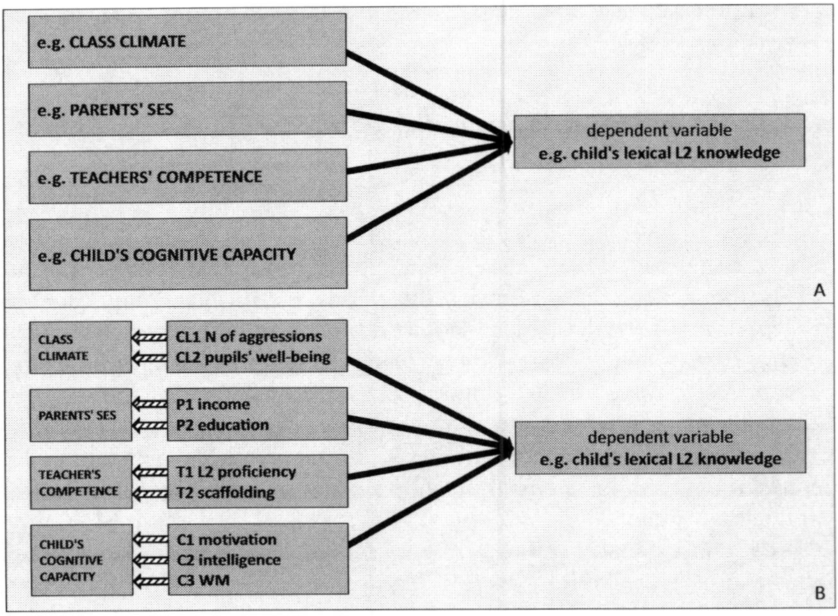

Figure 1.4 Examples of higher-order container variables (A) which are constituted by lower-order constituent variables but which do not exert an independent influence on DV (B). The relationship between the container variables and the constituent variables is that of *conceptual entailment* rather than of a causal (mediator) relationship: The respective container variable is *constituted* by the lower-level elements (thus, the relation between the different levels is conceptual, not causal; this is why the direction of the shaded arrows (4B) is reversed). This conceptual entailment can exist on all levels (example of analysis: multiple regression, multilevel analysis, structural equation model).

"gender" is a container comprising a huge variety of heterogeneous elements such as social expectations, physical strength, self-esteem, to name but a few. If in a given analysis in order to "explain," say, aggressive behavior, all these aspects (strength, self-esteem, expectations, gender, age) are introduced in a form depicted in Figure 1.1, it is less clear whether the authors have taken the conceptual relations into account. Figure 1.4, relation B depicts such constitutive relationships.

As the age example suggests, containers can and usually will be large. Certainly, "class climate" ($meso_e$ level) comprises, apart from individual perceptions (emotions and cognitions) of many persons, social rules and, in particular, social practices, i.e., concrete social micro-interactions, which the individual not only experiences but actively shapes, influences, or co-creates.[7] That means that not only are other IVs entailed in the IV "class climate," but they are (at least partly) also aspects of the DV (i.e., the pupils' behavior or competence).

Unfortunately, it is not always easy to recognize containers as mere conceptual umbrellas. An instructive sample case in point is intelligence. Several theoretical approaches conceptualize intelligence differently (Gardner, 2012). For instance, according to a Thurstonian view (Thurstone, 1938), intelligence is to be seen as comprising several *independent* basic components (such as verbal fluency, conclusive thinking, memory, etc.); in other words: intelligence is just the *container* of these components. From a Spearmanian perspective, however, the successful performance of any given intelligence-related task beyond task-specific competence is explained by a *common competence* (termed the g[general]-factor of intelligence by Spearman, 1904). In the latter theoretical tradition, (g-)intelligence, thus, is mainly a factor of its own potency, so to speak, *not* just an umbrella (container) term for independent factors.

Obviously, it depends on the theoretical perspective whether a certain variable is conceptualized as a container. Whether the particular theory claiming or denying the container status of a certain construct is true is, of course, an empirical question (although most difficult to solve). We will return to this aspect in the following section.

Such constitutive relations as described in these examples, in which complex levels of variables are embedded in a higher one, can be conceptualized on all different levels and with manifold interrelations. Thus, they often occur in *complex nested* structures of variables. These *nested structures* of hierarchical levels (Linck & Cunnings, 2015) are depicted in Figure 1.5.

For instance, the parents' socioeconomic status (SES) is a highly complex configuration of two people, their personal and intrapersonal structures, their belongings, their cognitive and material resources, their social interactions both with each other and with many other people (family, friends, colleagues) etc., which means that SES is constituted by these structures it entails. Likewise, class climate is not just constituted by the "elements" referred to earlier but also by the child's behavior, the

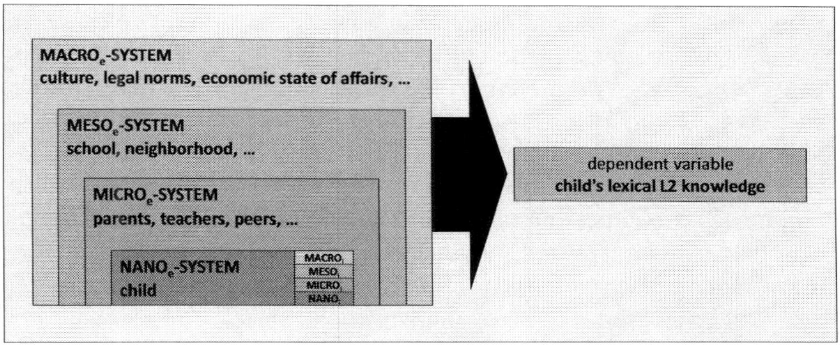

Figure 1.5 Nested structural depiction of variables of different levels (example of analysis: multilevel analysis)

teacher's behavior, the school's climate, etc., and each of these constituting structures are, again, composed of a variety of lower-level constituting structures (the cognitive resources of the parents, for instance, by their intelligence, their education, their motivation, etc., which, again, are constituted by their subpersonal [neural] processes; the teacher's behavior depends on a large variety of different factors as well.) Of course, there are manifold interactions between these different factors changing over time, which will be discussed in what follows.

The insight that there are nested dependencies among and across levels has led to the development of more complex statistical models such as multilevel analyses or mixed-method approaches (Linck & Cunnings, 2015; Windzio, 2008). For instance, if one container variable affects several lower-level elements in the same manner (e.g., the language competence of the teacher is *identical* for all pupils in the classroom), this will result in high intra-class correlations. This is what multilevel analyses in particular take into account. However, although these approaches do account for mutual interdependencies, even such complex multilevel approaches are blind to the problem of the *conceptual nature of the relations* between the different levels, i.e., they do not depict the *reasons* for a given intra-class correlation, which can be conceptual or causal.

Consequences for statistical models

The idea of a container variable assumes that if all relevant factors it contains are identified, the container variable, e.g., "age," would not have an additional effect of its own – for the exact reason that it was just an umbrella term. If the container variable functions just as a container (conceptual umbrella), an explanatory analysis must *either* calculate the *global* influence of the container (Figure 1.4, relation A) *or the singular effects* of its lower-level components (Figure 1.4, relation B). As mentioned, it can be an important and helpful strategy to decompose (and, hence, eliminate) the higher-level structure in particular if an explanatory approach is pursued. This holds for factors both outside and within the person. For instance, instead of measuring the global working memory capacity of an L2 learner, it could be useful to analyze the components of the WM (phonological loop, the visuospatial sketchpad, etc.) separately to arrive at a more precise understanding of mechanisms of how working memory components affect the acquisition of L2. To give another example, working memory, neural networks, and executive functions can be introduced into the analysis *in order to* "eliminate" the age effect (rather than to "investigate" whether age or working memory is the "stronger" predictor). It is our understanding that this procedure, the replacement of global container predictors (e.g., SES, migration background, etc.) by their more specific components leads to a deeper understanding of developmental phenomena and should, therefore, be the goal of theoretically informed empirical, explanatory research. It is a heuristically fruitful procedure if these conceptual relationships are taken into account (see Kersten, 2023, this volume, as an example).

Of course, this is not to claim that reductionism is the single appropriate way to success in scientific explanation. As will become clear in what follows, sometimes, the higher level may contribute to an explanation beyond the lower level components. This does neither hold, however, for higher-order predictors that are just containers (such as age, gender, SES, etc.) nor for higher-order predictors that are entailed by their lower-order constitutive elements.

Yet the procedure of eliminating higher-order predictors may prove problematic in several respects. If we analyzed, in a single multivariate analysis (Figure 1.1), the variables class climate, connectivity of pupils, number of aggressive actions per year, parents' SES, parents' education, parents' income, teacher's educational competence, teacher's language aptitude, variety of media applied in the classroom, the child's cognitive capacity, working memory capacity, and lexicon in order to eliminate those variables that do not significantly contribute to the prediction, we would ignore that *both conceptual* and *causal* reasons might explain why a certain predictor (IV) might show an effect.

A conceptual reason can be described, for example, as follows: if the distinction of constituency is disregarded, if for example the influence of SES is analyzed *together with* the L1 lexicon of the mother in a multivariate analysis (Figure 1.1), and if the L1 lexicon of the mother can be understood as a component of the family's SES, the container variable will always "win," i.e., have a stronger statistical impact than the lower-level variable: first, because SES contains many other component variables whose power is added up and included in the analysis, resulting in a much higher predictive power; and second, because the factor L1 lexicon is actually measured *twice* in the analysis: once as a separate variable and a second time *conceptually "hidden" within* the container of SES. For the same reason, to give another example, if working memory capacity ($meso_i$ level) and the capacity of the phonological loop ($micro_i$ level) are measured in the same multivariate analysis, working memory would probably absorb all variance and remain as the only predictor in the analysis. If this happens with a number of loosely defined, fuzzy constructs and their constituents within a statistical analysis, the predictive impact of the container, here SES or working memory, is blown out of proportion, and it is not possible to arrive at an exact explanation. In some cases, checking for multicollinearity might help to detect such fallacies, but this is not always the final remedy: correlations between variables might have measurement, causal, or conceptual reasons, which leads us back to the necessity of being theoretically clear. It would be incorrect, indeed, to conclude that the L1 lexicon of the mother or the phonological loop, as lower-level constituent variables, had no causal contribution to SLA.

In many studies, however, even after all of these attempts to eliminate a container variable and to replace it with its constituent lower-level factors, often, some variance of the DV remains unexplained. In such cases, however, it is unclear whether a constituting factor remained undetected in the analysis at hand or whether the conceptual relationship between the container and the constituent structures is not only that of constitution but is of a different nature. We will come back to this possibility in the following section when we discuss the phenomenon of *emergence*. Another problem could be that an effect remains invisible because there is not enough variation on the factor within a specific set of data. We will return to this issue in the section on sources of variance.

Consequences for prediction and explanation

The differentiation between cause and constitution does not necessarily need to be taken into account in a predictive approach. The size of the living room may statistically predict the size of the apartment in the same way as the capacity of the working memory may statistically predict intelligence. If it is the goal to identify factors which statistically (cross-sectionally or longitudinally) best predict, for example, the language competence of a child, it might not be necessary for that particular purpose to disentangle the different relations between these factors: If factors are only regarded competingly, the most potent predictor will "win."

From an explanatory perspective, however, the equal treatment of factors on different levels that might account for their statistical interaction but that disregards their conceptual relationship risks confounding a constitutive relation with a causal relation and thus contaminates the theoretical explanation (Smedslund, 2016). Studies that regard factors on different conceptual levels as equal and that do not analyze their conceptual relations will remain theoretically incoherent, and their interpretation will become misleading or, at worst, incorrect. It is therefore essential for an appropriate theoretical *explanation* of a developmental phenomenon to carry out a conceptual analysis of these relations in advance.

Thus, if we are to explain, not just predict, a certain developmental phenomenon, and if we include container and constituent variables at different conceptual social and individual levels in our analysis, we have to be aware of the "nested" order of these variables in order to avoid explanatory mistakes. It follows that we have to have a more systematically ordered theory in advance. If we are to analyze a given set of variables in order to explain L2 motivation, we have first to "locate" them at their proper conceptual level, e.g., according to the nested multilevel structure introduced earlier (Figure 1.5). Second, we have to clarify their conceptual relations before we pursue any analysis using these variables and discuss its results (see Kersten, 2023, this volume, for an example).

Emergence

Even if a container variable is constituted by its lower-level elements, it can have causal effects of its own that *go beyond the singular (added) effects of all of its constituents* (Figure 1.6). This claim that "the whole is greater than the sum of its parts," which is often attributed to an Aristotelian treatise, is called *emergence*[8] (Bedau & Humphreys, 2008; Juarrero & Rubino, 2010; Noordhof, 2010). To take up the example discussed in the previous section, can class climate be something more than the sum of perceptions of the climate of the class members?

It is possible that class climate has a causal impact on an individual learner's language development *above and beyond what this child perceives* of the class climate. While it is not self-evident that "the climate" actually is more than (or something beyond) the singular perceptions of the pupils in the class, it is easier for us to imagine such an emergent effect on the personal level. It is *the person* who talks, who is motivated, who has a certain intelligence and a state of consciousness and not the person's brain, even though we believe that neurophysiological processes constitute what we call "motivation," "language," or "consciousness." The person, her thoughts, her motivation, her language can therefore be regarded as *emergent* phenomena that seem to be more than just neural activities in the brain. In other words, a person can do things that each of the components can't do but that are nevertheless relevant for these components (to return to an example already mentioned: A person can decide to drink a bottle of red wine – an action which will not only influence his decisions but also the functioning of his central executive, his motor control, etc.).

The central idea of emergence, thus, means that in addition to the two possibilities discussed so far (i.e., (a) a mediator relationship, and

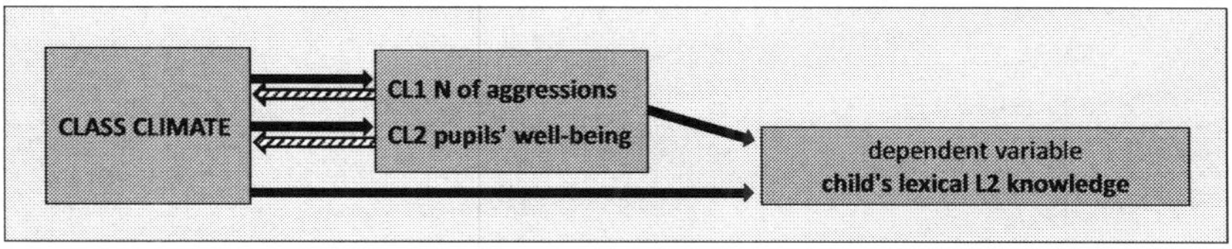

Figure 1.6 Higher-order container variables exert an influence on the DV that goes beyond the added impact of the lower-order constituent variables it entails *(emergence)*. (We cannot insert an example of analysis for the emergence phenomenon, since to establish an emergent relationship is a question in its own right. In any statistical model with unexplained variance, it is unclear whether a constituting factor remained undetected or whether the conceptual relationship between the container and the constituent structures is not that of constitution but of emergence.)

(b) a constitutive relationship between hierarchical factors), there might be a third possibility: (c) the higher-order container structure could have *emergent* characteristics *with an independent causal effect that goes beyond the impact of its constituents* (Figure 1.6). The phenomenon of emergence thus assumes that the impact of the whole is systematically different from the impact of the sum of its parts, without any additional elements or influences from the outside.

A thorough theoretical discussion of emergence is outside the scope of this chapter. With regard to the conceptual relation between personal versus subpersonal phenomena, the topic has been discussed as an essential facet of the mind–body problem for more than 2000 years with manifold variations and trends, but without a consensus, with questions such as: Is the personal realm really different from the subpersonal, physical (i.e., physiological) realm? Do personal phenomena *emerge* from physical processes, or are personal phenomena reducible to physical ones? If both realms are fundamentally different, do personal phenomena exert causal influences on physical phenomena? Moreover, the phenomenon of emergence (if it actually *is* a phenomenon) is, as our present discussion illustrates, not confined to the relationship between mind and body but refers (possibly) to all cross-level relationships and explanations.

Ultimately, the existence of emergent phenomena is, in a broader sense, an empirical question. They either exist or they do not exist. At present, however, it is undecidable in almost any particular case whether the phenomenon at hand actually is an emergent factor in its own right, as it were. If they exist, however, such phenomena need to be accounted for within the conceptual definitions of influencing variables.

Consequences for prediction and explanation

Apart from the question of whether emergence actually exists, the possible impact of emergent factors is of particular importance for explanatory approaches. If a container such as parents' SES is found to have an impact beyond other variables on the dependent variable, how can this impact be interpreted? Do we find it *because there is an emergent relation*, i.e., because SES has an additional independent contribution, or do we only witness an addition to the effect of the constituents that we have already taken into account? If we find a contribution of SES that goes beyond the addition of what we measure concerning its constituents, how can we be sure that the reason for this is an emergent phenomenon and not only our failure to identify all relevant constituents, let alone measure them adequately? This question is crucial for the theoretical modeling of developmental phenomena in the explanatory perspective, because its answer tells us whether we can interpret the relations between the different levels as *causal effects*.

In contrast to the section on container variables, however, this problem does concern the predictive perspective as well, at least to a certain degree. On the one hand, statistical prognoses can of course model the effect of working memory *and* SES *and* the phonological loop as (statistically) independent of each other. This statistical prognosis, however, is, to stress this again, only a necessary but not a sufficient condition for a *causal explanation*. On the other hand, if a certain factor actually *is* an emergent one, any prediction leaving it out (resting on the assumption that it is just a container) will be less successful.

Development across time ("horizontal perspective I")

So far, we have discussed the conceptual relation of factors on different hierarchical levels in what we have called the "vertical" perspective. Another complication of theoretical modeling is, however, that such relations manifest themselves, of course, *over time*. Ultimately, they can best be modeled in longitudinal designs, which can test chronological sequences (e.g., in "cross-lagged-designs"). Although cross-sectional designs, which are regularly used for pragmatic reasons or to avoid repeated-measure effects, often use the same terminology (independent variables are said to "predict" or "explain" the dependent one/s), causal interpretations of synchronic relations are difficult and vulnerable. At best, cross-sectional designs can *test* causal relations postulated by theoretical models. If a particular relationship between factors is not found in a synchronic measurement, a longitudinal effect would be unlikely.

In the section on container variables, we have already touched upon the fact that container variables (e.g., class climate) might comprise not only lower-level factors (e.g., pupils' emotions or perceptions) but real social (micro$_e$) interactions as well. As a consequence, the interactions between factors *over time* have to be taken into account for both predictive and explanatory purposes. Interrelations such as depicted in Figure 1.7 are what we are looking at in a "horizontal" perspective.

We can theoretically differentiate between several types of effects across time. Particularly important for our discussion are mediator effects (already introduced in Figure 1.3) and moderator effects. A mediator relationship identifies sequences of effects: V1 influences V2, and V2 influences the DV (Figure 1.7, relation A). In this case, V2 is the mediator of the effect of V1 on the DV. Again, in a predictive approach, the acknowledgment of this mediator effect is not necessary: The prediction of DV by V1 holds independently of the causal (explanatory) V1-V2-DV chain.

In contrast, a moderator relation denotes the "qualification" of an effect (the effect on an effect, so to say), i.e., the influence of a factor *(moderator)* on the *effect* of another factor (IV) on the dependent variable (Figure 1.7, relation B).[9] To illustrate this: The effect of a certain teaching strategy on the L2A of a student could be dependent on his attention or motivation to actually follow the classroom interaction.

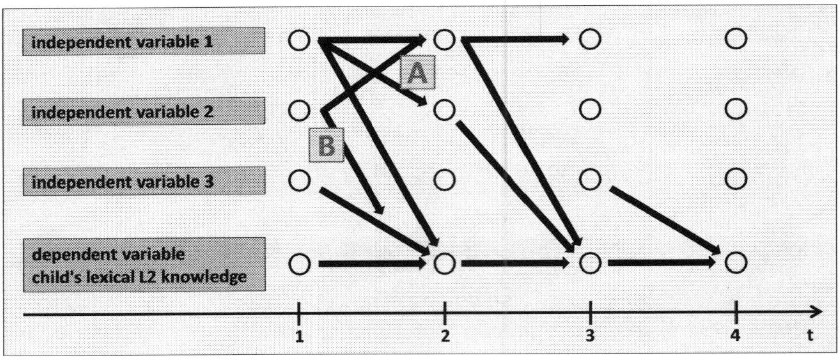

Figure 1.7 The interplay of different variables over time (example of analysis: multiple regression, structural equation, multilevel analysis)

A: *Mediator effect* – an independent $variable_1$ influences another independent $variable_2$, which influences the dependent variable ($variable_2$ mediates the relation between $variable_1$ and DV)

B: *Moderator effect* – an independent $variable_2$ influences (moderates) the impact of another independent $variable_3$ on the dependent variable

Certainly, more interrelations than these are possible and possibly important. Beyond self-stabilizing effects (V1 at t1 predicts V1 at t2), more complicated relations (e.g., recursive effects) might occur. For instance, V1 might influence V2, which has an effect on V3's relation to V1 (e.g., the teacher influences the pupil's motivation, which, in turn, increases the effect of the teaching materials on the pupil's L2A, which, in turn, increases the teacher's motivation to increase the pupil's motivation, etc.). Such types of effects are, of course, possible on and between all (sub)personal and social levels.

Obviously, then, beyond the acknowledgment of the conceptual relations of the factors involved, any coherent explanation needs to take into account the interactions of these factors across time. In fact, this is what any theoretical explanatory model aims for. In a predictive perspective, however, the acknowledgment of mediator effects does not necessarily increase the predictive value of the predictors, while the acknowledgment of a moderator effect might increase the precision of a prediction.

Dynamic processes across time ("horizontal perspective II")

When focusing on the interaction between different factors across time, the dynamic nature of this interaction is often neglected. However, it is plausible to assume that language acquisition results not just from many influencing conditions, not just from their interaction as captured by the general linear model (e.g., interaction in terms of an analysis of variance), but from complex and dynamic interactions between factors. In academic SLA discourse, it has recently been argued with increasing rigor that language development needs to be described as a dynamic system (DS) with all characteristics pertaining to it (de Bot, 2008, 2015; de Bot et al., 2007; Dörnyei, 2009, 2010; Ellis, 2007; Larsen-Freeman, 2007; Larsen-Freeman & Cameron, 2008; Lenzing, 2015). Language, speech communities, individuals, and subcomponents of individuals such as their brains have all been described as dynamic systems (Ellis, 2007), "from the social level to the neurological levels" (Larsen-Freeman & Cameron, 2008, p. 201). These characteristics are controversially debated in SLA, especially with regard to nonlinearity and predictability versus nonpredictability of DS. Indeed, the characteristics of DS, as we will discuss, pertain to both the explanatory and the predictive perspective on influencing factors in SLA.

While not all SLA researchers subscribe to DS approaches, the insight that interactions between the variables that contribute to the explanation of SLA often go beyond rigid linear relationships will hardly be disputed anymore. This is not the place to provide an overview of the discussion, but some aspects crucial for the purpose of this chapter will be addressed in the following (see also Lenzing et al., 2023, this volume).

Conceptual challenges

To our understanding, the terminology used in the SLA discourse deviates in some respects from the technical terminology in mathematical DS theories, and the mathematical bases of actual DS approaches are rarely applied in linguistics. In that vein, Lenzing et al. (2023, this volume) call for more conceptual clarity of linguistic positions. van Geert (2007, p. 47) calls this "the possible tension between formal and informal dynamic systems models," elaborating that "a formal model has a specific mathematical format . . . [while] an informal model is one that applies certain dynamic systems properties by analogy or similarity." Many characteristics of a dynamic approach (attractor states, butterfly effect, nonlinearity, self-organization, etc.) are often used in a rather metaphorical way. Even the question of whether mathematical or physical models can be directly applied to the development of language and speech has not yet been systematically clarified. In order to reconcile, for instance, universal grammar (UG) and DS theories, it might be acceptable to apply DS terminology in a metaphorical manner as an illustrating characterization of the phenomenon even though the linguistic discussion is still far from being able to model language development geometrically (van Geert, 2007, p. 49). This does not have to stand in the way of the heuristic function and fruitfulness of a DS approach in SLA, but it will not directly lead to a strict theoretical formalization of a theory of SLA, possibly making the systematic consideration of the questions addressed here more difficult.

Linearity

The elements of a DS are, in a systematic way, related to each other such that both the value of these variables and their interrelation change from step to step, i.e., over time (Dörnyei, 2010, p. 260).[10] DS can be linear or nonlinear. Linear DS have been well researched in mathematics. Here, as a rule, predictability is not excluded in general. However, the central tenet of many proponents of a DS approach in SLA (de Bot, 2008; Dörnyei, 2009) refers to the nonlinearity of the relations.

Stability

Nonlinear DS can be chaotic or nonchaotic. The term "chaotic" refers to the phenomenon that trajectories from two similar initial states can lead to very different future states. Thus, small initial changes may lead to large differences in effects (*butterfly effect*; Verspoor, 2015, p. 38). In contrast, in nonchaotic (sub)systems, small changes have small effects (Lenzing, 2015). If the model of a chaotic, nonlinear DS applies to certain empirical phenomena, future states may become almost unpredictable (given the limited accuracy of measurement required to assess the small differences between initial conditions).

However, this does not entail permanent changes and never-ending variability and variation. Rather, even these systems can run into stable states. Such stable end states toward which a system evolves are referred to, in mathematical terms, as "attractors" (Dörnyei, 2009, 2010; Hiver, 2015; Plaza-Pust, 2008). Such attractors are robust states that resist change and are recursively stable (i.e., they just (re-)produce their own state) so that the state of the system remains unchanged once the attractor state is reached. Attractors are, thus, "a relatively stable state of a system . . . [which] remains fixed for a long time (or forever, for that matter). An attractor state is insensitive to (small) perturbations" (van Geert, 2007, p. 47; see Ruhland & van Geert, 1998, for an application to language development).

DS applied to human phenomena (such as SLA) deal with finite phenomena, while DS in mathematical theories are not limited by time or space and, hence, are conceptualized as infinite. In the context of SLA, or of any limited human development for that matter, however, it would be useless, perhaps inappropriate to talk about indefinite stable states. In the social sciences, it thus makes sense to define DS terms such as stability and attractor states as finite concepts and discuss the applicability of a DS approach with respect to *temporary* stable and instable states. In this latter sense, attractor states are discussed within SLA discourse (Chan et al., 2015, p. 256; Larsen-Freeman & Cameron, 2008). Here, some authors use the term "attractor states" as indicating "stable *tendencies*, *solutions* or *outcomes* for dynamic systems" (Hiver, 2015, p. 20) or as "preferred patterns" that resist change over a sufficiently long period of time (Dörnyei, 2010). Dörnyei (2010, p. 261) suggests that higher-order variables of individual differences such as aptitude, emotional intelligence, or possible selves "can be seen as powerful attractors that act as stabilizing forces" (Dörnyei, 2010, p. 261), and Plaza-Pust, trying to reconcile UG and DS theories, proposes that UG parameter settings function as attractors and limit variability, while variation, according to her, is an indicator for a grammatical system in an unstable state in between different attractors (Plaza-Pust, 2008, p. 255f).

Consequences for prediction and explanation of SLA in a DS framework

To begin with, even a complex or chaotic nondeterministic dynamical system by no means escapes scientific analysis. Even if the individual state of the system cannot be predicted without knowledge of the initial state, and this initial state of even a finite number of system components cannot be determined with absolute accuracy, the behavior of the system can, in principle, be formally described. This is exactly the approach of the mathematical modeling of dynamical systems.

Concerning the question of whether explanation or prediction in the horizontal dynamic interplay of factors is possible, we have to differentiate between unstable phases of the system and stable ones (in the "informal" usage of these terms, as outlined earlier). While *theoretically possible* even for all parts of a deterministic system, prediction of *applied* DS will *in practice* be limited and depend on the characteristics of the specific constellation of empirical factors (i.e., on the appropriateness of the description of the empirical constellation *as a DS*) and on the precision of the measurement instruments available. Thus, they will be particularly difficult for instable parts and chaotic subsystems, as small differences in the initial state can lead to very different pathways and end states. If our knowledge of initial states is incomplete, and if measurement instruments are not precise enough to capture the relevant small initial differences (both of which are highly probable for the complex study of human development), prediction becomes a difficult endeavor. Moreover, any modeling of a highly complex reality (such as the empirical conditions of language development or SLA) through a DS will necessarily remain incomplete: the number of variables to be integrated into this model will be limited both by the boundaries of our knowledge and by the boundaries of the limited possibility to integrate a large number of variables into one model (given the sample sizes available). This incompleteness further restricts the precision of any empirical prediction.

For nonchaotic subsystems and for stable parts of nonlinear DS, however, this might be different. First, imprecise measurement of initial differences is much less relevant than for chaotic systems as they lead to similar consequences (Lenzing, 2015, p. 99; Figure 1.2). While empirical measurement of initial states is always limited by our research instruments, the precision of prediction will be much higher and closer to the theoretical prediction than for chaotic parts. Second, as stable parts endure over time (at least to some extent in human development), the chance for imprecise instruments to capture the main characteristics of the observed state is higher than in unstable parts and chaotic subsystems. It is a question that needs to be empirically corroborated (or falsified) – which parts within a DS under investigation are stable and which parts are not. We would therefore assume that prediction is easier (more precise) for the stable aspects of a DS within the practical constraints of a given research instrument but less so for chaotic DS.

Even for chaotic DS, beyond the formal constraints of a given *model* (here, of course, everything is "fixed"), any process to be modeled in a DS is restricted by certain constraints. Our physical environment, for example, is constrained by gravity. Thus, variation in the paths of falling balls in a DS limited by gravity will not include infinite upward movement. Likewise, language production of humans is constrained (among other things) by the structure of the articulatory apparatus. Thus, variation in the production of sounds will not include sounds beyond the possible spectrum. Accordingly, with respect to second language development, communication would break down if everything varied at the same time. Thus, communicative rules that govern speech communities need to be stable to a sufficiently high degree to ensure mutual comprehension (albeit nonstatic and subject to change). According to this view, variation within the learner's language or between learners does not occur randomly but follows certain laws and is constrained, at least to some extent, by universal developmental pathways a learner takes (and has taken in the past, limiting the possible trajectories in the future). The nature and number of variable linguistic items at a certain stage of interlanguage is not random in the absolute sense of the word but is restricted by the learner's cognitive apparatus: "[I]ndividual learner variation occurs *within the overall constraints of the developing L2 system*" (Lenzing, 2015, p. 100, italics by the authors), with "the range of structural options [being] . . . restricted by the processing constraints of a given stage of development delineated in Hypothesis Space" (Lenzing, 2015, p. 113; cf. Plaza-Pust, 2008, p. 266).

As a consequence, the cognitive (and other) influences on and constraints for language development can *theoretically* be described, as is being attempted in many different frameworks throughout SLA research. Such theories need to systematize and order what at first glance seemed to look like random variation (reduce the "degree of randomness"). It is theoretically possible to claim these elements to be predictable, as argued earlier, within the constraints of the context, the state and nature of the DS, and the limitations of the research instruments. On the other hand, one can make a case for *practical* unpredictability of variation during an unstable phase of restructuring in which small and undetectable differences lead to large differences that cannot be accounted for empirically.

How to model such complex dynamic processes in a predictive perspective statistically is, however, far beyond our expertise. Some researchers have proposed alternative, e.g., qualitative methodological approaches (Chan et al., 2015; Dörnyei, 2009, 2011; Larsen-Freeman & Cameron, 2008), but this discussion is outside the scope of this chapter.

Irrespective of the challenges and problems of an application of a DS approach to (S)LA, the problems discussed in the first part of this chapter remain important. The mathematical modeling of the dynamic nature of cross-temporal relations between factors is as neutral ("blind") with respect to the conceptual relations between these factors as any other (statistical) model. While mathematical models of dynamic or other systems are, of course, themselves conceptual models, the claim that the empirical dynamics of (S)LA development can be aptly described (albeit not always aptly measured) by a DS model presupposes that the modeled empirical relations are themselves not mere conceptual but rather causal relations. As a consequence of the discussion of the previous sections, any modeling of DS has to take into account the conceptual levels of the variables included in the model. The problems discussed can occur equally and have thus to be taken into account within this framework as well.

Dynamic systems and SLA

A controversy in SLA derives from different views on language development that "range from approaches that see L2 development as a highly variable and nonpredictable process . . . to those that view L2 development as both dynamic and rule-governed" (Lenzing, 2015, p. 91). Proponents of the first position claim, for instance, that universalities (i.e., developmental stages and sequences) do not exist and hence cannot be aptly modeled but rather occur as artificial consequences of the models or methods applied (Lenzing, 2015, p. 100). Even those variants of DS that claim unpredictability, nonlinearity, and nonperiodicality do not claim to entirely abandon any scientific attempt to explain, predict, and support SLA.

Certainly, DS *are* systematic models for a complex reality. Even if we are practically or in principle unable to predict certain states from the initial states in certain (sub)systems of a language or language development, this does not exclude the predictability of overall patterns. In a way, one important implication of such a DS approach in SLA may be that for the explanation of variation and change, the focus shifts from variables (causal factors) to processes: "it is not the possible causes but the degree of variability in itself (which may include systematic, free and unsystematic variation) that is taken as providing insight in the developmental process" (de Bot et al., 2007, p. 53).

From an explanatory point of view, however, it is probably essential to incorporate a DS approach into future theories of SLA. If the assumption that the interaction between factors within and between different levels is (as a rule) dynamic by nature should prove defendable, no explanation ignoring that can be true. Even complex (multilevel) models of interactions between a multitude of variables (Figure 1.7) will remain insufficient to truly depict the complex, dynamic nature of (second) language development.

Methodological challenges: Measurement, variance, and design

Independent of the conceptual problems discussed so far, an empirical investigation faces a number of methodological problems in a narrower, more technical sense. In the following sections, we will restrict ourselves to three basic practical aspects of empirical studies (of cognitive-linguistic factors in SLA) pertaining to the issues in question: problems of measurement, statistical premises, and research designs. We will not focus, however, on technical challenges of specific research instruments (e.g., for the measurement of neural processes) or specific statistical analyses (e.g. technical presuppositions of multilevel analyses).

Problems of measurement

Each construct that is part of a theoretical model requires an adequate model of measurement. In both vertical and horizontal perspectives, the construct needs to be reliably and validly captured, i.e., either directly measured or latently estimated (i.e., estimated from a number of manifest indicators).

In a first step, as argued already, this is a theoretical challenge: What "is" SES, what is intelligence, the social climate of a class, etc.? What is meant by these terms, what aspects do they include, and which aspects are not part of it? Is the parents' education, for instance, constitutive of their SES or only correlated with it? These conceptualizations need to be clarified theoretically before a measurement theory is applied.

In a second step, these theoretical constructs need to be operationalized. In empirical practice, that means that certain aspects or components of the construct need to be selected along with an adequate measuring instrument. More often than not, due to states of affairs in research and to practical restrictions, we will not be able to assess the construct to be investigated entirely without measurement error but will have to contend with procedures of estimation (e.g., by proxy variables). For instance, number of books at home might be useful as a proxy for the economic resources and the education level of a household. Naturally, each proxy requires an empirical corroboration of validity, which ultimately is based on the theoretical conceptualization of the construct in question.

Independent of whether a macro construct such as SES serves just as a container or is assumed to possess an emergent causal function, there are distinct problems connected with the indicators selected to represent the macro construct more or less directly. An indicator could, for instance, theoretically indicate other constructs in addition to the selected one. Number of books, which is often used as an indicator of SES, could also represent the *cultural background* of a family or a social group ("Do members read?"). This would have repercussions for the validity of the indicator, since "books" would not only measure SES und would thus contain partly invalid (but still possibly predictively relevant) information. In a statistical analysis, this could lead to methodological artefacts, if e.g., the indicator "number of books" could then be more powerful than a separate indicator for *culture*, so that the influence of the latter is underestimated or becomes invisible. These aspects would render the theoretical interpretation of the results difficult or impossible, but this only results from the operationalization, not from the theoretical problems discussed in this chapter.

One current methodological answer to this challenge is structural equation modeling (SEM) (see Kersten, 2023, this volume, for an example of an SEM application within this line of reasoning). The central point of this approach is to *estimate* a latent factor by calculating several manifest variables (in order to extract, in a way, measurement errors and other factors that reduce the latent factor's reliability and, hence, validity). Certainly, SEM is helpful and necessary both for the predictive and the explanatory paradigm (independent of the number and type of relations of the levels involved in the study). SEM could be used to model "container" relationships as well (the container can be modeled as the "latent" variable "behind" its "manifest" constituents). We have not referred to this approach in our discussion because all examples discussed so far (from Figure 1.1 to Figure 1.7, actually) can (and perhaps should) be calculated in a SEM frame even though a SEM approach is as insensitive to the problems discussed in this chapter as other statistical models mentioned so far.

Independent of these indicators and their problems of validity, the types of tools used to capture the respective variables differ widely for theoretical and practical reasons – self-report data (interviews, questionnaires), physiological measurements of brain structures or processes, functional subpersonal data (measurements of memory capacity, semantic associations, etc.), observations (field notes, semistructured and structured observations, e.g. of classroom interactions), or a combination of several of these. Hence, data are available in numerous qualitatively different formats, with a different degree of objectivity and different types of errors, all of which have a different effect on reliability. To give an example: "Social desirability" does not play a role when measuring reaction time, but it certainly does in interviews or questionnaires.

Since the success of both predictions and explanations depends on the quality of measurement of the variables included in a given analysis, predictions will often fail not because of a wrong theory but because of insufficiently precise measurement and, in addition, if samples are too small, as complex models require large samples. Although this problem is a serious (perhaps even unsolvable) obstacle for research, it is independent from the problems discussed in this chapter.

Sources of variance

Throughout this chapter, we have followed the (tacit) assumption that dependent variables can be predicted and/or explained by identifying the partial contributions of several IVs and their interactions, i.e., that factors have independent contributions to the variance of a DV (this assumption is also entailed in the INUS conception of a causal factor). This, however, the central idea that the contribution of each factor is *independent* and that their causal contributions are *added up*, is not necessarily correct. It is just a theoretical assumption (presupposition) and certainly not self-evident. We cannot delve into the epistemological debate of whether this idea of independent and additional causality (INUS) is defendable. It seems worth noting, however, that statistical approaches (for instance, those resting on analyses of variance, as do almost all approaches mentioned in this chapter) entail methodological and epistemological presuppositions.

Moreover, the identification of a relative (partial) weight of a certain variable in a given (statistical) prediction depends on the distribution of variances in the actual sample. As a consequence, the actual (causal) contribution of a certain variable may remain invisible (i.e., the IV would show no effect) if there is not enough variation of the factor within a specific set of data. An illustrative example would be the question of whether bipedalism in humans is genetically explainable. As there will be very little variation with respect to the relevant part of the genotype in humans but a broad variety of "environmental" influences (e.g., the loss of a leg due to injuries, accidents, etc.), analyses of variance will find (almost) no genetic effect on bipedalism. Yet the conclusion that bipedalism is not genetically influenced would be plain wrong. Analyses of variance can, thus, only detect the contribution of variance that is present in a data set. However, this problem is certainly independent from the theoretical problems discussed in this chapter (actually, it is no theoretical problem at all, just a methodological one).

Implications for design

In an explanatory approach, the actual aim of modeling is to investigate the causal impact on the developmental phenomenon in question (here: SLA), in other words, to *explain* the developmental stages or trajectories. Since this impact (causality) cannot be measured directly, however, its investigation is not only a question of how to capture a certain variable but of how to set up the research design. Some limitations of certain research designs (e.g., the impossibility of controlling certain variables such as education or gender in an experimental manner) can be reduced by using specific longitudinal analyses, e.g., cross-lagged designs. In addition to the operationalization of the variables, it is thus essential to clarify which *type of research design* is necessary to test the postulated causal relations in the explanatory model.

The "royal road" to test causal relations is the randomized experiment. This is often possible for the study of causal effects on the subpersonal level (e.g., the impact of cognitive factors on the [development of] L2 attainment). When conducted well, experiments increase the internal validity of the design and, thereby, support the causal/explanatory interpretation of the effect under investigation. For practical purposes, however, it has certain shortcomings. For one thing, an increase in internal validity is, as a rule, accompanied by a decrease of external validity. It is precisely the systematic control of conditions that leads to an artificial constellation, since it is impossible to include the complex factors and their interactions from real contexts in an experiment.

Second, the number of systematically controllable (and thus measurable) variables is inevitably limited in an experimental design. Randomization controls *all* other variables, of course, but at the same time, it renders their impact invisible. If a large number of variables is to be investigated at the same time, this cannot be modeled realistically in an experimental study. The alternative is to control them not experimentally but statistically – that is, to use a correlational design that just measures (instead of manipulates) the IVs to be investigated. This, however, leads to the confounding of variables, which is inevitable in quasi-experimental designs. Children, for instance, are seldom distributed randomly across different types of language programs. Their parents' motivation, their parents' own linguistic and educational background, their mobility, the schools' catchment area, and many other aspects will be confounded. Testing complex causal theories, therefore, yields considerable problems of design. For predictions and even for interventions, this does not necessarily need to be an obstacle (precisely because interventions can be successful even if they are based on [partly] incorrect theories).

As a consequence, a combination or triangulation of several research designs might be helpful to capture the complexity of the phenomenon under investigation (i.e., [second] language development). For the investigation of a particular causal process ("*How* does this particular IV influence the DV?"), an experimental approach might be most appropriate; to gain a broader picture of the dynamic interplay of a multitude of factors in the explanation of the DV, "correlational" approaches will be more suitable (see Dörnyei, 2011, for suggestions of an alternative qualitative research program).

Conclusion

The development of a learner's linguistic systems is intricately intertwined with the individual cognitive and emotional development and is embedded in his or her individual developmental process in general and in the interactions with the environment. Conducting and interpreting empirical research to explain cognitive and linguistic development, however, proves problematic in many respects and for different reasons. In this contribution, we tried to systematize two important groups of problems. First, the differentiation of conceptual layers into which factors are to be categorized and the differentiation of their mutual relations within and across layers. These are necessary prerequisites of any theoretically coherent (causal) explanation but not necessarily of a successful (statistical) prediction. We referred to these types of problems as the "vertical" perspective. Second, it is a necessary prerequisite for both coherent and true explanations/theories and for successful predictions and interventions to understand the dynamic interaction of conditions across time. We called this the "horizontal" perspective. While predictions are *theoretically* possible for such dynamic systems, they are practically limited for several reasons, in particular for instable parts and chaotic subsystems of the individual's developmental trajectories.

For some of these problems, statistical models provide solutions (for instance, structural equation models enhance the exactness of measurement, and multilevel models capture several facets of a nested structure of variables) if they employ a sufficiently differentiated measurement approach. Yet a statistical analysis of a model cannot test its *theoretical* coherence. Predictions, even if successful, do not "verify" a theory. Consequently, even advanced statistical methods, which may lead to successful cross-sectional and/or longitudinal predictions, are, in some respects, blind to differences between types of relations (i.e., causal vs. logical) between conceptual layers and thus may lead to misleading or even wrong interpretations. In other words, the adequacy of a given theory in this respect cannot be detected empirically.

This asks for greater accuracy in theory development and for more investment in the development of dynamic modeling of developmental trajectories as well as for a precise construction of the measurement applied to each variable in the model to be tested. This holds especially for the explanatory perspective, but if the complexity of (dynamic) interactions between developmental conditions is not sufficiently taken into account, both prediction and explanation will, as a rule, remain insufficient or fail altogether. If our arguments do not go wrong, a more careful consideration of the theoretical premises of our research on the one hand and progress in the application and refinement of dynamic models for developmental processes will advance the understanding of SLA in particular and individual development in general. Finally, this might also widen the potential for interventions to facilitate progress along developmental pathways for each individual learner.[11]

Notes

1. Of course, mediator and moderator relationships can be tested in synchronic cross-sectional analyses as well; the theoretical intention of these hypotheses, however, is a causal one and thus a relation across time.
2. The discussion of causality (as a theoretical concept) is beyond the scope of this chapter (for an overview, see Mackie, 1974). In the following, we will rely on an intuitive understanding of "cause" (for the independent variable) and "effect" (for the dependent variable). Neither will we enter the fundamental epistemological discussion of whether an objective "reality" can be captured by scientific methods at all, let alone the question of whether such a reality actually exists.
3. It is irrelevant for the current discussion whether the prediction is based on data collected in a cross-sectional or longitudinal design (*synchronic* versus *diachronic* prediction). Both approaches test whether and to what degree a dependent variable can be predicted by independent variables. Often, a predictive perspective has the second aim to change a current state with the help of an intervention and, thus, to predict that change. However, a longitudinal (diachronic) perspective is, as a rule, superior to cross-sectional designs for developmental processes, as the latter cannot depict the chronological sequence of the events under investigation.
4. This perspective is, of course, the one which we take intuitively in everyday life – but for the sake of completeness, it has to be mentioned that the debate of whether it denotes "real" phenomena *different* from, say, neurological ones or just expresses a view on these phenomena has been unresolved for more than two millennia (Metzinger, 2013).
5. It seems worth mentioning once more that the inclusion of the $nano_i$ level in this hierarchy (i.e., to conceptualize neurons as a sublevel of, say, motivation or even memory) ignores the mind–body problem. (This ignorance is statistically harmless but theoretically inappropriate.) Of course, this hierarchical structure repeats itself on many different levels. The neural level itself can, again, be subdivided into different cellular – or even atomic – components.
6. Certainly, there are many other forms of interrelations. For instance, an IV ($meso_e$) might have an influence on *the influence* of another IV ($micro_e$) on the DV (moderator effect; see Figure 1.7).
7. This means also that container factors such as class climate include not just lower-level constituents (e.g., class climate *consists of* individual perceptions of the climate in the class etc.) but real interactions between individuals. For instance, a teacher might react differently to a motivated student than to an inattentive one, and, dependent on that, the quality of her input and her interactions might change (de Bot, 2008; Ushioda, 2015). The teacher's reactions, in turn, are part of (i.e., co-constitute) the class climate. As a consequence, if we are to analyze the impact of class climate, the teacher's behavior, and the pupils' motivation (IVs) on the pupils' competence (DV), class climate (partly) comprises many other variables (including the DV) and their interactions. This argument entails, however, that the quality of these interactions has to be understood.
8. Note that the term *emergence* in this context is not identical with the emergence of a linguistic structure in the sense as it is used in the framework of Processability Theory (Pienemann, 1998; Pallotti, 2007).
9. Obviously, a simple moderator effect can only capture a small part of reality. In fact, there are countless interactions (i.e., moderator effects of a second, third, and even higher order) between countless variables. The "academic enterprise" boldly presupposes that a theoretical model with a manageable number of factors and their interactions allows for an adequate empirically testable depiction of reality.

10. For the remainder of this section, we will restrict our discussion to discrete (as opposed to continuous) dynamical systems for several reasons. In discrete systems, the measurement of its variables takes place at discrete points in time and is not carried out continually (even in dense longitudinal studies). At present, truly continuous measurements are empirically impossible (although they would sometimes be more appropriate from a theoretical point of view).

    It is worth noting that even if we restrict our models to discrete DS, the "temporal resolution," i.e., the narrowness of observation, the frequency of measurement, the magnitude of the focused time frame remains arbitrary. Do we model a dynamic developmental process over seconds or minutes, over hours or days, over weeks or months, over years or decades, or over generations? The acquisition of a language consists of years of influences; these in turn consists of weeks of schooling (among other things), these weeks consist of days, of seconds etc. (de Bot, 2015; Larsen-Freeman & Cameron, 2008). We cannot delve into the details of this problem, but the nestedness of processes (within processes etc.) seems to horizontally mirror the vertical nestedness of factor levels discussed earlier.

11. **Acknowledgments:** We are very grateful to Gabriele Pallotti and Adam Winsler for most valuable hints, objections, and suggestions. Any remaining errors and inconsistencies are solely ours.

References

Bedau, M. A., & Humphreys, P. (Eds.). (2008). *Emergence. Contemporary readings in philosophy and science*. MIT Press.

Bieri, P. (Ed.). (1981). *Analytische Philosophie des Geistes [Analytical philosophy of mind]*. Hain.

Brandtstädter, J. (Ed.). (1987). *Struktur und Erfahrung in der psychologischen Forschung [Structure and experience in psychological research]*. de Gruyter.

Bronfenbrenner, U. (2005). *Making human beings human: Bioecological perspectives on human development*. Sage.

Chan, A., Dörnyei, Z., & Alastair, H. (2015). Learner archetypes and signature dynamics in the language classroom: A retrodictive qualitative modelling approach to studying L2 motivation. In Z. Dörnyei & P. D. MacIntyre (Eds.), *Motivational dynamics in language learning* (pp. 238–259). Multilingual Matters. https://doi.org/10.21832/9781783092574-018

Cunnings, J. (2012). An overview of mixed-effects statistical models for second language researchers. *Second Language Research*, *28*(3), 369–382. https://doi.org/10.1177/0267658312443651

de Bot, K. (2008). Second language development as a dynamic process. *The Modern Language Journal*, *92*(2), 166–178. https://doi.org/10.1111/j.1540-4781.2008.00712.x

de Bot, K. (2015). Rates of change: Timescales in second language development. In Z. Dörnyei, P. D. MacIntyre, & A. Henry (Eds.), *Motivational dynamics in language learning* (pp. 29–37). Macmillan. https://doi.org/10.21832/9781783092574-006

de Bot, K., Lowie, W., & Verspoor, W. (2007). A dynamic view as a complementary perspective. *Bilingualism: Language and Cognition*, *10*(01), 51–55. https://doi.org/10.1017/S1366728906002811

Dennett, D. (1987). *The intentional stance*. MIT Press.

Dörnyei, Z. (2009). Individual differences: Interplay of learner characteristics and learning environment. *Language Learning*, *59*(1), 230–248. https://doi.org/10.1111/j.1467-9922.2009.00542.x

Dörnyei, Z. (2010). The relationship between language aptitude and language learning motivation: Individual differences from a dynamic systems perspective. In E. Macaro (Ed.), *Continuum companion to second language acquisition* (pp. 247–267). Continuum. https://doi.org/10.1111/j.1467-9922.2009.00542.x

Dörnyei, Z. (2011). Researching complex dynamic systems: 'Retrodictive qualitative modelling' in the language classroom. *Language Teaching*, *47*(1), 1–12. https://doi.org/10.1017/S0261444811000516

Ellis, N. C. (2007). Dynamic systems and SLA: The wood and the trees. *Bilingualism: Language and Cognition*, *10*(01), 23–25. https://doi.org/10.1017/S1366728906002744

Fuchs, T. (2018). *Ecology of the brain: The phenomenology and biology of the embodied mind*. Oxford University Press.

Gardner, M. K. (2012). *Theories of intelligence*. Oxford University Press.

Hiver, P. (2015). Attractor states. In Z. Dörnyei, P. D. MacIntyre, & A. Henry (Eds.), *Motivational dynamics in language learning* (pp. 20–28). Macmillan. https://doi.org/10.21832/9781783092574-005

Jordan, G. (2004). *Theory construction in second language acquisition*. Benjamins. https://doi.org/10.1075/lllt.8

Juarrero, A., & Rubino, C. A. (2010). *Emergence, complexity, and self-organization. Precursors and prototypes*. Emergent Publications.

Kersten, K. (2023, this volume). Proximity of Stimulation: Investigating the interplay of cognitive, linguistic and instructional factors in early language acquisition. In K. Kersten & A. Winsler (Eds.), *Understanding variability in second language acquisition, bilingualism, and cognition: A multi-layered perspective* (pp. 131–159). Routledge.

Larsen-Freeman, D. (2007). On the complementarity of chaos/complexity theory and dynamic systems theory in understanding the second language acquisition process. *Bilingualism: Language and Cognition*, *10*(01), 35–37. http://dx.doi.org/10.1017/S136672890600277X

Larsen-Freeman, D., & Cameron, L. (2008). Research methodology on language development from a complex systems perspective. *The Modern Language Journal*, *92*(2), 200–213. https://doi.org/10.1111/J.1540-4781.2008.00714.X

Lenzing, A. (2015). Exploring regularities and dynamic systems in L2 development. *Language Learning*, *65*(1), 89–122. https://doi.org/10.1111/lang.12092

Lenzing, A., Pienemann, M., & Nicholas, H. (2023, this volume). Lost in translation? On some key features of dynamical systems theorizing invoked in SLA research. In K. Kersten & A. Winsler (Eds.), *Understanding variability in second language acquisition, bilingualism, and cognition: A multi-layered perspective* (pp. 39–79). Routledge.

Lerner, R. M. (2013). *Concepts and theories of human development*. Taylor and Francis.

Linck, J. A., & Cunnings, I. (2015). The utility and application of mixed-effects models in second language research. *Language Learning*, *65*(S1), 185–207. https://doi.org/10.1111/lang.12117

Mackie, J. L. (1965). Causes and conditions. *American Philosophical Quarterly*, *2*(4), 245–264.

Mackie, J. L. (1974). *The cement of the universe: A study of causation*. Clarendon Press.

Metzinger, T. (2013). *Grundkurs Philosphie des Geistes (Band 2): Das Leib-Seele Problem [Basic Course Philosophy of Mind (Volume 2): The Body-Soul Problem]*. Mentis-Verlag.

Noordhof, P. (2010). Emergent causation and property causation. In C. Macdonald & G. Macdonald (Eds.), *Emergence in mind* (pp. 69–99). Oxford University Press. https://doi.org/10.1093/acprof:oso/9780199583621.003.0006

Pallotti, G. (2007). An operational definition of the emergence criterion. *Applied Linguistics*, *28*(3), 361–382. http://dx.doi.org/10.1093/applin/amm018

Pfenniger, S. E. (2021, August). *Questioning causality in applied linguistics*. Keynote presented at AILA 2021, University of Groningen.

Pienemann, M. (1998). *Language processing and second language development: Processability theory*. John Benjamins. https://doi.org/10.1075/sibil.15

Plaza-Pust, C. (2008). Dynamic systems theory and universal grammar: Holding up a turbulent mirror to development in grammars. *The Modern Language Journal*, *92*(2), 250–269. https://doi.org/10.1111/j.1540-4781.2008.00717.x

Ruhland, R., & van Geert, P. (1998). Jumping into syntax: Transitions in the development of closed class words. *British Journal of Developmental Psychology*, *16*(1), 65–95. http://dx.doi.org/10.1111/j.2044-835X.1998.tb00750.x

Ryle, G. (1949). *The concept of mind*. Hutchinson.

Shmueli, G. (2010). To explain or to predict? *Statistical Science*, *25*(3), 289–310. http://dx.doi.org/10.1214/10-STS330

Smedslund, J. (2016). Why psychology cannot be an empirical science. *Integrative Psychological & Behavioral Science*, *50*(2), 185–195. https://doi.org/10.1007/s12124-015-9339-x

Spearman, C. (1904). "General intelligence," objectively determined and measured. *The American Journal of Psychology*, *15*(2), 201–292. https://doi.org/10.2307/1412107

Thurstone, L. L. (1938). *Primary mental abilities*. University of Chicago Press.

Ushioda, E. (2015). Context and complex dynamic systems theory. In Z. Dörnyei, P. D. MacIntyre, & A. Henry (Eds.), *Motivational dynamics in language learning* (pp. 47–54). Multilingual Matters. https://doi.org/10.21832/9781783092574-008

van Geert, P. (1994). *Dynamic systems of development*. Harvester Wheatsheaf.

van Geert, P. (2007). Dynamic systems in second language learning: Some general methodological reflections. *Bilingualism: Language and Cognition*, *10*(01), 47–49. https://doi.org/10.1017/S136672890600280X

van Geert, P. (2008). The dynamic systems approach in the study of L1 and L2 acquisition: An introduction. *The Modern Language Journal*, *92*(2), 179–199. http://dx.doi.org/10.1111/j.1540-4781.2008.00713.x

van Geert, P. (2014). Dynamic modeling for development and education: From concepts to numbers. *Mind, Brain, and Education*, *8*(2), 57–73. http://dx.doi.org/10.1111/mbe.12046

Verspoor, M. (2015). Initial conditions. In Z. Dörnyei, P. D. MacIntyre, & A. Henry (Eds.), *Motivational dynamics in language learning* (pp. 38–46). Macmillan. https://doi.org/10.21832/9781783092574-007

Windzio, M. (2008). Social structures and actors: The application of multilevel analysis in migration research. *Romanian Journal of Population Studies*, *2*, 113–138.

2 Lost in translation? On some key features of dynamical systems theorizing invoked in SLA research

Anke Lenzing, Manfred Pienemann, and Howard Nicholas

Introduction

In this chapter, we reflect on the challenges involved in translating theorizing within the mathematical/physical sciences disciplinary approach of dynamical systems into the disciplinary framework of second language acquisition. We take as our core focus the issue of prediction that has emerged in association with recent writings grouped collectively as the "dynamic approach" (Dörnyei et al., 2014). Studies within this approach have sought to make use of concepts from mathematics to shape a research agenda for second language acquisition. In order to bring the issue of translation to the fore, we distinguish between "dynamic" and "dynamical" systems. We use the term "dynamical systems" to refer to the strand of theorizing based in mathematics. In contrast, we use the term "dynamic systems" to refer to the approach in SLA research that does not adhere to this mathematical framework.

The key claim that we explore in this chapter is that acknowledgement of dynamic aspects of systems makes prediction impossible. This claim has been made by SLA researchers such as de Bot (2008) and Larsen-Freeman (2009). We review foundational aspects of dynamical systems theorizing and use the analysis of those aspects to present evidence that the claims of the impossibility of prediction referred to above are not consistent with the mathematical foundations and key tenets of dynamical systems theory. The rationale underpinning our argument is that if prediction is, in fact, possible in dynamical systems, then the extensive bodies of work on variation in second language acquisition have relevance for future SLA work. However, we also point to some of the challenges involved in doing this, in particular how the underlying mathematical constructs are defined and operationalized.

We then turn our attention to selected studies that have made use of two core concepts from dynamical systems theorizing to point to translation issues that occur when attempting to bring concepts from one discipline into another. We identify some of the challenges that these studies

DOI: 10.4324/9781003155683-3

encountered in translating the original mathematical concepts. On the basis of this analysis, we suggest some key issues that SLA researchers will need to engage with if they wish to take advantage of the rich possibilities of dynamical systems thinking.

What is the dynamic approach to SLA?

In the past two or three decades, the field of second language acquisition (SLA) research has witnessed the emergence of a new approach that invokes findings and constructs from mathematics and the natural sciences to focus on the dynamics of SLA. The perception of this new approach by the research community has been summarized as follows by Dörnyei et al. (2014):

> When nonlinear system dynamics was introduced into SLA research – under various rubrics such as chaos theory (Larsen-Freeman, 1997), emergentism (Ellis & Larsen-Freeman, 2006), dynamic systems theory (de Bot et al., 2007) and complexity theory (Larsen-Freeman & Cameron, 2008) – the new approach, which may be seen as the 'dynamic turn' in SLA, resonated with many scholars because nonlinear system dynamics appeared to nicely describe several puzzling language learning phenomena.
>
> (p. 1)

The "dynamic turn" referred to in association with the dynamic approach reflects that its proponents define their view of SLA in contrast to what they perceive as "the traditional approach," which appears to subsume all other approaches to SLA (see de Bot & Larsen-Freeman, 2011). The dynamic turn means that proponents of the dynamic approach break with several traditions that they see as being incorrect in their underlying assumptions and counterproductive for the advancement of SLA research (de Bot et al., 2013; Larsen-Freeman, 2017). In this chapter, we will use the collective term "dynamic approach" in relation to the body of work that Dörnyei et al. (2014) analyze, albeit acknowledging that other researchers in (applied) linguistics have made use of alternative dynamic approaches (see Pienemann, 2007).

Larsen-Freeman (2019) attributes two key characteristics to the view of the learning process associated with the dynamic approach:

> There are two mechanisms in accounting for change in complex systems: iteration and co-adaptation. . . . In a complex system, what results from one iteration is used as the starting point for the next iteration. Thus the starting point or initial condition is always different, and the consequence is the system's mutability.
>
> (p. 67)

And using an L1 example for co-adaptation:

> As a child and its caregiver interact, the language resources of each are dynamically altered, as each adapts to the other. . . . Co-adaptation is an iterative process, with each partner adjusting to the other over and over again.
>
> (p. 67)

The emergence of the dynamic approach to SLA was accompanied by extensive references to popular accounts of the development of science in the 19th and early 20th centuries[1] (e.g., Briggs & Peat, 1989; Gleick, 1987) (for further details, see Pienemann et al., forthcoming). These authors (Briggs & Peat, 1989; Gleick, 1987), as well as academic accounts including those by Mitchell (2009) and Feldman (2019), report that the world of Newton's classical mechanics appeared to some contemporaries to be structured in its entirety by laws of nature that can be calculated to the point at which, ultimately, knowledge of all of the world's points derived from accurate measurement permits the prediction of all of its future states (Briggs & Peat, 1989; Gleick, 1987). An extension of this interpretation is that living creatures can be seen as biological machines whose behavior and metabolism can be calculated in the same way as the rest of the universe – as demonstrated aptly by the work of the 1904 Nobel Laureate Ivan Petrovitch Pavlov. According to popular accounts, this world of certainties was shattered late in the 19th and early in the 20th centuries when nonperiodic (i.e., nonrepeating) patterns were discovered in areas of science where regularity had been assumed. Key examples of this were when the long-term calculation of celestial mechanics (planetary movement) produced results that did not strictly repeat (Poincaré, 1993) and when Heisenberg identified the "uncertainty principle" in quantum mechanics in 1927. This principle reflected the insight that not all characteristics of a particle such as its position and momentum can be simultaneously measured, making features such as "location" uncertain. The uncertainty principle rendered impossible a foundational requirement of the attempt in Newtonian physics to measure precisely all characteristics of elements of a system (simultaneously). Recognition of this principle made it much more complex to model the behavior of certain kinds of systems.

The behavior of these special kinds of "complex-to-model" phenomena has been the subject of intense mathematical work since late in the 19th century. The mathematical principles that had been developed to model such complex long-term behavior of planets in Poincaré's work in the last 20 years of the 19th century (Poincaré, 1993) had meanwhile been transferred to various natural science disciplines and engineering, revealing similar underlying principles. Particularly complex aspects of this behavior received the popular name of "chaos" in association with the mathematical insights outlined in Li and Yorke (1975).

Based on popular accounts of the history of mathematics and science such as Gleick's, proponents of the dynamic approach to SLA (e.g., Larsen-Freeman, 2011, 2012, 2017) portrayed the various insights above as a rupture, a massive discontinuity from a world of certainty to a world of unpredictability. In contrast, however, historians of mathematics (e.g., Aubin & Dalmedico, 2002) saw this process as far more continuous, where principles such as classical mechanics that had been established earlier were not abolished but rather augmented by principles with a wider focus.

Nevertheless, the discontinuous view took priority in SLA work and, furthermore, was viewed as compatible with postmodernism and post-structuralism (see Larsen-Freeman, 2017). This sense of rupture can be seen in the way in which Larsen-Freeman (2017) portrayed Newtonian science:

> Complex dynamic systems . . . exhibit nonlinearity. Byrne and Callaghan (2014: 18) state that 'Linearity is foundational to 'Newtonian' science by which we mean scientific accounts in which we can describe a current state in terms of values of parameters . . . and have a universal specification [or law], which describes how that state will change if values in the parameters change.' By way of contrast, in a non-linear system, a small change in one parameter can have huge implications downstream, when a 'tipping point' is reached, so predictability is compromised.
>
> (pp. 16–17)

In this view, Newton's work is seen as something that limits the further development of science and research and as something that needs to be left behind, to be replaced by accounts of "nonlinear systems." We will return to the validity of this characterization of Newton's work and of nonlinear systems in the next section. To put that discussion in context, we now focus on the interpretation of selected dynamical features used in SLA research in association with the dynamic approach.

The interpretation of the dynamic approach that has emerged in SLA research is characterized by an antireductionist stance and, for some proponents (Larsen-Freeman, 2017), also by an association with postmodernism and post-structuralism:

> in common with CT [complexity theory] is post-structuralists' departure from the cornerstone of modernism, that of the goal of depicting an accurately reducible world. CT shares with post-modernism a rejection of reductionism, and with it, recognizes that our understandings can only be partial and provisional. As Derrida (1978: 270) proposes, 'There are forces at play which we can never completely predict or control.'
>
> (pp. 13–14)

The exact definition of reductionism that is implied in this approach remains unclear in this quotation as well as in the other accounts of the dynamic approach (for a more detailed analysis, see the review of the dynamic approach by Pienemann et al., forthcoming). Larsen-Freeman and other proponents of the dynamic approach have not been explicit about whether the focus of their antireductionist stance refers to ontological reductionism (the attempt to reduce a system to the smallest possible number of parts), methodological reductionism (the attempt to explain the workings of a system by reference to the smallest possible number of parts of the system – even if there are many parts), or theory reductionism (the attempt to develop a more general theory and to reduce a theory to more basic terms). Instead, as we exemplify in what follows, proponents of the dynamic approach articulate a general skepticism concerning any attempt to analyze specific parts of a system without considering all of the parts that potentially contribute to the system. This attitude is derived from their axiom of "complete interconnectedness" (de Bot et al., 2007, p. 8) that is postulated to be present in all systems: "all variables are interrelated, and therefore changes in one variable will have an impact on all other variables that are part of the system." de Bot et al. (2007) extended this principle to all subsystems and between components of subsystems and sub-subsystems "from sub-molecular particles to the universe" (p. 8). They have also assumed that due to "complete interconnectedness" "[i]n many complex systems, the outcome of development over time can . . . not be calculated exactly" (de Bot et al., 2007, p. 8).

In attempting to explain the nature of dynamic systems, de Bot et al. (2007) further make the following claims about features of dynamic systems, albeit without explicit reference to sources in science:

- *Attractor states*: "As they [i.e. dynamic systems] develop over time, dynamic sub-systems appear to settle in specific states, so-called ATTRACTOR STATES, which are preferred but not necessarily predictable. . . . Attractor states are by definition temporary and not fixed" (p. 8).
- *The butterfly effect*: "Because the development of some dynamic systems appears to be highly dependent on their initial state, minor differences at the beginning may have dramatic consequences in the long run" (p. 8).
- *Nonlinearity*: "Related to this [i.e., the butterfly effect] is the notion of non-linearity, which means that there is a non-linear relation between the size of an initial perturbation of a system and the effect it may have in the long run" (p. 8).
- *Self-reorganisation*: "Regardless of their initial states, systems are constantly changing. They develop through interaction with their environment and through internal self-reorganisation" (sic.) (p. 8).
- *Variation*: "Because systems are constantly in flow, they will show variation, which makes them sensitive to specific input at a given point in time and some other input at another point in time" (p. 8).

- *Resources*: "In natural systems, development is dependent on resources: . . . all natural systems will come to a still stand [sic.] when no additional energy is added to the system.[2]" (p. 8)

The proponents associated with the dynamic approach contrast these constructs with their assumptions about "traditional SLD [second language development] research" (van Dijk et al., 2011, p. 60). In their view, traditional approaches to SLA assume a predetermined order of acquisition that depends solely on a single factor (such as universal grammar or processing), whereas the dynamic approach brings with it the assumption that anything that connects with the learner's life (no matter how remotely) has the potential to influence development (in unforeseen ways) (de Bot & Larsen-Freeman, 2011, pp. 10–12). This specific view of how acquisition unfolds made it appear to proponents of the dynamic approach that traditional approaches uniformly assume that L2 development is "linear," which they interpret to mean that (all) traditional approaches to SLA assume that it follows a preprogrammed, one-dimensional trajectory (Lowie et al., 2011). Proponents of the dynamic approach argued that "most" traditional approaches try to "explain away" L2 variation (see de Bot et al., 2007). They claimed that what is needed is "a theory that does not regard real-life messy facts as 'noise' but as part of the 'sound' you get in real life" (de Bot et al., 2007, p. 7). In the arguments associated with the dynamic approach, the traditional approach has been described as having a static view of L2 development and making recourse to mental representations and innate ideas that are superfluous because the dynamics of the developmental process are sufficient to explain the emergence of new concepts and forms (for instance, Lowie, 2013).

The narrative of the dynamic approach glosses over substantial differences between different approaches to SLA. These differences can be seen, for instance, in the volume *Theories in Second Language Acquisition* (VanPatten et al., 2020) that surveys current approaches to SLA including functional, usage-based, skill-based, sociocultural, psycholinguistic, and other approaches. The substantial differences between various current approaches were not discussed in works advocating for the dynamic approach, and, in addition, the prior existence of many of the assumed innovations of the dynamic approach including the role of variation was not acknowledged (see Pienemann, 2007).

Larsen-Freeman (1997, 2011, 2017), de Bot et al. (2007), and other proponents of the dynamic approach argued for a new beginning in relation to SLA research. These authors invoked key notions from dynamical systems theory and used those notions to describe SLA phenomena in what they framed as a new and more appropriate "language." Their purpose in doing this was to gain new insights into SLA. One example of this redescription of SLA phenomena is related to fossilization/stabilization. de Bot et al. (2013) identify the so-called basic variety (Klein & Perdue,

1997) of an L2 as a linguistic system that has stopped developing, and they assumed that it had reached an attractor state. A second example is mentioned by Dörnyei et al. (2014, p. 1): "[T]he so-called 'butterfly effect' explained why language teaching input sometimes had considerable impact on the learners' progress, whereas at other times it led to only minimal, if any, uptake." However, this "rewording" of phenomena does not explain them. As Robertson et al. (1993) put it: "The danger lies in the temptation to naively adopt a new terminology or set of metaphors, to merely redescribe the phenomena we have been studying for so long, and then conclude that we have explained them" (p. 119).

In the lack of explicit definition and explicit consideration of how the ideas that have been discussed can move from the physical world to SLA, the view of dynamism that has become widespread is metaphorical rather than grounded in clear mathematical definitions. Nevertheless, the metaphors have led to a number of specific claims as to what can (or cannot) be achieved by SLA research. Two assumptions underpin these claims. The first assumption (see de Bot et al., 2007) is that all aspects of the language being acquired as well as features of the context of learners' acquisition are interconnected and capable of influencing one another (sometimes opaquely). This assumption has led to a core claim that we seek to engage with in this chapter, namely that predictions about language development and outcomes are impossible because many different features could potentially influence the process (e.g., Larsen-Freeman, 2017). The second assumption is presented in de Bot and Larsen-Freeman (2011, p. 12). This assumption is that the nonlinear nature of second language development has consequences for the issue of predictability. According to them, "nonlinearity is closely related to the interconnectedness of the system. The more components interact, the more problematic it becomes to predict how the system will change" (p. 12). In this context, Larsen-Freeman (2011, p. 11) called for a separation between explanation and prediction and argued that "the usual scientific method, which calls for making predictions and then testing them, is fraught with problems from a complexity theory perspective. Systems and behavior can of course be described retrospectively – once change has happened; in fact, this is the central work of complexity theory" (p. 61). But the approach proposed by Larsen-Freeman (2011) rules out predictions of any kind; an exclusion that we will return to later.

In a similar vein, de Bot (2016) sees the main focus of the dynamic approach as describing developmental processes rather than seeking to explain them (with the corollary of being unable to make predictions):

> A somewhat problematic characteristic of a DST approach is that language development cannot really be explained: the factors playing a role in development may all be known, but how their interaction will change in the course of development cannot be predicted and may in that sense be chaotic. A system develops in a certain way because that is how this system develops. On the one hand, this is

> not a very satisfactory situation, because traditionally research has been about hypothesis generation and hypothesis testing. The full interconnectedness of systems means that isolating single variables as explanatory may be unproductive because the impact of that variable on all the other variables is not taken into account. For the moment it seems wise to accept that we cannot explain development and to focus on adequate descriptions of developmental processes.
>
> (p. 130)

This interpretation requires further consideration. An attempt to predict does not have to be inherently an attempt to identify a single variable as a cause of everything. Similarly, a predicted outcome does not have to be a single point or path. Acknowledging this insight means that in principle, an application to SLA of core claims of dynamical systems theorizing put forward in science and mathematics could offer a fascinating challenge for SLA theorizing and research. However, in our view, any attempt to apply dynamical systems theory to SLA in a way that would enable SLA researchers to explain and predict second language development would need to go beyond a metaphorical approach/application and incorporate some of the key mathematical principles underlying dynamical systems theorizing. As we seek to show, the mathematical principles of dynamical systems theorizing do allow for a range of predictions concerning the development of dynamical systems, although not necessarily for all of their aspects. If the mathematical principles allow for prediction, the implications for SLA research are vast. If prediction is possible, SLA research is not restricted to description, and issues such as variation do not have to be positioned as random aspects of individual character or social setting. As a corollary, if the mathematics permit prediction, then SLA researchers will need to engage much more extensively and systematically with mathematical ways of working.

Identifying whether dynamical systems permit prediction, therefore, requires a careful examination of key aspects of such systems and whether they are all the same. In particular, it requires examination of the nature of dynamical systems and how aspects of some or all of them permit or limit predictions about either or both their short- and long-term behavior. One of the issues that underpins this discussion is clarifying how deterministic dynamical systems operate. To achieve this, we need to first consider how dynamical systems have been described and analyzed.

Some key features of dynamical systems theorizing invoked in the dynamic approach to SLA

The potential

Mitchell (2009, p. 15) pointed out that "Dynamical Systems Theory (or *dynamics*) concerns the description and prediction of systems that exhibit complex *changing* behavior at the macroscopic level, emerging from the collective actions of many interacting components." In order to be able to make predictions about these systems, dynamical systems are modeled mathematically. We now introduce some of the basic mathematical concepts underlying dynamical systems theory. We begin by briefly sketching out the origin and the tradition of dynamical systems work with a focus on the issue of predictability.

General problems and proposed solutions

The long history of the study of dynamical systems can be traced back to Aristotle, who developed a theory of motion (although, as pointed out by Mitchell (2009, p. 16), the two major principles that his theory was based on turned out to be wrong). Other prominent scholars who studied systems that change over time were Galileo and Kepler, who, in the 16th century, focused on planetary motion. Newton's work on what is known today as *classical mechanics* and his dynamic account of gravity published in 1687 in *Philosophiae Naturalis Principia Mathematica* are often considered as "the culmination or apotheosis of the scientific revolution" (Feldman, 2019, p. 46). As had Poincaré (1993) earlier, Mitchell (2009, p. 19) argued that "Newton's laws are the foundations of dynamics: they explain the motion of the planets, and everything else, in terms of the basic notions of force and mass." She maintains that Newton's contribution to dynamics – his universal law of gravity that "applies everywhere in the universe" – is "now the backbone of modern science" (Mitchell, 2009, p. 19). One consequence of Newton's insights was the emergence of a mechanistic worldview that portrayed the world as "machine-like" (Feldman, 2019, p. 47). In this mechanistic perspective of a "clockwork universe" the laws of physics mean that the universe's behavior can be ultimately explained and predicted by simple mathematical rules. This view of predictive determinism was articulated by the French mathematician Laplace. It entailed that "sufficient knowledge of the laws of nature and appropriate boundary conditions will enable a superior intelligence to predict the future states of the physical world and to retrodict its past states with infinite precision" (Falkenburg & Weinert, 2009, p. 307).

> The present state of nature is evidently a consequence of what it was in the preceding moment, and if we conceive of an intelligence which at a given instant comprehends of all the relations of the entities of this universe, it could state the respected positions, motions, and general effects of all these entities at any time in the past or future.
>
> (Laplace, 1776, as cited in Holton & May, 1993, p. 97)

The superior intelligence, also known as the Laplacean demon, would be able to make precise predictions about both the past and the future of the universe, as, according to Laplace, these are causally related: "We ought then to consider the present state of the universe as the effect of its previous state and as the cause of that which is to follow" (Laplace, 1995, p. 2).

This Laplacean worldview aligned with the view that it is, in principle, possible to obtain complete knowledge about the present state of a dynamical system in order to be able to make precise predictions about its future states. However, the principles underlying the view of perfect predictability were seriously challenged by two scientific discoveries. The first challenge came from Werner Heisenberg's work in quantum physics. He demonstrated that it is, in principle, not possible to precisely and simultaneously measure both the position and the momentum of a particle.

The second challenge relates to the importance of initial conditions for the subsequent development of dynamical systems. This issue had been articulated earlier by the mathematician Henri Poincaré, who is generally considered to be the father of the modern theory of dynamical systems. He had studied the so-called three-body problem in the context of a competition that celebrated the 60th birthday of the king of Sweden in 1889. Poincaré was awarded the prize for his work addressing the question of whether the orbits of the planets in the solar system were stable (Poincaré, 2017, p. vii).[3] Whereas Newton had solved the two-body problem – "the problem of calculating the motion of the earth around the sun, given the inverse-square law of gravitational attraction between them" (Strogatz, 2015, p. 2), the three-body problem turned out to be much more difficult to solve. As Strogatz (2015) observed, "[a]fter decades of effort, it was eventually realized that the three-body problem was essentially *impossible* to solve, in the sense of obtaining explicit formulas for the motions of the three bodies" (p. 2). In his attempt to find a solution to the complex three-body problem, Poincaré made the crucial observation that certain kinds of dynamical systems display *sensitivity to initial conditions*.

In the set of systems that show the kind of sensitivity to initial conditions observed by Poincaré, small differences in their initial conditions have huge consequences in the long run. This means that for these specific kinds of dynamical systems, accurate predictions of their long-term behavior are not possible:

> [I]t may happen that slight differences in the initial conditions produce very great differences in the final phenomena; a slight error in the former would make an enormous error in the latter. Prediction becomes impossible [. . .]
>
> (Poincaré, 1913, p. 398)

Poincaré's realization that not all dynamical systems seem to behave in the same way led to the discovery of what came to be called (mathematical) chaos, "in which a deterministic system exhibits aperiodic behavior that depends sensitively on the initial conditions, thereby rendering long-term prediction impossible" (Strogatz, 2015, p. 2). It is important to emphasize the "long-term" modification of "prediction" in this statement, because there can still be short-term predictions even in systems in which long-term modifications of behavior cannot be precisely predicted.

Chaos and dynamical systems

Li and Yorke (1975) specified the circumstances in which mathematical chaos could emerge in a system and gave the name "chaos" to this particular aspect of dynamical systems. The name was popularized by authors such as Gleick (1987) and Briggs and Peat (1989), and in the process, an interpretation emerged that equated the concept of mathematical chaos resulting from dynamical systems with the everyday meaning of the word and its association with a random, unorderly state. However, it is important to see the difference between the technical and the popular terms in order to appreciate the underlying principles of mathematical chaos and their implications for making predictions in dynamical systems. It is indeed possible to determine (and therefore predict) when chaos emerges and how this mathematical chaos relates to the behavior of dynamical systems. We will start unpacking these concepts by defining the key notion of a deterministic system.

Deterministic dynamical systems

Most references associated with the dynamic approach that refer to work on dynamical systems (including Gleick, 1987; Briggs & Peat, 1989) deal with what is known technically as "deterministic dynamical systems." While reference to deterministic dynamical systems is implicit in these accounts, it is made explicit in more academic accounts including those by Mitchell (2009) and Feldman (2019) as well as technical accounts by Devaney (2003) and Hasselblatt and Katok (2003). Feldman (2019) provided the following definition of a deterministic system:

> A system is deterministic if it follows a well defined, unambiguous rule. The same input always gives the same output. If a system is deterministic, the itinerary is completely determined by knowledge of the rule and the exact initial condition.
>
> (p. 97)

However, it can also be the case that a deterministic dynamical system produces behavior that, on first inspection, appears to be random, as the sequence (for instance of numbers) it produces seems to follow no pattern (Feldman, 2019, p. 98). But it turns out that the underlying pattern is the simple equation that produces the output. And this equation could be easily uncovered as an encryption method – in contrast to a truly random process that could be a more reliable basis for encryption. This rather puzzling finding that some deterministic systems can produce irregularity may initially seem counterintuitive. In order to fully appreciate the significance of this characteristic of some dynamical systems, we review the basic mathematical principles/operations underlying dynamical systems.[4]

Iterated functions as an example of a dynamical system

According to Feldman (2019, p. 1) "[a] *dynamical system* is any mathematical system that changes in time according to a well specified rule." In mathematics, one type of dynamical system is captured by *iterated functions*, and we will focus on these functions to introduce some key notions underlying dynamical systems theory.

Generally speaking, a function is a relation that associates a set of numbers with a second set of numbers as in the example in (1):

$$f(x) = \tfrac{1}{2}\,x + 2 \qquad (1)$$

In the case of an iterated function, this function is applied repeatedly. The output of the first application of the function is used as input to its next application. This process is called iteration, and an iterated function constitutes a dynamical system because it is "a mathematical entity that changes in time according to a well-defined rule" (Feldman, 2019, p. 2). The number that the function is first applied to is the initial condition, and the sequence of numbers that results from the repeated application of the function to its output is called the orbit or itinerary/trajectory. The initial condition is labeled x_0, the first value obtained by applying the function to x_0 is denoted x_1 and so on. However, not all iterated functions behave in the same way.

An iterated function with a fixed point

The outcomes of the iterative process discussed earlier are demonstrated in Table 2.1 with the function f in (1) and the value 2 as the starting point or initial condition. The first application of the function with $x_0 = 2$, yields the value 3 as output (i.e. $f(2) = \tfrac{1}{2}\,(2) + 2$). A second application of the function f to the output of the first application, $x_1 = 3$, yields 3.5, ($f(3) = \tfrac{1}{2}\,(3) + 2$). The repeated application of f to the obtained output yields the iterates displayed in Table 2.1 (for the first 10 applications):

The orbit of the function $f(x) = \tfrac{1}{2}\,x + 2$ with the initial condition $x_0 = 2$ can be plotted as a graph, as shown in the top plot in Figure 2.1.

The two plots in Figure 2.1 show that the orbits approach the value of 4 regardless of the initial condition. This value is called a fixed point of the function $f(x)$. When f is applied to 4, its value does not change: $f(4) = 4$, ($f(4) = \tfrac{1}{2}\,(4) + 2$). For this particular function, the long-term

Table 2.1 Orbit/trajectory for the function $f(x) = \frac{1}{2}x + 2$ with the initial condition $x_0 = 2$

t	x_t
0	2
1	3
2	3.5
3	3.875
4	3.9375
5	3.98675
6	3.993375
7	3.9966875
8	3.99834375
9	3,999171875
10	3.9995859375

behavior of the system approaches 4. This is true for different initial states, as illustrated in the bottom plot in Figure 2.1 for the three initial states 2, 6, and 10. The initial conditions that are larger than 4 produce output that gets smaller and the orbit gets closer and closer to 4. But the initial condition that is smaller than 4 produces output that gets larger and, as a result, also moves closer and closer to 4.

The fixed point at 4 is called an attractor, as "[n]earby orbits are pulled toward it; it attracts nearby points" (Feldman, 2019, p. 7). This kind of attractor is stable "because if one is at a fixed point and then a perturbation moves you a little bit away, you will return to the fixed point" (Feldman, 2019, p. 7). Feldman (2019, p. 9) provides the following definition of a stable fixed point: "A fixed point x is stable if there is an open interval around x such that any initial conditions in this interval get closer and closer to the fixed point x."

Dynamical systems, stability, and instability

Dynamical systems can also have more than one fixed point, as in the example function $f(x) = x$ from Feldman (2019, p. 5), which can be shown to have the fixed points 0 and 1. Introducing a further layer of complexity, not all fixed points are stable – unlike the one introduced in Figure 2.1. Feldman (2019, pp. 7–9) illustrated the phenomenon of instability in relation to the fixed point 0 of $f(x) = x$. This kind of fixed point is called unstable or repelling, as the orbit of an initial condition that is relatively close to 0 (e.g., 0.05) does not get closer to 0. The two types of fixed points are schematically illustrated in Figure 2.2.

A stable fixed point is illustrated by the position of the ball in a dip in (a). If the ball is subject to small perturbations resulting in it being moved around slightly, it will always return to the fixed point. The situation is

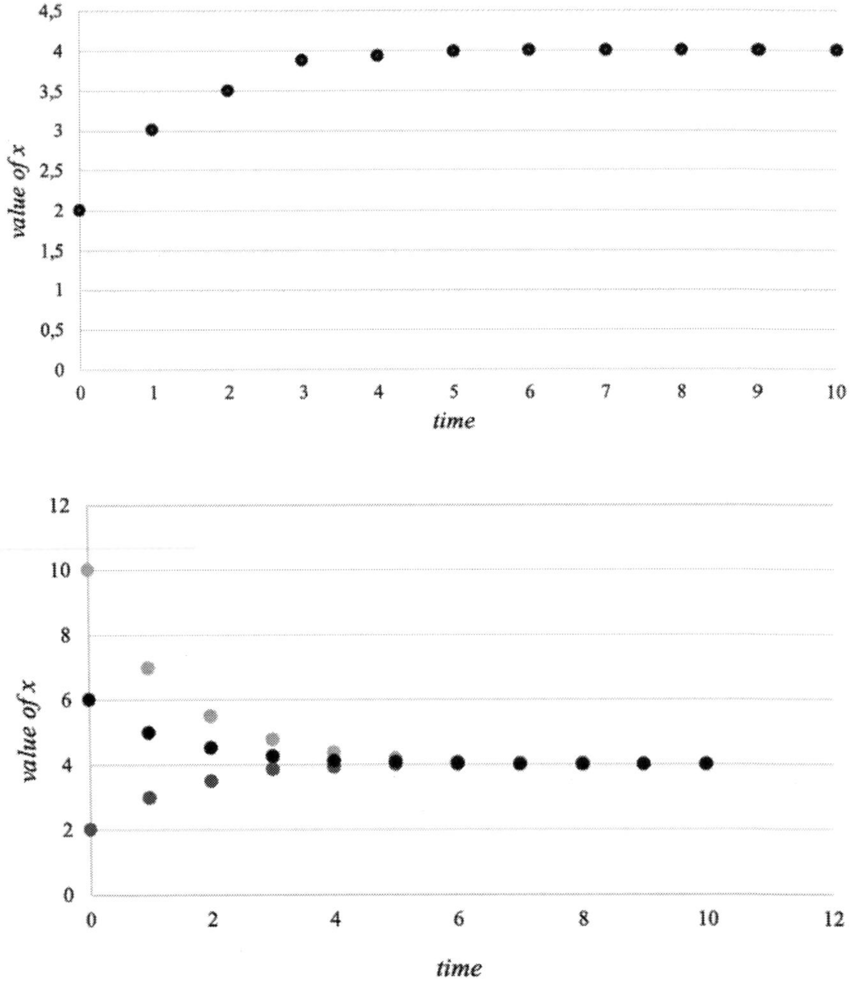

Figure 2.1 The top plot shows the orbit for $f(x) = ½\, x + 2$ with $x_0 = 2$; the bottom plot shows the orbits for three different initial states for the function $f(x) = ½\, x + 2$

Figure 2.2 Illustrations of (a) a stable (left) and (b) an unstable (right) fixed point

different for the unstable fixed point illustrated in relation to the ball on top of a mound in (b). If small perturbations cause the ball to move, it will not return to the unstable fixed point but instead will roll down the mound.

What is important in the context of the behavior of dynamical systems is that stable, fixed points are insensitive to initial conditions and small perturbations, such that if the system is slightly moved away from this point (e.g., due to external influences, such as wind), it will return to the fixed point over time. However, in contrast, unstable fixed points are sensitive to small changes such that a system that moves away from the fixed point will not return. Feldman (2019, p. 9) has pointed out that "[t]he upshot is that in dynamical systems one is particularly focused on stable behavior, as usually it is only stable behavior that is observed." In other words, the majority of dynamical systems that have been recognized are stable.

The possibilities of and limits on predictability – predicting stability and chaos

The iterated functions introduced here are all examples of deterministic dynamical systems. They adhere to specific, well-defined rules and they display specific types of predictable, long-term behavior. Thus, knowledge of the function and the initial condition of the system allows for predictions concerning its future states. However, not all deterministic dynamical systems behave in this way, as some display surprising and chaotic behavior.

The potential chaotic behavior of deterministic systems can be demonstrated with what is variably referred to as either a logistic equation or a logistic map, which constitutes a particular type of iterative function. According to Mitchell (2009, p. 27), the logistic map "is perhaps the most famous equation in the science of dynamical systems and chaos."

The logistic map has been used by population biologists to describe the growth of a population, including taking into account issues such as limited food supply and overcrowding. In our example, we consider a population of koalas whose development is monitored at discrete points in time, in our example once a year, over a specific time period. This allows us to describe the population by an iterated function, as in (2).

$$P_{n+1} = r(P_n) \qquad (2)$$

In this equation, P_n refers to the koala population at the first time of observation, P_{n+1} denotes their population one year later, and r constitutes the growth parameter of the population. One possible scenario is that the population grows constantly each year without any intervening factors. This would lead to an exponential growth, as illustrated in Figure 2.3 for an initial population of 300 koalas and a growth parameter

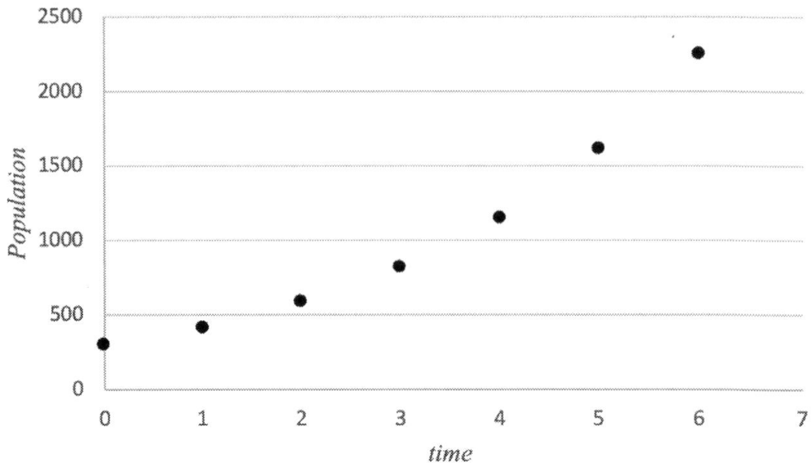

Figure 2.3 Exponential growth of koala population

of 1.4. This map would result in populations in subsequent years of 420, 588, 823, etc.

However, in order to model the development of the koala population more precisely, it makes sense to take factors into account apart from the population's birthrate, such as its death rate and the maximum *carrying capacity* of their habitat, i.e., the maximum number of koalas that a specific habitat can support (see Mitchell, 2009, p. 25).

These factors are taken into account in the logistic map given in (3).

$$x_{t+1} = rx_t (1 - x_t) \quad (3)$$

The rationale of the logistic map is described as follows by Mitchell (2009): x_t denotes the ratio of the current koala population to the maximum population that the habitat can support, the so-called fraction of carrying capacity (Mitchell, 2009, p. 305). The parameter r determines the growth rate, which accounts for the combined effect of the birth rate and the death rate. At $r < 1$, the population will get smaller, at $r = 1$ it will stay the same, and at $r > 1$ it will grow.[5] According to Feldman (2019), the logistic equation "is a qualitative model [. . .] used to capture in broad strokes possible features of the dynamics of a population that has some limits to its growth" (p. 67). As Feldman further noted, this "deceptively simple dynamical system" (p. 67) has a number of striking properties that illustrate the mathematical notion of chaos.

In what follows, we demonstrate the predictability of various dynamical systems, including showing how they vary with different initial conditions and showing the circumstances in which stability breaks down.

According to Feldman (2019, p. 70), the system can display two types of stable behavior, fixed points and cycles, depending on the value of the growth parameter *r*.

We illustrate the first type by choosing the growth parameter $r = 1.5$ and plotting the orbits for two different initial conditions that are specified by using the fractions of carrying capacity (the relationship between the current population and the potentially largest population that could be supported). The two hypothetical initial conditions are $x_0 = 0.05$ and $y_0 = 0.99$.[6] The orbits that emerge from these two initial conditions are shown in the upper plot in Figure 2.4 for the first 40 iterations.

The top plot in Figure 2.4 shows that the orbits of each of the two different initial conditions approach $x \approx 0.33$, which is the attracting fixed point of the system. This means that the system is stable, as the population will, over time, approach this value no matter the population's initial state or other external factors that might disturb the population at one point or another.

The second stable behavior of the system relates to cycles. This is the case for systems in which the growth parameter *r* ranges between about 3.0 and approximately 3.57. If $r = 3.2$, the system shows periodic behavior, as demonstrated in the middle plot in Figure 2.4 that displays the orbits for the same two initial conditions as in the top plot, $x_0 = 0.05$ and $y_0 = 0.99$.

The orbits in the middle plot in Figure 2.4 show that this system is stable, but instead of attracting to a single fixed point, it oscillates between two values (0.51304 and 0.79946). After a number of iterations, the system is pulled into this period-two cycle (see also Mitchell, 2009, pp. 29–30). This figure demonstrates that the koala population does not converge to one particular equilibrium value but instead oscillates between two values with a stable pattern of growth and decline, which repeats itself every second year and is identical for the two initial conditions after year 15.

A further qualitative change in the system can be observed at an *r* value between 3.4 and 3.5. Independent of the initial condition x_0, the period doubles, and the system now oscillates between four values, as can be seen in the bottom plot in Figure 2.4 with $r = 3.5$ and the two initial conditions of $x_0 = 0.9$ and $y_0 = 0.1$. In this system, it eventually takes four iterations for the koala population to repeat, and all initial conditions are pulled into the same period-four cycle with the values at approximately 0.875, 0.382, 0.826, and 0.500. A further increase of *r* closer to approximately 3.569946 leads to further changes in the system – at all transition points, the period doubles again, as will be further outlined when we introduce the notion of *bifurcations* and discuss the route from stable to unstable or chaotic systems.

The above examples clearly illustrate that for such stable systems – characterized by fixed points or cycles – predictions concerning their long-term behavior are possible. However, the logistic map also yields

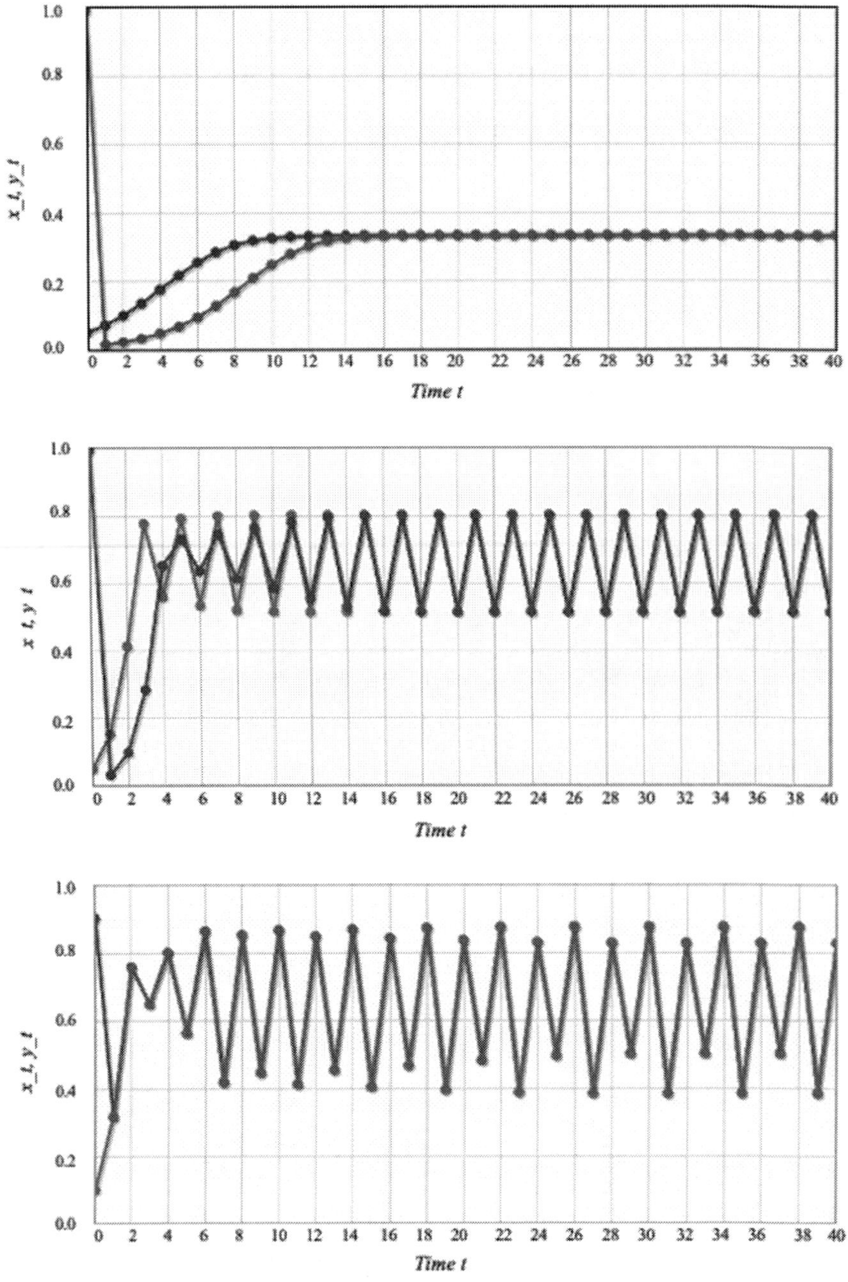

Figure 2.4 Orbits for the logistic equations for koala populations with different initial conditions and *r* values. This figure as well as the following ones were created with the program released by K. N. Springer. January 2014. © 2014 Santa Fe Institute (ComplexityExplorer.org)

systems that behave aperiodically. This seems to be the case with larger r values (starting from approximately 3.569946). The orbit for the equation with $r = 4$ shows this kind of aperiodic behavior. Two observations can be made related to the orbits for this logistic map. First, the population change does not become periodic but instead behaves chaotically in that it does not settle into a cycle but instead "continues to bounce around fairly irregularly" (Feldman, 2019, p. 71). This is not only the case for the first few iterations but applies to the system until infinity. Feldman (2019) pointed out that "one can show mathematically that the orbits of the logistic equation [. . .] are aperiodic" (p. 72). Second, it can be observed that this system is sensitive to initial conditions, i.e., a small change in the initial condition leads to a different trajectory. This is illustrated in two different ways in Figure 2.5 for the orbits of the logistic equation with $r = 4$ and two new initial conditions $x_0 = 0.3$ and the only very marginally

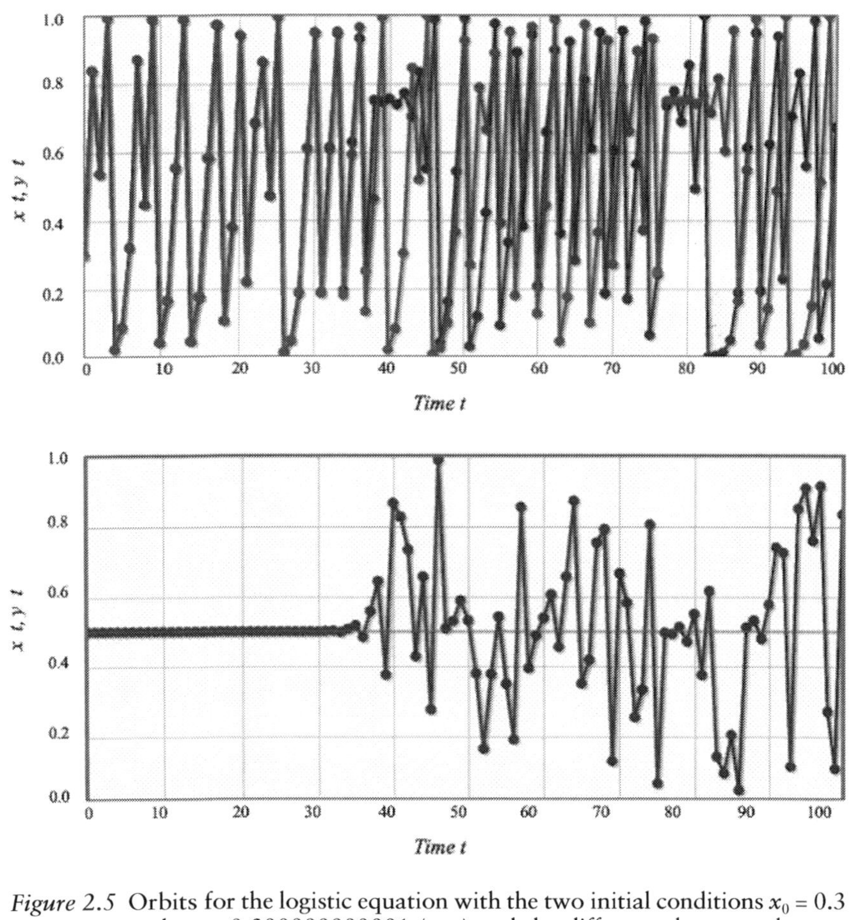

Figure 2.5 Orbits for the logistic equation with the two initial conditions $x_0 = 0.3$ and $y_0 = 0.300000000001$ (top) and the difference between the two orbits $(x_t - y_t)$ (bottom)

different $y_0 = 0.300000000001$. In the top plot in Figure 2.5, the trajectories of the two initial conditions are depicted, but the early course of the curve representing the initial condition $x_0 = 0.3$ is hidden by the curve for the initial condition $y_0 = 0.300000000001$ until about Time 34. Although the differences between the two initial conditions are only marginal and, initially, both curves behave in the same way, they start to slowly diverge after 22 iterations (even though this is not visible in the figure). This divergence becomes larger and larger over time, as the two orbits pull apart from each other. This is reflected in the curve in the bottom plot in Figure 2.5 that represents the difference between the two orbits ($x_t - y_t$).

This example shows that "complex or complicated behavior can emerge from a simple dynamical system" (Feldman, 2019, p. 73) and that in some cases, a deterministic dynamical system shows sensitive dependence on initial conditions such that "very small initial errors grow and become arbitrarily large" (Feldman, 2019, p. 78). This sensitivity to initial conditions is metaphorically known as the butterfly effect that was referred to earlier. The metaphorical notion of a butterfly flapping its wings in Brazil and causing a tornado in Texas relates to the title of a talk by the meteorologist Lorenz in 1972 to illustrate an unstable dynamical system's sensitive dependence on initial conditions (Hilborn, 2004, p. 425).

The dynamical systems whose orbits were given in Figure 2.5 might create the impression that chaotic systems behave in a random way involving elements of chance, as no long-term predictions are possible. However, this is not the case. Feldman (2019) stated that

> [a] dynamical system is chaotic if it is deterministic with bounded, aperiodic orbits that have sensitive dependence on initial conditions. [. . .] The mathematical use of the word chaos does not align that well with its everyday use, where chaos denotes something that is lawless and completely without order or structure. Mathematical chaos is exquisitely lawful; a chaotic dynamical system obediently follows a deterministic rule in perpetuity. In fact, this obedience is the source of the butterfly effect. The system follows its rules so precisely that it depends sensitively on its initial conditions. To underscore this point, chaos is sometimes referred to as *deterministic chaos*.
>
> (p. 84)

As we have sought to illustrate, the process involved in generating a particular sequence by a deterministic dynamical system is indeed not random because the system follows rules that are precisely spelled out. However, the outcome of chaotic deterministic systems can be unpredictable and seemingly random, as we discussed in relation to encryption. As Feldman (2019) puts it:

> The same orderly, deterministic system can produce both predictable periodic behavior and unpredictable chaotic behavior. So randomness

and order aren't completely different things that we need to think of in different ways. In a sense, they are two sides of the same coin.

(p. 104)

Chaos is a constrained element within dynamical systems

We return now to the implications of these findings for the ability to make predictions about the development of a dynamical system. It is certainly the case that the insight that there are systems that show sensitive dependence on initial conditions imposes restrictions on the ability to make precise long-term predictions. What is more, this challenge to prediction is not simply a practical issue that could be solved by gaining more accurate knowledge about their initial condition but rather seems to make prediction in principle impossible. Mitchell (2009, p. 33) claimed that "the presence of chaos in a system implies that perfect prediction *à la* Laplace is impossible not only in practice but also *in principle,* since we can never know x_0 to infinitely many decimal places." At quick glance, these insights could lead to the conclusion that predictions are impossible. However, this would be a much too simplistic view of dynamical systems.

As we have demonstrated, some of the basic mathematical notions underlying dynamical systems mean that by no means all deterministic systems are chaotic. Feldman (2019) argued that "[w]hile chaos is a common phenomenon, non-chaotic (and hence predictable) dynamical systems are very common as well" (p. 100). He also pointed to the finding that the unpredictability of the development of chaotic dynamical systems only applies to their long-term behavior: "chaotical systems *are* predictable – they're just not predictable for very long. How long they are predictable will vary, and in some cases the predictability window might be sufficient for whatever task is at hand" (p. 99).

And furthermore, even chaotic dynamical systems exhibit features that are stable and therefore do not show sensitivity to small perturbations or changes in the initial conditions, such as attractors (Feldman, 2019, pp. 101–102). Pondering on the question of whether the discovery of chaos necessarily needs us to radically revise our scientific understanding of the possibilities of making predictions, Feldman (2019) states that:

> [a]t one level, I think the phenomenon of chaos need not obligate us to fundamentally alter the Newtonian worldview. The dynamical systems we've been studying are deterministic; the world is still one of cause and effect. Rules are in place. However, these rules don't lead to order or predictability in the conventional sense. Chaos doesn't say that the world is ruleless, but it tells us that those rules can lead to random results. We can still imagine that we live in a mechanistic universe, but the gears are not as straightforward as we had imagined.
>
> (p. 102)

All chaotic systems share some characteristics

Finally, chaotic dynamical systems also display universal characteristics that can be observed across different systems. Mitchell (2009) maintains that "there turns out to be substantial order in mathematical chaos in the form of so-called *universal* features that are common to a wide range of chaotic systems" (p. 34). We will illustrate this rather surprising property of chaotic systems with the example of *bifurcations*, sudden transition points in the behavior of the system.

According to Feldman (2019, p. 106), "bifurcations are sudden qualitative changes in the behavior of a system as a parameter is varied continuously." When investigating these transition points, some remarkable regularities can be identified. One regularity relates to the so-called period-doubling route to chaos (e.g., Feldman, 2019, p. 143; Mitchell, 2009, p. 34). We will illustrate this characteristic of the systems' development by again using the logistic map. In our example of the logistic map, there are changes in the system's behavior that are related to the value of the growth parameter r. As we saw in the top plot in Figure 2.4, at r values less than approximately 3.0, the system is stable with a fixed-point attractor. In the top plot in Figure 2.4, the value of r was 1.5. The stability of this system means that independent of the initial conditions, the system approaches a fixed point (in this case $x \approx 0.33$). As the middle plot in Figure 2.4 illustrated, if r is between ≈ 3.0 and ≈ 3.5, the system is still considered to be stable but now oscillates in periodic cycles, as was shown for $r = 3.2$ and $r = 3.5$. Finally, as illustrated in the top plot in Figure 2.5 with $r = 4.0$, at r values larger than ≈ 3.569946, aperiodic cycles occur.

A closer look at the behavior of the system for the r values between 3.0 and 4.0 that were depicted in those figures shows that the system doubles its periods (or recurrence) at certain values of the parameter r. The cycle depicted in the middle plot in Figure 2.4 constitutes a period-two cycle, as the system oscillates between two points. This is also called a period-two attractor.

At an r value between 3.4 and 3.5, the cycle changes to a period-four oscillation, as the system now oscillates between four different values (see the bottom plot in Figure 2.4). As the r value increases, this period doubles again to 8 and continues to do so until the system comes to behave chaotically. This period-doubling behavior of the system can be seen in so-called bifurcation diagrams such as in Figure 2.6 for the logistic map with different r values. The vertical axis represents the final states of x and the horizontal axis gives the r values. In the diagram, the final attractor values of x are plotted for each r value (see Mitchell, 2009, p. 35).

Figure 2.6 shows that when r has the value of 2.6, x reaches a stable fixed-point attractor of 0.61538. At $r \approx 3.0$, a transition of the system occurs, and the system oscillates between two different values, i.e., a period-two attractor. This is shown by the change from a single line to

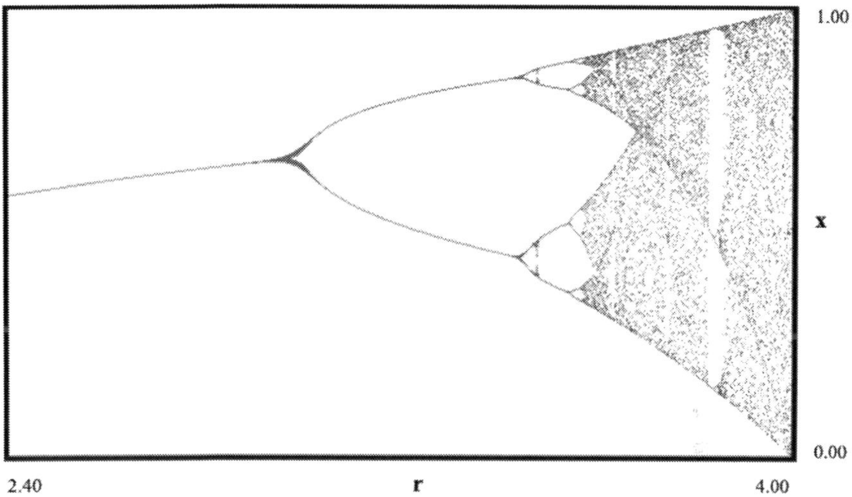

Figure 2.6 Bifurcation diagram for the logistic map. This figure was created with the program released by K. N. Springer. January 2014. © 2014 Santa Fe Institute (ComplexityExplorer.org)

two lines. A further transition in the system occurs at $r \approx 3.449$, when the period doubles to four (as shown by each of the two lines further dividing into two) and the attractor changes from a period-two to a period-four attractor. A further bifurcation can be observed at $r \approx 3.544$ with a change to a period-eight attractor. This process continues until chaos sets in at the value of $r \approx 3.569946$ (Mitchell, 2009, p. 35), where the system no longer oscillates only between a limited number of values. The significance of this is that it illustrates the technical meaning of "chaos" as "not random." There are limits and rules underpinning the behavior of this deterministic dynamical system that emerge at predictable points.

One example of this predictability is that the period-doubling bifurcations exhibit a universal characteristic that was discovered by Mitchell Feigenbaum in the 1970s. This characteristic is now known as the Feigenbaum constant. When investigating the *r* value at which the bifurcations occur, he observed that as the parameter value of *r* increases, the distance between the period-doubling bifurcations becomes smaller. This is captured in Table 2.2, which gives the approximate *r* values at which the first six bifurcations occur for the logistic map.

Feigenbaum noticed that with an increase in periods, the *r* values get closer together (Mitchell, 2009, p. 36). He also discovered that the rate at which the *r* values converge is constant at ≈ 4.669201609. Mitchell (2009) explained that "[w]hat this means is that as *R* increases, each new period doubling occurs about 4.6692016 times faster than the previous

Table 2.2 Approximate *r* values for the logistic map at which period-doubling bifurcations occur (Feldman, 2019, p. 145; Mitchell, 2009, p. 35)

Transition	*r*
1 → 2	3.00000
2 → 4	3.44949
4 → 8	3.54409
8 → 16	3.564407
16 → 32	3.568759
32 → 64	3.569692

one" (p. 36). She commented that "[t]his fact was interesting but not earth-shaking." What was striking, however, was the finding that this constant value – the Feigenbaum constant – is *universal*, as it is not restricted to the logistic map but is the same for all unimodal maps, i.e., maps "whose graph is parabola-shaped" (Mitchell, 2009, p. 35). A key point is that this relationship is not merely empirically observable but able to be written out as a mathematical definition and therefore used as a basis of predictions. Feigenbaum developed a theoretical approach to explain the universality of the constant value, using the so-called renormalization technique that originated in quantum field theory. This approach "has become a cornerstone in the understanding of chaos" (Mitchell, 2009, p. 36).

What makes these bifurcations extremely interesting in the study of dynamical systems is that the period-doubling route to chaos and the Feigenbaum constant are not restricted to mathematical systems but have also been observed in physical systems, such as electrical circuits, the laser, and specific chemical reactions or the flow of fluids (Mitchell, 2009, p. 36; Feldman, 2019, p. 149).

The implication of this mathematical understanding of dynamical systems is that certain predictions are possible. This applies in particular to those deterministic dynamical systems that behave conservatively and show stable behavior, either in terms of fixed-point or periodic cycle attractors. There are indeed systems that show sensitive dependence on initial conditions, and although these deterministic chaotic systems follow specific rules, their long-term behavior cannot be precisely predicted. Nevertheless, these systems also show aspects of stability as well as universal properties.[7]

In the logistic map that we have considered, we have shown that the system's behavior depends on the *r* value and that for the majority of *r* values, it is stable, which means that exact predictions can be made concerning the system's long-term development. As we have shown, if *r* is between 0 and about 3.5, the system is stable, and it does not exhibit sensitivity to initial conditions. If $r > 0$ and $< \approx 3.0$, the system approaches a fixed-point attractor, and if *r* is between ≈ 3.0 and 3.5, the attractor is

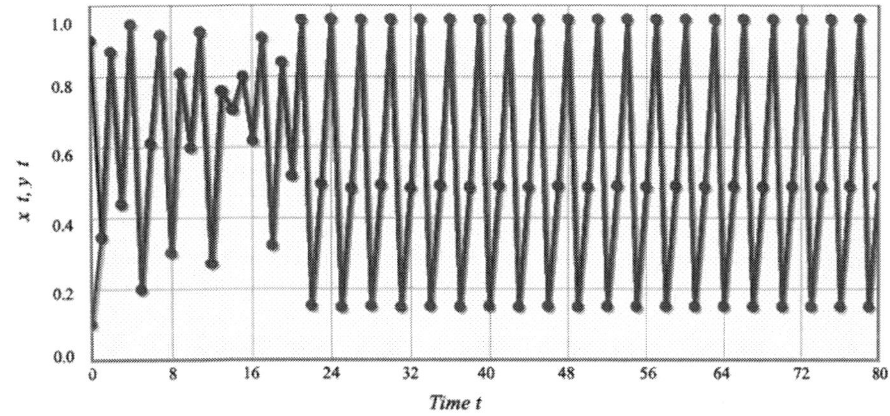

Figure 2.7 Orbits for the logistic equation with $r = 3.84$ and the two initial conditions $x_0 = 0.9$ and $y_0 = 0.1$

periodic (i.e., it recurs on a regular basis). It is only in the cases when r is between ≈ 3.569946 and 4.0 that the system behaves chaotically. And even in these cases, points of stability can be observed.

Strogatz (2015, p. 363) points out that for $r > \approx 3.569946$, "the orbit diagram reveals an unexpected mixture of order and chaos, with *periodic windows* interspersed between chaotic clouds of dots." One of these periodic windows begins near $r \approx 3.83$, where the system settles into a period-three cycle, oscillating between the approximate values 0.15, 0.49, and 0.96. At this point, it does not show sensitivity to initial conditions, as shown in Figure 2.7, which captures the first 80 iterations of the system with $r = 3.84$. As Figure 2.7 illustrates, for certain values, despite different initial conditions, initially unstable behavior eventually settles into a pattern of stable periodic behavior.

As Mitchell (2009) points out:

> [a]lthough the detailed behavior of a chaotic system cannot be predicted, there is some 'order in chaos' seen in universal properties common to large sets of chaotic systems, such as the period-doubling route to chaos and Feigenbaum's constant. Thus even though 'prediction becomes impossible' at the detailed level, there are some higher-level aspects of chaotic systems that are indeed predictable.
>
> (p. 38)

Interim conclusion

So far, we have sought to show that the mathematical underpinnings of dynamical systems theorizing are based in an understanding of order.

Even though that order is complex to perceive, there are ways in which it can be precisely and consistently calculated and the emergence (and disappearance) of chaos predicted. We have noted that chaos only appears in a minority of dynamical systems. These observations contrast with positions frequently associated with the dynamic approach that have become popular among SLA researchers. In other words, the assumption made by the dynamic approach that prediction is impossible is inconsistent with the mathematical foundations of dynamical systems theory.

The explanations of the mathematical foundations of dynamical systems theory that we have presented here do not conflict with the idea that systems are complex. Neither do they conflict with the claim that it is problematic to attempt to identify single causes or singular consequences of change. Equally, they do not require us to adopt a position on SLA research that distances it from key tenets of scientific research.

Instead, what the findings that we have presented point to is the possibility of acknowledging that the complexities of processes, systems, and relationships can be built into attempts to understand, explain, and, as a result, make testable predictions about features of learners' second language acquisition pathways. These pathways will not be single, straight lines or uniform in all respects for all learners. But neither does this mean that it will be, in principle, impossible to find commonalities and potentially also some features that all learners share.

How has the dynamic approach translated dynamical systems theory into SLA?

In this section, we will examine in more detail how two of the core assumptions of the dynamic approach introduced earlier in their mathematical context have been translated into the SLA context and how this translation process relates to the requirements of the mathematical theory from which the concepts have been adopted. We focus on the following key notions: (1) bifurcation and (2) attractor (state).

Bifurcation

As we pointed out, bifurcations are "sudden qualitative changes in the behavior of a system as a parameter is varied continuously" Feldman (2019, p. 106). These sudden changes affect transition points relating to attractors of a function, resulting in the so-called period-doubling route to chaos (e.g., Feldman, 2019, p. 143; Mitchell, 2009, p. 34). Bifurcation has appeared in SLA discussions since, at least, Larsen-Freeman (2006b, p. 613). More recently, the term has been invoked as an analytic tool by Evans and Larsen-Freeman (2020) in order to characterize "certain patterns in the flux" (Evans & Larsen-Freeman, 2020, p. 1) used by an untutored ESL learner in a 30-week longitudinal study. The study is a condensed version of some aspects of Evans' (2019) doctoral dissertation. Evans and Larsen-Freeman (2020) claim that:

> [t]he learner's ensuing second language development is characterized by a series of bifurcations, stemming from forms competing for the same functional terrain. Each bifurcation is accompanied by turbulence as the system moves from one attractor state to another. The transition is characterized by loss of stability, an increase in variability, and a period of dysfluency.
>
> (p. 1)

The analysis of what is referred to as bifurcation focuses on adverbial clauses introduced by "before." The informant is reported to show the following developmental pattern:

(1) before + infinitive ("before to tell"),
(2) either before + base ("before explain") or before + -ing ("before coming")
(3) before + -ing with backward anaphora

In the 2020 publication, these claims are not supported by the inclusion of any distributional analysis of the forms in the corpus for any section of the observational period nor of the functions they serve. Similarly, claims in relation to "turbulence," "attractor state," "loss of stability," and "variability" lack quantitative support in the paper. Evans and Larsen-Freeman (2020) nevertheless summarize the reported developmental pattern in a diagram with the caption "Bifurcation region of before-headed non-finite adverbial clauses" (p. 5), suggesting that the reported study represents a bifurcation analysis – as also announced in the title of the paper. This diagram shows branching lines reminiscent of those found in bifurcation diagrams such as the one displayed in Figure 2.6. However, they are not the result of any calculation. Instead, they serve to illustrate the following sequence of acquisition in which (2a) is claimed to appear concurrently with (2b), a transition that (gradually) replaces pattern (1), as shown in the progression from left to right in the direction of the arrow in the figure that follows later.

(2a) Before + ing ("before coming")
(1) Before + infinitive ("before to go")
(2b) Before + base ("before explain")

→

We illustrated in our earlier discussion that bifurcations arise in dynamical systems such as those generated by the logistic map as a result of varying system parameters. Evans and Larsen-Freeman (2020) do not present quantitative analyses using such a function. Nor have they identified a parameter that may cause sudden or other changes in the behavior of the system they refer to. The potentially intriguing observation related to the influence of two attractors in the assumed sequence of acquisition is also not supported by an analysis that would enable testing of the claim that it is an example of bifurcation in a mathematical sense.

In addition, Evans and Larsen-Freeman (2020) have not specified the term bifurcation in relation to a specific theory. As we have demonstrated earlier in this chapter, bifurcation occurs under different conditions depending on the mathematically defined nature of the system. We also pointed out that in deterministic dynamical systems, there is no phase of turbulent behavior between a single fixed attractor and a period-two attractor as assumed by Evans and Larsen-Freeman (2020). Instead, the transitions in these bifurcations are sudden – rather than being preceded by a period of instability.

Specifying the conditions for bifurcation in an SLA context is no simple task. As May (2004) points out, applying this approach to areas/disciplines outside mathematics would have to go beyond the mathematical model and connect the chosen parameters and the mathematical machinery to the substance of the phenomena to be modeled. To achieve this goal, we would need very complex levels of detail about the overall system being used by the learner and the relationships between the various parts of that system both for the learners and for other members of the community with whom they interact.

Attractor (state)

As pointed out earlier, a fixed point of a function is called an attractor, as "[n]earby orbits are pulled toward it; it attracts nearby points" (Feldman, 2019, p. 7). For stable attractors, the orbit stays on the attractor indefinitely. In contrast, de Bot et al. (2007) described this notion as follows:

> As they [i.e. dynamic systems] develop over time, dynamic subsystems appear to settle in specific states, so-called ATTRACTOR STATES (sic.), which are preferred but not necessarily predictable. . . . Attractor states are by definition temporary and not fixed. . .
> (p. 8)

This view of attractor states is inconsistent with dynamical systems theory. As we indicated in our comments earlier, Feldman (2019) discussed stable fixed points and cycles as the main categories of attractors (in the context of iterated functions) and pointed out that both are perfectly predictable. Stable attractors will stay on the fixed point and are insensitive to initial conditions and small perturbations. A different category of so-called strange attractors (Feldman, 2019, p. 189) is created by three-dimensional differential equations. However, these phenomena are not considered in the dynamic approach to SLA. A special type of attractors are so-called hidden attractors (Dudkowski et al., 2016). These are rare phenomena not discussed in the references quoted by de Bot et al. (2007) or by the other proponents of the dynamic approach nor by Feldman (2019), Devaney (2003), or Hasselblatt and Katok (2003) and are therefore not relevant in the context of this chapter.

Larsen-Freeman and de Bot have both made reference to attractors to explain fossilization. As we pointed out, de Bot et al. (2013) identify the so-called basic variety (Klein & Perdue, 1997) of an L2 as a linguistic system that has stopped developing, and they assume that it had reached an attractor state. However, Larsen-Freeman (2006a) claims that there are no final states in dynamical systems or SLA and that therefore, fossilization does not exist. This is inconsistent with the dynamical systems view that attractors are by definition final states. Substantial work would be required to define the particular patterns of L2 use that would conform to this definition and much more substantial work to demonstrate that a particular learner's pattern of use is consistent with this definition.

If claims are to be made about the role of attractors in fossilization, we need clear and theoretically justified relationships between the two terms (attractor and fossilization). And if SLA researchers are to use concepts from mathematics, then we must use them in ways consistent with their mathematical definitions.

Challenges in connecting variational data with "dynamical systems constructs"

As mentioned earlier in this chapter, the proponents of the dynamic approach to SLA promoted the allegation that "most" traditional approaches try to "explain away" L2 variation (see de Bot et al., 2007):

> Researchers in second language acquisition have traditionally attempted to explain away seemingly FREE VARIATION [sic.] by assuming full systematicity of variation in learner data. These explanations are often found in individual learner differences or in the learner's linguistic or situational environment, but also in an assumed innate language specific endowment. The systematicity of this innate system used to be hidden in a black box that arouses language structures in a fixed linear order.
>
> (p. 15–16)

As we also pointed out, in contrast, de Bot et al. (2007, p. 7) demanded "a theory that does not regard real-life messy facts as 'noise' but as part of the 'sound' you get in real life." Larsen-Freeman (2011) also claimed that other approaches treat variation as noise: "Variability pervades language production, its presence too profound to be relegated to noise and random performance factors" (pp. 56–57). And she continues that "Dörnyei (2009) . . . has recently suggested that the seemingly straightforward picture of individual differences based on stable and monolithic learner traits is part of an idealized narrative." In another paper, Larsen-Freeman (2006b, p. 601) claimed that "[t]raditionally, intraindividual variability was seen as a form of measurement error."

In such quotations, these proponents of the dynamic approach seem to be rewriting the history of SLA research in the shape of a homogenized narrative about L2 variation. This narrative glosses over substantial differences between a wide range of approaches to SLA that we mentioned in passing with reference to the volume *Theories in Second Language Acquisition* (VanPatten et al., 2020). A "minimalistic" summary of these approaches can be found in Pienemann (2007) covering the following key points:

> A substantial number of approaches to SLA were inspired by variationist linguistics as conceptualized by Labov (1972) and by the account of dynamic linguistic systems utilizing aspects of implicational scaling (Bickerton, 1971; DeCamp, 197[1]; Guttmann, 1944), of Labov's (1972) probabilistically weighted rules and of Bailey's (1973) wave model. This is evident, for instance, in the work of Klein and Dittmar (1979), Tarone (1979, 1985), Meisel, Clahsen and Pienemann (1981), Huebner (1983), Ellis (1985b), Preston (1993) and Pienemann (1998).
>
> Variable rules are designed to capture three different things:
>
> - the social context in which linguistic forms are being used,
> - the linguistic context, and
> - the probability of rule application.
>
> A variable rule typically makes the following kind of statement: *rule x (e.g. contraction of the copula) is used with probability X in social context Y given that the linguistic context is Z.*
>
> In applying this variationist approach to the study of SLA, Tarone (1979, 1982, 1983, 1985, 1988) and Ellis (1985a, b) focus on the social context and the probability of rule application.
>
> Pienemann (2007, p. 43)

Several approaches to L2 variation are rooted in a long tradition of research on the dynamics and variability of language identified in the quotation. In other words, dynamics and variability are by no means new concepts in the study of language and language acquisition; quite the opposite. Extensive frameworks for the description and explanation of the dynamics and variability of language and language acquisition have been developed, most of which have been only fleetingly engaged with by the proponents of the dynamic approach to SLA, including a whole branch of SLA research based on "variationist linguistics" (for a brief overview, see Bayley, 2005). The conceptualization of variation within processability theory (Pienemann, 1998) is an extension of this tradition (which complements its roots in psycholinguistics). In this framework, variation and development are treated as two separate but connected dimensions of "hypothesis space" that is modeled using an elaborated descriptive apparatus ensuring the integrity of the interwoven nature of the dimensions of hypothesis space.

As a contribution to *The Encyclopedia of Applied Linguistics* (Chapelle, 2013), Verspoor and van Dijk's (2013) paper on "Variability in a Dynamic Systems Theory Approach to Second Language Acquisition" can be expected to be reasonably representative of the handling of variation within the dynamic approach. Verspoor and van Dijk (2013) state that "there are still few studies that interpret patterns of variability from a dynamic systems perspective." (p. 5) and argue that

> . . . [a]ccording to dynamic systems theory (DST), variability is especially large during periods of rapid development because at that time the learner explores and tries out new strategies or modes of behavior that are not always successful and may therefore alternate with old strategies or modes of behavior (Thelen & Smith, 1994).
>
> (pp. 1–2)

To illustrate their approach, Verspoor and van Dijk (2013) present their reinterpretation of a study by Cancino et al. (1978) that focuses on the development of negative constructions by one learner (Jorge) and is augmented by a verbal reinterpretation of Cancino et al.'s (1978) findings from the other five *ab initio* longitudinal learners of ESL. Jorge's development of negative constructions is shown in Figure 2.8. Verspoor and van Dijk (2013) present this figure (p. 6) and interpret it (p. 5) as follows:

> Jorge, displayed a classic developmental pattern of variability . . . As Figure 2 illustrates, he used all four possible negative constructions. . . , from the first time he was interviewed, but early on the more advanced ones occurred only a few times. The nontarget *No* verb construction . . . had a . . . significant peak in session 3, then dropped down quickly but did not disappear completely until session 12. The *don't* verb construction, which is a target form in "I don't go" but a nontarget one in "he don't go" was significantly overused between sessions 7 and 9. At that same time, the use of the more advanced aux verb construction . . . had reached a small peak and then reached another peak around session 15. Meanwhile, the use of the most advanced analyzed *do* verb construction is slowly increasing and peaks in our data set in session 20, around which time a more target-like distribution of the negative constructions seems to emerge.
>
> To summarize, Jorge's negative constructions show a developmental hierarchy from less advanced constructions to more target-like ones. . .

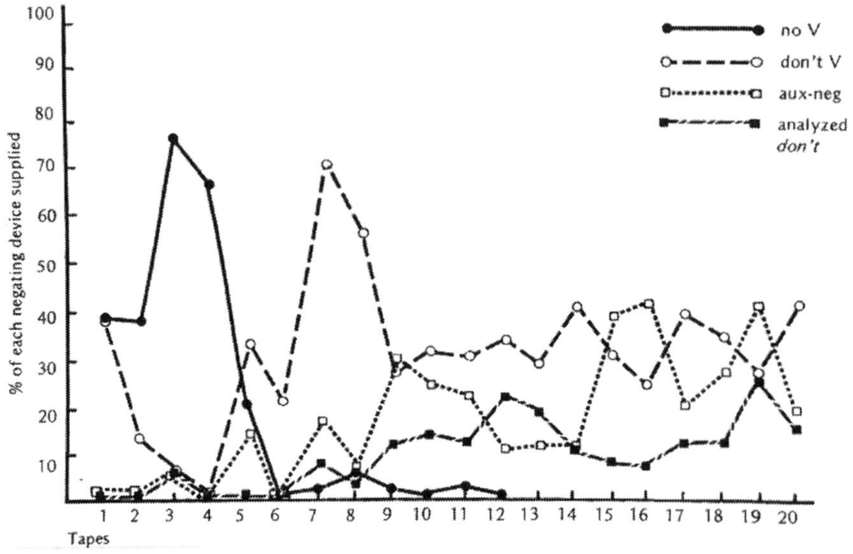

Figure 2.8 "Development of negation in Jorge showing proportion of each negating device to total negatives in each sample" taken from Cancino et al. (1978, p. 214)

Verspoor and van Dijk (2013, p. 5) draw the following conclusion from this and their re-interpretation of the other five informants:

> These findings together strongly suggest that the variability points to transitional stages and is indeed needed to progress.

This conclusion about the connection between variability and transitional stages appears to be the key hypothesis put forward by Verspoor and van Dijk (2013). Their analysis relies solely on visual inspection of Cancino et al.'s (1978) figure and the accompanying text. Therefore, it remains unclear according to which criteria Verspoor and van Dijk (2013) concluded that "Jorge's negative constructions show a developmental hierarchy from less advanced constructions to more target-like ones" (p. 5). Verspoor and van Dijk (2013) do not cite the discussion of methodological issues raised in Cancino et al. in 1978.

Verspoor and van Dijk (2013) appear to conceptualize variation as varying percentages of rule application, which raises the issue of how they can differentiate between percentage values as indicators of variation and as indicators of progress. These issues have been discussed over several decades (e.g., Meisel et al., 1981), and various solutions have been proposed. However, this and related discussions are not reported in

Verspoor and van Dijk (2013), who dispute the relevance of variationist approaches because such approaches are said to have the different objective of "focusing on the possible extraneous causes of variability" rather than connecting that variation with the course of longitudinal development (p. 4).

In a separate engagement with the issue of variation, Larsen-Freeman (2006b) announced her intention to analyze "The Emergence of Complexity, Fluency, and Accuracy in the Oral and Written Production of Five Chinese Learners of English." In relation to the issues we discuss here, she analyzed the written language productions of five high intermediate ESL learners from China on four parameters. Larsen-Freeman (2006b) used the following parameters as "indices . . . of second language development in writing":

> Fluency (average number of words per t-unit. . .), grammatical complexity (average number of clauses per t-unit), accuracy (the proportion of error-free t-units to t-units), and vocabulary complexity (a sophisticated type-token ratio – word types per square root of two times the words. . .).
>
> (p. 597)

Larsen-Freeman (2006b, p. 600) compared the figures obtained for the individual learners and noted that each set of scores is somewhat different from the other and different from the amalgamated scores for each parameter. In other words, amalgamated scores "cover up" individual differences. This insight was part of the early critique of the morpheme order studies (for instance, Andersen, 1977). Larsen-Freeman (2006b) goes on to calculate z-scores for each of the five learners and the four points of data collection relating to each of the four parameters to illustrate individual differences. In other words, the z-scores for each learner and parameter are based on four data points. This very small database limits the generalizability of the analysis. The z-scores amplify the differences between data points that appeared in the raw data. However, neither the raw data nor the z-scores reveal a specific trend over the four data points. In some cases, the scores increase, in some, they decrease, and in some, they are steady. Naturally, there are differences between the learners, as each of them has a different acquisition history. Based on this analysis, Larsen-Freeman (2006b) arrives at the following conclusion:

> although there is intraindividual variability from one time to the next, it is also possible to identify attractors or preferred paths within individual performances. This can best be seen by mapping the performance of the five participants on two of the indices.
>
> (Larsen-Freeman, 2006b, p. 601)

And she goes on to quote cases of specific comparisons:

> Plotting fluency against grammatical complexity . . . shows that participant L improved in fluency, subject U made more gains in grammatical complexity, and the others fell somewhere between.
> (Larsen-Freeman, 2006b, p. 602)

It remains unclear how Larsen-Freeman defines and identifies "attractors" and "preferred paths," as these terms are not operationalized or explicitly connected to the data presented in the paper.

These brief comments in relation to some aspects of research on variation within the dynamic approach to SLA suggest that it is not connected to the rich tradition of variationist linguistics nor to the equally rich body of research into L2 variation. Further, work within this dynamic approach seems to utilize concepts from dynamical systems theorizing, such as the notions of "attractor" and "bifurcation," without consistent attention to the ways in which dynamical systems theorizing has defined these concepts.

These observations suggest that attempts to connect dynamical systems theorizing and SLA research need very careful attention to both fundamental mathematical concepts and the extensive debates that have taken place in SLA research. Work in the mathematics of dynamical systems theorizing clearly indicates that predictions are, in principle, possible. The influences and constraints on this predictability, while extensive, are definable. SLA research has shown that there are identifiable but complex relationships between development and variation. This history offers ways of defining and operationalizing some ways of conceptualizing variation within and between learners and learner groups. In our analysis of the mathematical underpinnings of dynamical systems, we have shown that putting these varied approaches together can begin with the assumption that patterns that transcend individuals will be able to be identified and specific (kinds of) testable predications developed. However, we will need to work carefully and collaboratively to identify the circumstances and relationships entangled in those predictions.

Translating between disciplines: towards a roadmap

The approach taken in this chapter is different from the approach taken in Chapter 1 (Kersten & Greve, 2023, this volume). As with any emerging area of enquiry, this difference reflects the complex nature of the conceptual space that this volume engages with and the lack of consensus about how it should be best explored. Although both dynamics going back to DeCamp and dynamical systems going back to Poincaré have well-established histories in linguistics and mathematics respectively, attempts to bring them together create new challenges that require careful definition and extensive debate to clarify the principles that can best inform progress.

Our approach has been to highlight the need for careful attention to the mathematical basis of dynamical systems in their translation into the (for it) new domain of second language acquisition. We have argued for careful attention to (1) the application of the central features of the original mathematics and (2) acknowledgement of what SLA research has already documented in relation to the dynamics of second language systems. We indicated in our chapter that we can be confident that dynamical systems manifest predictable behaviors.

Nevertheless, the translation of dynamical systems from mathematics to SLA will require great thought in terms of the nature of the mathematical approaches that are used. The central aspect of the complexity that these approaches will need to engage with involves distinguishing between (1) language as a general construct, (2) different aspects of language and specific languages that will need to be learned, (3) the nuances of use and learning as well as (4) the processes involved in moments of communication and longer-term changes in both use and representations of the evolving language.

A second aspect of the complexity has been highlighted by Kersten and Greve in their discussion of the complexities involved in attempting to model individual and intraindividual aspects of variation. They have pointed to the challenge faced by SLA researchers in seeking to understand the different potential relationships between individual and situational variables and their interactions with one another.

These considerations mean that the *explanandum* that forms the focus of this volume is, therefore, not only the phenomenon itself (i.e., the learner's changing patterns of use of the second language in relationship to particular moments but also over time and across settings) but also the huge array of other potentially influencing variables that transcend individual learners to involve both their and their interlocutors' communities and histories (see Nicholas and Starks, 2014, 2019). As a dynamic perspective highlights, one of the key additional challenges is that we need to account not only for these "nonlinguistic" variables as influences on the course of second language acquisition but also build in ways of understanding how the course of the additional language development influences such individual and extended variables. As the history of SLA research into variation demonstrates, neither the constructs themselves nor their potential and shifting interrelationships have been easy to define or operationalize, let alone their dynamical characteristics.

We share the belief of Kersten and Greve that explanation is a key goal of second language researchers. The differences that we have indicated point to rich grounds for ongoing discussion about what is currently achievable and what developments are required in order for progress to be made. It may even be the case that we will not be able to rely on existing forms of mathematical/statistical analysis, and so SLA researchers may need to engage closely with mathematicians in the elaboration of developments in mathematics.

Notes

1. This is not true for de Bot and colleagues (e.g., de Bot et al., 2007), who refer to van Geert's work.
2. As Mitchell (2009, pp. 16f.) pointed out, this assumption was also made by Aristotle, and it was later demonstrated to be wrong by Galileo.
3. The three-body problem "is understood to be the problem of calculating the motion of three point-like masses which move under the sole influence of the mutual gravitational forces" (Schmid et al., 1988, p. 79).
4. In recent years, researchers in the natural sciences have added to nonlinear deterministic equations well-defined elements of randomness that mimic the "noise" that typically accompanies dynamical systems in natural processes such as neural development (for instance, Freeman et al., 2001). These approaches are formally known as "stochastic dynamical equations," as they contain a stochastic component, i.e., their modelling includes a random element. However, the stochastic component is constrained in such a way that the behavior of the resulting system is highly predictable even though only within narrow confines of a window of probability (see Sibani and Jensen, 2013). In this chapter, we will focus on deterministic dynamical systems, because for the purpose of the current discussion, stochastic and deterministic dynamical systems share many properties, in particular those related to predictability, and because the discussion of the dynamic approach has been based on deterministic dynamical systems even though this technical term as well as its mathematical formalisms have not been used within the dynamic approach.
5. It should be noted here that r must be < 4. This is demonstrated by May (1976). Equation (3) is based on a near-identical equation in May's (1976) influential publication in which the variable "r" in equation (3) was termed "a." May (1976, p. 460) explains why "r" (alias "a") must be $r < 4$:

   > F(X) in equation (3) [corresponding to equation (3) in this chapter] attains a maximum value of a/4 (at X = 1/2); the equation therefore possesses non-trivial dynamical behaviour only if $a < 4$. On the other hand, all trajectories are attracted to X = 0 if $a < 1$. Thus for non-trivial dynamical behaviour we require $1 < a < 4$; failing this, the population becomes extinct.
   >
   > May (1976, p. 460)

6. As x_t denotes the fraction of the carrying capacity, the current population is divided by the maximum carrying capacity. Therefore, the value of x_t is always between 0 and 1. For instance, if the current koala population is 200 and the maximum capacity of the habitat is 4,000, the value of x_t is 0.05. If the value of x_t is larger than 1, the population would be larger than the actual carrying capacity of the habitat. Thus, a value of $x_t = 2$ would mirror the unrealistic scenario of a koala population of 4,000 in a habitat that supports maximally 2,000 koalas. Feldman (2019, p. 68) points out that "the model breaks down at this point; the logistic equation gives a negative value."
7. Feldman shows that it is possible "to quantify the degree to which a dynamical system's behavior is sensitive to its initial conditions" (Feldman, 2019, p. 85). Mathematically, this is done by determining the Lyapunov exponents. For details, see, e.g., Feldman (2019, pp. 85–89).

References

Andersen, R. W. (1977). The impoverished state of cross-sectional morpheme acquisition/accuracy methodology (or: The leftovers are more nourishing than the main course). *Working Papers on Bilingualism*, *14*, 47–82.

Aubin, D., & Dalmedico, D. A. (2002). Writing the history of dynamical systems and chaos: Longue durée and revolution, disciplines and cultures. *Historia Mathematica*, *29*(3), 273–339. https://doi.org/10.1006/hmat.2002.2351
Bailey, C.-J. (1973). *Variation and linguistic theory*. Georgetown University Press.
Bayley, R. (2005). Second language acquisition and sociolinguistic variation. *Intercultural Communication Studies*, *XIV*(2), 1–13.
Bickerton, D. (1971). Inherent variability and variable rules. *Foundations of Language*, 7(4), 457–492. www.jstor.org/stable/25000558
Briggs, J., & Peat, F. D. (1989). *Turbulent mirror. An illustrated guide to chaos theory and the science of wholeness*. Harper and Row.
Byrne, D., & Callaghan, G. (2014). *Complexity theory and the social sciences*. Routledge.
Cancino, H., Rosansky, E., & Schumann, J. (1978). The acquisition of English negatives and interrogatives by native Spanish speakers. In E. Hatch (Ed.), *Second language acquisition: A book of readings* (pp. 207–230). Newbury House.
Chapelle, C. D. (Ed.). (2013). *The encyclopedia of applied linguistics*. Wiley-Blackwell. https://doi.org/10.1002/9781405198431
de Bot, K. (2008). Introduction: Second language development as a dynamic process. *The Modern Language Journal*, *92*(2), 166–178. www.jstor.org/stable/25173021
de Bot, K. (2016). Multi-competence and dynamic systems. In V. J. Cook & Li Wei (Eds.), *The Cambridge handbook of linguistic multi-competence* (pp. 125–141). Cambridge University Press.
de Bot, K., & Larsen-Freeman, D. (2011). Researching second language development from a dynamic systems perspective. In M. H. Verspoor, K. de Bot, & W. Lowie (Eds.), *A dynamic approach to second language development. Methods and techniques* (pp. 5–23). John Benjamins.
de Bot, K., Lowie, W., Thorne, S., & Verspoor, W. (2013). Dynamic systems theory as a comprehensive theory of second language development. In M. Mayo, M. Mangado, & M. Adrian (Eds.), *Contemporary approaches to second language acquisition* (pp. 199–220). John Benjamins.
de Bot, K., Lowie, W., & Verspoor, M. (2007). A dynamic systems theory approach to second language acquisition. *Bilingualism: Language and Cognition*, *10*(1), 7–21. https://doi.org/10.1017/S1366728906002732
DeCamp, D. (1971). Implicational scales and sociolinguistic linearity. *Linguistics*, *9*(73), 30–43. https://doi.org/10.1515/ling.1971.9.73.30
Derrida, J. (1978). *Writing and difference* (A. Bass, Trans.). University of Chicago Press (Original work published in 1967).
Devaney, R. L. (2003). *An introduction to chaotic dynamical systems* (2nd ed.). Westview Press.
Dörnyei, Z. (2009). *The psychology of second language acquisition*. Oxford University Press.
Dörnyei, Z., MacIntyre, P. D., & Henry, A. (2014). Introduction: Applying complex dynamic systems principles to empirical research on L2 motivation. In Z. Dörnyei, P. D. MacIntyre, & H. Alastair (Eds.), *Motivational dynamics in language learning* (pp. 1–7). Multilingual Matters.
Dudkowski, D., Jafari, S., Kapitaniak, T., Kuznetsov, N., Leonov, G., & Prasad, A. (2016). Hidden attractors in dynamical systems. *Physics Reports*, *637*(2016), 1–50. https://doi.org/10.1016/j.physrep.2016.05.002

Ellis, N. C., & Larsen-Freeman, D. (2006). Language emergence: Implications for applied linguistics – Introduction to the special issue. *Applied Linguistics*, *27*(4), 558–589. https://doi.org/10.1093/applin/aml028

Ellis, R. (1985a). *Understanding second language acquisition*. Oxford University Press.

Ellis, R. (1985b). Sources of variability in interlanguage. *Applied Linguistics*, *6*(2), 118–131. https://doi.org/10.1093/applin/6.2.118

Evans, D. R. (2019). *Bifurcations, fractals, and nonlinearity in second language development: A complex dynamic systems perspective*. (Publication No. 13861783) [Doctoral dissertation, State University of New York at Buffalo]. ProQuest Dissertations and Theses Global.

Evans, D. R., & Larsen-Freeman, D. (2020). Bifurcations and the emergence of L2 syntactic structures in a complex dynamic system. *Frontiers in Psychology (Open Access)*, *11*(574603), 1–12. https://doi.org/10.3389/fpsyg.2020.574603

Falkenburg, B., & Weinert, F. (2009). Indeterminism and determinism in quantum mechanics. In D. Greenberger, K. Hentschel, & F. Weinert (Eds.), *Compendium of quantum physics: Concepts, experiments, history and philosophy* (pp. 307–311). Springer.

Feldman, D. P. (2019). *Chaos and dynamical systems*. Princeton University Press.

Freeman, W. J., Kozma, R., & Werbos, P. J. (2001). Biocomplexity: Adaptive behavior in complex stochastic dynamical systems. *Biosystems*, *59*(2), 109–123. www.elsevier.com:locate:biosystems

Gleick, J. (1987). *Chaos: Making a new science*. Viking Press.

Guttmann, L. (1944). A basis for scaling qualitative data. *American Sociological Review*, *9*(2), 139–150. https://doi.org/10.2307/2086306

Hasselblatt, B., & Katok, A. (2003). *A first course in dynamics – with a panorama of recent developments*. Cambridge University Press.

Hilborn, R. C. (2004). Sea gulls, butterflies, and grasshoppers: A brief history of the butterfly effect in nonlinear dynamics. *American Journal of Physics*, *72*(4), 425–427. https://doi.org/10.1119/1.1636492

Holton, D., & May, R. M. (1993). Chaos and one-dimensional maps. In T. Mullin (Ed.), *The nature of chaos* (pp. 95–119). Oxford University Press.

Huebner, T. (1983). *A longitudinal analysis of the acquisition of English*. Karoma.

Kersten, K., & Greve, W. (2023, this volume). Investigating cognitive-linguistic development in SLA: Theoretical and methodological challenges for empirical research. In K. Kersten & A. Winsler (Eds.), *Understanding variability in second language acquisition, bilingualism and cognition – A multi-layered perspective* (pp. 3–38). Routledge.

Klein, W., & Dittmar, N. (1979). *Developing grammars*. Springer.

Klein, W., & Perdue, C. (1997). The basic variety (Or couldn't natural languages be much simpler?). *Second Language Research*, *13*(4), 301–347. https://doi.org/10.1191/026765897666879396

Labov, W. (1972). The internal evolution of linguistic rules. In R. P. Stockwell & R. K. S. Macauley (Eds.), *Linguistic change and generative theory* (pp. 101–171). Indiana University Press.

Laplace, P.-S. (1995). Philosophical essay on probabilities. In *Translated from the fifth French edition from 1825 by Andrew I. Dale. Sources in the History of Mathematics and Physical Sciences, 13*. Springer. https://doi.org/10.1007/978-1-4612-4184-3

Larsen-Freeman, D. (1997). Chaos/complexity science and second language acquisition. *Applied Linguistics*, *18*(2), 141–165. https://doi.org/10.1093/applin/18.2.141

Larsen-Freeman, D. (2006a). Second language acquisition and the issue of fossilization: There is no end, and there is no state. In Z. Han & T. Odlin (Eds.), *Studies of fossilization in second language acquisition* (pp. 189–200). Multilingual Matters.

Larsen-Freeman, D. (2006b). The emergence of complexity, fluency, and accuracy in the oral and written production of five Chinese Learners of English. *Applied Linguistics*, *27*(4), 590–619. https://doi.org/10.1093/applin/aml029

Larsen-Freeman, D. (2009). Prediction or retrodiction? The coming together of research and teaching. In C. Pearson, K. Losey, M. Pasquale, P. Bogart, & R. Anderson (Eds.), *"Spotlight on re-search: A new beginning". Selected proceedings of the 2008 Michigan Teachers of English to Speakers of Other Languages conference* (pp. 5–26). Eastern Michigan University. http://commons.emich.edu/mitesol/5

Larsen-Freeman, D. (2011). A complexity theory approach to second language development. In D. Atkinson (Ed.), *Alternative approaches to second language acquisition* (pp. 48–72). Routledge.

Larsen-Freeman, D. (2012). Complex, dynamic systems: A new transdisciplinary theme for applied linguistics. *Language Teaching*, *45*(2), 202–214. https://doi.org/10.1017/S0261444811000061

Larsen-Freeman, D. (2017). Complexity theory: The lessons continue. In L. Ortega & Z. H. Han (Eds.), *Complexity theory and language development. In celebration of Diane Larsen-Freeman* (pp. 11–50). John Benjamins.

Larsen-Freeman, D. (2019). On language learner agency: A complex dynamic systems theory perspective. *The Modern Language Journal*, *103*(Suppl. 2019), 61–79. https://doi.org/10.1111/modl.12536

Larsen-Freeman, D., & Cameron, L. (2008). Research methodology on language development from a complex systems perspective. *Modern Language Journal*, *92*(2), 200–213. https://doi.org/10.1111/j.1540-4781.2008.00714.x

Li, T-Y., & Yorke, J. (1975). Period three implies chaos. *The American Mathematical Monthly*, *82*(10), 985–992. http://links.jstor.org/sici?sici=0002-9890%28197512%2982%3A10%3C985%3APTIC%3E2.0.CO%3B2-H

Lowie, W. (2013). Dynamic systems theory approaches to second language acquisition. In C. A. Chapelle (Ed.), *The encyclopaedia of applied linguistics*. Wiley-Blackwell. https://doi.org/10.1002/9781405198431

Lowie, W., Caspi, T., van Geert, P., & Steenbeek, H. (2011). Modeling development and change. In M. Verspoor, K. de Bot, & W. Lowie (Eds.), *A dynamic approach to second language development: Methods and techniques* (pp. 99–121). John Benjamins.

May, R. M. (1976). Simple mathematical models with very complicated dynamics. *Nature*, *261*(5560), 459–467. https://doi.org/10.1038/261459a0

May, R. M. (2004). Uses and abuses of mathematics in biology. *Science*, *303*(5659), 790–793. https://doi.org/10.1126/science.1094442

Meisel, J. M., Clahsen, H., & Pienemann, M. (1981). On determining developmental stages in natural second language acquisition. *Studies in Second Language Acquisition*, *3*(2), 109–135. https://doi.org/10.1017/S0272263100004137

Mitchell, M. (2009). *Complexity. A guided tour*. Oxford University Press.

Nicholas, H., & Starks, D. (2014). *Language education and applied linguistics: Bridging the two fields*. Routledge.

Nicholas, H., & Starks, D. (2019). Using the Multiplicity framework to reposition and reframe the Hypothesis Space. In A. Lenzing, H. Nicholas, & J. Roos (Eds.), *Widening contexts for processability theory: Theories and issues* (pp. 157–183). John Benjamins.

Pienemann, M. (1998). *Language processing and second language development: Processability Theory*. John Benjamins.

Pienemann, M. (2007). Variation and dynamic systems in SLA. *Bilingualism: Language and Cognition*, *10*(1), 43–45. https://doi.org/10.1017/S1366728906002793

Pienemann, M., Lenzing, A., & Nicholas, H. (forthcoming). *Can dynamic systems theory explain SLA?* (Unpublished manuscript). University of Paderborn.

Poincaré, J. H. (1913). *The foundations of science: Vol 1: Science and hypothesis; Vol II the value of science; Vol III: Science and method* (G. Halsted, Trans.). The Science Press (Original works published in 1902 (Vol. I), 1905 (Vol. II), 1908 (Vol. III)).

Poincaré, J. H. (1993). *New methods of celestial mechanics, edited and introduced by Daniel Goroff. Vol I: Periodic and asymptotic solutions; Vol II: Approximations by series; Vol III: Integral invariants and asymptotic properties of certain solutions* (American Institute of Physics, Trans.). American Institute of Physics (Original works published 1892 (Vol. I), 1893 (Vol. II), 1899 (Vol. III).

Poincaré, J. H. (2017). *The three-body problem and the equations of dynamics. Poincaré's foundational work on dynamical systems theory* (B. Popp, Trans). Springer (Original work published in 1890).

Preston, D. R. (1993). Variation linguistics and SLA. *Second Language Research*, *9*(2), 153–172. https://doi.org/10.1177/026765839300900205

Robertson, S. S., Cohen, A. H., & Mayer-Kess, R. G. (1993). Behavioural chaos: Beyond the metaphor. In L. B. Smith & E. Thelen (Eds.), *A dynamic systems approach to development: Applications* (pp. 120–150). MIT Press.

Schmid, E. W., Spitz, G., & Lösch, W. (1988). *Theoretical physics on the personal computer* (A. Armstrong, Trans.). Springer.

Sibani, P., & Jensen, J. (2013). *Stochastic dynamics of complex systems: From glasses to evolution*. Imperial College Press.

Strogatz, S. H. (2015). *Nonlinear dynamics and chaos. With applications to physics, biology, chemistry and engineering* (2nd ed.). Westview Press.

Tarone, E. (1979). Interlanguage as a chameleon. *Language Learning*, *29*(1), 181–191. https://doi.org/10.1111/j.1467-1770.1979.tb01058.x

Tarone, E. (1982). Systematicity and attention in interlanguage. *Language Learning*, *32*(1), 69–82. https://doi.org/10.1111/j.1467-1770.1982.tb00519.x

Tarone, E. (1983). On the variability of interlanguage systems. *Applied Linguistics*, *4*(2), 142–163. https://doi.org/10.1093/applin/4.2.142

Tarone, E. (1985). Variability in interlanguage use: A study of style-shifting in morphology and syntax. *Language Learning*, *35*(3), 373–404. https://doi.org/10.1111/j.1467-1770.1985.tb01083.x

Tarone, E. (1988). *Variation in interlanguage*. Edward Arnold.

Thelen, E., & Smith, L. B. (1994). *A dynamic systems approach to the development of cognition and action*. MIT Press.

Van Dijk, M., Verspoor, M., & Lowie, W. (2011). Variability and DST. In M. Verspoor, K. de Bot, & W. Lowie (Eds.), *A dynamic approach to second language development: Methods and techniques* (pp. 55–84). John Benjamins.
VanPatten, B., Keating, G., & Wulff, S. (2020). *Theories in second language acquisition: An introduction* (3rd ed.). Routledge.
Verspoor, M., & van Dijk, M. (2013). Variability in a dynamic systems theory approach to second language acquisition. In C. A. Chapelle (Ed.), *The encyclopedia of applied linguistics*. Wiley-Blackwell. https://doi.org/10.1002/9781405198431.wbeal1251

3 How many moderators does it take till we know . . . that too many bilingual advantage effects have died?

Julia Festman, Sophia Czapka, and Adam Winsler

Introduction

Research findings have been mixed over the years regarding the presence of either a bilingual advantage or disadvantage in various aspects of cognitive performance. While early investigations tended to demonstrate a disadvantage or even "serious deficits" for bilingual individuals performing on intelligence tests compared to monolinguals (Feldman & Shen, 1971, p. 235), these early studies have been criticized, starting in the 1960s, foremost by Peal and Lambert (1962), regarding unfair group comparisons, failure to control for differences in socioeconomic status and education across groups and poor measurement or definitions of bilingualism, among other methodological flaws (Hakuta, 1986).

Over the last several decades, roughly an equal amount of evidence has piled up both for and against the bilingual advantage hypothesis, and numerous meta-analyses have attempted to provide a clearer picture of the state of the art of the bilingualism effects debate (Adesope et al., 2010; Lehtonen et al., 2018). However, the picture is still blurred, and most of all, it is clear that bilingual advantages apparently do not "come naturally," meaning that broad and easily detectable improvements in cognition and executive control do not develop quickly merely as a consequence of exposure to multiple languages for all bilingual individuals, broadly defined. Bilinguals vary tremendously in the history, timing, intensity, and context of their exposure to and use of multiple languages. At the same time, there are numerous cognitive processes, skills, and abilities at different levels of analysis involved that are tapped differentially by a wide variety of different tasks and assessments that have been used. In addition, there are large individual differences in both cognitive skills and language learning processes that can affect relations between cognition and bilingualism (de Bruin et al., 2021; Hartsuiker, 2015; Ware et al., 2020). Indeed, the more precise question, thus, seems to be under which specific circumstances a bilingual advantage appears in empirical investigations, for which kind of bilinguals, and on which cognitive skills/tasks (Hartsuiker, 2015; Leivada et al., 2021; Paap et al., 2015).

DOI: 10.4324/9781003155683-4

Researchers have recently called for the inclusion of individual differences in the bilingual profiles of participants and more consistent descriptions across studies of the bilingual individual and context (Byers-Heinlein et al., 2019; Surrain & Luk, 2017), challenging the illusion of a homogeneous group of bilinguals. Similarly, Grundy (2020) calls for attention to often "overlooked factors" causing failure of replication among studies on the bilingual advantage. This is partly due to the lack of a consensus as to how bilingual experience should be measured (see Bedore et al., 2012 on critically assessing language dominance) and the fact that the level of bilingualism of the participants tested is not reported consistently across studies (Byers-Heinlein et al., 2019). Influential variables that modulate bilinguals' performance on language and cognitive tasks are not yet clearly and well enough understood, owing to the complexity of bilingualism and multilingualism. The complex nature of bilingualism makes scholars even question whether bilingualism is effectively captured as a categorical variable and propose continuous measures of bilingualism instead (de Cat et al., 2018; Leivada et al., 2021). In this chapter, we attempt to provide an in-depth picture of the many influential and potentially *confounding* and/or *moderator variables* involved, with a focus on studies with children, for whom the bilingual advantage seems to be the most uncertain (Dick et al., 2019; Giovannoli et al., 2020; Gunnerud et al., 2020; Hilchey & Klein, 2011; Lowe et al., 2021).

Confounders and moderators in bilingualism research

Traditionally, research in the area of bilingual effects has involved fairly simple two-group comparisons between "monolingual" and "bilingual" participants (the independent variable [IV]) on some cognitive performance measure (the dependent variable [DV]), assuming that the speaker groups are well defined and homogeneous and only distinguished by the number of languages they speak or were exposed to. The extent to which researchers try to make the two groups equivalent (or statistically control for ways the groups are different) on a variety of other important variables or *confounding factors* or variables that are associated with both performance on the cognitive task and bilingualism varies from study to study. Obviously, and as was pointed out by Peal and Lambert (1962), if the bilingual group lives in poverty and has immigrant parents with limited education and income, while the monolingual English-speaking group consists of middle- to upper-class children, there is going to be a large effect favoring the monolingual group, since SES is strongly related to any test of cognitive skills, including IQ. Thus, confounding variables can lead researchers to falsely conclude that one group scores higher than the other when the reason for the performance differential has little or nothing to do with a child's language background as it is explained by other things. The bilingual advantage literature is full of such variables,

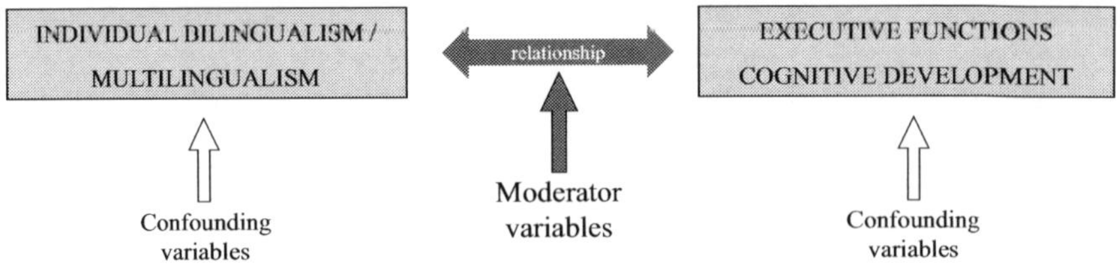

Figure 3.1 Graphical representation of confounder and moderator variables

and when crucial confounding variables are neglected, they bias and even distort results (Woumans et al., 2016).

Some confounding variables may or may not also be *moderator variables* (see Figure 3.1 for a graphical representation). A moderator is a third variable, say Z, that affects the strength or nature of the relationship between an independent variable (X – say bilingualism) and the dependent variable (Y – say cognitive processing or executive functioning). Moderators can be categorical (i.e., gender, type of bilingual – sequential vs. simultaneous, task type – inhibitory control vs. switching) or they can be continuous (i.e., age in years, degree of proficiency in L2). Such moderator variables are very common in the bilingual advantage literature, and they affect whether or not bilingual advantages are seen. For example, it could be that bilinguals show enhanced executive functions (EF) relative to monolinguals but only if the bilingual uses both languages frequently and switches back and forth between them a lot or only when the task used involves a certain type of EF.

This chapter reviews various confounding and moderator variables found to date in the bilingual advantage literature. It is important to note that moderators, confounding variables, independent variables, and dependent variables are determined in numerous ways. Sometimes they are researcher choices guided by theory, sometimes they are the result of particular statistical analyses run or not run, and sometimes they become clear only after studies are published (i.e., Study A controls for variable X and study B does not, and differences are seen in the results). Furthermore, what is a confounding variable in one study might be entered a priori as a moderator variable in another study. For these reasons, we use the terms "moderator" and "confounder variables" rather loosely to fit all situations concerning factors that potentially modulate a bilingual advantage across this large literature. Clearly, the presence of confounding variables, unmeasured systematic differences between the groups compared, and moderator variables would lead to mixed findings in the literature. Sometimes one observes a difference between bilinguals and monolinguals and sometimes not, depending on whether there is an unobserved/measured important variable present, insufficient control over a relevant confounding variable, or whether there is a hidden moderator at play. Many researchers have brought attention to these issues in research design and data analysis in research on bilingual effects (Leivada et al., 2021; Paap & Greenburg, 2013; Paap et al., 2014, 2015; Paap & Sawi, 2016; Valian, 2015).

Moderator variables in bilingual advantage research

Factors related to characteristics of languages/type of bilingualism

Age/timing of bilingualism

The first moderator we discuss here has to do with whether the bilingual individual is exposed to two languages from birth, whether the bilingual exposure and L2 language use happens during early childhood (ages 3–4), or whether bilingualism comes later after L1 is fully established. Infants exposed to two or more languages regularly from birth experience simultaneous bilingualism, or what has been called bilingual first language acquisition (BFLA; De Houwer, 2021). It is clear from a neurological language/information processing perspective that it is a very different and much more complex linguistic experience to encode, process, and make sense out of input from two languages from the beginning rather than one (Comishen et al., 2019; Sebastian-Galles & Santolin, 2020). Indeed, some have suggested that average bilingual input to babies functions the same way as rich, complex, monolingual linguistic infant-directed speech in terms of stimulating neuronal, language, and cognitive development (Brito, Troller-Renfree et al., 2020). Neuroscience research has confirmed that the organization of the brain for language (and other functions) is noticeably different for early simultaneous bilinguals compared to that of later, sequential L2 learners (Costa & Sebastián-Gallés, 2014; Hernandez & Li, 2007; Pliatsikas et al., 2020; Weisleder & Fernald, 2013). So one possibility is that (some kinds of) bilingual advantages might only be conferred to early simultaneous bilinguals and not later L2 learners. Another related question is whether early childhood bilingualism guarantees that a cognitive advantage will be detected during childhood or later, or alternatively phrased: Is mere (early) exposure enough (D'Souza et al., 2020), or do simultaneous early bilingual infants need to continue using both languages in certain ways later on to show bilingual cognitive effects?

Of course, it is quite a methodological challenge to investigate bilingual advantages in infancy due to restricted measurement options for the dependent variable – cognitive processing skills (see also the section later on age of child as a moderator). However, there has been interesting research on this. Some studies provide evidence of early bilingualism triggering different learning paths resulting in superior performance, while others have not reported an advantage related to bilingualism. The seminal studies by Kovács and Mehler (2009a on 7-month-olds; 2009b on 12-month-olds) suggested that bilingual babies are more flexible learners: they were able to learn two distinct syllabic structures (AAB and ABA), whereas the monolingual peers learned only one structure (AAB). Bilinguals were more flexible when learning speech structures than their monolingual peers. However, D'Souza et al. (2020) did not replicate these findings. They did show, however, that infants exposed to two languages were faster at disengaging attention to a known stimulus and shifting to a new one. They switched attention more frequently and oriented sooner to new stimuli compared to monolinguals. D'Souza et al. (2020) suggest that bilingual infants place less weight on consolidation of familiar information and are more interested in new information – which may be their way of adapting to their less predictable and more varied speech environment. The same pattern of results regarding faster disengagement of attention has been found for adults, but only for early and not for late bilinguals (D'Souza et al., 2021).

Singh (2021) suggested a fundamentally different way bilingual infants orientate in their speech environment regarding their distribution of attention. For bilingual infants, the core interest to attend to is novel information; they show broad interest and distribute attention for exploring their environment. Early sensory inputs due to bilingual exposure from birth have been shown to lead to distinct functional and structural changes in the brain (Berken et al., 2017; Vaquero et al., 2020). Although showing differential results, early bilinguals were not necessarily *better* word learners, as has been shown in a study with Spanish-English second graders (Alt et al., 2019). Indeed, several have recommended that rather than calling the phenomenon bilingual "advantage," we change the term to "bilingual effects," as it is clearer now that bilingual language processing, especially early on in life, is *different* from that of monolinguals, but it is less clear whether it is *better* (Leivada et al., 2021).

Some researchers have suggested that, in response to their increased communicative challenges demanding flexibility and greater attention to recognize and distinguish both languages, bilingual babies use referential cues differently than monolingual babies. Studies have revealed an advantage in integrating multiple communicative cues (e.g., gestural cues, contextual cues) for 3-year-olds (Yow & Markman, 2015), and 54-month-old English-Mandarin bilinguals and trilinguals were better able to use referential cues (i.e., following the gaze of an adult speaker) during a novel-object-word-pairing task compared to monolingual peers (Yow et al., 2017). Unique learning patterns and differences in memory generalization have been found in 18-month-olds dependent on early linguistic experience (exposure to two languages vs. one) which has been interpreted as a flexible adaptation of bilingual infants to environmental communicative cues (Brito, Greaves et al., 2020), and individual variability in this ability is linked to the amount of exposure to a second language (Brito & Barr, 2012).

Some studies shed light on differences between early bilinguals' ability to deal effectively with interference, a component of EF. Filippi et al. (2015) showed that 10-year-old early bilinguals (age 0–3) were better at focusing on the target voice and inhibiting distraction from verbal interference than monolingual peers. The authors suggested a bilingual advantage in interference control, which begins early in life. Luk et al. (2011) claimed that "more experience in being actively bilingual is associated with greater advantages in cognitive control and higher language proficiency" (p. 588). The early bilinguals in their study outperformed monolinguals and late bilinguals on a Flanker task. However, in Pelham and Abrams (2014), no such difference between early and late bilinguals was found on an attentional network task (ANT). Similarly, in Kapa and Colombo's study (2013) with early and late Spanish-English bilingual children, there was no difference on measures of inhibition.

To sum up, it appears that early bilinguals orient themselves in their more diverse linguistic environment to adapt flexibly to their surrounding languages and reduced input within each language, making it likely that there are differences between mono- and bilingual infants' and toddlers' language processing patterns and underlying neural structures. Acquiring two languages early on requires the build-up of a more common neural structure for both languages and greater language control demands (Yamasaki et al., 2018). Although some have found bilingual effects to be present in BFLA infants but not in later sequential bilinguals (Luk et al., 2011; Sabourin & Vīnerte, 2015), not all have even found bilingual effects within very young simultaneous bilinguals (Tao et al., 2011; Vega-Mendoza et al., 2015). Acquiring a second language later in life, just like other skills learned and trained, triggers reconfiguration of cognitive skills to deal with new tasks and may lead to salient transfer effects (Duñabeitia & Carreiras, 2015; Tao et al., 2011). Thus, it is unsurprising that the literature is full of mixed findings. This being said, the age at which an infant or child is first exposed to an additional language is quite certainly a moderator variable in research on bilingualism effects on cognition; its differential effects depending on age are, however, far from being clear (but see Tao et al., 2011).

L1/L2/L3 proficiency, language balance, and degree of bilingualism

A second common moderator in bilingualism research has to do with the degree of proficiency in L2 and/or in both languages. Simply put, how bilingual does one have to be, or how good does one have to get in L2, to see a bilingual advantage? Does taking two Spanish courses in secondary school qualify you to be called a "bilingual" even though you never use the L2? Or do you first have to attain almost perfect mastery of both languages before a bilingual advantage can appear? This has been operationalized in a couple of different ways – either degree of L2 competence (assuming native proficiency in a clear and dominant L1) and/or the degree of relative balance in facility shown by the bilingual between the two (or more) languages involved. Each one of these can be measured either continuously or categorically by classifying bilinguals into groups (high proficiency vs. low proficiency). The basic premise has been that one should see more bilingual cognitive advantages when the bilingual individual is quite good and/or balanced in their bilingual skills (Paap et al., 2014). This has been a large problem in the bilingual-effects literature, especially early on, because often, degree of proficiency in L1 and/or L2 was either not measured at all (and just assumed to be high), or measured poorly (i.e., via self- or other-report of proficiency in L2 as opposed to direct language assessments, which are now advised). It stands to reason that variance along this dimension in the studies would lead to failures to replicate and mixed results.

There is a fair amount of research indicating that enhanced EF is limited to bilingual children who are sufficiently proficient in both languages (Blom et al., 2017; Carlson & Meltzoff, 2008; Poarch & van Hell, 2012). Iluz-Cohen and Armon-Lotem (2013) found a positive relationship between level of language proficiency and inhibition and shifting abilities when assessing 43 sequential English-Hebrew bilingual preschool children classified as bilinguals with high (n = 33) or low (n = 10) language proficiency. Those with high proficiency were proficient in at least one of their languages (including balanced bilinguals with high language proficiency in both languages, or bilingual with higher proficiency in their second language = L2-dominant, or in their first = L1-dominant). High-language-proficiency bilinguals showed significantly better performance, in particular in resisting interference. Marton (2015) found highly proficient bilingualism to influence speed of processing and resistance to proactive interference in bilingual school-aged children. Chen et al. (2014) reported better cognitive flexibility of Chinese-English bilinguals between the ages of 7 and 10 (n = 223), but only when language proficiency was high in both languages. A similar finding in terms of better accuracy in the congruent condition was reported for 4-year-olds in a study by Gathercole et al. (2016), who tried to tease apart the differential impact of various factors including age and vocabulary size.

Slightly different from bilinguals being *highly* proficient in both languages is the issue of whether bilinguals' skills in their two languages are about the same (i.e., language balance). Language balance has been taken as a proxy for the ability of the individual to manage competition between the two languages (Macizo et al., 2012; Tao et al., 2011). The assumption of language balance in relation to competition is that if one language is mastered at a higher level (i.e., dominant language) than the other (i.e., nondominant language), interference from the nondominant language is weak, whereas if two languages are mastered at a similar level, they may influence one another to a similar degree requiring more inhibition due to more interference. In a longitudinal study over three years, Bosma et al. (2017) investigated the impact of degree of bilingualism (how balanced language proficiency was in both languages) on EF with 120 Frisian-Dutch 5- and 6-year-olds. Only at the beginning of the study did intensity of exposure to Frisian at home have an impact on one of the attention tasks (but not the others) and not later. Degree of bilingualism was a moderator in this relationship. More support for this pattern of influence was reported by Vega and Fernandez (2011). In their study with third- and fourth-grade Spanish-English bilinguals, performance on the Wisconsin Card Sort Task (WCST) and Stroop task was compared between a group with "more balanced" language skills to one "less balanced." There was a significant correlation between the degree of balance and error scores (perseveration errors) on the WCST (yet there were no group differences for the Stroop task – see task as moderator section in what follows). In a study with 8- to 9-year-old Spanish-English bilinguals, Thomas-Sunesson et al. (2018) found degree of bilingualism influenced EF performance: the more balanced the children were in their language skills, the better their performance on nonverbal tasks.

Another way to deal with this moderator is to either carefully match participants on proficiency or control for differential language proficiency statistically. A few studies have found a bilingual advantage when monolingual and bilingual children were matched on language ability in the language they shared (Okanda et al., 2010; Moreno-Stokoe & Damian, 2020) or when language skills were controlled for statistically (5- to 6-year-old bilinguals in Blom et al., 2014; Boerma & Blom, 2020; 4- to 6-year-olds in Carlson & Meltzoff, 2008). Finally, some studies did not reveal a bilingual advantage for unbalanced bilingual 8-year-olds on inhibitory control (Dimensional Change Card Sort – DCCS) when mono- and bilingual participants were matched on receptive vocabulary skills in the language they shared (Escobar et al., 2018); however, bilinguals outperformed their monolingual peers on a letter fluency task.

Until now, language proficiency as a moderator has been shown to have an impact on the bilingual effects on cognition observed, in particular for highly proficient bilinguals and to some degree as well for balanced bilinguals. The importance of this moderator is, however, still unclear, and one should not jump to early conclusions such that it is most important for highly proficient bilinguals, and less so for balanced bilinguals, given that the majority of published studies until now investigating this specific aspect included highly proficient bilinguals.

Manner of L2 acquisition, type of schooling, and the role of biliteracy

One of the many ways in which children learn an additional language is through formal schooling, and teachers in countries, school systems, and classrooms vary tremendously in their methods for second language teaching. Here, we examine how much type of schooling matters for the emergence of cognitive advantages related to bilingualism. In immersion schools, L2 is not taught as a foreign language subject, per se, but rather is used for teaching at least 50% of other academic subjects either by teachers having grown up with that language as their L1 or by individuals with high proficiency in the language. Immersion programs in two languages are offered to children who do not necessarily grow up with one (or both) of the languages in their family. Studies have aimed to determine if bilingualism stemming from immersion schooling, in particular, leads to cognitive advantages.

It is important to note that the *amount of time* spent on learning and using both languages can differ to a substantial degree depending on the type of immersion schooling. While some immersion models aim for an equal amount of time to be spent using both languages (50%–50% in two-way/double immersion) or a higher amount in the second language (up to 100% in full immersion), other types of bilingual programs (so-called CLIL programs – content and language integrated learning) use one language as the main language of instruction and only offer a few hours a week in the other language to teach content for example only in one or two subject areas. To complicate matters even further, there is also variance from program to program in how much literacy in both languages is emphasized. Language instruction in immersion schools often leads to *biliteracy*, as both languages are used as medium of instruction and thus children learn to read and write in both languages to some degree (see Festman, 2021, for review). A final potentially confounding factor to keep in mind is that many immersion schools are private, where parents often pay handsomely for their children to be enrolled in such special programs. Immersion studies are thus confronted with the problem of being based on more-advantaged, *self-selected samples* (Bruton, 2015), as such parents are typically academically motivated and usually come from high-socioeconomic-status (SES) backgrounds. For example, for English and Dutch immersion programs in Francophone Belgium where the L2 is a language of high prestige, presumably leading to increased motivation to learn it, "background analyses" including understanding and controlling for the SES of the families sending their children to immersion schools is vital to the interpretation of study results (Van Mensel et al., 2020).

The overall picture emerging from the studies investigating immersion schooling as a way to bilingualism and its effects on cognitive abilities is mixed. Studies differ in size of groups, children's age, languages involved, length of exposure, and daily time spent in the L2 in immersion schools as well as the tasks used to assess cognitive functions. Overall, however, a striking pattern has been observed. Studies that matched participants at the group level for background variables (commonly age, gender, SES, and sometimes intelligence) and that had *smaller sample sizes* (groups of

19–53 children) found a variety of specific immersion effects on single measures but not on a broad range of cognitive measures. For example, an immersion effect on nonverbal intelligence of 27 5-year-old French monolinguals after one year of immersion was found, but not on the Simon task (Woumans et al., 2016). Two studies point out an advantage for early bilingual children in immersion kindergarten (Carlson & Meltzoff, 2008 for a subgroup of 12 early-bilingual Spanish-English-speaking children with an advantage on a conflict task; Poarch & van Hell, 2012 for inhibitory control and attentional advantages in 20 5- to 8-year-old bilinguals).

A group of 53 first graders showed selective attention advantages but no advantage on a range of other attentional tasks (Barbu et al., 2019). English children acquiring Welsh (aged 4–6) in early formal education outperformed monolinguals in a task of attentional control (Kalashnikova & Mattock, 2012). Nicolay and Poncelet (2013, 2015) found advantages in attention and executive function tasks for 53 8-year-old French-English immersion children and for 51 third-graders, but only for those in high-exposure immersion). After only one year of immersion, children were found to perform faster on the selective attention task, whereas other effects were not observed in the same lab after three years (Nicolay & Poncelet, 2013, 2015). There was an immersion effect for 19 5- to 7-year-old children on working memory and word learning but not for shifting (DCCS) nor short term-memory (word-span) (Kaushanskaya et al., 2014).

Interestingly, studies that included background and moderator variables as covariates in their main analysis, had *larger* participant groups (50–500 children), and mostly looked at longer-term immersion effects did not find cognitive advantages for immersed bilingual children (Carlson & Meltzoff, 2008 for their larger group; Purić et al., 2017 for Spanish-English children with 2 years of immersion; Simonis et al., 2019, 2020 for EF tasks after 4 and 10 years of immersion, respectively). The only exception to this pattern was a recent study by Gillet et al. (2020), who included only gender as covariate in their oldest participant group (6 years of immersion) and found significant effects for cognitive flexibility and working memory. However, their younger participant groups (assessed after 1, 2, and 3 years of immersion) matched at the group level did not show cognitive advantages.

The available evidence on a bilingual immersion effect on cognition is mixed. Although some studies show single effects, there is also counterevidence, and broader cognitive assessments have not yet convincingly shown a bilingual effect on cognition. Immersion (or manner of bilingual schooling) likely plays a role as moderator variable, but the broadness of what has been subsumed under the umbrella-term "immersion" or "schooling" (amount of L1/L2, length and quality of exposure, degree of biliteracy, etc.) is not providing the grounds for clear conclusions yet.

Language distance/proximity, typology, bidialectism, and bimodal bilingualism

Does it matter for the appearance of bilingual effects on cognition whether the two languages involved are similar or different from one another? The degree of linguistic overlap between languages has led to discussions about whether bidialectism has effects on children's cognitive development (Alrwaita et al., 2020). Bidialectism refers to "two structurally, lexically similar, genetically related, and (to some degree) mutually intelligible linguistic varieties" (Antoniou et al., 2020, p. 1) such as Frisian and Dutch. Oschwald et al. (2018) proposed that language similarity may *increase* the language-related switching and control demands for bilinguals due to more frequent cross-language interference. Experiencing higher interference during language selection stages would lead to an increase of language control demands, which may train control networks and ultimately improve executive attention (Yamasaki et al., 2018). Alrwaita et al. (2020) reviewed the existing literature on the impact of bidialectism on children's and adults' cognition and stress the fact that speakers in bidialectical speech environments seem to have fewer opportunities for mixing or switching between the variants, potentially leading to different domain-general cognitive outcomes than those reported for bilingualism.

However, language similarity is also known to make language use easier due to an abundance of positive language transfer occasions and shared elements of grammar, phonology, and lexicality (see Festman, 2021, for review). As an example of high similarity across languages, Gonçalves et al. (2021) investigated bilingual (Brazilian Portuguese and Spanish) children, ages 6 to 8, regarding their language and EF skills, and observed a bilingual advantage in the bilinguals' reading and writing abilities compared to monolingual Brazilian Portuguese peers. The bilinguals, literate in Portuguese at school, grew up with both languages in their families (their parents being speakers of at least one of the languages as L1) and were immersed in both speech communities due to their place of residence, thereby being able to practice both languages daily and freely.

Various studies in which the bilinguals are immersed in both the regional dialect and the state's official language do show some single cognitive effects of bilingualism, but mainly when proficiency in the dialect is high and when the dialect is also used as a language of instruction at school. A few studies with bidialectal children showed some performance advantages, usually only on a singular measure within a broad range of tasks or sometimes only on intelligence measures or when analyzed as a composite EF score. Frisian-Dutch bilinguals ($N = 176$, 6- to 7-year-olds) outperformed their Dutch peers on a selective attention task, and the Frisian-speaking bilinguals outperformed Limburghish-speaking bilingual children with the former but not the latter being a language of instruction at school (Blom et al., 2017). Balanced Frisian-Dutch bidialectals showed superior performance in a working memory task (Bosma et al., 2017). Sardinian-Italian bidialectals showed a card-sorting and attention advantage (Garraffa et al., 2015; *n* = 40, 6- to 9-year-olds). Finally, Cypriot Greek-Standard Modern Greek bidialectals showed superior performance when composite scores of working memory and of inhibition were compared (Antoniou et al., 2016; *n* = 17 6- to 9-year-olds).

However, there are also studies on closely related language varieties that observe no cognitive effects, suggesting that language distance is not the decisive moderator for the appearance of cognitive advantages in bilingual children. For instance, no effects were observed in bidialectals with English and Dundonian, a regional variety of English spoken in the Northeast of Scotland (*N* = 147; ages 6–9) (Ross & Melinger, 2017). And no effects were found for Flanker task performance in Bosma et al. (2017), for interference suppression in Blom et al. (2017), or for DCCS in Garraffa et al. (2015) for the younger participant group.

A different and fascinating way of exploring whether language similarity matters for the appearance of bilingual effects is to examine bimodal bilinguals, that is, individuals who are proficient in both an aural language (say English) and a sign language (say, American Sign Language, ASL). There are neurological differences in the organization of spoken versus signed languages, especially when one of the languages is learned later in life (Emmorey et al., 2016). This, combined with the notion that there might be less interference and need for inhibition when the two languages involved are highly different from one another (Oschwald et al., 2018), and the observation that one doesn't necessarily have to turn "off" one of the languages when sign language is involved, explains perhaps why studies have *not* found bilingual advantages in EF for bimodal bilinguals but do find them for unimodal bilinguals (Emmorey et al., 2008).

Given the existent literature, there is no straightforward overarching bilingualism effect moderated by bidialectism or language proximity on cognition in bidialectal children. Bidialectism is related to issues of social stigmatization of one language with a higher prestige for the other language. This brings us to our next possible moderator variable: societal context and the perceived prestige of the languages involved.

Social aspects: heritage/minority speakers, prestige of languages, and multilingual societies

Do social aspects related to languages have the capacity to moderate the bilingual effects on cognition? Speakers of heritage languages (HL), often immigrants or children of immigrants (see section "Origin"), acquire an L1 that is different from the language(s) that is/are spoken by the speech community in their new country of residence. HL acquisition often entails changes in language contact, in language preferences, and language proficiency over time. Heritage speakers often experience a reduced language contact with their HL over time because only a small community or even only the core family uses it. This reduction in home-language use is, in some speech communities, not only linked to the reduced number of speakers of that language and the geographical distance to their country of origin but as well to issues of lower language prestige of the HL compared to the national language of the country, which may lead to a reluctance for openly using and wanting to learn the HL (Helmer, 2020).

Additionally, input dominance shifts with increasing language contact with the society language after entering the educational system, fostering specific languages to be learnt (i.e., the language of instruction, typically the national language, and other high-prestige foreign languages (such as English in Europe and Asia). Since input quality and quantity are decisive factors for stable language development (Hoff & Core, 2013; Gagarina & Klassert, 2018; Unsworth, 2016), the reduced input can result in a shift of language dominance in favor of the societal language (Polinsky & Scontras, 2020). A successful acquisition of an HL depends on numerous factors such as the family's SES (see section on SES) or family composition. For example, HL acquisition is more successful when both parents are speakers of HL than in a one-parent-one-language setting (Correia & Flores, 2017; Hoff et al., 2014). When older siblings prefer the society language, younger siblings often use this language with them, leading to changes over time in language dominance (Armon-Lotem et al., 2011).

The need to avoid using their HL in contexts outside of the family may lead to strong inhibition of that language and a focus on using only the "desired" language. Others who may have difficulties acquiring the new language likely feel outcast due to their lack of success. They might either avoid using the new language and stick to their HL or develop ways of mixing both languages. Whether HL-speaking children can feel proud about their HL and whether they can use it freely and enjoy that use is dependent on language policies in their countries of residence, attitudes of the direct speech communities, and school language policies (Helmer, 2020). Dixon et al. (2012) assessed children living in Singapore who speak an ethnic language, Chinese, Malay, or Tamil, and English as the societal language. They found that, amongst other aspects, the community influences lexicon development in the ethnic languages because some languages have more prestige, or certain communities consider their HL an important part of their identity and support its acquisition. These factors certainly influence children's language development in both languages and their language use, with a large range of effects and outcomes of unbalanced bilingualism and language attrition (Polinsky & Scontras, 2020). Children who can attend HL courses in their schools can move beyond informal language acquisition. Those who are allowed to develop biliteracy and who grow up in a respectful HL environment are found to outperform their bilingual and monoliterate peers on language development (Festman, 2021; Kremin et al., 2019).

Language policy decisions promoting national languages with high prestige typically lead to low prestige for the HL. Goriot et al. (2016)

found evidence that the perceived appreciation of a teacher towards a pupil's HL moderated the effects of a bilingual advantage in nonverbal working memory. Their study included groups of 23 monolingual Dutch, 25 German-Dutch children with higher teacher appreciation, and 23 Turkish-Dutch with lower appreciation. Higher appreciation led to a larger advantage.

Multilingual societies that also teach their languages in schools, e.g., Luxembourgish, Frisian, or languages in India, where not all individuals speak the surrounding languages, openly support multilingualism and plurilingual language use. In other countries such as Switzerland or Canada, mono- and bilingual speech communities coexist but do not necessarily mix.

Tsimpli et al. (2020) found evidence that beyond the impact of multilingualism, the sociolinguistic diversity of the environment can enhance children's EF. They compared 687 primary school children living in India (Delhi and Hyderabad), of which 41% were multilingual, i.e., growing up with two or more languages at home. This group outperformed monolinguals on working memory (n-back) and fluid intelligence, controlling for SES and other covariates. Higher sociolinguistic diversity was positively correlated with intelligence in monolinguals but negatively so in multilinguals.

In child studies on bilingual communities with, e.g., Catalan-Spanish, Basque-Spanish, Welsh-English speakers, no bilingual advantage in executive functions is found, nor in larger-scale studies of Welsh-English bilinguals (Gathercole et al., 2014) and Basque-Spanish bilinguals from immersion schools for simple inhibition tasks (Duñabeitia et al., 2014). These studies focused on communities in which the minority language has an officially recognized and protected status, yet no differences were reported.

To sum up, the majority of studies focusing on bilingual effects on cognition including social aspects linked to the languages under investigation did not reveal a bilingual effect moderated by social aspects. When embedded in a positive speaker environment toward the HL with a large speaker community of the HL, as well as the opportunity of formal schooling and biliteracy in the HL, successful acquisition of the heritage language is likely. While these characteristics are mainly related to language success (e.g., size of lexicon), they have not been found to extend to cognitive advantages. It needs to be said that HL use reduced to the core family and constant control of inhibiting HL use outside of home likely does not foster language development in HL and does not include frequent language switching, which is our next topic.

Experience-based factors: language usage in L1 versus L2 and language switching

Why might the sociolinguistic context serve as a moderator on the influence the bilingualism on EF development? One possibility is that the sociolinguistic context influences speakers' language usage, which in turn influences the development of EF (Blanco-Elorrieta & Pylkkänen, 2018). For example, growing up in a sociolinguistic context of trilingualism at home (Lx with mother, Ly with father, Lz with grandparents/nanny/at school; Festman et al., 2017) may help children to learn all three languages and to learn to use them appropriately with the specific interlocutor and thereby train EF. A community in which frequent switching between two languages is common and well accepted may lead to regular frequent language switching in the next generation of bilingual speakers (e.g., Catalan-Spanish; Basque-Spanish) with little language control needed and thus little training opportunity for EF linked to bilingualism.

While patterns of language use have long been the focus of sociolinguistics, it is only recently that cognitive psychologists, neuroscientists, and researchers of bilingualism have started to take bilingual experience and speech contexts more seriously into account. The current view is that the language control system has to cope with constraints caused by the specific interactional context (Blanco-Elorrieta & Pylkkänen, 2018). According to the adaptive control hypothesis (Green & Abutalebi, 2013), balanced bilinguals can be categorized based on the context of their interactions. Three contexts have been suggested: in a *dual-language context*, bilinguals use two languages within the same context (e.g., both L1 and L2 at home and work) – this requires a more taxing level of language control and reactive suppression of one language according to environmental cues and therefore should facilitate the development of adaptive cognitive-control skills. In the *single-language context*, there is a strict division between the languages used in contexts such that bilinguals speak only one language in one environment and therefore rarely switch languages (e.g., L1 at home and L2 at work). This clear functional division of languages requires only one language to be suppressed in each setting for long periods of time. Finally, the *dense code-switching context* allows bilinguals to routinely mix linguistic elements of two languages, e.g., within a single utterance. In this last context, no clear monitoring/inhibition of one language is necessary, as the languages mix more freely. Pot et al. (2018) concluded from the available evidence that for adults, the greatest cognitive benefits of bilingualism are observed in the dual-language context, presumably because language cues need to be closely monitored in order to inhibit and select the appropriate language. The continuous adjustment of the control mechanisms could train the brain to become more attentive and efficient in switching between languages.

Yow and Li (2015) examined the influence of the degree of bilingualism (i.e., language proficiency, frequency of use of two languages, and age of second language acquisition) on EF in 72 English-Mandarin bilingual adults (18–25 yrs.). They found that more *balanced use* (i.e., those who engage in language selection more frequently) and a more balanced level of proficiency in the two languages resulted in better EF performance, since regular switching seen as extensive practice in controlling attention to two language systems likely results in better inhibition of prepotent responses and global set-shifting. There was a positive association between age of second language acquisition and interference cost in the Stroop task and a significant effect of balanced bilingualism (balanced usage and proficiency in two languages) on the Stroop and number-letter task (mixing cost only). Woumans et al. (2015) revealed a correlation between language switching proficiency and cognitive conflict resolution in balanced bilinguals but not in unbalanced bilinguals and interpreters. Active and frequent language switching practice is claimed to lead to adults' better cognitive control (Woumans et al., 2019). In other studies with adults, cognitive benefits have been related to frequency of switching (Hartanto & Yang, 2016; Verreyt et al., 2016; Yow & Li, 2015).

With a focus on children, Verhagen et al. (2020) investigated language use in 37 2-year-old bilinguals and a control group. Compared to their monolingual peers, there was no advantage in parent-rated cognitive control (attentional focus, attention shifting, inhibitory control). The authors reported that children's degree of balanced language usage predicted cognitive control. Interestingly, toddlers with parents who were proficient only in one of the languages used at home were significantly better on selective attention compared to those with equally proficient parents. The authors suggested that conditions of having to use both languages actively and to switch between them for communication purposes with each parent triggered the bilingual advantage. This conclusion is in line with the findings of an earlier study with 200 bilingual and 829 monolingual 3-year-olds. Home language environment – in terms of language exposure – again played a crucial role: those bilingual children (n = 35) whose parents used different languages (their L1 and Dutch at home) outperformed their bilingual peers (with only L1 at home, n = 102) and monolingual peers (Dutch at home, n = 829) on a conflict task and a delay-of-gratification task (Verhagen et al., 2017).

Contrarily, less frequent code-switching in a single-language context was found to be associated with better inhibitory control skills in a longitudinal study with a sample of 29 French-English unbalanced bilingual preschoolers (Kuzyk et al., 2019). Guerrero et al. (2016) conducted a longitudinal study with 71 Spanish-English bilingual preschoolers to study growth in EF over time. Home bilingual language use (i.e., parents' ratings of their children's active daily use of two languages at home with higher proportions in Spanish) was revealed to foster development of EF, as it predicted EF performance on an ANT task.

With a broader approach, "experience-based" factors (EBF) of bilingualism, comprised of immersion in an L2 context, age of acquisition of L2, and L2 proficiency, emerged as factors to be considered in the bilingual experience (DeLuca et al., 2019). Their longitudinal study with highly proficient adult L2 English speakers reported on brain changes related to quantity and quality of the L2 immersion context. The results of the study demonstrate that specific EBFs predict specific brain adaptations. Duration of bilingual language use correlated with increased language processing efficiency, length of living in the L2 environment was related to increased automatization in language control, degree of L2 use in social settings positively related to better adaptations to increased demands on language control and selection, and active and sustained L2 use promoted efficiency in language regulation and processing.

On the behavioral level, in terms of response inhibition, no advantage could be found in a large-scale correlational analysis (Kałamała et al., 2020) between response inhibition and speaking contexts designed along the lines of the adaptive control hypothesis as suggested by Green and Abutalebi (2013). DeLuca et al. (2020) used duration and extent of bilingual language use, i.e., extent of using L2 at home and using it in broader social settings, as a proxy for EBF. On the behavioral Flanker performance of the adult bilingual participants, no impact of EBF could be observed, but it did affect patterns of neural recruitment during task performance: being immersed in a bilingual speech community resulted in more efficiency with language control. More exposure to L2 in social settings increased language control demands and was found to manifest as stronger use of networks for executing interference suppression. It is clear that bilingual language experiences change the brain in important ways (Costa & Sebastián-Gallés, 2014), but, as is a well-known and classic challenge in neuroscience, how such neurological changes map onto complex human behavior on tasks or in the natural environment over time is less clear (Hernandez et al., 2018).

Taken together, there are first promising findings from studies with adults suggesting a bilingual effect on cognition with bilingual experience/language use as a moderator variable. More specifically, balanced language use and balanced proficiency may enable the bilingual to frequently and actively use the languages and switch between them, as required in the dual-language context. Intense practice of control over and attention to language use may result from these demands, showing effects on cognition. As much as there seems to be support for this assumption for adults, for children, the available evidence is very scarce, even more so because measures of cognition are not always objective and reliable (i.e., parents' ratings).

Internal background variables

An individual's characteristics influence EF due to genetic predisposition and/or through activities that train or promote EF. The following examples – intelligence, activities that training EF skills, age, and gender – are by no means exhaustive, but they comprise known and prominent variables that are related to EF and to bilingualism and are therefore potential moderators for the bilingual advantage.

Intelligence

The concepts of intelligence and EF share some overlap. Higher-order EF, like problem-solving and reasoning, are similar to or even identical with fluid intelligence (Diamond, 2013; Roca et al., 2010). Working memory capacity (the ability to maintain information in short-term memory while processing tasks, and often measured with complex span tests similar to EF tasks) is closely related to intelligence, as they share certain cognitive control mechanisms in the prefrontal cortex (Conway et al., 2003; Kane & Engle, 2002). Unsworth et al. (2014) established that attentional control alongside memory capacity and long-term memory build the common ground between intelligence and working memory capacity. Updating (i.e., the ability to manipulate working memory content) and intelligence also share common variance. The other EF components, inhibition and shifting, are related to intelligence due to intercorrelations between them and updating ability (Friedman & Miyake, 2017).

Peal and Lambert (1962) described bilinguals as intellectually superior (p. 20) without drawing a causal relation between bilingualism and higher performance in tasks related to intelligence and mental flexibility. Until today, no study has investigated the independent effect of intelligence and bilingualism on EF. Woumans et al. (2016), however, investigated the effects of becoming bilingual by comparing 27 children (age 5 years) beginning to attend bilingual preschools with 27 controls attending monolingual preschools. These groups were matched on intelligence, SES, verbal fluency, and EF (accuracy and RTs in the Simon task). After one year, the bilingual group showed a significant increase in their intelligence scores (tested with the Raven's Colored Progressive Matrices), but both groups developed similarly in EF and verbal fluency. The absent effect on EF might be caused, for example, by the limited amount of bilingual experience in these children or the lower reliability of EF measures compared to standardized IQ scores. Evidence that bilingualism is related to intelligence and similar other concepts in children has been found, for example, for spatial reasoning (Greenberg et al., 2013), perspective taking (Kovács, 2009), and theory of mind (for a meta-analysis, see Schroeder, 2018). The causal relation between these effects remains unclear.

A related issue here is the fact that there are clearly bidirectional causal relationships between bilingualism and cognitive skills/intelligence. In this chapter, we have been discussing so far the idea that being/becoming bilingual enhances children's cognitive skills, but it is also the case that children with initially stronger cognitive and language processing skills are more likely to become bilingual or do so more quickly or with more ease (Winsler, 2023, this volume). Indeed, Peal and Lambert (1962) were among the first to suggest that it will be difficult for researchers to tease apart the direction of effect between cognition and bilingualism, since both affect the other. With regard to Woumans et al.'s study (2016), it is possible that the enriched educational experience in the bilingual group led to a faster increase in the intelligence measure compared to the inactive control group. As group assignment in such education circumstances is hardly ever random, parents with higher intelligence or a higher SES might more often seek language-learning opportunities for their children and thereby distort results (Kempe et al., 2015). There are individual differences in people's ability to process language input, both in L1 (Kidd et al., 2018) and in L2 acquisition (Darcy et al., 2015; Dörnyei, 2014; Serafini & Sanz, 2016). Those with better working memory and EF early on learn languages faster (Woodard et al., 2016). Winsler and colleagues (Kim et al., 2014; Winsler, 2023, this volume; Winsler et al., 2014) found that young dual-language learners in poverty who had stronger initial cognitive and self-control skills at age 4 learned English faster and were more likely to be classified as bilinguals later on in elementary school. Thus, better EF and initial general cognitive abilities might lead to higher language proficiency and more ease when acquiring additional languages (Yamasaki et al., 2018).

For this reason, many studies examining potential bilingual advantages in children have controlled for general IQ or cognitive skills by comparing these scores between language groups or including them in their analyses. No clear pattern emerges from them, as they both support (Barac et al., 2016; Czapka et al., 2020; Vega & Fernandez, 2011; Woumans et al., 2016) and falsify a bilingual advantage (Antón et al., 2014; Dick et al., 2019; Duñabeitia et al., 2014; Ladas et al., 2015) or show mixed findings (Naeem et al., 2018; Trebits et al., 2021). Studies that do not control for intelligence often comprise samples with a very young age for whom testing intelligence might be difficult due to age or experimental practicability (Verhagen et al., 2020, with 2-year olds; Brito Greaves et al. (2020) with 18-month olds; or Tran et al. (2018) and Bialystok et al. (2010) with 3- to 4-year-olds; see also section on culture). Studies with older samples that did not control for intelligence (including studies that only formulated an inclusion criterion with regard to normal intelligence) tend to find a bilingual advantage more often (Bialystok & Viswanathan, 2009; Crespo et al., 2019; Dicataldo & Roch, 2020; Kapa & Colombo, 2013; Krizman et al., 2016) than the opposite pattern (Haft et al., 2019; Moreno-Stokoe & Damian, 2020). This list, however, is not exhaustive.

As a general conclusion, we can state that relations between intelligence, bilingualism, and EF are complex, dynamic, and intertwined. Intelligence is clearly related to EF, bilingualism is linked to numerous enhanced cognitive skills implicated in intelligence (the topic of this section), intelligence and EF also contribute to bilingual language development (Winsler, 2023, this volume), and bilingualism, cognitive skills, and EF interact and influence each other in snowball fashion over time (Hernandez et al., 2018; Nguyen & Winsler, 2023, this volume). Therefore, intelligence is likely a confounding variable and/or a moderator variable for bilingual effects.

Activities that train/enhance EF

There is evidence that EF can be trained, and consequently, such experiences and activities that train or boost EF skills need to be controlled when monolinguals and multilinguals are compared. Little research exists that experimentally investigates the impact of different training activities and bilingualism. Therefore, we focus on meta-analyses or randomized controlled studies with control groups and child participants in this section.

The effects of *physical activity* on cognition are well studied (for recent meta-analyses, see de Greeff et al., 2018; Verburgh et al., 2014). In sum, de Greeff et al. (2018) and Verburgh et al. (2014) analyzed 37 studies including children between the ages of 6 and 12. They found a positive effect of acute (single bout) physical activity (cardiovascular exercise, yoga) on attention, and for longitudinal trainings a positive effect on attention, EF, and academic skills. Regarding specific EF components, longitudinal training interventions (e.g., to improve cardiorespiratory fitness, rope jumping, or playing team games) improved working memory and cognitive flexibility, while inhibition was significantly affected only by acute physical activity.

In adults, playing certain types of *computer games* is related to better information processing in general and executive functions specifically (for meta-analyses, see Bediou et al., 2018; Powers et al., 2013; Wang et al., 2016). However, little research exists for children. They show smaller or even no significant effects, in contrast to work with young adults (Bediou et al., 2018; Powers et al., 2013). A recent cross-sectional study including 119 preschoolers indicates that time spent playing certain types of computer games (but not game content) was positively related to EF (measured by different inhibition and planning tasks) when age, SES, and gender were controlled (Yang et al., 2020). Note that in this study, the type of electronic games, play time, and game content were revealed only by parents' responses on a questionnaire. The only study investigating the effect of bilingualism and playing computer games (Bialystok, 2006) revealed that young adult players exhibited a general processing speed advantage in inhibition tasks (a Simon and a Flanker task), while bilingualism only led to lower reaction times in the most demanding condition of the Flanker task. These results are probably not generalizable but indicate that playing computer games affects EF perhaps more than bilingualism and thus should be examined and controlled for in bilingual effects studies.

A recent randomized blind study assessed the effects of *musical training* on various aspects of cognition (Jaschke et al., 2018). Primary school children attended different trainings over two years and were assigned to one of two training groups receiving musical training, one with and one without prior music training, an active control group participating in an arts program, or an inactive control group. Both music groups improved in intelligence, planning, and inhibition, and the art group improved in visuospatial memory. The meta-analysis by Cooper (2020) found a medium effect size in school-aged children that became nonsignificant when moderator variables, like setting or type of control group, were controlled. The authors conclude that music training can effectively improve EF in children, but its heterogeneous impact is comparable to that of other cognitive interventions. Studies investigating the impact of musical training and bilingualism on EF have focused on adults and revealed either an advantage for musicians only (Moradzadeh et al., 2015) or similar behavioral patterns but different neural processing (Moreno et al., 2014; Vaquero et al., 2020). For example, in the study by Moreno et al. (2014), adult musicians and bilinguals exhibited similar behavioral patterns in an inhibition task (go/no go task that requires suppression of a motor response) but different neural responses in their ERP data. In summary, musical training can significantly alter EF performance in children and adults. Both bilingualism and musical training can alter neural structures and processing, but it remains unclear if and how both affect children.

Additional activities that can impact EF performance are *mindfulness training*, like yoga, or meditation, (for a meta-analysis, see Mak et al., 2018; Zelazo et al., 2018) and academic abilities, which reciprocally influence each other (Blair, 2016; Zelazo et al., 2018). Negative influence on EF can also stem from a lack of sleep, stress, and loneliness (Diamond & Lee, 2011). Of course, a complete review of factors that affect EF in children is beyond the scope of this chapter. We point to the mentioned factors simply to show that there are many potentially confounding variables to consider when comparing monolinguals and bilinguals and looking for group differences in EF. Best practice is, thus, to measure and control for such variables to help make the groups being compared as similar as possible on such confounding variables.

Age

The uncertainty of a bilingual advantage in children may owe some debt to maturation of cognitive functions and their orchestration in childhood. There is general agreement in the field that EF typically develops in a complex trajectory with slow development in early childhood, a peak in early adulthood, and a decline later in life (Best et al., 2011; Filippi et al., 2020; Zelazo & Lee, 2010). More specifically, all components, i.e., inhibition, switching, and working memory, are somewhat established at the age of 4 (Alloway et al., 2006; Zelazo et al., 2003). The preschool years (Hongwanishkul et al., 2005) and the ages of 6 to 13 (Brocki & Bohlin, 2004) are commonly related to important developmental gains in EF (de Cat et al., 2018). One of the crucial cognitive functions is inhibition. Park et al. (2018) conducted a longitudinal study with 8- to 12-year-old monolinguals and bilinguals. A strong increase in inhibition ability (Flanker task) but not in switching (Dimensional Change Card Sort) was observed for the bilingual but not the monolingual children. Thus, "bilingual experience may modulate the developmental rates of some components of EF but not others, resulting in specific EF performance differences between bilinguals and monolinguals only at certain developmental time points" (Park et al., 2018, p. 1842; see also Carlson & Meltzoff, 2008; Hartanto et al., 2019). This general conclusion of earlier bilingual EF development is specified in claims of superior EF performance when the bilingual child has (not yet) fully developed EF: enhanced performance on conflict tasks only manifests itself in early childhood when individuals have not yet reached peak performance on these tasks – later performance might be at ceiling (Bialystok & Martin, 2004), and bilingual advantages might not be easily detected.

There are mixed findings in terms of particular age groups in which the bilingual advantage is more likely to be observed. For example, cross-sectional studies comparing mono- and bilingual samples from childhood to late adulthood found no positive effect of bilingualism (Filippi et al., 2020; Gathercole et al., 2014). Both studies tested English monolinguals and compared them to either Welsh-English bilinguals with varying levels of language dominance (Gathercole et al., 2014) or simultaneous bilinguals with various language backgrounds (Filippi et al., 2020). Park et al. (2018), in contrast, carried out a longitudinal study assessing inhibition, updating, and shifting in Spanish-English bilinguals at the age of 9 and 10 years. In comparison to the monolingual English control group, reaction times in the incongruent block in the inhibition task decreased more steeply in bilinguals. In the shifting task, mixing costs were lower in bilinguals at both test points (measured at ages 9 and 10). The authors argue that both effects indicate superior monitoring abilities and that EF development might be accelerated by bilingualism.

Recent meta-analyses tend to find no bilingual advantage in young adults (Lehtonen et al., 2018; Ware et al., 2020). Exceptions are analyses by Grundy and Timmer (2017), who found evidence for an advantage in working memory tasks, and Donnelly et al. (2019), who found a very small effect size for a bilingual advantage in an interference inhibition task with no differences between children and young and older adults. For children, results are mixed too, but show a tendency toward a positive effect of bilingualism (Gunnerud et al., 2020; Hilchey et al., 2015; Lowe et al., 2021; Schirmbeck et al., 2020; Schroeder, 2018; Trebits et al., 2021; Ware et al., 2020). Gunnerud et al. (2020), for example, report a statistically significant but negligible effect size for EF performance overall in children younger than 18 years, and after correction for publication bias, a positive effect remained only for switching but not for inhibition and monitoring. In Lowe et al. (2021), the small but statistically significant effect of bilingualism on children disappeared after correction for publication bias. Ware et al. (2020) compared children and young and older adults and found the largest effect sizes in older adults. Regarding bilingual children, positive effects were found for accuracy and reaction times in both incongruent and congruent trials but not for interference. These effects, however, were not significantly different in a subgroup analysis taking age into account.

In conclusion, age is clearly an important factor, as EF and the tasks used to measure it vary as a function of age. It appears that bilingualism might accelerate EF development in childhood and perhaps retard/delay cognitive decline in late adulthood. Although beyond the scope of the current review, which focuses on children, a number of studies have shown bilingualism to be a buffering factor in late life, slowing dementia and cognitive decline (Mendez et al., 2020; Mukadam et al., 2017). Thus, participant age clearly serves as a moderator, affecting the probability of finding bilingual cognitive advantages.

Gender

Most studies ensure a similar number of males and females in their sample, or they match groups on gender, but whether gender influences EF development has not been studied in detail. Subramaniapillai et al. (2019) suggest the cognitive decline in middle-aged samples can affect women more strongly than men due to hormonal changes around menopause and environmental factors (e.g., psychosocial stress or greater number of major life roles as employee and caregiver). Bilingualism in their sample, acted as a protective factor in women. This study was conducted in Canada, but in a large American study, men showed a steeper decline in some cognitive measures (McCarrey et al., 2016). With regard to children, the review by Schirmbeck et al. (2020) indicates that there are some gender differences in EF performance, mostly indicating girls to outperform their male peers. The direction of this difference, however, depends on the country in which the study was conducted. To date, however, there is no evidence that gender moderates relations between bilingualism and EF.

External variables

Socioeconomic status (SES)

SES, either directly in terms of deprivation, stress, toxins, hunger, etc. or as a proxy for limited opportunities to engage in the cognitively stimulating and challenging activities and parent–child interactions that lead to better EF (Valian, 2015), is a central point in the discussion on confounding variables in bilingual advantage research, since it clearly influences EF (Calvo & Bialystok, 2014; Kishiyama et al., 2009; Morton & Harper, 2007). In infancy, there is no effect of SES on EF (Brito, Troller-Renfree et al., 2020), but from early childhood to primary school, child discrepancies in EF skills between low- and higher-SES families are constant (Hackman et al., 2015). Noble et al. (2005) showed that parental education and parental occupation (an index of SES) were responsible for more than 14% of the variance in EF outcomes in children. The meta-analysis from Lawson et al. (2018) found a small to medium effect of SES for EF. A composite measure including economic and educational aspects showed the largest effect. Consequently, it is important for future studies to assess SES precisely. Descriptive categorizations like "The communities in which the monolingual and bilingual children lived were geographically close and similar in socioeconomic status" (Bialystok & Martin, 2004, p. 328) are not sufficient to capture a child's family's educational and economic status.

Both SES and bilingualism independently influence EF (Calvo & Bialystok, 2014; Dicataldo & Roch, 2020; Naeem et al., 2018). Calvo and Bialystok (2014) did not find an interaction between SES and bilingualism (for similar results, see Krizman et al., 2016). Naeem et al. (2018), in contrast, found that the advantage of bilingual young adults compared to monolinguals on a Simon task was especially pronounced in their low-SES group. They conclude that SES impacts EF more strongly but that bilingualism can modulate this pattern, especially in disadvantaged groups. Support for a bilingual advantage in socioeconomically disadvantaged groups also comes from Hartanto et al. (2019), who found both SES and bilingualism to improve EF in a large sample of about 18,000 children between ages 5 and 7 years. This effect was especially pronounced in the lower-SES cohort. Studies focusing on lower-SES samples support this view (Engel de Abreu, Cruz-Santos et al., 2012; Calvo & Bialystok, 2014; Ladas et al., 2015). An opposite pattern, however, has also been found in Mezzacappa (2004), who found an advantage in higher-SES children. The meta-analysis from Gunnerud et al. (2020) support this view, as bilingual middle-class children, but not lower- and upper-class children, exhibited a bilingual advantage. Additionally, in group comparisons, in which multilinguals were disadvantaged with regard to SES compared to monolinguals, statistically controlling SES revealed a bilingual advantage (Blom et al., 2014; Czapka et al., 2020). Blom et al. used parental education and Czapka et al. (2020) mothers' education.

In conclusion, SES influences EF and needs to be controlled to avoid confounding results. Whether especially socioeconomically disadvantaged children benefit more from bilingualism needs to be determined by additional research.

Culture, location, and immigration

Variables that are unequal across bilingual and monolingual groups are often related to participants' origins. This includes the experience of migration (since bilinguals are often immigrants themselves or have a migration background), cultural differences, and the location/country of the study.

With regard to migration, both bilingualism and migration have been found to influence EF positively. The so-called *healthy migrant effect* describes the finding that immigration status can be associated with higher intelligence in comparison to native-born populations (Fuller-Thomson & Kuh, 2014). This might be caused by self-selection, because healthier and more competent people might be more driven, willing, and able to migrate, or by selection, through authorities only allowing certain people of higher-classes/education, etc. to immigrate to a particular country. Migrant and native populations, however, can also differ in the opposite way, with recent immigrant groups, especially those who may be refugees, fleeing war-torn countries, receiving asylum, and/or having experienced significant trauma during their migration experiences, having a lower SES, less income, lower education, and experienced more trauma. What is important is for bilingualism researchers to get good measures of family immigration experience, year/age of arrival, and country-of-origin information to help understand how such factor may relate to the EF skills of their bilingual individuals.

Cultural differences have also been discussed as an issue in bilingual advantage research. What is culture? It can entail religion, habits, attitude toward education, availability and type of learning opportunities, values, goals, and attitudes toward bilingualism. These aspects need to be considered, since they influence bilingual language acquisition and cognitive outcomes (Dixon et al., 2012). Dixon et al. compared 282 heritage speakers of Chinese, Malay, and Tamil who live in Singapore and spoke English as L2. The different language communities affected differential development of their heritage languages, and the impact of SES differed between the communities. There is considerable evidence that growing up in an Asian culture founded in Confucianism, in which a central aspect in cultural upbringing is self-control, strengthens EF. Two recent reviews (Samuel et al., 2018; Schirmbeck et al., 2020) support the view that growing up in an Asian culture can lead to superior EF compared to European or North American samples. Samuel et al. argue that the culture confound might have produced a number of false positive findings in the literature, as in 9 out of 10 studies between 2014 and 2018 that had a European and an Asian group showed bilingual advantages specifically for the Asian group. This pattern could be explained by culture alternatively. Studies on preschool children indicate specific effects of bilingualism on various EF components and of Asian culture on measures of self-control (Tran et al., 2018; Yang et al., 2011). Yang et al. (2011) revealed that 4- to 5-year-old children growing up in an Asian culture used a different strategy in the ANT, a test assessing different components of EF. While Korean-English bilinguals outperformed three groups of monolinguals (group sizes n = 13 to 15) in executive attention accuracy and overall RT, Korean monolinguals residing in Korea showed overall higher accuracy but at the cost of slower answers. Korean monolinguals residing in the US behaved similarly to English monolinguals from the US, indicating that acculturation to the host country transferred to EF. These findings indicate that the effect of culture (and in turn bilingualism) is not straightforward, i.e., better or worse EF, but EF training can focus on specific abilities, like being accurate, that can be traded for slower reactions (i.e., speed–accuracy-trade-off).

Another aspect of origin that has been found to matter for finding bilingual effects is *location*, either the geographical location of the sample or of the laboratory that runs the experiment. Meta-analyses come to different conclusions when geographical origin is taken into account as a factor for EF. Adesope et al. (2010) and Lowe et al. (2021) found only European but not American, Asian, or African samples to show a bilingual advantage. In the recent meta-analysis from Lehtonen et al. (2018), country moderated the effects of specific EF components, with the UK producing more bilingual advantages in attention than other countries. Geographical location is confounded with, among others, cultural, educational, and social aspects that need to be considered in research on the bilingual advantage. With regard to the laboratory's location, Gunnerud et al. (2020) found that the York lab (Bialystok's lab in Canada that produced the earliest and most evidence supporting a bilingual advantage) produced significantly more and stronger effects in favor of the bilingual advantage in children compared to other laboratories. This might have more to do with the personnel involved and the research methods used, however, than with geographical location.

Task-related factors

The cognitive task(s) used and the particular performance measures and variables analyzed can influence whether a bilingual advantage is detected. This is due to a number of reasons. The first is conceptual/theoretical. Executive function (EF) is a relatively new, notoriously complex, and challenging construct to define. There are multiple theoretical perspectives on EF, with little consensus in the field about how many subcomponents are involved (Friedman & Miyake, 2017; Posner & Digirolamo, 1998), how EF changes developmentally over time, and how best to measure it at different ages (Best & Miller, 2010). At the same time, within the field of bilingualism, there are limited and continually evolving theoretical assumptions as to *why* bilingualism would lead to specific changes in either brain function and/or cognition and *which* specific cognitive skills should be affected by what type of bilingual experience (Blanco-Elorrieta & Pylkkänen, 2018). In addition to the construct level, important variance is also seen at the task level and even at the level of the particular task performance measure(s) analyzed within a particular task. We will discuss each briefly in what follows.

Constructs/Theory. Most studies use a number of tasks to test different components of EF, and some have used factor analysis to identify underlying components. There seems to be good support for the Baddeley model for working memory for both monolingual and bilingual children between 8 and 12 years (Soliman, 2014; for an overview, see Baddeley, 2003). Soliman used 12 tests assessing the components of Baddeley's working memory model and found support for its components. Studies focusing on the components of EF, in contrast, have yielded heterogeneous results. Friedman and Miyake (2017) argue for the simultaneous unity and diversity of EF with a switching and updating component and either a common EF component or a separate inhibition component. These components seem to be established at the age of 4 (Alloway et al., 2006; Zelazo et al., 2003), but studies using factor analyses to corroborate this pattern in children rarely reflect this structure. For example, St Clair-Thompson and Gathercole (2006) used tests for updating, switching, and inhibition (following Miyake et al., 2000) and working memory with 51 children in England. Their factor analysis revealed two factors, one for working memory including updating tasks, and one for inhibition. Switching loaded partially on the updating factor. Engel de Abreu, Cruz-Santos, et al. (2012) used tasks to assess fluid intelligence, working memory, attention, and interference inhibition in monolingual Portuguese and bilingual Portuguese-Luxemburgish children at the age of 8 years. Their factor analysis revealed two factors assessing a "control," which could reflect a common EF component as it includes inhibition and selective attention, and a "representation" component, including working memory measures and fluid intelligence. Engel de Abreu et al. (2014) used a similar test battery with monolingual Portuguese children between 6 and 8 years residing in Brazil. This analysis revealed more fine-grained factors: working memory/cognitive flexibility, interference inhibition, selective attention, and response inhibition. In conclusion, neither the exact structure nor the timeframe of EF development has been conclusively clarified.

Tasks. Many different EF tasks have been used in the bilingual effects literature, and some tasks have been found to be more likely to reveal bilingual advantages; however, there is little consensus or consistency. In the meta-analysis from Ware et al. (2020), effect sizes of different tasks and their measures were compared. Only the attentional network task (ANT) revealed a consistent advantage, while tasks used to assess similar abilities, like the Stroop or Flanker task, did not consistently reveal group differences between mono- and multilinguals. Lehtonen et al. (2018) concluded from their meta-analysis with reference to adults that after correction for publication bias, no bilingual advantage exists. However, the effect sizes across different tasks differed widely, e.g., for shifting between $g = -0.01$ and $g = 0.55$ or for attention between $g = -0.16$ and $g = 0.72$. As the authors mention, the number of included studies influences effect sizes (e.g., the test of everyday attention with large effect sizes was used seven out of nine times in studies conducted in the UK), but still, this might indicate large differences between tasks.

The differences between tasks can at least partially be traced back to task impurity, i.e., the finding that tasks supposedly assessing the same EF component do not correlate (Friedman, 2016; Paap et al., 2015). The unavoidable impact of perceptual information (stimuli characteristics) and design components (response modality or dynamics) can conceal the common impact of specific EF demands (Valian, 2015).

Since task demands need to be high to find a bilingual advantage (Diamond, 2014), tasks need to be age appropriate. How *developmental* changes impact task performance can be illustrated, for example, for inhibition tasks. For young children, there is some evidence for a response inhibition advantage, which is somewhat confirmed by the age effect for response inhibition in the meta-analysis by Lowe et al. (2021). For older children and young adults, no impact of multilingualism on response inhibition is found. With regard to card-sorting tasks, which are used to assess switching, their complexity increases with increasing age of the assessed participants. In adult samples, the Wisconsin Card Sorting Test is often used, which comprises a complex design and trivalent stimuli (Festman & Münte, 2012). Even 9-year-old children can perform this test (Czapka & Festman, 2021), but with younger children, the complexity is reduced to, for example, one switch and bivalent stimuli as in the DCCS (Zelazo et al., 2003).

Studies that systematically varied task demands in EF tasks are rare (Qu et al., 2016). Costa et al. (2009) manipulated monitoring demands by varying the proportion of congruent and incongruent trials in a Flanker task. In the version with the highest monitoring demands, 50% of incongruent trials, a bilingual advantage was found. Ware et al. (2020) identified the ANT as an outstanding task, since it was the only task in their meta-analysis for which a bilingual advantage was consistently reported. This task (which was also used in Costa et al. (2009) might support the requirement for task difficulty or monitoring demands. Hernández et al. (2013) found that implicit (i.e., abstract symbols) in contrast to explicit cues (i.e., rule names, like "color") in a switching task increased cognitive demands and might have led to faster reaction times in their bilingual sample.

Measures. Performance on EF tasks can be determined through different measures, and a researcher's selection of the performance measure also matters and contributes to whether bilingual advantages will be found. For example, EF tasks are often assessed in terms of response latencies, but especially in children, accuracy is often used (Esposito et al., 2013; Tran et al., 2018). Esposito et al. (2013), for example, found 4-year-old Spanish-English bilinguals to answer more correctly on incongruent trials in an inhibition task than their monolingual peers. Czapka et al. (2020) used the same task, but with 9-year-old children living in Germany, and their multilinguals exhibited accuracy at ceiling and a global reaction time advantage. These differences are related to the developmental trajectories in EF: in early childhood, EF performance improves in accuracy, and only in later childhood do reaction times decrease (Best & Miller, 2010). In adults, accuracy in inhibition tasks does not seem to be an adequate measure of inhibition anymore (Rey-Mermet et al., 2019). The meta-analysis from Ware et al. (2020) supports the view that in different age groups, the bilingual advantage manifests itself in different performance measures. While smaller interference effects and reaction times in incongruent trials are found in adult samples, accuracy in incongruent trials and reaction times in congruent trials are similar between the age groups. Children were found to exhibit higher accuracy in congruent trials.

Interpreting different measures precisely remains challenging, as in the Wisconsin Card Sorting Test used to assess switching or higher-order executive functions (Miyake et al., 2000). Czapka and Festman (2021) used this task with 9-year-old children and discuss that global measures of task performance represent higher-order EF like problem solving and that no clear measure of switching performance could be identified in the classic version of the task. Finally, they found multilinguals to exhibit faster reaction times in one latent variable that represents monitoring abilities. They conclude that more studies need to identify the cognitive concepts that are represented by specific measures in EF tasks.

Additionally, statistical analysis strategies can influence study outcomes. Zhou and Krott (2016) found that data trimming of response latencies influenced outcomes, since bilinguals exhibited fewer long reaction times – their exclusion led more often to a similar performance of monolinguals and bilinguals. Struys et al. (2018) revealed that Dutch-French primary school children, but not their monolingual peers, showed a speed–accuracy trade-off in a Simon and a Flanker task. The authors interpret this pattern in the way that bilinguals were able to apply a specific strategy to reach the task's goal. But it shows that independent of age, task performance needs to be assessed carefully, and different strategies can change accuracy and reaction times.

Conclusion and implications

In this chapter, we have carefully looked at the empirical evidence for confounder and/or moderator variables in bilingual advantage research. The largest body of research focused on factors that are related to language and individual multilingualism. We looked into moderating effects of early bilingual upbringing and timing of first exposure to the second language, at level of proficiency in both languages, and whether it has a moderating effect if balanced proficiency or high proficiency in both languages has been attained. Type of schooling was our next moderator, together with the role of biliteracy, with the former being a very broad variable and difficult to capture due to worldwide differences in terms of the immersion; biliteracy seems to be a promising variable that needs more careful investigation. Next, we reviewed the studies on language proximity and bidialectism as well as social aspects related to languages, e.g., heritage language and prestige of languages. Finally, we checked if experience-based factors of language use play a role as moderator variable, in particular the setting of language use and the frequency of language switching. In the next section, we focused on internal background variables as moderator variables and summarized empirical findings for intelligence, activities that train or enhance EF, age, and gender as potential moderators. In the last section of our review, we considered a number of external variables, i.e., SES, culture, location of the study, immigration, and task-related factors.

In our attempt to review moderator and confounding variables in the currently available studies investigating bilingual effects on cognition in children, we come to the tentative, conservative conclusion that overall, the picture that emerged from the role of moderator variables is as vague as the appearance of the bilingual advantage itself. Like studies on the bilingual advantage, the scrutinized look at the moderator variables revealed both evidence and counterevidence for each moderator variable. While there was a clear impact of a number of factors suggesting ideal learning/acquisition conditions for bilingual children on attainment in their languages, this did not necessarily modulate the relation between bilingualism and EF performance but rather led the way to high proficiency in the languages. In the same vein, a number of confounding factors, mainly the internal and external background variables, have been shown to influence EF development, but not necessarily the relationship between language development and bilinguals' language performance.

However, it must be said that this conclusion – that there are no clear and consistent moderator effects in the bilingual advantage literature – is a very conservative one and one that is clinging to a very strict and perhaps unrealistic criterion – that moderator effects must *always* be found consistently in *all* studies and that they have to be in the *same direction and magnitude every time* they are studied in order to count. Nowhere in science is this really the case, as failures to replicate and nuance in findings are commonplace and indeed part of the empirical enterprise. Although the picture at present may not be as clear and consistent as one would like, it is in fact the case that *each* of the variables we have explored in this review (except for gender) has been found to moderate bilingual effects on EF at least once, and *each* of the variables reviewed here have been found to be related to EF and/or bilingualism, making them all at least *confounding variables* that should be considered in studies examining the effects of bilingualism on cognition.

What seems to be certain is that not all bilinguals show a bilingual advantage in EF performance. It could be that only a specific subgroup is able to reliably show superior performance, but to date, there is no single task that is continuously found to be best suited for revealing a bilingual advantage, nor has this specific subgroup been clearly identified. To find a clear bilingual advantage, it is necessary to compare different bilingual groups systematically. It would be advisable to develop hypotheses that are more specific than the general and broad bilingual advantage hypothesis, as it does not seem to hold for the bilingual speaker community of all ages worldwide.

To date, it seems that we have not yet been able to fully understand the direct relationship between bilingualism and cognitive development or the impact of moderator variables. What complicates matters (as well as conclusions) even further is the unresolved dilemma of directionality (Festman, 2021; Kersten & Greve, 2023, this volume; Winsler, 2023, this volume) – are smarter toddlers better able to learn two languages faster and more easily, or does exposure to two languages lead to children being smarter? Obviously, this question is put in an overly simplistic way. As this review has shown, there are many ways to improve language skills and foster bilingual acquisition, and there a many different activities to improve or even train EF and cognitive skills.

While research seems to have focused on corroborating or falsifying the bilingual advantage hypothesis, the parallelism and interplay of bilingualism and cognition (see Figure 3.2) seems to have been largely overlooked (Kersten, 2023, this volume). Most studies to date on the bilingual advantage are cross-sectional. A better understanding of this dynamic interplay over time, however, will require careful longitudinal research and strong theory.

With regard to how bilingualism should be captured, to date, no gold standard is available in terms of which information would be crucial and how it should be assessed/collected – the more so as tasks are dependent on the age of the participants (e.g., toddlers). It seems that the individual's history of language acquisition, the role and prestige of the languages, internal and external background variables for acquisition as well as current language use (in the context of exposure, switching frequency, society, and culture) would need to be included and preferably theoretically motivated (Kersten, 2023, this volume). This would be a first step toward nailing down the crucial speaker characteristics and the way to assess/capture them to be better able to describe the participants

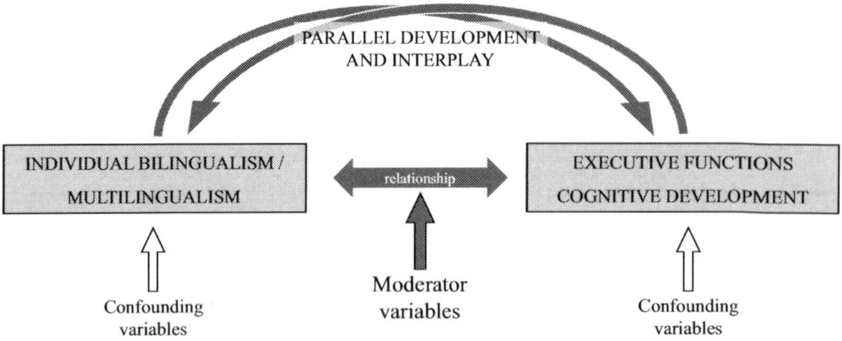

Figure 3.2 Graphical representation of confounder and moderator variables with dynamic interplay over time included

in order to make studies more easily comparable and to better determine the impact of possible moderators.

Given the complexity of bilingualism and the large number of speaker characteristics, we should not continue to compare groups of monolinguals to bilinguals, because they are not two homogenous groups that differ only in number of languages exposed to/acquired. Time and money for research might be better invested if we tried to understand bilingualism on its own rather than contrasting it with monolingualism. There are a number of fruitful, within-bilingual designs that have been used in which two meaningfully different bilingual groups are compared using a variety of different methodological approaches (Festman et al., 2010; Festman, 2012; Festman & Münte, 2012). Such methods show great promise for increasing our understanding of bilingualism and EF.

Concerning methodological and statistical issues, struggling with how bilingualism should be measured and operationalized is only one of several methodological issues that are important to consider. This issue of controlling statistically for relevant potentially confounding variables (like the ones discussed in this chapter) is paramount for studies examining bilingual effects, and to do so, such potentially confounding variables need to be measured. Obviously, as discussed in the section on task-related factors, the choice of EF task and the particular performance measures used matter for the appearance of bilingual effects. Regarding sample size and a potential publication bias, the field needs to move away from small-sample, two-group comparison designs that sometimes show huge effects and sometimes don't show any effects. One recent good development in the field is that journal editors, now cognizant of the problem of publication bias in bilingual advantage studies, are seeing the value of publishing null-effect studies, and those seem to be appearing more and more these days. Finally, researchers in the area of bilingualism and cognitive effects should more commonly embrace open science practices such as preregistration of studies, designs, hypotheses, and analyses (Shrout & Rodgers, 2018) to enhance theory and hypothesis building and to avoid post-hoc sense making when multiple tasks and measures are used.

In conclusion, it seems clear to us and to many in the field that *something* is different about the brains and cognitive skills of bilingual compared to monolingual individuals, and the field has been making fairly good progress in narrowing down the important components necessary for investigating this question. Good questions worth asking in science are rarely easy to answer, and results are not always clear. We hope that this chapter sheds at least some light on the important confounding and moderating variables that need to be considered in research on bilingual effects so the science in the area of bilingualism and executive functioning can move forward.

References

Adesope, O. O., Lavin, T., Thompson, T., & Ungerleider, C. (2010). A systematic review and meta-analysis of the cognitive correlates of bilingualism. *Review of Educational Research*, *80*(2), 207–245. https://doi.org/10.3102/0034654310368803

Alloway, T. P., Gathercole, S. E., & Pickering, S. J. (2006). Verbal and visuospatial short-term and working memory in children: Are they separable? *Child Development*, *77*(6), 1698–1716. https://doi.org/10.1111/j.1467-8624.2006.00968.x

Alrwaita, N., Houston-Price, C., & Pliatsikas, C. (2020). *The effects of using two variants of one language on cognition: Evidence from bidialectalism and diglossia* (Unpublished manuscript). https://doi.org/10.31234/osf.io/9c7df

Alt, M., Arizmendi, G. D., Gray, S., Hogan, T. P., Green, S., & Cowan, N. (2019). Novel word learning in children who are bilingual: Comparison to monolingual peers. *Journal of Speech, Language, and Hearing Research*, *62*(7), 2332–2360. https://doi.org/10.1044/2019_JSLHR-L-18-0009

Antón, E., Duñabeitia, J. A., Estévez, A., Hernández, J. A., Castillo, A., Fuentes, L. J., Davidson, D. J., & Carreiras, M. (2014). Is there a bilingual advantage in the ANT task? Evidence from children. *Frontiers in Psychology: Language Sciences*. https://doi.org/10.3389/fpsyg.2014.00398

Antoniou, K., Grohmann, K. K., Kambanaros, M., & Katsos, N. (2016). The effect of childhood bilectalism and multilingualism on executive control. *Cognition*, *149*, 18–30. https://doi.org/10.1016/j.cognition.2015.12.002

Antoniou, K., Veenstra, A., Kissine, M., & Katsos, N. (2020). How does childhood bilingualism and bi-dialectalism affect the interpretation and processing of pragmatic meanings? *Bilingualism: Language and Cognition*, *23*(1), 186–203. https://doi.org/10.1017/S1366728918001189

Armon-Lotem, S., Walters, J., & Gagarina, N. (2011). The impact of internal and external factors on linguistic performance in the home language and in L2 among Russian-Hebrew and Russian-German preschool children. *Linguistic Approaches to Bilingualism*, *1*(3), 291–317. https://doi.org/10.1075/lab.1.3.04arm

Baddeley, A. (2003). Working memory: Looking back and looking forward. *Nature Reviews Neuroscience*, *4*(10), 829–839. https://doi.org/10.1038/nrn1201

Barac, R., Moreno, S., & Bialystok, E. (2016). Behavioral and electrophysiological differences in executive control between monolingual and bilingual children. *Child Development*, *87*(4), 1277–1290. https://doi.org/10.1111/cdev.12538

Barbu, C., Gonzalez, A., Gillet, S., & Poncelet, M. (2019). Cognitive advantage in children enrolled in a second-language immersion elementary school program for one year. *Psychologica Belgica*, *59*(1), 416. http://doi.org/10.5334/pb.469

Bediou, B., Adams, D. M., Mayer, R. E., Tipton, E., Green, C. S., & Bavelier, D. (2018). Meta-analysis of action video game impact on perceptual, attentional, and cognitive skills. *Psychological Bulletin*, *144*(1), 77–110. https://doi.org/10.1037/bul0000130

Bedore, L., Pena, E., Summers, C., Boerger, K., Resendiz, M., Greene, K., Bohman, T. M., & Gillam, R. (2012). The measure matters: Language dominance profiles across measures in Spanish – English bilingual children. *Bilingualism: Language and Cognition*, *15*(3), 616–629. https://doi.org/10.1017/S1366728912000090

Berken, J. A., Gracco, V. L., & Klein, D. (2017). Early bilingualism, language attainment, and brain development. *Neuropsychologia*, *98*, 220–227. Https://doi.org/10.1016/j.neuropsychologia.2016.08.031

Best, J. R., & Miller, P. H. (2010). A developmental perspective on executive function. *Child Development*, *81*(6), 1641–1660. https://doi.org/10.1111/j.1467-8624.2010.01499.x.A

Best, J. R., Miller, P. H., & Naglieri, J. A. (2011). Relations between executive function and academic achievement from ages 5 to 17 in a large, representative national sample. *Learning and Individual Differences*, *21*(4), 327–336. https://doi.org/10.1016/j.lindif.2011.01.007

Bialystok, E. (2006). Effect of bilingualism and computer video game experience on the Simon task. *Canadian Journal of Experimental Psychology*, *60*(1), 68–79. https://doi.org/10.1037/cjep2006008

Bialystok, E., Barac, R., Blaye, A., & Poulin-Dubois, D. (2010). Word mapping and executive functioning in young monolingual and bilingual children. *Journal of Cognition and Development*, *11*(4), 485–508. https://doi.org/10.1080/15248372.2010.516420

Bialystok, E., & Martin, M. M. (2004). Attention and inhibition in bilingual children: Evidence from the dimensional change card sort task. *Developmental Science*, *3*(3), 325–339. https://doi.org/10.1111/j.1467-7687.2004.00351.x

Bialystok, E., & Viswanathan, M. (2009). Components of executive control with advantages for bilingual children in two cultures. *Cognition*, *112*(3), 494–500. https://doi.org/10.1016/j.cognition.2009.06.014

Blair, C. (2016). Executive function and early childhood education. *Current Opinion in Behavioral Sciences*, *10*(1), 102–107. https://doi.org/10.1016/j.cobeha.2016.05.009

Blanco-Elorrieta, E., & Pylkkänen, L. (2018). Ecological validity in bilingualism research and the bilingual advantage. *Trends in Cognitive Sciences*, *22*(12), 1117–1126. https://doi.org/10.1016/j.tics.2018.10.001

Blom, E., Boerma, T., Bosma, E., Cornips, L., & Everaert, E. (2017). Cognitive advantages of bilingual children in different sociolinguistic contexts. *Frontiers in Psychology*, *8*, 552. https://doi.org/10.3389/fpsyg.2017.00552

Blom, E., Küntay, A. C., Messer, M., Verhagen, J., & Leseman, P. (2014). The benefits of being bilingual: Working memory in bilingual Turkish-Dutch children. *Journal of Experimental Child Psychology*, *128*, 105–119. https://doi.org/10.1016/j.jecp.2014.06.007

Boerma, T., & Blom, E. (2020). Effects of developmental language disorder and bilingualism on children's executive functioning: A longitudinal study. *Research in Developmental Disabilities*, *107*, 103782. https://doi.org/10.1016/j.ridd.2020.103782

Bosma, E., Blom, E., & Versloot, A. (2017). Language balance and cognitive advantages in Frisian-Dutch bilingual children. In F. Lauchlan & M. C. Parafita Couto (Eds.), *Bilingualism and minority languages in Europe: Current trends and developments* (pp. 143–150). Cambridge Scholars Publishing.

Brito, N. H., & Barr, R. (2012). Influence of bilingualism on memory generalization during infancy. *Developmental Science*, *15*(6), 812–816. https://doi.org/10.1111/j.1467-7687.2012.1184.x

Brito, N. H., Greaves, A., Leon-Santos, A., Fifer, W. P., & Noble, K. G. (2020). Associations between bilingualism and memory generalization during infancy:

Does socioeconomic status matter? *Bilingualism: Language and Cognition*, *24*(2), 231–240. https://doi.org/10.1017/S1366728920000334

Brito, N. H., Troller-Renfree, S. V., Leon-Santos, A., Isler, J. R., Fifer, W. P., & Noble, K. G. (2020). Associations among the home language environment and neural activity during infancy. *Developmental Cognitive Neuroscience*, *43*, 100780. https://doi.org/10.1016/j.dcn.2020.100780

Brocki, K., & Bohlin, G. (2004). Executive functions in children aged 6 to 13: A dimensional and developmental study. *Developmental Neuropsychology*, *26*, 571–593. https://doi.org/10.1207/s15326942dn2602_3

Bruton, A. (2015). CLIL: Detail matters in the whole picture. More than a reply to J. Hüttner and U. Smit (2014). *System*, *53*, 119–128. https://doi.org/10.1016/j.system.2015.07.005

Byers-Heinlein, K., Esposito, A. G., Winsler, A., Marian, V., Castro, D. C., & Luk, G. (2019). The case for measuring and reporting bilingualism in developmental research. *Collabora: Psychology*. www.collabra.org/articles/10.1525/collabra.233

Calvo, A., & Bialystok, E. (2014). Independent effects of bilingualism and socioeconomic status on language ability and executive functioning. *Cognition*, *130*(3), 278–288. https://doi.org/10.1016/j.cognition.2013.11.015

Carlson, S. M., & Meltzoff, A. N. (2008). Bilingual experience and executive functioning in young children. *Developmental Science*, *11*(2), 282–298. https://doi.org/10.1111/j.1467-7687.2008.00675.x

Chen, S. H., Zhou, Q., Uchikoshi, Y., & Bunge, S. A. (2014). Variations on the bilingual advantage? Links of Chinese and English proficiency to Chinese American children's self-regulation. *Frontiers in Psychology*, *5*, 1069. https://doi.org/10.3389/fpsyg.2014.01069

Comishen, K. J., Bialystok, E., & Adler, S. A. (2019). The impact of bilingual environments on selective attention in infancy. *Developmental Science*, *22*(4), e12797. https://doi.org/0.1111/desc.12797

Conway, A. R. A., Kane, M. J., & Engle, R. W. (2003). Working memory capacity and its relation to general intelligence. *Trends in Cognitive Sciences*, *7*(12), 547–552. https://doi.org/10.1016/j.tics.2003.10.005

Cooper, P. K. (2020). It's all in your head: A meta-analysis on the effects of music training on cognitive measures in schoolchildren. *International Journal of Music Education*, *38*(3), 321–336. https://doi.org/10.1177/0255761419881495

Correia, L., & Flores, C. (2017). The role of input factors in the lexical development of European Portuguese as a heritage language in Portuguese – German bilingual speakers. *Languages*, *2*(4), 30. https://doi.org/10.3390/languages2040030

Costa, A., Hernández, M., Costa-Faidella, J., & Sebastián-Gallés, N. (2009). On the bilingual advantage in conflict processing: Now you see it, now you don't. *Cognition*, *113*(2), 135–149. https://doi.org/10.1016/j.cognition.2009.08.001

Costa, A., & Sebastián-Gallés, N. (2014). How does the bilingual experience sculpt the brain? *Nature Reviews Neuroscience*, *15*(5), 336–345. https://doi.org/10.1038/nrn3709

Crespo, K., Gross, M., & Kaushanskaya, M. (2019). The effects of dual language exposure on executive function in Spanish – English bilingual children with different language abilities. *Journal of Experimental Child Psychology*, *188*, 104663. https://doi.org/10.1016/j.jecp.2019.104663

Czapka, S., & Festman, J. (2021). Wisconsin card sorting test reveals a monitoring advantage but not a switching advantage in multilingual children. *Journal of Experimental Child Psychology*, *204*, 105038. https://doi.org/10.1016/j.jecp.2020.105038

Czapka, S., Wotschack, C., Klassert, A., & Festman, J. (2020). A path to the bilingual advantage: Pairwise matching of individuals. *Bilingualism: Language and Cognition*, *23*(2), 344–354. https://doi.org/10.1017/S1366728919000166

Darcy, I., Park, H., & Yang, C. L. (2015). Individual differences in L2 acquisition of English phonology: The relation between cognitive abilities and phonological processing. *Learning and Individual Differences*, *40*, 63–72. https://doi.org/10.1016/j.lindif.2015.04.005

de Bruin, A., Dick, A. S., & Carreiras, M. (2021). Clear theories are needed to interpret differences: Perspectives on the bilingual advantage debate. *Neurobiology of Language*, 1–46. https://doi.org/10.1162/nol_a_00038

de Cat, C., Gusnanto, A., & Serratrice, L. (2018). Identifying a threshold for the executive function advantage in bilingual children. *Studies in Second Language Acquisition*, *40*(1), 119–151. https://doi.org/10.1017/S0272263116000486

de Greeff, J. W., Bosker, R. J., Oosterlaan, J., Visscher, C., & Hartman, E. (2018). Effects of physical activity on executive functions, attention and academic performance in preadolescent children: A meta-analysis. *Journal of Science and Medicine in Sport*, *21*(5), 501–507. https://doi.org/10.1016/j.jsams.2017.09.595

De Houwer, A. (2021). *Bilingual development in childhood*. Cambridge University Press. https://doi.org/10.1017/9781108866002

DeLuca, V., Rothman, J., Bialystok, E., & Pliatsikas, C. (2020). Duration and extent of bilingual experience modulate neurocognitive outcomes. *NeuroImage*, *204*, 116222. https://doi.org/10.1016/j.neuroimage.2019.116222

DeLuca, V., Rothman, J., & Pliatsikas, C. (2019). Linguistic immersion and structural effects on the bilingual brain: A longitudinal study. *Bilingualism: Language and Cognition*, *22*(5), 1160–1175. https://doi.org/10.1017/S1366728918000883

Diamond, A. (2013). Executive functions. *Annual Review of Psychology*, *64*, 135–168. https://doi.org/10.1146/annurev-psych-113011-143750

Diamond, A. (2014). Want to optimize executive functions and academic outcomes? Simple, just nourish the human spirit. *Minnesota Symposia on Child Psychology*, *37*, 205–232.

Diamond, A., & Lee, K. (2011). Interventions shown to aid executive function development in children 4 to 12 years old. *Science*, *333*, 959–964. https://doi.org/10.1126/science.334.6054.311-d

Dicataldo, R., & Roch, M. (2020). Are the effects of variation in quantity of daily bilingual exposure and socioeconomic status on language and cognitive abilities independent in preschool children? *International Journal of Environmental Research and Public Health*, *17*(12), 1–23. https://doi.org/10.3390/ijerph17124570

Dick, A. S., Garcia, N. L., Pruden, S. M., Thompson, W. K., Hawes, S. W., Sutherland, M. T., . . . Gonzalez, R. (2019). No evidence for a bilingual executive function advantage in the nationally representative ABCD study. *Nature and Human Behavior*, *3*(9), 999. https://doi.org/10.1038/s41562-019-0609-3

Dixon, L. Q., Zhao, J., Quiroz, B. G., & Shin, J.-Y. (2012). Home and community factors influencing bilingual children's ethnic language vocabulary development. *International Journal of Bilingualism*, *16*(4), 541–565. https://doi.org/10.1177/1367006911429527

Donnelly, S., Brooks, P. J., & Homer, B. D. (2019). Is there a bilingual advantage on interference-control tasks? A multiverse meta-analysis of global reaction time and interference cost. *Psychonomic Bulletin and Review*, 1122–1147. https://doi.org/10.3758/s13423-019-01567-z

Dörnyei, Z. (2014). *The psychology of the language learner: Individual differences in second language acquisition*. Routledge.

D'Souza, D., Brady, D., Haensel, J. X., & D'Souza, H. (2020). Is mere exposure enough? The effects of bilingual environments on infant cognitive development. *Royal Society Open Science*, 7180191. https://doi.org/10.1098/rsos.180191

D'Souza, D., Brady, D., Haensel, J. X., & D'Souza, H. (2021). Early bilingual experience is associated with change detection ability in adults. *Scientific Reports*, *11*(1), 2068. https://doi.org/10.1038/s41598-021-81545-5

Duñabeitia, J. A., & Carreiras, M. (2015). The bilingual advantage: Acta est fabula. *Cortex*, *73*, 371–372. http://doi.org/10.1016/j.cortex.2015.06.009

Duñabeitia, J. A., Hernández, J. A., Antón, E., Macizo, P., Estévez, A., Fuentes, L. J., & Carreiras, M. (2014). The inhibitory advantage in bilnigual children revisited: Myth or reality? *Experimental Psychology*, *61*, 234–251. doi: 10.1027/1618-3169/a000243

Emmorey, K., Giezen, M. R., & Gollan, T. H. (2016). Psycholinguistic, cognitive, and neural implications of bimodal bilingualism. *Bilingualism: Language and Cognition*, *19*(2), 223–242. https://doi.org/10.1017/S1366728915000085

Emmorey, K., Luk, G., Pyers, J. E., & Bialystok, E. (2008). The source of enhanced cognitive control in bilinguals: Evidence From bimodal bilinguals. *Psychological Science*, *19*(12), 1201–1206. https://doi.org/10.1111/j.1467-9280.2008.02224.x

Engel de Abreu, P. M. J., Cruz-Santos, A., Tourinho, C. J., Martin, R., & Bialystok, E. (2012). Bilingualism enriches the poor: Enhanced cognitive control in low-income minority children. *Psychological Science*, *23*(11), 1364–1371. https://doi.org/10.1177/0956797612443836

Engel de Abreu, P. M. J., Puglisi, M. L., Cruz-Santos, A., Befi-Lopes, D. M., & Martin, R. (2014). Effects of impoverished environmental conditions on working memory performance. *Memory*, *22*(4), 323–331. https://doi.org/10.1080/09658211.2013.781186

Escobar, G. P., Kalashnikova, M., & Escudero, P. (2018). Vocabulary matters! The relationship between verbal fluency and measures of inhibitory control in monolingual and bilingual children. *Journal of Experimental Child Psychology*, *170*, 177–189. https://doi.org/10.1016/j.jecp.2018.01.012

Esposito, A. G., Baker-Ward, L., & Mueller, S. T. (2013). Interference suppression vs. response inhibition: An explanation for the absence of a bilingual advantage in preschoolers' Stroop task performance. *Cognitive Development*, *28*(4), 354–363. https://doi.org/10.1016/j.cogdev.2013.09.002

Feldman, C., & Shen, M. (1971). Some language-related cognitive advantages of bilingual five-year-olds. *The Journal of Genetic Psychology*, *118*(2), 235–244. https://doi.org/10.1080/00221325.1971.10532612

Festman, J. (2012). Language control abilities of late bilinguals. *Bilingualism: Language & Cognition*, *15*(3), 580–593. https://doi.org/10.1017/S1366728911000344

Festman, J. (2021). Learning and processing multiple languages: The more the easier? *Language Learning*, *71*(S1), 121–162. https://doi.org/10.1111/lang.12437

Festman, J., & Münte, T. F. (2012). Cognitive control in Russian-German bilinguals. *Frontiers in Psychology*, *3*(APR), 1–7. https://doi.org/10.3389/fpsyg.2012.00115

Festman, J., Poarch, G. J., & Dewaele, J.-M. (2017). *Raising multilingual children*. Multilingual Matters.

Festman, J., Rodriguez-Fornells, A., & Münte, T. F. (2010). Individual differences in control of language interference in late bilinguals are mainly related to general executive abilities. *Behavioral and Brain Functions*, *6*(5). www.behavioralandbrainfunctions.com/content/6/1/5

Filippi, R., Ceccolini, A., Periche-Tomas, E., & Bright, P. (2020). Developmental trajectories of metacognitive processing and executive function from childhood to older age. *Quarterly Journal of Experimental Psychology*, *73*(11), 1757–1773. https://doi.org/10.1177/1747021820931096

Filippi, R., Morris, J., Richardson, F., Bright, P., Thomas, M., & Karmiloff-Smith, A. M. V. (2015). Bilingual children show an advantage in controlling verbal interference during spoken language comprehension. *Bilingualism: Language and Cognition*, *18*(3), 490–501. https://doi.org/10.1017/S1366728914000686

Friedman, N. P. (2016). Research on individual differences in executive functions. *Linguistic Approaches to Bilingualism*, *6*(5), 535–548. https://doi.org/10.1075/lab.15041.fri

Friedman, N. P., & Miyake, A. (2017). Unity and diversity of executive functions: Individual differences as a window on cognitive structure. *Cortex*, *86*, 186–204. https://doi.org/10.1016/j.cortex.2016.04.023

Fuller-Thomson, E., & Kuh, D. (2014). The healthy migrant effect may confound the link between bilingualism and delayed onset of Alzheimer's disease. *Cortex*, *52*(1), 128–130. https://doi.org/10.1016/j.cortex.2013.08.009

Gagarina, N., & Klassert, A. (2018). Input dominance and development of home language in Russian-German bilinguals. *Frontiers in Communication*, *3*, 40.

Garraffa, M., Beveridge, M., & Sorace, A. (2015). Linguistic and cognitive skills in Sardinian – Italian bilingual children. *Frontiers in Psychology*, *6*, 1898. https://doi.org/10.3389/fpsyg.2015.01898

Gathercole, V. C. M., Thomas, E. M., Guasch, N. V., Kennedy, I., Prys, C., Young, N., . . . Jones, L. (2016). Teasing apart factors influencing executive function performance in bilinguals and monolinguals at different ages. *Linguistic Approaches to Bilingualism*, *6*(5), 605–647. https://doi.org/10.1075/lab.15051.gat

Gathercole, V. C. M., Thomas, E. M., Kennedy, I., Prys, C., Young, N., Guasch, N. V., . . . Jones, L. (2014). Does language dominance affect cognitive performance in bilinguals? Lifespan evidence from preschoolers through older adults on card sorting, Simon, and metalinguistic tasks. *Frontiers in Psychology*, *5*(FEB), 1–14. https://doi.org/10.3389/fpsyg.2014.00011

Gillet, S., Barbu, C. A., & Poncelet, M. (2020). Exploration of attentional and executive abilities in French-speaking children immersed in Dutch since 1, 2,

3, and 6 years. *Frontiers in Psychology*, *11*, 3547. https://doi.org/10.3389/fpsyg.2020.587574

Giovannoli, J., Martella, D., Federico, F., Pirchio, S., & Casagrande, M. (2020). The impact of bilingualism on executive functions in children and adolescents: A systematic review based on the PRISMA method. *Frontiers in Psychology*, *11*, 2398. https://doi.org/10.3389/fpsyg.2020.574789

Gonçalves, T. S., Viapiana, V. F., Fonseca, R. P., & Hübner, L. C. (2021). Literacy, metalinguistic, and executive functions processing in bilingual children speakers of similar typology languages in a border area. *Bilingualism: Language and Cognition*, *24*, 758–766. https://doi.org/10.1017/S1366728920000735

Goriot, C., Denessen, E., Bakker, J., & Droop, M. (2016). Benefits of being bilingual? The relationship between pupils' perceptions of teachers' appreciation of their home language and executive functioning. *International Journal of Bilingualism*, *20*(6), 700–713. https://doi.org/10.1177/1367006915586470

Green, D. W., & Abutalebi, J. (2013). Language control in bilinguals: The adaptive control hypothesis. *Journal of Cognitive Psychology*, *25*(5), 515–530. https://doi.org/10.1080/20445911.2013.796377

Greenberg, A., Bellana, B., & Bialystok, E. (2013). Perspective-taking ability in bilingual children: Extending advantages in executive control to spatial reasoning. *Cognitive Development*, *28*(1), 41–50. https://doi.org/10.1016/j.cogdev.2012.10.002

Grundy, J. G. (2020). The effects of bilingualism on executive functions: An updated quantitative analysis. *Journal of Cultural Cognitive Science*, *4*(9), 177–199. https://doi.org/10.1007/s41809-020-00062-5

Grundy, J. G., & Timmer, K. (2017). Bilingualism and working memory capacity: A comprehensive meta-analysis. *Second Language Research*, *33*(3), 325–340. https://doi.org/10.1177/0267658316678286

Guerrero, S. L., Smith, S., & Luk, G. (2016). Home language usage and executive function in bilingual preschoolers. In J. W. Schwieter (Ed.), *Cognitive control and consequences of multilingualism* (pp. 351–373). John Benjamins.

Gunnerud, H. L., ten Braak, D., Reikerås, E. K. L., Donolato, E., & Melby-Lervåg, M. (2020). Is bilingualism related to a cognitive advantage in children? A systematic review and meta-analysis. *Psychological Bulletin*, *146*(12), 1059–1083. https://doi.org/10.1037/bul0000301

Hackman, D. A., Gallop, R., Evans, G. W., & Farah, M. J. (2015). Socioeconomic status and executive function: Developmental trajectories and mediation. *Developmental Science*, *18*(5), 686–702. https://doi.org/10.1111/desc.12246

Hakuta, K. (1986). *The mirror of language: The debate on bilingualism*. Basic Books.

Haft, S. L., Kepinska, O., Caballero, J. N., Carreiras, M., & Hoeft, F. (2019). Attentional fluctuations, cognitive flexibility, and bilingualism in kindergarteners. *Behavioral Sciences*, *9*(5), 58. https://doi.org/10.3390/bs9050058

Hartanto, A., Toh, W. X., & Yang, H. (2019). Bilingualism narrows socioeconomic disparities in executive functions and self-regulatory behaviors during earlychildhood: Evidence from the early childhood longitudinal study. *Child Development*, *90*, 1215–1235. https://doi.org/10.1111/cdev.13032

Hartanto, A., & Yang, H. (2016). Disparate bilingual experiences modulate task-switching advantages: A diffusion-model analysis of the effects of interactional context on switch costs. *Cognition*, *150*, 10–19. https://doi.org/10.1016/j.cognition.2016.01.016

Hartsuiker, R. J. (2015). Why it is pointless to ask under which specific circumstances the bilingual advantage occurs. *Cortex*, *73*, 336–337. https://doi.org/10.1016/j.cortex.2015.07.018

Helmer, K. A. (2020). *Learning and not learning in the heritage language classroom: Engaging Mexican-origin students*. Multilingual Matters.

Hernandez, A. E., Claussenius-Kalman, H. L., Ronderos, J., & Vaughn, K. A. (2018). Symbiosis, parasitism and bilingual cognitive control: A neuroemergentist perspective. *Frontiers in Psychology*, *19*. https://doi.org/10.3389/fpsyg.2018.02171

Hernandez, A. E., & Li, P. (2007). Age of acquisition: Its neural and computational mechanisms. *Psychological Bulletin*, *133*(4) 638–650. https://doi.org/10.1037/0033-2909.133.4.638

Hernández, M., Martin, C. D., Barceló, F., & Costa, A. (2013). Where is the bilingual advantage in task-switching? *Journal of Memory and Language*, *69*(3), 257–276. https://doi.org/10.1016/j.jml.2013.06.004

Hilchey, M. D., & Klein, R. M. (2011). Are there bilingual advantages on nonlinguistic interference tasks? Implications for the plasticity of executive control processes. *Psychonomic Bulletin & Review*, *18*(4), 625–658. https://doi.org/10.3758/s13423-011-0116-7

Hilchey, M. D., Saint-Aubin, J., & Klein, R. M. (2015). Does bilingual exercise enhance cognitive fitness in traditional non-linguistic executive processing tasks? In J. W. Schwieter (Ed.), *The Cambridge handbook of bilingual processing* (pp. 586–613). Cambridge University Press. https://doi.org/http://dx.doi.org/10.1017/CBO9781107447257.026

Hoff, E., & Core, C. (2013). Input and language development in bilingually developing children. *Seminars in Speech and Language*, *34*(4) 215–226. https://doi.org/10.1055/s-0033-1353448

Hoff, E., Rumiche, R., Burridge, A., Ribot, K. M., & Welsh, S. N. (2014). Expressive vocabulary development in children from bilingual and monolingual homes: A longitudinal study from two to four years. *Early Childhood Research Quarterly*, *29*(4), 433–444. https://doi.org/10.1016/j.ecresq.2014.04.012

Hongwanishkul, D., Happaney, K. R., Lee, W., & Zelazo, P. D. (2005). Assessment of hot and cool executive function: Age-related changes and individual differences. *Developmental Neuropsychology*, *28*, 617–644. https://doi.org/10.1207/s15326942dn2802_4

Iluz-Cohen, P., & Armon-Lotem, S. (2013). Language proficiency and executive control in bilingual children. *Bilingualism: Language and Cognition*, *16*(4), 884–899. https://doi.org/10.1017/S1366728912000788

Jaschke, A. C., Honing, H., & Scherder, E. J. A. (2018, February). Longitudinal analysis of music education on executive functions in primary school children. *Frontiers in Neuroscience*, *12*. https://doi.org/10.3389/fnins.2018.00103

Kałamała, P., Szewczyk, J., Chuderski, A., Senderecka, M., & Wodniecka, Z. (2020). Patterns of bilingual language use and response inhibition: A test of the adaptive control hypothesis. *Cognition*, *204*, 104373. https://doi.org/10.1016/j.cognition.2020.104373

Kalashnikova, M., & Mattock, K. (2014). Maturation of executive functioning skills in early sequential bilingualism. *International Journal of Bilingual Education and Bilingualism*, *17*(1), 111–123. https://doi.org/10.1080/13670050.2012.746284

Kane, M. J., & Engle, R. W. (2002). The role of prefrontal cortex in working-memory capacity, executive attention, and general fluid intelligence: An individual-differences perspective. *Psychonomic Bulletin & Review*, *9*(4), 637–671. https://doi.org/10.3758/BF03196323

Kapa, L. L., & Colombo, J. (2013). Attentional control in early and later bilingual children. *Cognitive Development*, *28*(3), 233–246. http://doi.org/10.1016/j.cogdev.2013.01.011

Kaushanskaya, M., Gross, M., & Buac, M. (2014). Effects of classroom bilingualism on task-shifting, verbal memory, and word learning in children. *Developmental Science*, *17*(4), 564–583. https://doi.org/10.1111/desc.12142

Kempe, V., Kirk, N. W., & Brooks, P. J. (2015). Revisiting theoretical and causal explanations for the bilingual advantage in executive functioning. *Cortex*, *73*, 342–344. https://doi.org/10.1016/j.cortex.2015.07.021

Kidd, E., Donnelly, S., & Christiansen, M. H. (2018). Individual differences in language acquisition and processing. *Trends in Cognitive Sciences*, *22*(2), 154–169. https://doi.org/10.1016/j.tics.2017.11.006

Kim, Y. K., Curby, T. W., & Winsler, A. (2014). Child, family, and school characteristics related to English proficiency development among low-income, dual language learners. *Developmental Psychology*, *50*(12), 2600–2613. https://doi.org/10.1037/a0038050

Kishiyama, M. M., Boyce, W. T., Jimenez, A. M., Perry, L. M., & Knight, R. T. (2009). Socioeconomic disparities affect prefrontal function in children. *Journal of Cognitive Neuroscience*, *21*(6), 1106–1115. https://doi.org/10.1162/jocn.2009.21101

Kovács, Á. M. (2009). Early bilingualism enhances mechanisms of false-belief reasoning. *Developmental Science*, *12*, 48–54. https://doi.org/10.1111/j.1467-7687.2008.00742.x

Kovács, Á. M., & Mehler, J. (2009a). Cognitive gains in 7-month-old bilingual infants. *Proceedings of the National Academy of Sciences*, *106*(16), 6556–6560. https://doi.org/10.1073/pnas.0811323106

Kovács, Á. M., & Mehler, J. (2009b). Flexible learning of multiple speech structures in bilingual infants. *Science*, *325*(5940), 611–612. https://doi.org/10.1126/science.1173947

Kremin, L. V., Arredondo, M. M., Hsu, L. S. J., Satterfield, T., & Kovelman, I. (2019). The effects of Spanish heritage language literacy on English reading for Spanish – English bilingual children in the US. *International Journal of Bilingual Education and Bilingualism*, *22*(2), 192–206. https://doi.org/10.1080/13670050.2016.1239692

Krizman, J., Skoe, E., & Kraus, N. (2016). Bilingual enhancements have no socioeconomic boundaries. *Developmental Science*, *19*(6), 881–891. https://doi.org/10.1111/desc.12347

Kuzyk, O., Friend, M., Severdija, V., Zesiger, P., & Poulin-Dubois, D. (2019). Are there cognitive benefits of code-switching in bilingual children? A longitudinal study. *Bilingualism: Language and Cognition*, *23*(3), 1–12. https://doi.org/10.1017/S1366728918001207

Ladas, A. I., Carroll, D. J., & Vivas, A. B. (2015). Attentional processes in low-socioeconomic status bilingual children: Are they modulated by the amount of bilingual experience? *Child Development*, *86*(2), 557–578. https://doi.org/10.1111/cdev.12332

Lawson, G. M., Hook, C. J., & Farah, M. J. (2018). A meta-analysis of the relationship between socioeconomic status and executive function performance among children. *Developmental Science*, *21*(2), 1–22. https://doi.org/10.1111/desc.12529

Lehtonen, M., Soveri, A., Laine, A., Järvenpää, J., de Bruin, A., & Antfolk, J. (2018). Is bilingualism associated with enhanced executive functioning in adults? A meta-analytic review. *Psychological Bulletin*, *144*(4), 394–425. https://doi.org/10.1037/bul0000142

Leivada, E., Westergaard, M., Duñabeitia, J., & Rothman, J. (2021). On the phantom-like appearance of bilingualism effects on neurocognition: (How) should we proceed? *Bilingualism: Language and Cognition*, *24*(1), 197–210. https://doi.org/10.1017/S1366728920000358

Lowe, C. J., Cho, I., Goldsmith, S. F., & Morton, J. B. (2021). The bilingual advantage in children's executive functioning is not related to language status: A meta-analytic review. *Psychological Science*. https://doi.org/10.1177/0956797621993108

Luk, G., De Sa, E. R. I. C., & Bialystok, E. (2011). Is there a relation between onset age of bilingualism and enhancement of cognitive control? *Bilingualism: Language and cognition*, *14*(4), 588–595. https://doi.org/10.1017/S1366728911000010

Macizo, P., Bajo, T., & Paolieri, D. (2012). Language switching and language competition. *Second Language Research*, *28*(2), 131–149. https://doi.org/10.1177/0267658311434893

Mak, C., Whittingham, K., Cunnington, R., & Boyd, R. N. (2018). Efficacy of mindfulness-based interventions for attention and executive function in children and adolescents: A systematic review. *Mindfulness*, *9*(1), 59–78. https://doi.org/10.1007/s12671-017-0770-6

Marton, K. (2015, May). *Effects of language proficiency on speed of processing in executive function tasks in children*. Paper presented at the 10th International Symposium on Bilingualism. New Brunswick, New Jersey.

McCarrey, A. C., An, Y., Kitner-Triolo, M. H., Ferrucci, L., & Resnick, S. M. (2016). Sex differences in cognitive trajectories in clinically normal older adults. *Psychology and Aging*, *31*(2), 166–175. https://doi.org/10.1037/pag0000070

Mendez, M. F., Chavez, D., & Akhlaghipour, G. (2020). Bilingualism delays expression of Alzheimer's clinical syndrome. *Dementia and Geriatric Cognitive Disorders*, *48*(5–6), 281–289. https://doi.org/10.1159/000505872

Mezzacappa, E. (2004). Alerting, orienting, and executive attention: Developmental properties and sociodemographic correlates in an epidemiological sample of young, urban children. *Child Development*, *75*(5), 1373–1386. https://doi.org/10.1111/j.1467-8624.2004.00746.x

Miyake, A., Friedman, N. P., Emerson, M. J., Witzki, A. H., Howerter, A., & Wager, T. D. (2000). The unity and diversity of executive functions and their contributions to complex "frontal lobe" tasks: A latent variable analysis. *Cognitive Psychology*, *41*(1), 49–100. https://doi.org/10.1006/cogp.1999.0734

Moradzadeh, L., Blumenthal, G., & Wiseheart, M. (2015). Musical training, bilingualism, and executive function: A closer look at task switching and dual-task performance. *Cognitive Science*, *39*(5), 992–1020. https://doi.org/10.1111/cogs.12183

Moreno, S., Wodniecka, Z., Tays, W., Alain, C., & Bialystok, E. (2014). Inhibitory control in bilinguals and musicians: Event related potential (ERP) evidence for experience-specific effects. *PLoS One*, *9*(4), 1–8. https://doi.org/10.1371/journal.pone.0094169

Moreno-Stokoe, C. M., & Damian, M. F. (2020). Employing natural control for confounding factors in the hunt for the bilingual advantage in attention: Evidence from school children in Gibraltar. *Journal of Cognition*, *3*(1). https://doi.org/10.5334/joc.94

Morton, J. B., & Harper, S. N. (2007). What did Simon say? Revisiting the bilingual advantage. *Developmental Science*, *10*(6), 719–726. https://doi.org/10.1111/j.1467-7687.2007.00623.x

Mukadam, N., Sommerlad, A., & Livingston, G. (2017). The relationship of bilingualism compared to monolingualism to the risk of cognitive decline or dementia: A systematic review and meta-analysis. *Journal of Alzheimers Disease*, *58*(1), 45–54.

Naeem, K., Filippi, R., Periche-Tomas, E., Papageorgiou, A., & Bright, P. (2018, September). The importance of socioeconomic status as a modulator of the bilingual advantage in cognitive ability. *Frontiers in Psychology*, *9*, 1–9. https://doi.org/10.3389/fpsyg.2018.01818

Nicolay, A. C., & Poncelet, M. (2013). Cognitive advantage in children enrolled in a second-language immersion elementary school program for three years. *Bilingualism: Language & Cognition*, *16*(3), 597–607. https://doi.org/10.1017/S1366728912000375

Nicolay, A. C., & Poncelet, M. (2015). Cognitive benefits in children enrolled in an early bilingual immersion school: A follow up study. *Bilingualism: Language and Cognition*, *18*(4), 789–795. https://doi.org/10.1017/S1366728914000868

Nguyen, M. V. H., & Winsler, A. (2023, this volume). Early bilingualism increases the likelihood of taking (and mastering) foreign language courses later in secondary school. In K. Kersten & A. Winsler (Eds.), *Understanding variability in second language acquisition, bilingualism, and cognition: A multi-layered perspective*. Routledge.

Noble, K. G., Norman, M. F., & Farah, M. J. (2005). Neurocognitive correlates of socioeconomic status in kindergarten children. *Developmental Science*, *8*, 74–87. https://doi.org/10.1111/j.1467-7687.2005.00394.x

Okanda, M., Moriguchi, Y., & Itakura, S. (2010). Language and cognitive shifting: Evidence from young monolingual and bilingual children. *Psychological Reports*, *107*(1), 68–78. https://doi.org/10.2466/03.10.28.PR0.107.4.68-78

Oschwald, J., Schättin, A., von Bastian, C. C., & Souza, A. S. (2018). Bidialectalism and bilingualism: Exploring the role of language similarity as a link between linguistic ability and executive control. *Frontiers in Psychology*, *9*, 1997. https://doi.org/10.3389/fpsyg.2018.01997

Paap, K. R., & Greenburg, Z. I. (2013). There is no coherent evidence for a bilingual advantage in executive processing. *Cognitive Psychology*, *66*, 232–258. https://doi.org/10.1016/j.cogpsych.2012.12.002

Paap, K. R., Johnson, H. A., & Sawi, O. (2014). Are bilingual advantages dependent upon specific tasks or specific bilingual experiences? *Journal of Cognitive Psychology*, *26*(6), 615–639. https://doi.org/10.1080/20445911.2014.944914

Paap, K. R., Johnson, H. A., & Sawi, O. (2015). Bilingual advantages in executive functioning either do not exist or are restricted to very specific and undetermined circumstances. *Cortex*, *69*, 265–278. https://doi.org/10.1016/j.cortex.2015.04.014

Paap, K. R., & Sawi, O. (2016). The role of test-retest reliability in measuring individual and group differences in executive functioning. *Journal of Neuroscience Methods*, *274*, 81–93. https://doi.org/10.1016/j.jneumeth.2016.10.002

Park, J., Weismer, S. E., & Kaushanskaya, M. (2018). Changes in executive function over time in bilingual and monolingual school-aged children. *Developmental Psychology*, *54*(10), 1842–1853. https://doi.org/10.1037/dev0000562

Peal, E., & Lambert, W. (1962). The relation of bilingualism to intelligence. *Psychological Monographs: General and Applied*, *76*, 1–23.

Pelham, S. D., & Abrams, L. (2014). Cognitive advantages and disadvantages in early and late bilinguals. *Journal of Experimental Psychology: Learning, Memory, and Cognition*, *40*(2), 313. https://doi.org/10.1037/a0035224

Pliatsikas, C., Meteyard, L., Veríssimo, J., DeLuca, V., Shattuck, K., & Ullman, M. T. (2020). The effect of bilingualism on brain development from early childhood to young adulthood. *Brain Structure and Function*, *225*(7), 2131–2152. https://doi.org/10.1007/s00429-020-02115-5

Poarch, G. J., & Van Hell, J. G. (2012). Executive functions and inhibitory control in multilingual children: Evidence from second-language learners, bilinguals, and trilinguals. *Journal of Experimental Child Psychology*, *113*(4), 535–551. https://doi.org/10.1016/j.jecp.2012.06.013

Polinsky, M., & Scontras, G. (2020). Understanding heritage languages. *Bilingualism: Language and Cognition*, *23*(1), 4–20. https://doi.org/10.1017/S1366728919000245

Posner, M. I., & Digirolamo, G. J. (1998). Executive attention: Conflict, target detection, and cognitive control. In R. Parasuraman (Ed.), *The attentive brain* (pp. 401–423). MIT Press.

Pot, A., Keijzer, M., & de Bot, K. (2018). Intensity of multilingual language use predicts cognitive performance in some multilingual older adults. *Brain Sciences*, *8*, 92. http://dx.doi.org/10.3390/brainsci8050092

Powers, K. L., Brooks, P. J., Aldrich, N. J., Palladino, M. A., & Alfieri, L. (2013). Effects of video-game play on information processing: A meta-analytic investigation. *Psychonomic Bulletin & Review*, *20*(6), 1055–1079. https://doi.org/10.3758/s13423-013-0418-z

Purić, D., Vuksanović, J., & Chondrogianni, V. (2017). Cognitive advantages of immersion education after 1 year: Effects of amount of exposure. *Journal of Experimental Child Psychology*, *159*, 296–309. https://doi.org/10.1016/j.jecp.2017.02.011

Qu, L., Low, J. J. W., Zhang, T., Li, H., & Zelazo, P. D. (2016). Bilingual advantage in executive control when task demands are considered. *Bilingualism: Language and Cognition*, *19*(2), 277–293. https://doi.org/10.1017/S1366728914000376

Rey-Mermet, A., Gade, M., Souza, A. S., von Bastian, C. C., & Oberauer, K. (2019). Is executive control related to working memory capacity and fluid intelligence? *Journal of Experimental Psychology: General*, *148*(8), 1335–1372. https://doi.org/10.1037/xge0000593

Roca, M., Parr, A., Thompson, R., Woolgar, A., Torralva, T., Antoun, N., Manes, F., & Duncan, J. (2010). Executive function and fluid intelligence after frontal lobe lesions. *Brain*, *133*(1), 234–247. https://doi.org/10.1093/brain/awp269

Ross, J., & Melinger, A. (2017). Bilingual advantage, bidialectal advantage or neither? Comparing performance across three tests of executive function in middle childhood. *Developmental Science*, *20*(4), e12405. https://doi.org/10.1111/desc.12405

Sabourin, L., & Vīnerte, S. (2015). The bilingual advantage in the Stroop task: Simultaneous vs. early bilinguals. *Bilingualism: Language and Cognition*, *18*(2), 350–355. https://doi.org/10.1017/S1366728914000704

Samuel, S., Roehr-Brackin, K., Pak, H., & Kim, H. (2018). Cultural effects rather than a bilingual advantage in cognition: A review and an empirical study. *Cognitive Science*, *42*(7), 2313–2341. https://doi.org/10.1111/cogs.12672

Schirmbeck, K., Rao, N., & Maehler, C. (2020). Similarities and differences across countries in the development of executive functions in children: A systematic review. *Infant and Child Development*, *29*(1), 1–25. https://doi.org/10.1002/icd.2164

Schroeder, S. R. (2018, August). Do bilinguals have an advantage in theory of mind? A meta-analysis. *Frontiers in Communication*, *3*, 1–8. https://doi.org/10.3389/fcomm.2018.00036

Sebastian-Galles, N., & Santolin, C. (2020). Bilingual acquisition: The early steps. *Annual Review of Developmental Psychology*, *2*, 47–68. https://doi.org/10.1146/annurev-devpsych-013119-023724

Serafini, E. J., & Sanz, C. (2016). Evidence for the decreasing impact of cognitive ability on second language development as proficiency increases. *Studies in Second Language Acquisition*, *38*(4), 607–646. https://doi.org/10.1017/S0272263115000327

Shrout, P. E., & Rodgers, J. L. (2018). Psychology, science, and knowledge construction: Broadening perspectives from the replication crisis. *Annual Review of Psychology*, *69*, 487–510. https://doi.org/10.1146/annurev-psych-122216-011845

Simonis, M., Galand, B., Hiligsmann, P., & Szmalec, A. (2020). Attentional abilities of children enrolled in immersion education in French-speaking Belgium. *International Journal of Bilingual Education and Bilingualism*, 1–18. https://doi.org/10.1080/13670050.2020.1856033

Simonis, M., Van der Linden, L., Galand, B., Hiligsmann, P., & Szmalec, A. (2019). Executive control performance and foreign-language proficiency associated with immersion education in French-speaking Belgium. *Bilingualism: Language and Cognition*, *23*(2), 355–370. https://doi.org/10.1017/S136672891900021X

Singh, L. (2021). Evidence for an early novelty orientation in bilingual learners. *Child Development Perspectives*, *15*(2), 110–116. https://doi.org/10.1111/cdep.12407

Soliman, A. M. (2014). Bilingual advantages of working memory revisited: A latent variable examination. *Learning and Individual Differences*, *32*, 168–177. https://doi.org/10.1016/j.lindif.2014.02.005

St Clair-Thompson, H. L., & Gathercole, S. E. (2006). Executive functions and achievements in school: Shifting, updating, inhibition, and working memory. *Quarterly Journal of Experimental Psychology*, *59*(4), 745–759. https://doi.org/10.1080/17470210500162854

Struys, E., Duyck, W., & Woumans, E. (2018, September). The role of cognitive development and strategic task tendencies in the bilingual advantage controversy. *Frontiers in Psychology*, *9*, 1–11. https://doi.org/10.3389/fpsyg.2018.01790

Subramaniapillai, S., Rajah, M. N., Pasvanis, S., & Titone, D. (2019). Bilingual experience and executive control over the adult lifespan: The role of biological sex. *Bilingualism*, *22*(4), 733–751. https://doi.org/10.1017/S1366728918000317

Surrain, S. H., & Luk, G. (2017). Describing bilinguals: A systematic review of labels and descriptions used in the literature between 2005–2015. *Bilingualism: Language and Cognition*, *22*(2), 401–415. https://doi.org/10.1017/S1366728917000682

Tao, L., Marzecova, A., Taft, M., Asanowicz, D., & Wodniecka, Z. (2011). The efficiency of attentional networks in early and late bilinguals: The role of age of acquisition. *Frontiers in Psychology*, *2*, 123. https://doi.org/10.3389/fpsyg.2011.00123

Thomas-Sunesson, D., Hakuta, K., & Bialystok, E. (2018). Degree of bilingualism modifies executive control in Hispanic children in the US. *International Journal of Bilingual Education and Bilingualism*, *21*, 197–206. https://doi.org/10.1080/13670050.2016.1148114

Tran, C. D., Arredondo, M. M., & Yoshida, H. (2018). Early executive function: The influence of culture and bilingualism. *Bilingualism: Language and Cognition*, *22*(04), 714–732. https://doi.org/10.1017/S1366728918000160

Trebits, A., Koch, M. J., Ponto, K., Bruhn, A. C., Adler, M., & Kersten, K. (2021). Cognitive gains and socioeconomic status in early second language acquisition in immersion and EFL learning settings. *International Journal of Bilingual Education and Bilingualism*, 1–14. https://doi.org/10.1080/13670050.2021.1943307

Tsimpli, I. M., Vogelzang, M., Balasubramanian, A., Marinis, T., Alladi, S., Reddy, A., & Panda, M. (2020). linguistic diversity, multilingualism, and cognitive skills: A study of disadvantaged children in India. *Languages*, *5*(1), 10. https://doi.org/10.3390/languages5010010

Unsworth, N., Fukuda, K., Awh, E., & Vogel, E. K. (2014). Working memory and fluid intelligence: Capacity, attention control, and secondary memory retrieval. *Cognitive Psychology*, *71*(1), 1–26. https://doi.org/10.1016/j.cogpsych.2014.01.003

Unsworth, S. (2016). Quantity and quality of language input in bilingual language development. In E. Nicoladis & S. Montanari (Eds.), *Bilingualism across the lifespan* (pp. 103–122). De Gruyter Mouton.

Valian, V. (2015). Bilingualism and cognition: A focus on mechanisms. *Bilingualism: Language and Cognition*, *18*(1), 47–50. https://doi.org/10.1017/S1366728914000522

Van Mensel, L., Hiligsmann, P., Mettewie, L., & Galand, B. (2020). CLIL, an elitist language learning approach? A background analysis of English and Dutch CLIL pupils in French-speaking Belgium. *Language, Culture and Curriculum*, *33*(1), 1–14. https://doi.org/10.1080/07908318.2019.1571078

Vaquero, L., Rousseau, P. N., Vozian, D., Klein, D., & Penhune, V. (2020, February). What you learn & when you learn it: Impact of early bilingual & music experience on the structural characteristics of auditory-motor pathways.

NeuroImage, *213*, 116689. https://doi.org/10.1016/j.neuroimage.2020.116689

Vega, C., & Fernandez, M. (2011). Errors on the WCST correlate with language proficiency scores in Spanish-English bilingual children. *Archives of Clinical Neuropsychology*, *26*(2), 158–164. https://doi.org/10.1093/arclin/acq097

Vega-Mendoza, M., West, H., Sorace, A., & Bak, T. (2015). The impact of late, non-balanced bilingualism on cognitive performance. *Cognition*, *137*, 40–46. https://doi.org/10.1016/j.cognition.2014.12.008

Verburgh, L., Königs, M., Scherder, E. J. A., & Oosterlaan, J. (2014). Physical exercise and executive functions in preadolescent children, adolescents and young adults: A meta-analysis. *British Journal of Sports Medicine*, *48*(12), 973–979. https://doi.org/10.1136/bjsports-2012-091441

Verhagen, J., de Bree, E., & Unsworth, S. (2020). Effects of bilingual language use and language proficiency on 24-month-olds' cognitive control. *Journal of Cognition and Development*, *21*(1), 46–71. https://doi.org/10.1080/15248372.2019.1673752

Verhagen, J., Mulder, H., & Leseman, P. P. (2017). Effects of home language environment on inhibitory control in bilingual three-year-old children. *Bilingualism: Language & Cognition*, *20*(1), 114–127. https://doi.org/10.1017/S1366728915000590

Verreyt, N., Woumans, E. V. Y., Vandelanotte, D., Szmalec, A., & Duyck, W. (2016). The influence of language-switching experience on the bilingual executive control advantage. *Bilingualism: Language and Cognition*, *19*(1), 181–190. https://doi.org/0.1017/S1366728914000352

Wang, P., Liu, H. H., Zhu, X. T., Meng, T., Li, H. J., & Zuo, X. N. (2016). Action video game training for healthy adults: A meta-analytic study. *Frontiers in Psychology*, 7, 1–13. https://doi.org/10.3389/fpsyg.2016.00907

Ware, A. T., Kirkovski, M., & Lum, J. A. G. (2020). Meta-analysis reveals a bilingual advantage that is dependent on task and age. *Frontiers in Psychology*, *11*, 1–21. https://doi.org/10.3389/fpsyg.2020.01458

Weisleder, A., & Fernald, A. (2013). Talking to children matters: Early language experience strengthens processing and builds vocabulary. *Psychological Science*, *24*(11), 2143–2152. https://doi.org/10.1177/0956797613488145

Winsler, A. (2023, this volume). Becoming bilingual in Miami, USA: Predictors and outcomes of speed of English acquisition for low-income, dual-language learners. In K. Kersten & A. Winsler (Eds.), *Understanding variability in second language acquisition, bilingualism, and cognition: A multi-layered perspective*. Routledge.

Winsler, A., Kim, Y. K., & Richard, E. R. (2014). Socio-emotional skills, behavior problems, and Spanish competence predict the acquisition of English among English language learners in poverty. *Developmental Psychology*, *50*(9), 2242–2254. https://doi.org/10.1037/a0037161

Woodard, K., Pozzan, L., & Trueswell, J. C. (2016). Taking your own path: Individual differences in executive function and language processing skills in child learners. *Journal of Experimental Child Psychology*, *141*, 187–209. https://doi.org/10.1016/j.jecp.2015.08.005

Woumans, E., Ceuleers, E., Van der Linden, L., Szmalec, A., & Duyck, W. (2015). Verbal and nonverbal cognitive control in bilinguals and interpreters. *Journal of Experimental Psychology: Learning, Memory, and Cognition*, *41*(5), 1579–1586. https://doi.org/10.1037/xlm0000107

Woumans, E., Surmont, J., Struys, E., & Duyck, W. (2016). The longitudinal effect of bilingual immersion schooling on cognitive control and intelligence. *Language Learning*, *66*(S2), 76–91. https://doi.org/10.1111/lang.12171

Woumans, E., Van Herck, S., & Struys, E. (2019). Shifting gear in the study of the bilingual advantage: Language switching examined as a possible moderator. *Behavioral Sciences*, *9*(8), 86. https://doi.org/10.3390/bs9080086

Yamasaki, B. L., Stocco, A., & Prat, C. S. (2018). Relating individual differences in bilingual language experiences to executive attention. *Language, Cognition and Neuroscience*, *33*(9), 1128–1151. https://doi.org/10.1080/23273798.2018.1448092

Yang, S., Yang, H., & Lust, B. (2011). Early childhood bilingualism leads to advances in executive attention: Dissociating culture and language. *Bilingualism: Language and Cognition*, *14*(3), 412–422. https://doi.org/10.1017/S1366728910000611

Yang, X., Wang, Z., Qiu, X., & Zhu, L. (2020). The relation between electronic game play and executive function among preschoolers. *Journal of Child and Family Studies*, *29*(10), 2868–2878. https://doi.org/10.1007/s10826-020-01754-w

Yow, W. Q., & Li, X. (2015). Balanced bilingualism and early age of second language acquisition as the underlying mechanisms of a bilingual executive control advantage: Why variations in bilingual experiences matter. *Frontiers in Psychology*, *6*, 164. https://doi.org/10.3389/fpsyg.2015.00164

Yow, W. Q., Li, X., Lam, S., Gliga, T., Chong, Y. S., Kwek, K., & Broekman, B. F. (2017). A bilingual advantage in 54-month-olds' use of referential cues in fast mapping. *Developmental Science*, *20*(1), e12482. https://doi.org/10.1111/desc.12482

Yow, W. Q., & Markman, E. M. (2015). A bilingual advantage in how children integrate multiple cues to understand a speaker's referential intent. *Bilingualism: Language and Cognition*, *18*(3), 391–399. https://doi.org/10.1017/S1366728914000133

Zelazo, P. D., Forston, J. L., Masten, A. S., & Carlson, S. M. (2018, February). Mindfulness plus reflection training: Effects on executive function in early childhood. *Frontiers in Psychology*, *9*, 1–12. https://doi.org/10.3389/fpsyg.2018.00208

Zelazo, P. D., & Lee, W. S. (2010). Brain development: An overview. In R. M. Lerner (Ed.), *The handbook of life-span development* (pp. 89–114). Wiley.

Zelazo, P. D., Müller, U., Frye, D., Marcovitch, S., Argitis, G., Boseovski, J., . . . Carlson, S. M. (2003). The development of executive function in early childhood. *Monographs of the Society for Research in Child Development*, *68*(3). https://doi.org/10.1037/10522-163

Zhou, B., & Krott, A. (2016). Data trimming procedure can eliminate bilingual cognitive advantage. *Psychonomic Bulletin and Review*, *23*(4), 1221–1230. https://doi.org/10.3758/s13423-015-0981-6

Part II

The interplay of variables on macro, meso, and micro levels

4 The Proximity of Stimulation Hypothesis

Investigating the interplay of social and instructional variables with the cognitive-linguistic skills of young L2 learners

Kristin Kersten

Introduction

Research into factors that predict and explain second language acquisition (SLA) has traditionally focused on the relationship between two or only a few variables (Han, 2016). Studies have usually been situated within specific theoretical strands within SLA discourse. Lately, however, researchers have increasingly deplored the lack of a systems approach within SLA, as exemplified in this quote by Han (2019, Ch. 7, p. 7):

> the SLA field as a whole, despite its decades of existence, has come up short of a fuller and more credible understanding of the evolving nature of learning [. . .] in response to the changing configuration of interaction between learner-internal and learner-external resources.

Newer approaches call for a broader view on SLA as an interplay of various factors that have been identified in previous research and are situated in nested relationships. As language learning is strongly intertwined with cognitive processes and embedded in and shaped by the social environment, they point out the necessity to widen the scope of SLA research and go beyond the boundaries of our own field to include insights from research from adjacent fields such as psychology and sociology (Mitchell et al., 2019). According to Atkinson (2019, p. 115), "the continued lack of theoretical integration of the cognitive, the social, and the material is the single greatest barrier to transdisciplinarity in SLA studies," i.e., a barrier to a "viable transdisciplinary framework for SLA" (p. 119).

Following calls such as these, the last decade has seen an upsurge in interdisciplinary approaches to make sense of what is increasingly seen as a complex and dynamic system of factors shaping the (language) learning process (Mitchell et al., 2019). Only rather recently have attempts been made to develop more overarching frameworks that focus on the entanglement and interdependence of such factors. These approaches come

DOI: 10.4324/9781003155683-6

from very different strands of SLA including complex dynamic systems theory (Lenzing et al., 2023, this volume), the Douglas Fir Group (2016) and the research strand it has stimulated (Duff & Byrnes, 2019), or the systemic but more individual- and cognition-oriented Modular Cognition Framework (Truscott & Sharwood Smith, 2019).

These developments pose numerous theoretical and methodological challenges. Traditionally, studies including a restricted number of variables rely on the general linear model for data analysis. Yet a systemic view of influencing variables first of all needs to account theoretically for their complex relationships, i.e., their different conceptual levels, conceptual "distance" (distal and proximal external factors, internal factors), and their interdependence (i.e., container variables). Secondly, the complex nature of these interrelations calls for different analytical approaches (see Kersten & Greve, 2023, this volume, for a detailed discussion).

This chapter focuses on the interplay between external factors affecting internal linguistic and cognitive competences. In that sense, it is an empirical attempt to follow a line of thought outlined in Kersten and Greve (2023, this volume). It argues that effects of external on internal factors can best be described by proximal rather than distal external factors. This will be referred to as the *Proximity of Stimulation Hypothesis*. To that end, external factors need to be conceptually disentangled. Models on the interplay of external and internal factors will be introduced, and conceptual consequences for the operationalization of hierarchically ordered proximal and distal variables in empirical SLA studies will be discussed. Methodologically, the difference between statistical prediction for distal variables and causal explanation for proximal ones will be addressed.

The empirical study reported in the second part of the chapter is constructed, accordingly, to test predictions of the Proximity Hypothesis. Data on several exemplary distal, proximal external, and cognitive-linguistic internal variables for which strong predictive effects have been described in the literature were collected from 93 young German learners of English in primary school. These variables include socioeconomic status and type of school program (meso level), different measures of home parent–child interaction and teachers' L2 input quality in the classroom (micro level), cognitive skills (working memory, phonological awareness), and degree of multilingualism and L2 competence (nano level). Data were analyzed using structural equation modeling to account for the conceptual interplay of the variables. The goal of the study was, thus, to illustrate exemplary interrelationships of hierarchically structured variables rather than to give a near-complete overview of influencing external factors.

The interplay of external and internal factors in (language) learning

A number of models have been put forth in recent research that address the complex nature of intertwined factors.

Models
Model of Cognitive Growth and Language Development

In 1991, Paul van Geert pointed out the role of internal and external factors for the learning process, depicting learning as the growing of a cognitive system in an interplay of internal (biological) resources and resources in the external social environment. To describe this process, he differentiated between internal and external systems in his model, with four types of resources within these systems, respectively, i.e., *spatiotemporal*, *informational*, *motivational-energetic*, and *material* resources. More precisely, *internal* resources comprise:

- information processing capacity, time on task (spatiotemporal resources)
- prior knowledge and skills (informational resources)
- amount of energy, effort, activation during acquisition (motivational-energetic resources)
- physical properties, sensory/nervous system and beyond (material resources)

Analogously, *external* resources entail:

- spatial and temporal freedom in environment (spatiotemporal resources)
- type, amount, availability of information for learning (informational resources)
- reinforcement/payoffs provided by environment (motivational-energetic resources)
- objects, physical materials available to the learner (material resources)

According to this model, these resources constitute the relevant variables to be taken into account when explaining cognitive-linguistic development. In other words, in cognitive and linguistic development, learners draw from factors that are individual, i.e., internal to their own system, and from external factors in their immediate environment. To give an example relating to the study at hand, individual *internal informational resources* include, for instance, the prior world knowledge and the linguistic skills that a learner has already acquired, while external informational resources include available external linguistic input in the environment (provided by parents and teachers) that leads to language learning. What is notable and relevant here is that the model refers to external factors that *directly stimulate* the individual, which are referred to here as *proximal* external factors.

The Modular Cognition Framework

This immediate, proximal interaction of the individual with factors in the environment is also at the center of Sharwood Smith and Truscott's

Modular Cognition Framework (MCF) (Sharwood Smith & Truscott, 2014; Sharwood Smith, 2017).[1] The MCF describes in detail memory stores, their respective processors, and their connecting interfaces that form the *internal* basis for learning. In the internal context, cognitive systems comprise the auditory, somatosensory, visual, gustatory, and olfactory perceptual systems, complemented by the conceptual and affective systems and two linguistic systems for phonological and syntactic processing and storage, all of which are richly interconnected. Figure 4.1 depicts how external information that is encountered in the environment reaches the individual exclusively in the form of the different types of sensory stimuli, which are then further processed within the different cognitive systems.

With this focus on the immediate environment as a trigger of internal processes, both van Geert and Truscott and Sharwood Smith describe a *proximal view of resources*, i.e., those internal resources of both the learner and the external environment that are in direct interaction with each other. Two other influential models are compatible with this view

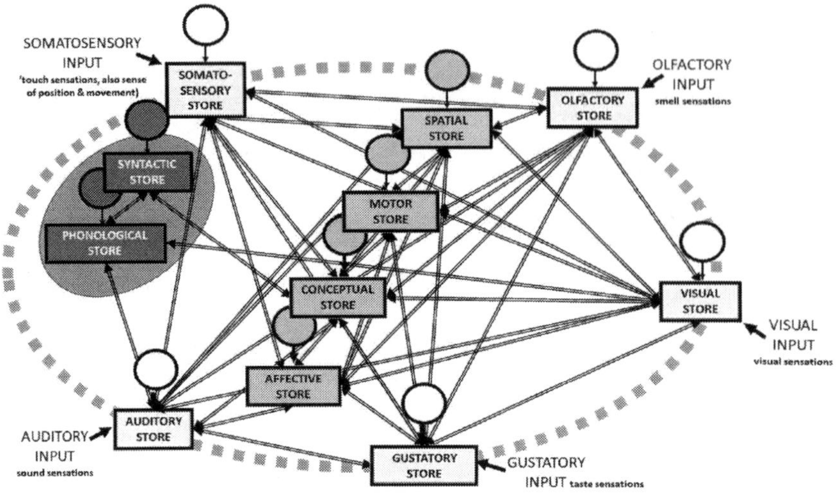

Figure 4.1 Interfaces of proximal external stimuli with internal memory stores and processors in the Modular Cognition Framework; interaction of internal context with external environment is expressed as a dotted line.

(This figure is taken from the homepage of The Modular Cognition Framework as Fig. 7, The MCF [stores, their respective processors and connecting interfaces between the stores], www.cognitionframework.com/home-1/mogul-architecture-the-basics/. It is slightly adapted from "Figure 12.1 – The MCF mind: The generator of internal context," Truscott, J. & Sharwood Smith, M., pp. 275, in "The Internal Context of Bilingual Processing" (2019) published by John Benjamins Publishing Company Amsterdam/Philadelphia; see https://benjamins.com/catalog/bpa.8. Reprinted with permission.)

but extend it to take into account additional more *distal layers* of external factors.

Developmental Conceptual View of Human Development

One such model from the field of psychology is Richard Lerner's (2002) Developmental Conceptual View of Human Development. His overarching model (p. 211) shows internal properties of the individual (cognitive, biological, personality, attitude, health, and other factors) depicted in immediate (i.e., proximal) contact with the direct social environment of *family members, peers, teachers (family/social/school network)* and in indirect contact with factors on higher external (distal) levels. These distal levels include different social contexts encompassing the central level in increasingly removed concentric circles of *community*, *society*, *culture*, and *designed and natural environments*. Double-headed arrows indicate that all of these factors are in dynamic interplay with each other and are all subject to change over time. Thus, in contrast to the two previous models, Lerner introduces various distal factors as several layers of higher-order factors, in addition to proximal ones that interact directly with the individual. These are depicted as conceptually further and further remote from the actual point of interaction between individual and environment.

Context dimensions in SLA: The Multifaceted Nature of Language Learning and Teaching

More recently, this comprehensive view has also been adopted by a transdisciplinary group of researchers in SLA that has come to be known as the Douglas Fir Group (2016), whose intention was "to integrate cognitive and social dimensions of language learning at several interconnected levels" (Mitchell et al., 2019, p. 373). According to the authors,

> [l]anguage learning is a complex, ongoing, multifaceted phenomenon that involves the dynamic and variable interplay among a range of individual neurobiological mechanisms and cognitive capacities and L2 learners' diverse experiences in their multilingual worlds occurring over their life spans and along three interrelated levels of social activity: the micro level of social action and interaction, the meso level of sociocultural institutions and communities, and the macro level of ideological structures.
>
> (The Douglas Fir Group, 2016, p. 36)

Their graphical illustration of these levels of activity (2016, p. 25) is compatible with the other views in that the individual neurobiological and cognitive basis represents the level of internal factors, the micro level of social activity in which "individuals are engaging with others" represents the first external *proximal* level of "multilingual contexts of action and interaction," while the meso level refers to the second, *distal*, level including families, schools, and social organizations. The third, distal, macro level includes, according to the model, the systems of beliefs and values in which sociocultural institutions are embedded. The model was partly developed by researchers within complex dynamic systems theory (Lenzing et al., 2023, this volume) and is compatible with it.

While tremendously helpful for conceptualizing the interrelations of different variables, the actual mechanisms of how they affect the learner and lead to changes of internal representations, i.e., learning, are yet to be described (Han, 2016). The approach outlined in this chapter aims to present one step toward this goal.

Conceptual consequences for the operationalization of proximal and distal variables in empirical (SLA) studies

These four models, which stem from different decades and different disciplines, have in common that they differentiate between different conceptual levels of variables, i.e., internal variables as well as several layers of external variables that are all closely intertwined. Such a framework to explain language learning processes has important theoretical and methodological implications. As pointed out before (Kersten & Greve, 2023, this volume), it is common practice to capture the influence of several variables on others in an additive way in multivariate analyses. We hold, however,

> that these types of analysis are often not sufficient to discover and/or confirm the causal effects of factors on different hierarchical levels, because they remain "blind," so to say, to a number of theoretical problems [. . .] [e.g.,] that factors may be related to each other in different conceptual ways. If these conceptual relations are disregarded, a prediction or a causal explanation can be incomplete or, at worst, downright wrong.
>
> (Kersten & Greve, 2023, this volume, p. 4)

Such conceptual relations include variables that are interrelated because they are conceptually "contained" in a higher-order variable on a more distal level. This practice, thus, raises several questions: What does it actually mean that a school program "influences" language acquisition or that socioeconomic status "affects" cognitive development? Who and what is it exactly that influences the learner? How can this influence be conceived of, both theoretically and practically? How can researchers methodologically account for effects of variables on different levels, which may or may not be contained within each other?

It is not reasonable to assume that a distal container variable such as type of school program or a family's socioeconomic status (SES)

– variables often used in regression analyses – exerts a direct influence on the individual. This holds for so-called proxies used for statistical analyses as well, such as the number of books in a family used as a proxy for SES. The question, then, arises as to which aspects contained within these distal variables actually have the power and chance to affect changes within the individual. Good, and frankly the only, candidates for this are interfaces where the learner experiences direct stimulation from environmental input. In other words, the immediate influence on a learning process manifests itself at the intersection of concrete, sensory experience and cognitive engagement, leading to individual knowledge construction (see Kersten, 2021). It is for that reason that Truscott and Sharwood Smith (2019, p. 10) define "input" in SLA as

> sights, including pointing and gesturing, sounds, smells, tastes, etc., in other words everything that contributes to the interpretation of an utterance and which can lead to further development of an individual's linguistic ability, i.e. all the relevant external contexts. This should be included in a comprehensive understanding of what input is.

It must therefore be assumed that externally induced change at the level of the individual can only be achieved by direct stimulation via the threshold of the sensory organs, which convey the stimuli of the outside world to the internal system.[2] Variables that describe these concrete interactions will be referred to as *proximal variables*. It follows that anything that does not describe an immediate interaction of the individual with the outside world is a variable of higher order, on a higher conceptual level further removed from the learner, i.e., a *distal* variable. Following this logic, distal variables can only exert an influence on the individual *via* proximal variables. This is a typical mediator relationship (Kersten & Greve, 2023, this volume). To give an example, a distal variable such as *parental education* can only exert an influence on the individual via a proximal variable such as the actual stimulating *interaction* of a parent with a child (Figure 4.2).

Distal factors such as *parental education* or *SES* are often used as proxies in statistical analyses. What complicates matters, however, is that such distal variables as parental education and parental SES are "container variables," which may contain numerous other variables on different conceptual levels. SES might, for example, be conceptualized as containing home resources in addition to parental education. Material resources, however, do not "exert any influence" through their mere presence but only if the learner interacts with them. This means that the presence of, for example, books in a home might be used as a proxy in an analysis, i.e., as an indicator of something else that actually impacts the child.

A container variable such as SES might involve several mediators on different conceptual levels (Figure 4.2). Consequently, each relationship

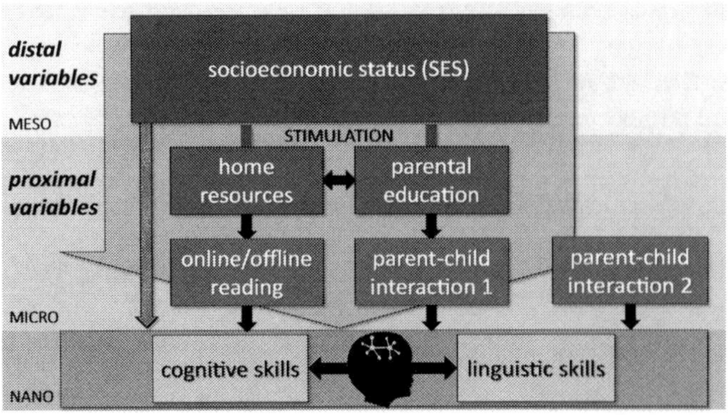

Figure 4.2 Variables on different conceptual levels affect the individual in different ways (proximal variables in direct interaction on the micro level; distal container variables in indirect interaction on the meso level)

would explain a part of the whole *(partial mediation)*. In addition, there might be other proximal variables that are not part of the container, i.e., are not predicted by the distal variables within the calculation – for example if mothers interact intensively with their children no matter what social background they come from (depicted as *parent–child interaction 2* in Figure 4.2).[3] Moreover, variables within the container might also be responsible for effects from so-called *emergent* phenomena (banded arrow) (Noordhof, 2010). Emergence cannot be explained by the sum of effects of single parts as is assumed in statistical analyses; rather, such effects emerge from a complex interplay of factors as something completely different, creating "something more" than just the sum of its parts. An example of emergent phenomena is consciousness. This line of thought is outside the scope of this chapter, but see Kersten and Greve (2023, this volume) for elaboration.

Methodological consequences for the operationalization of proximal and distal variables in empirical (SLA) studies

Consequently, one has to be aware that many of the factors that are often measured as independent predictors in competition with other ones in statistical models cannot be conceptualized on the same theoretical level. If these relationships are not disentangled prior to statistical analysis but are used concurrently as if belonging to the same level, this might have severe consequences for the interpretation of the results. Container variables, which consist of numerous different, proximal, micro-level predictors, can be assumed to have more statistical power than single proximal variables, even though the latter are, theoretically, the ones with the better or purer explanatory value. This can have a considerable influence on effect sizes (Kersten & Greve, 2023, this volume). In other words, if a distal factor instead of a proximal one is used in a calculation, the actual effect may be overestimated because the distal one may well include other mediators for the same behavior *(parallel mediation)*, but also various other variables for further proximal influences. Therefore, results could be biased when higher-order distal container variables are calculated in direct competition with proximal ones in a linear model, because the distal ones potentially contain more options of unmeasured effects and, therefore, will presumably achieve larger effect sizes. This renders explanatory interpretations difficult and imprecise because the actual cause is "hidden" within the large container, so to speak, and it is not apparent exactly which proximal factor is the determining factor for the effect. In other words, distal variables might function (well) as statistical predictors, while proximal variables have greater potential for causal explanation. To give an example from the current study, while (distal) type of L2 program might predict L2 attainment, (proximal) quantity and quality of L2 input the learners receive have greater potential to explain it.

For reasons such as these, it is helpful for a theoretical understanding of actual explanatory effects to define conceptual levels of variables involved in an investigation, to include proximal variables of direct interaction with the individual, and to account for their interrelated structure using appropriate techniques of analysis such as mediator or moderator analyses, structural equation models, or multilevel models for a nested structure of variables.[4] The *Proximity of Stimulation Hypothesis*, which takes these premises into account, will be formulated next.

Operationalizing the interplay of variables

Hierarchical model of SLA predictors

To enable the operationalization of variables affecting SLA on different conceptual levels, Figure 4.3 depicts central internal and external variables that have previously been found to be related to SLA. The illustration is derived from and compatible with the above-mentioned models by van Geert (1991), the Douglas Fir Group (2016), Lerner (2002, p. 211), Sharwood Smith (2017), and Truscott and Sharwood Smith (2019). The selection of variables is intended to be exemplary, not exhaustive, and can serve as a basis for research designs with different or additional variables.

Cultural environment is conceptualized on a *macro level* in this hierarchy, and social and institutional environments on the *meso level*. The level at which actual social interactions take place with family members, peers, and teachers in the classrooms is depicted as *micro level*.

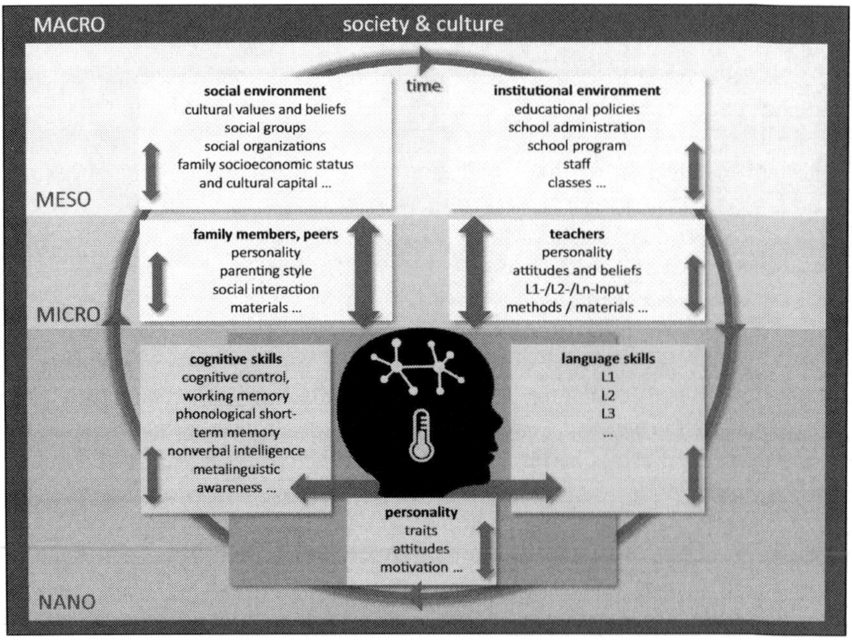

Figure 4.3 Hierarchical model of SLA predictors – exemplary representation of variables hypothesized to affect SLA on different conceptual levels (adapted from Kersten, 2020, p. 83), based on the Model of Cognitive Growth & Language Development (van Geert, 1991), the Modular Cognition Framework (Sharwood Smith, 2017), the Developmental Contextual View of Human Development (Lerner, 2002, p. 211), and the Multifaceted Nature of Language Learning & Teaching (Douglas Fir Group, 2016, p. 25)

Learner-internal variables such as personal traits, cognitive skills, affect, and language competences are seen at the *nano level*. The icon of a *thermometer* represents the perceived emotional atmosphere in which learning takes place. This can include, for example, stress levels in the family (Lawson et al., 2016) or the perceived emotional climate of the classroom (Dewaele, 2023, this volume). Across disciplines, all of these aspects have been used as variables in empirical studies and shown to predict learning and development in general and language learning in particular (for an overview, see Kersten, 2020).

From prediction to explanation: Proximity of stimulation

To sum up, the effect of a container variable on the learning process is mediated by proximal external variables, which induce a stimulus for the learner-internal system via direct interaction. It is only possible for an external stimulus to reach the learner if it passes the internal threshold via sensory organs to enter the internal system, as described in the modular cognition framework (Sharwood Smith, 2017). As an example, one might expect to find mediating effects of parent–child interaction for the effect of SES on language acquisition or of the form of classroom interaction for the effect of school program on language acquisition. To be sure, both distal and proximal factors can *predict* development in empirical studies. However, it should be the ambition of any theoretically driven empirical research to *explain* relationships. Only immediate proximal factors (i.e., as interaction with the environment) present stimuli for the learner, hence, exert influence, and could therefore be regarded as directly causal for a change in the internal system. If a distal factor predicts development, this influence must be mediated or moderated by proximal stimuli. Other proximal factors that do not depend on a distal one within a specific analysis may have additional independent effects.

Following this argumentation, it is assumed that in empirical studies, effects are *best explained using factors that describe the direct point of contact with the learner*, i.e., proximal factors. I call this the *Proximity of Stimulation Hypothesis*.

This approach predicts that

1. distal and proximal variables can be shown to have a (partial or full) mediator relationship, in which the proximal variable mediates the effect of the distal one ($V_{distal} \rightarrow V_{proximal} \rightarrow V_{dependent}$)
2. part of the variance within learner variables is likely explained by other, independent proximal factors that are not contained in the distal variables in a specific calculation.

For this purpose, the conceptual relationships of all variables within a research design first need to be identified and theoretically justified, which will be attempted in the empirical study discussed in what follows.

The current study

The study is part of the project Studies on Multilingualism in Language Education (SMILE), carried out from 2014 to 2019 at Hildesheim University, Germany. The aim of the project was to collect dense cross-sectional and longitudinal data from young learners of English that included individual information on all levels, as shown in Figure 4.4.

Following the Proximity of Stimulation Hypothesis, structural equation modeling was used to investigate the interplay of direct and mediator relationships between variables on the meso level (SES and L2 program), on the micro level (parent–child interaction [PCI] and teachers' L2 input quality), and on the nano level (cognitive skills, operationalized as working memory and phonological awareness, and receptive lexical and grammatical L2 attainment [L2A]) in a cross-sectional data set.

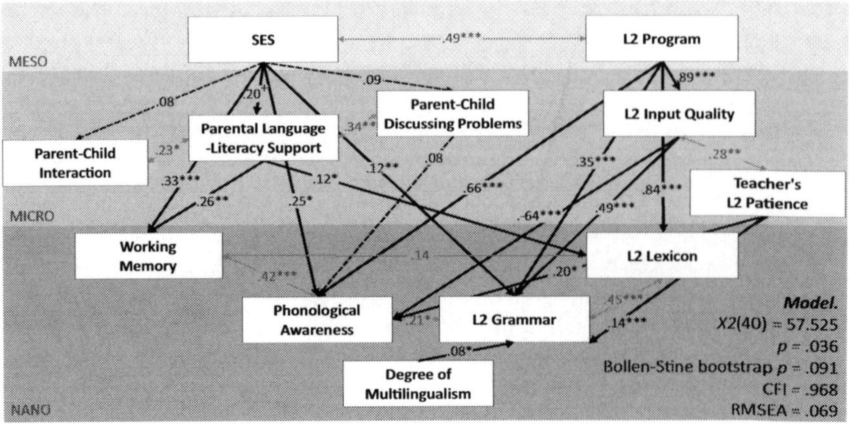

Figure 4.4 Structural equation model of distal meso-level variables, proximal micro-level variables, and internal nano-level variables ($N = 93$)

Note. $^*p < .05$; $^{**}p < .01$; $^{***}p < .001$; $^+p < .10$; standardized β regression weights (black single-headed regression arrows showing directional effects) and covariances (gray double-headed correlational arrows)

Research questions

The study investigates the following questions:

1. Do proximal variables in the data set (PCI, teachers' input quality) mediate the effect of distal container variables (SES, L2 program) on internal variables (cognition, L2A)?
2. Can part of the variance in learner variables be explained by independent proximal factors?

In line with the present argumentation, it was expected that main effects of distal SES and L2 program on cognitive and linguistic skills will be found, which will be mediated by some aspects of parent–child interaction and teachers' L2 input quality, respectively, while other aspects predict both internal skill sets independent of SES and L2 program.

While evidence for meso-level SES and type of L2 program as predictors of cognitive-linguistic skills is strong in reported studies (Hackman & Farah, 2009; Kersten et al., 2010; Kishiyama et al., 2009; Lawson et al., 2016 for SES; Sheridan et al., 2012; Trebits et al., 2021 for school program; Wesche, 2002), it is less clear which exact types of micro-level parental and teacher behavior exert the strongest influence on learner skills. As results in these strands of research are much more heterogeneous, no hypotheses were formed concerning the effect of particular micro-level variables.

Method

Participants

Cross-sectional data stem from 93 primary school L2 learners of English (43 female, mean age 9 years and 6 months, age range 7 years and 6 months to 11 years and 6 months) who took part in different types of primary foreign language programs with L2 English in Germany. Learners from three classes ($n = 31$) in three different schools took part in conventional foreign language programs (FLP) with typically two hours of L2 English per week. Students from six classes ($n = 62$) took part in two partial-immersion schools in which all subjects except for German language arts are taught through L2 English. L2 teachers in these programs are either native speakers of English or trained German foreign-language teachers with a very high command of English, while not all FLP teachers were trained as teachers of English.

Measures and procedures

A questionnaire on home language background, parents' education and occupation, and parent–child interaction (Kersten & Ponto, 2016)[5] was administered to the parents through the teachers. Schools were interviewed concerning the intensity and duration of their L2 programs.

Distal external variables (meso level)

L2 program was operationalized by the total number of lessons (45 minutes) in the L2 administered to the learners during their time in the primary school program. These values were calculated based on the number of lessons per week instructed in the L2 for the total of weeks at school per year for each grade level the students spent in the program (number of weekly lessons instructed in the L2 × number of weeks at school per year × grade level). Total number of lessons in the FLP schools ranged from 80 to 160 lessons, and for immersion classes from 1,296 to 4,212 lessons in the L2. To account for the fact that data were not normally distributed due to the two different school programs involved, Bollen-Stine bootstrapping was used in the structural equation modeling (see below).

Socioeconomic status (SES) was indicated using HISEI (Highest International Socio-Economic Index of Occupational Status, 2008 version, Ganzeboom, 2010), included in the parental background questionnaire (Kersten & Ponto, 2016).

Proximal external variables (micro level)

Parent–child interactions (PCI): Items operationalizing PCI stem from the parental questionnaire. The intention of the questionnaire was to gain differentiated information on various types of parental behavior in early and later childhood to measure their differential effects on learner development. Items were adapted from Deutscher Bundesverband für Logopädie (2020), Hertel et al. (2009), Lange et al. (1998), Linberg et al. (2019), the NICHD (2005, 2006), Safwat and Sheikhany (2014), Steinmetz and Hommers (2003) (for a detailed analysis of SMILE project data, see Fleitling, 2021). Item-based correlational analyses between types of parental behavior and learners' working memory scores[6] rendered a short scale of *parental language and literacy support* (Cronbach's $\alpha = .77$). Remaining items of general interactional behavior were subsumed under the scale of *parent–child interaction* (Cronbach's $\alpha = .84$).

Teachers' L2 input quality[7] was derived from videography of best practice videos of each teacher analyzed with the Teacher Input Observation Scheme (TIOS; Kersten et al., 2018a; Kersten, 2021). TIOS contains 41 items of L2 teaching techniques as part of four scales: Cognitively stimulating L2 task characteristics, verbal L2 input, nonverbal input, and support of L2 output.[8] A previous study (Kersten et al., 2019) found that interrater reliability of two raters tested on the basis of 18 videos of L2 teaching was high (Krippendorff's $\alpha = .88^{*}$ based on 687 cases, 1,374 decisions, item-based IRR Pearson's $r = .69^{**}$-1.00^{**}, $p < .05$), with an internal consistency of Cronbach's $\alpha = .91$ (for 38 items).

An item-based correlational analysis rendered a short scale of 13 L2 teaching techniques measured with the TIOS that correlated significantly with both L2 lexical and grammatical reception in the sample (*input quality short scale:* Cronbach's $\alpha = .90$).[9] TIOS video analysis was used for one best-practice lesson in the L2 of each L2 teacher ($n = 9$), i.e., the video with the highest score of each respective teacher. For one teacher, only one video was available, which was rated with a high total TIOS score. For the other teachers, up to five lessons could be videotaped and were selected according to a number of additional criteria to ensure comparability. Teacher consent had been collected beforehand. Teachers were aware of the overall project goal of the investigation of learner variables but had not been introduced to the specific goal of our classroom observation or to the observation instrument. Learners had already been familiarized with videography to reduce observer paradox. All sessions were general science lessons that were comparable in topic and structure, i.e., they contained an introductory phase, a main phase with a task or activity, and a final closing or consolidation phase, and were comparable in the proportion of teacher input in that all lessons included sections with observable teacher input and group work phases. For all videos, one teacher camera and another camera facing the students during the session were used. All videos were technically sound. All lessons were taped during the second half of a school year.

Internal variables (nano level)

Learner data were elicited during 2016–2017 with individual and group tests at the end of each school year. Group tests were carried out for L2 tests (BPVS 3 and ELIAS Grammar Test 2) during 45-minute lessons. Individual cognitive tests (WISC-IV and BAKO) were taken in a quiet room at school by two interviewers in the ambient language, German. One interviewer carried out the test while the other one recorded the results on a score sheet. Test instruments are introduced next.

Working memory was assessed using the WISC-IV, with the subscales *digit span* (digits forward, digits reversed) and *letter-number sequencing* (Petermann & Petermann, 2011).

Phonological awareness was assessed using BAKO 1–4 (Basiskompetenzen für Lese-Rechtschreibleistungen [Basic Competencies for Reading and Writing Skills], Stock et al., 2003), with the five subscales *segmentation of pseudo-words*, *vowel replacement*, *phoneme exchange*, *vowel length*, and *reversing words*.

L2 attainment: The British Picture Vocabulary Scale (BPVS) 3 (Dunn et al., 2009) was used for *receptive L2 lexicon* and the ELIAS Grammar Test 2 (Kersten et al., 2012, 2021) for *receptive L2 grammar*.

Learners' degree of multilingualism was operationalized as the sum of proficiency of all home languages as reported by parents in the parental questionnaire. Parents were asked to name all home languages of their child, the age of first contact with this language and with the majority language, German, if it was not listed among their home languages, and to describe their child's language competences in the majority language and up to three other home languages on a seven-point Likert scale ranging from "only a few words" to "native-like."

For statistical calculations, structural equation modeling (SEM) using SPSS (IBM SPSS Statistics 26) with the add-on AMOS was used. As not all variables were normally distributed, Bollen-Stine bootstrapping was carried out. To that end, missing data were imputed (single imputation using the expectation maximization algorithm), as AMOS needs a complete data set for this procedure.

Results and discussion

Figure 4.4 displays the results of the SEM, which tests whether hypothesized effects of the two distal container variables (SES, L2 program) on internal variables (working memory, phonological awareness, receptive lexical and grammatical L2 skills, degree of multilingualism) were mediated by proximal factors (parent–child interaction, teacher input).

Structural equation modeling shows the mutual interdependency of numerous variables and is thus suitable to test the conceptual predictions based on hierarchical ordering of the data in line with a *Proximity of*

Stimulation focus (Figure 4.3). The model had a good model fit (Bollen-Stine bootstrap p-value > .05, CFI > .95, RMSEA < .07; Hu & Bentler, 1999) and yielded a number of other interesting relations between variables. The number of participants is small for SEM analysis, however.

Testing proximity of stimulation predictions: Mediation effects and additional effects of proximal variables

With regard to RQ1, Figure 4.4 shows three partial mediations:

(1) *The effect of SES on working memory is partially mediated by proximal parental language and literacy support at home.* (The path of *SES → parental language and literacy support* is marginally significant at $p = .052$.) The effect of SES on working memory capacities of the child (which was also found on phonological awareness [PA]) corroborates what has been shown in numerous studies before (Waters et al., 2021, for WM; McDowell et al., 2007; Zhang et al., 2013, for PA, Bruhn et al., 2023, this volume). As argued, however, SES as a higher-order construct cannot be assumed to exert a direct influence on the learner's mind and might encompass a large number of other factors associated with high social class. This is why a large effect of the distal variable is to be expected. Effects of proximal variables as immediate points of contact would thus be expected to be much smaller but to contain explanatory value. It is thus surprising that the effect of *parental language/literacy support* on WM is comparable to that of SES on WM, corroborating the assumption that early linguistic interactions with a child are strong predictors of their working-memory development (Valcan et al., 2018). This finding lends some support to the Proximity approach, but it will need to be confirmed in larger longitudinal studies with more statistical power, since the cross-sectional design does not allow for a causal interpretation of the direction of the effect.

(2) *The effect of the L2 program on grammar comprehension is partially mediated by proximal teachers' L2 input quality.* The main effect of L2 program (on both language variables) supports a well-known finding in SLA research (Sun et al., 2015). The mediation, however, shows that in the more intensive programs, teachers use significantly more stimulating L2 input techniques and that this input quality is crucial for L2A. Part of this difference could be explained by the fact that the more intensive L2 programs are content-based immersion programs in which a meaningful use of language for purposes other than language learning itself is inherent. Teaching of subject matter in bilingual programs requires a particularly intensive use of L2 instructional techniques to render content comprehensible to the learners. Bilingual teachers might therefore make stronger use of such

techniques. There might also be some self-selection of teachers with good L2 knowledge and high methodological competence and motivation who choose to teach in bilingual programs (Wegner, 2021). However, as I have pointed out elsewhere (Kersten, 2020, 2021), bilingual teaching is not based on "special" teaching approaches. The TIOS was developed based on theories of foreign language teaching in instructed second language acquisition. The difference in the use of teaching techniques can thus not necessarily be derived from the programs' approaches to foreign language teaching. Even though we showed that trained L2 teachers in conventional programs are as capable as immersion teachers of scoring highly on TIOS scales (Kersten, 2019, 2020), the influence of the program type is apparent. These are crucial questions for teaching practice in conventional and bilingual programs which need to be investigated further.

This finding confirms, at least in part, that the learning context in which the L2 is encountered, i.e., the actual proximal stimulation of the learners through activities, input, and interactions, impacts their level of L2 competence. This is in line with models on the effect of input processing such as Gass et al.'s (2020) Model of Second Language Acquisition, Leow's (2015) Model of the L2 Learning Process in ISLA, Kormos' (2011) Model of Bilingual Speech Production, Truscott and Sharwood Smith's (2019) Modular Cognition Framework, and Li and Jeong's (2020) Social Brain of Language Learning (Kersten, 2021). These results also support the wide range of studies on the effectiveness of immersion teaching (Wesche, 2002; Kersten & Rohde, 2015).

(3) *The effect of L2 program on phonological awareness is partially mediated by L2 input.* This last mediation has a very strong main effect of *program* → *PA* and of *program* → *L2 input* quality and a negative regression weight for *L2 input quality* → *PA*. A possible explanation might be that PA is highly susceptible to the amount and frequency of L2 encounters, as operationalized in the *program* variable (number of accumulated lessons of L2 contact). In other words, learners in the bilingual programs who experience the language with a much higher intensity significantly outperform learners in low-intensity conventional programs in PA. The additional negative impact of *input quality* might indicate the phenomenon that teachers tend to use more scaffolding techniques for learners with lower linguistic capacities than for more advanced learners – in fact, they reduce scaffolding as a function of learners' comprehension ("fading," van de Pol et al., 2010).

This points to a chicken-and-egg relationship in cross-sectional data sets in which the causal direction of relationships cannot be established. It is, in other words, possible that the data indicate that within both programs, teachers use fewer L2 input techniques for more advanced learners with inherently higher PA and not that (as the data seem to suggest) L2 input quality has a negative effect on learners' PA (compare van de Pol et al., 2010). A longitudinal design is needed to shed more light on this question, which we are currently working on.

In addition, *parental language/literacy support* also predicts L2 lexical skills, but not L2 grammatical reception. While L2 lexicon is, beyond that, only dependent on the school program, i.e., the intensity in which the L2 is provided, L2 grammar reception seems to be much more susceptible to input quality and the learner's degree of multilingualism, which supports research showing that previous experiences with multiple languages can facilitate metalinguistic awareness such as pattern recognition in an additional language (Adesope et al., 2010; Maluch et al., 2015). Grammar reception, which also correlates with PA (see what follows) thus seems to be more susceptible to instructional quality and different cognitive abilities than the L2 lexicon, which is more strongly dependent on the intensity of the input, a finding that supports the results of Kersten et al. (2018b) in bilingual preschools.

These findings are in line with the Proximity of Stimulation Hypothesis, which posits that effects of higher-order (distal) container variables in a data set are mediated by the proximal variables they comprise and which affect a learner directly, and that additional variance might be predicted by proximal variables that are independent of the distal container.

Pertaining to RQ2, however, not all immediate stimuli – here, not all types of parental or teacher behavior – were either dependent on SES/school program or, in turn, predictive for cognitive and linguistic skills. No additional PCI variable was found to predict cognitive skills independently of SES, but not all PCI variables were predicted by SES, as was found for general PCI and the single-item variable of *discussing problems*. This shows that parental behavior has to be viewed and assessed in a much more fine-grained way than only using SES as a proxy. Even though SES (measured as education and occupation) might often strongly predict PCI, this relationship is not obligatory. Behavior underlies numerous factors and intentional changes. Some parents will interact with and cognitively stimulate their children even though they do not have a high educational degree or a high-paying job. In order to detect and capture these effects, it is necessary to look at proximal variables of direct stimulation in much more detail. If only higher-order variables are included, these actual stimulating effects become blurred and are reduced to background noise. As specific parent–child interactions seem to be carried out by parents no matter which social class they belong to, this calls for a differentiated view on parental behavior and a much more fine-grained analysis of types of parental behavior, which may translate into item-based rather than cluster-based statistical analyses. It also stresses that including a container variable such as SES as a proxy in empirical studies falls short of identifying which actual types of parental stimulation might explain child development.

Moreover, teachers' patience to wait for student answers also predicted L2 grammar and phonological awareness independently of L2 program, which supports the hypothesis that stimulating proximal (and thus potentially causal) factors are not necessarily included in distal containers and should therefore be measured separately.

Additional correlational effects

Finally, a number of correlations between the included variables were found within the different levels. As is to be expected, variables that belong to the same larger construct correlate with each other. This holds for the three PCI variables, the two teacher input variables, the two cognitive skills (working memory and phonological awareness), and the two linguistic variables (L2 grammar and lexical reception).

SES and school program also show a strong positive correlation. This hints at a social selection effect, which has often been reported in special programs such as immersion. One of the two immersion schools is a private school that provided certain funding for socially disadvantaged families but is still prone to attract a majority of more affluent families. Selection effects are also known in public schools where motivated parents compete for a place in the bilingual strand for their children. Controlling for this correlation means, however, that the remaining effects are independent of this selection bias.

In addition, phonological awareness and L2 grammar reception were correlated significantly and positively, in line with Engel de Abreu and Gathercole (2012). Correlations in cross-sectional data do not allow the interpretation of causal direction. Individual cognitive abilities are considered an important factor in the L2 acquisition process (Dörnyei, 2005; Dörnyei & Ryan, 2015), and thus the relationship between cognitive and L2 skills corresponds to various studies that find predictor effects in both directions (Kersten, 2020). Research into effects of bilingual language competence on cognitive skills, on the other hand, has focused on the so-called bilingual advantage debate (Festman et al., 2023, this volume), which claims that high L2 skills and frequent L2 usage, as present in the immersion programs, can lead to an increase in cognitive skills. Effects of bilingual competences on metalinguistic awareness, of which phonological awareness is a part, were shown by Bialystok and Barac (2012), Laurent and Martinot (2010), and Trebits et al. (2021). Effects on working memory were found by Bialystok et al. (2009), Trebits et al. (2021), as well as several meta-analyses (Adesope et al., 2010; Grundy & Timmer, 2017), while Lehtonen et al. (2018) do not find working memory effects in their meta-analytical review. Trebits et al. (2021) also found in a longitudinal study of 39 fourth graders in conventional and immersion schools that PA is more malleable than WM, and that effects of degree of bilingualism on PA are found earlier and are stronger. While advantages of PA were present in third grade and increased in fourth grade,

WM scores were the same in third grade, but at the end of fourth grade, immersion students had developed a significant advantage. The findings in the current data set thus lend some support to the bilingual advantage hypothesis with regard to L2 grammar skills and PA and, albeit just as a tendency, for L2 lexical skills and working memory. This also calls for a detailed view on differential relationships between specific linguistic and cognitive abilities. However, as pointed out before, whether degree of bilingualism represents a stronger predictor on cognitive abilities or the other way round cannot be determined with this type of cross-sectional data. For that purpose, longitudinal data and a different research design (e.g., cross-lagged panel or growth models) are needed.

This chapter mainly focuses on exemplifying the theoretical assumptions of the Proximity of Stimulation Hypothesis using selected constructs at the distal, proximal, and internal levels. To sum up, several mediating relationships identified in the data lend support to the assumption that the proximal level of direct stimuli provides a more differentiated view on immediate effects on learners' cognitive-linguistic skills than variables at the distal level in which proximal variables are conceptually contained. As argued, they can provide much more detailed information about what exactly stimulates and hence shapes the learners' internal systems.

Limitations

There are obviously numerous limitations to the study. With respect to the data set, a larger number of participants is needed to achieve higher statistical power and more reliable results. As it is, a full set of variables was not available for all participants in the project due to illness and missing parental responses. This is a general risk of data sets with such dense descriptions of participants.

Moreover, data were collected cross-sectionally, which means that the direction of the observed effects cannot be determined. Longitudinal or experimental data are preferable to investigate causal effects. The project at large includes longitudinal data for a subset of the participants; however, analysis of these data is still in progress.

The current sample is not homogenous concerning age and school program, which increases the risk that several factors might be confounded. Only the immersion program included participants in second grade. In conventional FLT programs in Germany, English is introduced in grade 3, so no grade 2 data were available. On the other hand, this has an intended positive effect in that L2 competence in immersion programs is considerably higher than in conventional programs so that L2 attainment in lower immersion grades can be assumed to be more comparable to older learners in conventional programs. Including second-grade data adds to the heterogeneity and variance in the data. The inclusion of age as a covariate was tested in the SEM but did not contribute to the model.

More reliable scores for teachers' instructional quality as measured with the TIOS could be achieved using several classroom videos with comparable lesson structures per teacher. This was, however, not possible to elicit due to the permissions of the schools and teachers.

The parental questionnaire only elicits parents' self-reported behavior as an indicator of parent–child interactions, which might be biased due to social desirability. Actual observations of parental behavior would be preferable but were out of the scope of this project.

Conclusion

Human cognitive and linguistic development are intrinsically intertwined and take place within a nested structure of conceptual levels. Proximal levels contain variables that present concrete stimuli to the learner, while variables at distal conceptual levels only exert indirect effects and often represent container variables made up of numerous proximal ones. Research on the combined and differential effects of these variables that takes these different levels into account is still scarce. Major difficulties lie in the assumed nature of effects and statistical representations (Kersten & Greve, 2023, this volume). This chapter took a Proximity of Stimulation focus which holds that since distal variables, logically, exert only indirect effects mediated by proximal factors, effects are best explained using factors that have an immediate effect on the learner. Such stimuli induce and condition intake and processing, activate associative networks, and are thus crucial for storage of the information within the learner's internal system (Li & Jeong, 2020; Kersten, 2021). This is in line with overarching models on layers of contextual factors (Lerner, 2002; Douglas Fir Group, 2016).

In this vein, this study investigated the impact of an exemplary selection of potentially influencing variables on different levels on L2 acquisition and cognitive skills. To do so, it attempted to unpack container variables and to disentangle conceptual and causal hierarchies, accounting for mediating relationships between the different variables and analyzing their differential contributions. Variables included in the analysis were social status and school programs with different amounts of L2 teaching (distal, meso-level), types of parent–child interaction and types of teacher behavior/input (proximal, micro-level), and working memory, phonological awareness, and L2 grammar and lexical reception (internal, nano-level). Structural equation modeling was used to account for the hierarchical data structure of 93 L2 learners of English in German conventional and bilingual primary schools.

Results showed that, as hypothesized within the Proximity of Stimulation focus, the effect of both distal container variables (social status and school program) on the internal cognitive and linguistic variables was partially mediated by proximal variables, i.e., parental language and literacy support and teacher's input quality, respectively. The L2 program also strongly predicted L2 lexical comprehension and phonological awareness without a mediating effect of the included proximal variables, pointing to the effectiveness of bilingual teaching programs as compared to conventional school programs with regard to L2 acquisition and aspects of cognition.

Additional independent effects that were not predicted by the higher-level distal variables were found for parental language/literacy support on L2 lexical comprehension, for teachers' allowing time and space with respect to L2 utterances ("teachers' patience") for L2 grammar comprehension and phonological awareness, and, internally, children's degree of multilingualism on their L2 grammar.

Moreover, correlations were found for SES with school program, pointing to selection effects of more engaged or affluent parents in the bilingual programs. As expected, further correlations were shown between variables belonging to the same constructs (PCI variables, teacher behavior variables, cognitive skills, and L2 skills, respectively). Finally, phonological awareness correlated with L2 grammar, and working memory showed a correlational tendency with L2 lexicon, showing that cognitive and linguistic development are intertwined and lending at least some support to a cognitive advantage hypothesis (Grundy & Timmer, 2017; Laurent & Martinot, 2010).

Lexical and grammar comprehension were thus predicted by different stimuli. Phonological awareness was predicted much more strongly by numerous external variables in family and school contexts and seems therefore much more malleable than working memory, which was mainly related to social variables. These results also confirm the importance of a differential view on factors that shape different linguistic and cognitive skills.

As the data presented in this chapter suggest, to shed light on the interplay of various variables relevant to SLA, it might be promising for future studies to elicit dense and detailed information on types of distal and proximal factors for each participant. To best understand the actual driving forces of SLA and their interconnections with cognitive development in individual learning trajectories, it seems necessary to disentangle conceptual levels of variables included in the respective analysis and to pay specific attention to proximal stimuli for learning processes. It will also be necessary to further develop suitable instruments to elicit this type of data. As we experienced in this project, eliciting a multitude of variables has practical consequences in terms of both capacities of the research team and of individuals and institutions involved in the study. Desired background information has to be balanced with length of questionnaires, for instance, so as not to reduce response rates. In addition, disadvantages of self-reports have to be carefully weighed against the workload necessary for more objective observations of behavior within classrooms and families. The Teacher Input Observation Scheme (Kersten et al., 2018a) used in this study for L2 input quality operationalized observation of proximal instructional variables, while the parental background questionnaire (Kersten & Ponto, 2016) relied on parents' self-reports. This type of elicitation should be refined in future studies. To corroborate both the theoretical views as well as preliminary findings of the study presented here, longitudinal data are necessary to determine the causal direction of a relationship between variables. Further methodologies and more refined statistical analyses need to be explored to account for the complex systemic nature of (language) learning, including longitudinal growth models. In terms of practical relevance, findings regarding effective types of behavior in families and instructional contexts may serve as a basis for recommendations for educational institutions that work closely together with parents and thus increase the chance to foster the linguistic and cognitive development of young learners within families (Niklas et al., 2018) and school systems.[10]

Notes

1. For recent updates of the framework, see www.cognitionframework.com/.
2. There are exceptions to this reasoning that affect the individual as a whole not via sensory organs, such as gravity or magnetism, but those are beyond the scope of the current focus.
3. Unfortunately, almost all of these variables can, theoretically, be further deconstructed to ever-lower levels – as a system within a system.
4. It has to be pointed out that even with a mediation analysis a causal relationship cannot be inferred from cross-sectional data. However, a presumed mediator relationship can be refuted. Longitudinal data and experiments with randomized subjects allow for causal interpretations.
5. The questionnaire elicits data concerning individual factors such as age and gender of the child as well as linguistic background/s of the family. The full questionnaire is available at www.researchgate.net/publication/348760402_Elternfragebogen_zum_familiaren_und_sprachlichen_Hintergrund.
6. Items were included that correlated up to an alpha level of .10 to avoid a type 2 error and to make sure that all potential predictors were regarded (Ellis, 2010, p. 82; Larson-Hall, 2012, p. 249; see what follows). The scale comprised the following types of parental behavior (translated from German): *Explaining events to the child that are difficult to understand, listening to the child, playing with letters in early childhood, playing word games in early childhood, repeating the young child's utterances in simple, whole sentences, singing songs in early childhood, talking about daily events, playing word or language games*, and *encouraging the child to write postcards, letters*, etc.
7. See Kersten (2021) and Kersten et al. (2021) for a definition and background of the construct of input quality.
8. The instrument can be downloaded at www.researchgate.net/publication/340096869_Teacher_Input_Observation_Scheme_TIOS_and_Manual.
9. The short scale on teachers' input quality includes the following TIOS items: *Cognitively Stimulating Tasks/Activities: 1 (tasks/activities focus on meaningful content goals), 5 (tasks/activities are explicitly linked to their specific learning goals/learning objectives), 7 (tasks/activities require active problem-solving by the learners), 8 (tasks/activities are based on the prior world knowledge of the learners (i.e., their everyday experiences)), 11 (tasks/*

activities provide opportunities for genuine output (language use) of the learners), 12 (tasks/activities are based on authentic materials / realia / texts / auditory displays); Verbal Input: 14 (the teacher has a high language proficiency in the L2), 15 (the teacher exclusively uses the L2 in class), 16 (the teacher provides a high amount of L2 input (i.e., uses L2 a lot to accompany all actions)), 17 (the teacher uses varied L2 input), 25 (the teacher uses comprehension checks); Non-Verbal Input: 26 (the teacher uses body language); Support of Learners' Output: 31 (the teacher asks questions that promote open answers).

10. **Acknowledgments** This chapter was funded by a grant from the Ministry for Science and Culture of the State of Lower Saxony (VW Vorab, grant number 12.3–76251–99–55/14). The study is part of the project Studies on Multilingualism in Language Education (SMILE) on variables influencing SLA in primary school and conducted in close cooperation with Werner Greve. The thoughts presented in this chapter are largely the result of numerous discussions and would not have been possible without his inspiring input and advice. I am exceedingly grateful to Katharina Ponto and Ann-Christin Bruhn for an extraordinary job of project coordination, Martin Koch for his invaluable support with statistical analysis, and Laureen Gallwitz and numerous student research assistants for their help with data collection. This study would not have been possible without them.

References

Adesope, O. O., Lavin, T., Thompson, T., & Ungerleider, C. (2010). A systematic review and meta-analysis of the cognitive correlates of bilingualism. *Review of Educational Research*, *80*(2), 207–245. http://dx.doi.org/10.3102/0034654310368803

Atkinson, D. (2019). Second language acquisition beyond borders? The Douglas Fir Group searches for transdisciplinary identity. *The Modern Language Journal*, *103*, 113–121. https://doi.org/10.1111/modl.12530

Bialystok, E., & Barac, R. (2012). Emerging bilingualism: Dissociating advantages for metalinguistic awareness and executive control. *Cognition*, *122*, 67–73. https://doi.org/10.1016/j.cognition.2011.08.003

Bialystok, E., Craik, F. I. M., Green, D. W., & Gollan, T. H. (2009). Bilingual minds. *Psychological Science*, *10*(3), 89–129. https://doi.org/10.1177/1529100610387084

Bruhn, A.-C., Miller, L., Ponto, K., Kersten, K., & Mähler, C. (2023, this volume). Can type of schooling compensate for low SES? Investigating effects of instruction and SES on cognitive skills. In K. Kersten & A. Winsler (Eds.), *Understanding variability in second language acquisition, bilingualism, and cognition – A multi-layered perspective* (pp. 292–320). Routledge.

Deutscher Bundesverband für Logopädie e.V. (2020). *Wie unterstützen Eltern den Spracherwerb ihrer Kinder? Tipps, die Eltern dabei helfen können, die Sprachentwicklung ihres Kindes zu unterstützen.* Retrieved April 15, 2021, from www.dbl-ev.de/logopaedie/foerderung-der-sprachentwicklung/sprachfoerderung-beim-spracherwerb/wie-unterstuetzen-eltern-den-spracherwerb-ihrer-kinder.html/

Dewaele, J.-M. (2023, this volume). The interplay between learner-internal variables and levels of anxiety and enjoyment among Spanish EFL learners. In K. Kersten & A. Winsler (Eds.), *Understanding variability in second language acquisition, bilingualism, and cognition – A multi-layered perspective* (pp. 217–239). Routledge.

Dörnyei, Z. (2005). *The psychology of the language learner: Individual differences in second language acquisition.* Erlbaum. http://dx.doi.org/10.4324/9781410613349

Dörnyei, Z., & Ryan, S. (2015). *The psychology of the language learner revisited.* Routledge. https://doi.org/10.4324/9781315779553

Douglas Fir Group. (2016). A transdisciplinary framework for SLA in a multilingual world. *The Modern Language Journal*, *100*(Suppl 1), 19–47. https://doi.org/10.1111/modl.12301

Duff, P. A., & Byrnes, H. (2019). SLA across disciplinary borders: Introduction to the special issue. *The Modern Language Journal*, *103*, 3–5.

Dunn, L. M., Dunn, D. M., Styles, B., & Sewell, J. (2009). *The British Picture Vocabulary Scale* (3rd ed.). GL Assessment.

Ellis, P. D. (2010). *The essential guide to effect sizes. Statistical power, meta-analysis, and the interpretation of research results.* Cambridge University Press. https://doi.org/10.1017/CBO9780511761676

Engel de Abreu, P. M., & Gathercole, S. E. (2012). Executive and phonological processes in second language acquisition. *Journal of Educational Psychology*, *104*(4), 974–986. https://doi.org/10.1037/a0028390

Festman, J., Czapka, S., & Winsler, A. (2023, this volume). How many moderators does is take till we know . . . that too many bilingual advantage effects have died? In K. Kersten & A. Winsler (Eds.), *Understanding variability in second language acquisition, bilingualism, and cognition – A multi-layered perspective* (pp. 80–127). Routledge.

Fleitling, V. (2021). *Indicators and consequences of parent-child interaction* (Unpublished Master's Thesis). Hildesheim University.

Ganzeboom, H. B. G. (2010). *A new international socio-economic index (ISEI) of occupational status for the inter-national standard classification of occupation 2008 (ISCO-08) constructed with data from the ISSP 2002–2007.* Paper presented at the Annual Conference of International Social Survey Programme.

Gass, S. M., Behney, J., & Plonsky, L. (2020). *Second language acquisition: An introductory course* (5th ed.). Routledge. https://doi.org/10.4324/9781315181752

Grundy, J. G., & Timmer, K. (2017). Bilingualism and working memory capacity: A comprehensive meta-analysis. *Second Language Research*, *33*(3), 325–340. https://doi.org/10.1177/0267658316678286

Hackman, D. A., & Farah, M. J. (2009). Socioeconomic status and the developing brain. *Trends in Cognitive Sciences*, *13*(2), 65–73. https://doi.org/10.3389/fnins.2014.00276

Han, Z. (2016). A "reimagined SLA" or an expanded SLA? A rejoinder to The Douglas Fir Group (2016). *The Modern Language Journal*, *100*(4), 736–740. https://doi.org/10.1111/modl.12378

Han, Z. (2019). Researching CDST: Promises and pitfalls. In Z. Han (Ed.), *Profiling learner language as a dynamic system.* Multilingual Matters. http://ebookcentral.proquest.com; created from teacherscollege-ebooks on 2019-10-10 11:30:17. https://doi.org/10.21832/9781788922807-009

Hertel, S., Hochweber, J., Mildner, D., Steinert, B., & Jude, N. (Eds.). (2009). *PISA 2009 Skalenhandbuch.* Waxmann.

Hu, L., & Bentler, P. M. (1999). Cutoff criteria for fit indexes in covariance structure analysis: Conventional criteria versus new alternatives. *Structural Equation Modeling*, 6, 1–55. https://doi.org/10.1080/10705519909540118
Kersten, K. (2019). Einflussfaktoren im bilingualen Fremdsprachenerwerb. In A. Rohde & A. K. Steinlen (Eds.), *Sprachenvielfalt als Ressource begreifen: Mehrsprachigkeit in bilingualen Kindertagesstätten und Schulen* (Band II) (pp. 35–70). Dohrmann.
Kersten, K. (2020). Der Zusammenhang von kognitiven Fähigkeiten und Zweisprachigkeit im frühen L2-Erwerb: Individuelle und externe Faktoren [The relationship between cognitive abilities and bilingualism in early L2 acquisition: Individual and external factors]. In H. Böttger, J. Festman, & T. Müller (Eds.), *Language education & acquisition research: Blick auf den frühen Spracherwerb [Focusing early language acquisition]* (pp. 81–118). Klinkhardt.
Kersten, K. (2021). L2 input and characteristics of instructional techniques in early foreign language classrooms – Underlying theory and pedagogical practice. *The European Journal of Applied Linguistics and TEFL, 10*(2), 27–59.
Kersten, K., Rohde, A., Schelletter, C., & Steinlen, A. K. (Eds.). (2010). *Bilingual preschools. Vol. I: Learning and development*. WVT.
Kersten, K., Piske, T., Rohde, A., Steinlen, A. K., Weitz, M., Couve de Murville, S., & Kurth, S. (2012). ELIAS grammar test II. *Studies on Multilingualism in Language Education, 1*, Hildesheim University. http://dx.doi.org/10.13140/RG.2.2.35027.32806/1
Kersten, K., & Greve, W. (2023, this volume). Investigating influencing factors of cognitive-linguistic development in SLA: Challenges for empirical research. In K. Kersten & A. Winsler (Eds.), *Interplay of Variables in Cognitive-Linguistic Development – A Multi-Layered Perspective* (pp. 3–38). Routledge.
Kersten, K., & Ponto, K. (2016). Fragebogen zum familiären und sprachlichen Hintergrund [Parental questionnaire on socioeconomic and linguistic background of language learners]. *Studies on Multilingualism in Language Education, 3*, Hildesheim University. http://dx.doi.org/10.13140/RG.2.2.20734.61760
Kersten, K., & Rohde, A. (2015). Immersion teaching in English with young learners. In J. Bland (Eds.), *Teaching English language to young learners: Critical issues in language teaching with 3–12 year olds* (pp. 71–89). Bloomsbury.
Kersten, K., Bruhn, A.-C., Ponto, K., Böhnke, J., & Greve, W. (2018a). Teacher input observation scheme (TIOS). *Studies on Multilingualism in Language Education, 4*, Hildesheim University. https://doi.org/10.13140/RG.2.2.22467.35368
Kersten, K., Schelletter, C., Bruhn, A.-C., & Ponto, K. (2021). Quality of L2 input and cognitive skills predict L2 grammar comprehension in instructed SLA independently. *Languages, 6*(3), 124. https://doi.org/10.3390/languages6030124
Kersten, K., Steinlen, A.-K., & Schüle, C. (2018b). *The effect of L2 input and cognitively stimulating tasks on second language acquisition*. Paper presented at EUROSLA 28, University of Münster.
Kersten, K., Bruhn, A.-C., Koch, M., & Schriek, J. (2019). *The effect of L2 input and cognitively stimulating tasks on second language acquisition*. Paper presented at EUROSLA 29, Lund University.
Kishiyama, M. M., Boyce, W. T., Jimenez, A. M., Perry, L. M., & Knight, R. T. (2009). Socioeconomic disparities affect prefrontal function in children.

Journal of Cognitive Neuroscience, *21*(6), 1106–1115. https://doi.org/10.1162/jocn.2009.21101

Kormos, J. (2011). Speech production and the cognition hypothesis. In P. Robinson (Ed.), *Second language task complexity* (pp. 39–60). Benjamins. https://doi.org/10.1075/tblt.2.06ch2

Lange, A., Blonk, R., & Wiers, R. W. (1998). The parent-child interaction questionnaire, PACHIQ. *Clinical Psychology & Psychotherapy: An International Journal of Theory and Practice*, *5*(3), 187–198.

Larson-Hall, J. (2012). How to run statistical analyses. In A. Mackey & S. G. Gass (Eds.), *Research methods in second language acquisition* (pp. 245–274). Wiley-Blackwell. https://doi.org/10.1002/9781444347340

Laurent, A., & Martinot, C. (2010). Bilingualism and phonological awareness: The case of bilingual (French – Occitan) children. *Reading and Writing*, *23*(3), 435–452. https://doi.org/10.1007/S11145-009-9209-3

Lawson, G. M., Hook, C. J., Hackman, D. A., & Farah, M. J. (2016). Socioeconomic status and the development of executive functions: Behavioral and neuroscience approaches. In J. A. Griffin, P. McCardle, & L. S. Freund (Eds.), *Executive function in preschool-age children: Integrating measurement, neurodevelopment, and translational research*. American Psychological Association. http://dx.doi.org/10.1037/14797012

Lehtonen, M., Soveri, A., Laine, A., Järvenpää, J., de Bruin, A., & Antfolk, J. (2018). Is bilingualism associated with enhanced executive functioning in adults? A meta-analytic review. *Psychological Bulletin*, *144*(4), 394–425. https://doi.org/10.1037/bul0000142

Lenzing, A., Pienemann, M., & Nicholas, H. (2023, this volume). Lost in translation? On some key features of dynamical systems theorizing invoked in SLA research. In K. Kersten & A. Winsler (Eds.), *Understanding variability in second language acquisition, bilingualism, and cognition – A multi-layered perspective* (pp. 39–79). Routledge.

Leow, R. P. (2015). *Explicit learning in the L2 classroom*. Routledge. https://doi.org/10.4324/9781315887074

Lerner, R. M. (2002). *Concepts and theories of human development*. Erlbaum.

Li, P., & Jeong, H. (2020). The social brain of language: Grounding second language learning in social interaction. *NPJ Science of Learning*, *5*(8). https://doi.org/10.1038/s41539-020-0068-7

Linberg, A., Mann, D., Attig, M., Vogel, F., Weinert, S., & Roßbach, H.-G. (2019). *Quality of parent-child-interactions. Assessment of interactions with the macro-analytic rating system of parent-child-interactions in the National Educational Panel Study at the child's age of 7, 17, and 26 months (NEPS Survey Paper No. 51)*. Leibniz-Institut für Bildungsverläufe, Nationales Bildungspanel.

Maluch, J. T., Kempert, S., Neumann, M., & Stanat, P. (2015). The effect of speaking a minority language at home on foreign language learning. *Learning and Instruction*, *36*, 76–85.

McDowell, K. D., Lonigan, C. J., & Goldstein, H. (2007). Relations among socioeconomic status, age, and predictors of phonological awareness. *Journal of Speech, Language, and Hearing Research*, *50*(4), 1079–1092. https://doi.org/10.1044/1092-4388(2007/075)

Mitchell, R., Myles, F., & Marsden, E. (2019). *Second language learning theories*. Routledge. https://doi.org/10.4324/9781315617046

National Institute of Child Health and Human Development. (2005). *Child care and child development – results from the NICHD study of early child care and youth development*. The Guilford Press.

National Institute of Child Health and Human Development. (2006). *The NICHD study of early child care and youth development (SECCYD): Findings for children up to age 4 ½ years*. U.S. Government Printing Office.

Niklas, F., Cohrssen, C., & Tayler, C. (2018). Making a difference to children's reasoning skills before school-entry: The contribution of the home learning environment. *Contemporary Educational Psychology*, *54*, 79–88. https://doi.org/10.1016/j.cedpsych.2018.06.001

Noordhof, P. (2010). Emergent causation and property causation. In C. Macdonald & G. Macdonald (Eds.), *Emergence in mind* (pp. 69–99). Oxford University Press. https://doi.org/10.1093/acprof:oso/9780199583621.003.0006

Petermann, F., & Petermann, U. (Eds.). (2011). *Wechsler intelligence scale for children (WISC-IV)*. Pearson Assessment. https://doi.org/10.1007/978-0-387-79061-9_3066

Safwat, R. F., & Sheikhany, A. R. (2014). Effect of parent interaction on language development in children. *The Egyptian Journal of Otolaryngology*, *30*(3), 255.

Sharwood Smith, M. (2017). *Introducing language and cognition: A map of the mind*. Cambridge University Press. https://doi.org/10.1017/9781316591505

Sharwood Smith, M., & Truscott, J. (2014). *The multilingual mind: A modular processing perspective*. Cambridge University Press. https://doi.org/10.1017/CBO9781139644044

Sheridan, M. A., Sarsour, K., Jutte, D., D'Esposito, M., & Boyce, W. T. (2012). The impact of social disparity on prefrontal function in childhood. *PloS One*, 7(4), e35744. https://doi.org/10.1371/journal.pone.0035744

Steinmetz, M., & Hommers, W. (2003). Das "Parent-Child Relationship Inventory" als deutschsprachiges Eltern-Diagnostikum [The "Parent-Child Relationship Inventory" as German parent diagnostic]. *Diagnostica*, *49*(3), 120–128.

Stock, C., Marx, P., & Schneider, W. (2003). *BAKO 1–4. Basiskompetenzen für Lese-Rechtschreibleistungen. Ein Test zur Erfassung der phonologischen Bewusstheit vom ersten bis vierten Grundschuljahr [Basic competencies for reading and spelling performance. A test to assess phonological awareness from the first to the fourth year of primary school]*. Beltz Test GmbH.

Sun, H., Steinkrauss, R., Tendeiro, J., & de Bot, K. (2015). Individual differences in very young children's English acquisition in China: Internal and external factors. *Bilingualism: Language and Cognition*, *19*(3), 550–566. https://doi.org/10.1017/S1366728915000243

Trebits, A., Koch, M., Ponto, K., Bruhn, A.-C., Adler, M., & Kersten, K. (2021). Cognitive gains and socioeconomic status in early second language acquisition in immersion and EFL learning settings. *International Journal of Bilingual Education and Bilingualism*. https://doi.org/10.1080/13670050.2021.1943307

Truscott, J., & Smith, M. S. (2019). *The internal context of bilingual processing*. John Benjamins. https://doi.org/10.1075/bpa.8

Valcan, D. S., Davis, H., & Pino-Pasternak, D. (2018). Parental behaviours predicting childhood executive functions: A meta-analysis. *Educational Psychology Review*, *30*, 607–649. https://doi.org/10.1007/s10648-017-9411-9

van de Pol, J., Volman, M., & Beishuizen, J. (2010). Scaffolding in teacher-student Interaction: A decade of research. *Educational Psychology Review*, *22*(3), 271–296. https://doi.org/10.1007/S10648-010-9127-6

van Geert, P. (1991). A dynamic systems model of cognitive and language growth. *Psychological Review*, *98*(1), 3–53. https://doi.org/10.1037/0033-295X.98.1.3

Waters, N. E., Ahmed, S. F., Tang, S., Morrison, F., & Davis-Kean, P. (2021). Pathways from socioeconomic status to early academic achievement: The role of specific executive functions. *Early Childhood Research Quarterly*, *54*, 321–331. https://doi.org/10.1016/j.ecresq.2020.09.008

Wegner, A. (2021). *Die Implementation von CLIL (Content and Language Integrated Learning) in der Grundschule: Eine methodenintegrierende Untersuchung zu Einflussfaktoren bei der Umsetzung bilingualer Unterrichtskonzepte [The Implementation of CLIL (Content and Language Integrated Learning) in Elementary Schools: A Method-Integrating Study of Factors Influencing the Implementation of Bilingual Teaching Concepts]*. Universitätsverlag Hildesheim.

Wesche, M. B. (2002). Early French immersion: How has the original Canadian model stood the test of time? In P. Burmeister, T. Piske, & A. Rohde (Eds.), *An integrated view of language development. Papers in honor of Henning Wode* (pp. 357–379). WVT.

Zhang, Y., Tardif, T., Shu, H., Li, H., Liu, H., McBride-Chang, C., Liang, W., & Zhang, Z. (2013). Phonological skills and vocabulary knowledge mediate socioeconomic status effects in predicting reading outcomes for Chinese children. *Developmental Psychology*, *49*(4), 665–671. https://doi.org/10.1037/a0028612

5 Becoming bilingual in Miami, USA

Predictors and outcomes of speed of English acquisition for low-income, dual-language learners

Adam Winsler

Introduction

There are many ways of becoming bilingual. When researchers use the term "bilingual," although it might seem like this refers to a coherent, well-defined group of people, the reality is that variability, heterogeneity, and diversity are the rules when it comes to second (and third+) language acquisition. One can be exposed to two (or more) languages at the same time consistently from birth, known as *simultaneous* bilingualism, or bilingual first language acquisition (BFLA; De Houwer, 1990). One can be exposed to and acquire only one language at home early on (L1) but then get significant exposure to and learn another language (L2) during the preschool years, often by attending some kind of early childhood educational (ECE) setting where a different, typically the majority/societal language is used. This is often referred to as early second language acquisition (ESLA, De Houwer, 1990, 2021), an early form of *sequential* bilingualism whereby one masters a primary language first before acquiring a second one. Obviously, the line between ESLA and BFLA becomes thin the earlier and more significant the exposure to the second language appears.

When older monolingual children and adults get exposed to a second language, often explicitly in the context of second language classes in school, this type of later potential sequential bilingualism is called second language acquisition (SLA; De Houwer, 1990, 2021). However, learning a second language formally in elective or required foreign language courses later in school can be very different and often more explicit compared to learning a language in the natural context of immersive use of language being required for survival and communicating with others. This raises another level of heterogeneity and complexity among bilinguals – namely, the context/setting in which the additional language is learned and used. Such variance in terms of the timing and setting of second language acquisition has consequences in terms of individuals'

DOI: 10.4324/9781003155683-7

brain organization and processing of language stimuli (Pliatsikas et al., 2017). Ultimate language outcomes of SLA vary greatly and depend on the individual's motivation for learning the L2 and their continued exposure to and use of the L2. Indeed, many if not most individuals whose exposure to an additional language is limited to SLA classroom settings never reach full proficiency in the L2 (Dewaele & Thirtle, 2009; MacIntyre, 2002).

Finally, the larger sociocultural, economic, and sociolinguistic contexts of the bilingual experience also matter for language trajectories and outcomes over time. *Additive bilingualism* refers to the situation in which a monolingual speaker of the dominant societal language (i.e., English in the US) adds a new language to their repertoire (say Spanish) with varying degrees of eventual success and language permanence depending on continued use over time. This is seen as a bonus and a strength, and there is no fear that the individual will stop speaking or eventually lose their L1. *Subtractive bilingualism*, on the other hand, refers to the situation whereby an L1 speaker of a nondominant language in the society (i.e., Spanish or Arabic in the US) learns the dominant language (say, English in the US) and because of both strong pressure from peers and the community to use English and strong disincentives if not overt punishment that children receive for speaking an unvalued, low-status, minority language, the child stops using their L1 and eventually loses facility in their L1. In such cases, L2 takes over as their dominant language over time (Roberts, 2010). The notion that one language might be stronger than the other for a bilingual individual at any given time (or context) brings up yet another example of variability in bilingualism – the degree of balance between the languages. One can be a *balanced bilingual* when both languages are used relatively equally and often or an *unbalanced bilingual* who has considerably better facility in one language than the other. Dynamic change over time within the individual is the final level of complexity/variability, since depending on the language context, use, motivation, and demand, an individual's skills in multiple languages can and will change over time.

This volume is all about understanding variability at multiple levels in bilingualism and SLA. I give the overview of different types of bilinguals and contexts for bilingualism to show the larger context into which the current work's population of interest falls. In this chapter, I focus on young dual-language learners (DLLs) largely living in poverty in the southern Florida city of Miami, USA. These children fall into the ESLA, early sequential second language learner category, since they speak mostly Spanish (L1) at home and are enrolled in primarily English-using preschool settings (L2) at age 4 and later go on to attend technically "English-only" public school settings (except for a few immersion bilingual education programs). Different than most cities in the US where the larger sociolinguistic context supports only English to be used as the lingua franca, however, Miami-Dade County Florida is home for many Cuban, Caribbean, and Central/South American immigrants, so there is strong community support for Spanish. Spanish is the self-reported primary language for 65% of the city's population (U.S. Census Bureau, 2017), and it is common to hear more Spanish than English on the streets and in businesses. So although this would technically still be a subtractive bilingualism setting since English (L2) is the dominant language in the country as a whole, in Miami, it is much less likely for students to lose their L1 Spanish skills than in other locations.

Importantly, it is worth noting that much of the research on bilingualism has been conducted in very different contexts with different populations. Much SLA research has been conducted in additive bilingualism contexts with ethnic majority individuals with full command of the societal L1 learning an L2 say in Canada, Europe, or the US (often privileged middle-class college students and adults – those who sign up for research studies) and often in laboratory settings or SLA classrooms. Thus, although we know a lot about, for example, middle-class, English-French bilingual college students and adults in Quebec and Ontario, Canada, much less is known about bilingualism over time for the large number of young, ethnic-minority DLLs in poverty in the US learning English as L2 while attempting to navigate the public school system – this is the population for the present work and the group introduced in more detail next.

Dual-language learners in the USA

Dual-language learners (DLLs) are defined as students who are learning English in school settings and speak a language other than English almost exclusively at home (AIR, 2014). This is a rapidly growing segment of the school-age population in the US, making up about 10% of school-age students nationally (much higher in some states) and 17% of kindergarten children (NCELA, 2011; NCES, 2017; Wolf et al., 2008). Spanish is the home language for about 77% of DLLs in the US, with Arabic, Chinese, and Vietnamese being the next most common home languages (NCES, 2017). Importantly, DLLs are much more likely than others to be living in poverty (66%; NEA, 2008).

In terms of how well DLLs in the US do in school, this depends on how long the student has lived in the US (if they come from an immigrant family) and their degree of English proficiency (Reardon & Galindo, 2007; Rozell et al., 2021). It is of no surprise given that instruction and assessment are typically in English that overall, DLL students do not perform as well as native English-speaking children, even after controlling for socioeconomic status (SES) (Kieffer, 2008). However, it is important to distinguish here between *DLL status* (speaking mostly a non-English language at home) and *English proficiency* (how proficient the student is in English), and it is degree of English proficiency that is critical for academic success. English proficiency is strongly correlated with *concurrent* performance in school (*r*'s = .45–.70) (Beal et al., 2010; Butler & Castellon-Wellington, 2000; Henry et al., 2014; Parker et al., 2009), and early proficiency in English for DLLs predicts *later* performance as well (Halle et al., 2012; Reardon & Galindo, 2007; Reese et al., 2000; Rozell et al., 2021; Serafini et al., 2019).

Importantly, former DLLs, those who are bilingual with native proficiency in their home language and who have full English proficiency relatively early in schooling (before first grade) actually not only outperform other DLLs who are still developing in English, but they also often do better in school than their monolingual English-speaking peers (Ardasheva et al., 2012; Halle et al., 2012; Rozell et al., 2021), even after controlling for SES. This is impressive and suggests that (a) there is nothing about being a DLL per se that is a risk factor for academic achievement – it is more SES and English proficiency that matters, but also that (b) controlling for other relevant factors, being bilingual might convey an advantage in terms of children's academic performance in school, which leads to our next topic.

Bilingual advantage

The idea of a potential bilingual advantage for certain cognitive and metacognitive skills is not new. In fact, the issue of whether bilingualism is linked to particular cognitive skills (or deficits) has had an interesting and sordid past. For the first half of the 20th century, researchers, enamored with the emergence of standardized IQ tests around 1900 and ideas of eugenics, and an anti-immigrant and racist political climate, were quick to point out that "bilingual" individuals in the US (i.e., darker-skinned individuals who spoke a different language than English and who were living in poverty in poor, recent-arrival immigrant neighborhoods), when given a standardized IQ test (in their new L2, English!) scored notably lower than White, middle-class, monolingual English-speaking individuals (Crawford, 1999; Darcy, 1963; Gould, 1981; Hakuta, 1986). Such data were used to flame public fears that certain immigrants were cognitively inferior and not worthy of being in the country (Fuller, 2019; Gould, 1981; Leeman, 2004). Thus, early on, those who were bilinguals (i.e., those who were still learning English with a different L1) were seen as cognitively disadvantaged and confused (Darcy, 1963; Hakuta, 1986). The problem was that the early research failed to include appropriate statistical controls (SES, education, health status) to make sure that the bilingual and monolingual group comparisons were fair (Hakuta, 1986). Also, the early researchers failed to verify and rather just assumed that the "bilinguals" were fully proficient in English and another language, typically lacking direct proficiency assessments in either language. Sampling was also an issue in that bilinguals were sometimes selected on the basis of one's ethnic-sounding last name or from the barrio in which they lived with little knowledge of the participants' actual language background (Darcy, 1963; Hakuta, 1986; Peal & Lambert, 1962).

It was not until 1962, when the first well-designed study, appeared that appropriately tested whether well-sampled and verified bilingual individuals showed cognitive processing differences compared to a reasonably matched group of monolinguals in terms of age, education, and income (Peal & Lambert, 1962). This study, along with many others to follow over the next several decades, found that fully bilingual adults and children who use both languages in reasonable quantities often (but not always) show enhanced skills in certain areas of cognitive processing, such as metalinguistic awareness (understanding the arbitrary nature of language word referents), executive control (switching from one strategy, goal, or focus to another), and inhibition (inhibiting irrelevant stimuli/information to focus on current relevant information) (Bialystok, 2007; Calvo et al., 2016; Iluz-Cohen & Armon-Lotem, 2013; Leeuw & Bogulski, 2016; Saint-Aubin et al., 2018). The exact mechanism is still unclear, but the theory is that bilingual individuals have extra practice inhibiting a language system and switching back and forth from one language to another (because both languages are always "active" in the brain), and this exercises executive functioning (EF) cognitive processes and skills that transfer to other cognitive and perhaps behavioral tasks that require EF (Bialystok, 2007; Green, 1998). It is clear that *something* is different neurologically about the minds of individuals who manage two or more complex linguistic systems in their brains (Pliatsikas & Luk, 2016; Rahmani et al., 2017), and the age and manner of L2 acquisition relative to L1 matters in terms of the changes seen in neurological anatomy and functioning (Pliatsikas et al., 2017). However, given the variability and complexity discussed earlier about how different bilingual language experiences and contexts can be, research is still quite far from isolating one or more central mechanisms involved. Also, it is not clear how neurological changes found with L2 acquisition map onto behavioral differences observed in the lab on various EF tasks (Leivada et al., 2021; Pliatsikas & Luk, 2016).

Indeed, although many studies show bilingual effects on cognition, there are many failures to replicate and other studies finding no differences between the EF skills of monolingual and bilingual individuals (Leivada et al., 2021). Sometimes even meta-analyses disagree on their conclusions about bilingual effects even after reviewing similar groups of papers (Lehtonen et al., 2018; Paap et al., 2015). Needless to say, there is currently intense scholarly debate concerning the conditions under which bilingual effects are found, as they appear to depend on many factors, including the age of participants, the types or breadth of EF tasks used, the language history and age of exposure of the bilingual person, the degree of proficiency or balance between the two languages, the type of bilingual immersion educational program experienced, and the frequency with which bilingual participants actively use and switch between their two languages in daily use (Festman et al., in press; Kalia et al., 2014; Kersten, 2020; Leivada et al., 2021: Paap et al., 2015; Tse & Arriba, 2015; Yow & Li, 2015).

Another complication in the literature on potential cognitive advantages of bilingualism, and one that even Peal and Lambert (1962) acknowledged would be a problem more than 50 years ago, is that it is difficult to tease apart the directionality of effect. That is, is it becoming bilingual that leads to cognitive and neurological differences in the brain, or are there certain types of individuals with initial cognitive and other skills that are more likely to become bilingual, or are both causal directions in play (Kersten & Greve, 2023, this volume)? Not much research has examined this particular question, since large-scale longitudinal studies are needed to get at this. There is the second language acquisition (SLA) literature involving adolescents and adults learning L2 formally in high school and college courses showing that a variety of individual differences are associated with second language performance and course grades (Dörnyei & Ryan, 2015). Such factors include gender (favoring females – Andreou et al., 2005), social skills and personality (favoring those who are outgoing and socially competent – MacIntyre et al., 1998), motivation, emotion, and anxiety (favoring those with less anxiety, more positive emotions, and more motivation – Dewaele et al., 2018; Dewaele, 2023, this volume; Horwitz et al., 1986; MacIntyre, 2017; Segalowitz, 1997), and children's prior L1 competence (favoring those with stronger L1 skills – Bhatia & Ritchie, 1999; Ordóñez et al., 2002). However, this research is typically with older students sequentially learning an L2 in a classroom setting. Little is known about (1) how long it takes young DLLs in poverty to reach English proficiency and (2) which child and school factors longitudinally predict the speed of acquisition of L2 English in young DLLs in the US in natural settings. The current chapter addresses these two questions related to potential bidirectional causal links between cognitive (and other) skills linked to the development of bilingualism over time. In addition, the chapter covers two additional research questions that link bilingual language development for DLLs to later academic performance and educational practices. Namely, (3) whether earlier acquisition of English L2 is linked to better academic performance over time for DLLs (after controlling for other relevant variables) and (4) whether L2 acquisition speed and later performance at the end of elementary school is associated with the school's bilingual/ESOL program model and whether it supports L1 maintenance[1].

The current studies

This chapter summarizes work from the Miami School Readiness Project (MSRP). The MSRP is a large-scale longitudinal research and program evaluation project, which was a partnership between universities (George Mason University [Adam Winsler] and Florida International University

[Charles Bleiker]) and the community (Early Learning Coalition of Miami-Dade/Monroe, Miami-Dade County Public Schools [MDCPS], and South Florida's early childhood task force) (Winsler et al., 2008, 2014). For 5 years/cohorts, from 2002 to 2006, the community wanted to assess the school readiness of all 4-year-old children in the county living in poverty who received childcare subsidies to attend either center-based or family childcare in the community and all those who attended public school prekindergarten programs. The community also wanted longitudinal follow-up information on the sample to see how well the students were doing later on in elementary school. Thus, a very large (*N* > 30,000), ethnically diverse (about 60% Latino, 33% Black, 7% White/Asian/other), linguistically diverse (almost 60% spoke a home language other than English – mostly Spanish), and predominantly low-income sample was followed longitudinally from age 4 throughout school.

Here, I summarize results from four published works. The first is Winsler et al. (2014), in which one cohort (*n* = 2059) of the sample was followed from age 4 through the end of Kindergarten. The goal of this paper was to examine age-4 predictors of being later classified at the end of kindergarten (the first formal year of public education in the US) as either a monolingual English speaker, a dual-language learner (DLL) who was still developing their L2 English skills, or an early bilingual student who was fully proficient in English according to the school system at the end of kindergarten. The second paper is Kim et al. (2014), in which a large group of just DLLs (those classified by the school district as an English language learner *n* = 18,532) was followed from age 4 throughout all of elementary school (i.e., through fifth grade in the U.S.) to see factors that predict speed of acquisition of L2 English. The third work is Rozell et al. (2021), in which the full group of DLLs (*n* = 20,870) was followed from kindergarten through fifth grade, and the question there was how much speed of English acquisition mattered for students' academic achievement at the end of elementary school. The final paper is Serafini et al. (2020), in which the same group of DLLs was examined through fifth grade with special attention given to the type of "bilingual" or English as a second/other language (ESOL) educational program model(s) offered by the child's school to see if that was related to both the speed of English acquisition for the child and achievement at the end of elementary school.

Method

Participants

As described, participants were various subsets of students from the larger MSRP sample, ranging from 2,059 to 20,870, depending on the particular study, with the 20,870 figure representing all DLL students in the sample and the smaller numbers being a subset of the same DLLs (depending on cohort/year), and, in the case of Winsler et al. (2014), an additional matched comparison group of monolingual English-speaking students. About 52% of the overall MSRP sample were considered dual-language learners (DLLs) by the school district based on parent-reported home language use and English proficiency assessments given to the children (described in what follows). The DLL sample was 48% female, and the majority were from low-income families (80% qualified for free or reduced-price lunch at school, a government benefit for families in or near poverty in the US) and was linguistically and ethnically diverse (60% Latino, 33% Black, 7% White/Asian/other, with the vast majority of DLLs speaking Spanish at home). For Winsler et al. (2014), all the students identified as Latino, including the monolingual English-speaking group, which was comparable in terms of income status.

Procedures and measures

Children were assessed directly for school readiness skills in their pre-kindergarten year by the research team with assessments selected by the county's multiagency early childhood assessment task force. For the direct child assessment, bilingual (Spanish-English) assessors from the community with MA degrees in educational, school, developmental psychology or social work, and the public-school pre-K teachers were trained on the instrument over a 2-day period in workshops conducted by the instrument authors/publishers and the local university. Children were assessed for cognitive, language, motor, behavior, and social skills in the beginning and end of their prekindergarten year (September/October and then April/May). After entering elementary school the following year, deidentified, confidential student school record data were given to the researchers each year with the assistance and consent of the school system, parents, and the university and school system's ethical review board.

School readiness at age 4

The Learning Accomplishment Profile-Diagnostic (LAPD; Nehring et al., 1992) was completed individually by children in a separate room of the child's center/school. Bilingual assessors chose the best language (English or Spanish) to use for the assessment using both teacher report of the child's strongest language and their own impression of the child's stronger language after talking with the child in both languages and establishing rapport. Resources were not available to assess the child in both English and Spanish. The LAPD has good internal consistency reliability within the original norming sample (alphas of .76–.92) and good content validity and construct validity (Nehring et al., 1992). Internal consistency reliability for the LAPD within the MSRP sample was between .92 and .95 for the cognitive (matching and counting) and language (naming, comprehension) subscales (Winsler et al., 2008).

Children's social skills and behavior concerns were also measured at age 4 (at the same time intervals as the LAPD) via preschool teacher report using the Devereux Early Childhood Assessment (DECA; LeBuffe & Naglieri, 1999). The Initiative scale measures the child's ability to use independent thought and action to meet his/her needs. The Self-Control scale measures the child's ability to regulate emotion and communicate both verbally and behaviorally in a socially appropriate way. The Attachment scale measures mutual, strong, and long-lasting relations between a child and adults in general. The Initiative, Self-Control, and Attachment scales combine for a Total Protective Factors (TPF) scale, with higher scores indicating greater socio-emotional strengths. The Behavior Concerns scale describes child behaviors of concern to parents and teachers, and higher scores indicate poorer child behavior.

Teachers had the option of completing the DECA in either English or Spanish, and 50% of the preschool teachers completed the Spanish form. Internal consistency reliability within the MSRP sample ranged from .81 (behavior concerns) to .94 (TPF), and reliability of the DECA within this population was consistent across language of form (Crane et al., 2011).

Early language status and English proficiency

Student language status was determined by parent-reported home language at school entry as well as whether they were enrolled in the English for speakers of other languages (ESOL) program in kindergarten. Those with a home language other than English complete a yearly English proficiency assessment, either the Miami-Dade County Oral Language Proficiency Scale-Revised ([M-DCOLPS-R]; Abella et al., 2005) and/or the Comprehensive English Language Learning Assessment ([CELLA], Florida Department of Education [FDOE], 2015) depending on the year (the district changed the assessment over time). Students are classified into one of five English proficiency levels by the school system: Novice (Level 1), Low Intermediate (Level 2), High Intermediate (Level 3), Advanced (Level 4), and Independent (Level 5). At Level 5, the student is considered proficient in English enough to exit the ESOL program and no longer receives bilingual/ESOL education services.

For studies 2 through 4, the students' tested ESOL level (1–5) each year/grade and/or the grade/year at which the student reached Level 5 for English proficiency was used as a measure of the speed of English L2 acquisition. For the first study (Winsler et al., 2014), children of Latino/Hispanic ethnicity were categorized into three groups according to their language background and L2 acquisition trajectory over time from preschool to kindergarten. Children were classified as being in the *monolingual English group* (ME) if they were assessed on the LAPD in English at age 4, the parent reported English as the home language at school entry, and they were never considered DLL or tested for English proficiency in kindergarten. Students were categorized in the *predominantly*

Spanish-speaking group (PS) if Spanish was their strongest language at age 4 (indicated by the LAPD being given in Spanish) and then, at the end of kindergarten, the child still tested at only the beginner or intermediate level in English according to the school district's standards. Children were considered in the *emergent bilingual group* (EB) if Spanish was their strongest language at age 4 (LAPD given in Spanish) and then, at the end of kindergarten, the children tested at the advanced (4) or independent level (5) in English according to the school's assessment.

Fifth-grade academic achievement

Our end-of-elementary school measures of academic performance included the teacher-assigned grades that students received at the end of their fifth-grade year in all subjects (math, social studies, science, etc.) averaged together in the form of a grade-point average (GPA). Grades from each subject were converted from letters to numeric values (i.e. 1 = "F" to 5 = "A"). Second, we used standardized reading and math test scores in fifth grade based on the high-stakes Florida Comprehensive Assessment Test (FCAT; Florida Department of Education [FDOE], 2009) that students begin taking in 3rd grade. The FCAT yields a continuous standard score as well as an ordinal proficiency score ranging from 1 (little success with the challenging content) to 5 (success with the most challenging content).

School bilingual education model

In paper 4 (Serafini et al., 2020), a variable was created to show whether the school the child was enrolled in had a language/ESOL education program involving support for the home/partner language (0 = school did not have an education program that involved home language support [sheltered or mainstream English only where the goal was to learn English as soon as possible], or 1 = school did have a bilingual education program supporting home language, such as one-way [OWI] or two-way immersion programs [TWI]). Schools often offered more than one type of language program, preventing us from knowing which type of program was actually experienced by the child; thus, bilingual education for this variable included whether one-way or two-way immersion programs were available, regardless of the partner language and the home language of our participants. OWI programs only contained DLL students, and TWI programs contained both DLLs and native English speakers in the classrooms. For most but not all of the immersion programs, the languages were Spanish and English, and most followed a 50/50 model, but some were 60/40 or 90/10 in L1 with increasing amounts of English used as the grade increases. To further isolate the effects of TWI, a second variable was created to indicate if participants were at a school that exclusively offered a two-way immersion program, as opposed to schools that did not offer a two-way immersion program or had a two-way immersion program along with other types of programs (0 = school did not have a two-way immersion program or had other ESOL models in addition to a two-way immersion program, 1 = school only offered a two-way immersion program). This variable identifies children who were definitely enrolled in a two-way immersion program in elementary school (because that is all the school offered).

Demographics and other covariates

The covariates included varied somewhat from paper to paper but at some point included gender (female, male), ethnicity (Hispanic/Latino, African American/Black, White/Other), poverty status (qualify for free/reduced-priced lunch = 1), type of preschool/childcare at age 4 (public school pre-K, community-based center/family childcare), and a variety of elementary school-level variables such as percentage of teachers and students that are Hispanic, percentage of beginning teachers, size of school, average class size, total number of ESOL students, and percentage of students receiving reduced/free lunch.

Summary of analyses

Analyses varied depending on the particular project but included ANOVA and multiple regression models, longitudinal growth curve analyses via hierarchical linear modeling (with English proficiency/ESOL level as the DV), and discrete-time survival analysis (with the grade at which the student exited ESOL/bilingual programs as the dependent variable). Type of analysis used is discussed in what follows, in turn.

Results and discussion

Results are presented in order of the research questions provided at the end of the introduction, which span the four studies listed (Kim et al., 2014; Rozell et al., 2021; Serafini et al., 2020; Winsler et al., 2014).

Question (1) How long does it take for DLLs in the Miami School Readiness Project (MSRP) to reach full English proficiency (i.e., exit ESOL programs) as defined by the school system?

As a reminder, the DLLs we are talking about here are ESLA early sequential bilinguals who spoke mostly Spanish at home and likely started experiencing serious exposure to L2 English in their preschool settings around age 3 or 4, and by design, all children in the sample were attending some kind of pre-K/center/childcare arrangement at age 4. Our measure of English proficiency is a fairly limited one – namely, in which school grade did the child reach ESOL Level 5 and exit ESOL services in the school? It should be noted that this is a rather low bar and does not indicate that the child has full native-like command of L2 necessary for optimum academic learning. Descriptive and survival analyses revealed that almost a third (29%) of the sample reached this threshold by the end of Kindergarten, and by first grade, 52% had exited the ESOL program. By third grade, 85% had reached proficiency (which includes passing the high-stakes English reading standardized test), and by the end of elementary school, fifth grade, 90% of the DLL students had reached the school district's criterion for English proficiency. Those DLLs who did not reach the proficiency threshold by fifth grade tended to be those with language disorders or other disabilities (35%) and those struggling to pass the high-stakes standardized English reading assessment (78%). Thus, DLLs in poverty overall, even in this community in which there is strong societal support for L1 Spanish, are becoming proficient in English relatively quickly as a group (Kim et al., 2014). However, there were important individual differences in the speed of L2 acquisition, which leads us to the second research question.

Question (2) Which child and school factors longitudinally predict the speed of acquisition of English (L2) in young DLLs in the natural setting in Miami?

This question was tackled in two different ways. First, it was examined categorically – placing children into three different groups on their language status at the end of Kindergarten – monolingual English [ME], DLLs still predominantly Spanish-speaking [PS], and emergent bilinguals [EB] who had reached full English proficiency by the end of kindergarten – and then we examined early, preexisting predictors of group membership via ANOVAs or regression (Winsler et al., 2014). Second, the research question was examined continuously using either English skills at school entry (Winsler et al., 2014) or the grade in which full proficiency was obtained (Kindergarten through grade 5) as the dependent measure as predicted by various child- and school-level factors using growth curve modeling or survival analysis (Kim et al., 2014).

In terms of group membership on the basis of early language status, a variety of demographic and early school readiness skills was associated with the child's classification at the end of kindergarten. In terms of demographics, girls, older children, and those with parents who were US-born were more likely to fall in the emerging bilingual group. More importantly, early child competence in the areas of cognitive, language, social skills, and behavior assessed 18 months before classification was associated with language status at the end of kindergarten. Figure 5.1 shows the child's age-4 readiness assessments plotted by language status group. As can be seen, those children who went on to become fully proficient in English by the end of kindergarten, the emergent bilingual

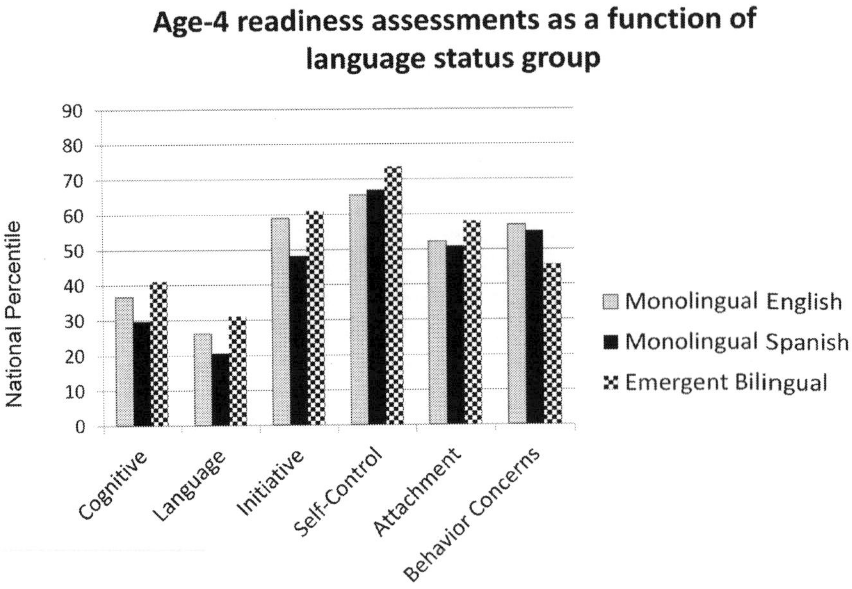

Figure 5.1 Prior age-4 skills plotted as a function of language grouping at the end of kindergarten. Children who go on to become bilingual in kindergarten were those with stronger socioemotional and cognitive skills earlier in preschool.

(EB) group (blue bars), were consistently stronger in cognitive, language (L1), and social skills and showed fewer behavior problems 18 months earlier when they were assessed in preschool. The (preschool teacher-reported) self-control and behavior problems subscales of the DECA are the two closest real-world/behavioral measures of executive function (EF) that we have in the sense that those with EF difficulties tend to show externalizing behavior problems and poor impulse control/inhibition (Berlin et al., 2004; Winsler et al., 2007). Importantly, the emergent bilingual group was already showing strengths in these areas before they became proficient enough in English to be considered a bilingual. This suggests bidirectional relations between cognitive (and social) skills and bilingualism – here, it was the children with high EF, behavioral, and cognitive and L1 language skills in the first place that went on later to become fully bilingual, as assessed in the real world of the school setting (Winsler et al., 2014).

In terms of the continuous measures of English proficiency, we had English LAPD language scores at age 4 and the DLL's ESOL level upon school entry as measures of *initial status*, and we had the grade/year the DLL reached full English (L2) proficiency and/or the student's ESOL level each year as measures of *growth over time* or speed of L2 acquisition

(Kim et al., 2014). Correlational, multiple regression, growth curve modeling, and survival analyses revealed that the following variables were positively associated with the DLL's initial status on English (L2) skills at school entry: (a) L1 (Spanish) proficiency at age 4, (b) being female, (c) not being in poverty, and (d) having high social skills and few behavioral concerns in preschool. School-level factors that were significantly positively associated with initial Kindergarten L2 English skills included attending public school pre-K programs at age 4 (compared to childcare in the community) and attending an elementary school that was larger and had fewer DLLs. Factors associated with steeper growth over time and faster exit from ESOL programs included (a) children's higher initial English skills upon school entry, (b) stronger initial L1 Spanish skills, (c) higher cognitive, language, and social skills as a preschooler, (d) not being in poverty, (e) increased parental education, and (f) child ethnicity (White/other students were faster than Latinos who were faster than Black students).

The fact that DLLs with stronger skills in L1 (Spanish) showed faster growth in L2 (English) is an important finding, as it shows that rather than competing for resources, a strong foundation in L1 only aids in L2 development. This is consistent with Cummins's (1991) interdependence and transfer model, showing that DLLs use their L1 in important ways for guiding L2 development (Ordóñez et al., 2002; Parra et al., 2011). This finding also has implications for early childhood bilingual education programs in that it shows that maintaining a strong L1 only helps in L2 learning and that support for the home language can be a positive thing, assuming sufficient exposure to L2 is present (Howes et al., 2011; Lindholm-Leary, 2001; Winsler et al., 1999).

Our findings pertaining to gender and L2 growth are interesting. Replicating studies with sequential, older, and typically societal L1 speakers learning an L2 in formal classroom settings (Andreou et al., 2005; Dörnyei & Ryan, 2015), we saw that among this young ESLA DLL sample, girls showed more advanced English skills early on and faster growth in L2. However, and of particular note, this effect disappeared when child social and behavioral skills were factored in. This means that it is enhanced social skills and behavioral strengths (which are present more in girls on average, both in general and in this sample (Hartman & Winsler, 2017), rather than gender per se) that help young female DLLs acquire L2, presumably due to increased access to L2 speaking and socialization opportunities with their peers.

It is clear from the studies reported on here that not all DLLs will acquire full proficiency in L2 English at the same rates. Some students may need additional support, and a one-size-fits-all approach may not be warranted. We found here that those in poverty, those with parents with less education and not US-born, and Black DLLs showed slower growth in L2 English. Such students may need additional supports and/or need additional institutional barriers and inequalities removed in order to grow to their potential in L2 acquisition. Some have found that school districts vary in how quickly they reclassify DLLs as proficient even when criteria are met and that teacher discretion and parental requests are also part of the equation (Estrada & Wang, 2018).

Question (3) To what extent is earlier/faster acquisition of English (L2) linked to better academic performance over time for DLLs (after controlling for other relevant variables)?

In the previous sections, we have asked how long it takes DLLs largely in poverty to gain mastery of L2 English and what factors predict speed of acquisition. Now we turn to the issue of whether faster/earlier mastery of English matters for DLLs' academic achievement throughout elementary school. In fifth grade, we had students' standardized math and reading test scores (both continuous and categorized into pass/fail) and their teacher-assigned grades received (overall GPA across all of their subjects). These we analyzed as dependent measures in a series of ANOVAs as a function of the grade in which the DLLs exited the ESOL program as the independent variable, as well as in multiple regression models that controlled for gender, ethnicity, poverty status, and preschool cognitive, social, and behavioral skills (Rozell et al., 2021).

As expected, DLLs' performance in fifth grade (G5) was significantly consistently related to how quickly they exited the ESOL program, with those students who were proficient in English by the end of kindergarten getting the highest test scores and GPAs later on and performance declining in a fairly linear manner with each year/grade's delay in becoming fully proficient in English (i.e., first grade > second grade > third grade etc.). The students who were still not proficient in English according to school district standards in fifth grade performed particularly poorly on all measures in fifth grade. Of DLLs who were proficient in English by kindergarten, 80% of them passed the high-stakes reading exam in G5; however for those who did not reach proficiency until G5, only 63% passed the exam. Even after controlling for the abovementioned demographic variables and school readiness, each year's delay in reaching ESOL level 5 was associated with about a 20% reduction in the odds that the DLL would perform at grade level on the fifth-grade reading test. Thus, our findings support prior work showing that DLLs who are proficient in English early on, especially in kindergarten or first grade, do much better is school compared to DLLs whose proficiency in L2 arrives later (Halle et al., 2012; Reardon & Galindo, 2007; Reese et al., 2000).

The facts that (a) the initial L2 English skill that DLLs enter school with was a strong predictor of L2 growth and thus faster exit from ESOL services and (b) that earlier attainment of L2 English proficiency is strongly related to elementary school academic performance, with earlier being better, together suggest that early access to English (with continuing support for L1) before formal schooling begins is essential and would be helpful for DLLs in the US. Increased access to universal and subsidized pre-K programs is helping low-income DLL families with finding affordable child care (Bassok & Galdo, 2015; Phillips et al., 2018). However, there are many options for organized childcare/preschool, and these vary in quality and exposure to cognitively stimulating English L2. Indeed, other work shows that DLLs who attend high-quality public school–based pre-kindergarten programs at age 4 are not only more academically ready for school, but they also are farther along in the English L2 development compared to DLLs who attend center-based or family childcare in the community on childcare subsidies (Ansari et al., 2017; Conger et al., 2019). Although getting a start on English exposure in pre-K programs is indeed helpful academically down the road for DLLs, this L2 goal needs to be weighted together with other family, cultural, and L1 maintenance goals and opportunities for and culturally responsive childcare needs and choices for DLL and immigrant families (Li-Grining & Coley, 2006; Vesely, 2013). Finding a language program that supports home language use in addition to L2 English acquisition can be a challenge and is the topic of the next section.

Question (4) Is L2 acquisition speed and later performance at the end of elementary school associated with the school's bilingual/ESOL program model and whether it supports L1 maintenance?

The final question explored here is how L2 English growth and academic performance is related to the elementary school's bilingual education program model. Serafini et al. (2020) examined this question with the same MSRP DLL sample. As described, the data available to us were only at the school level rather than the child or classroom level, so we don't actually know for each child in our sample what kind of ESOL/language education program support they experienced in any given grade. However, we knew which school the child attended in any given year and what that school offered in terms of ESOL/language education. Instructional models in this district varied from sheltered English programs where only DLLs were present in the classroom and only English was used for instruction to mainstream inclusion classrooms where DLLs and native speakers of English were together in English-only classrooms, to one-way developmental bilingual immersion (OWI) programs where only DLLs were present in the classroom but both the home language (L1) and English (L2) were used for instruction, to two-way immersion programs (TWI) where native English speakers and DLLs occupied the classrooms together and both the home language and English were used. The latter two programs (OWI and TWI) were classified by us as having support for the home language, and the other programs were classified as little support for home language. Some schools only offered TWI programs, so in those cases, it was known that the DLL experienced TWI (Serafini et al., 2020).

As described, numerous child and demographic variables predicted how quickly the DLL students learned English (gender, ethnicity, poverty, cognitive and social skills at age 4), so these important covariates were included in multiple regression analyses predicting first speed of L2 acquisition, and then fifth-grade academic performance, with the main predictor of interest being whether the school attended by the DLL had either (a) bilingual programs that included some support for L1 (TWI or OWI programs) or (b) were TWI only. We found that controlling for all other factors mentioned associated with speed of L2 acquisition, DLLs who attended schools with TWI programs that supported home language actually learned English L2 somewhat *faster* than those whose schools emphasized English-only education programs. Also, fifth-grade academic performance (GPA and math and reading test scores) was higher for DLLs who attended schools that offered at least some home language support in their ESOL instructional models compared to English-only programs, controlling for all other important child factors linked to better school performance. Finally, given that speed of English acquisition was the strongest predictor of fifth-grade academic performance, and students in TWI-only schools learned English faster, we ran mediational analyses and found speed of English acquisition mediated the effect of TWI programs on fifth-grade performance (GPA). That is, TWI programs may have increased the speed of L2 English development, and that helps explain why DLLs in TWI bilingual programs did better in school (Serafini et al., 2020). Thus, in addition to child-level "nano" variables predicting speed of L2 acquisition as found in the earlier sections in this chapter, more macro school-level variables (such as ESOL educational model) are also important in mediating and explaining SLA outcomes, which is fully consistent with the multilevel theoretical framework proposed in Chapter 1 of this volume (Kersten & Greve, 2023, this volume).

In terms of the limitations of the studies reported here, the current work was restricted to administrative school record data, which did not allow us to get qualitative information about the experiences of our DLLs progressing through school. Also, we do not have information on L1 development and/or loss over time. Our Miami sample consisting of mostly Latino and Black students and DLLs is a strength in the sense that Black DLLs are an understudied group. However, our findings are likely not generalizable to other DLL groups with other L1 experiences outside of Miami and the US. Finally, we did not have access to details on the types of or quality of the ESOL/bilingual education programs experienced by our DLLs. As discussed elsewhere in this volume (Kersten, 2020), the types of bilingual language program experienced by second language learners can change the nature and quality of teacher–child interactions and scaffolding for learning the student receives, which can alter academic trajectories.

Summary and conclusions

This volume explores different types of variability in the process through which individuals acquire a second language. In this chapter, I summarized results from the Miami School Readiness Project, in which a very large sample of predominantly Latino and Black DLLs, largely in poverty, were longitudinally followed from preschool through the end of elementary school (fifth grade). Here, the DLLs were experiencing what can be described as early second language acquisition (ESLA, De Houwer, 2002, in that for most, their home L1 was Spanish and they were exposed to considerable L2 English, the societal language, during their early childhood preschool settings. Although the setting was the US, Miami is a unique community with considerable sociolinguistic support for Spanish. In this context, we examined the length of time until DLLs reached the school system's definition of English proficiency, predictors of speed of L2 acquisition, and academic outcomes associated with both the speed of L2 learning and the ESOL or bilingual program model used at the school (Kim et al., 2014; Rozell et al., 2021; Serafini et al., 2020; Winsler et al., 2014).

We found that our DLLs who started attending English ECE programs at age 4 learned English quickly, with more than half of them graduating out of bilingual education services by the end of first grade, and almost all (about 90%) of them did so by or shortly after third grade. It is worth noting that the small group of DLLs who did not exit ESOL services by fifth grade were particularly at risk for poor academic performance, and many had been diagnosed with a disability by fifth grade. We recommend that any DLL who has been in the school system since kindergarten who is not yet proficient in English by third grade be slated to receive extra supports. Indeed, we found that the earlier DLLs reach proficiency in the L2 language of instruction, the better they do in terms of later academic performance, with those who exit ESOL services by kindergarten or first grade doing much better than those who do so later, but every year mattered.

In terms of factors linked with speed of L2 acquisition, we found that those with higher cognitive skills, social skills, and behavioral control in preschool, those with stronger L1 Spanish skills early on, and those not in poverty reached full English proficiency faster than other children. On a practical level, this means that teachers and interventionists need to understand that not all DLLs will progress in L2 development at the same rate, and some children may need additional supports. From a research standpoint, the fact that those with higher initial cognitive and behavioral control skills in the first place are those more likely/faster to become fully bilingual suggests that in addition to bilingualism perhaps leading individuals to develop advanced executive functioning skills, there appears to be a causal pathway in the other direction as well – those with high self-control and cognitive skills early on have an advantage over time in becoming bilingual and reaching full proficiency in L2. This observation is critical to the ongoing debate about the presence of bilingual effects on cognition (Leivada et al., 2021). The other critical finding here, with implications for early child bilingual education programs and home language maintenance efforts, is that children with higher L1 Spanish skills showed better and faster L2 English development. Also related to maintenance of the home language, we found that students who went to schools that offered language education models that involved at least some instruction in L1 reached English proficiency earlier and did better in fifth grade on some measures than those whose language education programs involved English-only instruction. Further research is needed to identify more malleable factors that can be leveraged to help DLLs (and all students) become fully bilingual.

Note

1. Here, I use the term "bilingual" or "ESOL" education in the broadest sense when describing language educational models and experiences of DLLs in US schools, acknowledging that many of these are not technically bilingual programs at all, as they may just focus on L2/English learning at the expense of L1.

References

Abella, J., Urrita, J., & Schneiderman, A. (2005). An examination of the validity of English-language achievement test scores in an English language learner population. *Bilingual Research Journal*, *29*, 127–144. https://doi:10.1080/15235882.2005.10162827

American Institutes for Research. (2014). *Common ELL terms and definitions*. www.air.org/resource/common-ell-terms-and-definitions

Andreou, G., Vlachos, F., & Andreou, E. (2005). Affecting factors in second language learning. *Journal of Psycholinguistic Research*, *34*, 429–438. https://doi:10.1007/s10936-005-6202-0

Ansari, A., López, M., Manfra, L., Bleiker, C., Dinehart, L. H. B., Hartman, S. C., & Winsler, A. (2017). Differential third grade outcomes associated with attending publicly funded preschool programs for low-income, Latino children. *Child Development*, *88*(5), 1743–1756. https://doi.org/10.1111/cdev.12663

Ardasheva, Y., Tretter, T. R., & Kinney, M. (2012). English language learners and academic achievement: Revisiting the threshold hypothesis. *Language Learning*, *62*, 769–812. https://doi:10.1111/j.1467-9922.2011.00652.x

Bassok, D., & Galdo, E. (2016). Inequality in preschool quality? Community-level disparities in access to high-quality learning environments. *Early Education and Development*, *27*(1), 128–144. https://doi.org/10.1080/10409289.2015.1057463

Beal, C. R., Adams, N. M., & Cohen, P. R. (2010). Reading proficiency and mathematics problem solving by high school English language learners. *Urban Education*, *45*, 58–74. https://doi:10.1177/0042085909352143

Berlin, L., Bohlin, G., & Rydell, A-M. (2004). Relations between inhibition, executive functioning, and ADHD symptoms: A longitudinal study from age

5 to 8½ years. *Child Neuropsychology*, 9, 225–266. https://doi.org/10.1076/chin.9.4.255.23519

Bhatia, T. K., & Ritchie, W. C. (1999). The bilingual child: Some issues and perspectives. In W. C. Ritchie & T. K. Bhatia (Eds.), *Handbook of child language acquisition* (pp. 569–646). Academic Press.

Bialystok, E. (2007). Cognitive effects of bilingualism: How linguistic experience leads to cognitive change. *International Journal of Bilingual Education and Bilingualism*, *10*(3), 210–223. https://doi.org/10.2167/beb441.0

Butler, F. A., & Castellon-Wellington, M. (2000). Students' concurrent performance on tests of English language proficiency and academic achievement. In *The validity of administrating large-scale content assessments to English language learners: An investigation from three perspectives*. National Center for Research on Evaluation, Standards, and Student Testing. University of California.

Calvo, N., Ibáñez, A., & García, A. M. (2016). The impact of bilingualism on working memory: A null effect on the whole may not be so on the parts. *Frontiers in Psychology*, *7*, 265. https://doi.org/10.3389/fpsyg.2016.00265

Conger, D., Gibbs, C. R., Uchikoshi, Y., & Winsler, A. (2019). New benefits of public-school pre-kindergarten programs: Early school stability, reduced retention, and early exit from ELL programs. *Early Childhood Research Quarterly*, *48*, 26–35. https://doi.org/10.1016/j.ecresq.2018.10.015

Crane, J., Mincic, M., & Winsler, A. (2011). Parent-teacher agreement and reliability on the Devereux early childhood assessment (DECA) in English and Spanish for ethnically diverse children living in poverty. *Early Education and Development*, *22*, 520–547. https://doi.org/10.1080/10409289.2011.565722

Crawford, J. (1999). *Bilingual education: History, politics, theory, and practice*. Bilingual Educational Services.

Cummins, J. (1991). Interdependence of first- and second-language proficiency in bilingual children. In E. Bialystok (Ed.), *Language processing in bilingual children* (pp. 70–89). Cambridge University Press.

Darcy, N. T. (1963). Bilingualism and the measurement of intelligence: Review of a decade of research. *Journal of Genetic Psychology*, *103*, 259–282. https://doi.org/10.1080/00221325.1963.10532521

De Houwer, A. (1990). *The acquisition of two languages from birth: A case study*. Cambridge University Press.

De Houwer, A. (2021). *Bilingual development in the first decade of life*. Cambridge University Press.

Dewaele, J.-M. (2023, this volume). The interplay between learner-internal variables and levels of anxiety and enjoyment among Spanish EFL learners. In K. Kersten & A. Winsler (Eds.), *Understanding variability in second language acquisition, bilingualism, and cognition: A multi-layered perspective*. Routledge.

Dewaele, J.-M., & Thirtle, H. (2009). Why do some young learners drop foreign languages? A focus on learner-internal variables. *International Journal of Bilingual Education and Bilingualism*, 12(6), 635–649. https://doi.org/10.1080/13670050802549656

Dewaele, J.-M., Witney, J., Saito, K., & Dewaele, L. (2018). Foreign language enjoyment and anxiety in the FL classroom: The effect of teacher and learner variables. *Language Teaching Research*, 22(6), 676–697. https://doi.org/10.1177/1362168817692161

Dörnyei, Z., & Ryan, S. (2015). *The psychology of the second language learner revisited*. Routledge.

Estrada, P., & Wang, H. (2018). Making English learner reclassification to fluent English proficient attainable or elusive: When meeting criteria is and is not enough. *American Educational Research Journal*, *55*, 207–242. https://doi.org/10.3102/0002831217733543

Festman, J., Czapka, S., & Winsler, A. (in press). How many moderators does is take till we know . . . that too many bilingual advantage effects have died? In K. Kersten & A. Winsler (Eds.), *Understanding variability in second language acquisition, bilingualism, and cognition: A multi-layered perspective*. Routledge.

Florida Department of Education. (2009). *District plan for services to English language learners (ELLs)*. www.fldoe.org/aala/ELLPlans/2009/Miamidade09.pdf

Florida Department of Education: Bureau of Student Achievement Through Language Acquisition. (2015). *2015 comprehensive English language learning assessment (CELLA) frequently asked questions*. www.fldoe.org/core/fileparse.php/7583/urlt/06-05-152015-CELLA-FAQs.pdf

Fuller, J. M. (2019). Ideologies of language, bilingualism, and monolingualism. In A. De Houwer & L. Ortega (Eds.), *The Cambridge handbook of bilingualism* (pp. 119–134). Cambridge University Press.

Gould, S. J. (1981). *The mismeasure of man*. W. W. Norton & Company.

Green, D. W. (1998). Mental control of the bilingual Lexico-semantic system. *Bilingualism: Language and Cognition*, *1*(2), 67–81. https://doi.org/10.1017/S1366728998000133

Hakuta, K. (1986). *Mirror of language*. Basic Books.

Halle, T., Hair, E., Wandner, L., McNamara, M., & Chien, N. (2012). Predictors and outcomes of early versus later English language proficiency among English language learners. *Early Childhood Research Quarterly*, *27*, 1–20. https//doi.org:10.1016/j.ecresq.2011.07.004

Hartman, S. C., & Winsler, A. (2017). Behavioral concerns among low-income ethnically diverse children in child care: Importance for school readiness and kindergarten achievement. *Early Education and Development*, *28*, 255–273. https://doi.org/10.1080/00220671.2016.1145095

Henry, D., Nistor, N., & Baltes, B. (2014). Examining the relationship between math scores and English language proficiency. *Journal of Educational Research and Practice*, *4*(1), 11–29. https://doi:10.5590/JERAP.2014.04.1.02

Horwitz, E. K., Horwitz, M. B., & Cope, J. (1986). Foreign language classroom anxiety. *Modern Language Journal*, *70*, 125–132. https://doi:10.1111/j.1540-4781.1986.tb05256.x

Howes, C., Downer, J., & Pianta, R. C. (Eds.). (2011). *Dual language learners in the early childhood classroom*. Brookes.

Iluz-Cohen, P., & Armon-Lotem, S. (2013). Language proficiency and executive control in bilingual children. *Bilingualism: Language and Cognition*, *16*, 884–899. https://doi.org/10.1017/S1366728912000788

Kalia, V., Wilbourn, M. P., & Ghio, K. (2014). Better early or late? Examining the influence of age of exposure and language proficiency on executive function in early and late bilinguals. *Journal of Cognitive Psychology*, *26*, 699–713. https://doi.org/10.1080/20445911.2014.956748

Kersten, K. (2020). Der Zusammenhang von kognitiven Fähigkeiten und Zweisprachigkeit im frühen L2-Erwerb: Individuelle und externe Faktoren. In H. Böttger, J. Festman, & T. Müller (Hrsg.), *Language education and acquisition research: Focusing early language learning* (pp. 82–116). Klinkhardt.

Kersten, K., & Greve, W. (2023, this volume). Investigating influencing factors of cognitive-linguistic development in SLA: Challenges for empirical research. In K. Kersten & A. Winsler (Eds.), *Interplay of variables in cognitive-linguistic development – a multi-layered perspective.*

Kieffer, M. (2008). Catching up or falling behind? Initial English proficiency, concentrated poverty, and the reading growth of language minority learners in the United States. *Journal of Educational Psychology, 100*, 851–868. https://dx.doi.org/10.1037/0022-0663.100.4.851

Kim, Y. K., Curby, T. W., & Winsler, A. (2014). Child, family, and school characteristics related to English proficiency development among low-income dual language learners (DLLs). *Developmental Psychology, 50*, 2600–2613. https://doi.org/10.1037/a0038050

LeBuffe, P. A., & Naglieri, J. A. (1999). *Devereux early childhood assessment.* Kaplan Press.

Leeman, J. (2004). Racializing language: A history of linguistic ideologies in the US census. *Journal of Language and Politics, 3*(3), 507–534.

Leeuw, E. D., & Bogulski, C. A. (2016). Frequent L2 language use enhances executive control in bilinguals. *Bilingualism: Language and Cognition, 19*, 907–913. https://doi.org/10.1017/S1366728916000201

Lehtonen, M., Soveri, A., Laine, A., Järvenpää, J., de Bruin, A., & Antfolk, J. (2018). Is bilingualism associated with enhanced executive functioning in adults? A meta-analytic review. *Psychological Bulletin, 144*(4), 394–425. https://doi.org/10.1037/bul0000142

Leivada, E., Westergaard, M., Duñabeitia, J. A., & Rothman, J. (2021). On the phantom-like appearance of bilingualism effects on neurocognition: (How) should we proceed? *Bilingualism: Language and Cognition, 24*, 197–210. https://doi.org/10.1017/S1366728920000358

Li-Grining, C. P., & Coley, R. L. (2006). Child care experiences in low-income communities: Developmental quality and maternal views. *Early Childhood Research Quarterly, 21*(2), 125–141. https://doi.org/10.1016/j.ecresq.2006.04.001

Lindholm-Leary, K. J. (2001). *Dual language education.* Multilingual Matters.

MacIntyre, P. D. (2002). Motivation, anxiety and emotion in second language acquisition. In P. Robinson (Ed.), *Individual differences and instructed language learning* (pp. 45–68). John Benjamins.

MacIntyre, P. D. (2017). An overview of language anxiety research and trends in its development. In C. Gkonou, M. Daubney, & J.-M. Dewaele (Eds.), *New insights into language anxiety: Theory, research and educational implications* (pp. 11–30). Multilingual Matters.

MacIntyre, P. D., Clément, R., Dörnyei, Z., & Noels, K. A. (1998). Conceptualizing willingness to communicate in a L2: A situational model of L2 confidence and affiliation. *Modern Language Journal, 82*, 545–562. https://doi:10.1111/j.1540-4781.1998.tb05543.x

National Center for Education Statistics. (2017). *Digest of education statistics.* https://nces.ed.gov/programs/digest/d16/tables/dt16_204.20.asp

National Clearinghouse for English Language Acquisition. (2011). *The growing numbers of English learner students, 1997/98–2007/08*. www.ncela.us/files/uploads/9/growingLEP_0809.pdf

National Education Association, NEA Education Policy and Practice Department. (2008). *An NEA policy brief: English language learners face unique challenges*. www.nea.org/assets/docs/HE/ELL_Policy_Brief_Fall_08_(2).pdf

Nehring, A. D., Nehring, E. F., Bruni, J. R., & Randolph, P. L. (1992). *Learning accomplishment profile – Diagnostic standardized assessment*. Kaplan Press.

Ordóñez, C. L., Carlo, M. S., Snow, C. E., & McLaughlin, B. (2002). Depth and breadth in vocabulary in two languages: Which vocabulary skills transfer? *Journal of Educational Psychology*, *94*, 719–728. https://doi:10.1037/0022-0663.94.4.719

Paap, K. R., Johnson, H. A., & Sawi, O. (2015). Bilingual advantages in executive functioning either do not exist or are restricted to very specific and undetermined circumstances. *Cortex*, *69*, 265–278. https://doi.org/10.1016/j.cortex.2015.04.014

Parker, C. E., Louie, J., & O'Dwyer, L. (2009). *New measures of English language proficiency and their relationship to performance on large-scale content assessments*. U.S. Department of Education, Institute of Education Sciences, National Center for Education Evaluation and Regional Assistance, Regional Educational Laboratory Northeast and Islands.

Parra, M., Hoff, E., & Core, C. (2011). Relations among language exposure, phonological memory, and language development in Spanish-English bilingually-developing two-year-olds. *Journal of Experimental Child Psychology*, *108*(1), 113–125. https://doi:10.1016/j.jecp.2010.07.011

Peal, E., & Lambert, W. E. (1962). The relation of bilingualism to intelligence. *Psychological Monographs*, *76*(27, Whole No. 546).

Phillips, D. A., Anderson, S., Datta, A. R., & Kisker, E. E. (2018). The changing landscape of publicly-funded center-based child care: 1990 and 2012. *Children and Youth Services Review*, *91*, 94–104. https://doi.org/10.1016/j.childyouth.2018.05.029

Pliatsikas, C., & Luk, G. (2016). Executive control in bilinguals: A concise review on fMRI studies. *Bilingualism: Language and Cognition*, *19*, 699–705. https://doi.org/10.1017/S1366728916000249

Pliatsikas, C., Moschopoulou, E., & Saddy, D. (2017). Immersive late bilingualism reshapes the core of the brain. *Brain Structure and Function*, *222*(4), 1785–1795. https://doi.org/10.1007/s00429-016-1307-9

Rahmani, F., Sobhani, S., & Aarabi, M. H. (2017). Sequential language learning and language immersion in bilingualism: Diffusion MRI connectometry reveals microstructural evidence. *Experimental Brain Research*, *235*, 2935–2945. https://doi.org/10.1007/s00221-017-5029-x

Reardon, S. F., & Galindo, C. (2007). Patterns of Hispanic students' math skill proficiency in the early elementary grades. *Journal of Latinos & Education*, 6(3), 229–251. https://doi:10.1080/15348430701312883

Reese, L., Garnier, H., Gallimore, R., & Goldberg, C. (2000.) Longitudinal analysis of the antecedents of emergent Spanish literacy and middle-school English reading achievement of Spanish-speaking students. *American Educational Research Journal*, *37*, 633–662.

Roberts, C. A. (2010). Bilingual education program models: A framework for understanding. *Bilingual Research Journal, 19*, 369–378. https://doi.org/10.1080/15235882.1995.10162679

Rozell, N., Winsler, A., & Norvell, G. (2021). *Elementary school outcomes associated with faster English language acquisition for dual language learners.* Manuscript submitted for publication. Manuscript submitted for publication.

Saint-Aubin, J., Hilchey, R., Mishra, N., Singh, D., Savoie, D., Guitard, D., & Klein, R. M. (2018). Does the relation between the control of attention and second language proficiency generalize from India to Canada? *Canadian Journal of Experimental Psychology*, 72(3), 208–218. https://doi.org/10.1037/cep0000151

Segalowitz, N. (1997). Individual differences in second language acquisition. In A. M. B. de Groot & J. F. Kroll (Eds.), *Tutorials in bilingualism: Psycholinguistic perspectives* (pp. 85–112). Psychology Press.

Serafini, E. J., Rozell, N., & Winsler, A. (2020). Academic and English language outcomes for DLLs as a function of school bilingual education model: The role of two-way immersion and home language support. *International Journal of Bilingual Education and Bilingualism.* http://dx.doi.org/10.1080/13670050.2019.1707477

Tse, C. S., & Arriba, J. A. (2015). Local and global task switching costs in bilinguals who vary in second language proficiency. *American Journal of Psychology, 128*(1), 89–106. https://doi.org/10.5406/amerjpsyc.128.1.0089

U.S. Census Bureau. (2017). *Language spoken at home of Miami-Dade County, Florida, 2013–2017 American community survey 5-year estimates.* https://factfinder.census.gov/

Vesely, C. K. (2013). Low-income African and Latina immigrant mothers' selection of early childhood care and education (ECCE): Considering the complexity of cultural and structural influences. *Early Childhood Research Quarterly, 28*, 470–486. https://doi.org/10.1016/j.ecresq.2013.02.001

Winsler, A., Abar, B., Feder, M., Rubio, D. A., & Schunn, C. (2007). Private speech and executive functioning among high functioning children with autistic spectrum disorders. *Journal of Autism and Developmental Disabilities, 37*, 1617–1635. https://doi.org/10.1007/s10803-006-0294-8

Winsler, A., Diaz, R. M., Espinosa, L., & Rodriguez, J. L. (1999). When learning a second language does not mean losing the first: Bilingual language development in low-income, Spanish-speaking children at- tending bilingual preschool. *Child Development, 70*, 349–362. https://doi: 10.1111/1467-8624.t01-1-00026 \

Winsler, A., Kim, Y. K., & Richard, E. (2014). Socio-emotional skills, behavior problems, and Spanish competence predict the acquisition of English among English language learners in poverty. *Developmental Psychology, 50*, 2242–2254. https://doi.org/10.1037/a0037161

Winsler, A., Tran, H., Hartman, S., Madigan, A., Manfra, L., & Bleiker, C. (2008). School readiness gains made by ethnically-diverse children in poverty attending center-based childcare and public school pre- kindergarten programs. *Early Childhood Research Quarterly, 23*, 314–329. https://doi:10.1016/j.ecresq.2008.02.003

Wolf, M. K., Kao, J., Griffin, N., Herman, J. L., Bachman, P. L., Chang, S. M., & Farnsworth, T. (2008). *Issues in assessing English language learners: English language proficiency measures and accommodation uses*. CRESST Report 732. National Center for Research on Evaluation, Standards, and Student Testing.

Yow, W. Q., & Li, X. (2015). Balanced bilingualism and early age of second language acquisition as the underlying mechanisms of a bilingual executive control advantage: Why variations in bilingual experiences matter. *Frontiers in Psychology*, 6, 164. https://doi.org/10.3389/fpsyg.2015.00164

6 Immigrant achievement and language use across countries

The role of family background and education systems

Janna Teltemann, Maximilian Brinkmann, Nora Huth-Stöckle, and Reinhard Schunck

Introduction

As immigrant populations are growing in many countries, the challenge of long-term integration becomes more pressing. Successful educational attainment of immigrants – and, as a prerequisite, language acquisition – is a keystone of integration processes. A sociological perspective can help understand the process of language acquisition and integration, as it is one of the fundamental tasks of sociology to analyze how new members of a society acquire required (linguistic and cultural) knowledge (Berger & Luckmann, 1966). Sociology has pointed out that understanding integration processes requires an understanding of immigration (Portes & Böröcz, 1989; Waldinger & Catron, 2016), as the causes and trajectories of immigration are likely to affect paths of integration. A broader perspective on the conditions for language acquisition, thus, requires a sociological analysis of immigration and integration processes, with immigrant education at the core of this process.

Issues of immigrant education have been discussed intensively in recent years, and a preliminary conclusion might be that migrants underperform relative to nonimmigrants in most receiving countries. This picture, however, is incomplete. Throughout the last 25 years, the availability of international school assessment data such as the OECD PISA and other large-scale studies (e.g., TIMMS & PIRLS) allowed researchers to compare immigrants' and nonimmigrants' educational outcomes across various countries. It turns out that matters of immigrant achievement are much more nuanced. In some countries, first-generation migrants perform (much) lower than native-born individuals without a migration background, but in others, they do not, or they even outperform their native-born counterparts (Levels & Dronkers, 2008; Schnepf, 2007). The relative performance of migrants seems not only to differ between destination countries but also between migrants from different regions of origin (Levels & Dronkers, 2008). A similar pattern was found for native-born

DOI: 10.4324/9781003155683-8

students whose parents are born abroad (second generation): in some countries, the second generation outperforms the nonimmigrant students, but in many other countries, they are less successful in school than majority students (Heath et al., 2008; Levels & Dronkers, 2008; Marks, 2005; Schnepf, 2007; Teltemann & Schunck, 2016). This is an intriguing finding. In this chapter, we aim to illustrate how individual, familial, and contextual factors shape language use and educational achievement of immigrants and their offspring as a part of immigrant integration.

The remainder of this chapter is structured as follows. In the first part, we provide a short theoretical framework that serves as a heuristic for presenting previous findings from sociological research about educational inequalities. Here, we will explore typical mechanisms explaining unequal educational achievement between immigrants and nonimmigrants within a given country. The established sociological knowledge about immigrants' educational achievement elucidates why there often is a gap between (children of) immigrants and nonimmigrants. Part of the explanation is that immigrants and their children control fewer resources that could help them meet the education system's demands, including language skills. Nevertheless, we will also see that migrants usually have one advantage on their side: their high motivation (Glick & White, 2004; Kao & Tienda, 1995). In the second part of this chapter, we present findings from PISA 2018 that illustrate key aspects laid out in the first part. In our discussion, we turn to issues that are still under scientific scrutiny and pertain to structural elements of an education system and the way it interacts with immigrant students. We will discuss important factors hypothesized to diminish or even close the achievement gap between immigrants and natives.

Migration and integration: the importance of language

During the last decades, an increasing number of countries have been facing the challenge of integrating growing immigrant populations (IOM, 2019; OECD/European Union, 2018). Likewise, research on immigrant integration and its determinants has raised increased attention. Commonly, scholars conceive immigrant integration as an intergenerational and multidimensional process. We can distinguish at least four dimensions of integration: cultural, social, structural, and emotional integration (Berry, 1980; Esser, 2008). The cultural dimension includes the process of acculturation, i.e., endowment with cultural knowledge. The social dimension relates to interaction with members of the host society. Structural integration refers to participation in education and the labor market as well as the endowment with rights, and emotional integration involves identification as a member of the host society. Mastering the language of the host society is at the heart of these four aspects (Esser, 2006). Therefore, understanding the process of language acquisition is a key to understanding integration in more general terms.

Sociological theory on immigrant integration has pointed out the fact that integration takes time. Most researchers agree that integration is an intergenerational process (Alba & Nee, 1997). So-called first-generation immigrants, in particular if they arrive as adults, are often deprived of resources like sufficient skills in the host-country language or needed educational certificates. Even if they have educational credentials, it may be that they are not recognized in the receiving country's labor market. In contrast, their children, the so-called second-generation, are brought up in the receiving country and thus, at least theoretically, have the opportunity to acquire the same skills and resources as nonimmigrant children. However, research has shown that second-generation immigrants show substantially different integration outcomes in different countries, underscoring that immigrant integration depends, among other things, on the receiving countries' societal conditions (van Tubergen et al., 2004; van Tubergen, 2006). Understanding the process of integration and the underlying factors involved requires, first, an understanding of the process of immigration, as it shapes the fundamental prerequisites for integration. In that respect, it is necessary to comprehend *why people move*. Theoretical accounts of migration decision-making have revealed that voluntary migration is never random or without due consideration. Migration is led by strong motives and mostly follows a deliberate evaluation of the opportunities and chances of realizing the aims of migration (De Jong & Gardner, 1981). It is a risky, costly decision that is directed, most basically, toward increasing one's chances in life. Thus, in general, voluntary migration involves the willingness to engage with the host society and to integrate. As a group, immigrants are, on average, ambitious and strive for upward mobility (Feliciano & Lanuza, 2016; Ogbu, 1978; but see Polavieja et al., 2018). Though not the focus of our chapter, it is noteworthy that these claims are more nuanced when it comes to involuntary migration (Sheikh & Anderson, 2018). Refugees, for instance, are also often found to hold high educational aspirations (Molla, 2019; Stevenson & Willott, 2007) or motivations to acculturate (Strang & Ager, 2010). However, since the migration is involuntary, refugees often face additional obstacles like psychological distress (Turrini et al., 2019), loss of educational certificates, or documents in receiving countries that do not offer them a long-term perspective (Strang & Ager, 2010).

Still, migration usually implies a loss of resources, especially with regard to the command of language, and human capital in general, as well as social capital (Chiswick, 1978; Friedberg, 2000). Having fewer individual resources is a central disadvantage that migrants and their children face in most receiving countries. These aspects, high motivation and deprivation, constitute two basic conditions of immigrant integration – and of language acquisition as the foundation of this process. They are, however, not the only factors affecting language learning, educational success, and finally, the integration of immigrants. In order to better understand the processes at stake, we present a short conceptual framework that captures some general conditions and mechanisms.

A framework for understanding language acquisition, education, and integration of immigrants

In this section, we present a framework that summarizes a major sociological approach to understanding immigrant integration, language acquisition, and educational success (see Figure 6.1). It consists of four blocks: (1) *elementary needs*, (2) *viable strategies* to pursue these needs, (3) *individual resources*, and (4) the *institutional setup*.

(1) Elementary needs constitute the first block, the "engine" of this framework. What makes people (we will call them actors from now on) act? Or, with respect to our example, why might some immigrants do better than others with regard to language learning and educational success? A well-established sociological perspective argues that two universal needs drive human behavior: physical well-being and social recognition (Esser, 1999; Lindenberg, 1984). Note the implication: actors (e.g., migrants and nonmigrants) all share these universal needs. This is not to say that all actors are the same in every regard but merely that they all strive to fulfill similar goals. To pursue these needs, however, actors need to exert (2) *viable strategies*. For example, it might be a strategy to strive for a high educational degree, which promises a good occupation and a stable income, which can be used to acquire goods, health care, and status symbols (Merton, 1938). Yet if all actors have the same needs and pursue them with viable strategies, how can there be systematic differences in outcomes between social groups, e.g., in educational degrees

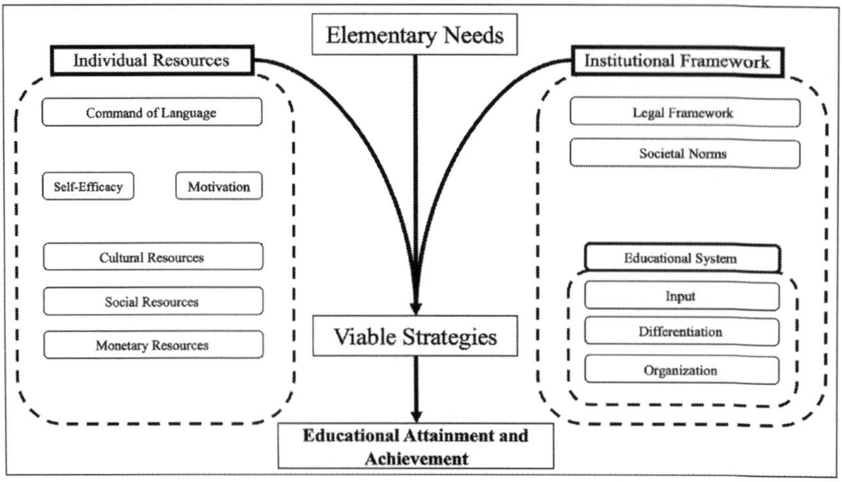

Figure 6.1 A framework for understanding immigrants' educational success

and labor market positions? This has to do with the last two blocks of the model, (3) *individual resources* and (4) *the institutional setup*. The interaction between individual resources and the institutional setup shapes the strategies viable in a given social context for a given actor.

Most (modern) societies are in some sense stratified in that different actors are differently endowed with (3) *individual resources*. For instance, college-educated parents will likely have (on average) more money to spend on their child's college education or tutoring, as compared to parents who are high-school dropouts. Differences in resources go beyond economic resources; children benefit when their parents hold high educational degrees, as these entail more knowledge about the explicit and implicit demands of an educational system. High-status families also have a higher likelihood of having friends and acquaintances who are well positioned themselves, which can be a resource in itself (McPherson et al., 2001). For instance, entering the labor market is easier if one has personal ties that can "open a door." The endowment with different resources is an indicator of the socioeconomic status (SES) of a person. Empirically, SES measures usually draw on information on education, occupation, income, and cultural possessions of a person or their family (Watermann et al., 2016).

However, the importance of personal resources might vary, depending on (4) *the institutional setup* of a country. Here, we can think about durable modes of coordination of action that shape the social life and are often formalized (Scott, 2014). Examples include education systems, laws, or strong societal norms. From the perspective of an individual actor, the institutional framework is given. For instance, suppose an educational system demands to have a certain degree or grade average to apply for a university. In that case, an individual may like or dislike it, but the institution defines the "rules of the game" (Merton, 1938). The institutional framework therefore sets boundaries to what can be considered a viable strategy and modifies the value and usability of individual resources (Merton, 1938).

These institutional setups differ between countries. Different societies exhibit different ideas about which behavior is appropriate or desirable in a given situation. Differing values (e.g., about desirable goods) and norms of behavior are part of a society's culture – which, however, does not imply that receiving societies are themselves homogenous units (Portes et al., 2005; Portes & Zhou, 1993). This implies that the strategies for reaching the basic aims (physical well-being and social recognition) vary across cultures (and can vary within societies). Immigration often implicates a change of cultures and therefore involves the demand to navigate a set of unknown rules of behavior. As the process of acculturation, e.g., the acquisition of the norms and knowledge of the host society, takes time, "old" values might be maintained for a certain time. This might involve norms about goals in life as well as the perception of desirable goods such as education. Further, certain institutions in the host society might ease or hinder the acculturation process. For example, the general openness of the receiving society toward immigrants and other cultures, as well as support structures (e.g., language courses, recognition of educational credentials) can differ between receiving countries and affect the process of acculturation (Reitz, 1998). Furthermore, differences in the transparency regarding determinants of success within a certain area (such as education) might affect the acculturation process (Portes & Rumbaut, 2006).

With regard to education as part of integration, the institutional setup of the host society's education system plays a crucial role. Public and mandatory education systems are prevalent in practically every country; however, modern education systems vary with regard to central aspects. According to Esser (2016), education systems can be characterized by three major aspects, each of which combines a multitude of attributes and variables: *input, differentiation*, and *organization*. The education systems' *input* refers to all institutionally organized resources. This includes aspects such as public educational expenditures, the schools' quality, the proliferation and quality of preschools, and teachers' qualifications. The *differentiation* of education systems refers to the extent to which the educational pathway is divided into different types of schools and tracks. Differentiation relates to characteristics such as the future opportunities associated with the different tracks and school types and the time at which students are sorted into different tracks. *Organization* includes aspects that characterize the internal organization of the education system and the relationship toward external actors, such as parents and other institutions. For example, the degree of an education system's standardization (as it is reflected in the proliferation of school autonomy and the centralization of school-exit exams) is part of the organizational dimension of education systems.

Hence, elementary needs, viable strategies, individual resources, and the institutional framework together constitute a framework that helps to understand the actions of individuals and, consequently, different outcomes of groups of people. In the next section, we focus on education as a keystone of immigrant integration processes. We lay out theoretical accounts that explain why educational outcomes differ between groups in general and between immigrants and nonimmigrants in particular.

Sociological approaches to educational inequality

According to our framework (Figure 6.1), unequal educational achievements of students can be conceived as the result of an *interaction between students' individual resources* and the *educational environment* they encounter. In most education systems, at some point during an educational trajectory, decisions have to be made. When and to what extent these decisions are necessary depends on the specifics of a country's educational system. Many European countries, like Germany, Austria, or the Netherlands, have *differentiated systems* in which students are sorted into different types of schools after attending a comprehensive primary school. Other countries, like the U.S. or Canada, have *integrated systems*, but even here, education-related decisions have to be made, for example, whether to take advanced courses and whether to go to college after high school or choose a vocational pathway instead.

Varying endowment with individual resources affects both students' achievement within a given school and the decisions they face when transitioning from one school to another. This is captured by the theoretical differentiation of so-called *primary and secondary effects* (Boudon, 1974). *Primary effects* reflect the degree to which differences in individual resources are associated with differences in students' achievement. *Secondary effects* reflect the degree to which educational decisions are associated with differences in resources. Further effects arise from factors at the level of schools, for example through their composition.

Primary effects

Primary effects incorporate a multitude of effects that lead to differences in students' abilities and achievements due to unequal familial endowment with resources. Examples include differences in the quality of parent–child interactions or leisure-time activities that stimulate a child's development. Generally, the endowment with cultural, economic, and social resources creates a certain environment in which socialization takes place. A higher endowment with resources often creates more favorable conditions for child development. Further effects arise from sociobiological processes like health behavior, which is related to the availability of resources (Batty et al., 2006; Delpisheh et al., 2006). Empirically, primary effects are reflected in (strong) associations between primary school achievement and family resources (Karlson, 2013). Yet empirical support also comes from other sources like summer break studies, which have repeatedly shown that students' achievement diverges during summer break depending on familial resource availability (Alexander et al., 2001). During school time, differences in resources between families have a less strong effect, as children spend less time at home. Further evidence for primary effects is provided by positive statistical associations between preschool education and achievement, which are particularly pronounced for students from households with fewer resources (Roßbach et al., 2009; Schlotter & Wößmann, 2010). Achievement differences due to socioeconomic factors can be self-reinforcing. Two equally capable students who differ in academic achievement due to primary effects may develop different rates of self-efficacy, which can be a resource for future education in itself (Multon et al., 1991).

Altogether, *primary effects cause differences in educational achievements independent of students' actual capabilities*. However, some primary effects are specific to students of immigrant families and thus explicitly contribute to ethnic educational inequality. With regard to the situation of immigrant students, primary effects are mainly driven by language skills (Heath et al., 2008; Jackson et al., 2012). The command of the instructional language is a key resource for children's learning process in schools. Children need good proficiency in the instructional language to follow classes and understand the teacher's lectures and assigned tasks. Furthermore, parents with limited command of the instructional language may have a harder time supporting their children in studying and doing their homework. Accordingly, a lower language proficiency of immigrant parents and children often causes underachievement (Schnepf, 2007). A minority language background and low proficiency in the instructional language affect not only reading achievement but also other (nonlanguage) domains such as math and science (Agirdag & Vanlaar, 2018; Schnepf, 2007). This also applies to second-generation students, who often speak a language other than the majority language at home (Marks, 2005; Winsler, 2023, this volume; Nguyen & Winsler, 2023, this volume). Thus, proficiency in the instructional language is crucial not only for language-specific educational outcomes but for educational success in general. Beyond the importance of the instructional language for educational achievement, bilingualism is a resource from which children can benefit. For example, bilingualism may lead to cognitive benefits such as a higher capacity to learn an additional language (Ngyuen & Winsler, this volume; Edele et al., 2018; Hopp et al., 2019). Further, migration is often accompanied by a devaluation of immigrants' social and cultural capital and a lack of transferability of immigrants' resources to the receiving country (Chiswick, 1978). For example, immigrants tend to have less strategic knowledge about the country-specific school and education system (Antony-Newman, 2019). Since many immigrants attended school in another country, it may be challenging to familiarize themselves with the new and often complex educational system their children attend. Likely, parents with less information about the education system cannot support their children to the same extent as parents who are familiar with the country-specific determinants of educational success. Accordingly, the lack of information about how to successfully navigate their children through the school system is another immigrant-specific primary effect. Moreover, immigrants in many countries are particularly affected by social deprivation, as the devaluation of resources after migration allocates immigrants to lower socioeconomic status positions. As a result, further adverse primary effects arise for immigrants and their offspring's achievement.

Secondary effects

Primary effects affect ability and achievement. Differences in educational outcomes, however, are also shaped by *secondary effects*. These come into effect when students and their families face decisions about future educational pathways. Secondary effects comprise differences in decision-making between (groups of) students *with the same grades or competencies* but varying resources. These differences in decision-making can be explained by differences in the subjectively expected costs and benefits of different educational pathways (Erikson & Jonsson, 1996). An important factor that determines the subjectively expected benefits is the expected probability of success of a given educational pathway. This probability is actually higher if parents have more resources, e.g., money for private tutoring. As costs for education are relatively lower and probabilities of success are higher for higher-status families, they are more likely to choose more ambitious educational pathways (Kersten, 2023, this volume).

A second factor determining educational choices is the *expected loss of status*. It is assumed that families strive for intergenerational status maintenance (Breen & Goldthorpe, 1997). In other words, parents want their children to attain at least the same social status that they have. This implies that depending on their socioeconomic status position, families have to make different educational decisions. Students whose parents are not college educated will incur no loss of status if they do not acquire a college education. Given their lower resources, they are more likely to make risk-averse (i.e., safe) decisions. Higher-status families, however, have "more to lose" and also can afford to make risky choices. Accordingly, they might choose more ambitious alternatives, irrespective of their child's actual achievement (Becker & Hecken, 2009; Stocké, 2007).

Empirical support for the existence of secondary effects has been established by a number of studies. Data from Germany, for instance, show an inverse relationship between socioeconomic status and competencies in math, reading, and science when it comes to the transition to the most ambitious school track, the Gymnasium (Stubbe et al., 2011). This means that students from the most affluent households need the lowest competencies in order to "convince" both their teachers and parents to send them to the Gymnasium. Reversely, those with the lowest SES need to show the highest competencies. Similar results have been found for other countries (Erikson & Rudolphi, 2010; Jackson et al., 2007; Kloosterman et al., 2009).

From a theoretical perspective, secondary effects may differ for immigrant families. On the one hand, the negative primary effects of immigrants reduce their average probabilities of success. The probability of underachievement due to lower resource endowments increases the likelihood of making less ambitious educational choices (Jackson et al., 2012). Further, a lower resource endowment increases the relative costs of making long-term investments in education and of being enrolled in a higher education track (Becker & Tomes, 1986). On the other hand, immigrant families have often been characterized by high educational aspirations (Ditton et al., 2005; Glick & White, 2004; Rosenbaum & Rochford, 2008; Salikutluk, 2016). As described earlier, migration is usually driven by high ambitions and is associated with a higher willingness to take risks (Kao & Tienda, 1995). Furthermore, immigrant parents may respond to social barriers caused by discrimination in the education system and labor market with higher aspirations to compensate for lower educational returns (Heath et al., 2008). Both high aspiration and risk-taking are also important for educational decision-making in that they increase the likelihood of ambitious educational choices of immigrants. In addition, immigrants often have to make decisions based on lower strategic knowledge about the national education system. Lower familiarity with the education system could cause an inadequate track allocation, as parents have less capacity to adequately assess their children's chances in a higher track (Kao & Tienda, 1998).

A number of studies have also provided evidence for secondary effects of immigrant origin, i.e., ambitious choices of immigrants, particularly if achievement and SES are controlled for (Dollmann & Weißmann, 2019; Jackson et al., 2012; Kilpi-Jakonen, 2011; Kristen et al., 2008; Relikowski et al., 2010; Van De Werfhorst & Van Tubergen, 2007). These findings illustrate that immigrants tend to have higher educational aspirations and make more ambitious choices in various countries. However, other studies indicate that immigrant students do not always benefit from ambitious educational choices, as they face higher risks of dropping out of the more demanding tracks (Dollmann & Weißmann, 2019; Tjaden & Hunkler, 2017).

Effects of school composition

Further effects on educational achievement may arise from school composition. Students are not randomly allocated to schools; they rather tend to visit schools in their neighborhood. Depending on the characteristics of a neighborhood, the composition of schools may differ. This link might give rise to the creation of "differential learning environments" (Maaz et al., 2008) and can have adverse effects especially for low-achieving students, who often are of lower socioeconomic status and attend schools with lower average status. As low-status schools often have fewer resources (because parents cannot supply them), learning conditions are poorer (Baird, 2012). Further, as low socioeconomic status is frequently associated with stresses and strains within families, students may be more distracted and teachers more challenged (O'Donnell et al., 2008; Palardy et al., 2015). Composition effects may be particularly pronounced for immigrants due to ethnic residential segregation, which is a common pattern in many host societies (Johnston et al., 2007). As immigrants tend to live in neighborhoods with higher proportions of immigrants, they often visit schools with larger shares of other immigrant students.

The literature on composition effects has pointed to different mechanisms through which the proportion of immigrants in classrooms, schools, or neighborhoods affects educational outcomes. First, effects on achievement can arise from exposure: with larger shares of foreign-language students, opportunities for learning the receiving-country language decline. As a result, actual learning goals and tasks will be harder to accomplish, resulting in lower achievement. As a consequence, teachers might adapt their standards and lower their expectations, leading to fewer learning gains for students in classes or schools with higher shares of immigrants (Blanchard & Muller, 2015). Lower average achievement, however, might have actual positive effects on educational aspirations. Building on Davis (1966), one could argue that comparisons with low-achieving students are more favorable and help to raise self-esteem and academic self-perception (the so-called "big-fish-little-pond-effect"). Schools and classes with higher shares of immigrants and lower performance thus shield the students from the "complete spectrum of competition" (Frost, 2007, p. 60). Further, there can be a positive effect of a larger share of immigrant students in schools or classrooms, as the whole school culture and the teachers' practices might be more adjusted to the special needs of immigrants, providing a supportive learning environment (Van Houtte & Stevens, 2010). Most previous research on immigrant or ethnic composition focuses on achievement and has yielded mixed results, depending on controlled class or school characteristics (Szulkin & Jonsson, 2007; Van der Slik et al., 2006). Even less conclusive evidence exists when it comes to effects on educational attainment (Fekjaer & Birkelund, 2007).

Taken together, there are a variety of mechanisms through which ethnic educational inequality can arise (see Figure 6.2). In the next section, we illustrate the extent to which achievement gaps exist between second-generation immigrant and nonimmigrant students in different receiving countries. We examine the degree to which the immigrant–nonimmigrant gap can be attributed to differences in socioeconomic status and the language/s spoken at home. Further, we assess whether not speaking the majority language at home affects competence acquisition and test the previously established assumption that children of immigrants tend to be highly motivated.

Data and methods

To illustrate differences in educational achievement between immigrant and native students, we draw on student data from the most recent OECD PISA study 2018 (OECD, 2019). The OECD PISA study is the most comprehensive standardized achievement survey at the secondary education level. Its research design is oriented toward international comparability of the competencies of 15-year-old students and determinants of these competences. PISA is administered every three years starting in 2000 with changing foci on three key competence domains: reading, mathematics, and science. Not only OECD member states but a growing number of partner countries participate in the survey. The hitherto biggest study in

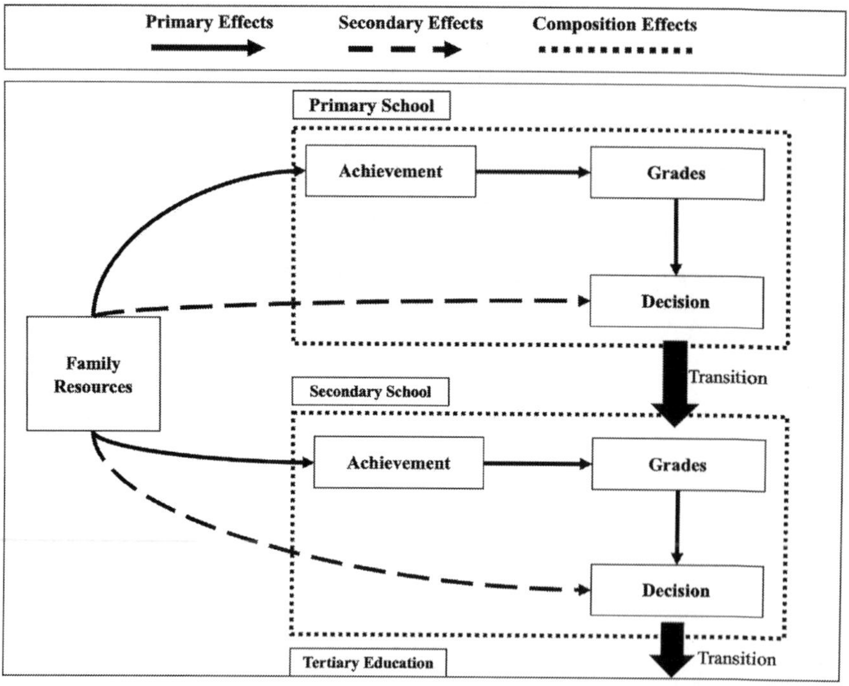

Figure 6.2 Family resources and their effects on ability and decision-making in education

2018 assessed about 600,000 students in 79 countries. The survey design provides a representative sample of the 15-year-old (school) population in a country. Students that participate in the cognitive tests additionally fill in an extensive background questionnaire. A further questionnaire is administered to the leaders of the sampled schools. The resulting data pool is publicly available via the OECD website (www.oecd.org/pisa).

Immigrant status is measured by questions on the country of birth of the student and parents. Based on this information, we distinguish two groups: nonimmigrants (students and both parents born in the country of the test) and second-generation immigrants (students born in the country of test, parents born abroad). We do not include first-generation immigrants in our analyses, as this group might have quite different characteristics in different countries, e.g., with regard to the duration of stay in the receiving country. Children from interethnic parents, i.e., one parent born abroad and one parent born in the country of the test, are categorized as nonimmigrant. We believe that it makes a significant difference when at least one parent was born in the country of the test and thus likely speaks the societal language of the country. Further, we do not know the age of arrival of the parents, so interethnic parents may be parents who immigrated as children and, given that they married partners who were born in the country of the test, are well acculturated.

We illuminate three relevant aspects of immigrant education: language use at home (majority language vs. another language), gaps in reading achievement, and, as an indicator of immigrants' motivation, educational expectations. We take into account the importance of socioeconomic status for differences with regard to these aspects. For language use, we differentiate between students who speak the majority language of the survey country at home and students who speak a language other than the national majority language at home. The dummy variable, language use, is based on a question asking whether the majority language (i.e., the language of the test = 0) or another language is spoken predominantly at home (another language = 1). In the following, we refer to the test language of the survey country as TL (test language) and a language other than the test language as other language (OL). While language use is not a reliable indicator of actual TL skills, PISA's measure of reading achievement can be used as one. According to PISA, "Reading literacy is understanding, using, evaluating, reflecting on and engaging with texts in order to achieve one's goals, to develop one's knowledge and potential and to participate in society" (OECD, 2019, p. 28). Clearly, language skills in the test language are required to develop reading literacy in this regard. Reading literacy is measured on a standardized scale that has a mean value (across all OECD countries) of 500 points. Table 6.1 gives descriptive information about the number of (immigrant) students per country.

Educational expectations are measured by a question about the highest educational degree a student expects to acquire. We created a dummy variable that indicates that a student expects to complete tertiary education (1 = yes). Tertiary education refers to postsecondary education received at universities or similar institutions. As our sample includes only OECD countries, this measure adequately reflects high educational expectations. The OECD has put efforts into fostering tertiary education within its member countries, as tertiary education is seen as a "major driver of economic competitiveness in an increasingly knowledge-driven global economy" (OECD, 2008, 13).

Students' socioeconomic background is measured through parental education (measured through the international ISCED scale), family wealth possessions (measured through the "wealth" index in PISA), cultural possessions (measured through the "cultposs" index in PISA), and home educational resources (measured through the "hedres" index in PISA) (see OECD, 2017, p. 339). The indices are derived from student information on the availability of 16 houschold items at their home including three country-specific items that were seen as local measures of family resources. In addition, students reported the number of possessions and books at home. Table 6.2 shows descriptive information for the variables included in the analysis.

Table 6.1 Sample statistics (unweighted)

Country	N	*Proportion nonimmigrant*	*Proportion second-generation*
Australia (AUS)	11,701	0.890	0.110
Austria (AUT)	6,198	0.870	0.130
Belgium (BEL)	7,935	0.910	0.090
Canada (CAN)	16,390	0.880	0.120
Switzerland (CHE)	4,951	0.780	0.220
Czech Rep. (CZE)	6,304	0.980	0.020
Germany (DEU)	5,015	0.880	0.120
Denmark (DNK)	6,116	0.820	0.180
Spain (ESP)	5,785	0.980	0.020
Estonia (EST)	5,359	0.900	0.100
Finland (FIN)	5,519	0.980	0.020
France (FRA)	5,424	0.920	0.080
United Kingdom (GBR)	10,999	0.950	0.050
Greece (GRC)	5,101	0.930	0.070
Hungary (HUN)	5,312	0.980	0.020
Ireland (IRL)	4,729	0.960	0.040
Israel (ISR)	5,411	0.870	0.130
Italy (ITA)	10,524	0.970	0.030
Luxembourg (LUX)	3,783	0.610	0.390
Latvia (LVA)	4,673	0.960	0.040
Netherlands (NLD)	4,886	0.920	0.080
Norway (NOR)	4,766	0.930	0.070
New Zealand (NZL)	3,254	0.880	0.120
Portugal (PRT)	6,780	0.970	0.030
Slovenia (SVN)	5,835	0.950	0.050
Sweden (SWE)	4,581	0.900	0.100
United States (USA)	4,904	0.830	0.170

We restricted the analyses to second generation and nonimmigrant students in member countries of the Organisation for Economic Co-operation and Development (OECD, $N = 248{,}620$). Students were excluded if they had missing values on any variable (listwise deletion, see Table 6.2 for proportions)[1]. After listwise deletion, we further excluded countries with fewer than 50 immigrant students in the multivariate sample – this led to the exclusion of Estonia, Japan, Korea, Latvia, Poland, and Turkey. The final sample comprises 172,235 students (of which 15,605 are immigrant students), nested in 7,576 schools, from 27 OECD countries.

The predicted probabilities for the outcomes in Figures 6.3, 6.5, and 6.6 are based on linear probability models that account for the three-level structure of the data (students nested in schools nested in countries) and correct the standard errors accordingly (see Teltemann & Schunck, 2020, for more information on a similar modeling approach). Achievement gaps (Figure 6.4.) were estimated via linear models that account for two-way clustering in countries and schools and adjust the standard errors accordingly (Correia, 2016). The observations have been weighted by the

Table 6.2 Sample statistics (unweighted)

	Mean	*SD*	*Min*	*Max*	*Proportion missing*
Plausible values reading					
PV 1	506.75	93.81	95.96	861.85	0.000
PV 2	506.48	94.10	60.74	879.05	0.000
PV 3	506.60	94.05	50.36	874.01	0.000
PV 4	506.61	94.13	84.62	854.44	0.000
PV 5	507.06	94.01	79.44	865.09	0.000
PV 6	506.37	93.98	35.36	870.75	0.000
PV 7	506.43	93.85	23.56	898.02	0.000
PV 8	506.48	93.99	0.00	863.84	0.000
PV 9	507.09	93.89	0.00	864.96	0.000
PV 10	507.00	94.08	55.74	855.82	0.000
Immigrant status					0.033
Nonimmigrant	0.91		0.00	1.00	
Second-generation	0.09		0.00	0.00	
Language of test spoken at home	0.11		0.00	1.00	0.018
Parental education					0.033
None	0.00		0.00	1.00	
ISCED 1	0.01		0.00	1.00	
ISCED 2	0.06		0.00	1.00	
ISCED 3b,c	0.08		0.00	1.00	
ISCED 3a,4	0.23		0.00	1.00	
ISCED 5b	0.18		0.00	1.00	
ISCED 5a,6	0.42		0.00	1.00	
Index of home possessions	0.21	0.87	-9.26	5.99	0.017
Index of cultural possessions	0.03	1.00	-1.84	2.63	0.033
Index of home educational resources	0.08	0.96	-4.39	1.18	0.022
Index of family wealth possessions	0.23	0.89	-7.44	4.44	0.021
N	172,235				

Source: OECD PISA 2018; proportion missing with respect to full sample

so-called senate weights, which ensure that despite different sample sizes, each country makes an equal contribution to the analysis. All analyses were carried out using Stata 17.0. Code for reproducing the analysis has been archived on the Open Science Framework (https://osf.io/78sgz/).

Results

In a first step, we present analyses that illustrate the probability among immigrant students of speaking a language other than the test language (OL) at home (adjusted for parental education, resources, and wealth). As we have laid out in the first part of our chapter, language is at the core of the general integration process. The choice of the family language is

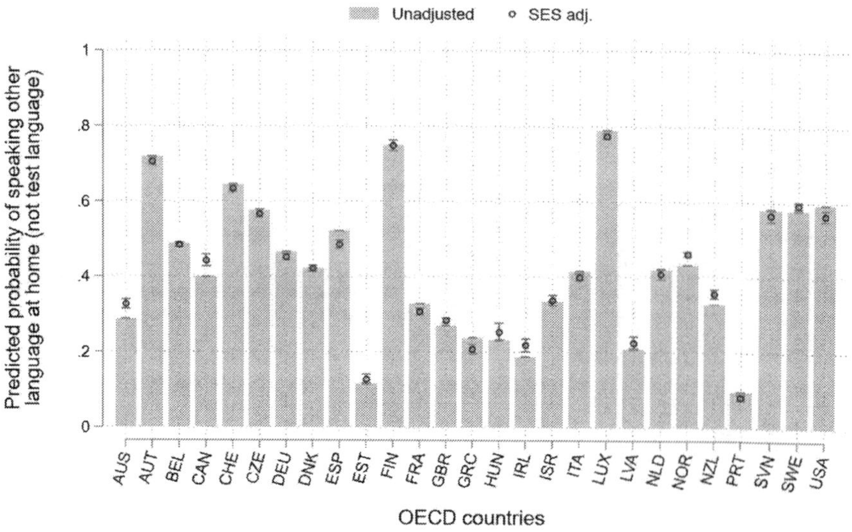

Figure 6.3 Probability of speaking other language (OL) at home (Source: PISA 2018 database, own calculations)

Note: Predicted probabilities are based on linear probability models for second-generation immigrant students from the multivariate sample (N = 15,605). Estimations weighted by normalized student weights (senate weights). Standard errors adjusted for clustering in countries; bars indicate 95% confidence interval. Bars show unadjusted predictions. Adjusted predictions (circles) control parental education, index of home possessions, index of cultural possessions, index of home educational resources, and index of family wealth possessions.

an indicator of the orientation and acculturation of a family. In a second step, we display the (adjusted) reading achievement of immigrant students in relation to nonimmigrant students. Reading achievement is an indicator for actual language skills. Last, we examine university expectations of immigrants and nonimmigrants as an indicator for immigrants' (higher) educational motivations.

Figure 6.3 shows the probability of speaking OL at home, as indicated by the gray bars. The y-axis gives the probability, which can also be read as percentages when multiplied by 100 (e.g., in the USA, about 60% of second-generation immigrants indicated speaking a language other than the test language at home). This probability varies substantially across countries, between about 10% (in Portugal) and 80% (in Luxembourg). In about half of the countries, around or more than 40% of second-generation immigrant students mainly speak a language other than the test language at home. Clearly, language use depends on the composition of the immigrant population and also the language of the receiving country. However, English-speaking countries are not among the countries with the lowest shares. Also, there are differences between countries with

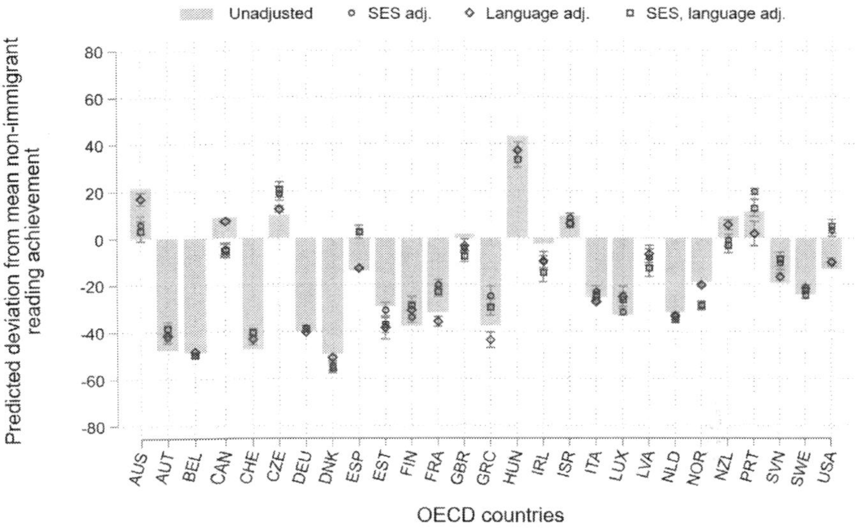

Figure 6.4 Reading achievement gaps between nonimmigrant and immigrant students (Source: PISA 2018 database, own calculations)

Note: Predictions show deviations of mean immigrant reading achievement from the mean of the nonimmigrants in a country. Values are based on linear models for second-generation immigrant students from the multivariate sample (N = 15,605). Estimations weighted by normalized student weights (senate weights). Standard errors adjusted for clustering in countries; bars indicate 95% confidence interval. Bars show unadjusted predictions. SES-adjusted predictions (circles) control parental education, index of home possessions, index of cultural possessions, index of home educational resources, and index of family wealth possessions. Language-adjusted predictions (rhombuses) control language use at home. SES and language adjusted predictions (squares) control both sets of variables.

relatively similar immigrant compositions, such as Germany, the Netherlands, and Austria. The figure also shows that the probability of OL use at home does not depend substantially on the socioeconomic status of the family. The black circles show how the probability of speaking a language other than the test language changes if socioeconomic status is accounted for. Apparently, immigrants who mainly speak the test language (TL) at home and those who do not do not differ substantially with regard to socioeconomic status, as the probabilities do not change substantively.

To investigate differences in educational achievement, we compared the mean reading performance of the nonimmigrants and second-generation immigrants in each country (Figure 6.4). We calculated the difference between the mean score of nonimmigrant students and the reading scores of the second-generation students for each country. The gray bars in Figure 6.4 show the gross, unadjusted differences. Bars above the zero axis indicate relatively better reading achievement of immigrant students compared to nonimmigrant students. Accordingly, bars below the zero axis indicate relative lower reading achievement of immigrant students. In 7 of 27 countries, immigrants score better in reading than nonimmigrants, with the highest outperformance of immigrant students found in Hungary. Among the other countries, the achievement gaps are negative, with the largest gap in Denmark and only small disadvantages in Latvia and Ireland.

Earlier in this chapter, we identified socioeconomic resources and language skills as crucial determinants of achievement. In the next step of our illustrating analyses, we examine whether these factors account for the achievement gaps. The circles denote the immigrant–nonimmigrant achievement gaps adjusted for the students' socioeconomic resources, the rhombuses show the gaps adjusted for language use at home, and the squares show the achievement gaps adjusted for both SES and language use. These symbols can be interpreted as follows: If the symbols lie within the gray bars, this indicates that the observed achievement gap is (partly) driven by the respective individual characteristic. If a symbol lies outside a bar, this means that observed differences between immigrants and nonimmigrants are not due to differences in socioeconomic and cultural composition.

Adjusting for effects of socioeconomic status of parents (indicated by the circles in Figure 6.4) reveals that immigrants are not always of lower socioeconomic status. In Canada, for example, the results suggest that the migrant population has a higher average SES compared to the nonmigrant Canadian (see CAN in Figure 6.4). This might explain why migrants outperform nonimmigrant Canadians. When we compare migrants to nonimmigrant Canadians with similar resources, we find that they have slightly lower reading skills. This is indicated by the square (CAN in Figure 6.4) below the zero axis. Likewise, in Australia, Estonia, Denmark, Ireland, Israel, Latvia, Hungary, Norway, and New Zealand, the results of immigrant students decrease if socioeconomic status is held constant. In some countries, these factors do not explain much of the immigrant–nonimmigrant achievement gap: in Germany, Italy, and Sweden, for example, the results do not change much if SES and foreign language use are controlled for. The achievement gaps between immigrant and nonimmigrant students seem to be mainly driven by differences in socioeconomic status and language use in Australia, Spain, and the USA. Here, the gaps (almost) completely disappear when we control for these characteristics (indicated by the squares)

Overall, the adjusted achievement gaps show that socioeconomic status and language use at home – i.e., individual characteristics of immigrant students – account for a part of reading achievement gaps between immigrants and nonimmigrants in most countries. However, in the vast majority of countries, the gaps remain substantive even when these important individual characteristics are controlled for. We discuss potential explanations for these residual effects of immigrant status – and their variation across countries – in the last section.

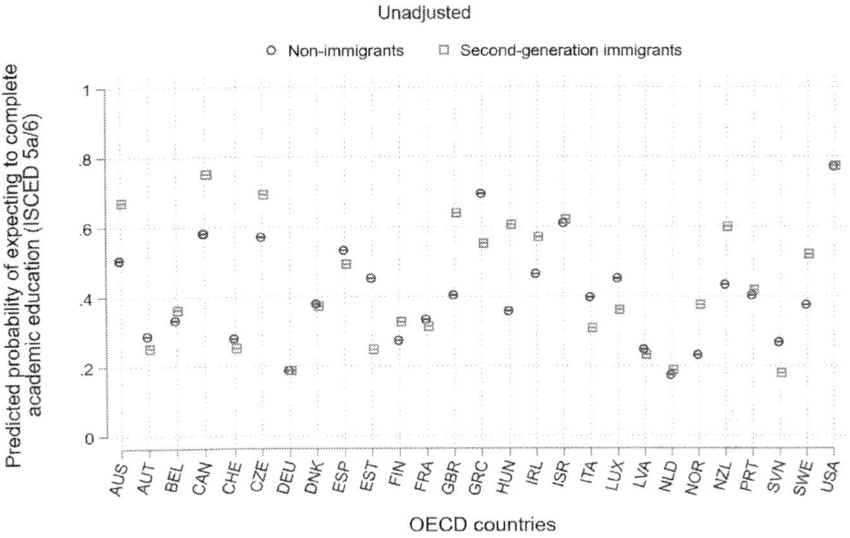

Figure 6.5 Expectation to complete tertiary education (Source: PISA 2018 database, own calculations)

Note: Predicted probabilities are based on a linear probability model for nonimmigrant and second-generation immigrant students from the multivariate sample (N = 172,235). Estimations weighted by normalized student weights (senate weights). Standard errors adjusted for clustering in countries; bars indicate 95% confidence interval. Circles show unadjusted predicted probabilities for nonimmigrant and squares for second-generation immigrant students.

Before we come to the discussion, we examine the second factor we previously identified as distinctive for immigrant groups, namely their high motivation. Figure 6.5 shows students' expectations (unadjusted) to complete tertiary education – our indicator of motivation – for nonimmigrants (circles) and second-generation immigrants (squares). Again, the symbols here denote probabilities or percentages (when multiplied with 100). For example, in Canada (CAN), almost 60% of nonimmigrants expect to complete a university education (indicated by the circle). Among the nonimmigrant students, around 75% expect to complete the academic education (indicated by the square). In 8 of our 27 countries, second-generation immigrants show lower aspirations than nonimmigrants. In another eight countries, no differences between the two groups can be established. In Germany (DEU), around 20% of both nonimmigrants and second-generation immigrants expect to complete an academic education. In contrast to that, around 80% of US-American students (both nonimmigrants and second-generation immigrants) expect to complete a university education. In 11 countries, immigrants show higher aspirations. In seven countries (Germany, Denmark, France,

Israel, Latvia, Netherlands, and Portugal), nonimmigrants and second-generation immigrants do not differ significantly with regard to their expectations (circles and squares overlap).

This picture becomes even more pronounced when socioeconomic status and reading achievement is accounted for (Figure 6.6). Now, immigrants have higher aspirations in 20 of 27 countries. The highest expectations can still be observed in the US; however, now, immigrants show even higher aspirations than nonimmigrants. In Germany, by contrast, expectations are rather low, especially for nonimmigrant students. Only in Estonia, Latvia, and Greece are there lower expectations for tertiary education of immigrants. In Italy, Israel, Portugal, and Slovenia, the groups do not differ, as the overlapping symbols indicate.

These results confirm our previous arguments: immigrants are, on average, highly aspiring. Overall, we have seen that speaking a language other than the test language is a typical pattern even for second-generation immigrants. This, however, is not the main reason for their (on average) lower reading performance when compared to nonimmigrants. Speaking a language other than the test language may simply be a necessity

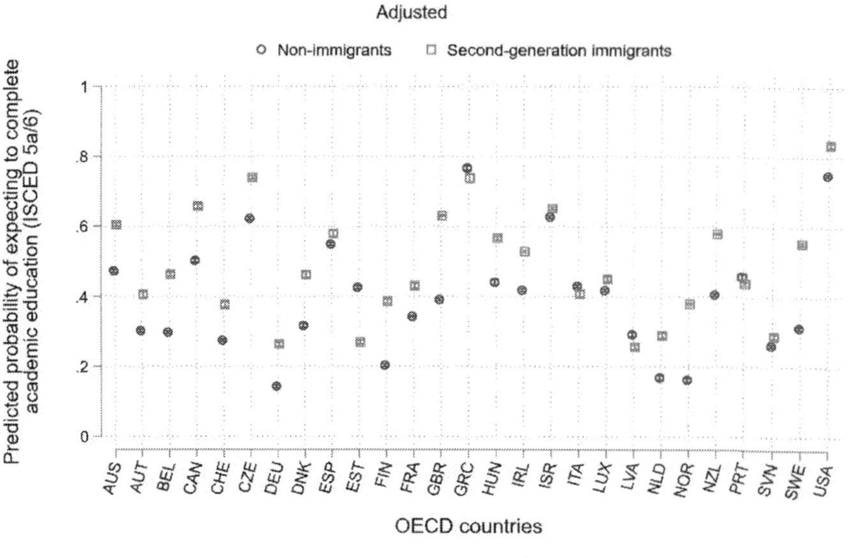

Figure 6.6 Expectation to complete tertiary education, adjusted (Source: PISA 2018 database, own calculations)

Note: Predicted probabilities are based on a linear probability model for nonimmigrant and second-generation immigrant students from the multivariate sample (N = 172,235). Estimations weighted by normalized student weights (senate weights). Standard errors adjusted for clustering in countries; bars indicate 95% confidence interval. Model controls parental education, index of home possessions, index of cultural possessions, index of home educational resources, index of family wealth possessions, and reading achievement. Circles show adjusted predicted probabilities for nonimmigrant and squares for second-generation immigrant students.

for communicating with family members. Obviously, lower endowment with resources and language use are not sufficient to understand reading achievement gaps between nonimmigrants and immigrants. In the last section, we now turn to potential explanations for the remaining gaps and for differences across countries.

Discussion

Although immigrants have relatively higher educational aspirations in almost all countries (as shown in Figures 6.5 and 6.6), this advantage does not translate into higher educational achievements everywhere. In many countries, we can still identify achievement gaps between immigrant and nonimmigrant students. The observed differences in immigrant–nonimmigrant achievement gaps across countries raise the question of why immigrants have better educational opportunities in some countries than in others. Recent research suggests two factors explaining country differences. The first factor is closely related to immigrant students' family background and language proficiency, which are, as we laid out earlier in this chapter, essential for students' achievement. As the selectivity of immigration varies between destination countries, the characteristics of the immigrant populations vary. The selectivity of immigration is partly determined by immigration laws but also by other (e.g., macroeconomic) characteristics of receiving countries. The resulting differences in immigrant populations pertain also to characteristics that are central to students' academic success, e.g., parents' educational and socioeconomic background and command of national languages (Cobb-Clark et al., 2012; Entorf & Minoiu, 2005; Fuchs & Wößmann, 2007; Van de Werfhorst, 2019; Washbrook et al., 2012). Thus, differences in the composition of the migrant population can lead to differences in educational achievement.

However, immigrant population characteristics cannot fully explain the international variance in immigrant students' achievement and college expectations – as we have shown, thereby confirming the findings of a number of previous studies (Azzolini et al., 2012; Dustmann et al., 2012; Schnepf, 2007; Van de Werfhorst & Heath, 2019). We illustrated this in Figure 6.4. Countries vary on how much the reading achievement of immigrants and nonimmigrants differ, and when we control for language use and family characteristics, this achievement gap is only marginally reduced. This indicates that a major part of the differences cannot be explained by the composition of migrants in different countries. This leads us to the second factor that may explain variation across countries with regard to achievement: differences in receiving country institutions, and here most importantly, in education systems. We already pointed at the importance of institutions in our conceptual framework at the beginning of this chapter. In Figure 6.1, we referred to education systems and their input, differentiation, and organization as relevant characteristics.

The education system sets the "rules of the game" through its norms, regulations, and laws. By setting specific incentives or restrictions, educational institutions can address previously existing inequalities. For example, in the context of the education system's input, preschools proved to be an important factor related to primary effects. Participation in early childhood education can compensate somewhat for low resource endowments. Studies suggest that early enrollment in preschool mitigates the negative primary effect of a low socioeconomic background (Sierens et al., 2020). Furthermore, findings show that preschools foster skills in the instruction language at an early age and, thus, mitigate negative primary effects of immigrant origin (Becker, 2006, 2010; Conger et al., 2019; Magnuson et al., 2006). However, whether immigrant children benefit *more* from preschools than native children is still unclear, and the overall results in this regard are mixed (Sierens et al., 2020).

Further, an education system's differentiation into tracks of lower and higher degree (stratification) has been identified as a critical contextual factor affecting educational inequality (Allmendinger, 1989; Kerckhoff, 2001). Since socioeconomic background affects children's ability through primary effects, ability tracking commonly increases socioeconomic segregation between schools, which, in turn, might foster educational inequalities due to associated differences in school quality, equipment, and learning environment (Dronkers et al., 2012, see the section on composition effects previously mentioned).

Studies analyzing the impact of education systems' differentiation on immigrants' scholastic achievement reveal a somewhat mixed picture. Whereas Ruhose and Schwerdt (2016) found no association between stratification and migrant–native achievement gaps, Borgna and Contini (2014) show that stratification is linked to lower average achievement of second-generation immigrants due to a higher concentration of this group in poorly equipped schools. Furthermore, Teltemann and Schunck (2016) show that migrant students can benefit from a school's internal differentiation, particularly in countries with a high degree of ethnic segregation in schools.

Studies investigating the link between immigrant achievement and aspects of an education system's organization, and in particular standardization, also yield mixed results. Whereas Schneeweis (2011) and Wößmann (2005) found a positive association between external student assessments and the school performance of first- and second-generation immigrant students, Cobb-Clark and colleagues' (2012) findings do not support this link. Moreover, Teltemann and Schunck (2020) show that standardized achievement tests alone are not associated with risks of low performance. In fact, making the test results available to the public, and thus decreasing information asymmetries for parents, is associated with decreased risks of low performance, particularly among first-generation immigrant students (Teltemann & Schunck, 2020, p. 7).

So far, research on immigrant–nonimmigrant differences in educational expectations and their interplay with institutional differences is scarce. The small number of studies in this research area focuses on the impact of an education system's differentiation, particularly tracking. Chykina (2019) has shown that first-generation immigrants have lower educational expectations in tracked systems as compared to nontracked systems. Nygård (2017) analyzed immigrants' educational expectations in Sweden (late tracking) and the Netherlands (early tracking). He expected expectations to be lower in a system with early tracking. These findings were confirmed with data from a study with low-achieving students. However, results show that this finding holds for "realistic" aspirations (an indicator for expectations) but not for "idealistic" aspirations, a distinction that is commonly being made in research on educational aspirations and expectations (Stocké, 2013). Hadjar and Scharf (2019) conclude from their study of immigrant expectations in four European countries that institutional settings seem to be less important than expected. The institutional variation with four countries, however, is too small to derive conclusions about the impact of single institutional factors. The limited and inconclusive results indicate a research gap with regard to institutional determinants of differences in educational expectations between immigrants and nonimmigrants. However, researching effects on institutional factors in education is demanding in terms of data and methods, which partly explains the rare and inconclusive results.

Conclusion

Empirically, the different aspects of education systems and their respective manifestations create a variety of institutional patterns across different countries. A challenge of most previous studies in this area is that they are mostly based on cross-sectional data. Based on cross-sectional data, it is hardly possible to model the complex relationships between country characteristics, educational systems, and individual characteristics of immigrant and native students. For example, institutional characteristics beyond education systems, such as integration and other social policies, might also play a crucial role – however, they are seldom observed in educational surveys. Thus, cross-sectional data entail the problem of unobserved heterogeneity, meaning that we cannot draw reliable conclusions about the causality of effects (Kersten & Greve, 2023, this volume). A solution to this problem might be the utilization of repeated cross-sectional studies. Several cross-sectional surveys on school achievement are being conducted repeatedly and allow for an examination of changes over time at least at the country level. However, as this analytical aim is not an actual focus of studies such as PISA and PIRLS, longitudinal analyses of these data require careful and often complex data preparation. The effort could be worth it, as the application of a longitudinal perspective enables scholars to not only examine differences *between* countries but also investigate how changes in the education system *within* countries affect immigrant achievement. This approach brings us closer to a deeper understanding of how the education system can reduce (or increase) inequalities, as we can control confounders at the country level.

The focus on institutions of education systems and their role in shaping (ethnic) educational inequalities and integration processes in the long run is promising, as these institutions are malleable to some extent. Educational reform that focuses on students with special needs, such as immigrant students, may yield favorable long-term effects and avoid substantial societal costs. However, in order to choose adequate policies and interventions, robust scientific knowledge on their effects is required. The sociological rational-choice perspective, which conceives institutions as incentives, opportunities, or restrictions, thereby shaping the individual evaluations of the consequences of action (Esser, 2016), is an efficient theoretical framework that enables the deduction of testable hypotheses on the interplay of individual resources and institutional setups. A sociological perspective thus can provide insight into the broader conditions of language acquisition, educational success, and integration processes of immigrants.

Note

1. In general, reading competencies covaried statistically significantly with presence of missing values. That is, students with missing values on the study variables had lower values of reading achievement than students who did not have missing values. Thus, a (multiple) imputation approach would be preferable. However, combining multiple imputation with the use of plausible values in achievement scores is not trivial, and there is currently not a validated approach available in Stata.

References

Agirdag, O., & Vanlaar, G. (2018). Does more exposure to the language of instruction leads to higher academic achievement? A cross-national examination. *International Journal of Bilingualism*, *22*(1), 123–137. https://doi.org/10.1177/1367006916658711

Alba, R., & Nee, V. (1997). Rethinking assimilation theory for a new era of immigration. *The International Migration Review*, *31*(4), 826–874. doi:10.2307/2547416

Alexander, K. L., Entwisle, D. R., & Olson, L. S. (2001). Schools, achievement, and inequality: A seasonal perspective. *Educational Evaluation and Policy Analysis*, *23*(2), 171–191. https://doi.org/10.3102/01623737023002171

Allmendinger, J. (1989). Educational systems and labor market outcomes. *European Sociological Review*, *5*(3), 231–250.

Antony-Newman, M. (2019). Parental involvement of immigrant parents: A meta-synthesis. *Educational Review*, *71*(3), 362–381. https://doi.org/10.1080/00131911.2017.1423278

Azzolini, D., Schnell, P., & Palmer, J. R. B. (2012). Educational achievement gaps between immigrant and native students in two "New" immigration countries: Italy and Spain in comparison. *The Annals of the American Academy of Political and Social Science*, *643*(1), 46–77. https://doi.org/10.1177/0002716212441590

Baird, K. (2012). Class in the classroom: The relationship between school resources and math performance among low socioeconomic status students in 19 rich countries. *Education Economics*, *20*(5), 484–509. https://doi.org/10.1080/09645292.2010.511848

Batty, G. D., Der, G., & Deary, I. J. (2006). Effect of maternal smoking during pregnancy on offspring's cognitive ability: Empirical evidence for complete confounding in the US national longitudinal survey of youth. *Pediatrics*, *118*(3), 943–950. https://doi.org/10.1542/peds.2006-0168

Becker, B. (2006). Der Einfluss des Kindergartens als Kontext zum Erwerb der deutschen Sprache bei Migrantenkindern [The influence of preschool as a context for the acquisition of the German language by immigrant children]. *Zeitschrift für Soziologie*, *35*(6), 449–464. https://doi.org/10.1515/zfsoz-2006-0602

Becker, B. (2010). Wer profitiert mehr vom Kindergarten? [Who profits more from preschool attendance?]. *KZfSS Kölner Zeitschrift für Soziologie und Sozialpsychologie*, *62*(1), 139–163. https://doi.org/10.1007/s11577-010-0090-5

Becker, G. S., & Tomes, N. (1986). Human capital and the rise and fall of families. *Journal of Labor Economics*, *4*(3), 1–39.

Becker, R., & Hecken, A. E. (2009). Higher education or vocational training? An empirical test of the rational action model of educational choices suggested by Breen and Goldthorpe and Esser. *Acta Sociologica*, *52*(1), 25–45. https://doi.org/10.1177/0001699308100632

Berger, P., & Luckmann, T. (1966). *The social construction of reality. A treatise in the sociology of knowledge*. Doubleday.

Berry, J. W. (1980). Acculturation as varieties of adaptation. In A. M. Padilla (Ed.), *Acculturation: Theory, models and some new findings* (pp. 9–25). Westview Press.

Blanchard, S., & Muller, C. (2015). Gatekeepers of the American dream: How teachers' perceptions shape the academic outcomes of immigrant and language-minority students. *Social Science Research*, *51*, 262–275. https://doi.org/10.1016/j.ssresearch.2014.10.003

Borgna, C., & Contini, D. (2014). Migrant achievement penalties in western Europe: Do educational systems matter? *European Sociological Review*, *30*(5), 670–683. https://doi.org/10.1093/esr/jcu067

Boudon, R. (1974). *Education, opportunity, and social inequality: Changing prospects in western society*. Wiley.

Breen, R., & Goldthorpe, J. H. (1997). Explaining educational differentials: Towards a formal rational action theory. *Rationality and Society*, *9*(3), 275–306. https://doi.org/10.1177%2F104346397009003002

Chiswick, B. R. (1978). The effect of Americanization on the earnings of foreign-born men. *Journal of Political Economy*, *86*(5), 897–921.

Chykina, V. (2019). Educational expectations of immigrant students: Does tracking matter? *Sociological Perspectives*, *62*(3), 366–382. https://doi.org/10.1177/0731121419828397

Cobb-Clark, D. A., Sinning, M., & Stillman, S. (2012). Migrant youths' educational achievement: The role of institutions. *The Annals of the American*

Academy of Political and Social Science, *643*(1), 18–45. https://doi.org/10.1177/0002716212440786

Conger, D., Gibbs, C. R., Uchikoshi, Y., & Winsler, A. (2019). New benefits of public-school pre-kindergarten programs: Early school stability, grade promotion, and exit from ELL services. *Early Childhood Research Quarterly*, *48*, 26–35. https://doi.org/10.1016/j.ecresq.2018.10.015

Correia, S. (2016). *A feasible estimator for linear models with multi-way fixed effects*. http://scorreia.com/research/hdfe.pdf

Davis, J. A. (1966). The campus as a frog pond: An application of the theory of relative deprivation to career decisions of college men. *American Journal of Sociology*, *72*(1), 17–31. https://doi.org/10.1086/224257

De Jong, G. F., & Gardner, R. W. (Eds.). (1981). *Migration decision making: Multidisciplinary approaches to microlevel studies in developed and developing countries*. Pergamon Press.

Delpisheh, A., Kelly, Y., Rizwan, S., & Brabin, B. J. (2006). Socio-economic status, smoking during pregnancy and birth outcomes: An analysis of cross-sectional community studies in Liverpool (1993–2001). *Journal of Child Health Care*, *10*(2), 140–148. https://doi.org/10.1177/1367493506062553

Ditton, H., Krüsken, J., & Schauenberg, M. (2005). Bildungsungleichheit – der Beitrag von Familie und Schule [Educational disparities and the contribution of family and school]. *Zeitschrift für Erziehungswissenschaft*, *8*(2), 285–304. https://doi.org/10.1007/s11618-005-0138-x

Dollmann, J., & Weißmann, M. (2019). The story after immigrants' ambitious educational choices: Real improvement or back to square one? *European Sociological Review*, 32–47. https://doi.org/10.1093/esr/jcz042

Dronkers, J., Van Der Velden, R., & Dunne, A. (2012). Why are migrant students better off in certain types of educational systems or schools than in others? *European Educational Research Journal*, *11*(1), 11–44. https://doi.org/10.2304/eerj.2012.11.1.11

Dustmann, C., Frattini, T., & Lanzara, G. (2012). Educational achievement of second-generation immigrants: An international comparison. *Economic Policy*, *27*(69), 143–185. https://doi.org/10.1111/j.1468-0327.2011.00275.x

Edele, A., Kempert, S., & Schotte, K. (2018). Does competent bilingualism entail advantages for the third language learning of immigrant students? *Learning and Instruction*, *58*, 232–244. https://doi.org/10.1016/j.learninstruc.2018.07.002

Entorf, H., & Minoiu, N. (2005). What a difference immigration policy makes: A comparison of PISA scores in Europe and traditional countries of immigration. *German Economic Review*, *6*(3), 355–376. https://doi.org/10.1111/j.1468-0475.2005.00137.x

Erikson, R., & Jonsson, J. (1996). *Can education be equalized? The Swedish case in comparative perspective*. Westview Press.

Erikson, R., & Rudolphi, F. (2010). Change in social selection to upper secondary school-primary and secondary effects in Sweden. *European Sociological Review*, *26*(3), 291–305. https://doi.org/10.1093/esr/jcp022

Esser, H. (1999). *Soziologie. Spezielle Grundlagen Bd. 1 [Sociology: Special foundations Volume 1]*. Campus.

Esser, H. (2006). Migration, language and integration. *AKI Research Review, 4*. Wissenschaftszentrum Berlin für Sozialforschung

Esser, H. (2008). Assimilation, ethnische Schichtung oder selektive Akkulturation? Neuere Theorien der Eingliederung von Migranten und das Modell der intergenerationalen Integration [Assimilation, ethnic stratification, or selective acculturation? Recent theories of immigrant integration and the model of intergenerational integration]. *Kölner Zeitschrift Für Soziologie und Sozialpsychologie: KZfSS. Sonderhefte*, *60*(48), 81–107.

Esser, H. (2016). Bildungssysteme und ethnische Bildungsungleichheiten [Education systems and ethnic educational inequality]. In C. Diehl, C. Hunkler, & C. Kristen (Eds.), *Ethnische Ungleichheiten im Bildungsverlauf [Ethnic inequalities over the educational trajectory]* (pp. 331–396). Springer Fachmedien.

Fekjaer, S. N., & Birkelund, G. E. (2007). Does the ethnic composition of upper secondary schools influence educational achievement and attainment? A multilevel analysis of the Norwegian case. *European Sociological Review*, *23*(3), 309–323. https://doi.org/10.1093/esr/jcm003

Feliciano, C., & Lanuza, Y. R. (2016). The immigrant advantage in adolescent educational expectations. *International Migration Review*, *50*(3), 758–792. https://doi.org/10.1111/imre.12183

Friedberg, R. M. (2000). You can't take it with you? Immigrant assimilation and the portability of human capital. *Journal of Labor Economics*, *18*(2), 221–251. https://doi.org/10.1086/209957

Frost, B. (2007). Texas students' college expectations: Does high school racial composition matter? *Sociology of Education*, *80*(1), 43–65. https://doi.org/10.1177/003804070708000103

Fuchs, T., & Wößmann, L. (2007). What accounts for international differences in student performance? A re-examination using PISA data. *Empirical Economics*, *32*(2–3), 433–464. https://doi.org/10.1007/s00181-006-0087-0

Glick, J. E., & White, M. J. (2004). Post-secondary school participation of immigrant and native youth: The role of familial resources and educational expectations. *Social Science Research*, *33*(2), 272–299. https://doi.org/10.1016/j.ssresearch.2003.06.001

Hadjar, A., & Scharf, J. (2019). The value of education among immigrants and non-immigrants and how this translates into educational aspirations: A comparison of four European countries. *Journal of Ethnic and Migration Studies*, *45*(5), 711–734. https://doi.org/10.1080/1369183X.2018.1433025

Heath, A. F., Rothon, C., & Kilpi, E. (2008). The second generation in western Europe: Education, unemployment, and occupational attainment. *Annual Review of Sociology*, *34*(1), 211–235. https://doi.org/10.1146/annurev.soc.34.040507.134728

Hopp, H., Vogelbacher, M., Kieseier, T., & Thoma, D. (2019). Bilingual advantages in early foreign language learning: Effects of the minority and the majority language. *Learning and Instruction*, *61*, 99–110. https://doi.org/10.1016/j.learninstruc.2019.02.001

IOM. (2019). *World Migration Report*. International Organization for Migration.

Jackson, M., Erikson, R., Goldthorpe, J. H., & Yaish, M. (2007). Primary and secondary effects in class differentials in educational attainment: The transition to A-level courses in England and Wales. *Acta Sociologica*, *50*(3), 211–229. https://doi.org/10.1177/0001699307080926

Jackson, M., Jonsson, J. O., & Rudolphi, F. (2012). Ethnic inequality in choice-driven education systems: A longitudinal study of performance and choice in

England and Sweden. *Sociology of Education*, *85*(2), 158–178. https://doi.org/10.1177/0038040711427311

Johnston, R., Poulsen, M., & Forrest, J. (2007). The geography of ethnic residential segregation: A comparative study of five countries. *Annals of the Association of American Geographers*, 97(4), 713–738. https://doi.org/10.1111/j.1467-8306.2007.00579.x

Kao, G., & Tienda, M. (1995). Optimism and achievement: The educational performance of immigrant youth. *Social Science Quarterly*, *76*(1), 1–19.

Kao, G., & Tienda, M. (1998). Educational aspirations of minority youth. *American Journal of Education*, *106*(3), 349–384.

Karlson, K. B. (2013). Summarizing primary and secondary effects. *Research in Social Stratification and Mobility*, *33*, 72–82. https://doi.org/10.1016/j.rssm.2013.01.001

Kerckhoff, A. C. (2001). Education and social stratification processes in comparative perspective. *Sociology of Education*, *74* (Extra Issue: Current of Thought: Sociology of Education at the Dawn of the 21st Century), 3–18.

Kersten, K. (2023, this volume). Proximity of stimulation: Investigating the interplay of cognitive, linguistic, and instructional factors at play in early second language acquisition. In K. Kersten & A. Winsler (Eds.), *Understanding variability in second language acquisition, bilingualism, and cognition – A multi-layered perspective*. Routledge.

Kersten, K., & Greve, W. (2023, this volume). Investigating cognitive-linguistic development in SLA – Theoretical and methodical challenges for empirical research. In K. Kersten & A. Winsler (Eds.), *Understanding variability in second language acquisition, bilingualism, and cognition – A multi-layered perspective*. Routledge.

Kilpi-Jakonen, E. (2011). Continuation to upper secondary education in Finland: Children of immigrants and the majority compared. *Acta Sociologica*, *54*(1), 77–106. https://doi.org/10.1177/0001699310392604

Kloosterman, R., Ruiter, S., De Graaf, P. M., & Kraaykamp, G. (2009). Parental education, children's performance and the transition to higher secondary education: Trends in primary and secondary effects over five Dutch school cohorts (1965–99): Social selection in Dutch secondary education. *The British Journal of Sociology*, *60*(2), 377–398. https://doi.org/10.1111/j.1468-4446.2009.01235.x

Kristen, C., Reimer, D., & Kogan, I. (2008). Higher education entry of Turkish immigrant youth in Germany. *International Journal of Comparative Sociology*, *49*(2–3), 127–151. https://doi.org/10.1177/0020715208088909

Levels, M., & Dronkers, J. (2008). Educational performance of native and immigrant children from various countries of origin. *Ethnic and Racial Studies*, *31*(8), 1404–1425. https://doi.org/10.1080/01419870701682238

Lindenberg, S. (1984). Normen und die Allokation sozialer Wertschätzung [Norms and the allocation of social esteem]. In D. Dörner & H. Todt (Eds.), *Normengeleitetes Verhalten in den Sozialwissenschaften [Norm-guided behavior in the social sciences]* (pp. 169–191). Duncker & Humblot.

Maaz, K., Trautwein, U., Lüdtke, O., & Baumert, J. (2008). Educational transitions and differential learning environments: How explicit between-school tracking contributes to social inequality in educational outcomes. *Child Development Perspectives*, 2(2), 99–106. https://doi.org/10.1111/j.1750-8606.2008.00048.x

Magnuson, K., Lahaie, C., & Waldfogel, J. (2006). Preschool and school readiness of children of immigrants. *Social Science Quarterly*, *87*(5), 1241–1262. https://doi.org/10.1111/j.1540-6237.2006.00426.x

Marks, G. N. (2005). Accounting for immigrant non-immigrant differences in reading and mathematics in twenty countries. *Ethnic and Racial Studies*, *28*(5), 925–946. https://doi.org/10.1080/01419870500158943

McPherson, M., Smith-Lovin, L., & Cook, J. M. (2001). Birds of a feather: Homophily in social networks. *Annual Review of Sociology*, *27*(1), 415–444. https://doi.org/10.1146/annurev.soc.27.1.415

Merton, R. K. (1938). Social structure and anomie. *American Sociological Review*, *3*(5), 672. https://doi.org/10.2307/2084686

Molla, T. (2019). Educational aspirations and experiences of refugee-background African youth in Australia: A case study. *International Journal of Inclusive Education*, 1–19. https://doi.org/10.1080/13603116.2019.1588924

Multon, K. D., Brown, S. D., & Lent, R. W. (1991). Relation of self-efficacy beliefs to academic outcomes: A meta-analytic investigation. *Journal of Counseling Psychology*, *38*(1), 30–38. https://doi.org/10.1037/0022-0167.38.1.30

Nguyen, M. V. H., & Winsler, A. (2023, this volume). Early bilingualism increases the likelihood of taking (and mastering) foreign language courses later in secondary school. In K. Kersten & A. Winsler (Eds.), *Understanding variability in second language acquisition, bilingualism, and cognition – A multi-layered perspective*. Routledge.

Nygård, O. (2017). Early tracking and immigrant optimism: A comparative study of educational aspirations among students in disadvantaged schools in Sweden and the Netherlands. *Comparative Migration Studies*, *5*(20). https://doi.org/10.1186/s40878-017-0063-1

O'Donnell, M., Lambert, R. G., & McCarthy, C. J. (2008). School poverty status, time of year, and elementary teachers' perceptions of stress. *The Journal of Educational Research*, *102*(2), 152–160. https://doi.org/10.3200/JOER.102.2.152-160

OECD. (2008). *Tertiary education for the knowledge society: Volume 1 and Volume 2*. OECD. https://doi.org/10.1787/9789264046535-en

OECD. (2017). *PISA 2015 technical report*. OECD Publishing.

OECD. (2019). *PISA 2018 assessment and analytical framework*. OECD. https://doi.org/10.1787/b25efab8-en

OECD/European Union. (2018). *Settling in 2018: Indicators of immigrant integration*. OECD Publishing/European Union. https://doi.org/10.1787/9789264307216-en

Ogbu, J. U. (1978). *Minority education and caste: The American system in cross-cultural perspective*. Academic Press.

Palardy, G., Rumberger, R., & Butler, T. (2015). The effect of high school socioeconomic, racial, and linguistic segregation on academic performance and school behaviors. *Teachers College Record*, *117*(12), 1–52.

Polavieja, J. G., Fernández-Reino, M., & Ramos, M. (2018). Are migrants selected on motivational orientations? Selectivity patterns amongst international migrants in Europe. *European Sociological Review*, *34*(5), 570–588. https://doi.org/10.1093/esr/jcy025

Portes, A., & Böröcz, J. (1989). Contemporary immigration: Theoretical perspectives on its determinants and modes of incorporation. *International Migration Review*, *23*(3), 606–630. https://doi.org/10.1177/019791838902300311

Portes, A., Fernández-Kelly, P., & Haller, W. (2005). Segmented assimilation on the ground: The new second generation in early adulthood. *Ethnic and Racial Studies*, *28*(6), 1000–1040. https://doi.org/10.1080/01419870500224117

Portes, A., & Rumbaut, R. G. (2006). *Immigrant America: A portrait* (3rd ed.). University of California Press.

Portes, A., & Zhou, M. (1993). The new second generation: Segmented assimilation and its variants. *The ANNALS of the American Academy of Political and Social Science*, *530*(1), 74–96. https://doi.org/10.1177/0002716293530001006

Reitz, J. G. (1998). *Warmth of the welcome: The social causes of economic success for immigrants in different nations and cities*. Westview Press.

Relikowski, I., Schneider, T., & Blossfeld, H.-P. (2010). Primäre und sekundäre Herkunftseffekte beim Übergang in das gegliederte Schulsystem [Primary and secondary effects of origin in the transition to secondary education]. In T. Beckers, K. Birkelbach, J. Hagenah, & U. Rosar (Eds.), *Komparative empirische Sozialforschung [Comparative empirical social research]* (pp. 143–167). VS Verlag für Sozialwissenschaften. https://doi.org/10.1007/978-3-531-92472-4_6

Roßbach, H.-G., Kluczniok, K., & Kuger, S. (2009). Auswirkungen eines Kindergartenbesuchs auf den kognitiv-leistungsbezogenen Entwicklungsstand von Kindern [Effects of attending kindergarten on the cognitive development of children]. In H.-G. Roßbach & H.-P. Blossfeld (Eds.), *Frühpädagogische Förderung in Institutionen [Early childhood education in institutions]* (pp. 139–158). VS Verlag für Sozialwissenschaften. https://doi.org/10.1007/978-3-531-91452-7_10

Rosenbaum, E., & Rochford, J. A. (2008). Generational patterns in academic performance: The variable effects of attitudes and social capital. *Social Science Research*, *37*(1), 350–372. https://doi.org/10.1016/j.ssresearch.2007.03.003

Ruhose, J., & Schwerdt, G. (2016). Does early educational tracking increase migrant-native achievement gaps? Differences-in-differences evidence across countries. *Economics of Education Review*, *52*, 134–154. https://doi.org/10.1016/j.econedurev.2016.02.004

Salikutluk, Z. (2016). Why do immigrant students aim high? Explaining the aspiration – achievement paradox of immigrants in Germany. *European Sociological Review*, *32*(5), 581–592. https://doi.org/10.1093/esr/jcw004

Schlotter, M., & Wößmann, L. (2010). Frühkindliche Bildung und spätere kognitive und nichtkognitive Fähigkeiten: Deutsche und internationale Evidenz [Early childhood education and later cognitive and non-cognitive skills: German and international evidence]. *Vierteljahrshefte Zur Wirtschaftsforschung*, *79*(3), 99–120. https://doi.org/10.3790/vjh.79.3.99

Schneeweis, N. (2011). Educational institutions and the integration of migrants. *Journal of Population Economics*, *24*(4), 1281–1308. https://doi.org/10.1007/s00148-009-0271-6

Schnepf, S. V. (2007). Immigrants' educational disadvantage: An examination across ten countries and three surveys. *Journal of Population Economics*, *20*(3), 527–545. https://doi.org/10.1007/s00148-006-0102-y

Scott, W. R. (2014). *Institutions and organizations: Ideas, interests, and identities* (4th ed.). Sage.

Sheikh, M., & Anderson, J. R. (2018). Acculturation patterns and education of refugees and asylum seekers: A systematic literature review. *Learning and Individual Differences*, *67*, 22–32. https://doi.org/10.1016/j.lindif.2018.07.003

Sierens, S., Van Avermaet, P., Van Houtte, M., & Agirdag, O. (2020). Does preschooling contribute to equity in education? Participation in universal pre-school and fourth-grade academic achievement. *European Educational Research Journal*, *19*(6), 564–586. https://doi.org/10.1177/1474904120925981

Stevenson, J., & Willott, J. (2007). The aspiration and access to higher education of teenage refugees in the UK. *Compare: A Journal of Comparative and International Education*, *37*(5), 671–687. https://doi.org/10.1080/03057920701582624

Stocké, V. (2007). Explaining educational decision and effects of families' social class position: An empirical test of the Breen Goldthorpe model of educational attainment. *European Sociological Review*, *23*(4), 505–519. https://doi.org/10.1093/esr/jcm014

Stocké, V. (2013). Bildungsaspirationen, soziale Netzwerke und Rationalität [Educational aspirations, social networks and rationality]. In R. Becker & A. Schulze (Eds.), *Bildungskontexte. Strukturelle Voraussetzungen und Ursachen ungleicher Bildungschancen [Contexts of eduation. Structural conditions and causes of unequal educational chances]* (pp. 269–298). Springer VS.

Strang, A., & Ager, A. (2010). Refugee integration: Emerging trends and remaining agendas. *Journal of Refugee Studies*, *23*(4), 589–607. https://doi.org/10.1093/jrs/feq046

Stubbe, T. C., Bos, W., & Euen, B. (2011). Der Übergang von der Primar-in die Sekundarstufe [The transition from primary to secondary education]. In W. Bos, I. Tarelli, A. Bremerich-Vos, & K. Schwippert (Eds.), IGLU 2011 *Lesekompetenzenvon Grundschulkindern in Deutschland im internationalen Vergleich [PIRLS 2011 Reading achievement of German primary school students in comparison]* (pp. 209–226). Waxmann.

Szulkin, R., & Jonsson, J. O. (2007). Ethnic segregation and educational outcomes in Swedish comprehensive schools. *SULCIS Working Paper Series*, *2*. www.su.se/polopoly_fs/1.55483.1321514485!/SULCISWP2007_2.PDF

Teltemann, J., & Schunck, R. (2016). Education systems, school segregation, and second-generation immigrants' educational success: Evidence from a country-fixed effects approach using three waves of PISA. *International Journal of Comparative Sociology*, *57*(6), 401–424. https://doi.org/10.1177/0020715216687348

Teltemann, J., & Schunck, R. (2020). Standardized testing, use of assessment data, and low reading performance of immigrant and non-immigrant students in OECD countries. *Frontiers in Sociology*, *5*, 1–12. https://doi.org/10.3389/fsoc.2020.544628

Tjaden, J. D., & Hunkler, C. (2017). The optimism trap: Migrants' educational choices in stratified education systems. *Social Science Research*, *67*, 213–228. https://doi.org/10.1016/j.ssresearch.2017.04.004

Turrini, G., Purgato, M., Acarturk, C., Anttila, M., Au, T., Ballette, F., . . . Barbui, C. (2019). Efficacy and acceptability of psychosocial interventions in asylum seekers and refugees: Systematic review and meta-analysis. *Epidemiology and Psychiatric Sciences*, *28*(4), 376–388. Cambridge Core. https://doi.org/10.1017/S2045796019000027

Van de Werfhorst, H. G. (2019). Early tracking and social inequality in educational attainment: Educational reforms in 21 European countries. *American Journal of Education*, *126*(1), 65–99. https://doi.org/10.1086/705500

Van de Werfhorst, H. G., & Heath, A. (2019). Selectivity of migration and the educational disadvantages of second-generation immigrants in ten host societies. *European Journal of Population*, *35*(2), 347–378. https://doi.org/10.1007/s10680-018-9484-2
Van De Werfhorst, H. G., & Van Tubergen, F. (2007). Ethnicity, schooling, and merit in the Netherlands. *Ethnicities*, 7(3), 416–444. https://doi.org/10.1177/1468796807080236
Van der Slik, F. W. P., Driessen, G. W. J. M., & De Bot, K. L. J. (2006). Ethnic and socioeconomic class composition and language proficiency: A longitudinal multilevel examination in Dutch elementary schools. *European Sociological Review*, 22(3), 293–308. https://doi.org/10.1093/esr/jci058
Van Houtte, M., & Stevens, P. A. J. (2010). School ethnic composition and aspirations of immigrant students in Belgium. *British Educational Research Journal*, *36*(2), 209–237. https://doi.org/10.1080/01411920902802180
van Tubergen, F. (2006). Occupational status of immigrants in cross-national perspective: A multilevel analysis of seventeen Western societies. In C. A. Parsons & T. M. Smeeding (Eds.), *Immigration and the transformation of Europe* (pp. 147–171). Cambridge University Press. https://doi.org/10.1017/CBO9780511493577.006
van Tubergen, F., Maas, I., & Flap, H. (2004). The economic incorporation of immigrants in 18 Western societies: Origin, destination, and community effects. *American Sociological Review*, *69*(5), 704–727. https://doi.org/10.1177/000312240406900505
Waldinger, R., & Catron, P. (2016). Modes of incorporation: A conceptual and empirical critique. *Journal of Ethnic and Migration Studies*, *42*(1), 23–53. https://doi.org/10.1080/1369183X.2015.1113742
Washbrook, E., Waldfogel, J., Bradbury, B., Corak, M., & Ghanghro, A. A. (2012). The development of young children of immigrants in Australia, Canada, the United Kingdom, and the United States. *Child Development*, *83*(5), 1591–1607. https://doi.org/10.1111/j.1467-8624.2012.01796.x
Watermann, R., Maaz, K., Bayer, S., & Roczen, N. (2016). Social background. In S. Kuger, E. Klieme, N. Jude, & D. Kaplan (Eds.), *Assessing contexts of learning* (pp. 117–145). Springer. https://doi.org/10.1007/978-3-319-45357-6_5
Winsler, A. (2023, this volume). Becoming bilingual in Miami, USA: Predictors and outcomes of speed of English acquisition for low-income, dual-language learners. In K. Kersten & A. Winsler (Eds.), *Understanding variability in second language acquisition, bilingualism, and cognition – A multi-layered perspective*. Routledge.
Wößmann, L. (2005). The effect heterogeneity of central exams: Evidence from TIMSS, TIMSS-Repeat and PISA. *Education Economics*, *13*(2), 143–169. https://doi.org/10.1080/09645290500031165

7 The interplay between learner-internal variables and levels of anxiety and enjoyment among Spanish EFL learners

Jean-Marc Dewaele

Introduction

Dörnyei and Ryan (2015) pointed out that research into emotions in second language acquisition (SLA) was scarce, which they attributed to the dominant cognitivist orientation of the field, and they admitted that the previous version of their own book (Dörnyei, 2005) had paid little attention to emotions: "Affective issues were only discussed under the rubric of 'emotion control strategies' within the chapters on motivation and learning strategies" (p. 10).

They regret the earlier omission and acknowledge the importance of emotions in SLA:

> Perhaps the greatest omission of the classic ID [individual differences] paradigm is that it barely acknowledges the central role of emotions in human thought and behavior, even though affect is an unavoidable component of any attempt to understand the nature of learner characteristics. Feelings and emotions play a huge part in all our lives, yet they have been shunned to a large extent by both the psychology and the SLA literature. "Shunned" does not mean fully "ignored," though, because there is a significant body of research looking at emotions in both fields; but affect has been considered at best a poor relation to rational thinking.
>
> (p. 9)

Interest in emotion in SLA is not exactly new (Dewaele, 2005, 2011; MacIntyre, 2002), but it was boosted by the introduction of positive psychology in the field (MacIntyre & Gregersen, 2012). Positive psychologists argue that general psychology has concentrated for too long on the negative aspects of life, ignoring its positive aspects. Positive psychologists do not deny the existence of problems, but they defend a more

DOI: 10.4324/9781003155683-9

holistic perspective on humans in which the negative and the positive are balanced. Seeing the glass as half full rather than half empty is particularly important in a foreign language classroom, where positive emotions can foster greater engagement and more success, while negative emotions can be linked to poor performance and withdrawal (MacIntyre & Mercer, 2014). The arrival of positive psychology in SLA has led to a flowering of research on learners' positive attributes such as flow, hope, courage, well-being, optimism, creativity, happiness, grit, resilience, and laughter as well as learner emotions (Dewaele, Chen et al., 2019). This increased interest is reflected in a growing number of special issues and edited books on the topic (Berdal-Masuy, 2018; Berdal-Masuy & Pairon, 2019; Budzińska & Majchrzak, 2021; Dewaele, 2018a; Li, 2020b; Padilla et al., 2019).

Discussing the theoretical and methodological challenges in SLA research, Kersten and Greve (2023, this volume) point out that it is fine to identify potential factors affecting SLA but that this needs to be complemented by research into their causal and conceptual interrelations. In other words, researchers can investigate the differences between conceptual layers of both internal (individual) and external factors, as well as the different types of relationships (causal, constitutive, or emergent) between factors (Kersten & Greve, 2023, this volume). The present study will attempt this by focusing on the effect of learner-internal "nano-level" independent variables such as sociobiographical and learner profiles and learner-external "micro-level" independent variables (such as peers and teachers) on the dependent variable, learner emotions, more specifically foreign language enjoyment (FLE) and foreign language classroom anxiety (FLCA) (Dewaele & Li, 2020; Dewaele & MacIntyre, 2014).

Previous research suggests that different independent variables are linked to FLE and FLCA and that some confounding micro- and meso-level variables, such as the status of languages in the classroom, school, and society at large may also have an effect (Dewaele & Proietti Ergün, 2020; Resnik & Dewaele, 2020). Although the assumption is that "nano-level" (i.e., unique to the individual) learner-internal variables such as performance in the foreign language (FL), attitudes toward the FL, and toward the FL teacher may affect learners' FLE and FLCA, we do not exclude the possibility that the causal relationship could also go the other way (Botes et al., 2020). The present study takes this research forward by focusing on the interplay between different "nano-level" learner-internal variables and the FLE and FLCA of 207 adult Spanish EFL learners.

Literature review

Foreign language classroom anxiety

Early research on language learning anxiety in SLA, which MacIntyre (2017) named the confounded approach, produced confusing results, since the concept of language anxiety was not yet clearly defined. Horwitz et al. (1986) inaugurated a second phase, the so-called specialized approach (MacIntyre, 2017), in which FLCA was defined as "a distinct complex of self-perceptions, beliefs, feelings and behaviors related to classroom learning arising from the uniqueness of the language learning process" (Horwitz et al., 1986, p. 128). Reflecting about FLCA, Horwitz stated recently that students who face FLCA "have the trait of feeling state anxiety when participating in language learning and/or use" (Horwitz, 2017, p. 33). By this, she means that FLCA is not a personality trait that learners are born with. It develops gradually among those who have a tendency to be anxious in the FL class, comes from multiple sources, and coalesces into situation-specific FLCA. Horwitz (2017) argues that the main cause of FL learners' FLCA is the "distress at their inability to be themselves and to connect authentically with other people through the limitation of the new language" (p. 41). MacIntyre (2017) pointed out that FLCA is now in its third phase, the so-called dynamic approach, with a focus on interacting factors that affect acquisition and performance in the FL. It fluctuates constantly over different timescales and interacts with a wide range of variables:

> This new, emerging tradition emphasizes situating anxiety among the multitude of interacting factors that affect language learning and development. Anxiety is continuously interacting with a number of other learner, situational and other factors including linguistic abilities, physiological reactions, self-related appraisals, pragmatics, interpersonal relationships, specific topics being discussed, type of setting in which people are interacting and so on.
>
> (MacIntyre, 2017, p. 23)

FLCA has a range of negative effects on learners' performance and can be "highly detrimental to the learning process" (MacIntyre, 2017, p. 150). It can even push learners to abandon the learning of the FL (Dewaele & Thirtle, 2009). It can disrupt their concentration during classes and limit their potential language input (MacIntyre & Gregersen, 2012). FLCA smothers learners' willingness to communicate in the classroom because silence is seen as preferable to the potential shame of making an error in public (Dewaele, 2019; Dewaele & Dewaele, 2018; Khajavy et al., 2018).

A more holistic take on learner emotions

MacIntyre and Gregersen (2012) suggested that positive emotions can undo the effects of negative emotions. Learners interacting in a positive emotional atmosphere acclimatize more easily to the events in the classroom and absorb more language input. These repeated positive classroom emotions have longer-term consequences, as they boost social cohesion as well as learners' long-term resilience and hardiness, also strengthening their sense of exploration and linguistic risk-taking. MacIntyre et al. (2019) wondered to what extent the positive and negative emotions that 907 FL learners reported having experienced in the preceding week were linked to their longer-term attitudes and motivation. Correlation analyses revealed strong relationships between 10 positive and 10 negative emotions, and 11 dimensions from Gardner's Attitudes and Motivation Test Battery (Gardner, 2004). Attitudes toward the learning situation, the teacher, the course, desire to learn the FL, attitudes toward learning, attitudes toward FL-speaking people, and interest in FLs were strongly correlated with positive emotions. Similarly, the language anxiety cluster was correlated with 15 emotions. The authors conclude that learners' relatively fleeting emotions may sustain attitudes toward the FL learning situation, integration, and motivation.

The first study to juxtapose FLCA and a positive emotion, foreign language enjoyment (FLE), with the same research design was Dewaele and MacIntyre (2014). The authors collected data through closed and open questions from 1,746 FL learners aged between 11 and 75 and from different parts of the world. The authors introduced a new FLE scale which included Likert scales of 21 items combined with an 8-item FLCA scale extracted from Horwitz et al.'s (1986) scale. FLE was defined as a complex emotion that "occurs when people not only meet their needs but exceed them to accomplish something new or even unexpected" (Dewaele & MacIntyre, 2016, p. 217). Dewaele and MacIntyre (2014) found that FLE and FLCA were moderately negatively correlated ($r = -.36$, $p < .0001$), suggesting that they are fundamentally independent dimensions. In other words, they are not in a see-saw relationship: a lower degree of FLCA does not automatically imply a higher level of FLE. Participants who reported higher levels of FLE and lower levels of FLCA reported knowing more languages, were more confident about their classroom performance, more proficient, older, and Western (rather than Asian). Female participants scored significantly higher than male participants on both FLE and FLCA (though the effect size was small). Feedback from participants on episodes of enjoyment in the FL class revealed the importance of the social dimension, namely supportive peers and teachers. Judicious praise and encouragement, combined with humor, trust, and respect, were common themes in the episodes. FLE levels were also linked to classroom activities that gave students a degree of autonomy.

In order to gain a better understanding of the gender differences, Dewaele et al. (2016) carried out an item-level analysis on the same corpus. The FLCA items on which female participants scored higher than male participants referred to mild rather than more extreme symptoms of anxiety. More specifically, female participants reported more fun and more pride in their FL performance than the male peers. However, they were more worried about making errors, and they were less confident than their male peers.

In an effort to control confounding variables and include teacher-centered variables, Dewaele et al. (2018) collected data from 189 secondary school pupils in two London schools, two-thirds of whom were studying French as an FL. A moderate negative correlation emerged between FLE and FLCA ($r = -.194, p < .007$) (p. 683). FLCA was found to be much less connected to teacher-centered variables than FLE. Indeed, higher levels of FLCA were linked to being less advanced in the FL, having lower perceived relative standing among peers in the FL, and having more negative attitudes toward the FL. In contrast, higher levels of FLE were linked to more positive attitudes toward the FL and the FL teacher, frequency of use of the FL by the teacher, the opportunity to speak in class, having attained a higher level of mastery in the FL, and teacher unpredictability in class. The authors thus encouraged teachers to boost their students' enjoyment in a friendly, positive classroom atmosphere without being overly worried about students' FLCA. A follow-up study by Dewaele and Dewaele (2020) on a subsample of 40 students who had two teachers for the same FL focused on the extent to which FLE and FLCA were teacher specific. FLCA was found to be identical with the main teacher and a second teacher, but FLE was significantly lower with the latter. Unsurprisingly, typical positive predictors of FLE such as attitude toward the teacher, teacher's frequency of use of the FL in class, and unpredictability were significantly stronger for the main teacher than for the second teacher (with $p < .003$, $p < .0029$, and $p < .033$, respectively) (p. 55). One possible explanation is that the main teacher was typically more experienced and may have developed the ability to regulate the emotional "temperature" in the classroom.

In a mixed-methods study that focused on 564 Chinese undergraduate EFL learners, Jiang and Dewaele (2019) found the expected moderate negative correlation between FLE and FLCA ($r = -.44, p < .0001$) (p. 18). As in previous studies, FLE was found to be predicted by teacher-related variables while FLCA was predicted by learner-internal variables. Qualitative analysis of reports on episodes of high FLE and FLCA showed that the teacher was mentioned more frequently in relation to FLE than in relation with FLCA.

Generally similar patterns emerged in the Dewaele, Özdemir et al. (2019) study of 592 Kazakh learners of FL Turkish. One exception was the finding of a weak **positive** correlation between FLE and FLCA ($r = .082, p < .045$) (p. 12). Just like in Dewaele et al. (2018), where the FL was not English, attitude toward the FL was found to be a strong predictor of FLE, explaining 18% of variance (p. 15). Other predictors of FLE included higher teacher friendliness (3.1% of variance), higher frequency of use of the FL (1.8% of variance), lower strictness (1% of variance), more positive attitude toward the teacher (0.8% of variance), higher participant's age (0.7% of variance), and higher FL exam results (0.8% of variance) (p. 15). Another divergence from previous studies was that FLCA was only weakly predicted by learner-internal variables: FL exam results (3.1% of variance), attitude toward the FL (0.7% of variance), as well as teacher-centered variables: teacher friendliness (1.9% of variance) and strictness (1.3% of variance) (p. 15).

Dewaele and MacIntyre (2019) expanded the number of independent variables with potential links to FLE and FLCA. They included personality traits and teacher characteristics such as strictness, friendliness, and joking. Quantitative and qualitative data were collected from 750 FL learners from around the world via an online questionnaire. A moderate negative correlation was found between FLE and FLCA. Multiple regression analyses revealed that teacher-related variables and cultural empathy were the strongest predictors of FLE, explaining 40% of variance (p. 275), while two personality traits, emotional stability and social initiative, were strong negative predictors of FLCA, followed by relative standing in the group in terms of proficiency, multilingualism, FL level, and attitude toward the teacher, explaining 44% of variance (p. 275). A search for causes of FLE and FLCA in participants' descriptions of classroom episodes in which they had experienced intense FLE and FLCA showed that teachers were most frequently mentioned in relation to FLE, while the self was most frequently mentioned in FLCA episodes. The quantitative and qualitative analyses thus independently confirmed that FLE and FLCA are not the two faces of Janus (Dewaele & MacIntyre, 2014) but rather conceptually different dimensions.

Focusing exclusively on the effect of teacher characteristics on FLE and FLCA, Dewaele, Franco Magdalena et al. (2019) collected data from 207 EFL learners from Spain.[1] Teacher characteristics were found to explain twice as much variance in FLE (20% of variance) as in FLCA. Teacher friendliness was the strongest positive predictor of FLE, while the teacher's strong foreign accent in English was a weaker negative predictor of FLE. Teacher's younger age, strictness, and limited use of English in class were weaker predictors of FLCA. A small but significant negative correlation was found between FLE and FLCA ($r = -.212, p < .002$) (p. 7).

The relation between meso- and macro-level variables and FLE and FLCA

In a study on the effect of broader societal and political factors on learners' FLE and FLCA, De Smet et al. (2018) collected data from 896 primary- and secondary-level pupils in French-speaking Belgium. Pupils were in both content and language integrated learning (CLIL) schools in which English or Dutch were used in addition to French and non-CLIL schools where French was the sole school language. The researchers found higher levels of FLE and lower levels of FLCA for English than for Dutch, a language perceived as less useful by Francophones and associated with the Flemish community, with whom Belgian Francophones have a strained relationship (De Smet et al., 2018). A follow-up study by the same authors showed similar patterns for language attitudes and motivation, with a growing gap between English and Dutch at the start of secondary education (De Smet et al., 2019).

Dewaele and Proietti Ergün (2020) considered the effect of the target language on classroom emotions, attitudes, and motivation of the same learners studying two FLs simultaneously in an Italian immersion school in Turkey. Participants were 110 Turkish teenagers studying Italian and English. A positive relationship was found between FLE in both languages, but none existed for FLCA and attitudes/motivation. Within-FL analyses showed that FLE and attitudes/motivation were positively correlated in both FLs and that FLCA was negatively correlated with FLE and with attitudes/motivation in both FLs. The authors speculated that the differences between both FLs could be linked to the fact that Italian has a higher status within the school but that English has more prestige in Turkish society. Other mediating variables may be the teaching style in the Italian and English FL classes.

Change of FLE and FLCA over time

Dewaele and Dewaele (2017) reused the data from Dewaele et al. (2018) for a cross-sectional "pseudo-longitudinal" study to examine changing values of FLE and FLCA over three age groups (with presumably greater proficiency with age) (12–13 years old; 14–15 years old; 16–18 years old). The authors found moderately higher values for FLE in the oldest age group but no differences by age in FLCA. Regression analyses revealed that predictors of FLE and FLCA were different for the three age groups and that they explained different amounts of variance: fewer learner-internal and teacher-centered variables predicted FLE and FLCA for the youngest age group (relative standing explained 28% of variance for FLE, and language level explained 25% of variance for FLCA) and the oldest age group (attitude toward the teacher for FLE: 45% of variance), and relative standing (21% of variance) and teacher predictability (8% of variance) for FLCA), compared to the middle age group (attitude toward the FL, attitude toward the teacher, teacher predictability, and multilingualism predicted a total of 44% of variance for FLE, and relative standing and teacher predictability predicted 20% of variance in FLCA) (p. 18). The authors suggested that sources of FLE shift from peers to teachers, while sources of FLCA shift from self to peers with increasing age/FL proficiency.

Boudreau et al. (2018) showed that FLE and FLCA also fluctuate on a second-by-second basis during speech production. Idiodynamic software allowed 10 Anglo-Canadian students to indicate their levels of FLE and FLCA when observing a videorecording of themselves performing a 2-minute speaking task in French L2. After completing the ratings, a graph of the participant's ratings was printed, and the researcher asked about potential causes of the spikes and dips in ratings. The patterns of FLE and FLCA were sometimes negatively correlated, sometimes positively correlated, and often unconnected. Fluctuations were linked to linguistic problems or dis-/interest in the topic.

The relationship between FLE, FLCA, and FL performance

A number of studies have also investigated the effect of both positive and negative emotions on FL performance. Dewaele and Alfawzan (2018) examined the relationship between FLE, FLCA, and the test results of 189 British secondary school pupils from Dewaele et al. (2018), and the relationship between FLE, FLCA, and the performance in English of 152 Saudi university students in Saudi Arabia. The effect size of the significant positive relationship between FLE and test results (Rho = .34, p < .0001) was found to be greater than the effect size of the significant negative relationship between FLCA and test results (Rho = –.30, p < .0001) among British pupils (p. 34). A similar pattern emerged in the group of Saudi EFL learners, with a significant positive relationship between FLE and performance (Rho = .242, p < .003), but the negative relationship between FLCA and performance was only marginally significant (Rho = –.145, p = .075) (p. 36).

Further confirmation of the role of positive emotions on L2 performance emerged in Jin and Zhang (2018). Cross-sectional path analysis showed that 320 Chinese EFL high school pupils' enjoyment of English learning had a direct positive "effect" on their English achievement. On the other hand, enjoyment of teacher and student support (i.e., social dimensions of enjoyment) only had an indirect effect. The authors argue that a range of internal and external variables influence learners' FLE and that one key source of FLE is learners' authentic liking of FL learning.

Li, Dewaele et al. (2020) also looked at the link between FLE, FLCA, and proficiency among 1,307 Chinese EFL university students. The significant negative relationship between FLCA and self-perceived EFL proficiency turned out to be stronger than the significant positive relationship with FLE. The relationship between classroom emotions and proficiency was found to be different among those with low, medium, and high proficiency: FLE had a stronger relationship with proficiency (r = .396, p < .00001) than FLCA in the low-proficiency group (r = –.324, p < .00001), but FLCA had a stronger relationship with proficiency in the medium- and high-proficiency groups (r = –.502 and –.392, p < .00001 respectively), compared to FLE (r = .347 and .285, p < .00001, respectively). Interviews with 64 students revealed that bad results in English tests and fear of criticism by the teachers for bad test results were the most common sources for FLCA. Good test results, higher relative standing in the group, and teacher praise were frequently mentioned sources for FLE.

Li (2018, 2020a) added trait emotional intelligence (TEI) to her research design, to investigate its direct and indirect effect on FLE and on both self-perceived and actual English proficiency of 1,307 Chinese high school pupils. Mediation analysis revealed that TEI and FLE were positively linked to both self-perceived and actual English proficiency. Li (2020a) speculates that students with high TEI are better able to exploit their emotional competence to manage their FLCA and to generate more FLE. A study by Li and Xu (2019) on 1,718 Chinese high school pupils confirmed the significant positive relationship between TEI and FLE ($r = .313$, $p < .0001$) and the even stronger negative relationship with FLCA ($r = -.389$, $p < .0001$) (p. 8). Analysis of written feedback from 55 participants showed that they drew on facets of TEI to cope with stressful negative classroom emotions. This included forcing their focus away from the source of anxiety and making a conscious effort to feel more positive by thinking of things in English associated with happy memories.

The relationship between TEI and classroom emotions was confirmed in Resnik and Dewaele (2020). Participants were 768 secondary school and university students studying German (L1) and English (FL) in the German-speaking world. Anxiety was found to be negatively correlated with enjoyment in both German L1 classes and EFL classes ($r = -.120$, $p < .001$ and $r = -.282$, $p < .0001$, respectively). Participants who scored high on TEI reported higher levels of L1 and FL enjoyment ($r = .235$, $p < .0001$ and $r = .284$, $p < .0001$, respectively) and suffered less from L1 and FL anxiety ($r = -.340$, $p < .0001$ and $r = -.386$, $p < .0001$, respectively) (p. 10). Analysis of learner feedback about their emotions experienced in the German and English classes revealed that they experienced more fun and less boredom in their EFL classes.

Finally, classroom emotions, combined with motivation factors, were found to have a significant effect on improved comprehensibility in Saito et al. (2018). Participants were 108 Japanese high school pupils in EFL classes. The amount of progress over three months was primarily linked with high FLE and low FLCA and secondarily with motivational dispositions. Higher levels of the private subdimension of FLE and a stronger Ideal L2 Self predicted comprehensibility gains in English (explaining 7.5% and 2.7% of variance, respectively). FLCA was not a significant predictor of gains (p. 733).

To conclude, the literature review suggests that research on FLCA and FLE is flowering but that the picture on sources and causality is still incomplete and that further confirmation of observed relationships is necessary, with different language combinations, in different contexts, with longitudinal research designs that allow causal interpretation, combined with the inclusion of new independent variables. The present study will present a further step in this direction, exploring the relationship between Spanish EFL learner variables and their FLE and FLCA.

The current study Research questions

The following research questions were explored in this study:

RQ1. What is the effect of Spanish EFL learners' sociobiographical background variables such as the type of institution where the learner is enrolled, age, gender, and degree of multilingualism on their FLE and FLCA? We hypothesize that all these factors might have an effect, considering the previous literature.

RQ2. What is the relationship between classroom-specific learner variables, such as test results, attitude toward English, and attitude toward the teacher, and how are they linked to FLE and FLCA? We hypothesize that positive relationships will exist between test results, attitude toward English, attitude toward the teacher, and FLE. Conversely, we expect that test results, attitude toward English, and attitude toward the teacher will be negatively linked to FLCA.

Method

Participants and procedure

Data were collected through snowball sampling, which is a form of non-probability sampling (Ness Evans & Rooney, 2013). An open-access anonymous online questionnaire was used. Calls for participation were sent through emails to Spanish colleagues and informal contacts asking them to forward the link to colleagues and their students. The questionnaire remained online for 2 months in 2018. The questionnaire was anonymous. The research design and questionnaire obtained approval from the ethics committee in the author's research institution. Participants' consent was obtained at the start of the survey that was posted online using Google Docs.

A total of 207 participants (149 females, 57 males, 1 preferred not to say) completed the online questionnaire. Participants ranged from 15 to 63 years old, with 54% in the age range 18 to 22 (Mean age = 25.63, *SD* = 9.18). Almost all the participants had Spanish nationality and resided in Spain. A number of items inquired about participants' language profiles. All of them had Spanish as an L1, sometimes combined with other L1s, such as: Armenian, Basque, Catalan, Galician, Italian, Korean, Portuguese, Romanian, Russian, and Valencian. They also listed a wide variety of languages acquired later in life. Based on this self-reported information, we established that the sample consisted of 60 bilinguals, 83 trilinguals, 53 quadrilinguals, 9 pentalinguals, and 2 sextalinguals. All participants were EFL students at different levels of education, with two-thirds (n = 136) at university, a quarter (n = 52) at secondary school, and the remaining 9% of participants (n = 19) in official languages school, *Escuela Oficial de Idiomas*.

Participants reported their attitude toward English on a five-point Likert scale ranging from "very unfavorable" to "very favorable."

Because only six participants reported "very unfavorable" and "unfavorable" attitude toward English, they were merged with participants who reported a "neutral" attitude, and the resulting group was labeled "neutral or less" (n = 22). Fifty-five participants had a favorable attitude, and the remaining 130 participants had a "very favorable" attitude. A similarly worded item enquired about the attitude toward the teacher. Here also, 19 participants with "very unfavorable" and "unfavorable" attitudes toward their English teacher were merged with the 41 who had a "neutral" attitude, and the resulting group was labeled "neutral or less" (n = 60). Ninety-three participants had a favorable attitude toward their teacher, and the remaining 54 participants had a "very favorable" attitude. These ordinal variables were treated continuously in the analyses. Finally, 177 participants reported results on their "last major English test" (with the details of the test varying from school to school) on a 100-point scale as was done in Dewaele et al. (2018). The average grade was 77.8% (SD = 15.5), which suggests they were good students, on average.

The online questionnaire started with a demographics section from which the information mentioned was retrieved. Participants then completed 10 items extracted from the original FLE questionnaire, selected to capture the reliability of the original scale without sacrificing the reliability of the measurement (see Dewaele & MacIntyre, 2014, 2016). Participants were asked to what extent they agreed with statements such as "I enjoy it," "The peers are nice." Possible responses ranged from "strongly disagree" (1), "disagree" (2), "undecided" (3), "agree" (4) to "strongly agree" (5). All items were positively phrased. A scale analysis revealed high internal consistency (Cronbach's alpha = .87). FLE values ranged from 1.9 to 5, with mean score of 3.91 (SD = 0.54). The eight items were extracted from the FLCAS reflecting physical symptoms of anxiety, nervousness, and lack of confidence (Horwitz et al., 1986) and were the same as the ones used in Dewaele and MacIntyre (2014). Two FLCA items reflected low anxiety and six reflected medium to high anxiety. Items included: "I always feel that the other students speak the Foreign language better than I do," "I can feel my heart pounding when I'm going to be called on in foreign language class." Positively oriented items were reverse coded so that all scores reflect anxiety. A scale analysis of the whole data set revealed high internal consistency (Cronbach's alpha = 0.85). The mean score was 2.85 (SD = 1.02).

A one-sample Kolmogorov-Smirnov test revealed that the distribution was close to normal for FLE (KS = .96, p < .001) and for FLCA (KS = .65, p = .035). The calculation of Q-Q plots suggests that they follow a normal distribution reasonably well except for the extreme tail for FLCA (values below 1) and the region below 2.5 for FLE. We thus opted for the more powerful parametric statistics, namely Pearson correlation analyses, independent t-tests, and analyses of variance (ANOVA) for independent variables that had three levels, followed by post-hoc tests.

Results

Institution

A one-way ANOVA revealed that participants' institution (secondary school, university, or Escuela Oficial de Idiomas[2]) had no effect on levels of FLE ($F(2, 204) = .10$, $p = .90$) nor on levels of FLCA ($F(2, 204) = .38$, $p = .68$).

Age

Pearson correlation analyses revealed no relationship between age and FLE ($r(206) = .044$, $p = .52$) nor between age and FLCA ($r(206) = -.015$, $p = .82$).

Gender

An independent *t*-test revealed that gender had no effect on levels of FLE (*Mean* Females = 3.93, *SD* = .49; *Mean* Males = 3.85, *SD* = .65; $t(81.026) = .79$, $p = .43$, Cohen's $d = .139$) but that the 149 female participants reported more FLCA than the 57 male peers (*Mean* Females = 3.03, *SD* = 1.02; *Mean* Males = 2.39, *SD* = .89; $t(204) = 4.146$ $p < .0001$, Cohen's $d = .668$). This is close to a medium effect size (.70) for Plonsky and Oswald (2014).

Number of languages known

A one-way ANOVA revealed that participants' degree of multilingualism (two, three, or four+ languages) had no effect on levels of FLE ($F(2, 204) = .65$, $p = .52$) nor on levels of FLCA ($F(2, 204) = .86$, $p = .42$).

A series of Pearson correlation analyses, with Bonferroni correction for multiple testing ($p < .01$), shows that FLE is significantly correlated with all other variables and that the only negative relationship is with FLCA (Table 7.1). Effect sizes are mostly small ($r = .25$), with a few reaching a medium size ($r = .40$) (Plonsky & Oswald, 2014). FLCA

Table 7.1 Inter-correlations between the variables (Pearson *r*)

	2	*3*	*4*	*5*
1. FLE	–.21*	.36**	.21*	.44**
2. FLCA		–.25*	–.28**	–.10
3. Test results			.24*	.16
4. Attitude toward English				.41**
5. Attitude toward teacher				1

*$p < .01$, **$p < .001$

is significantly negatively correlated with most positively oriented variables. Test results are further positively correlated with attitude toward English. Attitude toward English is similarly significantly positively correlated with the positively oriented variables and significantly negatively correlated with FLCA. Attitude toward the teacher is also significantly positively correlated with the positively oriented variables but unrelated to FLCA.

Attitude toward English

A one-way ANOVA revealed that participants' attitude toward English (neutral or less, favorable, very favorable) had a significant effect on levels of FLE ($F(2, 204) = 6.92$, $p < .001$, $eta^2 = .063$). The effect size would be considered medium according to Cohen's (1988) criteria but would be considered very large in Wei and Hu's (2018) new benchmark system for interpreting the effects of sociobiographical variables.[3] Tukey HST post-hoc tests revealed that only the difference between the "neutral or less" group and the "very favorable" group was significant ($p < .002$) (see Figure 7.1). Participants' attitude toward English had an even stronger effect on levels of FLCA ($F(2, 204) = 11.38$, $p < .0001$, $eta^2 = .100$). This represents a medium effect size for Cohen (1988) and a very large one for Wei and Hu (2018). Tukey HST post-hoc tests revealed that the difference was not significant between the "neutral or less" and "favorable" groups but that the difference between the "neutral or less" group and the "favorable" group ($p < .003$), and between the "neutral or less" and the "very favorable" groups ($p < .0001$) were significant (see Figure 7.1).

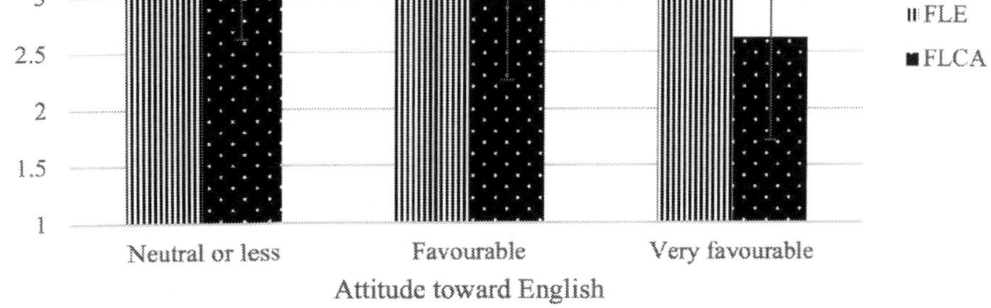

Figure 7.1 Graph showing the effect of attitude toward English on FLE and FLCA

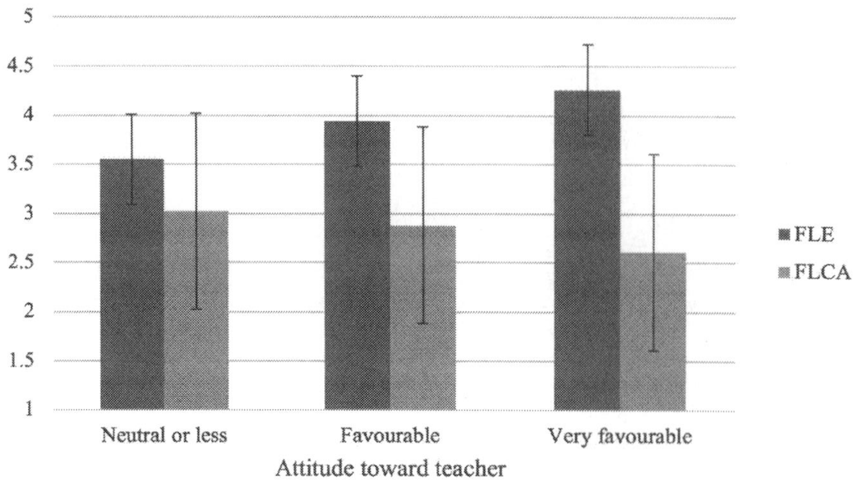

Figure 7.2 Graph showing the effect of attitude toward the English teacher on FLE and FLCA

A one-way ANOVA revealed that participants' attitude toward their English teacher (neutral or less, favorable, very favorable) had a significant effect on levels of FLE ($F(2, 204) = 33.59$, $p < .0001$, $eta^2 = .248$). This represents a large effect size for Cohen (1988) and a huge one for Wei and Hu (2018). Tukey HST post-hoc tests revealed significant differences between the three groups (all $p < .0001$) (see Figure 7.2). A final one-way ANOVA revealed that participants' attitude toward their English teacher had no significant effect on levels of FLCA ($F(2, 204) = 2.45$, $p = .088$, $eta^2 = .023$). Tukey HST post-hoc tests revealed no significant differences between the three groups (the difference between the "neutral or less" and the "very favorable" groups was $p = .077$).

Discussion

The first research question focused on the relationship between sociobiographical background variables and Spanish EFL learners' FLE and FLCA, and the first hypothesis was broadly rejected. The first variable, type of institution, showed no effect. In other words, levels of FLE and FLCA were not dissimilar in secondary schools, universities, or in the *Escuela Oficial de Idiomas*. Learners' age was also unrelated to FLE and FLCA. Both findings are slightly unexpected, as Dewaele and MacIntyre (2014) found that older students in tertiary education were more likely to have higher levels of FLE and lower levels of FLCA. A gender effect was found in the expected direction for FLCA (a small effect size), with female participants reporting more FLCA, but no significant difference emerged for FLE. This partly confirms previous research (Dewaele & MacIntyre, 2014; Dewaele et al., 2016) and should not be overinterpreted given the small effect size. The finding that the number of languages known by participants was unrelated to their levels of FLE and FLCA differs markedly from the finding that degree of multilingualism was linked to more FLE and less FLCA in Dewaele and MacIntyre (2014). It is possible that the effect of multilingualism depends on the specific profile of the participants, which was quite different in the current study from that in Dewaele and MacIntyre (2014), where slightly over half of the participants did not study English as FL and where participants had 90 different nationalities. Both samples do not differ much in terms of age, degree of multilingualism, and gender distribution.

The second research question focused on the relationship between "nano-level" learner variables and FLE and FLCA, and the hypothesis on links between independent and dependent variables was largely confirmed. Interestingly, the positive relationship between FLE and test results seemed stronger than the negative relationship between FLCA and test results. However, an analysis of the difference between the two correlation coefficients revealed that it was not significant ($z = 1.23$, $p = .22$) (Soper, 2021). The positive link between FLE and test results and the negative link between FLCA and test performance confirms the findings of previous studies (Dewaele & Alfawzan, 2018; Dewaele & Proietti Ergün, 2020; Li, 2018, 2020a). As has been pointed out before, causality can run in both directions (Botes et al., 2020; Dewaele & Dewaele, 2017; Dewaele et al., 2018). On the one hand, strong FLE may push the learner to work harder, resulting in linguistic progress and better test results. On the other hand, good test results may push learners to re-evaluate their relative standing in the class, which may in turn boost their levels of FLE and engagement in the learning process. Similarly, high FLCA may indirectly or directly affect FL test performance, but good test performance may also gradually lower levels of FLCA (MacIntyre, 2017). Jin and Zhang (2018) point out that FLE can have a positive effect of learners' cognition, broadening their horizon, pushing them to try multiple learning strategies, increasing learning efficiency, and resulting in better achievement. Finally, as Kersten and Greve (2023, this volume) point out, causal interpretations of synchronic relations are especially difficult and vulnerable in cross-sectional designs like ours.

The second learner-internal variable explored was attitude toward English, which turned out to have a significant relationship with FLE and an even stronger significant negative relationship with FLCA (very large effect size). This mirrors the patterns uncovered in Dewaele et al. (2018) and Dewaele, Özdemir et al. (2019). Having a positive attitude toward the FL increases the chances of enjoying the class, of having a greater willingness to communicate (Dewaele, 2019; Khajavy et al., 2018), of being more motivated and having more positive attitudes (MacIntyre et al., 2019), greater engagement (MacIntyre & Mercer, 2014), more resilience in the face of difficulty, and more confidence in the ability to do well. This would also explain why a positive attitude is linked to lower FLCA. It could help learners overcome their perceived inability to be authentic in the FLE and to connect authentically with peers (Horwitz, 2017). Of course, the picture could be flipped round, with a negative attitude toward the FL linked to lower FLE and more FLCA. Having to learn something that is not valued is unlikely to be enjoyable and more likely to be anxiety provoking. It is likely that language attitudes and classroom emotions reinforce each other, positively or negatively (De Smet et al., 2018).

The relationship between attitude toward the teacher and classroom emotions was slightly different. Positive attitudes toward the teacher were linked to a much higher FLE (a huge effect size), but they had no effect on FLCA. This again confirms previous research that the teacher plays a central role in learners' FLE but has little or no effect on their FLCA (Dewaele & Dewaele, 2017, 2020; Dewaele et al., 2018; Dewaele, Franco Magdalena, et al., 2019; Dewaele, Özdemir et al., 2019; Dewaele & MacIntyre, 2019; Jiang & Dewaele, 2019). A good teacher who can get the emotional temperature right in the classroom and who can get learners in a state of flow (Dewaele & MacIntyre, 2021, to appear) will make the class enjoyable. On the other hand, a teacher who is not as well regarded by students, because of some deficit in professional or emotional skills, will struggle to get students into a state of flow, and as a result, the class will be generally less enjoyable to both teacher and students. Why then is a well-loved foreign language linked to lower FLCA and not a well-loved teacher? A possible explanation is that the attitude toward the FL is stable and long term, with the potential to inspire confidence in FL use over a wide range of contexts. Attitude toward the teacher might matter relatively less in reducing FLCA because a specific teacher's role in the FL learning is typically restricted to a single school year and is restricted in the contexts in which the FL can be used.

At this point, it is worth remembering that teacher characteristics (micro-level variables) also explained a good deal of variance in FLE and much less variance in FLCA in the current sample (Dewaele, Franco Magdalena et al., 2019). Teacher's gender had no effect, but participants who had a teacher who was a L1 user of English reported significantly more FLE and less FLCA. Teacher's friendliness was a strong positive predictor of FLE, while teacher's strong foreign accent in English (which could be an indicator of limited proficiency) was a weaker negative predictor of FLE, explaining together 20% of the variance of FLE. In contrast, lower teacher age, higher strictness, and lower use of English in class predicted only 8.4% of variance in FLCA (p. 9). The authors concluded that "teachers who create a positive emotional atmosphere in their FL classroom, allowing flow to occur, are like gardeners preparing the soil of a well-situated garden: They allow learners to develop deep roots and grow rapidly toward the sun" (Dewaele, Franco Magdalena et al., 2019, p. 13).

The main limitation of the current study is the use of snowball sampling that affects the generalizability of the findings (Dewaele, 2018b). This technique is widely used in applied linguistics when target participants are scattered geographically and cannot be reached via institutional channels. Some degree of self-selection bias is inevitable, as good and enthusiastic FL learners are more likely to fill out a 20-minute questionnaire rather than weak and disappointed learners who balk at their negative EFL experience. The advantage of self-selection is that the quality of the feedback is higher than that of captive samples (Wilson & Dewaele, 2010). Nevertheless, there is sufficient variation in the data of the self-selected sample to allow some degree of generalization. Also, to constitute a truly random sample of FL learners, researchers would need the services of a specialized polling institute, which, unfortunately, falls outside the financial means of typical researchers in applied linguistics (Dewaele, 2018b).

Conclusion

The aim of the present study was to focus on the relationships between learner-internal "nano-level" independent variables on FLE and FLCA among Spanish EFL learners, complementing an earlier study on micro-level variables with the same participants, namely the unique effect of teacher characteristics on their FLE and FLCA (Dewaele, Franco Magdalena et al., 2019). Sociobiographical background variables turned out to have a much weaker effect than in previous studies (Dewaele & MacIntyre, 2014). High test results were found to be linked to higher FLE (small-to-medium effect size) and lower FLCA (small effect size), and it was argued that causality was likely to be bidirectional. This finding again confirmed previous findings (Dewaele et al., 2018). The most interesting finding was that positive attitudes toward English and toward the teacher were linked to significantly higher levels of FLE. More positive attitudes toward English were also linked to lower levels of FLCA, but more positive attitudes toward the English teacher were not connected to lower FLCA. It thus seems that having a positive attitude toward the FL – presumably built up over years of learning – transcends that of attitude toward the teacher, whose contribution to the FL learning journey is restricted in time. It is highly likely that here also, causality is bidirectional, with attitudes reinforcing classroom emotions in either positive or negative ways and being shaped by the classroom emotions. The results confirm and expand previous research that showed that a positive attitude toward the FL plays an important part in FLE and FLCA and that teachers play a crucial role in increasing FLE but have limited power in reducing learners' FLCA (Dewaele et al., 2018).

The pedagogical implication of the present study, in addition to the importance of the teacher creating an optimal emotional atmosphere in the classroom (Dewaele, 2015), is that teachers should help learners develop a positive attitude toward the FL and its culture. Such an attitude will help sustain engagement in FL learning over a longer term. It means that learners should be made aware, first, that the FL is much more than unappealing grammar rules and dry vocabulary lists that have to be mastered to obtain a passing grade. Second, that the FL is more than a communication tool allowing the user to ask the way to the station. It is also the key to a treasure chest of linguistic and cultural delights. It is a key that every learner needs to forge for her/himself with the assistance of the teacher. After turning the key in the metaphorical keyhole, the FL learning turns into an adventure game that will expand the learners' mind, identity, and personality (see Pascal Mercier's (2008) novel *Night Train to Lisbon*, in which the main character's learning of Portuguese is a journey of discovery and self-discovery). It is clear that more effort is needed by education authorities and teachers around the world to inform students about the multiple benefits of FL learning beyond short-term instrumental goals that do not appeal to learners' imaginations. Crucially, teachers can help awaken learners' curiosity in the FL and culture.[4]

Notes

1. The present study is based on unused data in Dewaele, Franco Magdalena, et al. (2019).
2. As this type of institution is unique to Spain, we will use the Spanish term.
3. Wei and Hu (2018) argue that given the topic-specific nature of effect size, Cohen's (1988) traditional interpretation is inadequate for the effects of sociobiographical variables in applied linguistic research. They suggest to lower the Cohen's threshold values so "that .005, .01, .02, and .09 be used respectively as the small, typical (medium), large, and very large benchmarks for the effect size R^2 when interpreting the influence of sociobiographical variables" (Wei & Hu, 2018, p. 8).
4. **Acknowledgments:** We would like to thank our participants for providing us with precious data and the editors and reviewers for their excellent feedback.

References

Berdal-Masuy, F. (Ed.). (2018). *Emotissage. Les émotions dans l'apprentissage des langues* [*Emotissage: Emotions in language learning*]. Presses Universitaires de Louvain.

Berdal-Masuy, F., & Pairon, J. (Eds.). (2019). Emo-langages: Vers une approche transversale des langages dans leurs dynamiques émotionnelles et créatives (Emo-language: Towards a transversal approach to languages in their emotional and creative dynamics). *Travaux interdisciplinaires sur la parole et le langage*, *35*.

Botes, E., Dewaele, J.-M., & Greiff, S. (2020). The power to improve: Effects of multilingualism and perceived proficiency on enjoyment and anxiety in foreign language learning. *European Journal of Applied Linguistics*, *8*(2), 1–28. https://doi.org/10.1515/eujal-2020-0003

Boudreau, C., MacIntyre, P. D., & Dewaele, J.-M. (2018). Enjoyment and anxiety in second language communication: An idiodynamic approach. *Studies in Second Language Learning and Teaching*, *8*, 149–170. https://doi.org/10.14746/ssllt.2018.8.1.7

Budzińska, K., & Majchrzak, O. (Eds.). (2021). *Positive psychology in second and foreign language education*. Springer.

Cohen, J. (1988). *Statistical power analysis for the behavioral sciences* (2nd ed.). Erlbaum.

De Smet, A., Mettewie, L., Galand, B., Hilingsmann, P., & Van Mensel, L. (2018). Classroom anxiety and enjoyment in CLIL and non-CLIL: Does the target language matter? *Studies in Second Language Learning and Teaching*, *8*(1), 47–71. https://doi.org/10.14746/ssllt.2018.8.1.3

De Smet, A., Mettewie, L., Galand, B., Hilingsmann, P., & Van Mensel, L. (2019). Does CLIL shape language attitudes and motivation? Interactions with target languages and instruction levels. *International Journal of Bilingual Education and Bilingualism*. https://doi.org/10.1080/13670050.2019.1671308

Dewaele, J.-M. (2005). Investigating the psychological and the emotional dimensions in instructed language learning: Obstacles and possibilities. *The Modern Language Journal*, *89*, 367–380. https://doi.org/10.1111/j.1540-4781.2005.00311.x

Dewaele, J.-M. (2011). Reflections on the emotional and psychological aspects of foreign language learning and use. *Anglistik. International Journal of English Studies*, *22*, 23–42.

Dewaele, J.-M. (2015). On emotions in foreign language learning and use. *The Language Teacher*, *39*, 13–15.

Dewaele, J.-M. (Ed.). (2018a). Emotions in SLA. [Special Issue] *Studies in Second Language Learning and Teaching*, *8*.

Dewaele, J.-M. (2018b). Online questionnaires. In A. Phakiti, P. De Costa, L. Plonsky, & S. Starfield (Eds.), *The Palgrave handbook of applied linguistics research methodology* (pp. 269–286). Palgrave Macmillan.

Dewaele, J.-M. (2019). The effect of classroom emotions, attitudes toward English, and teacher behaviour on willingness to communicate among English foreign language learners. *Journal of Language and Social Psychology*, *38*(4), 523–535. https://doi.org/10.1177/0261927X19864996

Dewaele, J.-M., & Alfawzan, M. (2018). Does the effect of enjoyment outweigh that of anxiety in foreign language performance? *Studies in Second Language Learning and Teaching*, *8*(1), 21–25. https://doi.org/10.14746/ssllt.2018.8.1.2

Dewaele, J.-M., Chen, X., Padilla, A. M., & Lake, J. (2019). The flowering of positive psychology in foreign language teaching and acquisition research. *Frontiers in Psychology. Language Sciences*, *10*, 2128. https://doi.org/10.3389/fpsyg.2019.02128

Dewaele, J.-M., & Dewaele, L. (2017). The dynamic interactions in Foreign Language Classroom Anxiety and Foreign Language Enjoyment of pupils aged 12 to 18: A pseudo-longitudinal investigation. *Journal of the European Second Language Association*, *1*, 11–22. http://doi.org/10.22599/jesla.6

Dewaele, J.-M., & Dewaele, L. (2018). Learner-internal and learner-external predictors of willingness to communicate in the FL classroom. *Journal of the European Second Language Association*, *2*, 24–37. http://doi.org/10.22599/jesla.37

Dewaele, J.-M., & Dewaele, L. (2020). Are foreign language learners' enjoyment and anxiety specific to the teacher? An investigation into the dynamics of learners' classroom emotions. *Studies in Second Language Learning and Teaching*, *10*, 45–65. https://doi.org/10.14746/ssllt.2020.10.1.3

Dewaele, J.-M., Franco Magdalena, A., & Saito, K. (2019). The effect of perception of teacher characteristics on Spanish EFL Learners' Anxiety and Enjoyment. *Modern Language Journal*, *103*(2), 412–427. https://doi.org/10.1111/modl.12555

Dewaele, J.-M., & Li, C. (2020). Emotions in Second Language Acquisition: A critical review and research agenda. In C. Li (Ed.), A positive psychology perspective on emotions in SLA. [Special Issue] *Foreign Language World* [Chinese 外语界], *196*(1), 34–49.

Dewaele, J.-M., & MacIntyre, P. D. (2014). The two faces of Janus? Anxiety and enjoyment in the foreign language classroom. *Studies in Second Language Learning Teaching*, *4*, 237–274. https://doi.org/10.14746/ssllt.2014.4.2.5

Dewaele, J.-M., & MacIntyre, P. D. (2016). Foreign language enjoyment and foreign language classroom anxiety: The right and left feet of FL learning? In P. D. MacIntyre, T. Gregersen, & S. Mercer (Eds.), *Positive psychology in SLA* (pp. 215–236). Multilingual Matters.

Dewaele, J.-M., & MacIntyre, P. D. (2019). The predictive power of multicultural personality traits, learner and teacher variables on Foreign Language Enjoyment and Anxiety. In M. Sato & S. Loewen (Eds.), *Evidence-based second language pedagogy: A collection of instructed second language acquisition studies* (pp. 263–286). Routledge.

Dewaele, J.-M., & MacIntyre, P. D. (2021). El flujo en el aula de Español como lengua extranjera. In M. del Carmen Méndez Santos & J. Andoni Duñabeitia Landaburu (Eds.), *Factores cognitivos y afectivos en la enseñanza del español como LE/L2 – Cognitive and affective factors in Spanish as FL/L2 teaching* (pp. 303–330). Thomson Reuters Aranzadi.

Dewaele, J.-M., & MacIntyre, P. D. (to appear). Do flow, enjoyment and anxiety emerge equally in English foreign language classrooms as in other foreign language classrooms? *Revista Brasileira de Linguística Aplicada*, doi:10.1590/1984-6398202218487

Dewaele, J.-M., MacIntyre, P. D., Boudreau, C., & Dewaele, L. (2016). Do girls have all the fun? Anxiety and enjoyment in the foreign language classroom. *Theory and Practice of Second Language Acquisition*, *2*, 41–63.

Dewaele, J.-M., Özdemir, C., Karci, D., Uysal, S., Özdemir, E. D., & Balta, N. (2019). How distinctive is the foreign language enjoyment and foreign language classroom anxiety of Kazakh learners of Turkish? *Applied Linguistics Review*. https://doi.org/10.1515/applirev-2019-0021

Dewaele, J.-M., & Proietti Ergün, A. L. (2020). How different are the relations between enjoyment, anxiety, attitudes/motivation and course marks in pupils' Italian and English as Foreign languages? *Journal of the European Second Language Association*, *4*, 45–57. https://doi.org/10.22599/jesla.65

Dewaele, J.-M., & Thirtle, H. (2009). Why do some young learners drop foreign languages? A focus on learner-internal variables. *International Journal of Bilingual Education and Bilingualism*, *12*(6), 635–649. https://doi.org/10.1080/13670050802549656

Dewaele, J.-M., Witney, J., Saito, K., & Dewaele, L. (2018). Foreign language enjoyment and anxiety in the FL classroom: The effect of teacher and learner variables. *Language Teaching Research*, *22*(6), 676–697. https://doi.org/10.1177/1362168817692161

Dörnyei, Z. (2005). *The psychology of the language learner: Individual differences in second language acquisition*. Erlbaum.

Dörnyei, Z., & Ryan, S. (2015). *The psychology of the second language learner revisited*. Routledge.

Gardner, R. (2004). *Attitude/motivation test battery: International AMTB research project*. The University of Western Ontario. https://publish.uwo.ca/~gardner/docs/englishamtb.pdf

Horwitz, E. K. (2017). On the misreading of Horwitz, Horwitz and Cope (1986) and the need to balance anxiety research and the experiences of anxious language learners. In C. Gkonou, M. Daubney, & J.-M. Dewaele (Eds.), *New insights into language anxiety: Theory, research and educational implications* (pp. 31–50). Multilingual Matters.

Horwitz, E. K., Horwitz, M., & Cope, J. (1986). Foreign language classroom anxiety. *Modern Language Journal*, *70*, 125–132. https://doi.org/10.1111/j.1540-4781.1986.tb05256.x

Jiang, Y., & Dewaele, J.-M. (2019). How unique is the foreign language classroom enjoyment and anxiety of Chinese EFL learners? *System*, *82*, 13–25. https://doi.org/10.1016/J.SYSTEM.2019.02.017

Jin, Y., & Zhang, L. J. (2018). The dimensions of foreign language classroom enjoyment and their effect on foreign language achievement. *International Journal of Bilingual Education and Bilingualism*. https://doi.org/1080/13670050.2018.1526253

Kersten, K., & Greve, W. (2023, this volume). Investigating cognitive-linguistic development in SLA – theoretical and methodical challenges for empirical research. In K. Kersten & A. Winsler (Eds.), *Understanding variability in second language acquisition, bilingualism, and cognition: A multi-layered perspective*. Routledge.

Khajavy, G. H., MacIntyre, P. D., & Barabadi, E. (2018). Role of the emotions and classroom environment in willingness to communicate: Applying doubly latent multilevel analysis in second language acquisition research. *Studies in Second Language Acquisition*, *40*, 605–624. https://doi.org/10.1017/S0272263117000304

Li, C. (2018). *A positive psychology perspective on Chinese students' emotional intelligence, classroom emotions, and EFL learning achievement* (Unpublished doctoral dissertation). Xiamen University, China.

Li, C. (2020a). A positive psychology perspective on Chinese EFL students' trait emotional intelligence, foreign language enjoyment and EFL learning achievement. *Journal of Multilingual and Multicultural Development*, *41*, 246–263. https://doi.org/10.1080/01434632.2019.1614187

Li, C. (Ed.). (2020b). A positive psychology perspective on emotions in SLA. [Special Issue] *Foreign Language World* [Chinese 外语界], *196*(1).

Li, C., Dewaele, J.-M., & Jiang, G. (2020). The complex relationship between classroom emotions and EFL achievement in China. *Applied Linguistics Review*, *11*(3), 485–510. https://doi.org/10.1515/applirev-2018-0043

Li, C., & Xu, J. (2019). Trait emotional intelligence and classroom emotions: A positive psychology investigation and intervention among Chinese EFL learners. *Frontiers in Psychology. Language Sciences*, *10*, 2453. https://doi.org/10.3389/fpsyg.2019.02453

MacIntyre, P. D. (2002). Motivation, anxiety and emotion in second language acquisition. In P. Robinson (Ed.), *Individual differences and instructed language learning* (pp. 45–68). John Benjamins.

MacIntyre, P. D. (2017). An overview of language anxiety research and trends in its development. In C. Gkonou, M. Daubney, & J.-M. Dewaele (Eds.), *New insights into language anxiety: Theory, research and educational implications* (pp. 11–30). Multilingual Matters.

MacIntyre, P. D., Dewaele, J.-M., Macmillan, N., & Li, C. (2019). The emotional underpinnings of Gardner's attitudes and motivation test battery. In A. Al-Hoorie & P. D. MacIntyre (Eds.), *Contemporary language motivation theory: 60 years since Gardner and lambert (1959)* (pp. 57–79). Multilingual Matters.

MacIntyre, P. D., & Gregersen, T. (2012). Emotions that facilitate language learning: The positive broadening power of the imagination. *Studies in Second Language Learning and Teaching*, *2*, 193–213.

MacIntyre, P. D., & Mercer, S. (2014). Introducing positive psychology to SLA. *Studies in Second Language Learning and Teaching*, *4*, 153–172.

Mercier, P. (2008). *Night train to Lisbon*. Grove Press.

Ness Evans, A., & Rooney, B. J. (2013). *Methods in psychological research* (3rd ed.). Sage Publications.

Padilla, A. M., Chen, X., & Lake, J. (Eds.). (2019). Positive psychology, second language learning and third language learning. [Special Issue] *Frontiers in Psychology. Language Sciences*, *10*.

Plonsky, L., & Oswald, F. L. (2014). How big is 'big'? Interpreting effect sizes in L2 research. *Language Learning*, *64*, 878–912. https://doi.org/10.1111/lang.12079

Resnik, P., & Dewaele, J.-M. (2020). Trait emotional intelligence, anxiety and enjoyment in first and foreign language classes. *System*, *94*. https://doi.org/10.1016/j.system.2020.102324

Saito, K., Dewaele, J.-M., Abe, M., & In'nami, Y. (2018). Motivation, emotion, learning experience and second language comprehensibility development in classroom settings. *Language Learning*, *68*, 709–743. https://doi.org/10.1111/lang.12297

Soper, D. S. (2021). *Significance of the difference between two correlations calculator [Software]*. www.danielsoper.com/statcalc.

Wei, R., & Hu, Y. (2018). Exploring the relationship between multilingualism and tolerance of ambiguity: A survey study from an EFL context. *Bilingualism: Language and Cognition*, 22, 1209–1219. https://doi.org/10.1017/S1366728918000998

Wilson, R., & Dewaele, J.-M. (2010). The use of web questionnaires in second language acquisition and bilingualism research. *Second Language Research*, 26, 103–123. https://doi.org/10.1177/0267658309337640

Appendix
Background information

Gender:
Age:
Is your school: a secondary school/ university?
Nationality:
Which languages do you know? (chronological order from birth; for your first language, L1, you can give more than one if you grew up in a multilingual family: L1a, L1b), by "knowing" I mean the ability to have at least a basic exchange in the language

a. L1a_____________
b. L1b_____________
c. L1c_____________
d. L2_____________
e. L3_____________
f. L4_____________
g. L5_____________

Other languages (please specify) _____________
What is your attitude towards English? 1 = Very unfavourable; 2 = Unfavourable, 3 = Neutral, 4 = Favourable, 5 =Very favourable
What was the result on your last major English test (in %)?
What is your attitude towards your English teacher? (if you have several, focus on one only) 1 = Very unfavourable; 2 = Unfavourable, 3 = Neutral, 4 = Favourable, 5 =Very favourable

8 Early bilingualism increases the likelihood of taking (and mastering) foreign language courses later in secondary school

My Viet Ha Nguyen and Adam Winsler

Introduction

Bilingualism involves the use and proficiency of two languages (Skutnabb-Kangas & McCarty, 2008). While some researchers adopt a relatively inclusive description, where "bilinguals do not necessarily need to have perfect knowledge of all the languages they know to be considered as such" (Fabbro, 2001, p. 201), others distinguish between *second-language learners* and *bilinguals*, with the latter strictly referring to those who learn and use both languages from birth (Poarch & van Hell, 2012). In general, bilinguals are quite heterogeneous, as individuals vary greatly in their level of proficiency, usage, exposure, age of acquisition, culture, and context (Baker, 2011). In the U.S., terminologies such as EL (English learners), ELL (English language learners), and DLL (dual-language learners) are widely used in the fields of education, psychology, and second language acquisition (SLA) to refer to children learning English during their schooling (for an extended discussion, refer to Winsler, 2023, this volume). In the present chapter, "bilingual" refers to children who speak a different language at home but reach the school system's definition of English proficient early, by the end of the kindergarten school year, and "DLL" refers to children who speak another language at home but were not deemed proficient in English by the school system until first grade or later (Winsler et al., 2014).

Many factors influence the acquisition of two languages, from the individual child level to the larger social context (Kersten & Greve, 2023, this volume; Larsen-Freeman & Cameron, 2008). Whether these effects transfer to the acquisition of a third language or beyond is less studied, although bilingualism has been implicated in L3 acquisition in contexts where bilingual children who know a nonsocietal home language enroll in immersion programs (Cenoz, 2013; Hirosh & Degani, 2018). A few recent studies explore populations of bilinguals who speak a minority home language and acquire the societal language as their L2 through it

DOI: 10.4324/9781003155683-10

being the main instructional language in school. Results suggested that early bilingual experience fosters novel (L3) language learning, although this effect is dependent on the student's proficiency in L2, i.e., the societal language (Edele et al., 2018; Maluch et al., 2015, 2016; Hopp et al., 2019).

This book focuses on the interplay between many factors influencing second language acquisition from multiple perspectives. Our chapter contributes to this effort by examining child characteristics that influence later foreign language learning in a unique sample of low-income bilingual and monolingual children in Miami, Florida, USA – a unique location due to a majority language being Spanish (U.S. Census Bureau, 2017). Furthermore, we seek to extend the work on bilingualism and foreign language learning of second and third languages in a linguistically and ethnically diverse population, looking at the interplay between early cognitive abilities and bilingual experience in influencing later additional language learning in secondary school. The current study includes a group of bilingual children characterized by what has been called early second language acquisition (ESLA; De Houwer, 1990, 2021). Specifically, children master their first language (L1) at home from birth and then receive significant exposure to the second language (L2; English, in this case) when attending English-speaking early childcare settings at the age of 3 or 4. Eventually, DLLs acquire sufficient proficiency in English and are no longer considered DLL by the school system. We first discuss relevant findings pertaining to links between various factors and then present empirical evidence from our longitudinal study and highlight how this complements prior findings, providing insights into these relationships.

Early experience-dependent bilingual neural development and novel language learning

It is well documented that even in adulthood, gaining new skills is associated with neural plasticity, as the brain exhibits adaptation both structurally and functionally to accommodate new experiences (Wenger et al., 2017). Thus, it is no surprise that brain development is experience dependent, especially during early stages of life (Ismail et al., 2017). Specifically, early language exposure has been associated with strengthened language skills later in life in both typical (Weisleder & Fernald, 2013) and atypical development (Mayberry et al., 2002; Swanson et al., 2019). This effect is further evidenced in early multiple language exposure, where the age of L2 acquisition matters (Hernandez & Li, 2007), and second language acquisition is associated with both structural and functional changes in the brain (Costa & Sebastián-Gallés, 2014).

Within the first few years of development, the brain undergoes dramatic changes, and children gradually decrease in the ability to distinguish between different phonemes in nonnative languages (Kuhl, 2010). Due to being exposed to a variety of phonetic stimuli early in development, there seems to be an advantage for bilingual and multilingual infants and for phoneme discrimination later when they are adults (Petitto et al., 2012; Singh, 2018), which can facilitate additional language learning later in life (Antoniou et al., 2015). Neuroimaging evidence suggests that during L3 acquisition, bilinguals employ both their L1 and L2 (Bartolotti & Marian, 2017), and those who are proficient in both languages earlier are more receptive to the addition of an L3 (Kaiser et al., 2015).

Interestingly, in the literature on sequential multilinguals, there exist neurological differences in neural adaptation between those who learn an L3 after acquiring two languages (early sequential or simultaneous bilinguals who learn an L3) and those who learn two new languages sequentially later (monolinguals who learn the L2 first then the L3 shortly after but later in life), even when these groups have similar ages of L3 acquisition (Hämäläinen et al., 2017, 2018). It seems that additional language acquisition is dependent upon early language experience, and the acquisition of a third language or beyond induces similar structural brain changes as the sequential acquisition of an L2 (Pliatsikas, 2020). Thus, it is reasonable to compare monolinguals during L2 acquisition to bilinguals during L3 acquisition, as often practiced in research on L3 acquisition in children (Edele et al., 2018; Maluch et al., 2015, 2016; Hopp et al., 2019). It must be noted that the bilingual groups in the research typically consist of children with a minority home language who learn the societal/instructional language as their L2. In other words, these children learned their second language through consistent exposure in the environment (classroom, society), and the L3 is acquired in a foreign language class, whereas monolinguals in the US generally learn their L2 rather explicitly in foreign language classroom settings, unless they are in some special and rare two-way language immersion program in school that tries to make L2 learning more implicit/natural (Tedick & Wesely, 2015). Overall, the bilingual experience promotes L3 learning, as bilinguals typically outperform monolinguals in learning a novel language within artificial language learning environments (Maluch et al., 2015).

Notably, sequential bilinguals with a minority home language who learn the majority language through the education system and societal exposure are neurologically different from second language learners with limited experience (e.g., college students enrolling in FL classes) (Pliatsikas, 2020). The former group resembles early simultaneous bilinguals, and the length of exposure positively corresponds to structural changes in the brain (Pliatsikas et al., 2017; Rahmani et al., 2017). Furthermore, bilinguals with a minority home language sometimes have a more dominant L2 than L1, with balanced receptive and productive skills in the majority language (L2) but stronger receptive than productive skills in their L1 (Gibson et al., 2012; Hurtado & Vega, 2004). This helps explain findings in sequential bilingual children's L3 learning, with L1 proficiency being a better predictor than L2 for L3 development early in elementary school (Hopp et al., 2019) but L2 proficiency – the instructional language – being a better predictor of L3 learning by late elementary and middle school (Edele et al., 2018; Hopp et al., 2019; Maluch et al., 2016). In the case of bilingual experience, not only does early exposure matter, but continuous experience in either or both languages also matters for additional language learning. Indeed, biliterate bilinguals outperform monoliterate bilinguals in L3 learning, and both groups outperform monolinguals (Keshavarz & Astaneh, 2004; Sanz, 2000; Schwartz et al., 2007). In sum, early bilingual and multilingual experience appears beneficial for language learning in general and additional (L3) language learning in particular.

Individual differences in language learning and cognitive abilities

While external factors such as being exposed to multiple languages in the environment influence language learning, individuals also differ in their ability to acquire and process languages (Kidd et al., 2018). This is evident in research in monolinguals, showing that individual differences (IDs) are stable across development, and IDs in a sublinguistic component reliably predict IDs in another one. For instance, phonological awareness and memory significantly correlated with vocabulary in Lonigan et al.'s (2009) study, which, in turn, is associated with grammatical development (Brinchmann et al., 2019). Furthermore, IDs in first language acquisition are also related to various aspects of cognition, including working memory (Jones et al., 2007) and executive function (Novick et al., 2014; Woodard et al., 2016). Indeed, it is reasonable to assume that children with superior cognitive abilities might have an advantage in language learning in general (Kidd et al., 2018). Individual differences also exist in second language acquisition (Dörnyei, 2014), and IDs in cognitive abilities also contribute to second language acquisition (SLA) in different contexts (Faretta-Stutenberg & Morgan-Short, 2018). Specifically, there is a positive correlation between general cognitive capabilities and acquiring an L2 (Darcy et al., 2015; Kim et al., 2014; Winsler et al., 2014), although this effect was shown to be moderated by individuals' L2 proficiency level and language aptitude in some studies (Li, 2015; Serafini & Sanz, 2016).

One body of literature that has received much attention in the past decade focuses on a potential *bilingual advantage* in selective cognitive control (Bialystok, 2007). According to the *inhibitory control theory* (Green, 1998), bilinguals must continuously suppress one language while using the other, and this in turn increases their overall ability to inhibit irrelevant information – a key component of executive function. Prior research showed that bilinguals outperform monolinguals in a variety of tasks concerned with verbal fluency (Friesen et al., 2015), attentional control

(Saint-Aubin et al., 2018), interference control and response inhibition (Leeuw & Bogulski, 2016), set shifting (Iluz-Cohen & Armon-Lotem, 2013), and working memory (Calvo et al., 2016). However, recent meta-analyses have called this effect into question, noting the inconsistencies across different aspects of executive function, and many instances where no group differences are found between bilingual and monolingual individuals (Lehtonen et al., 2018; Paap et al., 2015, see also Festman et al., 2023, this volume). One of the key reasons for such inconsistencies may stem from the heterogeneity of the executive functions measured and the ways bilinguals are defined, since the effect is often not straightforward even within research that demonstrates a bilingual advantage (Kaushanskaya & Prior, 2015; Luk & Bialystok, 2013). Various factors may influence the appearance of bilingual advantages in executive function, including degree of L2 proficiency (Tse & Arriba, 2015), age of L2 acquisition (Kalia et al., 2014), or degree of relative proficiency in the two languages (Yow & Li, 2015). Thus, the degree to which bilinguals cognitively benefit from their bilingual experience appears dependent on both individual differences and environmental factors, such as language use and exposure in the environment.

A snowball effect on language learning?

It appears there may exist not a unidirectional but rather a bidirectional relationship between bilingualism and cognitive abilities, and both of these factors may influence additional language learning. This is fully consistent with the multivariate model presented by Kersten (2023, this volume). Indeed, children with stronger initial cognitive skills are more likely to become bilingual in the first place, but on the other hand, being bilingual also may provide certain cognitive benefits, as discussed previously (Bialystok, 2007; Kim et al., 2014; Winsler, 2023, this volume). A recent review suggests that multilingualism influences novel language acquisition both directly and indirectly, with the latter pathway including cognitive factors as a mechanism allowing bilinguals and multilinguals to learn new languages effectively (Hirosh & Degani, 2018). Based on this framework, and combined with research on the relationship between bilingualism and cognitive abilities, there may exist a snowball effect, in which children with higher cognitive abilities become proficient in multiple languages earlier, which then shapes their experience, allowing for constant exercising of various components of executive function, which influences additional language learning, and the effect is repeated and grows over time like a snowball rolling down a hill in the snow.

This proposed snowball effect is consistent with the *neuroemergentist* perspective, positing a dynamic interaction between the individual and their environment in the context of language learning (Hernandez et al., 2018). More specifically, according to this theory, bilingualism and cognitive control interact throughout development and show nonlinear growth in cognitive processing. Such nonlinear growth is also evidenced at the brain level, with genetic differences accounting for variation in L2 acquisition along with other variables (Mamiya et al., 2016), which, in turn, is associated with neural adaptation for learning within subcortical regions of the brain, allowing for bilinguals to be more adept in learning new rules as applicable to both cognitive control and language processing (Stocco et al., 2014; Stocco & Prat, 2014). This, too, is aligned with the snowball effect proposed here. This is somewhat evident in research in dual-language learners (DLLs) with a minority home language, with both L1 proficiency and cognitive skills predicting both initial level and speed of becoming proficient in the L2 societal/instructional language (Blom, 2019; Kim et al., 2014). In turn, the rate at which DLLs achieve L2 proficiency predicts elementary school academic performance, whereby becoming proficient earlier in the societal language is associated with superior achievement (Halle et al., 2012; Rozell et al., 2018; Winsler, 2023, this volume). The current chapter explores the final part of the snowball effect, i.e., how relationships between early cognitive skills, academic achievement, and early language experience in conjunction have implications for later additional language learning.

Foreign language learning in the United States

In the US, foreign language (FL) learning is typically not required in middle school and high school. Thus, there is scarce FL research at these school levels, and the few studies that do explore this found that various factors contribute to enrollment, including the school context (Finn, 1998), student characteristics (Corra et al., 2011; Pratt, 2012; Sparks et al., 2016), and student academic interest (Lemke, 1993). For example, male students and Black students are less likely to enroll in FL courses compared to their peers (Corra et al., 2011; Pratt, 2012), and students placed in "higher" academic tracks are more likely to enroll in FL courses (Finn, 1998). Despite later academic benefits from learning FL, less than 20% of students between K–12 in the US enroll in FL courses (American Councils for International Education [ACIE], 2017), which is much lower than in European countries (Eurostat, 2017). L3 research is typically conducted in countries where learning English as a foreign language is required; thus, as the majority of the US population's first (and only) language is English, FL courses are deemed elective choices, leading to relatively low percentages of enrollment.

As previously mentioned, L3 research is usually conducted in bilingual samples with a minority home language in a majority instructional L2 context (e.g. L1 = Hebrew, L2 = German, L3 = English in Germany). The current study we report on here takes place in the unique context of Miami-Dade County Florida in the US, where the majority language is actually Spanish (65.3% of the county population; U.S. Census Bureau, 2017) rather than English, despite the instructional (and larger societal) language being English. This creates a unique language-learning environment, as students can have a majority home language (L1 = Spanish), learn the instructional language in school (L2 = English), then choose to take either Spanish or another additional language (L3 ≠ Spanish) later in school. They can also have a minority home language (L1 = Hebrew, L2 = English), then choose to take a majority language (L3 = Spanish) or another unfamiliar language in the environment (L3 = Italian). Thus, the current chapter takes place in a linguistically complex environment and seeks to explore whether earlier findings regarding the relationship between early bilingualism and secondary school FL learning (Hopp et al., 2019; Maluch et al., 2016) replicate in this context.

The current study

Here, we use data from the Miami School Readiness Project (MSRP), which is a large-scale (*N* > 30,000) longitudinal research and program evaluation project started in 2002, a university (George Mason University [Adam Winsler] and Florida International University [Charles Bleiker]) – community (Early Learning Coalition of Miami-Dade/Monroe, Miami-Dade County Public Schools [MDCPS], and South Florida's early childhood task force) partnership (Winsler et al., 2008, 2014). The sample in this project is majority low income (> 80%), is linguistically and ethnically diverse (60% Latino, 33% Black, 7% White/Asian/other, about 60% have a home language other than English). Children were assessed for school readiness at 4 years of age and followed through high school, with academic information for grades K–12 supplied by the MDCPS. (For more details on the MSRP, see Winsler et al., 2008, 2014, 2023, this volume)

The current chapter explores the following questions:

1. What is the rate of enrollment in foreign language courses in middle school and high school for the MSRP sample?
2. Does children's language status (monolingual, DLL, and bilingual) in kindergarten predict foreign language learning (both enrollment and performance) after accounting for various child-level covariates (demographic information, early school readiness, and prior elementary school academic achievement)?
3. Does cognitive ability at age 4 moderate the relationship between students' early language status and secondary school enrollment and performance in foreign language courses?

Method

Participants

Participants (*N* = 33,247) are a subset of students from the larger MSRP sample. The sample is 48% female, majority low-income (82% received free or reduced-price lunch in sixth grade, a government benefit given to families below or close to the federal poverty line in the US), and ethnically diverse (58.8% Hispanic/Latinx, 33.4% Black/African American, and 6.8% White/Asian/other). Inclusion criteria include (1) student must have school course-taking data anytime between 6th and 12th grades, and (2) student language status at age 4 could be determined (described in what follows).

Measures

Language status

Student language status was determined by parent-reported home language at school entry as well as whether they were enrolled in the English for speakers of other languages (ESOL) program in kindergarten. Those with a home language different from English completed a yearly English proficiency assessment either the Miami-Dade County Oral Language Proficiency Scale-Revised ([M-DCOLPS-R]; Abella et al., 2005) and/or the Comprehensive English Language Learning Assessment ([CELLA], Florida Department of Education [FDOE], 2015) depending on the school year. Regardless of the test taken, students are classified into one of five English proficiency levels: Novice (Level 1), Low Intermediate (Level 2), High Intermediate (Level 3), Advanced (Level 4), and Independent (Level 5) – at which point they exit the ESOL program.

Children whose home language was English and who never received ELL services were considered monolinguals (n = 13,794; 41.5%). Those with a home language different from English and still enrolled in ESOL by the end of kindergarten were considered DLLs (n = 14,274; 42.9%), and those ELLs who either did not enroll in ESOL or had exited the program by the end of kindergarten (ESOL Level 5) were considered bilinguals (n = 5,179; 15.6%).

Demographics

Various demographic information was included in our analyses, including gender (0 = female, 1 = male), race/ethnicity (1 = White/Asian/other, 2 = Hispanic, 3 = Black), whether the student qualified for free or reduced lunch (0 = not qualified, 1 = qualified), and disability status (0 = does not have a disability, 1 = has a disability).

School readiness

School readiness includes child cognitive and socioemotional skills obtained prior to school entry. *Cognitive skills* were assessed by the cognitive subscale of the Learning Accomplishment Profile-Diagnostic (LAP-D; Nehring et al., 1992), given in the child's strongest language as determined by their teachers or the assessor (M = 51.97, SD = 30.38). *Socioemotional skills and behavior* were measured by parents and preschool teachers reporting children's strengths on the Devereux Early Childhood Assessment (DECA; LeBuffe & Naglieri, 1999). The DECA is a frequently used scale that has been shown to retain its integrity in low-income and ethnically diverse samples, and internal consistency alphas for the current sample ranged from .71 to .94 (Crane et al., 2011). The 37 items of DECA were classified into two subscales, with 27 items assessing initiation, attachment, and self-control comprising the total socioemotional protective factors (TPF, M = 58.79, SD = 28.09) and 10 items identifying behavioral concerns (BC, M = 48.88, SD = 29.54), with both subscales included in various analyses.

Elementary school academic performance

Fifth-grade *standardized test scores* and *GPA* were used to index prior academic achievement. Students complete a high-stakes, statewide test – the Florida Comprehensive Assessment Test (FCAT) – beginning in third grade, and were given both a standard score and a 1-to-5 scale proficiency score (FDOE, 2019a). Notably, the state of Florida changed the test from FCAT to the FCAT-2 in the 2010–2011 school year, which had a very different standard scale but an identical ordinal proficiency scale (FDOE, 2019a). In this sample, 53.4% of the students took FCAT-1 (n = 16,262), and 46.6% took FCAT-2 (n = 14,182) in fifth grade. For this reason, we used the 1-to-5 ordinal proficiency FCAT score in analyses, for both math (M = 2.08, SD = 1.28) and reading (M = 2.10, SD = 1.27) as covariates (included in separate models due to the two being highly correlated with each other, r = .84, p < .001). Student fifth-grade GPA was obtained from school records and converted from an A–F letter scale to a 5-point of 4-to-0 numeric scale (M = 3.18, SD = .53).

Foreign language (FL) learning

FL learning was the primary outcome of interest, consisting of two constructs: *enrollment* and *performance*. Course information (course/subject names) was retrieved from yearly school transcripts. Between 6th and 12th grade, students could be flagged as having enrolled in (1) a general FL course (any foreign language course), (2) a Spanish course, (3) any non-Spanish FL course, and (4) any novel FL, which is L2 for monolinguals and L3 for DLLs and bilinguals. Novel FLs were determined to be languages that differed from both the students' home language and the instructional language (English). Thus, for English monolinguals, the flag for this category is the same as the general FL course flag, but for DLLs and bilinguals, the flag differs by whether their home language was Spanish or non-Spanish. It must be noted that these categories are not mutually exclusive. For instance, a student whose home language is Spanish and who took French in middle school was flagged as having taken a general FL course, a non-Spanish FL course, and a novel FL course. Performance variables were determined in similar categories (general FL, Spanish, non-Spanish FL, and novel FL), calculated as the average grade (0–4 GPA scale) the student received across all FL courses even taken across middle school and high school.

Summary of analyses

Enrollment in FL courses was determined using simple frequencies. We ran a series of hierarchical regression analyses (logistic regression for binary outcomes (enrollment Y or N), multiple regression for continuous GPA) to predict enrollment and performance in FL courses. Child language status was the predictor of interest, and we gradually added in covariates to various blocks of the models (demographic information, school readiness, and elementary academic performance). Categorical variables (race/ethnicity, language status) were dummy coded, and additional analyses were run flipping the reference groups. For instance, a first set of analyses returned results for the Hispanic/White and Black/White contrasts and an additional set of results give the Hispanic/Black contrast. Finally, we ran a series of moderation analyses using IBM SPSS (www.ibm.com/analytics/spss-statistics-software) and R (www.r-project.org/) predicting enrollment and performance by the interaction term of student language status by early cognitive skills.

Results and discussion

In general, we found significant effects of early bilingualism on secondary school language learning, even after accounting for various child-level covariates. Specifically, bilinguals had the highest performance and enrollment rates, followed by DLLs and monolinguals. A detailed description of the findings is found in what follows.

Foreign language enrollment in secondary school

Table 8.1 shows the frequency of student enrollment in FL courses in middle and high school in our sample. In the present sample, 59% of students between 6th and 12th grade enrolled in at least one FL course. Further broken down by school level, around 27% of middle schoolers and 66% of high schoolers in our sample enrolled in FL classes. While these findings exhibit similar trends to national data in the percentage of enrollment in middle school (36% – 2008 data; Pufahl & Rhodes, 2011), compared to high school (88.5% – 2009 data; NCES, 2018), our sample had a lower percentage of enrollment at both school levels. A potential explanation for such a discrepancy might come from the low-income and majority Latinx and Black nature of the current sample. For elective FL

Table 8.1 Proportion of ever enrollment in foreign language courses in secondary school by type of language

	Middle School		*High School*		*Ever Secondary School*	
Total	*32,779*		*25,060*		*33,247*	
Type of Language	N	%	N	%	N	%
General FL	8,873	27.1%	16,463	65.7%	19,752	59.4%
Spanish	6,763	20.6%	12,700	51.6%	15,840	47.7%
Non-Spanish	2,924	8.9%	4,658	19.5%	6,600	19.9%
Novel FL*	5,154	15.7%	9,924	40.8%	12,498	37.6%

Notes*:* *Novel FL = L2 for monolinguals, L3 for DLLs and bilinguals
Enrollment is not mutually exclusive between language types.

courses (Met & Brandt, 2017; FDOE, 2019b), these students may not consider these types of classes a priority, leading to low enrollment rates. Indeed, as described next, students in poverty who qualified for free or reduced-price lunch had significantly lower odds of enrollment compared to those not in poverty across many types of FL courses.

Consistent with our expectation, Spanish was favored as a FL course, as 80% of students who enrolled in some type of FL chose the Spanish language. These results resemble national findings, as Spanish is both the most popular FL course (69% enrolled between K–12) and is the most widely taught FL across the country (ACIE, 2017). Furthermore, taking Spanish might create an advantage for communication in the context of the present community, as the majority language of Miami is also Spanish. Other languages enrolled in by students included French, German, Russian, Italian, Portuguese, Greek, Japanese, Chinese, Hebrew, and Latin.

Student characteristics and foreign language learning

While a detailed discussion of how student demographics influence student foreign language learning is beyond the scope of the current chapter (see Nguyen & Winsler, 2021, for more details), it's worth noting that gender, ethnicity, poverty status, and disability status were all significant predictors in the first steps of most models, although some effects went away when early skills and prior academic performance were included in the models (Table 8.2). Male students, Black students, students in poverty, and students with a disability had lower odds of enrolling in FL courses, and they did not perform as well in such courses compared to their counterparts. These results are consistent with prior research, showing that certain groups of students are less likely to enroll in FL classes and underperform compared to their peers, perhaps due to assumptions

Table 8.2 Multiple regression analyses predicting general foreign language learning (FL course enrollment and performance) in secondary school

	Enrollment (OR)			*Performance (β)*		
	Model 1	*Model 2*	*Model 3*	*Model 1*	*Model 2*	*Model 3*
Demographic						
[a] Ethnicity						
Hispanic/White	.856	.898	1.014	-.081***	-.063***	-.025
Black/White	.634***	.686***	.928	-.132***	-.107***	-.010
Hispanic/Black	1.350***	1.310***	1.093	.060***	.050***	-.015
Male	.827***	.873***	.990	-.215***	-.198***	-.150***
[b] Received FRL	.631***	.682***	.895	-.136***	-.114***	-.056***
Special Education	.331***	.381***	.525***	-.056***	-.035***	.002
[a] **Language Status**						
DLL/Monolingual	1.606***	1.685***	1.677***	.072***	.092***	.087***
Bilingual/Monolingual	1.824***	1.777***	1.561***	.092***	.086***	.061***
DLL/Bilingual	.548***	.948	1.074	-.040***	-.013	.012
School Readiness at age 4						
LAP-D Cognitive Skills		1.004***	1.001		.102***	.024*
DECA Social Skills		1.001	.999		.035**	.009
DECA Behavior Concerns		.996***	.997***		-.058***	-.023*
Elementary academic performance						
GPA in 5th grade			2.124***			.370***
[c] Reading 5th grade			1.411***			.034***
[c] Math in 5th grade			1.408***			.040***

Note. $*p < .05$, $**p < .01$, $***p \leq .001$.
a To analyze the third ethnicity (Hispanic/Black) and language status (DLL/Bilingual) contrast, additional analyses were run by flipping the reference group.
b FRL = free or reduced-price lunch
c Math and Reading scores were run in different models to avoid multicollinearity.

by both counselors and the students themselves about their ability to succeed in these courses and not necessarily due to actual language-learning ability (Baggett, 2016; van der Slik et al., 2015; Sung et al., 2006; Sparks, 2016). We argue that educators should encourage students, especially those underrepresented in these courses, to take foreign language classes due to their potential cognitive, social, and cultural benefits (Bordia & Bordia, 2015; Knutson, 2006; Le Pichon et al., 2010).

School readiness, elementary school achievement, and FL learning

Cognitive skills prior to school entry significantly predicted both enrollment and performance in FL courses in secondary school, while early social skills only predicted performance (Table 8.2). Thus, our results demonstrate the role of cognitive abilities in language learning, such that those with higher initial skills were more likely to take on, as well as performed better at, later FL learning compared to their peers. More importantly, once elementary school grades and test scores were included in the analyses, most of these early skills were no longer significant predictors. While it is likely that children with high initial skills would also do well academically in elementary school (*OR* ranges from .997 to 1.001, β ranges from .009 to .024), performance in fifth grade is a better predictor of both enrollment and performance in FL classes in middle school and high school (*OR* ranges from 1.408 to 2.124, β ranges from .034 to .370). The students who are already doing well in school are the ones more likely to take FL courses. Interestingly, as previously mentioned, due to the highly correlated nature of math and reading standardized test scores, we ran separate models including only one of these variables at a time. Results showed that they account for virtually the same amount of variance in the outcomes across different models, suggesting that perhaps later language learning is not only associated with language/reading skills but rather more general cognitive abilities (Ellis, 2004).

A notable result is that child behavior concerns at 4 years old consistently negatively predicted FL learning for most FL language outcomes, even when elementary school achievement was included. Earlier findings using the same dataset revealed the role of behavior concerns in second language acquisition for DLLs (Winsler et al., 2014), and the current work provides support for a potential long-lasting effect on later language learning as well. Behavior concerns can be considered a proxy for children's self-regulatory skills, and within the MSRP, behavior concerns were negatively correlated with both social skills and cognitive skills (Crane et al., 2011). This is consistent with the social-cognitive perspective on attaining self-regulation, as children must engage in an effortful cognitive process to regulate their behavior after receiving feedback from the environment (Zimmerman, 2000). Thus, children with advanced inhibitory control skills may become more successful at controlling multiple languages earlier (Kim et al., 2014), which then allows them to further exercise their cognitive skills (Rozell et al., 2018) and once again allows them to be proficient in language learning later on – the snowball effect. Indeed, these findings not only imply that language learning is influenced by cognitive abilities but rather that there is an interplay between early cognitive skills and early language experience on multiple language learning.

Language background and foreign language learning

A primary goal of the current research was to examine whether student language background, reflecting children's early language experience, influences later FL learning. We found that even after all relevant covariates were included in the models, language status in kindergarten consistently predicted both performance and enrollment in FL classes (Table 8.2). In general, bilinguals had the highest enrollment rates and performance, followed by DLLs and monolinguals. Notably, differences in performance between bilinguals and DLLs only existed before early skills and academic achievement were taken into account; by the last model, they performed similarly, with both outperforming monolinguals in foreign language courses. These findings are relatively consistent across various language types (Spanish vs. non-Spanish), suggesting a long-lasting positive effect of early bilingual experience on later multiple language learning (not tabled here, but detailed results found in Nguyen, 2020). Furthermore, bilinguals and DLLs are also likely bicultural (e.g., having Spanish-speaking parents/grandparents at home practicing their culture, but also getting exposed to and immersed in the U.S. English-speaking culture with friends and in settings outside the home), leading to personal motivation for language learning (Thompson, 2017). Indeed, within the bilingual and DLL groups, students whose home language was Spanish were more likely to take Spanish courses and less likely to enroll in an L3 class compared to their monolingual counterparts, perhaps demonstrating a will to learn their heritage language (Leeman, 2015). Regardless, early bilingual experience seems to have a pronounced effect on FL learning.

Due to the unique nature of the present sample and community, language outcomes were explored separately for Spanish and non-Spanish courses (Nguyen, 2020). We found that monolinguals in our sample actually had comparable odds of FL enrollment to both DLLs and bilinguals, possibly showing gains in language learning interest due to being in a majority Spanish-speaking environment – Miami-Dade County, Florida. This finding somewhat implies the influence of being consistently exposed to multiple languages in the environment, regardless of whether individuals are proficient in all of those languages. Since knowing Spanish would be considered an advantage in Miami, it is reasonable that this would motivate monolinguals to take these language classes. Notably,

DLLs and bilinguals showed greater performance in Spanish classes, once again suggesting a long-lasting effect of early multiple language exposure. Indeed, these bilingual groups also enrolled more than and outperformed monolinguals in non-Spanish classes, showing that the effect of language background extends to unfamiliar languages in the environment, as well.

Particularly interesting findings emerged when we examined novel language learning, defined as L2 for monolinguals and L3 for DLLs and bilinguals (Nguyen, 2020; Nguyen & Winsler, 2021). Prior research on L3 learning typically focuses on comparing monolinguals' performance in their L2 to bilinguals' performance in an L3 and has found that while home-language proficiency is the better predictor for L3 acquisition earlier in development, proficiency in the instructional language is the better predictor by later elementary and early middle school (Edele et al., 2018; Hopp et al., 2019). Our results are consistent with these patterns, showing similar performance across different language groups in novel language learning, with fifth-grade (English) reading scores being a significant predictor for FL performance. In addition, it is possible that monolinguals in our sample benefited in language learning from living in a linguistically diverse context, consistent with findings by Bice and Kroll (2019). Interestingly, within the bilingual and DLL groups, those who had a non-Spanish home language performed significantly better than those with a Spanish home language at learning an L3, which is Spanish for them. It is possible that those with non-Spanish home language were also exposed to Spanish in their environment and became familiar with this language, further indicating the importance of multiple language exposure in the community for language learning.

The interplay between early cognitive ability and language background on FL learning

To further examine how early cognitive skills and language experience together influence middle school and high school foreign language learning, we ran a series of moderation analyses on every language outcome (enrollment and performance by language type, see Table 8.3).

Similar to previously described findings, cognitive skills at age 4 and language status significantly predicted both enrollment and performance in all FL types. Notably, cognitive skills significantly moderated the relationship between bilingual status and performance but not enrollment for overall FL courses. In particular, for students with high initial cognitive skills, performance was comparable across language groups; however, for students with lower initial cognitive skills at age 4, wider differences existed between monolinguals and students exposed to multiple languages early in development (DLLs and bilinguals) (Figure 8.1; shaded regions denote standard error). Indeed, these findings indicate evidence of an interplay between cognitive skills and early language experience in influencing FL learning in secondary school, consistent with

Table 8.3 Moderation analyses predicting FL enrollment and performance

	Enrollment		*Performance*	
	OR	*SE(B)*	*B*	*SE(B)*
Total FL				
DLL/Monolingual	1.935***	0.034	0.182***	0.018
Bilingual/Monolingual	2.579***	0.049	0.293***	0.024
Cognitive Skills at Age 4	1.014***	< .001	0.007***	< .001
Cognitive * DLL/Monolingual	0.998	0.001	-0.001*	< .001
Cognitive * Bilingual/Monolingual	0.997+	0.002	-0.002**	< .001
Spanish Courses				
DLL/Monolingual	1.390***	0.031	0.236***	0.020
Bilingual/Monolingual	1.711***	0.044	0.321***	0.026
Cognitive Skills at Age 4	1.012***	0.001	0.006***	< 0.001
Cognitive * DLL/Monolingual	.996***	0.001	-0.001*	< 0.001
Cognitive * Bilingual/Monolingual	.993***	0.001	-0.002	< 0.001
Non-Spanish Courses				
DLL/Monolingual	2.548***	0.040	0.146***	0.038
Bilingual/Monolingual	2.760***	0.053	0.282***	0.049
Cognitive Skills at Age 4	1.007***	0.001	0.008***	0.001
Cognitive * DLL/Monolingual	0.999	0.001	-0.002	0.001
Cognitive * Bilingual/Monolingual	0.998	0.002	-0.003	0.002
Novel Language Courses				
DLL/Monolingual	0.404***	0.031	-0.005	0.024
Bilingual/Monolingual	0.510***	0.045	0.143***	0.034
Cognitive Skills at Age 4	1.013***	< 0.001	0.007***	< 0.001
Cognitive * DLL/Monolingual	0.993***	0.001	-0.0004	< 0.001
Cognitive * Bilingual/Monolingual	0.992***	0.001	-0.002+	0.001

Note. DLL = dual language learners; +$p < .10$ *$p < .05$, **$p < .01$, ***$p \leq .001$.

our earlier explanation for results. It is possible that for children who have high cognitive skills early in life, early language exposure has less of an influence for adolescent choice to take languages. However, for children with low to average cognitive skills early on, having a bilingual experience is important for them to keep seeking out language-learning opportunities later on.

Interestingly, cognitive skills significantly moderated the effect of language status on particularly Spanish enrollment. Specifically, students enrolled at similar rates across language status for those with high early cognitive skills, while bilinguals and DLLs had significantly higher odds of enrollment compared to monolinguals at lower initial skills (Figure 8.2). As the majority of our bilingual and DLL sample have a Spanish home language (85%), it is likely that they choose to take this course regardless of cognitive skills due to prior knowledge. However, monolinguals may only feel confident taking Spanish courses if they have strong

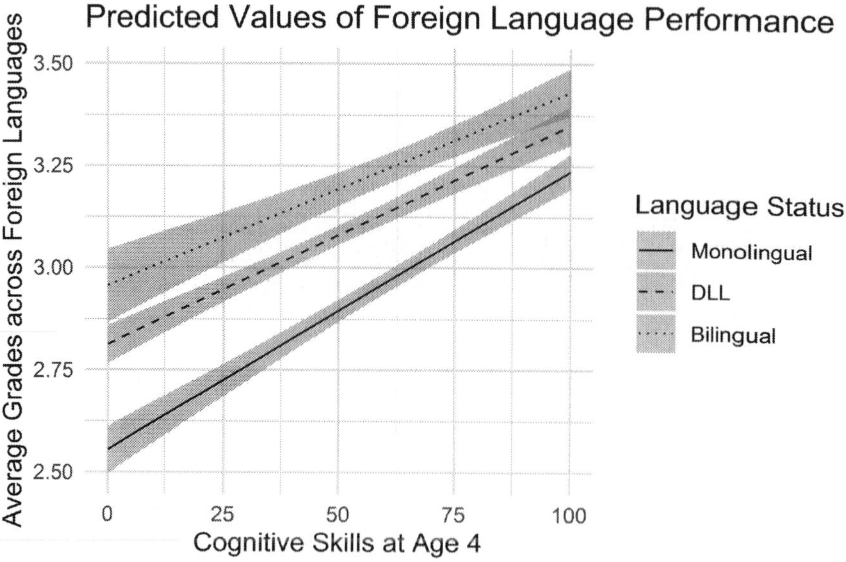

Figure 8.1 Moderation effect of early cognitive skills on the relationship between student language status and average grade across all foreign language courses

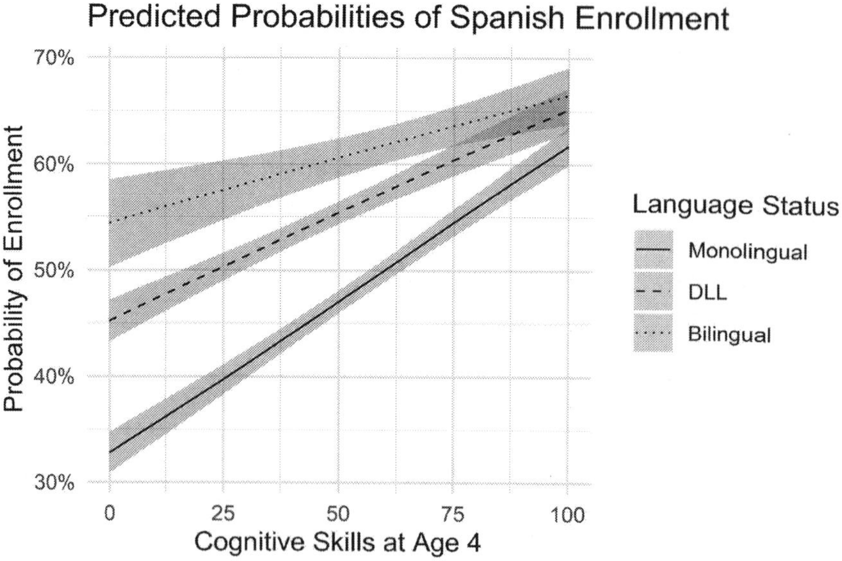

Figure 8.2 Moderation effect of early cognitive skills on the relationship between student language status and probability of enrollment in Spanish

cognitive abilities, reflected in their doing well academically. Another possible explanation might be that when DLLs/bilinguals choose to take a FL course, those with lower cognitive skills feel less confident with a novel FL and want to rely on their Spanish knowledge. This would be similar to monolinguals not enrolling in novel FL classes if they have lower cognitive skills, as reflected in earlier results.

The moderating effect of early cognitive skills also existed for FL performance. Although bilinguals and DLLs had significantly higher grades in Spanish classes than monolinguals, bilinguals and monolinguals had more similar trajectories to each other than to DLLs. It is possible that bilinguals in our sample are more *simultaneous* bilinguals, while DLLs represent more *sequential* bilinguals, and neuroimaging research shows that the former group has more similar cortical patterns to monolinguals than the latter group (Pliatsikas, 2020). Thus, for monolinguals and bilinguals in our sample, cognitive skills might affect language learning more similarly. Another possible explanation may lie in how Spanish classes are taught, as students might need to learn the information explicitly through translation from English. Given that the majority of our DLL and bilingual sample had Spanish as their home language, they might perform similarly if they enroll in *heritage language* courses rather than *foreign language* courses (Kelleher, 2010). Unfortunately, we do not have information on whether the Spanish classes were heritage language courses, so this question remains open for future research.

The interaction between language status and early cognitive skills was not significant for enrollment and performance in non-Spanish classes. When looking at L3 learning, early cognitive skills significantly moderate the relationship between language status and novel language enrollment (Figure 8.3). Specifically, bilinguals and DLLs exhibited similar patterns of enrollment, and both showed a positive relationship between cognitive skills and enrollment. However, the moderating effect of cognitive skills was much stronger for monolinguals than for both of the other groups, demonstrated in the steeper increase of odds of enrollment by cognitive skill (Figure 8.3). Hence, for children who are not exposed to multiple languages earlier in development, cognitive skills seem to play an important role in whether they enroll in foreign language classes at all later on.

Interestingly, monolinguals and DLLs had similar performance in novel FL classes (L2 for monolinguals, L3 for bilinguals and DLLs), and bilinguals outperformed both groups, with wider differences found for those with lower cognitive skills, although the moderating relationship was only trending toward significance in this case ($p = .07$) (Figure 8.4). These findings lend support to research suggesting that early proficiency in multiple languages makes the brain become more receptive to learning additional languages (Kaiser et al., 2015).

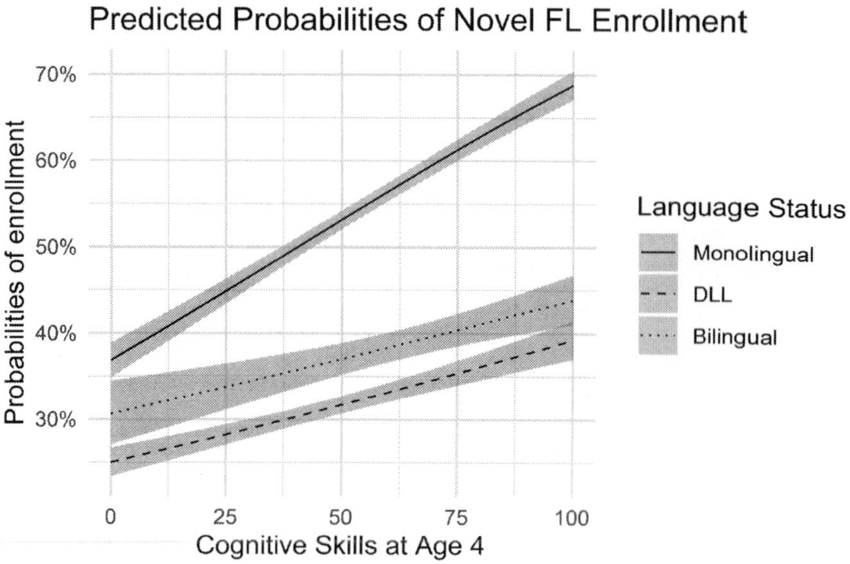

Figure 8.3 Moderation effect of early cognitive skills on the relationship between student language status and enrollment in novel foreign language courses

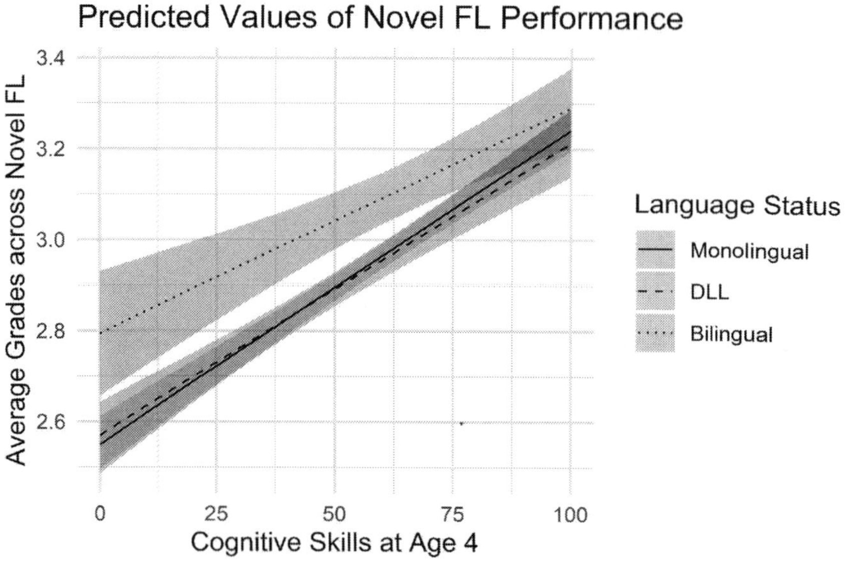

Figure 8.4 Moderation effect of early cognitive skills on the relationship between student language status and average grades in novel foreign language courses

Conclusions

This chapter provided an overview of research on the role of early language experience and cognitive abilities in multiple language learning in the public-school context while presenting some novel findings from our ongoing work with a low-income, ethnically and linguistically diverse population in a unique language learning context. Using academic information supplied by public schools in Miami-Dade County, Florida, USA, in conjunction with early assessment scores of school readiness and child characteristics as reported by the parents, we answered questions pertaining to (a) student enrollment of foreign language in middle school and high school and (b) how early cognitive skills and language experience work together to influence later language learning.

In general, students with higher cognitive and academic skills early in life were more likely to take FL classes and performed better in them compared to their counterparts. Notably, language background played a significant role in later language learning, remaining a significant predictor after many covariates were considered. Bilingual students by kindergarten had the highest odds of enrolling in FL courses and had the highest performance in FL courses, followed by DLLs and monolinguals. Results support the benefit of early multiple language exposure and lend support to the importance of maintaining a minority home language for children. Furthermore, findings demonstrate that cognitive abilities and language experience may work together in a sort of snowball effect, with higher skills early in development leading to the successful acquisition of multiple languages prior to school entry, which then provide children with the opportunity to exercise their mental capabilities, once again providing an advantage for later language learning. Thus, our research offers rich information and insight into the process of multiple language acquisition, especially in a less studied population – DLLs in poverty in the US. Findings lend support to previous research and theories on bilingualism as well as foreign language learning and education (Baggett, 2016; Bialystok, 2007; Finn, 1998; Hernandez & Li, 2007; Hirosh & Degani, 2018; Met & Brandt, 2017).

While it's beyond the scope of the current chapter, we found discrepancies in student enrollment in FL courses due to children's characteristics – gender, SES, ethnicity, and disability status (Nguyen, 2020; Nguyen & Winsler, 2021). Foreign language learning is beneficial for students in various ways, as it not only can increase students' metacognitive awareness (Le Pichon et al., 2010) and is associated with academic performance (Cooper, 1987), but it can also be useful to gain social and cultural advantages (Wight, 2015). Thus, we believe educators should encourage students to take foreign language courses, especially in groups of students who have historically been underrepresented in these classes.

References

Abella, J., Urrita, J., & Schneiderman, A. (2005). An examination of the validity of English language achievement test scores in an English language learner population. *Bilingual Research Journal*, *29*(1), 127–144. https://doi.org/10.1080/15235882.2005.10162827

American Councils for International Education. (2017). *The national K-12 foreign language enrollment survey report*. www.americancouncils.org/

Antoniou, M., Liang, E., Ettlinger, M., & Wong, P. C. (2015). The bilingual advantage in phonetic learning. *Bilingualism: Language and Cognition*, *18*(4), 683–695. https://doi.org/10.1017/S1366728914000777

Baggett, H. C. (2016). Student enrollment in world languages: L'Égalité des chances? *Foreign Language Annals*, *49*(1), 162–179. https://doi.org/10.1111/flan.12173

Baker, C. (2011). *Foundations of bilingual education and bilingualism*. Multilingual Matters.

Bartolotti, J., & Marian, V. (2017). Bilinguals' existing languages benefit vocabulary learning in a third language. *Language Learning*, *67*(1), 110–140. https://doi.org/10.1111/lang.12200

Bialystok, E. (2007). Cognitive effects of bilingualism: How linguistic experience leads to cognitive change. *International Journal of Bilingual Education and Bilingualism*, *10*(3), 210–223. https://doi.org/10.2167/beb441.0

Bice, K., & Kroll, J. F. (2019). English only? Monolinguals in linguistically diverse contexts have an edge in language learning. *Brain and Language*, *196*, 104644. https://doi.org/10.1016/j.bandl.2019.104644

Blom, E. (2019). Domain-general cognitive ability predicts bilingual children's receptive vocabulary in the majority language. *Language Learning*, *69*(2), 292–322. https://doi.org/10.1111/lang.12333

Bordia, S., & Bordia, P. (2015). Employees' willingness to adopt a foreign functional language in multilingual organizations: The role of linguistic identity. *Journal of International Business Studies*, *46*(4), 415–428. https://doi.org/10.1057/jibs.2014.65

Brinchmann, E. I., Braeken, J., & Lyster, S. A. H. (2019). Is there a direct relation between the development of vocabulary and grammar? *Developmental Science*, *22*(1), e12709. https://doi.org/10.1111/desc.12709

Calvo, N., Ibáñez, A., & García, A. M. (2016). The impact of bilingualism on working memory: A null effect on the whole may not be so on the parts. *Frontiers in Psychology*, *7*, 265. https://doi.org/10.3389/fpsyg.2016.00265

Cenoz, J. (2013). The influence of bilingualism on third language acquisition: Focus on multilingualism. *Language Teaching*, *46*(1), 71–86. https://doi.org/10.1017/S0261444811000218

Cooper, T. C. (1987). Foreign language study and SAT-verbal scores. *The Modern Language Journal*, *71*(4), 381–387. https://doi.org/10.2307/328467

Corra, M., Carter, J. S., & Carter, S. K. (2011). The interactive impact of race and gender on high school advanced course enrollment. *The Journal of Negro Education*, *80*(1), 33–46.

Costa, A., & Sebastián-Gallés, N. (2014). How does the bilingual experience sculpt the brain? *Nature Reviews Neuroscience*, *15*(5), 336–345. https://doi.org/10.1038/nrn3709

Crane, J., Mincic, M. S., & Winsler, A. (2011). Parent-teacher agreement and reliability on the Devereux early childhood assessment (DECA) in English and Spanish for ethnically diverse children living in poverty. *Early Education & Development*, *22*(3), 520–547. https://doi.org/10.1080/10409289.2011.565722

Darcy, I., Park, H., & Yang, C. L. (2015). Individual differences in L2 acquisition of English phonology: The relation between cognitive abilities and phonological processing. *Learning and Individual Differences*, *40*, 63–72. https://doi.org/10.1016/j.lindif.2015.04.005

De Houwer, A. (1990). *The acquisition of two languages from birth: A case study*. Cambridge University Press.

De Houwer, A. (2021). *Bilingual development in the first decade of life*. Cambridge University Press.

Dörnyei, Z. (2014). *The psychology of the language learner: Individual differences in second language acquisition*. Routledge.

Edele, A., Kempert, S., & Schotte, K. (2018). Does competent bilingualism entail advantages for the third language learning of immigrant students? *Learning and Instruction*, *58*, 232–244. https://doi.org/10.1016/j.learninstruc.2018.07.002

Ellis, R. (2004). Individual differences in second language learning. In A. Davies & C. Elder (Eds.), *The handbook of applied linguistics* (pp. 525–571). Blackwell Publishing.

Eurostat. (2017). *Pupils by education level and number of modern foreign languages studied – absolute numbers and % of pupils by number of languages studied*. https://ec.europa.eu/eurostat/

Fabbro, F. (2001). The bilingual brain: Bilingual aphasia. *Brain and Language*, *79*(2), 201–210. https://doi.org/10.1006/brln.2001.2480

Faretta-Stutenberg, M., & Morgan-Short, K. (2018). The interplay of individual differences and context of learning in behavioral and neurocognitive second language development. *Second Language Research*, *34*(1), 67–101. https://doi.org/10.1177/0267658316684903

Festman, J., Czapka, S., & Winsler, A. (2023, this volume). How many moderators does is take till we know . . . that too many bilingual advantage effects have died? In K. Kersten & A. Winsler (Eds.), *Understanding variability in second language acquisition, bilingualism, and cognition – A multi-layered perspective*. Routledge.

Finn, J. D. (1998). Taking foreign languages in high school. *Foreign Language Annals*, *31*(3), 287–306. https://doi.org/10.1111/j.1944-9720.1998.tb00577.x

Florida Department of Education. (2019a). *FCAT historical*. www.fldoe.org/accountability/assessments/k-12-student-assessment/archive/fcat/

Florida Department of Education. (2019b). *World languages (Foreign Languages)*. www.fldoe.org/core/fileparse.php/7583/urlt/06-05-152015-CELLA-FAQs.pdf

Florida Department of Education: Bureau of Student Achievement Through Language Acquisition. (2015). *2015 Comprehensive English language learning assessment (CELLA) frequently asked questions*. www.fldoe.org/academics/eng-language-learners/world-languages-foreign-languages.stml

Friesen, D. C., Luo, L., Luk, G., & Bialystok, E. (2015). Proficiency and control in verbal fluency performance across the lifespan of monolinguals and bilinguals. *Language, Cognition, and Neuroscience*, *30*(3), 238–250. https://doi.org/10.1080/23273798.2014.918630

Gibson, T. A., Oller, D. K., Jarmulowicz, L., & Ethington, C. A. (2012). The receptive-expressive gap in the vocabulary of young second-language learners: Robustness and possible mechanisms. *Bilingualism: Language and Cognition*, *15*(1), 102–116. https://doi.org/10.1017/S1366728910000490
Green, D. W. (1998). Mental control of the bilingual lexico-semantic system. *Bilingualism: Language and Cognition*, *1*(2), 67–81. https://doi.org/10.1017/S1366728998000133
Halle, T., Hair, E., Wandner, L., Mcnamara, M., & Chien, N. (2012). Predictors and outcomes of early versus later English language proficiency among English language learners. *Early Childhood Research Quarterly*, *27*, 1–20. https://doi.org/10.1016/j.ecresq.2011.07.004
Hämäläinen, S., Joutsa, J., Sihvonen, A. J., Leminen, A., & Lehtonen, M. (2018). Beyond volume: A surface-based approach to bilingualism-induced grey matter changes. *Neuropsychologia*, *117*, 1–7. https://doi.org/10.1016/j.neuropsychologia.2018.04.038
Hämäläinen, S., Sairanen, V., Leminen, A., & Lehtonen, M. (2017). Bilingualism modulates the white matter structure of language-related pathways. *NeuroImage*, *152*, 249–257. https://doi.org/10.1016/j.neuroimage.2017.02.081
Hernandez, A. E., Claussenius-Kalman, H. L., Ronderos, J., & Vaughn, K. A. (2018). Symbiosis, parasitism and bilingual cognitive control: A neuroemergentist perspective. *Frontiers in Psychology*, *9*, 2171. https://doi.org/10.3389/fpsyg.2018.02171
Hernandez, A. E., & Li, P. (2007). Age of acquisition: Its neural and computational mechanisms. *Psychological Bulletin*, *133*(4), 638. https://doi.org/10.1037/0033-2909.133.4.638
Hirosh, Z., & Degani, T. (2018). Direct and indirect effects of multilingualism on novel language learning: An integrative review. *Psychonomic Bulletin & Review*, *25*(3), 892–916. https://doi.org/10.3758/s13423-017-1315-7
Hopp, H., Vogelbacher, M., Kieseier, T., & Thoma, D. (2019). Bilingual advantages in early foreign language learning: Effects of the minority and the majority language. *Learning and Instruction*, *61*, 99–110. https://doi.org/10.1016/j.learninstruc.2019.02.001
Hurtado, A., & Vega, L. A. (2004). Shift happens: Spanish and English transmission between parents and their children. *Journal of Social Issues*, *60*(1), 137–155. https://doi.org/10.1111/j.0022-4537.2004.00103.x
Iluz-Cohen, P., & Armon-Lotem, S. (2013). Language proficiency and executive control in bilingual children. *Bilingualism: Language and Cognition*, *16*(4), 2013, 884–899. https://doi.org/10.1017/S1366728912000788
Ismail, F. Y., Fatemi, A., & Johnston, M. V. (2017). Cerebral plasticity: Windows of opportunity in the developing brain. *European Journal of Paediatric Neurology*, *21*(1), 23–48. https://doi.org/10.1016/j.ejpn.2016.07.007
Jones, G., Gobet, F., & Pine, J. M. (2007). Linking working memory and long-term memory: A computational model of the learning of new words. *Developmental Science*, *10*(6), 853–873. https://doi.org/10.1111/j.1467-7687.2007.00638.x
Kaiser, A., Eppenberger, L. S., Smieskova, R., Borgwardt, S., Kuenzli, E., Radue, E. W., Nitsch, C., & Bendfeldt, K. (2015). Age of second language acquisition in multilinguals has an impact on gray matter volume in language-associated brain areas. *Frontiers in Psychology*, *6*, 638. https://doi.org/10.3389/fpsyg.2015.00638

Kalia, V., Wilbourn, M. P., & Ghio, K. (2014). Better early or late? Examining the influence of age of exposure and language proficiency on executive function in early and late bilinguals. *Journal of Cognitive Psychology*, *26*(7), 699–713. https://doi.org/10.1080/20445911.2014.956748

Kaushanskaya, M., & Prior, A. (2015). Variability in the effects of bilingualism on cognition: It is not just about cognition, it is also about bilingualism. *Bilingualism: Language and Cognition*, *18*(1), 27–28. http://doi.org/10.1017/S1366728914000510

Kelleher, A. (2010). *Heritage briefs. Center for applied linguistics: Heritage languages in America*. www.cal.org/heritage/research/briefs.html

Kersten, K. (2023, this volume). The proximity of stimulation hypothesis: Investigating the interplay of social and instructional variables with the cognitive-linguistic skills of young L2 learners. In K. Kersten & A. Winsler (Eds.), *Understanding variability in second language acquisition, bilingualism, and cognition – A multi-layered perspective*. Routledge.

Kersten, K., & Greve, W. (2023, this volume). Investigating influencing factors of cognitive-linguistic development in SLA: Challenges for empirical research. In K. Kersten & A. Winsler (Eds.), *Interplay of variables in cognitive-linguistic development – A multi-layered perspective*. Routledge.

Keshavarz, M. H., & Astaneh, H. (2004). The impact of bilinguality on the learning of English vocabulary as a foreign language (L3). *International Journal of Bilingual Education and Bilingualism*, *7*(4), 295–302. https://doi.org/10.1080/13670050408667814

Kidd, E., Donnelly, S., & Christiansen, M. H. (2018). Individual differences in language acquisition and processing. *Trends in Cognitive Sciences*, *22*(2), 154–169. https://doi.org/10.1016/j.tics.2017.11.006

Kim, Y. K., Curby, T. W., & Winsler, A. (2014). Child, family, and school characteristics related to English proficiency development among low-income, dual language learners. *Developmental Psychology*, *50*(12), 2600–2613. https://doi.org/10.1037/a0038050

Knutson, E. (2006). Cross-cultural awareness for second/foreign language learners. *Canadian Modern Language Review*, *62*(4), 591–610. https://doi.org/10.1353/cml.2006.0037

Kuhl, P. K. (2010). Brain mechanisms in early language acquisition. *Neuron*, *67*(5), 713–727. https://doi.org/10.1016/j.neuron.2010.08.038

Larsen-Freeman, D. L., & Cameron, L. (2008). Research methodology on language development from a complex systems perspective. *The Modern Language Journal*, *92*(2), 200–213. https://doi.org/10.1111/j.1540-4781.2008.00714.x

Le Pichon, E., de Swart, H., Vorstman, J., & van den Bergh, H. (2010). Influence of context of learning a language on the strategic competence of children. *International Journal of Bilingualism*, *14*(4), 447–465. https://doi.org/10.1177/1367006910370921

LeBuffe, P. A., & Naglieri, J. A. (1999). The Devereux early childhood assessment (DECA): A measure of within-child protective factors in preschool children. *NHSA Dialog: A Research-to-Practice Journal for the Early Intervention Field*, *3*(1), 75–80. https://doi.org/10.1207/s19309325nhsa0301_10

Leeman, J. (2015). Heritage language education and identity in the United States. *Annual Review of Applied Linguistics*, *35*, 100–119. https://doi.org/10.1017/S0267190514000245

Leeuw, E. D., & Bogulski, C. A. (2016). Frequent L2 language use enhance executive control in bilinguals. *Bilingualism: Language and Cognition*, *19*(5), 907–913. https://doi.org/10.1017/S1366728916000201

Lehtonen, M., Soveri, A., Laine, A., Järvenpää, J., de Bruin, A., & Antfolk, J. (2018). Is bilingualism associated with enhanced executive functioning in adults? A meta-analytic review. *Psychological Bulletin*, *144*(4), 394–425. https://doi.org/10.1037/bul0000142

Lemke, L. A. (1993). *Foreign language enrollment and the attrition rates in the Grand Blanc community schools*. https://files.eric.ed.gov/fulltext/ED366212.pdf

Li, S. (2015). The associations between language aptitude and second language grammar acquisition: A meta-analytic review of five decades of research. *Applied Linguistics*, *36*(3), 385–408. https://doi.org/10.1093/applin/amu054

Lonigan, C. J., Anthony, J. L., Phillips, B. M., Purpura, D. J., Wilson, S. B., & McQueen, J. D. (2009). The nature of preschool phonological processing abilities and their relations to vocabulary, general cognitive abilities, and print knowledge. *Journal of Educational Psychology*, *101*(2), 345. https://doi.org/10.1037/a0013837

Luk, G., & Bialystok, E. (2013). Bilingualism is not a categorical variable: Interaction between language proficiency and usage. *Journal of Cognitive Psychology*, *25*(5), 605–621. https://doi.org/10.1080/20445911.2013.795574

Maluch, J. T., Kempert, S., Neumann, M., & Stanat, P. (2015). The effect of speaking a minority language at home on foreign language learning. *Learning and Instruction*, *36*, 76–85. https://doi.org/10.1016/j.learninstruc.2014.12.001

Maluch, J. T., Neumann, M., & Kempert, S. (2016). Bilingualism as a resource for foreign language learning of language minority students? Empirical evidence from a longitudinal study during primary and secondary school in Germany. *Learning and Individual Differences*, *51*, 111–118. https://doi.org/10.1016/j.lindif.2016.09.001

Mamiya, P. C., Richards, T. L., Coe, B. P., Eichler, E. E., & Kuhl, P. K. (2016). Brain white matter structure and COMT gene are linked to second-language learning in adults. *Proceedings of the National Academy of Sciences*, *113*(26), 7249–7254. http://doi.org/10.1073/pnas.1606602113

Mayberry, R. I., Lock, E., & Kazmi, H. (2002). Linguistic ability and early language exposure. *Nature*, *417*(6884), 38–38. https://doi.org/10.1038/417038a

Met, M., & Brandt, A. M. (2017). Foreign language learning in K-12 classrooms in the USA. In N. Van Deusen-Scholl & S. May (Eds.), *Second and foreign language education* (3rd ed., pp. 357–370). Springer International Publishing. https://doi.org/10.1007/978-3-319-02246-8_17

National Center for Education Statistics. (2018). *Digest of education statistics*. https://nces.ed.gov/programs/digest/d17/tables/dt17_204.20.asp

Nehring, A. D., Nehring, E. F., Bruni, J. R., & Randolph, P. L. (1992). *Learning accomplishment profile – Diagnostic standardized assessment*. Kaplan Press.

Nguyen, M. V. H. (2020). *Early bilingualism and foreign language learning in secondary school* (Master thesis), George Mason University. Mason Archival Repository Service. http://hdl.handle.net/1920/11932

Nguyen, M. V. H., & Winsler, A. (2021). *Early bilingualism and foreign language learning in secondary school* [Manuscript submitted for publication]. Department of Psychology, George Mason University.

Novick, J. M., Hussey, E., Teubner-Rhodes, S., Harbison, J. I., & Bunting, M. F. (2014). Clearing the garden-path: Improving sentence processing through cognitive control training. *Language, Cognition and Neuroscience*, *29*(2), 186–217. https://doi.org/10.1080/01690965.2012.758297

Paap, K. R., Johnson, H. A., & Sawi, O. (2015). Bilingual advantages in executive functioning either do not exist or are restricted to very specific and undetermined circumstances. *Cortex*, *69*, 265–278. https://doi.org/10.1016/j.cortex.2015.04.014

Petitto, L. A., Berens, M. S., Kovelman, I., Dubins, M. H., Jasinska, K., & Shalinsky, M. (2012). The "perceptual wedge hypothesis" as the basis for bilingual babies' phonetic processing advantage: New insights from fNIRS brain imaging. *Brain and Language*, *121*(2), 130–143. https://doi.org/10.1016/j.bandl.2011.05.003

Pliatsikas, C. (2020). Understanding structural plasticity in the bilingual brain: The dynamic restructuring model. In *Bilingualism* (Vol. 23, Issue 2, pp. 459–471). Cambridge University Press. https://doi.org/10.1017/S1366728919000130

Pliatsikas, C., Moschopoulou, E., & Saddy, D. (2017). Immersive late bilingualism reshapes the core of the brain. *Brain Structure and Function*, *222*(4), 1785–1795. https://doi.org/10.1007/s00429-016-1307-9

Poarch, G. J., & van Hell, J. G. (2012). Executive functions and inhibitory control in multilingual children: Evidence from second-language learners, bilinguals, and trilinguals. *Journal of Experimental Child Psychology*, *113*(4), 535–551. https://doi/org/10.1016/j.jecp.2012.06.013

Pratt, C. (2012). Are African-American high school students less motivated to learn Spanish than other ethnic groups? *Hispania*, *95*(1), 116–134. https://doi.org/10.2307/41440366

Pufahl, I., & Rhodes, N. (2011). Foreign language instruction in U.S. schools: Results of a national survey of elementary and secondary schools. *Foreign Language Annals*, *44*(2), 258–288. https://doi.org/10.1111/j.1944-9720.2011.01130.x

Rahmani, F., Sobhani, S., & Aarabi, M. H. (2017). Sequential language learning and language immersion in bilingualism: Diffusion MRI connectometry reveals microstructural evidence. *Experimental Brain Research*, *235*(10), 2935–2945. https://doi.org/10.1007/s00221-017-5029-x

Rozell, N., Winsler, A., & Serafini, E. (2018). *Elementary school outcomes associated with faster English language acquisition for dual language learners*. Poster presented at the National Conference on Undergraduate Research (NCUR).

Saint-Aubin, J., Hilchey, M. D., Mishra, R., Singh, N., Savoie, D., Guitard, D., & Klein, R. M. (2018). Does the relation between the control of attention and second language proficiency generalize from India to Canada? *Canadian Journal of Experimental Psychology/Revue Canadienne de Psychologie Expérimentale*, *72*(3), 208–218. https://doi.org/10.1037/cep0000151

Sanz, C. (2000). Bilingual education enhances third language acquisition: Evidence from Catalonia. *Applied Psycholinguistics*, *21*(1), 23–44. https://doi.org/10.1017/S0142716400001028

Schwartz, M., Geva, E., Share, D. L., & Leikin, M. (2007). Learning to read in English as third language: The cross-linguistic transfer of phonological processing skills. *Written Language & Literacy*, *10*(1), 25–52. https://doi.org/10.1075/wll.10.1.03sch

Serafini, E. J., & Sanz, C. (2016). Evidence for the decreasing impact of cognitive ability on second language development as proficiency increases. *Studies in Second Language Acquisition*, *38*(4), 607–646. https://doi.org/10.1017/S0272263115000327

Singh, L. (2018). He said, she said: Effects of bilingualism on cross-talker word recognition in infancy. *Journal of Child Language*, *45*(2), 498–510. https://doi.org/10.1017/S0305000917000186

Skutnabb-Kangas, T., & McCarty, T. L. (2008). Key concepts in bilingual education: Ideological, historical, epistemological, and empirical foundations. *Encyclopedia of Language and Education*, *5*(17), 1466–1482.

Sparks, R. L. (2016). Myths about foreign language learning and learning disabilities. *Foreign Language Annals*, *49*(2), 252–270. https://doi.org/10.1111/flan.12196

Stocco, A., & Prat, C. S. (2014). Bilingualism trains specific brain circuits involved in flexible rule selection and application. *Brain and Language*, *137*, 50–61. http://doi.org/10.1016/j.bandl.2014.07.005

Stocco, A., Yamasaki, B., Natalenko, R., & Prat, C. S. (2014). Bilingual brain training: A neurobiological framework of how bilingual experience improves executive function. *International Journal of Bilingualism*, *18*(1), 67–92. http://doi.org/10.1177/1367006912456617

Sung, H., Padilla, A. M., & Silva, D. M. (2006). Foreign language education, academic performance, and socioeconomic status: A study of California schools. *Foreign Language Annals*, *39*(1), 115–130. https://doi.org/10.1111/j.1944-9720.2006.tb02253.x

Swanson, M. R., Donovan, K., Paterson, S., Wolff, J. J., Parish-Morris, J., Meera, S. S., Watson, L. R., Estes, A. M., Marrus, N., Elison, J. T., Shen, M. D., McNeilly, H. B., MacIntyre, L., Zwaigenbaum, L., St. John, T., Botteron, K., Dagger, S., & Piven, J. (2019). Early language exposure supports later language skills in infants with and without autism. *Autism Research*, *12*(12), 1784–1795. https://doi.org/10.1002/aur.2163

Tedick, D. J., & Wesely, P. M. (2015). A review of research on content-based foreign/second language education in US K-12 contexts. *Language, Culture and Curriculum*, *28*(1), 25–40. https://doi.org/10.1080/07908318.2014.1000923

Thompson, A. S. (2017). Language learning motivation in the United States: An examination of language choice and multilingualism. *The Modern Language Journal*, *101*(3), 483–500. https://doi.org/10.1111/modl.12409

Tse, C. S., & Arriba, J. A. (2015). Local and global task switching costs in bilinguals who vary in second language proficiency. *American Journal of Psychology*, *128*(1), 89–106. https://doi.org/10.5406/amerjpsyc.128.1.0089

U.S. Census Bureau. (2017). *Language spoken at home of Miami-Dade County, Florida, 2013–2017 American community survey 5-year estimates*. https://factfinder.census.gov/

van der Slik, F. W., van Hout, R. W., & Schepens, J. J. (2015). The gender gap in second language acquisition: Gender differences in the acquisition of Dutch among immigrants from 88 countries with 49 mother tongues. *PloS One*, *10*(11), e0142056. https://doi.org/10.1371/journal.pone.0142056

Weisleder, A., & Fernald, A. (2013). Talking to children matters: Early language experience strengthens processing and builds vocabulary. *Psychological Science*, *24*(11), 2143–2152. https://doi.org/10.1177/0956797613488145

Wenger, E., Brozzoli, C., Lindenberger, U., & Lövdén, M. (2017). Expansion and renormalization of human brain structure during skill acquisition.

Trends in Cognitive Sciences, *21*(12), 930–939. https://doi.org/10.1016/j.tics.2017.09.008

Wight, M. C. S. (2015). Students with learning disabilities in the foreign language learning environment and the practice of exemption. *Foreign Language Annals*, *48*(1), 39–55. https://doi.org/10.1111/flan.12122

Winsler, A. (2023, this volume). Becoming bilingual in Miami, USA: Predictors and outcomes of speed of English acquisition for low-income, dual-language learners. In K. Kersten & A. Winsler (Eds.), *Understanding variability in second language acquisition, bilingualism, and cognition – A multi-layered perspective*. Routledge.

Winsler, A., Kim, Y. K., & Richard, E. R. (2014). Socio-emotional skills, behavior problems, and Spanish competence predict the acquisition of English among English language learners in poverty. *Developmental Psychology*, *50*(9), 2242. https://doi.org/10.1037/a0037161

Winsler, A., Tran, H., Hartman, S. C., Madigan, A. L., Manfra, L., & Bleiker, C. (2008). School readiness gains made by ethnically diverse children in poverty attending center-based childcare and public school pre-kindergarten programs. *Early Childhood Research Quarterly*, *23*(3), 314–329. https://doi.org/10.1016/j.ecresq.2008.02.003

Woodard, K., Pozzan, L., & Trueswell, J. C. (2016). Taking your own path: Individual differences in executive function and language processing skills in child learners. *Journal of Experimental Child Psychology*, *141*, 187–209. https://doi.org/10.1016/j.jecp.2015.08.005

Yow, W. Q., & Li, X. (2015). Balanced bilingualism and early age of second language acquisition as the underlying mechanisms of a bilingual executive control advantage: Why variations in bilingual experiences matter. *Frontiers in Psychology*, 6, 164. https://doi.org/10.3389/fpsyg.2015.00164

Zimmerman, B. J. (2000). Attaining self-regulation: A social cognitive perspective. In *Handbook of self-regulation* (pp. 13–39). Elsevier Inc. https://doi.org/10.1016/B978-012109890-2/50031-7

9 From differential to dynamic

The role of working memory in second language (L2) learning

Ellen J. Serafini

Introduction

In instructed settings, two learners may be exposed to a similar quality and quantity of input in a second language (L2) and have comparable opportunities to engage in communicative practice and output, but their learning trajectories and outcomes are likely to look quite different. This variability contrasts sharply with acquiring a first language (L1) under naturalistic, "optimal" conditions, which typically involves rich, meaningful, and sustained exposure to language and results in a relatively uniform ability to understand and use that language across contexts and for a variety of purposes. With this in mind, language acquisition researchers have endeavored to theorize and explain the "logical problem" (Bley-Vroman, 1989) of language learning in both childhood and adulthood, though the nature of the problem differs in each case. In L1 acquisition, the question arises from the fact that the linguistic data to which children are exposed cannot fully account for their ultimate knowledge and attainment (i.e., they do not simply repeat what they hear); on the other hand, the root of the "problem" in instructed L2 learning lies in explaining why learners vary so much in their ability to understand and use the target language, no matter how similar the learning conditions.

In this sense, variability is the rule rather than the exception, which has prompted decades of second language acquisition (SLA) research seeking to address the "differential success" question (Larsen-Freeman, 2001, 2018). A driving focus to emerge out of this line of research has been the extent to which learner individual differences (IDs) are related to and can explain this variability (see, for example, many scholarly overviews on the topic – Ackerman, 2003; Altman, 1980; Bowden et al., 2005; Dörnyei, 2005; Dörnyei & Ryan, 2015; Dörnyei & Skehan, 2003; Ellis, 2008; Gardner & Lambert, 1972; Granena et al., 2016; Larsen-Freeman & Long, 1991; Miyake & Friedman, 1998; Roberts & Meyer, 2012; Robinson, 2001, 2002; Sagarra, 2013; Saito et al., 2020; Sanz, 2005; Sawyer & Ranta, 2001; Skehan, 1991, 1998, 2002, 2012).

Most of the learner IDs investigated in SLA originate in cognitive and educational psychology and are broadly viewed as a systematic and

DOI: 10.4324/9781003155683-11

stable deviation from some norm, or "dimensions of enduring personal characteristics that are assumed to apply to everybody and on which people differ by degree" (Dörnyei, 2005, p. 4). In SLA, IDs matter not only for theory but also for research and practice as they refine our hypotheses and predictions about language-related phenomena (Skehan, 1991). Also incorporating them as in-/dependent variables in our research designs can increase the validity, reliability, and generalizability of findings, which can be used to more effectively differentiate L2 instruction based on differences in learners' cognitive resources (Roberts & Meyer, 2012).

While early studies aimed to construct "good language learner" profiles based on successful language learning strategies (Rubin, 1975), over time, it has become clear that there are multiple routes to language learning success (Griffiths, 2008) and a multitude of factors that constrain L2 attainment (Saito et al., 2020). To date, the two most researched and powerful IDs to emerge in terms of consistent and robust relationships with L2 development are *L2 motivation* (Gardner, 1985, 2001, 2010; Gardner & Lambert, 1972; Dörnyei, 2005, 2009a; Dörnyei & Ushioda, 2009) and *L2 aptitude* (Carroll & Sapon, 1959; Li, 2016; Robinson, 2002, 2005; Sawyer & Ranta, 2001; Skehan, 1998, 2012). The core components of the latter, traditionally defined as rote learning, phonetic coding, and grammatical sensitivity, have come to be dominantly viewed in terms of the key construct of working memory (WM) capacity, broadly defined as "those mechanisms or processes that are involved in the control, regulation, and active maintenance of task-relevant information in the service of complex cognition" (Miyake & Shah, 1999, p. 450).

The current chapter provides a critical synthesis of the evidence for the relationship between WM and L2 development based on 30 years of empirical inquiry. While the majority of studies report relatively strong or moderate effects, others report weak relationships or no effects. This differential impact has been attributed to moderating factors like L2 proficiency (Serafini, 2021; Serafini & Sanz, 2016) and the nature of the learning context (Grey et al., 2015). However, little research has investigated the role of WM in L2 learning from a dynamic perspective that views WM as a complex, ever-changing, context-dependent construct embedded within other complex dynamic systems (Jackson, 2020; Serafini, 2017; Simmering & Perone, 2013). It is argued here that conceptual tools afforded by complex dynamic systems theory (CDST) (Larsen-Freeman, 1997, 2002, 2012; Larsen-Freeman & Cameron, 2008a; van Geert, 2008; Verspoor et al., 2008, 2011) can shed light on and reframe these "contradictory" findings. The chapter concludes by recommending future directions in research that advances calls to focalize the dynamic properties of learner IDs (Dörnyei, 2009b, 2010, 2017; Dörnyei & Ryan, 2015; Gurzynski-Weiss, 2020) and implement longitudinal research designs that align with CDST principles (Hiver & Al-Hoorie, 2016, 2020; Hiver et al., 2021).

L2 learning as complex cognition

Before considering the role of WM in L2 development, it is useful to first consider the aspects that make language learning a complex cognitive process. Similar to acquiring an L1, L2 learners must perceive, remember, attend to, analyze, and generalize different aspects of incoming input and process linguistic sequences or chunks in a linear fashion (Ellis, 1996, 2001). However, while carrying out these tasks in the L1 is relatively automatic and happens without conscious awareness, L2 learning is more effortful, controlled, and, many would argue, a partly conscious process that is constrained by adult L2 learners' cognitive maturity and limited capacity to process input (McLaughlin, 1987). These characteristics make it similar to learning other complex cognitive skills that become more automatic over time with sufficient practice and sustained opportunities to use the target language in instructed and authentic contexts (DeKeyser, 1997, 2015), similar to learning to drive a car.

Most influentially conceived as a mental workspace where we code, store, process, and retrieve verbal information (Baddeley, 2000, 2007, 2010; Baddeley & Hitch, 1974), working memory (WM) has been posited as a key mechanism underlying the ability to simultaneously comprehend and produce language (Miyake & Friedman, 1998), whether in the L1, L2, L3, etc. However, many scholars in SLA have argued that, in contrast to acquiring a "native" language or languages, L2 learners experience a greater cognitive load in processing and producing the L2, and thus IDs in cognitive resources play a more prominent role (McLaughlin, 1987; Miyake & Friedman, 1998).

Since Harrington and Sawyer (1992) first reported a significant association between WM and L2 reading comprehension, following Daneman and Carpenter's (1980) seminal study of the role of WM in L1 reading comprehension, an active line of empirical research has developed, culminating in several reviews (Granena et al., 2016; Juffs & Harrington, 2011; Sagarra, 2013; Sanz & Serafini, 2018; Wen, 2012; Williams, 2012, 2015), meta-analyses and systematic research syntheses (Adesope et al., 2010; Linck et al., 2014; Shin, 2020; Watanabe & Bergsleithner, 2006), and books devoted to the topic (e.g., Wen, 2016; Wen et al., 2015). The following section briefly considers the main theoretical models and measurements of WM in SLA research, followed by a critical synthesis of previous research.

Dominant models of working memory

Like many ID constructs, the theoretical models of WM that are dominant in SLA originate within the fields of cognitive and developmental psychology. All models posit that the construct of WM underlies everyday tasks that involve the processing, storing, and retrieving of information necessary for carrying out complex cognitive actions (Miyake,

2001; Miyake & Shah, 1999; Sagarra, 2013; Wen, 2012, 2016; Wen et al., 2015). However, as Sagarra (2013) notes, among the multiple WM models that have emerged since the 1960s, key differences lie in whether WM is conceived to be a domain-specific or a domain-general construct and how cognitive resources are allocated.

Domain-specific models include Baddeley and colleagues' multiple-resource model (Baddeley, 1986, 2000, 2003, 2007, 2010; Baddeley & Hitch, 1974; Baddeley & Logie, 1999) and Just and Carpenter's (1992) capacity theory. In contrast to Just and Carpenter, who posit a trade-off between processing and storage due to competing for a shared and limited pool of resources, the Baddeleyan model posits specialized, independent processing and storage components consisting of two domain-specific storage systems, the phonological loop (i.e., phonological working memory, PWM) that handles phonological and verbal information and has a span of about 1 to 2 seconds (Baddeley, 1986, 2003) and a visuospatial sketchpad that processes visual and spatial information. A domain-general central executive system (i.e., executive function, EF) is responsible for directing attention and controlling information in each store, including inhibiting, switching, and ignoring information. An episodic buffer communicates with storage components and encodes and retrieves information from long-term memory.

Domain-general, or domain-free, models such as Cowan's embedded-processes model (Cowan, 2005) and Engle and colleagues' controlled-attention model (Engle, Kane et al., 1999; Engle, Tuholski et al., 1999) rely on a domain-general attentional construct to explain limitations in WM that constrain L2 learning (for a summary, see Jackson, 2020, p. 92). Specifically, attentional resources are controlled and allocated or regulated by a central element; if not actively rehearsed, information is subject to interference or decay (Miyake, 2001; Miyake & Shah, 1999). In each model, an executive attentional control mechanism plays a key role in determining which external stimuli become focalized and enter conscious awareness (Cowan's model) and in carrying out controlled processing or maintaining focus on task-relevant information in the presence of interfering or distracting stimuli (Engle and colleagues' model).

While models differ in what they conceive as the main source(s) of variance in an individual's WM capacity, Wen (2012) notes key similarities across models in that the construct of WM is not unitary but has a structure; WM has a limited capacity to perform its functions; and WM interacts with long-term memory, essentially acting as a "gateway" (p. 3). In SLA, the most influential and durable model over the years is arguably the domain-specific, multiple-resource system developed by Baddeley and colleagues, particularly the role of EF and PWM, which are the two most widely researched WM components in terms of their effects on L2 development (Wen et al., 2015). Importantly, variation in these WM components is greatly influenced by how they are measured, and variable methodological features of WM tasks have been reported to moderate the relationship between WM and different facets of L2 development, such as L2 reading comprehension (Shin, 2020).

Dominant measures of working memory

In both cognitive psychology and SLA, variation in WM is typically measured via complex span tasks with dual-task demands that aim to push a learner's WM to its limit. Dual-task demands are argued to more sufficiently capture variation (Logie, 2011) and accurately indicate the amount of available resources that remain after meeting the processing requirements of the task (Miyake, 2001). As opposed to short-term memory tasks such as the word span or digit span that require participants to passively store target items in memory, complex span tasks impose simultaneous processing and storage demands that align with the construal of WM as an active workspace where task-relevant processing and storage activities dynamically take place (Miyake & Shah, 1999).

To tap the EF component of WM, many L2 studies have adopted complex span tasks from cognitive psychology (Conway et al., 2005). Complex span tasks can require subjects to maintain target items (a word like Cat or a letter like A) in memory while processing the meaning of sentences they read or hear, as in the verbal Reading and Listening span tasks (RSpan/LSpan – Daneman & Carpenter, 1980; Waters & Caplan, 1996), or calculating a simple mathematical operation (e.g., 4 + 4 = 8 >> Yes/No) as required by the nonverbal Operation span (OSpan – Turner & Engle, 1989; Unsworth et al., 2005).

The language in which a complex span task is administered is a key aspect to consider given that carrying out a complex span task in one's L2 could lead to a confound with L2 proficiency (Van den Noort et al., 2006). That is, if someone is skilled at language processing and has high proficiency, then fulfilling the concurrent processing requirement of the RSpan or OSpan task will consume a smaller amount of resources, enabling her to allocate more leftover resources to maintaining target items (e.g., letters) in memory. In contrast, someone with lower L2 proficiency will be significantly taxed by the processing requirement, making the complex span task a measure of their language skills rather than their WM capacity. Further, nonverbal tasks like the OSpan are argued to be preferable to verbal tasks like the RSpan to avoid a potential confound with verbal processing (Engle, 2002; Wen, 2012).

To measure PWM, or the ability to encode and store acoustic sounds in the target language, repetition tasks aim to assess the ability to form and maintain a mental representation of spoken material so that it can be immediately accessed and accurately repeated back aloud or silently rehearsed (Service, 1992). More recent studies have begun to employ a version of the nonword span task (Gathercole, 2006), which involves recognition followed by repetition. Many L2 studies have also used the nonverbal digit span or word span task which involves the immediate serial recall of numbers or words. As Wen (2012) and others argue, the nonword span task better "approximates the complex nature of the construct of PWM" (p. 5) by also tapping into the articulatory component of PWM.

Overall, variation and inconsistencies in the measurement of these components across studies lead to mixed findings regarding the magnitude of WM effects in L2 development. For example, Sagarra (2017) reported that WM was only a significant predictor of L2 grammar and reading development when a taxing processing component was incorporated in the WM test. One key issue with WM measurement is that most L2 studies only measure it at one point in time rather than longitudinally. As Jackson (2020) argues, "longitudinal studies of WM and L2 outcomes, which are relatively scarce, have typically measured WM at a fixed time point, using repeated measures only for the L2 variable" (p. 100). As will be argued in a subsequent section, this is a limited construal of WM as a static, fixed construct and obscures its sensitivity to context, change, and its dynamic interrelationships with other ID constructs (Serafini, 2017).

Working memory and L2 development: critically considering the evidence

As reviewed earlier, processing and communicating information in a nonprimary language is initially a slow and effortful process that speeds up and gets more efficient over time given sufficient frequency and quality of practice and contextualized use (DeKeyser, 2015; Segalowitz, 2003). The ability to attend to both form and meaning in the input is key in determining what is potentially restructured and internalized into the developing language system (Leow, 2015). Thus, it is not surprising that many researchers subscribe to some form of the *more is better* hypothesis (Miyake & Friedman, 1998) under the logic that "the more WM you have, presumably the more attentional resources you possess and the more you can potentially learn, because you have enough memory to process form together with meaning" (Juffs & Harrington, 2011, p. 147).

Over the last few decades, an impressive body of cumulative research has investigated whether the *more is better* hypothesis holds true in relation to a range of aspects of L2 development. Table 9.1 provides a comprehensive look at the various strands of inquiry that have developed over the years along with a representative sample of research that has investigated these phenomena.

In these various lines of inquiry, most studies, but not all (Grey et al., 2015; Juffs, 2005), report positive effects of WM in facilitating L2 development. Further, the different components of WM (PWM and EF) are found to be differentially involved with different aspects of L2 performance and development (vocabulary, grammar acquisition) and with the development of specific L2 skills (e.g., listening, reading, speaking, writing) (Wen, 2012). One of the most prominent areas of research has

Table 9.1 Areas of inquiry into the role of WM in L2 development

WM & Area of L2 Development	*Representative Studies*
L2 reading comprehension	(Alptekin & Erçetin, 2010; Alptekin et al., 2014; Harrington & Sawyer, 1992; Leeser, 2007; Shin, 2020*; Shin et al., 2019)
L2 morphosyntax	(Coughlin & Tremblay, 2013; Dussias & Piñar, 2010; Foote, 2011; Grey et al., 2015; Havik et al., 2009; Juffs, 2004, 2005; Kempe & Brooks, 2008; Kempe et al., 2010; Linck et al., 2014*; Linck & Weiss, 2011; Nowbakht, 2019; Sagarra, 2017; Sagarra & Herschensohn, 2010; Serafini & Sanz, 2016; Williams & Lovatt, 2003)
Corrective oral or written L2 feedback	(Goo, 2012; Kim et al., 2015; Li & Roshan, 2019; Mackey et al., 2002 et al., 2010; Mackey & Sachs, 2012; Sagarra, 2007)
L2 listening comprehension	(Andringa et al., 2012)
L2 pronunciation or accent	(Mattys & Baddeley, 2019; Simard et al., 2020)
L2 oral proficiency or oral production	(Fehringer & Fry, 2007; Gilabert & Muñoz, 2010; Granena & Yilmaz, 2019; O'Brien et al., 2006; Park et al., 2020; Payne & Ross, 2005; Wen, 2012)
L2 lexical comprehension or production	(Cheung, 1996; Grey et al., 2015; Linck et al., 2008; Sunderman & Kroll, 2009; Tokowicz et al., 2004)
L2 writing	(Abu-Rabia, 2003; Johnson, 2020; Michel et al., 2019)
L2 vocabulary	(Lee et al., 2020; Martin & Ellis, 2012; Perez, 2020; Ruíz et al., 2019)
L2 pragmatic abilities	(Ahmadian, 2020; Li, 2017; Taguchi, 2008)
Type of instructional condition	(Ahmadian, 2020; Ruíz et al., 2019; Sanz et al., 2014)
L2 task features (complexity, modality, planning)	(Li & Fu, 2018; Zabildea, 2017; Zabildea & Sanz, 2020)
Overall L2 abilities as measured on general proficiency or placement tests	(Gilabert & Muñoz, 2010; Hummel, 2009; Kormos & Sáfár, 2008; Winke, 2005)

Note: * denotes a meta-analysis.

Note: Other lines of research not included in Table 9.1 have investigated the existence of a bilingual advantage, or whether language experience or degree of bilingualism impacts cognitive ability (WM, executive function, inhibitory control; see Festman et al. in the current volume) as well as the question of WM trainability (see Jackson, 2020 for an overview).

focused on the role of WM in the acquisition of L2 morphosyntax. In particular, researchers have explored to what extent variation in the ability to temporarily store and process incoming information (i.e., the EF component) and to code and store acoustic sounds (i.e., PWM) underlies the ability to process word order or different syntactic movements (i.e., *wh-* movement in question formation) or to accurately understand or produce gender and number agreement in Romance languages like Spanish or case marking in Slavic languages like Russian. These areas can be especially challenging for learners whose L1 does not have those same features, potentially increasing a reliance on WM which is posited to underlie the chunking of linguistic sequences (Ellis, 1996). However, several methodological and learner variables have been shown to mediate this relationship.

Linck et al. (2014) published the first meta-analysis on the topic and specifically investigated which variables may moderate the relationship between WM and L2 comprehension and production. They analyzed 748 correlation effect sizes reported in 79 published and unpublished studies (N = 3,707 participants) and included covariates such as specific characteristics of cognitive tasks (e.g., verbal vs. nonverbal), criterion measures (e.g., skills tested), and participants (e.g., less proficient vs. highly proficient). The meta-analysis showed a robust positive association between WM and L2 processing and proficiency outcomes (estimated population effect size, ρ = .255), meaning the more efficient the WM resources a learner has, the better their language outcomes. The covariate analyses also revealed larger effect sizes for the executive function component of WM and for verbal (vs. nonverbal) measures of WM. Importantly, however, effect sizes were similar across lower and higher levels of L2 proficiency. Nonetheless, the authors confirmed previous critiques (Tremblay, 2011) that studies included in the meta-analysis differed greatly in how they described and/or quantified the construct of L2 proficiency in their samples and called for more empirical research to clarify the contributions of WMC at earlier and later stages of L2 learning.

Few studies to date specifically address the question of the differential impact of WM according to L2 proficiency, and even fewer do so from a longitudinal perspective with a focus on within-learner variability. Serafini and Sanz (2016) is one exception that investigated whether the strength of the relationship between WM and L2 learning declines with increasing proficiency. Specifically, the study examined whether EF and PWM components predict the morphosyntactic development of L2 Spanish during and after a semester of instruction for learners at three levels of proficiency (beginning, intermediate, advanced), determined based on both institutional status and the results of an internal placement test. Findings revealed robust relationships, particularly with the PWM component at the two lower proficiency levels only. Further, the impact of cognitive ability was found to be dynamic and variable within the same learners over time, decreasing in strength overall at the end of instruction. At advanced proficiency, WM was not found to play a meaningful role in performance.

Other studies have also reported stronger effects of PWM at lower levels of proficiency. In a study conducted with adult L1 French-L2 English learners, Hummel (2009) found moderate positive correlations between

L1 PWM and L2 English proficiency as measured on a standardized TOEFL-like test tapping L2 vocabulary, grammar, and reading comprehension. Learners were determined to be relatively proficient based on a mean score of 75%, but when learners were divided into higher and lower-proficiency subgroups using a median split, PWM was a significant predictor for low-proficiency learners only.

In contrast, other studies have found a more powerful role for EF but not PWM at beginning levels of proficiency. In a study conducted with adolescent beginning and pre-intermediate L2 learners, Kormos and Sáfár (2008) reported moderate correlations between L1 PWM and overall performance and several subcomponents of a standardized English exam for pre-intermediate L1 Hungarian-L2 English adolescent learners at the end of a one-year intensive program. For the beginning group, the executive function component (EF) but not PWM significantly related to overall performance and to listening, speaking, and reading components (but not writing) and accounted "for as much as 30.25% of the variance in the performance of the complete language test" (p. 266). However, the English test was not administered at the beginning of the study, only at the end, which makes it cross-sectional rather than longitudinal in nature.

At high proficiency, some studies have reported a narrower role for WM. For example, Winke (2005) analyzed beginning and advanced L2 Chinese learners' performance on a Chinese proficiency test and found significant positive relationships between L1 PWM and writing, speaking, and reading abilities for beginners, but only with listening ability for advanced learners. This finding may be attributed, at least in part, to the difficulty of aural comprehension in the target language (L2 Chinese). Other aptitude components (i.e., rote learning, phonetic coding, and grammatical sensitivity) also significantly related to performance at beginning but not advanced L2 proficiency, indicating a broader, more comprehensive role for IDs in cognitive ability for L2 learners at beginning levels of proficiency. In Gilabert and Muñoz (2010), who investigated L1 Spanish/Catalan-L2 English learners' oral production via a film retelling task, no significant relationships were found between L1 WM and overall proficiency (measured via the standardized Oxford Placement Test), but a weak correlation obtained between WMC and fluency and lexical complexity in learner oral narratives. Interestingly, a split-level analysis separating learners into higher and lower levels of proficiency revealed moderate correlations between lexical complexity and WMC only for the higher-proficiency group.

In terms of morphosyntactic development, several studies have not found facilitative effects of WM in advanced learners. For example, Foote (2011) investigated native-like English-Spanish late bilinguals' ability to process subject–verb number and noun–adjective gender agreement errors and reported that L2 WMC did not account for differential sensitivity, though all groups showed similar sensitivity to grammaticality as a function of number and gender agreement distance, which limited variation in reading time scores and thus lessened the likelihood of yielding significant relationships. Juffs (2004, 2005) investigated the processing of temporary syntactic ambiguities and *wh-* movements in L1 Chinese-, Japanese-, and Spanish-L2 English speakers and did not find relationships with either L1 or L2 WMC although low WMC scores (based on storage) were associated with slower reading times. However, the results of learners' standardized test performance were not clearly interpreted and thus the test scores, which varied considerably across L1 groups (Juffs, 2004), do not clearly align with L2 proficiency.

Finally, in one of the few studies to examine the effects of WMC in a study-abroad context (Sunderman & Kroll, 2009), Grey et al. (2015) reported significant gains in morphosyntactic and lexical accuracy and latency in advanced L1 English-L2 Spanish learners over a five-week study-abroad experience but these gains were not related to learners' L1 EF or L1 and L2 PWM. In addition to learners' advanced level of proficiency, the authors attributed this finding to the naturalistic, immersion-like setting, which may have lessened or neutralized the impact of WM.

Future directions in L2 ID research from a complex dynamic perspective

As the current synthesis has shown, there is significant evidence supporting the *more is better* hypothesis in various areas of L2 development. However, findings are not unequivocal, and some have asserted that the importance of WM in L2 learning is overstated (Juffs, 2004). Many researchers have attributed contradictory findings to methodological differences in the studies' design, measurement tasks used, and characteristics of the learner population and learning context. The current chapter argues for moving beyond trying to "explain" disparate findings and moving toward a broader, more holistic approach that reframes the goal of solving the "logical problem" of L2 learning and prompts us to rethink the "differential success" question itself.

A first key step in this endeavor requires questioning traditional conceptualizations of learner IDs as modular (i.e., discrete, separate, isolated), stable, and context-independent traits (Dörnyei, 2009b, 2010; Dörnyei & Ryan, 2015; Larsen-Freeman, 1997, 2001; Jackson, 2020; Serafini, 2017). The principles and conceptual tools afforded within complex dynamic systems theory (CDST) provide crucial guidance in this endeavor under the view that language, cognition, and language learners themselves are complex, dynamic, adaptive systems within which all factors interact and affect one another (Beckner et al., 2009; de Bot et al., 2007a; Larsen-Freeman, 2002, 2015; Larsen-Freeman & Cameron, 2008a; Verspoor et al., 2011).

A complex dynamic system is defined as "a set of variables that mutually affect each other's changes over time" (van Geert, 1994, p. 50). Diane

Larsen-Freeman (1997) was one of the first to propose viewing L2 development as a complex adaptive system that shares many parallel characteristics with complex systems in the natural world, such as a forest ecosystem. In other words, they are "dynamic, complex, nonlinear, chaotic, unpredictable, sensitive to initial conditions, open, self-organizing, feedback sensitive, and adaptive" (p. 142). A key principle of CDST is that the behavior of the whole emerges from the interactions of its parts, which questions "traditional scientific approaches that analyze systems into their components and study them individually" (Larsen-Freeman, 2002, p. 38). Thus, research designs must account for the multiple ways IDs interact with the external environment (Dörnyei, 2010) and with one another (de Bot, 2008; Verspoor et al., 2011), leading to a conceptualization of IDs as higher-order integrated wholes with the potential to act as "powerful attractors" or "stabilizing forces" (Dörnyei, 2010, p. 261).

While research informed by a CDST perspective has increasingly accumulated over the past 25 years (see Hiver et al., 2021, for a recent scoping review), very few studies have applied dynamic principles to understanding interrelationships among IDs. Serafini (2017) is one exception that explored the interconnectedness of learner IDs, specifically working memory and L2 motivation, in instructed L2 learners of Spanish at beginning, intermediate, and advanced proficiency over a semester of instruction. Motivated by the hypothesis that learner resources, or growers (van Geert, 1995), are limited by nature and may amplify and/or compete with one another's effects, Serafini investigated whether relationships among focal IDs were (a) *supportive* (i.e., growers develop in unison because they mutually support and reinforce each other), (b) *competitive* (i.e., growers develop in unison because they compete with one another), (c) *conditional* (i.e., a minimal level of one grower is a necessary precondition for another grower to develop), or (d) *compensatory* (i.e., a low level in one grower can be compensated for by a higher level in another grower) (de Bot, 2008; Verspoor et al., 2011).

Results revealed differential involvement of IDs at different levels of proficiency as well as stability and fluctuation in their interactional patterns. Specifically, the PWM component of WM was more relevant for the two lower-proficiency groups, while EF was significantly related to L2 motivation for advanced learners. Further, all relationships between cognitive and motivational IDs were supportive for the intermediate group and compensatory for the advanced group, while relationships were more variable for beginners, oscillating between conditional and supportive in nature. This key difference was interpreted as the potential emergence of attractor states, or stable states in system behavior, at higher L2 proficiency, resulting from "the propensity to self-organize" (Larsen-Freeman, 2012, p. 209), whereas more fluctuating relationships at low proficiency likely indicate a transitional phase in the developing system (de Bot et al., 2007b; Verspoor et al., 2008).

A few key limitations in the design of this exploratory study can inform future research. First, WM was only measured once at the beginning of instruction, which assumes that this particular cognitive ability is a stable trait that does not fluctuate or interact with contextual variables or other internal or external variables. This stands in contrast to other cognitive abilities such as phonological awareness that are conceived to be less stable and more malleable, as reflected in their measurement (Trebits et al., 2021). Second, relationships were probed over a macro-timescale (i.e., a semester) only, which obscures how relationships may change for individuals over a more micro-level (e.g., seconds, minutes, hours, days, or weeks). Finally, the results do not provide a clear picture of the context dependence of learner IDs in terms of both the more immediate pedagogical context and the broader social context of learning. These methodological shortcomings within a dynamic perspective of learner IDs can be addressed and improved upon by consulting systematic, accessible, guidelines provided by Hiver and Al-Hoorie (2016, 2020) and others (Byrne & Callaghan, 2014; Larsen-Freeman & Cameron, 2008a; Verspoor et al., 2011). In spite of this growing body of methodological resources, see a critique of CDST applications in SLA research in Lenzing et al. (2023, this volume), which typically lack formal mathematical operationalizations of the dynamical systems processes discussed.

In terms of WM, Jackson (2020) builds on work by Simmering and Perone (2013) to provide a provocative discussion that lays out key arguments for conceptualizing and researching WM as a complex, dynamic system. One key area of critique is the tendency in SLA studies to only focus on narrow learner populations (e.g., high school or college-age learners) and to implement cross-sectional designs (Ortega & Byrnes, 2008; Ortega & Iberri-Shea, 2005), which does not "reflect the long-term trajectory of WM development" over the lifespan (Jackson, 2020, p. 90). Thus, Jackson calls for more longitudinal ID research conducted at multiple timescales that probes the context dependence of WM, particularly its prevalence in explicit learning contexts; that underscores the interrelationships between WM and other variables; and that documents variability in WM capacity not only in childhood and adolescence but throughout adulthood. The study also considers how a dynamic perspective of WM can shed light on long-standing, controversial empirical questions such as the bidirectionality issue, traditionally framed as a chicken-or-egg dilemma (i.e., do more efficient WM resources enhance language development or does language learning experience enhance WM function?), and the existence of a "bilingual advantage" in cognition. Jackson urges a broader framing of these issues, one that does not assume or search for simple causal relationships but emphasizes the interconnectedness of all systems, meaning that "when one component changes, another component will change too, and the other way around" (Verspoor & van Dijk, 2011, p. 85, c.f., Jackson, 2020, p. 99).

In sum, the conceptual groundwork is laid for L2 learner ID research to proceed within a CDST framework, but more research is needed that puts these principles into practice. Future studies should endeavor to move beyond the standard approach of controlling for the effects of one ID variable in order to isolate the effects of the other and comparing group-level data with only one or two measurement points. More research is needed that conceptualizes and measures WM holistically, as part of complex ID composites or higher-order trait complexes (Ackerman, 2003; Dörnyei, 2010). More longitudinal case studies are also needed that collect data for all variables of interest with frequent, dense measurement points (Verspoor & Van Dijk, 2011), which allows for complex intraindividual variability to emerge over both macro- and micro-level timescales or primary and secondary scales (Byrne & Callaghan, 2014; de Bot, 2008; de Bot et al., 2007a; Larsen-Freeman & Cameron, 2008b; Verspoor et al., 2008). Some useful methods for analyzing longitudinal data are moving correlation plots (Verspoor et al., 2011), moving min-max graph plots (van Geert & van Dijk, 2002), qualitative modeling (Dörnyei, 2009b; Larsen-Freeman & Cameron, 2008a), and multivariate analyses (Larsen-Freeman, 1997; Saito et al., 2020). As I have argued elsewhere (Serafini, 2021), applying CDST principles and analytical methods in our research design will aid in moving from a focus on explaining differential effects of learner IDs to a focus on highlighting their dynamic, context-dependent, interconnected characteristics with the goal of better understanding their changing role over the course of L2 development.

References

Abu-Rabia, S. (2003). The influence of working memory on reading and creative writing processes in a second language. *Educational Psychology*, *23*(2), 209–222. https://doi.org/10.1080/01443410303227

Ackerman, P. L. (2003). Aptitude complexes and trait complexes. *Educational Psychologist*, *38*, 85–93. https://doi.org/10.1207/S15326985EP3802_3

Adesope, O. O., Lavin, T., Thompson, T., & Ungerleider, C. (2010). A systematic review and meta-analysis of the cognitive correlates of bilingualism. *Review of Educational Research*, *80*(2), 207–245. https://doi.org/10.3102/0034654310368803

Ahmadian, M. J. (2020). Explicit and implicit instruction of refusal strategies: Does working memory capacity play a role? *Language Teaching Research*, *24*(2), 163–188. https://doi.org/10.1177/1362168818783215

Alptekin, C., & Erçetin, G. (2010). The role of L1 and L2 working memory in literal and inferential comprehension in L2 reading. *Journal of Research in Reading*, *33*(2), 206–219. https://doi.org/10.1111/j.1467-9817.2009.01412.x

Alptekin, C., Erçetin, G., & Ozemir, O. (2014). Effects of variation in reading task design on the relationship between working memory capacity and second language reading. *The Modern Language Journal*, *98*(2), 536–552. https://doi.org/10.1111/j.1540-4781.2014.12089.x

Altman, H. (1980). Foreign language teaching: Focus on the learner. In H. Altman & C. Vaughan James (Eds.), *Foreign language teaching: Meeting individual needs* (pp. 1–16). Pergamon.

Andringa, S., Olsthoorn, N., van Beuningen, C., Schoonen, R., & Hulstijn, J. (2012). Determinants of success in native and non-native listening comprehension: An individual differences approach. *Language Learning*, *62*(s2), 49–78. https://doi.org/10.1111/j.1467-9922.2012.00706.x

Baddeley, A. (1986). *Working memory*. Oxford University Press.

Baddeley, A. (2000). The episodic buffer: A new component of working memory? *Trends in Cognitive Sciences*, *4*(11), 417–423. https://doi.org/10.1016/S1364-6613(00)01538-2

Baddeley, A. (2003). Working memory: Looking back and looking forward. *Nature Reviews Neuroscience*, *4*, 829–839. https://doi.org/10.1038/nrn1201

Baddeley, A. (2007). *Working memory, thought, and action*. Oxford University Press. https://doi.org/10.1093/acprof:oso/9780198528012.001.0001

Baddeley, A. (2010). Working memory. *Current Biology*, *20*(4), R136–R140. https://10.1016/j.cub.2009.12.014

Baddeley, A., & Hitch, G. (1974). Working memory. In S. Dornic (Ed.), *Recent advances in learning and motivation* (Vol. VII, pp. 47–89). Academic Press. http://dx.doi.org/10.1016/s0079-7421(08)60452-1

Baddeley, A., & Logie, R. (1999). Working memory: The multiple-component model. In A. Miyake & P. Shah (Eds.), *Models of working memory: Mechanisms of active maintenance and executive control* (pp. 28–61). Cambridge University Press. https://doi.org/10.1017/CBO9781139174909.005

Beckner, C., Blythe, R., Bybee, J., Christiansen, M. H., Croft, W., Ellis, N. C., Holland, J., Ke, H., Larsen-Freeman, D., & Schoenemann, T. (2009). Language is a complex adaptive system: Position paper. *Language Learning*, *59*(s1), 1–26. https://doi.org/10.1111/j.1467-9922.2009.00533.x

Bley-Vroman, R. (1989). What is the logical problem of foreign language learning? In S. M. Gass & J. Schachter (Eds.), *Linguistic perspectives on second language acquisition* (pp. 41–68). Cambridge University Press. https://doi.org/10.1017/CBO9781139524544.005

Bowden, H. W., Sanz, C., & Stafford, C. A. (2005). Individual differences: Age, sex, working memory, and prior knowledge. In C. Sanz (Ed.), *Mind and context in adult second language acquisition: Methods, theory, and practice* (pp. 105–140). Georgetown University Press.

Byrne, D., & Callaghan, G. (2014). *Complexity theory and the social sciences: The state of the art*. Routledge and Taylor & Francis.

Carroll, J. B., & Sapon, S. M. (1959). *Modern language aptitude test (MLAT)*. Psychological Corporation.

Cheung, H. (1996). Nonword span as a unique predictor of second-language vocabulary language. *Developmental Psychology*, *32*(5), 867–873. https://doi.org/10.1037/0012-1649.32.5.867

Conway, A. R. A., Kane, M. J., Bunting, M. F., Hambrick, D. Z., Wilhelm, O., & Engle, R. W. (2005). Working memory span tasks: A methodological review and a user's guide. *Psychonomic Bulletin and Review*, *12*(5), 769–786. https://doi.org/10.3758/BF03196772

Coughlin, C. E., & Tremblay, A. (2013). Proficiency and working memory-based explanations for nonnative speakers' sensitivity to agreement in sentence processing. *Applied Psycholinguistics*, *34*(3), 615–646. https://doi.org/10.1017/S0142716411000890

Cowan, N. (2005). *Working memory capacity*. Psychology Press. https://doi.org/10.4324/9780203342398

Daneman, M., & Carpenter, P. (1980). Individual differences in working memory and reading. *Journal of Verbal Learning and Verbal Behavior*, *19*, 450–466. https://doi.org/10.1016/S0022-5371(80)90312-6

de Bot, K. (2008). Introduction: Second language development as a dynamic process. *Modern Language Journal*, *92*(2), 166–178. https://doi.org/10.1111/j.1540-4781.2008.00712.x

de Bot, K., Lowie, W., & Verspoor, M. (2007a). A dynamic systems theory approach to second language acquisition. *Bilingualism: Language and Cognition*, *10*(1), 7–21. https://doi.org/10.1017/S1366728906002732

de Bot, K., Lowie, W., & Verspoor, M. (2007b). A dynamic view as a complementary perspective. *Bilingualism: Language and Cognition*, *10*(1), 51–55. https://doi.org/10.1017/S1366728906002811

DeKeyser, R. (1997). Beyond explicit rule learning: Automatizing second language morphosyntax. *Studies in Second Language Acquisition*, *19*(2), 195–221. https://doi.org/10.1017/S0272263197002040

DeKeyser, R. (2015). Skill acquisition theory. In B. VanPatten & J. Williams (Eds.), *Theories in second language acquisition: An introduction* (pp. 94–112). Routledge.

Dörnyei, Z. (2005). *The psychology of the language learner: Individual differences in second language acquisition*. Lawrence Erlbaum.

Dörnyei, Z. (2009a). The L2 motivational self system. In Z. Dörnyei & E. Ushioda (Eds.), *Motivation, language identities and the L2 self* (pp. 9–42). Multilingual Matters.

Dörnyei, Z. (2009b). Individual differences: Interplay of learner characteristics and learning environment. *Language Learning*, *59*(1), 230–248. https://doi.org/10.1111/j.1467-9922.2009.00542.x

Dörnyei, Z. (2010). The relationship between language aptitude and language learning motivation: Individual differences from a dynamic systems perspective. In E. Macaro (Ed.), *Continuum companion to second language acquisition* (pp. 247–267). London: Continuum. https://doi.org/10.5040/9781474212397.ch-009

Dörnyei, Z. (2017). Conceptualizing L2 learner characteristics in a complex, dynamic world. In L. Ortega & Z. Han (Eds.), *Complexity theory and language development: In celebration of Diane Larsen-Freeman* (pp. 79–96). John Benjamins. https://doi.org/10.1075/lllt.48.05dor

Dörnyei, Z., & Ryan, S. (2015). *The psychology of the language learner revisited*. Routledge.

Dörnyei, Z., & Skehan, P. (2003). Individual differences in second language learning. In C. J. Doughty & M. Long (Eds.), *The handbook of second language acquisition* (pp. 589–630). Blackwell.

Dörnyei, Z., & Ushioda, E. (2009). *Motivation, language identities and the L2 self*. Multilingual Matters.

Dussias, P. E., & Piñar, P. (2010). Effects of reading span and plausibility in the reanalysis of wh- gaps by Chinese-English second language speakers. *Second Language Research*, *26*(4), 443–472. https://doi.org/10.1177/0267658310373326

Ellis, N. C. (1996). Sequencing in SLA: Phonological memory, chunking, and points of order. *Studies in Second Language Acquisition*, *18*, 91–126. https://doi/org/10.1017/S0272263100014698

Ellis, N. C. (2001). Memory for language. In P. Robinson (Ed.), *Cognition and second language instruction* (pp. 33–68). Cambridge University Press. https://doi.org/10.1017/CBO9781139524780.004

Ellis, R. (2008). Individual learner differences and second language learning. In R. Ellis (Ed.), *The study of second language acquisition* (2nd ed., pp. 643–720). Oxford University Press.

Engle, R. W. (2002). Working memory capacity as executive attention. *Current Directions in Psychological Science*, *11*, 19–23. https://doi.org/10.1111/1467-8721.00160

Engle, R. W., Kane, M. J., & Tuholski, S. W. (1999). Individual differences in working memory capacity and what they tell us about controlled attention, general fluid intelligence, and functions of the prefrontal cortex. In A. Miyake & P. Shah (Eds.), *Models of working memory: Mechanisms of active maintenance and executive control* (p. 102–134). Cambridge University Press. https://doi.org/10.1017/CBO9781139174909.007

Engle, R. W., Tuholski, S. W., Laughlin, J. E., & Conway, A. R. A. (1999). Working memory, short-term memory, and general fluid intelligence: A latent-variable approach. *Journal of Experimental Psychology: General*, *128*(3), 309–331. https://doi.org/10.1037/0096-3445.128.3.309

Fehringer, C., & Fry, C. (2007). Hesitation phenomena in the language production of bilingual speakers: The role of working memory. *Folia Linguistica: Acta Societatis Linguisticae Europaeae*, *41*(1–2), 37–72. https://doi.org/10.1515/flin.41.1-2.37

Foote, R. (2011). Integrated knowledge of agreement in early and late English-Spanish bilinguals. *Applied Psycholinguistics*, *32*(1), 187–220. https://doi.org/10.1017/S0142716410000342

Gardner, R. C. (1985). *Social psychology and second language learning: The role of attitudes and motivation.* Edward Arnold. https://doi.org/10.1037/h0083787

Gardner, R. C. (2001). Integrative motivation and second language acquisition. In Z. Dörnyei & R. Schmidt (Eds.), *Motivation and second language acquisition* (pp. 1–19). University of Hawaii Press.

Gardner, R. C. (2010). *Motivation and second language acquisition: The socio-educational model.* Peter Lang.

Gardner, R. C., & Lambert, W. E. (1972). *Attitudes and motivation in second language learning.* Newbury House.

Gathercole, S. E. (2006). Nonword repetition and word learning: The nature of the relationship. *Applied Psycholinguistics*, *27*(4), 513–543. https://doi.org/10.1017/S0142716406060383

Gilabert, R., & Muñoz, C. (2010). Differences in attainment and performance in a foreign language: The role of working memory capacity. *International Journal of English Studies*, *10*(1), 19–42. https://doi.org/10.6018/ijes/2010/1/113961

Goo, J. (2012). Corrective feedback and working memory capacity in interaction-driven L2 learning. *Studies in Second Language Acquisition*, *34*(3), 445–474. https://doi.org/10.1017/S0272263112000149

Granena, G., Jackson, D. O., & Yilmaz, Y. (2016). Cognitive individual differences in second language learning and processing. In G. Granena, D. O. Jackson, & Y. Yilmaz (Eds.), *Cognitive individual differences in second language processing and acquisition* (pp. 1–14). John Benjamins. https://doi.org/10.1075/bpa.3

Granena, G., & Yilmaz, Y. (2019). Phonological short-term memory capacity and L2 oral performance. *Journal of Second Language Studies*, *2*(2), 317–335. https://doi.org/10.1075/jsls.19005.gra

Grey, S., Cox, J., Serafini, E. J., & Sanz, C. (2015). The role of individual differences in the study abroad context: Cognitive capacity and language development during short-term intensive language exposure. *The Modern Language Journal*, *99*(1), 137–157. https://doi.org/10.1111/modl.12190

Griffiths, C. (Ed.). (2008). *Lessons from good language learners*. Cambridge University Press.

Gurzynski-Weiss, L. (2020). Editorial. In L. Gurzynski-Weiss (Ed.), Investigating the dynamic nature of learner individual differences in L2 learning [Special issue]. *Studies in Second Language Learning and Teaching*, *10*(1), 15–19. https://doi.org/10.14746/ssllt.2020.10.1.1

Harrington, M., & Sawyer, M. (1992). L2 working memory capacity and L2 reading skill. *Studies in Second Language Acquisition*, *14*(1), 25–38. https://doi.org/10.1017/S0272263100010457

Havik, E., Roberts, L., van Hout, R., Schreuder, R., & Haverkort, M. (2009). Processing subject – object ambiguities in the L2: A self-paced reading study with German L2 learners of Dutch. *Language Learning*, *59*(1), 73–112. https://doi.org/10.1111/j.1467-9922.2009.00501.x

Hiver, P., & Al-Hoorie, A. H. (2016). A dynamic ensemble for second language research: Putting complexity theory into practice. *Modern Language Journal*, *100*(4), 741–756. https://doi.org/10.1111/modl.12347

Hiver, P., & Al-Hoorie, A. H. (2020). *Research methods for complexity theory in applied linguistics*. Multilingual Matters. https://doi.org/10.21832/HIVER5747

Hiver, P., Al-Hoorie, A. H., & Evans, R. (2021). Complex dynamic system theory in language learning: A scoping review of 25 years of research. *Studies in Second Language Acquisition*. https://doi.org/10.1017/S0272263121000553.

Hummel, K. M. (2009). Aptitude, phonological memory, and second language proficiency in non-novice adult learners. *Applied Psycholinguistics*, *30*(2), 225–249. https://doi.org/10.1017/S0142716409090109

Jackson, D. (2020). Working memory and second language development: A complex, dynamic future? *Studies in Second Language Learning and Teaching*, *10*(1), 89–109. https://doi.org/10.14746/ssllt.2020.10.1.5

Johnson, M. D. (2020). Planning in L1 and L2 writing: Working memory, process, and product. *Language Teaching*, *53*(4), 433–445. https://doi.org/10.1017/S0261444820000191

Juffs, A. (2004). Representation, processing and working memory in a second language. *Transactions of the Philological Society*, *102*(2), 199–225. https://doi.org/10.1111/j.0079-1636.2004.00135.x

Juffs, A. (2005). The influence of first language on the processing of wh-movement in English as a second language. *Second Language Research*, *21*(2), 121–151. https://doi.org/10.1191/0267658305sr255oa

Juffs, A., & Harrington, M. (2011). Aspects of working memory in L2 learning. *Language Teaching*, *44*(2), 137–166. https://doi.org/10.1017/S0261444810000509

Just, M. A., & Carpenter, P. (1992). A capacity theory of comprehension: Individual differences in working memory. *Psychological Review*, *99*(1), 122–149. https://doi.org/10.1037/0033-295x.99.1.122

Kempe, V., & Brooks, P. J. (2008). Second language learning of complex inflectional systems. *Language Learning*, *58*(4), 703–746. https://doi.org/10.1111/j.1467-9922.2008.00477.x

Kempe, V., Brooks, P. J., & Kharkhurin, A. (2010). Cognitive predictors of generalization of Russian grammatical gender categories. *Language Learning*, *60*(1), 127–153. https://doi.org/10.1111/j.1467-9922.2009.00553.x

Kim, Y. J., Payant, C., & Pearson, P. (2015). The intersection of task-based interaction, task complexity, and working memory: L2 question development through recasts in a laboratory setting. *Studies in Second Language Acquisition*, *37*(3), 549–581. http://dx.doi.org/10.1017/S0272263114000618

Kormos, J., & Sáfár, A. (2008). Phonological short-term memory, working memory and foreign language performance in intensive language learning. *Bilingualism: Language and Cognition*, *11*(2), 261–271. https://doi.org/10.1017/S1366728908003416

Larsen-Freeman, D. (1997). Chaos/complexity science and second language acquisition. *Applied Linguistics*, *18*, 140–165. https://doi.org/10.1093/APPLIN/18.2.141

Larsen-Freeman, D. (2001). Individual cognitive/affective learner contributions and differential success in second language acquisition. In M. Breen (Ed.), *Learner contributions to language learning: New directions in research* (pp. 12–24). Routledge.

Larsen-Freeman, D. (2002). Language acquisition and language use from a chaos/complexity theory perspective. In C. Kramsch (Ed.), *Language acquisition and language socialization* (pp. 33–46). Continuum.

Larsen-Freeman, D. (2012). Complex, dynamic systems: A new transdisciplinary theme for applied linguistics? *Language Teaching*, *45*(2), 202–214. https://doi.org/10.1017/S0261444811000061

Larsen-Freeman, D. (2015). Ten lessons from CDST: What is on offer. In Z. Dörnyei, P. MacIntyre, & A. Henry (Eds.), *Motivational dynamics in language learning* (pp. 11–15). Bristol, UK: Multilingual Matters.

Larsen-Freeman, D. (2018). Looking ahead: Future directions in, and future research into, second language acquisition. *Modern Language Journal*, *51*(1), 55–72. https://doi.org/10.1111/flan.12314

Larsen-Freeman, D., & Cameron, L. (2008a). *Complex systems and applied linguistics*. Oxford University Press.

Larsen-Freeman, D., & Cameron, L. (2008b). Research methodology on language development from a complex systems perspective. *Modern Language Journal*, *92*(2), 200–213. https://doi.org/10.1111/j.1540-4781.2008.00714.x

Larsen-Freeman, D., & Long, M. (1991). *An introduction to second language acquisition research*. Longman.

Lee, H., Warchauer, M., & Lee, J. H. (2020). Toward the establishment of a data-driven learning model: Role of learner factors in corpus-based second language vocabulary learning. *The Modern Language Journal*, *104*(2), 345–362. https://doi.org/10.1111/modl.12634

Leeser, M. J. (2007). Learner-based factors in L2 reading comprehension and processing grammatical form: Topic familiarity and working memory. *Language Learning*, *57*(2). 229–270. https://doi.org/10.1111/j.1467-9922.2007.00408.x

Lenzing, A., Pienemann, M., & Nicholas, H. (2023, this volume). Lost in Translation? On some key features of dynamical systems theorizing invoked in SLA research. In K. Kersten & A. Winsler (Eds.), *Understanding variability in second language acquisition, bilingualism, and cognition – A multi-layered perspective*. Routledge.

Leow, R. (2015). *Explicit learning in the L2 classroom: A student-centered approach*. Routledge. https://doi.org/10.4324/9781315887074

Li, S. (2016). The construct validity of language aptitude: A meta-analysis. *Studies in Second Language Acquisition*, *38*(4), 801–842. https://doi.org/10.1017/S027226311500042X

Li, S. (2017). An exploratory study on the role of foreign language aptitudes in instructed pragmatics learning in L2 Chinese. *Chinese as a Second Language Research*, *6*(1), 103–128. https://doi.org/10.1515/caslar-2017-0005

Li, S., & Fu, M. (2018). Strategic and unpressured within-task planning and their associations with working memory. *Language Teaching Research*, *22*(2), 230–253. https://doi.org/10.1177/1362168816684367

Li, S., & Roshan, S. (2019). The associations between working memory and the effects of four different types of written corrective feedback. *Journal of Second Language Writing*, *45*(2), 1–15. https://doi.org/10.1016/j.jslw.2019.03.003

Linck, J. A., Hiroshino, N., & Kroll, J. (2008). Cross-language lexical processes and inhibitory control. *Mental Lexicon*, *3*(3), 349–374. https://doi.org/10.1075/ml.3.3.06lin

Linck, J. A., Osthus, P., Koeth, J. T., & Bunting, M. F. (2014). Working memory and second language comprehension and production: A meta-analysis. *Psychonomic Bulletin & Review*, *21*(4), 861–883. https://doi.org/10.3758/s13423-013-0565-2

Linck, J. A., & Weiss, D. J. (2011). Working memory predicts the acquisition of explicit L2 knowledge. In C. Sanz & R. P. Leow (Eds.), *Implicit and explicit language learning: Conditions, processes, and knowledge in SLA and bilingualism* (pp. 101–113). Georgetown University Press. https://doi.org/10.5860/choice.48-6736

Logie, R. H. (2011). The functional organization and capacity limits of working memory. *Current Directions in Psychological Science*, *20*(4), 240–245. https://doi.org/10.1177/0963721411415340

Mackey, A., Adams, R., Stafford, C., & Winke, P. (2010). Exploring the relationship between modified output and working memory capacity. *Language Learning*, *60*(3), 501–533. https://doi.org/10.1111/j.1467-9922.2010.00565.x

Mackey, A., Philp, J., Egi, T., Fujii, A., & Tatsumi, T. (2002). Individual differences in working memory, noticing of interactional feedback and L2 development. In P. Robinson (Ed.), *Individual differences and instructed language learning* (pp. 181–209). Benjamins. https://doi.org/10.1075/lllt.2.12mac

Mackey, A., & Sachs, R. (2012). Older learners in SLA research: A first look at working memory, feedback, and L2 development. *Language Learning*, *62*(3), 704–740. https://doi.org/10.1111/j.1467-9922.2011.00649.x

Martin, K. I., & Ellis, N. C. (2012). The roles of phonological short-term memory and working memory in L2 grammar and vocabulary learning. *Studies in Second Language Acquisition*, *34*(3), 379–413. https://doi.org/10.1017/S0272263112000125

Mattys, S. L., & Baddeley, A. (2019). Working memory and second language accent acquisition. *Applied Cognitive Psychology*, *33*(6), 1113–1123. https://doi.org/10.1002/acp.3554

McLaughlin, B. (1987). *Theories of second language learning*. Edward Arnold. https://doi.org/10.1017/S0142716400000503

Michel, M., Kormos, J., Brunfaut, T., & Ratajczak, M. (2019). The role of working memory in young second language learners' written performances. *Journal of Second Language Writing*, *45*, 31–45. https://doi.org/10.1016/j.jslw.2019.03.002

Miyake, A. (2001). Individual differences in working memory: Introduction to the special section. *Journal of Experimental Psychology: General*, *130*(2), 163–168. https://doi.org/10.1037/0096-3445.130.2.163

Miyake, A., & Friedman, N. P. (1998). Individual differences in second language proficiency: Working memory as language aptitude. In A. Healy & L. Bourne (Eds.), *Foreign language learning: Psycholinguistic studies on training and retention* (pp. 339–365). Lawrence Erlbaum. https://doi.org/10.4324/9780203774670

Miyake, A., & Shah, P. (Eds.). (1999). *Models of working memory: Mechanisms of active maintenance and executive control*. Cambridge University Press. https://doi.org/10.2307/1423383

Nowbakht, M. (2019). The role of working memory, language proficiency, and learners' age in second language English learners' processing and comprehension of anaphoric sentences. *Journal of Psycholinguistic Research*, *48*(2), 353–370. https://doi.org/10.1007/s10936-018-9607-2

O'Brien, I., Segalowitz, N., Freed, B., & Collentine, J. (2006). Phonological memory predicts oral fluency gains. *Studies in Second Language Acquisition*, *29*(4), 557–582. https://doi.org/10.1017/S027226310707043X

Ortega, L., & Byrnes, H. (2008). The longitudinal study of advanced L2 capacities: An introduction. In L. Ortega & H. Byrnes (Eds.), *The longitudinal study of advanced L2 capacities* (pp. 3–20). Routledge. https://doi.org/10.4324/9780203871652

Ortega, L., & Iberri-Shea, G. (2005). Longitudinal research in second language acquisition: Recent trends and future directions. *Annual Review of Applied Linguistics*, *25*, 26–45. https://doi.org/10.1017/S0267190505000024

Park, H. I., Solon, M., Henderson, C., & Dehghan-Chaleshtori, M. (2020). The roles of working memory and oral language abilities in elicited imitation performance. *The Modern Language Journal*, *104*(1), 133–151. https://doi.org/10.1111/modl.12618

Payne, S. J., & Ross, B. M. (2005). Synchronous CMC, working memory, and L2 oral proficiency development. *Language Learning and Technology*, *9*(3), 35–54. http://dx.doi.org/10125/44031

Perez, M. M. (2020). Incidental vocabulary learning through viewing video: The role of vocabulary knowledge and working memory. *Studies in Second Language Acquisition*, *42*(4), 749–773. https://doi.org/10.1017/S0272263119000706

Roberts, L., & Meyer, A. (2012). Individual differences in second language learning: Introduction. *Language Learning*, *62*(s2), 1–4. https://doi.org/10.1111/j.1467-9922.2012.00703.x
Robinson, P. (2001). *Cognition and second language instruction*. Cambridge: Cambridge University Press. https://doi.org/10.1017/CBO9781139524780
Robinson, P. (2002). Effects of individual differences in intelligence, aptitude and working memory on incidental SLA. In P. Robinson (Ed.), *Individual differences and instructed language learning* (pp. 211–251). Philadelphia: Benjamins. https://doi.org/10.1075/lllt.2
Robinson, P. (2005). Aptitude and second language acquisition. *Annual Review of Applied Linguistics*, *25*, 46–73. https://doi.org/10.1017/S0267190505000036
Rubin, J. (1975). What the "good language learner" can teach us. *TESOL Quarterly*, *9*(1), 41–51. https://doi.org/10.2307/3586011
Ruíz, S., Rebuschat, P., & Meurers, D. (2019). The effects of working memory and declarative memory on instructed second language vocabulary learning: Insights from intelligent CALL. *Language Teaching Research*, *25*(4), 510–539. https://doi.org/10.1177/1362168819872859
Sagarra, N. (2007). From CALL to face-to-face interaction: The effect of computer-delivered recasts and working memory on L2 development. In A. Mackey (Ed.), *Conversational interaction in second language acquisition: A series of empirical studies* (pp. 229–248). Oxford University Press.
Sagarra, N. (2013). Working memory in second language acquisition. In C. A. Chapelle (Ed.), *The encyclopedia of applied linguistics*. John Wiley and Sons, Ltd. https://doi.org/10.1002/9781405198431.wbeal1286
Sagarra, N. (2017). Longitudinal effects of working memory on L2 grammar and reading abilities. *Second Language Research*, *33*(3), 341–363. https://doi.org/10.1177/0267658317690577
Sagarra, N., & Herschensohn, J. (2010). The role of proficiency and working memory in gender and number agreement processing in L1 and L2 Spanish. *Lingua*, *120*(8), 2022–2039. https://doi.org/10.1016/j.lingua.2010.02.004
Saito, K., Macmillan, K., Mai, T., Suzukida, Y., Sun, H., Magne, V., . . . Murakami, A. (2020). Developing, analyzing and sharing multivariate datasets: Individual differences in L2 learning revisited. *Annual Review of Applied Linguistics*, *40*, 9–25. https://doi.org/10.1017/S0267190520000045
Sanz, C. (2005). *Mind and context in adult second language acquisition*. Georgetown University Press.
Sanz, C., Lin, H-J., Lado, B., Bowden, H. W., & Stafford, C. A. (2014). One size fits all? Learning conditions and working memory capacity in *Ab initio* language development. *Applied Linguistics*, *37*(5), 669–692. https://doi.org/10.1093/applin/amu058
Sanz, C., & Serafini, E. J. (2018). La cognición y las lenguas no nativas: El papel de las diferencias individuales en el aprendizaje de lenguas extranjeras con especial atención a la memoria operativa [Cognition and non-native languages: The role of individual differences in foreign language learning with a focus on working memory]. In E. Ortiz-Preuss & I. Finger (Eds.), *A dinâmica do processamento bilíngue* [*The dynamics of bilingual processing*] (pp. 233–267). Pontes Editores.
Sawyer, M., & Ranta, L. (2001). Aptitude, individual differences, and instructional design. In P. Robinson (Ed.), *Cognition and second language*

instruction (pp. 319–353). Cambridge University Press. https://doi.org/10.1017/CBO9781139524780

Segalowitz, N. (2003). Automaticity and second language. In C. Doughty & M. H. Long (Eds.), *Handbook of second language acquisition* (pp. 382–408). Blackwell. https://doi.org/10.1002/9780470756492

Serafini, E. J. (2017). Exploring the dynamic long-term interaction between cognitive and psychosocial resources in adult second language development at varying proficiency. *Modern Language Journal*, *101*(2), 369–390. https://doi.org/10.1111/modl.12400

Serafini, E. J. (2021). Advancing notions of advancedness: Clarifying the role of individual differences in learners across the second language proficiency spectrum. In P. Malovrh & M. Menke (Eds.), *Advancedness in second language Spanish: Definitions, challenges and possibilities* (pp. 351–366). John Benjamins' Issues in Hispanic and Lusophone Linguistics series. https://doi.org/10.1075/ihll.31

Serafini, E. J., & Sanz, C. (2016). Evidence for the decreasing impact of cognitive ability on second language development as proficiency increases. *Studies in Second Language Acquisition*, *38*(4), 607–646. https://doi.org/10.1017/S0272263115000327

Service, E. (1992). Phonology, working memory, and foreign language learning. *Quarterly Journal of Experimental Psychology*, *45*(1), 21–50. https://doi.org/10.1080/14640749208401314

Shin, J. (2020). A meta-analysis of the relationship between working memory and second language reading comprehension: Does task type matter? *Applied Psycholinguistics*, *41*(4), 873–900. https://doi.org/10.1017/S0142716420000272

Shin, J., Dronjic, V., & Park, B. (2019). The interplay between working memory and background knowledge in L2 reading comprehension. *TESOL Quarterly*, *53*(2), 320–347. https://doi.org/10.1002/tesq.482

Simard, D., Molokopeeva, T., & Zhang, Y. Q. (2020). The contribution of working memory to L2 French pronunciation among adult language learners. *Canadian Modern Language Review*, *76*(1), 50–69. https://doi.org/10.3138/cmlr.2018-0223

Simmering, V. R., & Perone, S. (2013). Working memory capacity as a dynamic process. *Frontiers in Psychology*, *3*, Article 567. https://doi.org/10.3389/fpsyg.2012.00567

Skehan, P. (1991). Individual differences in second-language learning. *Studies in Second Language Acquisition*, *13*(2), 275–298. https://doi.org/10.1017/S0272263100009979

Skehan, P. (1998). *A cognitive approach to language learning*. Oxford University Press. https://doi.org/10.1093/elt/54.4.398

Skehan, P. (2002). Theorising and updating aptitude. In P. Robinson (Ed.), *Individual differences and instructed language learning* (pp. 69–95). John Benjamins. https://doi.org/10.1075/lllt.2

Skehan, P. (2012). Language aptitude. In S. Gass & A. Mackey (Eds.), *The Routledge handbook of second language acquisition* (pp. 381–395). Routledge. https://doi.org/10.4324/9780203808184

Sunderman, G., & Kroll, J. F. (2009). When study-abroad experience fails to deliver: The internal resources threshold effect. *Applied Psycholinguistics*, *30*(1), 79–99. https://doi.org/10.1017/S0142716408090048

Taguchi, N. (2008). The effect of working memory, semantic access, and listening abilities on the comprehension of conversational implicatures in L2 English. *Pragmatics & Cognition*, *16*(3), 517–539. https://doi.org/10.1075/pc.16.3.05tag

Tokowicz, N., Michael, E. B., & Kroll, J. (2004). The roles of study-abroad experience and working memory capacity in the types of errors made during translation. *Bilingualism: Language and Cognition*, *7*(3), 255–272. https://doi.org/10.1017/S1366728904001634

Trebits, A., Koch, M., Ponto, K., Bruhn, A-C., Adler, M., & Kersten, K. (2021). Cognitive gains and socioeconomic status in early second language acquisition in immersion and EFL learning settings. *International Journal of Bilingual Education and Bilingualism*, 1–14. https://doi.org/10.1080/13670050.2021.1943307

Tremblay, A. (2011). Proficiency assessment standards in second language acquisition research. *Studies in Second Language Acquisition*, *33*(3), 339–372. https://doi.org/10.1017/S0272263111000015

Turner, M. L., & Engle, R. W. (1989). Is working memory capacity task dependent? *Journal of Memory and Language*, *28*(2), 127–154. https://doi.org/10.1016/0749-596X(89)90040-5

Unsworth, N., Heitz, R. P., Schrock, J. C., & Engle, R. W. (2005). An automated version of the operation span task. *Behavior Research Methods*, *37*, 498–505. https://doi.org/10.3758/BF03192720

Van den Noort, M., Bosch, P., & Hugdahl, K. (2006). Foreign language proficiency and working memory capacity. *European Psychologist*, *11*(4), 289–296. https://doi.org/10.1027/1016-9040.11.4.289

van Geert, P. L. C. (1994). *Dynamic systems of development: Change between complexity and chaos*. Harvester Wheatsheaf.

van Geert, P. L. C. (1995). Growth dynamics in development. In R. F. Port & T. van Gelder (Eds.), *Mind as motion: Explorations in the dynamics of cognition* (pp. 313–338). Bradford Books and The MIT Press.

van Geert, P. L. C. (2008). The dynamic systems approach in the study of L1 and L2 acquisition: An introduction. *Modern Language Journal*, *92*(2), 179–199. https://doi.org/10.1111/j.1540-4781.2008.00713.x

van Geert, P. L. C., & van Dijk, M. (2002). Focus on variability: New tools to study intra-individual variability in developmental data. *Infant Behavior & Development*, *25*, 340–374. https://doi.org/10.1016/S0163-6383(02)00140-6

Verspoor, M., de Bot, K., & Lowie, W. (Eds.). (2011). *A dynamic approach to second language development: Methods and techniques*. John Benjamins. https://doi.org/10.1075/lllt.29

Verspoor, M., Lowie, W., & Van Dijk, M. (2008). Variability in second language development from a dynamic systems perspective. *Modern Language Journal*, *92*(2), 214–231. https://doi.org/10.1111/j.1540-4781.2008.00715.x

Verspoor, M., & van Dijk, M. (2011). Visualizing interaction between variables. In M. Verspoor, K. de Bot, & W. Lowie (Eds.), *A dynamic approach to second language development: Methods and techniques* (pp. 85–96). John Benjamins. https://doi.org/10.1075/lllt.29

Watanabe, Y., & Bergsleithner, J. M. (2006). A systematic research synthesis of L2 WM measurements. In Z. Madden-Wood & K. Ueki (Eds.), *Selected papers from the tenth college-wide conference for students in languages, linguistics, and literature* (pp. 47–60). College of Languages, Linguistics, and Literature, University of Hawaii.

Waters, G. S., & Caplan, D. (1996). The measurement of verbal working memory capacity and its relation to reading comprehension. *The Quarterly Journal of Experimental Psychology*, *49A*(1), 51–79. https://doi.org/10.1080/713755607

Wen, Z. (2012). Working memory and second language learning. *International Journal of Applied Linguistics*, 22(1), 1–22. https://doi.org/10.1111/j.1473-4192.2011.00290.x

Wen, Z. (2016). *Working memory and second language learning: Towards an integrated approach*. Multilingual Matters.

Wen, Z., Mota, M. B., & McNeill, A. (Eds.). (2015). *Working memory in second language acquisition and processing*. Multilingual Matters. https://doi.org/10.21832/9781783093595

Williams, J. N. (2012). Working memory and SLA. In S. M. Gass & A. Mackey (Eds.), *The Routledge handbook of second language acquisition* (pp. 427–441). Routledge. https://doi.org/10.4324/9780203808184

Williams, J. N. (2015). Working memory in SLA research: Challenges and prospects. In Z. Wen, M. B. Mota, & A. McNeill (Eds.), *Working memory in second language acquisition and processing* (pp. 301–307). Multilingual Matters. https://doi.org/10.21832/9781783093595

Williams, J. N., & Lovatt, P. (2003). Phonological memory and rule learning. *Language Learning*, *53*(1), 67–121. https://doi.org/10.1111/1467-9922.00211

Winke, P. (2005). *Individual differences in adult Chinese second language acquisition: The relationships among aptitude, memory and strategies for learning* (Unpublished doctoral dissertation). Georgetown University.

Zabildea, J. (2017). "One task fits all"? The roles of task complexity, modality, and working memory capacity in L2 performance. *Modern Language Journal*, *101*(2), 335–352. https://doi.org/10.1111/modl.12389

Zabildea, J., & Sanz, C. (2020). Does learner cognition count on modality? Working memory and L2 morphosyntactic achievement across oral and written tasks. *Applied Psycholinguistics*, *41*(5), 1171–1196. https://doi.org/10.1017/S0142716420000442

10 Can type of schooling compensate for low SES? Investigating effects of instruction and SES on cognitive skills

Ann-Christin Bruhn, Lisa Miller, Claudia Mähler, Katharina Ponto, and Kristin Kersten

Introduction

Learners' development is influenced by a vast number of external factors, such as the family and the social environment with their respective resources, as well as the educational institutional environment in which a child grows up. However, the actual influence of these factors on the developmental process depends on many conditions and varies greatly, since learners themselves also have different individual abilities (i.e., cognitive and linguistic abilities) and personality traits (i.e., motivation, attitudes), which interact with external resources (Kersten, 2019).

Diversity in the social and institutional backgrounds of young children manifests in numerous individual differences even before school entry. Aspects of diversity pertain to genetics, family education and income, and type of preschool program. Even within the first years of life, such differences have been found to predict children's cognitive (Hackman & Farah, 2009; Lawson et al., 2018) and linguistic skills (Brooks-Gunn & Duncan, 1997; Hart & Risley, 1995; Pace et al., 2017). Cognitive and linguistic skills at school entry, in turn, are essential predictors of later academic achievement in school (Alloway & Alloway, 2010). These skills are closely intertwined and develop interdependently. It is therefore vital for any type of early instructional program to create a learning environment that fosters cognitive and linguistic development to help level the playing field for young children from low-income backgrounds. In this chapter, we take a closer look at the interplay of external resources such as children's socioeconomic background and type of institutional education in preschool and their relevance for the development of learners' internal cognitive skills. To that end, we present results from two studies in two different preschool programs that were designed to foster cognitive-linguistic development. In this context, it is important to note that the term "preschool" is used in this chapter to refer to the institution

DOI: 10.4324/9781003155683-12

in the German education system that children attend between the ages of three and six before they enter the first grade of formal schooling in elementary school. The first study focuses on a preschool phonological awareness training program, and the second study investigates the impact of bilingual preschool experiences compared to monolingual programs. The overall main objective of both studies is to examine whether such programs may compensate for cognitive disadvantages in preschool linked to low socioeconomic status.

Internal cognitive resources

A growing body of literature has shown cognitive skills to be of considerable predictive value for children's development (Alloway & Alloway, 2010; Huschka et al., 2020; Robson et al., 2020). Traditionally, the role of cognitive skills has been viewed under the scope of their contribution to academic achievement. In this regard, specifically, nonverbal intelligence, working memory, and phonological awareness are considered crucial skills to develop before entering school (Roth et al., 2015; Schuchardt et al., 2008; Schneider, 1989).

Nonverbal intelligence: Amid numerous disparate theories of intelligence (for an overview, see Sternberg, 2018), Spearman's structural notion of the g factor remains among the most prominent (Spearman, 1904). Nonverbal intelligence (NVI) is assessed to gather children's general ability to process information without the need to rely on language competencies.

Working memory: A useful and widely accepted theoretical framework for the functioning of short-term processing has been provided by Baddeley and Hitch (1974). The multicomponent model assumes that working memory consists of three parts: the central executive, the phonological loop, and the visuospatial sketchpad. The central executive is the main component of the model, while the other two work as slave systems (Baddeley, 1994). The visuo-spatial sketchpad processes visual material, while the phonological loop stores and rehearses verbal and acoustic information. The higher-level attentional control system, the central executive, monitors the slave systems' capacities and regulates the flow of information as well as the interaction between the systems. In a revision of the original model, Baddeley (2000) includes the episodic buffer, a third system that functions as an interface between the other systems, the central executive, and long-term storage.

Phonological awareness: As one of the three components of phonological information processing (the others being phonological recoding in lexical access and phonetic recoding in working memory), phonological awareness (PA) refers to the awareness and manipulation of the phonetic (sound) structure of language. It represents the ability to focus attention on the formal linguistic aspects of language independently of the content or meaning of what is said (Fröhlich et al., 2010). Skowronek and Marx (1989) differentiate between two subconstructs: PA in a broad and narrow sense. Regularly, the majority of preschoolers are able to process general units of language, such as syllables and rhymes, implicitly in play before school entry. PA in a narrow sense requires a more conscious application of phonetic knowledge. It enables children to recognize phonemes in particular words and to operate with these. For instance, this ability is necessary to synthetize multiple phonemes into a word – a crucial skill for literacy.

As indicated before, all of the cognitive resources described are crucial predictors for future academic success. However, it has been shown that in addition to children's abilities, environmental aspects may affect developmental and academic paths substantially, which is illustrated as follows.

External social and institutional resources

Socioeconomic status

The social-economic environment is an important context in which human development is shaped. Children's background includes factors such as parental occupation and education, family income, social prestige, cultural capital, and other cultural aspects. Many of these are often comprised within the concept of socioeconomic status (SES), which is one of the most widely studied constructs in social science and is often used as a predictor variable in empirical studies (Hackman & Farah, 2009; Lawson et al., 2016). There is universal agreement that children from higher-SES backgrounds have access to more beneficial resources for their social and cognitive development than children from lower-SES backgrounds (Bornstein & Bradley, 2012). There is no consensus, however, on how to best operationalize family SES, as it is a container variable that encompasses diverse proximal factors (Kersten & Greve, 2023, this volume). Each of these different factors included in SES indices represents a different resource that might foster children's cognitive development in different ways (Bradley & Corwyn, 2002; Duncan & Magnuson, 2012). Despite uncertainty about the optimal index, the relationship between SES and cognitive and language development is robust enough to occur across different measurement approaches (Pace et al., 2017). For a long period of time, maternal education appeared to be the most commonly used component of SES that was most strongly associated with child outcomes (Rindermann & Baumeister, 2015). However, according to Hoffmeyer-Zlotnik and Geis (2003), education and income seem to have lost importance as indicators compared to occupation. A frequently used scale to measure SES in cross-national comparative studies (e.g., OECD's PISA) is the International Socio-Economic Index of Occupational Status (ISEI) developed by Ganzeboom (2010). In this study, the Highest

International Socio-Economic Index of Occupational Status among parents (HISEI; Ganzeboom, 2010) was used to represent the family's SES.

Numerous studies demonstrate that SES is a reliable predictor of many facets of children's development, with effects beginning prior to birth and continuing into adulthood (Bradley & Corwyn, 2002). Children from educationally disadvantaged and low-income families typically face many barriers to learning due to fewer educational resources such as books, games, and cognitively stimulating materials in their households. In contrast, socioeconomically advantaged students are more likely to get financial support and home resources for individual learning that promote cognitive development (Sirin, 2005). It is therefore not surprising that a strong link between children's development and intelligence and their family background is becoming increasingly apparent (Brooks-Gunn & Duncan, 1997; Gottfried et al., 2012).

Moreover, a growing body of research demonstrates that childhood SES is positively related to executive functions (Hackman et al., 2015; Noble et al., 2007; Rosen et al., 2020; Sarsour et al., 2011). Executive functions, including working memory, inhibition, and attention shifting, have been shown to partially mediate the relation between SES and academic achievement in early (Lawson et al., 2016) and later childhood (Lawson & Farah, 2017). In a meta-analysis of the relationship between SES and executive function performance among children, Lawson and colleagues (2018) confirm SES differences in learners' executive function ranging from small to medium effects, depending on the measurement method. Rosen et al. (2020) identified the amount of cognitive stimulation in the home environment as an underlying mechanism explaining the SES-related differences in executive function performance. This is in line with Kersten's findings (2023, this volume), which showed that SES strongly predicted working memory in primary school children and that this effect was partially mediated by parental language support and literacy support at home. Similarly, Hackman et al. (2015) found that the role of early childhood characteristics of the home and family environment partially explained the relation between SES and executive functions. In addition, recent findings indicate SES differences in prefrontal function and cortical structure over the course of childhood (Kishiyama et al., 2009; Sheridan et al., 2012). Kishiyama et al. (2009) associate these alterations in prefrontal cortex function in children from lower-SES backgrounds with higher levels of stress and lack of access to cognitively stimulating materials and experiences, whereas Sheridan et al. (2012) identify the home language environment and stress and adversity exposure as two underlying mechanisms. Recent research confirms that socioeconomically advantaged children tend to experience greater quantity and quality of linguistic input and more social and cognitive stimulation from their caregivers and home environment than children from families with lower social status (Pace et al., 2017). Therefore, it is not surprising that sensitive parenting is associated with positive outcomes for children, including early language and literacy development (Noble et al., 2006).

Although it is quite clear that phonological awareness and SES contribute to individual differences in reading ability, very few studies have addressed the issue of the influence of SES on PA (Noble et al., 2006). A number of studies report that lower-SES children show lower levels of phonological awareness than middle- to high-SES children (Bowey, 1995; Lonigan et al., 1998; McDowell et al., 2007; McIntosh et al., 2007; Zhang et al., 2013). A large-scale meta-analysis of phonological awareness intervention studies by Ehri and colleagues (2001) reported that children with low SES benefited from phonological awareness training as much as middle- to high-SES children. These findings indicate that phonological awareness is teachable and modifiable, demonstrating the potential for interventions focused on improving children's early phonological awareness (McIntosh et al., 2007; Lundberg et al., 2012).

Institutional environments

The two studies reported in this chapter both investigate preschool programs, which are thought to foster early cognitive-linguistic development. While one program consists of a specific and time-limited intervention carried out by trained preschool teachers, the other program type implements foreign language exposure with various stimulating scaffolding techniques in everyday routines in bilingual preschools over the full course of preschool attendance.

Program 1: Training of phonological awareness

Training programs for PA are of particular relevance in preschools since phonological abilities have been shown to be important precursors for literacy, and thus, academic achievement. A pioneering Scandinavian study administered a 9-month PA training in the final year of preschool, showing large effects for phoneme segmentation and small effects on rhyming and tasks involving word and syllable manipulation (Lundberg et al., 1988). An early meta-analysis of experimental training studies indicates that training PA may account for approximately 12% of variance in word-identification skills and greater effects if paired with letter training (Bus & Ijzendoorn, 1999). Additional studies and meta-analyses corroborate the value of PA interventions (Fälth et al., 2017; Fischer & Pfost, 2015; Kjeldsen et al., 2014).

The vast majority of PA trainings focus on implementing programs for several months, instructing preschool teachers to administer them to children of the specific age group. *Hören, Lauschen, Lernen* [Hearing, Listening, Learning] (HLL), a 20-week program with daily 10-minute training sessions, is widely used in Germany (Küspert et al., 1999; Küspert & Schneider, 2018). The training provides a playful approach to attentional listening, rhyming, structures of words and sentences, syllables, initial sounds, and phonemes. Jäger (2018) summarizes several evaluation studies outlining the heterogeneity of effects, especially in relation to the transfer of phonological skills to the acquisition of literacy. However, the author shows sustainable training effects until the second year of school for both reading and writing skills. Since additive training formats entail great effort and expense of resources, Jörns and colleagues (2017) developed a training program conceptualized as a board game (*ZIK – Zuhören im Kindergarten* [Listening in Preschool]). The design is expected to promote PA in a playful manner without fixed schedules, integrating the training into daily routines while deriving the ideas from HLL and therefore covering substantial components of PA. In a first evaluation study, ZIK has shown promising short-term efficacy, while long-term effects have not been found (Jörns et al., 2017).

Program 2: Bilingual education in preschools

As a result of the European Commission's goal to promote language learning to the extent that every citizen is fluent in at least two languages in addition to their mother tongue, an increasing number of pre- and primary schools have implemented bilingual programs (European Commission, 2017). In bilingual preschools, usually, one preschool teacher uses the ambient language (L1; e.g., German in the German educational context), while another (preferably a native speaker) uses the target foreign language (L2) exclusively in all interactions with the children (One Person-One Language approach; de Houwer, 2009, p. 107; Döpke, 1992). This way, the children receive a large part of their daily language input in the L2. The advantage of this approach for language acquisition lies, among other things, in the intensive, context-bound, and natural use of language as well as the comprehension-promoting strategies of illustration. As long as children have limited or no knowledge of their L2, L2 preschool teachers need to find strategies to foster and stimulate children's development by contextualizing the new language as much as possible and making it comprehensible (i.e., using gestures, facial expressions, visualization, and real objects) (Kersten et al., 2010; Weitz et al., 2010; Weitz, 2015). These scaffolding techniques are often related to linguistic input quality, which includes how teachers modify verbal and nonverbal L2 input, create authentic communicative activities and interactions, vary the type of feedback, focus on form, and provide opportunities for learners' L2 output, all to ensure comprehension and cognitive stimulation during L2 acquisition and facilitate long-term retention (Kersten, 2019).

Recent studies indicate that teachers in bilingual programs outperform monolingual teachers regarding the cognitive stimulation and scaffolding children receive, their drive to improve their own teaching, and investing time and implementing innovations (Kersten et al., 2019; Wegner, 2022).

Positive results for different aspects of input quality have been found in various studies (for overviews, see Graham et al., 2017; Loewen & Sato, 2018; Weitz et al., 2010). In addition to input quality, numerous studies have also shown that the quantity of input in another language, i.e., intensive bilingual school contexts, has positive effects on the linguistic development of young learners' L1 and L2 (Graham et al., 2017; Unsworth et al., 2014) and can yield positive cognitive effects (Nicolay & Poncelet, 2015; Woumans et al., 2016).

Recent research focuses increasingly on the effects of bilingualism on cognitive skills. Positive results are mainly explained by the fact that learners with bilingual exposure continuously switch between languages and monitor this process during communication (Bialystok et al., 2008; Bialystok et al., 2009; Costa et al., 2009). The bulk of the studies carried out on the so-called bilingual advantage hypothesis (Bialystok et al., 2009) has focused on bilingual first language acquisition (BFLA – when children learn two languages simultaneously from birth; de Houwer, 2009), and one of the most important predictors is the speakers' degree of bilingualism (Bialystok et al., 2009; Bialystok & Barac, 2012). Strong skills in two languages are assumed to contribute to the development of cognitive skills. Meta-analyses suggest that bilingualism is reliably associated with increased working memory, attentional control, metalinguistic awareness, and abstract and symbolic representational abilities (Adesope et al., 2010).

While the degree of bilingualism in BFLA is much higher on average than in bilingual institutions where L2 input is reduced to limited contact time with the L2 teacher, several studies find positive effects of early institutional L2 acquisition on cognitive abilities such as attention, executive control, working memory, or metalinguistic abilities (Bialystok & Barac, 2012; Nicolay & Poncelet, 2015; Woumans et al., 2016; Trebits et al., 2021). Likewise, Kersten (2023, this volume) finds a strong effect of a bilingual L2 program on PA in fourth graders. However, the influence of bilingualism on cognitive skills is currently the subject of controversial discussions within the bilingual advantage debate (Antón et al., 2014; De Bruin et al., 2015; Duñabeitia et al., 2014; Lehtonen et al., 2018; Paap et al., 2017; Festman et al., 2023, this volume). According to Dicataldo and Roch (2020), many differences in the results depend in particular on the degree of bilingual exposure.

As the discussion has shown, both SES and degree of bilingualism have been shown to influence children's linguistic and cognitive abilities when considered independently. However, much less is known about the relationship between these two environmental factors (Meir & Armon-Lotem, 2017). Calvo and Bialystok (2014) found no significant interaction between SES (indexed by maternal education) and bilingualism but only significant independent influences of both factors on 6- to 7-year-old learners' working memory performance and inhibitory control tasks. Specifically, higher-SES children outperformed lower-SES children, and bilingual children outperformed monolingual children on all executive function tasks. In contrast, Hartanto et al. (2019) report that SES predicted verbal working memory scores and that bilingualism moderated the effects of SES in their longitudinal study by mitigating the negative consequences of low SES on executive functions. A similar assumption was made by Engel de Abreu et al. (2012), who found a bilingual advantage in executive control among children growing up in economically disadvantaged families in their study. Based on their findings, the authors suggest that "bilingualism might also provide protection against the adverse cognitive effects that are associated with poverty. From this perspective, regular use of more than one language is a mentally stimulating activity that provides the opportunity to strengthen executive control mechanisms that build a defense to counteract the negative impact of poverty on cognition" (Engel de Abreu et al., 2012, p. 1369). Moreover, Kersten (2020) found that the relation between SES and working memory was moderated by type of bilingual school program: The higher the intensity of bilingual teaching at the school, the lower was the effect of SES on working memory. Similarly, Trebits et al. (2021) reported that SES has a higher impact on children participating in a monolingual school program than on children in a bilingual program. These data indicate that intensive bilingual programs have the potential to exert a strong influence on children's development, raising the question of whether negative effects of low socioeconomic background can be partially mitigated by programs that provide linguistic and cognitive support.

In summary, research has provided evidence that low SES affects children's language and cognitive development, even though the underlying mechanisms have yet to be identified. These effects can be observed even in young children. However, previous research also suggests that language-sensitive interventions may be able to help mitigate effects of families' SES on their children's life outcomes.

The current studies

In this chapter, we address the question of whether purportedly negative effects of low SES could be mitigated or alleviated by specific language support programs in preschool. For this purpose, this chapter presents two new cross-sectional studies that investigate the relationship of socioeconomic status and different types of preschool interventions on cognitive skills. Both studies focus on subsets of two longitudinal research projects FRISCH – Early Inclusion in Literacy Acquisition (Study 1) and FLINK – Foreign Language Learning in Inclusive Contexts (Study 2), which are part of the research network Inclusive Educational Research in Early Childhood as a Multidisciplinary Challenge [Inklusive Bildungsforschung der frühen Kindheit als multidisziplinäre Herausforderung] of the Competence Center Early Childhood Lower Saxony [Kompetenzzentrum Frühe Kindheit Niedersachsen] at the University of Hildesheim (see www.uni-hildesheim.de/inklusive-bildungsforschung/inklusive-bildungs forschung-der-fruehen-kindheit-als-multidisziplinaere-herausforderung).

Research questions

Specifically, we address the following research questions:

1. Does SES predict young learners' cognitive skills?
2. If so, is this influence moderated by different types of language support programs?

To answer these questions, children were tested at the end of their last year in preschool over a 3-month period (April–June) in 2018 in different language-supporting preschool programs. Participants from traditional preschools serve as comparison groups. Study 1 reports on the efficacy of phonological awareness intervention programs. Study 2 focuses on the influence of bilingual school programs, which are characterized by specific foreign language input scaffolding techniques to foster comprehension, interaction, and language production. We expected to find an effect of SES on learners' cognitive skills across both samples, as well as a moderating effect of language-supporting preschool programs on this relationship. Identical measures were used for both projects. Procedures and results will be described first for Study 1, subsequently for Study 2. Results of both studies will be discussed in combination.

Method

Participants

Participants Study 1: The sample consisted of $N = 171$ children from 21 preschools in urban and suburban German areas. Children were already enrolled in the particular preschool when the respective programs were introduced. Hence, all groups are naturally occurring groups; thus, we could not randomly assign kids to intervention and control groups. A total of $n = 80$ children (45% female) participated in PA training programs (age in months: $M = 75.68$, $SD = 4.30$). The control group sample consisted of $n = 91$ children (45% female) and did not partake in any kind of phonological training (age in months: $M = 74.54$, $SD = 3.80$). The participants were assessed within the last 3 months of the particular year of preschool and were between 66 and 89 months old ($M = 75.07$, $SD = 4.16$).

Participants Study 2: The study investigated $N = 43$ children (26 female, 17 male; age in months: $M = 75$, $SD = 4.57$) enrolled in 10 regular monolingual (German) preschools ($n = 29$; 18 female, 11 male; $M = 74.66$, $SD = 4.16$) and two bilingual (German-English) preschools ($n = 14$; 8 female, 6 male; $M = 75.71$, $SD = 5.41$) in urban and suburban areas of Germany. All children attending bilingual preschools had spent at least 3 years in the institution.

In contrast to the monolingual preschools, the bilingual preschools were characterized by an intensive bilingual approach, which means that in addition to the German-speaking educator, a foreign language teacher spent the whole day with the children and exclusively used the foreign language English (One Person-One Language principle). The two bilingual preschools were private preschools, while the monolingual preschools were state-run. However, except for the bilingual approach, all preschools were almost identical in terms of their structural features, organization, and resources.

Measures and procedures in Study 1 and 2

Learners' cognitive abilities were assessed with a battery of standardized tests conducted in German. All cognitive tests were administered individually in the prescribed standardized way by trained research assistants in 20- to 30-minute sessions. All assessments took place in quiet rooms within the preschool building. In addition, all parents and guardians were asked to complete a questionnaire on the family's linguistic and socioeconomic background. Informed consent for participation in the study was obtained from preschool administrations, parents, and children.

Socioeconomic status: Information about the parents' current occupation or employment was obtained from responses to open-ended questions. The indicator used for SES was the International Socioeconomic Index of Occupational Status (ISEI; Ganzeboom, 2010), which combines occupational activity with information on income and education (Hoffmeyer-Zlotnik & Geis, 2003). The ISEI is constructed as a continuous metric variable and can take values between 16 and 90. For the following analyses, the highest ISEI (HISEI) of both parents or the only available parent's ISEI value was used to represent the family's SES. For Study 1, only a subset of our participants from all preschools ($N = 134$) provided data on their HISEI.

Nonverbal intelligence: NVI was assessed using Raven's Coloured Progressive Matrices, which were designed as a language-free test for young children aged 5 to 11 years and older adults (Raven et al., 2006). Measuring the children's fluid intelligence (ability to think clearly and make sense of complexity), the test contains three sets of matrices, with 12 items per set. According to Raven's standardized procedure, children were asked to choose the missing element from six options in a drawing. One point was given for each correct answer, and the total score was the sum of the correct answers, with a maximum score of 36. For the analyses of this chapter, the raw scores were converted to IQ scores.

Working memory: Four sub-tests of the standardized computer-based AGTB 5–12 (Arbeitsgedächtnistestbatterie für Kinder von 5 bis 12 Jahren [Working memory test battery for children aged 5 to 12], Hasselhorn et al., 2012) were used to measure storage capacity of the phonological loop and central executive, according to Baddeley's working memory model (Baddeley, 2000). Instructions for each task were given acoustically by the interviewer. Depending on the task, children were asked to respond by tapping on a touchscreen monitor or by responding verbally. *Phonological loop* measures included a nonword repetition task (Kunstwörter [pseudo words]), consisting of the repetition of 24 three- to five-syllable nonwords (e.g., "karflumen", "fradorlucke", or "grappenfegalit"), and a one-syllable word span task (Wortspanne einsilbig), in which sequences of monosyllables had to be repeated in chronological order. For assessment of *central executive functioning*, the subtests color span backwards test (Farben rückwärts) and complex span task (Objektspanne) were used. During the former task, the children had to repeat an ascending sequence of different colors in the reverse order of their appearance. The latter consists of sequences of different pictures (e.g., cheese, apple, key) shown on the screen. The children were asked to say whether the item in the picture was edible or not by answering yes/no. At the end of the sequence, children were asked to recall the correct order of the items. To obtain the final scores for both scales, the mean of the standardized scores of the respective subtests was calculated.

Phonological awareness: Several aspects of PA were estimated using five subtests of the German *Würzburger Vorschultest* [Würzburg preschool test] (WVT, Endlich et al., 2017). The scale Phonological Awareness comprises the scales Phonological Awareness in a broad sense (two tasks) and Phonological Awareness in a narrow sense (three tasks). Each task contains a number of ten items, hence the possible maximum score for the scale is a value of 50. First, in the subtest *Anlauterkennung* [identification of initial sounds], the children heard singular words and were then asked to identify their initial sound. Subsequently, the children were presented with sequences of single phonemes and were asked to pick the corresponding word out of three choices (subtest *Phonemsynthese* [phoneme synthesis]). In the third assignment, this task was inverted. Children were shown a picture and were asked to recite the correct sequence of phonemes for each corresponding word (*Phonemanalyse* [phoneme analysis]). The following task required children to decide whether a presented phoneme was audible in a specific word (*Silbe-zu-Wort* [syllable to word]). At last, children were presented with a sequence of four words and were asked to identify the single word that does not rhyme with the remaining three words (*Reimaufgabe* [rhyming task]). Each subtest consisted of 10 items. The order of presentation was standardized and identical for all participants. The tasks syllable-to-word and rhyming were used to compile a scale for PA in a broad sense, while the scale for PA in a narrow sense comprises the subtest *identification of initial sounds*, *phoneme synthesis*, and *phoneme analysis*. Both scales were added together to a total score of PA with a possible maximum score of 50.

Study 1: Specific procedures, analyses and results

The primary objective of Study 1 was to explore everyday incidental chances to facilitate the introduction to literacy for children with low cognitive skills specifically important for the acquisition of written language. We expected children who participated in training of phonological awareness to have significantly higher levels of PA than children who did not receive a specific training as such. Furthermore, we expected a significant interaction of children's SES and their respective participation in a training program with regard to the correlation of SES and cognitive skill level.

During the 3 preceding months before the point of measurement, *N* = 85 children received phonological awareness training, either ZIK (Jörns et al., 2017) or HLL (Küspert & Schneider, 2008). While we implemented the training (ZIK) in some of the participating preschools, others already regularly performed phonological awareness training (HLL) before regardless of project participation. Thus, children were assigned to the training group ex post. The training procedures focused on phonological awareness in a broad as well as in a narrow sense, containing elements for rhyming, segmenting of syllables, identification of initial sounds, and analysis of phonemes. Trainings were instructed as well as supervised by preschool teachers. While increasing in difficulty over the course of time, the attention focus shifts to increasingly smaller units of language.

Analyses Study 1

Descriptive data were generated for all dependent variables using SPSS 27. We opted against data imputation for missing values since for the cognitive variables, the maximum number of missing cases per task did not exceed 10 children. For SES analyses, we only included completed questionnaires due to concerns regarding the imputation of parents' professions and occupation. After inspecting bivariate correlations, *t*-tests for independent samples were conducted, followed by moderated hierarchical regression analyses with standardized dependent variables.

Results Study 1

Descriptive statistics as well as bivariate correlations for the dependent variables for the entire sample are presented in Table 10.1.

T-tests for independent variables were conducted to examine differences between the children who have received phonological training and children who have not partaken in specific additional training. The results are depicted in Table 10.2. It is evident that groups differ significantly from each other regarding all scales of PA. They do not differ from each other in NVI, working memory, and SES.

Table 10.1 Descriptive statistics and correlations for study variables

Variable	*n*	*M*	*SD*	*NVI*	*CE*	*PL*	*PA*	*PA_B*	*PA_N*	*SES*
Nonverbal Intelligence (NVI)	170	101.31	13.72	–	.284**	.154*	.369**	.377**	.280**	.115
Central Executive (CE)	164	48.87	8.46		–	.221**	.357**	.250**	.333**	.220*
Phonological Loop (PL)	165	49.98	7.07			–	.342**	.282**	.297**	.144
Phonological Awareness Total (PA)	168	22.01	7.33				–	.690**	.929**	.286**
PA in a broad sense (PA_B)	169	12.03	2.92					–	.375**	.213*
PA in a narrow sense (PA_N)	168	9.95	5.72						–	.263**
Socioeconomic Status (SES)	134	54.27	15.51							–

Note. Phonological Awareness Total (PA) comprises the scales Phonological Awareness in a broad sense and Phonological Awareness in a narrow sense.
$^{+}p < .10$; $^{*}p < .05$; $^{**}p < .01$

Table 10.2 Results of independent samples *t*-tests

	Control Group		*Intervention Group*		*t*	*df*	*p*
	M	*SD*	*M*	*SD*			
Nonverbal Intelligence	100.76	14.57	101.94	12.73	–0.557	168	.578
Central Executive	48.69	8.51	49.06	8.46	–0.281	162	.683
Phonological Loop	49.49	6.50	48.44	7.64	0.953	163	.128
Phonological Awareness Total	20.69	6.94	23.53	7.52	–2.54	166	.012*
PA in a broad sense	11.60	3.00	12.52	2.77	–2.06	167	.041*
PA in a narrow sense	9.09	5.32	10.95	6.03	–2.12	166	.035*
Socioeconomic Status	54.18	16.56	54.35	14.54	–0.064	132	.949

Note. $^{+}p < .10$; $^{*}p < .05$; $^{**}p < .01$

To examine the impact of SES on cognitive skills as well as the cross-sectional interaction between SES and the participation in a training of PA in regard to children's cognitive skill level, moderated hierarchical regression analyses were conducted. For cognitive variables significantly correlating with SES, the results of the moderated hierarchical regression analyses are depicted in Tables 10.3 to 10.6.

SES significantly predicts the central executive, while training participation does not explain further variance and, hence, does not moderate the relation between SES and the central executive (see Table 10.3).

Table 10.3 Hierarchical moderated regression analysis predicting central executive with PA training program as moderator

	B	SE_B	β	t	p	R^2	ΔR^2
Model 1						.040	.048
(Constant)	.057	.087		0.654	.514		
SES	.215	.087	.220	2.46	.015*		
Model 2						.036	.004
(Constant)	–.011	.129		–0.082	.934		
SES	.212	.088	.217	2.422	.017*		
PA training program	.126	.175	.064	0.717	.475		
Model 3						.028	.000
(Constant)	–.010	.129		–0.079	.937		
SES	.216	.122	.222	1.77	.079+		
PA training program	.125	.176	.064	0.711	.478		
SES x PA training	–.009	.176	–.006	–0.052	.959		

Note. (N = 121)
+$p < .10$; *$p < .05$; **$p < .01$
Model 1: $F(1,119) = 6.04$, $p = .015$; Model 2: $F(2,118) = 3.27$, $p = .042$; Model 3: $F(3,117) = 2.16$, $p = .096$

Table 10.4 Hierarchical moderated regression analysis predicting phonological awareness (total) with program as moderator

	B	SE_B	β	t	p	R^2	ΔR^2
Model 1						.075	.082
(Constant)	.093	.085		1.09	.277		
SES	.281	.085	.286	3.30	.001**		
Model 2						.106	.038
(Constant)	–.102	.119		–0.853	.395		
SES	.278	.084	.284	3.33	.001**		
PA training program	.382	.167	.195	2.29	.024*		
Model 3						.107	.009
(Constant)	–.105	.119		–0.882	.380		
SES	.193	.113	.197	1.70	.092+		
PA training program	.388	.167	.198	2.32	.022*		
SES x PA training	.187	.168	.129	1.12	.266		

Note. (N = 124)
+$p < .10$; *$p < .05$; **$p < .01$
Model 1: $F(1,122) = 10.90$, $p = .001$; Model 2: $F(2,121) = 8.26$, $p = .000$; Model 3: $F(3,120) = 5.94$, $p = .001$

To assess the influence of PA training on the relation between SES and PA, first, hierarchical moderated regression was conducted for the total score of PA as the dependent variable. SES significantly predicts PA. While the participation in PA training explains differences between the children regarding PA, it does not influence the impact of SES on PA itself (Table 10.4).

To inspect influences on PA more closely, separate analyses were conducted for PA in a broad sense and PA in a narrow sense as dependent variables, respectively. SES predicts PA in a broad as well as narrow sense significantly ($B = .189$, $p < .05$, $R^2 = .036$; $B = .262$, $p < .01$, $R^2 = .096$). Training participation neither explains variance in the dependent variable nor does it moderate the relation between SES and PA in a broad sense ($B = .134$, *n.s.*, $R^2 = .096$; $B = .114$, *n.s.*, $R^2 = .032$). Training participation does explain variance in PA in a narrow sense. However, it does not moderate the relation between SES and the dependent variable ($B = .409$, $p < .01$, $R^2 = .096$; $B = .186$, *n.s.*, $R^2 = .097$).

Study 2: Specific procedures, analyses, and results

Study 2 investigated whether intensive bilingual preschool programs, which aim to foster skills in a foreign language using numerous comprehension-promoting and cognitively stimulating scaffolding techniques, are beneficial for the development of cognitive skills and are able to compensate somewhat for negative effects of SES. Learners in monolingual and bilingual preschools in Germany were examined in their last year of preschool with regard to their central executive, phonological loop, and nonverbal intelligence as described. In contrast to Study 1, this study did not assess phonological awareness. We expected a correlation between the learners' SES and their cognitive skills in both school programs, and we assumed that children who participated in the bilingual program would perform better on all cognitive tasks. Furthermore, we predicted a moderating effect of program on the relationship between SES and cognitive skills.

Analyses Study 2

Analogous to Study 1, identical analyses were performed in Study 2. Based on information from the parent questionnaire on the family's linguistic background and language use at home, children who grew up bilingual, i.e., learned two languages at home or in the social environment from birth or before preschool, were excluded from the initial dataset to avoid interactions between bilingual first language acquisition and the bilingual institutional intervention. Accordingly, for all participants in this study, German was the first and only language acquired before entering preschool. For the children of the intervention group, English was added as a second language at the beginning of preschool. Only participants who completed all corresponding tests and returned the parent questionnaire with information on their language background and HISEI were included.

Results Study 2

Descriptive statistics and bivariate correlations between SES and cognitive variables for the total sample are presented in Table 10.5. A weak

Table 10.5 Descriptive statistics and correlations for study variables

Variable	*n*	*M*	*SD*	*NVI*	*CE*	*PL*	*SES*
Nonverbal Intelligence (NVI)	43	108.16	12.12	–	.171	.149	.281⁺
Central Executive (CE)	41	52.41	8.06		–	.287⁺	.142
Phonological Loop (PL)	41	56.29	8.12			–	.081
Socioeconomic Status (SES)	43	60.28	18.48				–

Note. ⁺$p < .10$; $^{*}p < .05$; $^{**}p < .01$

Table 10.6 Results of independent samples *t*-tests

	Monolingual Preschool		*Bilingual Preschool*		*t*	*df*	*p*
	M	*SD*	*M*	*SD*			
Nonverbal Intelligence	108.59	12.03	107.29	12.71	0.326	41	.746
Central Executive	51.78	8.48	53.64	7.30	−0.698	39	.489
Phonological Loop	53.96	7.63	60.79	7.30	−2.755	39	.009**
Socioeconomic Status	57.07	20.78	66.93	10.13	−2.091	40.968	.043*

Note. ⁺$p < .10$; $^{*}p < .05$; $^{**}p < .01$

Table 10.7 Hierarchical moderated regression analysis predicting nonverbal intelligence with program as moderator

	B	SE_B	β	*t*	*p*	R^2	ΔR^2
Model 1						.079	.079
(Constant)	5.428E-16	0.148		0.000	1.000		
SES	0.281	0.150	.281	1.876	.068⁺		
Model 2						.095	.016
(Constant)	0.089	0.183		0.489	.628		
SES	0.314	0.155	.314	2.020	.050⁺		
Bilingual program	−0.275	0.328	−.130	−0.838	.407		
Model 3						.100	.005
(Constant)	0.085	0.185		0.462	.647		
SES	0.291	0.165	.291	1.756	.087		
Bilingual program	−0.347	0.368	−.165	−0.942	.352		
SES x Bilingual program	0.235	0.525	.082	0.448	.657		

Note. ($N = 43$)
⁺$p < .10$; $^{*}p < .05$; $^{**}p < .01$
Model 1: $F(1,41) = 3.52$, $p = .068$; Model 2: $F(2,40) = 2.10$, $p = .136$; Model 3: $F(3,39) = 1.44$, $p = .247$

positive correlation between SES and NVI was found at a 10% alpha level ($r = .28$, $p < .10$).

Independent samples *t*-tests were performed comparing the mean scores of monolingual and bilingual preschoolers on cognitive abilities and SES, with the bilingual group coming from a significantly higher social background. Statistically significant differences between the two groups were found only for performance on phonological loop tasks, on which the children who attended bilingual schools performed better (Table 10.6).

Contrary to expectations, a hierarchical moderated regression analysis did not show that program moderated the effect between SES and NVI significantly (see Table 10.7). However, regression analysis predicting NVI revealed that at a 10% significance level, SES ($B = 0.281$, $t = 1.876$, $p = .068$) did predict NVI.

Discussion

The presented studies addressed the question of which cognitive skills are predicted by SES in our samples and whether purported negative effects of low SES could be buffered by two different cognitive-linguistic interventions in preschool. To that end, our studies examined the relationship between different types of preschool interventions (i.e., Study 1: phonological awareness interventions; Study 2: bilingual education) and SES on cognitive skills. Although the two interventions differ in their objectives and intensity, both share the common goal of promoting cognitive and linguistic skills.

Relevance of socioeconomic status

In Study 1, SES correlated strongly with aspects of processing of speech sounds, i.e., all subtests of phonological awareness, and with the central executive. These results are in line with past research indicating that PA is significantly influenced by children's family background and that high SES correlates with an efficiently functioning prefrontal cortex, which, in turn, navigates working memory capability (Lundberg et al., 2012; Sheridan et al., 2012). However, nonverbal intelligence was not predicted by SES. This is contrary to the results of Study 2, in which only NVI correlated with SES (at the 10% level), while no correlations were found for central executive and the phonological loop. We interpreted results at a 10% level following a recommendation by Ellis (2010). As he cautions, effects are generally small in the social sciences, which leads to an inherent risk of a type 2 error, i.e., the risk of missing a small effect due to low statistical power. As one of several remedies, he suggests relaxing the alpha criterion to an $\alpha = .10$ level, especially for small sample studies (Larson-Hall, 2012).

On the surface level, mean values and correlations differed between the two studies. Furthermore, sample sizes differed from each other. Hence, significant effects may prevail in Study 1 due to larger sample size and, therefore, stronger statistical power. As for parental influence on cognitive skills, it is important to note the SES difference within and between the samples. Thus, disparities in results possibly reflect sample variance regarding parental background.

Relevance of preschool programs/cognitive-linguistic interventions

To check whether the influence of programs might be relevant as a possible moderator for SES effects on cognition (RQ2), main effects of program were calculated in the form of group differences between intervention and control groups. *T*-tests showed that learners in the Study 1 intervention group differed significantly from the controls in all aspects of phonological awareness and in Study 2 for the subtest phonological loop. As Trebits et al. (2021) argue, phonological awareness seems more malleable and susceptible to training influences than central executive functions or intelligence (Kersten, 2023, this volume). These results also match those observed in earlier studies (Schneider et al., 2000; Jörns et al., 2017). We would expect to find a similar result for phonological awareness in bilingual versus monolingual preschools (Trebits et al., 2021); it would thus be recommendable to include PA in subsequent studies with a similar design.

These group differences have, however, to be treated with caution, as data are only cross-sectional, and a baseline test is missing. To establish causal relationships, a pretest-posttest and random assignment design is necessary and advisable for future studies. Another indicator for cautious interpretation is the fact that in Study 2, intervention and control groups also differed in SES. The groups differ in HISEI by 9.86 units. One reason could be the clientele of bilingual private schools, which draw families from more educationally advantaged households.

However, no effects of program were found for intelligence and central executive. This might be for a number of reasons. In both studies, it is yet unclear to what extent children were given enough opportunities to consolidate and transfer knowledge acquired during the training processes. In Study 1, before cognitive skill assessment, children had participated in a specific training for a duration of 3 months. It is possible that this time span was insufficient for training effects to manifest. In Study 1, children participating in the ZIK training autonomously determined the frequency of playing the games. Hence, only a few children reached training intensity as high as children participating in trainings conducted by preschool teachers on a daily basis. Since previous evaluations have shown ZIK to effectively increase phonological awareness (Jörns et al., 2017), future studies should advise preschool teachers to administer fixed playtimes in order to achieve sufficient training intensity. As this may play a crucial role to training efficacy, it can be argued that either children need more persuasive incentives to play the games more often voluntarily or a stricter administration by teachers is necessary.

In Study 2, children participated in a bilingual schooling program. Even though L2 speakers were present in the bilingual groups at all times, children were able to choose whether they would like to interact with and take part in the activities offered by the L2 personnel. Analyses did not account for such interindividual differences in exposure to the second language. Future studies should consider including these differences in their analysis. Furthermore, this result is not entirely surprising as cognitive benefits often emerge after children have participated in a high-intensity bilingual program for an extended period of time (Trebits et al., 2021).

Taken together, no definitive conclusions can be drawn from these studies as to whether the interventions were successful, since no baseline for cognitive skills was elicited, and numerous other factors may have influenced the children's development. Thus, we were not able to control whether the intervention groups had higher cognitive abilities from the beginning or whether their advantage developed as a result of the intervention experience.

The relationship between parental SES, school type, and cognitive abilities

In past research, summarized earlier, both PA training and bilingual education have been shown to have positive impact on specific cognitive skills (Fischer & Pfost, 2015; Bialystok, 2018; Nicolay & Poncelet, 2015; Woumans et al., 2016; Trebits et al., 2021). Since such promotion is especially crucial for children from low-SES backgrounds, in this chapter, we aimed for a closer look at the possibility that trainings might mitigate SES impacts on cognitive skills.

Based on the assumption that cognitively stimulating intervention programs could strengthen cognitive processes and the findings on cognitive benefits for socially disadvantaged children (Engel de Abreu et al., 2012; Hartanto et al., 2019; Kersten, 2020; Trebits et al., 2021), we expected a moderating effect of the programs (i.e., PA training and the bilingual education) on the relationship between SES and cognitive abilities. Contrary to expectations, no moderating effect of preschool cognitive-linguistic support programs on the association between SES and cognitive variables was found. This might partly be due to the fact that the independent cognitive variables did not show strong variation in the sample. On the other hand, with regard to Study 2, the results are in line with those studies critical of the bilingual advantage hypothesis that do not find effects of degree of bilingualism on cognition (Simonis et al., 2019). Although we expected different results (Kersten, 2020), these findings are consistent with other previous studies documenting strong effects of parental influence on children's cognitive as well as academic development (Niklas & Schneider, 2017). Strong parental influence may, in turn, be associated with skills resistant to short trainings. This does, however, not exclude the possibility that a moderation effect could be found in a larger data set with more statistical power, in longer and more intensive interventions, and in samples that do not differ in their SES in the first place.

Oftentimes, although children spend a majority of their time in educational institutions, additive as well as incidental trainings do not reach the intensity of parent–child interactions. While there is evidence for additive trainings to be effective (Schneider et al., 1997), it has also been shown that cognitive skills are stable to a large extent (Hoekstra et al., 2007; Schneider et al., 2014). Furthermore, relevant findings imply an extensive role of family environment in regard to learning, even after the consideration of children's cognitive skills and their socioeconomic background (Niklas & Schneider, 2010). Niklas and colleagues (2018) point out the potential of promoting children's home learning environment by offering parents training in dialogic reading. Since children experience a substantial amount of learning experiences at home, it is possible that training children's parents may provide additional effects along with training children in preschool, who may have difficulties transferring knowledge without constant guidance at a young age. Thus, the relatively short duration (and, in the case of Study 1, low intensity) of our training programs may have been insufficient to contribute to performance above and beyond children's socioeconomic status. In prior studies, training effects have been shown in the longer term (Ise et al., 2012). For this reason, it is recommendable that future studies should consider points of measurements later in school.

As a final aspect of consideration, SES is a distal container variable that is used as a proxy for numerous other effects that were not controlled for in this study (Kersten & Greve, and Kersten, 2023, this volume). As a consequence, it exerts stronger statistical power in analyses than proximal external variables such as specific types of teacher behavior or parent–child interaction. The latter, however, describe the actual point of stimulation of the learner. While it is more difficult to detect the impact of such proximal variables, they are logically the better predictors as they have actual explanatory value for changes in the learners' minds (Proximity Hypothesis, Kersten, 2023, this volume). This might be another reason we find correlations between the central executive, phonological awareness, and nonverbal intelligence with SES across both data sets but no moderation of the instructional programs.

Limitations of the studies

Finally, a number of important limitations need to be considered. Due to high organizational complexity and limited resources, not all children in both studies could be tested with all test instruments. For a more comprehensive view, it would be helpful to include more learners with data for each variable. The missing values are particularly noticeable in the participation in the parents' questionnaire. Unfortunately, there was a low response rate to the parent questionnaires (especially in Study 2), so for future studies, we will need to recruit a larger number of participants to ensure the reliability and generalizability of our results. Additionally, the question arises as to whether a kind of preselection had already taken place by filling out the parent questionnaire, since parents from better-educated households may be more likely to participate in this type of questionnaire than parents from lower-educated households. Furthermore, the parent questionnaire is a self-report of occupational or socioeconomic status, which may lead to response bias due to social desirability.

For those reasons, caution must be applied to the interpretation of the results due to small sample sizes, especially in Study 2. In addition, larger samples would provide more statistical power. However, the most important limitation lies in the fact that cross-sectional data, such as those used in these studies, do not allow for causal interpretation. For future studies, longitudinal designs that also include baselines for cognitive variables and control for additional domestic variables are needed.

Conclusion and future directions

The aim of this study was to examine whether the relationship between parental SES and cognitive abilities is moderated by the type of schooling in preschool (two different cognitive-linguistic interventions: phonological awareness intervention and bilingual education). The presented cross-sectional studies were able to provide initial insights to the chances and limitations of preschool trainings regarding diverse cognitive skills. While the given theoretical assumptions behind the trainings imply promising results, they are not reflected in the data of our respective studies. In neither of these were interactions between training and socioeconomic status found. Although correlations were found between SES and phonological awareness as well as central executive, a playful training of phonological awareness could not moderate this relationship and thus was not effective in order to support children with low SES (Study 1), nor was the positive correlation of SES and nonverbal intelligence influenced by bilingual education in preschool (Study 2).

We suggest that future studies and analyses should, first, account for additional variables such as home learning environment and different degrees of bilingualism. Second, a longitudinal perspective is crucial to inspect the efficacy of the training programs. Finally, we would expect that the impact of educational training programs emerges gradually as a function of quality, intensity, and duration of the intervention and differentially for different cognitive skills.

Funding

Research within the research association Inclusive Educational Research in Early Childhood as a Multidisciplinary Challenge [Inklusive Bildungsforschung der frühen Kindheit als multidisziplinäre Herausforderung] was funded by the Lower Saxony Ministry of Science and Culture ("Niedersächsisches Vorab").

References

Adesope, O. O., Lavin, T., Thompson, T., & Ungerleider, C. (2010). A systematic review and meta-analysis of the cognitive correlates of bilingualism. *Review of Educational Research*, *80*(2), 207–245. https://doi.org/10.3102/0034654310368803

Alloway, T. P., & Alloway, R. G. (2010). Investigating the predictive roles of working memory and IQ in academic attainment. *Journal of Experimental Child Psychology*, *106*(1), 20–29. https://doi.org/10.1016/j.jecp.2009.11.003

Antón, E., Duñabeitia, J. A., Estévez, A., Hernández, J. A., Castillo, A., Fuentes, L. J., Davidson, D. J., & Carreiras, M. (2014). Is there a bilingual advantage in the ANT task? Evidence from children. *Frontiers in Psychology*, *5*, 398. https://doi.org/10.3389/fpsyg.2014.00398

Baddeley, A. D. (1994). The magical number seven: Still magic after all these years? *Psychological Review*, *101*(2), 353–356. https://doi.org/10.1037/0033-295X.101.2.353

Baddeley, A. D. (2000). The episodic buffer: A new component of working memory? *Trends in Cognitive Sciences*, *4*(11), 417–423. https://doi.org/10.1016/S1364-6613(00)01538-2

Baddeley, A. D., & Hitch, G. (1974). Working memory. In G. H. Bower (Ed.), *Psychology of learning and motivation* (Vol. 8, pp. 47–89). Elsevier. https://doi.org/10.1016/S0079-7421(08)60452-1

Bialystok, E. (2018). Bilingual education for young children: Review of the effects and consequences. *International Journal of Bilingual Education and Bilingualism*, *21*(6), 666–679. https://doi.org/10.1080/13670050.2016.1203859

Bialystok, E., & Barac, R. (2012). Emerging bilingualism: Dissociating advantages for metalinguistic awareness and executive control. *Cognition*, *122*(1), 67–73. https://doi.org/10.1016/j.cognition.2011.08.003

Bialystok, E., Craik, F. I. M., Green, D. W., & Gollan, T. H. (2009). Bilingual minds. *Psychological Science in the Public Interest*, *10*(3), 89–129. https://doi.org/10.1177/1529100610387084

Bialystok, E., Craik, F. I. M., & Luk, G. (2008). Cognitive control and lexical access in younger and older bilinguals. *Journal of Experimental Psychology: Learning, Memory, and Cognition*, *34*(4), 859–873. https://doi.org/10.1037/0278-7393.34.4.859

Bornstein, M. H., & Bradley, R. H. (Eds.). (2012). *Socioeconomic status, parenting, and child development*. Psychology Press Taylor & Francis Group.

Bowey, J. A. (1995). Socioeconomic status differences in preschool phonological sensitivity and first-grade reading achievement. *Journal of Educational Psychology*, *87*(3), 476–487. https://doi.org/10.1037/0022-0663.87.3.476

Bradley, R. H., & Corwyn, R. F. (2002). Socioeconomic status and child development. *Annual Review of Psychology*, *53*(1), 371–399. https://doi.org/10.1146/annurev.psych.53.100901.135233

Brooks-Gunn, J., & Duncan, G. J. (1997). The effects of poverty on children. *The Future of Children*, *7*(2), 55. https://doi.org/10.2307/1602387

Bus, A. G., & van Ijzendoorn, M. H. (1999). Phonological awareness and early reading: A meta-analysis of experimental training studies. *Journal of Educational Psychology*, *91*(3), 403–414. https://doi.org/10.1037/0022-0663.91.3.403

Calvo, A., & Bialystok, E. (2014). Independent effects of bilingualism and socioeconomic status on language ability and executive functioning. *Cognition*, *130*(3), 278–288. https://doi.org/10.1016/j.cognition.2013.11.015

Costa, A., Hernández, M., Costa-Faidella, J., & Sebastián-Gallés, N. (2009). On the bilingual advantage in conflict processing: Now you see it, now you don't. *Cognition*, *113*(2), 135–149. https://doi.org/10.1016/j.cognition.2009.08.001

De Bruin, A., Treccani, B., & Della Sala, S. (2015). Cognitive advantage in bilingualism: An example of publication bias? *Psychological Science*, *26*(1), 99–107. https://doi.org/10.1177/0956797614557866

De Houwer, A. (2009). *Bilingual first language acquisition*. Multilingual Matters. https://doi.org/10.21832/9781847691507

Dicataldo, R., & Roch, M. (2020). Are the effects of variation in quantity of daily bilingual exposure and socioeconomic status on language and cognitive abilities independent in preschool children? *International Journal of Environmental Research and Public Health*, *17*(12). https://doi.org/10.3390/ijerph17124570

Döpke, S. (1992). *One parent – one language: An interactional approach*. John Benjamins Publishing Company.

Duñabeitia, J. A., Hernández, J. A., Antón, E., Macizo, P., Estévez, A., Fuentes, L. J., & Carreiras, M. (2014). The inhibitory advantage in bilingual children revisited: Myth or reality? *Experimental Psychology*, *61*(3), 234–251. https://doi.org/10.1027/1618-3169/a000243

Duncan, G. J., & Magnuson, K. (2012). Socioeconomic status and cognitive functioning: Moving from correlation to causation. *Wiley Interdisciplinary Reviews. Cognitive Science*, *3*(3), 377–386. https://doi.org/10.1002/wcs.1176

Ehri, L. C., Nunes, S. R., Willows, D. M., Schuster, B. V., Yaghoub-Zadeh, Z., & Shanahan, T. (2001). Phonemic awareness instruction helps children learn to read: Evidence from the National Reading Panel's Meta-Analysis. *Reading Research Quarterly*, *36*(3), 250–287. https://doi.org/10.1598/RRQ.36.3.2

Ellis, P. D. (2010). *The essential guide to effect sizes: Statistical power, meta-analysis, and the interpretation of research results*. Cambridge University Press.

Endlich, D., Berger, N., Küspert, P., Lenhard, W., Marx, P., Weber, J., & Schneider, W. (2017). *WVT. Würzburger Vorschultest. Erfassung schriftsprachlicher und mathematischer (Vorläufer-)Fertigkeiten und sprachlicher Kompetenzen im letzten Kindergartenjahr [Würzburg preschool test: Assessment of literacy and mathematical (precursor) abilities and linguistic competencies in the last year of preschool]* (1st ed.). Hogrefe.

Engel de Abreu, P. M. J., Cruz-Santos, A., Tourinho, C. J., Martin, R., & Bialystok, E. (2012). Bilingualism enriches the poor: Enhanced cognitive control in low-income minority children. *Psychological Science*, *23*(11), 1364–1371. https://doi.org/10.1177/0956797612443836

European Commission. (2017). *Key data on teaching languages at school in Europe – 2017 edition. Eurydice report*. Publications Office of the European Union.

Fälth, L., Gustafson, S., & Svensson, I. (2017). Phonological awareness training with articulation promotes early reading development. *Education*, *137*(3), 261–276.

Festman, J., Czapka, S., & Winsler A. (2023, this volume). How many moderators does is take till we know . . . that too many bilingual advantage effects have died? In K. Kersten & A. Winsler (Eds.), *Interplay of variables in cognitive-linguistic development – A multi-layered perspective*. Routledge.

Fischer, M. Y., & Pfost, M. (2015). Wie effektiv sind Maßnahmen zur Förderung der phonologischen Bewusstheit? [How effective are interventions to promote phonological awareness?]. *Zeitschrift für Entwicklungspsychologie und Pädagogische Psychologie [Journal of Developmental and Educational Psychology]*, *47*(1), 35–51.

Fröhlich, L. P., Metz, D., & Petermann, F. (2010). *Förderung der phonologischen Bewusstheit und sprachlicher Kompetenzen. Das Lobo-Kindergartenprogramm [Promoting phonological awareness and language skills. The Lobo-preschool program]*. Hogrefe.

Ganzeboom, H. B. G. (2010). *A new international socio-economic index (ISEI) of occupational status for the international standard classification of occupation 2008 (ISCO-08) constructed with data from the ISSP 2002–2007: With an analysis of quality of occupational measurement in ISSP*. Annual Conference of the International Social Survey Programme.

Gottfried, A. W., Gottfried, A. E., Bathurst, K., Guerin, D. W., & Parramore, M. M. (2012). Socioeconomic status in children's development and family environment: Infancy through adolescence. In M. H. Bornstein & R. H. Bradley (Eds.), *Socioeconomic status, parenting, and child development* (pp. 189–207). Psychology Press and Taylor & Francis Group.

Graham, S., Courtney, L., Marinis, T., & Tonkyn, A. (2017). Early language learning: The impact of teaching and teacher factors. *Language Learning*, *67*(4), 922–958. https://doi.org/10.1111/lang.12251

Hackman, D. A., & Farah, M. J. (2009). Socioeconomic status and the developing brain. *Trends in Cognitive Sciences*, *13*(2), 65–73. https://doi.org/10.1016/j.tics.2008.11.003

Hackman, D. A., Gallop, R., Evans, G. W., & Farah, M. J. (2015). Socioeconomic status and executive function: Developmental trajectories and mediation. *Developmental Science*, *18*(5), 686–702. https://doi.org/10.1111/desc.12246

Hart, B., & Risley, T. R. (1995). *Meaningful differences in the everyday experience of young American children*. Paul H Brookes Publishing.

Hartanto, A., Toh, W. X., & Yang, H. (2019). Bilingualism narrows socioeconomic disparities in executive functions and self-regulatory behaviors during early childhood: Evidence from the early childhood longitudinal study. *Child Development*, *90*(4), 1215–1235. https://doi.org/10.1111/cdev.13032

Hasselhorn, M., Schumann-Hengsteler, R., Gronauer, J., Grube, D., Mähler, C., Schmid, I., Seitz-Stein, K., & Zoelch, C. (2012). *AGTB 5–12. Arbeitsgedächtnistestbatterie für Kinder von 5 bis 12 Jahren* [*Working memory test battery for children aged 5 to 12*]. Hogrefe.

Hoekstra, R. A., Bartels, M., & Boomsma, D. I. (2007). Longitudinal genetic study of verbal and nonverbal IQ from early childhood to young adulthood. *Learning and Individual Differences*, *17*(2), 97–114.

Hoffmeyer-Zlotnik, J. H. P., & Geis, A. J. (2003). Berufsklassifikation und Messung des beruflichen Status/Prestige [Occupational classification and measurement of occupational status/prestige]. *ZUMA Nachrichten*, *27*(52), 125–138.

Huschka, S. S., Emde, K. R., & Brandenburg, J. (2020). Zur Vorhersage der Schriftsprache durch vorschulische Kompetenzen [On the prediction of written language by preschool skills]. *Frühe Bildung [Early Education]*, *9*(4), 193–202.

Ise, E., Engel, R. R., & Schulte-Körne, G. (2012). Was hilft bei der Lese-Rechtschreibstörung? [What helps with dyslexia?]. *Kindheit und Entwicklung [Childhood and Development]*, *21*(2), 122–136.

Jäger, D. (2018). *Zur pädagogischen Legitimation des Würzburger Trainingsprogrammes Hören, lauschen, lernen: Trainingseffekte und Trainereffekte* [*On the pedagogical legitimacy of the Würzburg training program hearing, listening, learning: Training effects and trainer effects*] (Doctoral dissertation). Universität Würzburg.

Jörns, C., Schuchardt, K., Grube, D., Barkam, L. V., & Mähler, C. (2017). ZIKZAK – Profitieren Kindergartenkinder von Gesellschaftsspielen zur Förderung numerischer Kompetenzen und phonologischer Bewusstheit? [ZIKZAK – Do preschool children benefit from board games to promote numerical skills and phonological awareness?]. *Unterrichtswissenschaft [Teaching Science]*, *45*, 220–238.

Kersten, K. (2019). Einflussfaktoren im bilingualen Fremdsprachenerwerb [Influencing factors in bilingual foreign language acquisition]. In A. Rohde & A. K. Steinlen (Eds.), *Sprachenvielfalt als Ressource begreifen: Mehrsprachigkeit in bilingualen Kindertagesstätten und Schulen [Understanding linguistic diversity as a resource: Multilingualism in bilingual preschools and schools]* (Vol. 2, pp. 35–70). Dohrmann Verlag.

Kersten, K. (2020, January). *The interplay of cognitive, linguistic and instructional factors in early language acquisition*. Paper presented at the Interdisciplinary symposium: Variables affecting (language) learning processes, Hildesheim University.

Kersten, K. (2023, this volume). Proximity of stimulation: Investigating the interplay of cognitive, linguistic and instructional factors in early language acquisition. In K. Kersten & A. Winsler (Eds.), *Interplay of variables in cognitive-linguistic development: A multi-layered perspective*. Routledge.

Kersten, K., Bruhn, A.-C., Koch, M., & Schriek, J. (2019, August). *The effect of L2 input and cognitively stimulating tasks on second language acquisition*. Paper presented at EuroSLA 29, Lund University.

Kersten, K., & Greve, W. (2023, this volume). Investigating influencing factors of cognitive-linguistic development in SLA: Challenges for empirical research. In K. Kersten & A. Winsler (Eds.), *Interplay of variables in cognitive-linguistic development: A multi-layered perspective*. Routledge.

Kersten, K., Rohde, A., Schelletter, C., & Steinlen, A. K. (2010). *Bilingual preschools: Learning and development* (Vol. 1). Wissenschaftlicher Verlag Trier.

Kishiyama, M. M., Boyce, W. T., Jimenez, A. M., Perry, L. M., & Knight, R. T. (2009). Socioeconomic disparities affect prefrontal function in children. *Journal of Cognitive Neuroscience*, *21*(6), 1106–1115. https://doi.org/10.1162/jocn.2009.21101

Kjeldsen, A. C., Kärnä, A., Niemi, P., Olofsson, Å., & Witting, K. (2014). Gains from training in phonological awareness in kindergarten predict reading comprehension in grade 9. *Scientific Studies of Reading*, *18*(6), 452–467.

Küspert, P., & Schneider, W. (2008). *Hören, lauschen, lernen – Anleitung: Sprachspiele für Kinder im Vorschulalter – Würzburger Trainingsprogramm zur Vorbereitung auf den Erwerb der Schriftsprache [Hearing, listening, learning – instructions: Language games for preschool children – Würzburg training program to prepare for the acquisition of written language]*. Vandenhoeck & Ruprecht.

Küspert, P., & Schneider, W. (2018). *Hören, lauschen, lernen – Anleitung: Sprachspiele für Kinder im Vorschulalter – Würzburger Trainingsprogramm zur Vorbereitung auf den Erwerb der Schriftsprache [Hearing, listening, learning. Language games* for *preschoolers. Würzburg training program for the preparation of literacy. Acquisition]*. Vandenhoeck & Ruprecht.

Küspert, P., Schneider, W., & Plume, E. (1999). *Hören, lauschen, lernen [Hearing, listening, learning]*. Vandenhoeck & Ruprecht.

Larson-Hall, J. (2012). Our statistical intuitions May be misleading us: Why we need robust statistics. *Language Teaching*, *45*(4), 460–474. https://doi.org/10.1017/S0261444811000127

Lawson, G. M., & Farah, M. J. (2017). Executive function as a mediator between SES and academic achievement throughout childhood. *International Journal of Behavioral Development*, *41*(1), 94–104. https://doi.org/10.1177/0165025415603489

Lawson, G. M., Hook, C. J., & Farah, M. J. (2018). A meta-analysis of the relationship between socioeconomic status and executive function performance among children. *Developmental Science*, *21*(2). https://doi.org/10.1111/desc.12529

Lawson, G. M., Hook, C. J., Hackman, D. A., & Farah, M. J. (2016). Socioeconomic status and the development of executive function: Behavioral and neuroscience approaches. In P. D. McCardle, J. A. Griffin, & L. Freund (Eds.), *Executive function in preschool-age children: Integrating measurement, neurodevelopment, and translational research* (pp. 259–278). American Psychological Association. https://doi.org/10.1037/14797-012

Lehtonen, M., Soveri, A., Laine, A., Järvenpää, J., De Bruin, A., & Antfolk, J. (2018). Is bilingualism associated with enhanced executive functioning in adults? A meta-analytic review. *Psychological Bulletin*, *144*(4), 394–425. https://doi.org/10.1037/bul0000142

Loewen, S., & Sato, M. (2018). Interaction and instructed second language acquisition. *Language Teaching*, *51*(3), 285–329. https://doi.org/10.1017/S0261444818000125

Lonigan, C. J., Burgess, S. R., Anthony, J. L., & Barker, T. A. (1998). Development of phonological sensitivity in 2- to 5-year-old children. *Journal of Educational Psychology*, *90*(2), 294–311. https://doi.org/10.1037/0022-0663.90.2.294

Lundberg, I., Frost, J., & Petersen, O. P. (1988). Effects of an extensive program for stimulating phonological awareness in preschool children. *Reading Research Quarterly*, 263–284.

Lundberg, I., Larsman, P., & Strid, A. (2012). Development of phonological awareness during the preschool year: The influence of gender and socioeconomic status. *Reading and Writing*, *25*(2), 305–320. https://doi.org/10.1007/s11145-010-9269-4

McDowell, K. D., Lonigan, C. J., & Goldstein, H. (2007). Relations among socioeconomic status, age, and predictors of phonological awareness. *Journal of Speech, Language, and Hearing Research*, *50*(4), 1079–1092. https://doi.org/10.1044/1092-4388(2007/075)

McIntosh, B., Crosbie, S., Holm, A., Dodd, B., & Thomas, S. (2007). Enhancing the phonological awareness and language skills of socially disadvantaged preschoolers: An interdisciplinary programme. *Child Language Teaching and Therapy*, *23*(3), 267–286. https://doi.org/10.1177/0265659007080678

Meir, N., & Armon-Lotem, S. (2017). Independent and combined effects of socioeconomic status (SES) and bilingualism on children's vocabulary and verbal short-term memory. *Frontiers in Psychology*, *8*, 1442. https://doi.org/10.3389/fpsyg.2017.01442

Nicolay, A. C., & Poncelet, M. (2015). Cognitive benefits in children enrolled in an early bilingual immersion school: A follow up study. *Bilingualism: Language and Cognition*, *18*(4), 789–795.

Niklas, F., Cohrssen, C., & Tayler, C. (2018). Making a difference to children's reasoning skills before school-entry: The contribution of the home learning environment. *Contemporary Educational Psychology*, *54*, 79–88. https://doi.org/10.1016/j.cedpsych.2018.06.001

Niklas, F., & Schneider, W. (2010). Der Zusammenhang von familiärer Lernumwelt mit schulrelevanten Kompetenzen im Vorschulalter [The association of family learning environments with school-relevant competencies in preschool.]. *Zeitschrift für Soziologie der Erziehung und Sozialisation [Journal for Sociology of Education and Socialization]*, *30*(2), 149–165.

Niklas, F., & Schneider, W. (2017). Home learning environment and development of child competencies from kindergarten until the end of elementary school. *Contemporary Educational Psychology*, *49*, 263–274. https://doi.org/10.1016/j.cedpsych.2017.03.006

Noble, K. G., Farah, M. J., & McCandliss, B. D. (2006). Socioeconomic background modulates cognition-achievement relationships in reading. *Cognitive Development*, *21*(3), 349–368. https://doi.org/10.1016/j.cogdev.2006.01.007

Noble, K. G., McCandliss, B. D., & Farah, M. J. (2007). Socioeconomic gradients predict individual differences in neurocognitive abilities. *Developmental Science*, *10*(4), 464–480. https://doi.org/10.1111/j.1467-7687.2007.00600.x

Paap, K. R., Myuz, H. A., Anders, R. T., Bockelman, M. F., Mikulinsky, R., & Sawi, O. M. (2017). No compelling evidence for a bilingual advantage in switching or that frequent language switching reduces switch cost. *Journal of Cognitive Psychology*, *29*(2), 89–112. https://doi.org/10.1080/20445911.2016.1248436

Pace, A., Luo, R., Hirsh-Pasek, K., & Golinkoff, R. M. (2017). Identifying pathways between socioeconomic status and language development. *Annual Review of Linguistics*, *3*(1), 285–308. https://doi.org/10.1146/annurev-linguistics-011516-034226

Raven, J., Raven, J. C., & Court, J. H. (2006). *Manual zu Raven's Progressive Matrices and Vocabulary Scales (Deutsche Bearbeitung und Normierung von S. Bulheller und H. Häcker) [Manual for Raven's progressive matrices and vocabulary scales (German editing and standardization by S. Bulheller and H. Häcker)]*. Harcourt Test Services.

Rindermann, H., & Baumeister, A. E. (2015). Parents' SES vs. parental educational behavior and children's development: A reanalysis of the Hart and Risley study. *Learning and Individual Differences*, *37*, 133–138. https://doi.org/10.1016/j.lindif.2014.12.005

Robson, D. A., Allen, M. S., & Howard, S. J. (2020). Self-regulation in childhood as a predictor of future outcomes: A meta-analytic review. *Psychological Bulletin*, *146*(4), 324–354. https://doi.org/10.1037/bul0000227

Rosen, M. L., Hagen, M. P., Lurie, L. A., Miles, Z. E., Sheridan, M. A., Meltzoff, A. N., & McLaughlin, K. A. (2020). Cognitive stimulation as a mechanism linking socioeconomic status with executive function: A longitudinal investigation. *Child Development*, *91*(4), e762–e779. https://doi.org/10.1111/cdev.13315

Roth, B., Becker, N., Romeyke, S., Schäfer, S., Domnick, F., & Spinath, F. M. (2015). Intelligence and school grades: A meta-analysis. *Intelligence*, *53*, 118–137.

Sarsour, K., Sheridan, M., Jutte, D., Nuru-Jeter, A., Hinshaw, S., & Boyce, W. T. (2011). Family socioeconomic status and child executive functions: The roles of language, home environment, and single parenthood. *Journal of the International Neuropsychological Society: JINS*, *17*(1), 120–132. https://doi.org/10.1017/S1355617710001335

Schneider, W. (1989). Möglichkeiten der frühen Vorhersage von Leseleistungen im Schulalter [Opportunities for early prediction of school-age reading achievement]. *Zeitschrift für Pädagogische Psychologie [Journal of Educational Psychology]*, *3*(2), 157–168.

Schneider, W., Küspert, P., Roth, E., Visé, M., & Marx, H. (1997). Short- and long-term effects of training phonological awareness in kindergarten: Evidence from two German studies. *Journal of Experimental Child Psychology*, *66*(3), 311–340. https://doi.org/10.1006/jecp.1997.2384

Schneider, W., Niklas, F., & Schmiedeler, S. (2014). Intellectual development from early childhood to early adulthood: The impact of early IQ differences on stability and change over time. *Learning and Individual Differences*, *32*, 156–162. https://doi.org/10.1016/j.lindif.2014.02.001

Schneider, W., Roth, E., & Ennemoser, M. (2000). Training phonological skills and letter knowledge in children at risk for dyslexia: A comparison of three kindergarten intervention programs. *Journal of Educational Psychology*, *92*(2), 284–295. https://doi.org/10.1037/0022-0663.92.2.284

Schuchardt, K., Maehler, C., & Hasselhorn, M. (2008). Working memory deficits in children with specific learning disorders. *Journal of Learning Disabilities*, *41*(6), 514–523.

Sheridan, M. A., Sarsour, K., Jutte, D., D'Esposito, M., & Boyce, W. T. (2012). The impact of social disparity on prefrontal function in childhood. *PloS One*, *7*(4). https://doi.org/10.1371/journal.pone.0035744

Simonis, M., Van der Linden, L., Galand, B., Hiligsmann, P., & Szmalec, A. (2019). Executive control performance and foreign-language proficiency associated with immersion education in French-speaking Belgium. *Bilingualism: Language and Cognition*, *23*(2), 355–370.

Sirin, S. R. (2005). Socioeconomic status and academic achievement: A meta-analytic review of research. *Review of Educational Research*, *75*(3), 417–453. https://doi.org/10.3102/00346543075003417

Skowronek, H., & Marx, H. (1989). The Bielefeld longitudinal study on early identification of risks in learning to read and write: Theoretical background and first results. In M. Brambring, F. Lösel, & H. Skowronek (Eds.), *Children at risk: Assessment, longitudinal research, and intervention* (pp. 268–294). Walter De Gruyter.

Spearman, C. (1904). The proof and measurement of association between two things. *The American Journal of Psychology*, *15*(1), 72–101. https://doi.org/10.2307/1412159

Sternberg, R. J. (2018). Theories of intelligence. In S. I. Pfeiffer, E. Shaunessy-Dedrick, & M. Foley-Nicpon (Eds.), *APA handbook of giftedness and talent* (pp. 145–161). American Psychological Association. https://doi.org/10.1037/0000038-010

Trebits, A., Koch, M. J., Ponto, K., Bruhn, A.-C., Adler, M., & Kersten, K. (2021). Cognitive gains and socioeconomic status in early second language acquisition in immersion and EFL learning settings. *International Journal of Bilingual Education and Bilingualism*, 1–14. https://doi.org/10.1080/13670050.2021.1943307

Unsworth, S., Argyri, F., Cornips, L., Hulk, A., Sorace, A., & Tsimpli, I. (2014). The role of age of onset and input in early child bilingualism in Greek and Dutch: S. Unsworth, F. Argyri, L. Cornips, A. Hulk, A. Sorace, I. Tsimpli. *Applied Psycholinguistics*, *35*(4), 765–805. https://doi.org/10.1017/S0142716412000574

Wegner, A. (2022). *Die Implementation von CLIL (Content and Language Integrated Learning) in der Grundschule: Eine methodenintegrierende Untersuchung zu Einflussfaktoren bei der Umsetzung bilingualer Unterrichtskonzepte [The implementation of CLIL in elementary school: A method-integrating study of factors influencing the implementation of bilingual instructional concepts]*. Universitätsverlag Hildesheim. https://doi.org/10.18442/191

Weitz, M. (2015). *Die Rolle des L2-Inputs in bilingualen Kindergärten [The role of L2 input in bilingual preschools]*. Peter Lang.

Weitz, M., Pahl, S., Mattson, A. F., Buyl, A., & Kalbe, E. (2010). The input quality observation scheme (IQOS): The nature of L2 input and its influence on L2 development in bilingual preschools. In K. Kersten, A. Rohde, C. Schelletter, & A. K. Steinlen (Eds.), *Bilingual preschools, Volume I: Learning and development* (pp. 5–44). Wissenschaftlicher Verlag Trier.

Woumans, E., Surmont, J., Struys, E., & Duyck, W. (2016). The longitudinal effect of bilingual immersion schooling on cognitive control and intelligence. *Language Learning*, *66*(S2), 76–91. https://doi.org/10.1111/lang.12171

Zhang, Y., Tardif, T., Shu, H., Li, H., Liu, H., McBride-Chang, C., Liang, W., & Zhang, Z. (2013). Phonological skills and vocabulary knowledge mediate socioeconomic status effects in predicting reading outcomes for Chinese children. *Developmental Psychology*, *49*(4), 665–671. https://doi.org/10.1037/a0028612

Part III

Synthesis

11 Commentary on *Understanding Variability in Second Language Acquisition, Bilingualism, and Cognition*

A second language acquisition perspective

Gabriele Pallotti

Introduction

No one doubts that second language acquisition (SLA) is a complex process, involving many aspects and depending on many factors, as the chapters in this volume attest. Clearly, no single book can encompass an entire field of study, much less can a short chapter like this one. Therefore, my aim will not be to provide a comprehensive synthesis but to elaborate some methodological and epistemological reflections on the very enterprise of conceiving SLA research in an organic way – in other words, to see the "interplay of variables" also as an "interplay of researchers."

SLA began to be studied systematically as a research field around the 1960s (for an extensive historical summary, see Ellis, 2008). Prior to that time, the little research on second language learning was closely associated with the practical purposes of teaching, which explains why for a long time, and to some extent still today, SLA research was regarded as a branch of applied linguistics, that is, linguistics applied to more effective teaching.

Early studies in the 1970s were essentially descriptive in nature and sought to track the order in which language structures were acquired, the role of the first language, the interactions between native and nonnative speakers, and the strategies the latter employ when learning and using a new language. Toward the end of that decade, Krashen (1982) presented his "monitor model." Although it was subsequently criticized for its vagueness and nonfalsifiability, it nevertheless had an enormous influence in setting the research agenda. Much of the research of the 1980s, in fact, had the more or less explicit purpose of empirically testing some of Krashen's statements, such as the role of comprehensible input, the presence of an "affective filter" impacting learning outcomes, and of a

DOI: 10.4324/9781003155683-14

conscious "monitor," which leads to the distinction between (spontaneous) acquisition and (guided) learning. The latter aspect, in particular, prompted a number of studies in the 1980s and 1990s comparing learners who only had "natural" exposure to the input and learners who received various forms of focus on form, such as explicit or implicit instruction, controlled practice, and error correction.

Those years also saw a proliferation of studies seeking to determine whether Universal Grammar (UG) is accessible and in what ways when acquiring languages subsequent to the first. The debate was lively, but the conclusions were not so clear-cut given the variety of operational definitions of key constructs, different experimental methodologies, and the theoretical-descriptive apparatus of generative grammar, which was updated several times (for a historical overview and a balance of what can presently be considered the best-established facts, see Rothman & Slabakova, 2018). This kind of research, based on controlled experimental methodologies, formal descriptive categories, and the assumption that language learning rests on innate cognitive mechanisms, was opposed in increasingly polemical ways by scholars emphasizing the social nature of language and the role of communicative functionality as a key explanatory factor.

At the end of the 1990s, SLA research was already quite diversified in terms of objects of investigation, methodologies, and theoretical frameworks. However, in the last decades, the growth has been exponential, and many areas that two or three decades ago were considered neglected Cinderellas (e.g., the lexicon, phonology, or positive emotions, as discussed by Dewaele, 2023, this volume) are now widely investigated, with hundreds of new publications every year. In addition to the number of published papers, the areas of study, the variables analyzed, and the level of detail have increased: the question is no longer whether instruction is effective or not but which types of pedagogical intervention impact which aspects of competence and to what extent effects are mediated by individual variables such as working memory, level of education, or proficiency (Loewen & Sato, 2017).

Methodological tools have also multiplied. Early research described the *products of L2 acquisition*, such as the texts produced by learners, or their responses to tests of comprehension or grammatical acceptability. In addition to this type of data, today, *language use processes* may be directly observed too: eye-tracking, event-related potentials (ERP), and functional magnetic resonance (fMRI) allow us to observe a person's eyes or brain at the precise moment they are using the new language. Statistical analysis techniques are also much more varied and sophisticated than in the past (Gass et al., 2021).

The range of populations investigated has also expanded, now including participants with different levels of socioeconomic status and education, learners of third, fourth, and other additional languages, and multilingual speakers who began to be exposed to two or more languages at various ages. In addition, large-scale studies involving hundreds of participants and teams of several researchers are becoming increasingly common (Berthele & Udry, 2021; de Jong et al., 2012).

Several chapters in this volume bear witness to these trends and offer new insights. For instance, Winsler (2023, this volume) and Nguyen and Winsler (2023, this volume) tracked the development of language competences and attitudes and their associated socio-cognitive skills in a sample of more than 30,000 pupils in Miami (USA) from pre-school to secondary education. They show that early linguistic experiences, such as family bilingualism and multilingual educational programs, have a long-lasting effect on later academic achievement, mastery of additional languages, and positive attitudes toward language learning. These studies, together with the chapters by Bruhn et al. (2023, this volume) and Teltemann et al. (2023, this volume), also address a wider sense of "context" than what is used in most other studies on SLA and multilingualism by including factors such as the family socioeconomic status (SES), the country's educational system, or multilingual practices at the societal level. In so doing, they represent a concrete answer to Serafini's (2023, this volume) call to employ multiple time scales and granularity levels in the investigation of micro, meso, and macro factors, which are all related in complex and dynamic ways. Festman et al. (2023, this volume), too, take a very broad perspective on one of the most debated questions in the field, that is, whether multilingualism impacts more general cognitive skills. Their conclusion is that many variables come into play to moderate this relationship, and research to date has not yet been able to fully determine which ones have a systematic role. In any case, these authors suggest going beyond the simplistic monolingual/bilingual dichotomy, treating different degrees of multilingualism as an area of study in its own right. This is becoming a more widespread attitude in the field, now increasingly framing SLA in the wider context of multilingualism rather than in the traditional terms of L1 versus L2 acquisition.

Complication, fragmentation, and/or disintegration?

This multiplication of variables, approaches, methods, and objects of study certainly results in a considerable complication and fragmentation of SLA studies, to the point that some have wondered if, in the end, this may lead to a disintegration of the field. For example, Cook (2017) feared that applied linguistics may become a "second-hand psychology," looking only at the results of controlled experiments and losing its roots in the study of linguistic data produced in real communicative exchanges. DeKeyser (2010, p. 647) similarly speculates that "(SLA) research will be absorbed completely into psycholinguistics or cognitive psychology, on the one hand, and anthropology or sociology, on the other hand."

Concerns such as these led Hulstijn (2013) to title an article "Is the Second Language Acquisition Discipline Disintegrating?" His conclusions, however, are not pessimistic: "the study of SLA has developed from a mainly linguistic discipline to one with a wider scope, including socio-psychological, neuro-cognitive and social perspectives. SLA, in my view, is not a separate, independent scientific discipline, or is so only in a limited sense" (p. 512). I agree, and I would even add that SLA is not a "discipline" but an object of study, that is, the ways people learn and use languages other than the first, thus one of the many human behaviors in need of an explanation. Human behavior can be explained, in general, by referring to neurobiological, cognitive, or social factors; as for their description, in the case of linguistic behaviors, the categories of descriptive linguistics may be used. This awareness that SLA is not a discipline but a phenomenon to be studied with the means of linguistics, psychology, neurobiology, sociology, anthropology (these are indeed "disciplines" born before researchers began to systematically investigate SLA) does not seem to involve any problem.

Another possible source of complication is the multiplicity of levels of observation: from the individual to small groups such as a class to large social aggregates such as an entire society. Temporal granularity can also range from the order of fractions of a second for certain (neuro)cognitive processes to the hours, weeks, and years of an experimental treatment, a language course, an academic pathway, or an entire lifetime (see chapters by Nguyen & Winsler, 2022; Serafini, 2022; Winsler, 2023, this volume). These different levels are usually represented with concentric circles, as in Kersten's (2022) chapter in this volume. Here again, I don't see any risk of disintegration – on the contrary, the integration of multiple levels allows a greater understanding of the phenomena, as is the case in biology with the study of cells, tissues, organs, organisms, and ecosystems.

Perhaps a more realistic concern is that the multiplication of variables and aspects under investigation may make it more difficult to gain an overall view. Today's SLA researchers are increasingly specialized in particular areas, and this, according to DeKeyser (2010, p. 647), "contributes to a narrowing of our field of vision, rather paradoxical in these times of much-vaunted interdisciplinarity." This is certainly true, and each time a piece is added to the puzzle, this becomes more complicated and difficult to grasp in its entirety. On the other hand, this is also a sign of the vitality and progress of a field of research and responds to the unanimous demand to include as many variables as possible in the big picture. Something similar has happened in medicine (a sort of applied human biology), where specializations have multiplied: today we have experts in gastroenterology, orthopedics, ophthalmology, etc., but this has not made general practitioners useless. Everyone acknowledges the importance of a holistic view of the human body and its (mal)functioning, and finding the right balance between the understanding of specific phenomena and their role within general mechanisms is one of the fundamental objectives of contemporary medical science. It is not easy, of course, but the solution does not seem to be to abandon every specialization and turn every physician into a general practitioner. Similarly, in the study, more or less applied to solving concrete problems, of the processes of language acquisition, we have specialists in certain fields (phonology, lexicon, attention to form, interaction), who should strive to show how their piece of the puzzle fits in with the others, and, at the same time, generalist scholars who can integrate the different fields to answer perhaps very general, but not illegitimate questions such as "What works best in language teaching?" "What factors contribute most to vocabulary development?" or "What learner characteristics favor the learning of a new language, or some more specific aspects?"

A final risk of disintegration, and in my opinion the most concrete, is related to researchers' individualism and the premature formulation of theories, models, and hypotheses. I will give just one example, in an area I am more familiar with. At the turn of the 2000s, a series of studies began to appear on the relationships between the characteristics of communicative tasks, in particular their "complexity," and the linguistic forms that are produced during their performance, in particular their complexity, accuracy, and fluency (CAF). Many of these studies were aimed at testing the validity of two competing models, by Skehan (1998) and Robinson (2001) that made different predictions about these relationships. I cannot account here for the richness of the debate and research findings, which are certainly interesting though rather controversial and difficult to interpret, as also evidenced in the meta-analyses by Jackson and Suethanapornkul (2013) and Johnson (2017). What is of interest for the present discussion is that about a decade later, some theoretical-critical studies appeared (Bulté & Housen, 2012; Norris & Ortega, 2009; Pallotti, 2009, 2015) highlighting how some key constructs used in this research, such as "complexity," had been poorly defined at the theoretical and operational levels, were underrepresented (e.g., measuring "language complexity" only as a subordination ratio) or redundantly assessed (e.g., by including measures that gauged essentially the same dimension, such as the number of clauses per unit together with the subordination ratio), or resulted in spurious constructs mixing structural complexity with cognitive difficulty. Moreover, almost every study used different types of tasks, making comparisons particularly difficult, and only after some time were attempts made to empirically validate whether the "more complex" versions of the tasks were really such, i.e., whether they required more cognitive effort (Révész et al., 2016).

I do not intend to criticize these seminal investigations, which certainly had the merit of initiating a lively and interesting debate, but I believe that important lessons can be learned for the future. A good research program should not start with theoretical assumptions to be confirmed or confuted (Is Skehan or Robinson right? Or, 20 years earlier, is Krashen right or wrong?) but from an explicit and shared definition of the constructs under investigation (What are language and task complexity?), of the measures to be used (How do we measure language and task complexity?) and of the instruments to be used (Which tasks display more or less complexity?).

Attempts toward synthesis and integration

Researchers have always been aware of these risks of fragmentation, and several attempts have been made toward synthesis and integration. On a conceptual-theoretical level, one of the first models was perhaps that of Gass (1988), who provided a coherent view of the cognitive factors involved in transforming linguistic input into interlinguistic representations, which in turn generate L2 productions, or output. More recent models, such as those by the Douglas Fir Group (2016) or Kersten (2023, this volume), are even broader because they also include a number of social factors, with a scope ranging from the nano to the micro and the macro.

While it is relatively easy to draw graphs displaying as many aspects and variables as possible, it is far more difficult to conduct empirical studies showing how all of these variables interact with each other and impact second language acquisition and use. In this volume, Kersten (2022) uses structural equation modeling to assess the impact of several more or less proximal variables on L2 English acquisition; other applications of this approach are discussed by Schoonen (2015). Studies such as these require large samples in order to establish, in a statistically reliable way, the contribution of so many interacting variables. Furthermore, as Kersten and Greve (2022) note in this volume, it is not enough to include as many variables as possible in a model and simply look at which ones explain the most variance, but it is essential to critically reflect on the hierarchical relationships among variables, which once again shows how preliminary conceptual reflections are indispensable before rushing to presenting and discussing results.

Another way of providing a unified picture is via research syntheses, which now appear regularly in the form of articles, essays, and volumes, portraying the entirety of SLA research or more specific areas, such as focus on form, interaction, or vocabulary. Meta-analyses have also become extremely common in recent years, reflecting the rapid growth of studies and variables, which require some form of integrated assessment. This, in turn, has had methodological consequences: in order to be included in a meta-analysis, studies must report the results and methods in an explicit and clear way, which nowadays happens more regularly than in the past, when many works could not be included in meta-analyses for methodological deficiencies.

Meta-analyses thus contribute to sensitizing the field toward the importance of designing research and reporting results in ways that promote knowledge sharing and accumulation. This is coherent with the principles of the open science movement, whose aim is to make the research process as transparent as possible by making research tools and data publicly available (Marsden, 2019; Marsden & Plonsky, 2018). These practices also serve to bolster replication studies, which are another way of demonstrating the maturity of a field of inquiry, with its need to consolidate acquired findings (Marsden et al., 2018a; Porte, 2012).

Meta-analyses assemble together the results of studies that have already been conducted, which can imply two risks. First, the studies may not be fully comparable; second, research not achieving significant results may not adequately circulate because of publication bias. A solution to the first problem may be multisite research (MSR; Moranski & Ziegler, 2021; Morgan-Short et al., 2018), i.e., a series of parallel replications of the same research protocol in different contexts, which makes results statistically more reliable and ecologically more valid, as they are not limited to one single context. Registered reports (Marsden et al., 2018b), on the other hand, contribute to reducing publication bias: authors submit a well-defined research protocol, and the journal agrees to accept the article regardless of the results obtained, provided that the protocol was rigorously followed. Here, too, research quality is assessed first and foremost in terms of the adequacy of methodological choices rather than in terms of how results are "significant" for verifying or falsifying a given theory or hypothesis.

Real risks of disintegration

Thus, the fact that the SLA field is becoming more complex and diverse does not necessarily imply its disintegration: indeed, as we have seen, several initiatives have been undertaken in recent decades to promote greater unity. What these initiatives have in common is a willingness to collaborate, to integrate results, to see research as a collective and cumulative endeavor – not easy but certainly possible.

The real risk of disintegration seems to be not so much on the level of content, methods, and results but of the underlying attitudes toward scientific research as a common enterprise. For example, we increasingly hear about "turns" in our field: one of the earliest and most cited is Block's (2003) volume *The Social Turn in Second Language Acquisition*, which emphasized that SLA research must move beyond the dominant cognitivist perspective to include a whole range of social factors. As Prior (2019, p. 517) notes, this has since been followed by others, such as the "identity" turn, the "critical" turn, the "interpretive" turn, the "narrative" or "(auto)biographic" turn, the "multilingual" turn, the "affective" turn, and so on. He observes that all these announcements of new turns give the impression that research carried out thus far is wrong, that it is necessary to radically change direction and start again from scratch. However, this is almost never true: most of these so-called breakthroughs are actually additions of small pieces to the puzzle, the consolidation of preexisting research lines that perhaps did not have much impact, and sometimes not even that, but just rhetorical proclamations of pseudo-news, with some terminological tweaking and, sometimes, a good dose of ignorance or ingratitude towards those who preceded us. Moreover, the comparison between different research approaches and fields, such as the cognitive and the social, the experimental and the descriptive, is often presented as a clash of paradigms, so that "these academic turf wars have tended to reify rather than address or transform the binary divides the various camps claim to be challenging" (Prior, 2019, p. 518).

Terminology plays an important role in this respect. Introducing new terms is sometimes useful and necessary, but sometimes it only serves to establish and sclerotize academic identities, resulting in a form of "academic branding" (Pavlenko, 2018). For example, as Lenzing et al. (2022) note in this volume, CDST often borrows terms from the mathematical-natural sciences to rename well-known concepts in SLA research (e.g., "attractor state" for fossilization/stabilization) and to emphasize and radicalize differences with other approaches. These phenomena should be observed with the eye of the sociology of science. SLA researchers, like all others, are subject to the logic of academic competition, which, at least in certain fields, rewards (self-styled) originality more than consolidation work, strong and confrontational identities more than humble interdisciplinary collaboration.

These "alternative" approaches, in their attack on "traditional" or "mainstream" science, may also question its epistemological foundations, thus approaching relativistic and postmodern positions. The real fracture then becomes not that between micro and macro, between cognitive and social, or between qualitative descriptions and quantitative analysis. All these distinctions can be recomposed into a unitary framework, seeing micro and macro as different levels of granularity, cognitive and social as different explanatory perspectives, and qualitative and quantitative as different moments of a research process, moving from the observation and interpretation of individual cases to the formulation of general hypotheses. True incommunicability occurs between those who "play the game" (in Wittgenstein's sense) of science as it has come to be over the past four centuries, with its practices of generalization, formulation of predictive hypotheses, and attempts at falsification or corroboration through statistical inference, and those who systematically question this game, its rules, and its assumptions (Cook, 2015; DeKeyser, 2014; Hulstijn, 2013). There is nothing wrong with practicing cultural-historical hermeneutics, social activism, or mystical contemplation of the universe in all its details, but starting from these positions to criticize those who do science because they deal with something else would be like a soccer player nagging a chess player because she is not concerned with penalty kicks.

Of course, I am not suggesting that every criticism of the status quo and every proposal for innovation should be censored. I am just saying that terminological and methodological reforms or the opening of new research areas should not be heralded every time as scientific revolutions, as "radically different" breakthroughs from a mainstream caricaturally represented as the cradle of dullness. More often than not, these are small course adjustments, short steps forward, tweaks to the big picture, all of which the field certainly needs. What is not needed, however, are specious polemics, useless wars, and academic fouls to score a few points in the race for the highest citation score.

Recommendations for interdisciplinary and cooperative SLA research

To conclude, I would like to list some principles for conducting constructive and collaborative work aimed at integrating research and researchers across disciplinary boundaries, levels of inquiry, and methodological approaches.

The first recommendation is ethical and concerns appropriate attitudes, which must be inspired by modesty. In order to accomplish any difficult task, such as climbing Mount Everest, winning the World Cup, or discovering the cure for a new disease, one does not need a group of stars acting on their own, each with the main objective of showing off and diminishing the others' role, but people who know how to collaborate, each making a contribution to a challenge that they feel belongs to everyone. The same is true for research on a complex phenomenon such as SLA: one cannot pay lip service to interdisciplinarity and then remain with one's own academic tribe, trying to demolish the others. It is necessary to make an effort to underline the similarities, not the differences, let alone to invent differences and call them radical when in reality they are modest terminological reforms or slight shifts of accent (an exemplary attempt in this direction is the article by Rothman and Slabakova (2018), who show how generative approaches are complementary rather than opposed to other approaches, without denying nontrivial differences that may be resolved through empirical investigation). From this point of view, the example of Galileo, one of the fathers of modern science, may be useful. To express his ideas, he always preferred to use already-existing terms, often taken from everyday language, rather than coining new ones. For him, the role of the scientist is mainly to define in an exact and rigorous way the existing terms in view of sharing them with others, not to create new, often ill-defined, labels that generate more confusion and incommunicability.

This modest attitude also translates into an appreciation of descriptive research not necessarily aimed at confirming theories or hypotheses. The latter are certainly useful in scientific progress, but they run the risk of stiffening positions and creating affiliative attitudes for which the guiding question is not "What is the case?" but "Who is right and who is wrong?" with the implication that "we (the supporters of this theory) must be right and we must at all costs prove others wrong". I find these theoretical disputes, which frequently boil down to nuances such as "factor A is not so/is very important" tedious and counterproductive, and sometimes anti-educative to young researchers, who are socialized into uncritical loyalty to their own group and fallacious argumentation. In short, the field needs more good-quality normal science, with its patient, humble, puzzle-solving work, than continuous announcements of scientific revolutions.

This modesty must, however, be accompanied by a general optimism about the feasibility of the enterprise. Those who announce revolutions and paradigm shifts often end up being rather pessimistic in their critique of the mainstream. The warning that one cannot make perfectly accurate and long-term predictions, that one cannot take into account all possible variables because there could always be some butterfly producing unexpected effects, that no sample can ever be perfectly representative of the population because all individuals are different, often lead to the conclusion that research must be limited to describing individual events, retrospectively explaining their causes without venturing to the further step of generalizing and making predictions for other similar cases. All these caveats are right but also obvious: the conclusion, however, must be that we should strive to improve current research rather than self-imposing limitations to avoid the risk of making mistakes (Pallotti, 2021; Lenzing et al., 2023, this volume).

Moving from ethics to practice, the last few decades have suggested several ways in which cooperative and cumulative research can be achieved. Transparency is key: procedures, measures, analyses, and anything that allows a study to be replicated or included in a meta-analysis must be made accessible (to this end, the IRIS repository was specifically developed for SLA studies: www.iris-database.org). Sharing of data, particularly production data, is also crucial: many learner corpora are publicly available today, allowing on the one hand to conduct studies with greater statistical power and on the other hand to study multiple aspects for the same group of participants.

Another requirement is that of standardization: researchers should strive to use a limited number of data elicitation procedures and analytical measures, making sure that the latter are clear and based on well-defined constructs (from this point of view, language testing research may be a valuable source of insight). This may be achieved by the replication of previous studies or, even better, by conceiving shared research programs from the beginning. Multisite replication is certainly a good starting point, but more ambitious steps could also be envisaged, such as launching collective campaigns to study a certain phenomenon or answer a certain question, which would require a large number of scholars to work together and share their methods and objectives as much as possible. For example, one of the main problems of the research on linguistic and task complexity discussed earlier was that dozens of different tasks were used. In the future, couldn't we dare to act in a more coordinated way and choose only a few tasks that may be looked at from a variety of perspectives to gain a comprehensive view of how their characteristics impact language performance under the influence of several moderating factors? The same applies to measures of linguistic complexity, which now number in the hundreds in online analysis tools: here too, it would be advisable to establish a small set to be included in all studies, adding others only to answer more specific research questions (Pallotti, 2015).

Admittedly, it is difficult, on a practical level, to imagine how a scientific community might move to pursue such large-scale research programs: in SLA, as in other fields, there are no overarching regulatory bodies, and the very idea of a "central research committee" sounds a bit disconcerting. It is more likely to imagine that the methodological sensitivity developed in recent decades will make researchers more aware of past errors and limitations, such as dispersing efforts on a variety of fronts, opened somewhat haphazardly.

Greater cooperation among SLA researchers would also have beneficial effects at the practical level. When trying to translate research into teaching advice, we often have to admit that very few conclusions are firm and generalizable, and this may partly be due to the methodological fragmentation discussed earlier. Obviously, not all research should be driven by the single question "What works?" but it is also true that such a question should not be ignored, if only because taking it into consideration could also lead to improving the quality of research itself.

The chapters in this volume demonstrate that this is feasible and show several ways in which theoretical and practical concerns can inform research on SLA and multilingualism. Micro-level variables such as working memory, classroom anxiety, and foreign language enjoyment; meso-level variables such as instructional practices; and macro-level variables like socioeconomic status, language policies, and educational systems are all taken into consideration within and across chapters, displaying an exceptionally wide viewpoint. This broad perspective should not be seen by practitioners as intimidating, but rather, it should enable them to answer questions that regularly come up in the discussion of how to foster multilingualism and better educational opportunities for all.

References

Berthele, R., & Udry, I. (Eds.). (2021). *Individual differences in early instructed language learning: The role of language aptitude, cognition, and motivation*. Language Science Press.

Block, D. (2003). *The social turn in second language acquisition*. Edinburgh University Press.

Bruhn, A.-C., Miller, L., Mähler, C., Ponto, K., & Kersten, K. (2023, this volume). Can type of schooling compensate for low SES? Investigating effects of instruction and SES on cognitive skills. In K. Kersten & A. Winsler (Eds.), *Understanding variability in second language acquisition, bilingualism, and cognition: A multi-layered perspective*. Routledge.

Bulté, B., & Housen, A. (2012). Defining and operationalising L2 complexity. In A. Housen, F. Kuiken, & I. Vedder (Eds.), *Dimensions of L2 performance and proficiency – Investigating complexity, accuracy and fluency in SLA* (pp. 21–46). Benjamins.

Cook, G. (2015). Birds out of dinosaurs: The death and life of applied linguistics. *Applied Linguistics*, *36*(4), 425–433. https://doi.org/10.1093/applin/amv038

Cook, V. (2017). Review of S. E. Pfenninger & J. Navracsics (Eds.). (2017). Future research directions for applied linguistics. *International Journal of Applied Linguistics*, 27(3), 712–713. https://doi.org/10.1111/ijal.12190

de Jong, N. H., Steinel, M. P., Florijn, A. F., Schoonen, R., & Hulstijn, J. H. (2012). Facets of speaking proficiency. *Studies in Second Language Acquisition*, *34*(1), 5–34. https://doi.org/10.1017/S0272263111000489

DeKeyser, R. (2010). Where is our field going? *The Modern Language Journal*, *94*(4), 646–647. https://doi.org/10.1111/j.1540-4781.2010.01100.x

DeKeyser, R. (2014). The philosophy of science and the social-cognitive dichotomy in research in language learning and teaching. *Studies in Second Language Acquisition*, *36*(3), 365–368. https://doi.org/10.1017/S0272263114000035

Dewaele, J.-M. (2023, this volume). The interplay between learner-internal variables and levels of anxiety and enjoyment among Spanish EFL learners. In K. Kersten & A. Winsler (Eds.), *Understanding variability in second language acquisition, bilingualism, and cognition: A multi-layered perspective*. Routledge.

The Douglas Fir Group. (2016). A transdisciplinary framework for SLA in a multilingual world. *The Modern Language Journal*, *100*(S1), 19–47. https://doi.org/10.1111/modl.12301

Ellis, R. (2008). *The study of second language acquisition* (2nd ed.). Oxford University Press.

Festman, J., Czapka, S., & Winsler, A. (2023, this volume). How many moderators does is take till we know . . . that too many bilingual advantage effects have died? In K. Kersten & A. Winsler (Eds.), *Understanding variability in second language acquisition, bilingualism, and cognition – A multi-layered perspective*. Routledge.

Gass, S. (1988). Integrating research areas: A framework for second language studies. *Applied Linguistics*, *9*(2), 198–217. https://doi.org/10.1093/applin/9.2.198

Gass, S., Loewen, S., & Plonsky, L. (2021). Coming of age: The past, present, and future of quantitative SLA research. *Language Teaching*, *54*(2), 245–258. https://doi.org/10.1017/S0261444819000430

Hulstijn, J. H. (2013). Is the second language acquisition discipline disintegrating? *Language Teaching*, *46*(4), 511–517. https://doi.org/10.1017/S0261444811000620

Jackson, D. O., & Suethanapornkul, S. (2013). The cognition hypothesis: A synthesis and meta-analysis of research on second language task complexity. *Language Learning*, *63*(2), 330–367. https://doi.org/10.1111/lang.12008

Johnson, M. D. (2017). Cognitive task complexity and L2 written syntactic complexity, accuracy, lexical complexity, and fluency: A research synthesis and meta-analysis. *Journal of Second Language Writing*, *37*, 13–38. https://doi.org/10.1016/j.jslw.2017.06.001

Kersten, K. (2023, this volume). The proximity of stimulation hypothesis: Investigating the interplay of social and instructional variables with the cognitive-linguistic skills of young L2 learners. In K. Kersten & A. Winsler (Eds.), *Understanding variability in second language acquisition, bilingualism, and cognition – A multi-layered perspective*. Routledge.

Kersten, K., & Greve, W. (2023, this volume). Investigating cognitive-linguistic development in SLA: Theoretical and methodological challenges for empirical research. In K. Kersten & A. Winsler (Eds.), *Understanding variability in second language acquisition, bilingualism, and cognition – A multi-layered perspective*. Routledge.

Krashen, S. D. (1982). *Principles and practice in second language acquisition*. Pergamon.

Lenzing, A., Pienemann, M., & Nicholas, H. (2023, this volume). Lost in Translation? On some key features of dynamical systems theorizing invoked in SLA research. In K. Kersten & A. Winsler (Eds.), *Understanding variability in second language acquisition, bilingualism, and cognition – A multi-layered perspective*. Routledge.

Loewen, S., & Sato, M. (2017). Instructed second language acquisition (ISLA): An overview. In S. Loewen & M. Sato (Eds.), *The Routledge handbook of instructed second language acquisition* (pp. 1–12). Routledge.

Marsden, E. (2019). Methodological transparency and its consequences for the quality and scope of research. In J. McKinley & H. Rose (Eds.), *The Routledge handbook of research methods in applied linguistics* (1st ed., pp. 15–28). Routledge. https://doi.org/10.4324/9780367824471-2

Marsden, E., Morgan-Short, K., Thompson, S., & Abugaber, D. (2018a). Replication in second language research: Narrative and systematic reviews and recommendations for the field. *Language Learning*, *68*(2), 321–391. https://doi.org/10.1111/lang.12286

Marsden, E., Morgan-Short, K., Trofimovich, P., & Ellis, N. C. (2018b). Introducing registered reports at Language Learning. *Language Learning*, *68*(2), 309–320. https://doi.org/10.1111/lang.12284

Marsden, E., & Plonsky, L. (2018). Data, open science, and methodological reform in second language acquisition research. In A. Gudmestad & A. Edmonds (Eds.), *Critical reflections on data in second language acquisition* (Vol. 51, pp. 219–228). Benjamins. https://doi.org/10.1075/lllt.51.10mar

Moranski, K., & Ziegler, N. (2021). A case for multisite second language acquisition research: Challenges, risks, and rewards. *Language Learning*, *71*(1), 204–242. https://doi.org/10.1111/lang.12434

Morgan-Short, K., Marsden, E., Heil, J., Issa II, B. I., Leow, R. P., Mikhaylova, A., Mikołajczak, S., Moreno, N., Slabakova, R., & Szudarski, P. (2018). Multisite replication in second language acquisition research: Attention to form during listening and reading comprehension. *Language Learning*, *68*(2), 392–437. https://doi.org/10.1111/lang.12292

Nguyen, M. V. H., & Winsler, A. (2023, this volume). Early bilingualism increases the likelihood of taking (and mastering) foreign language courses later in secondary school. In K. Kersten & A. Winsler (Eds.), *Understanding variability in second language acquisition, bilingualism, and cognition – A multi-layered perspective*. Routledge.

Norris, J. M., & Ortega, L. (2009). Towards an organic approach to investigating CAF in instructed SLA: The case of complexity. *Applied Linguistics*, *30*(4), 555–578. https://doi.org/10.1093/applin/amp044

Pallotti, G. (2009). CAF: Defining, refining and differentiating constructs. *Applied Linguistics*, *30*(4), 590–601. https://doi.org/10.1093/applin/amp045

Pallotti, G. (2015). A simple view of linguistic complexity. *Second Language Research*, *31*(1), 117–134. https://doi.org/10.1177%2F0267658314536435

Pallotti, G. (2021). Cratylus' silence: On the philosophy and methodology of complex dynamic systems theory in SLA. *Second Language Research*. https://doi.org/10.1177/0267658321992451

Pavlenko, A. (2018). Superdiversity and why it isn't: Reflections on terminological innovation and academic branding. In B. Schmenk, S. Breidbach, & L. Küster (Eds.), *Sloganization in language education discourse* (pp. 142–168). Multilingual Matters. https://doi.org/10.21832/9781788921879-009

Porte, G. (Ed.). (2012). *Replication research in applied linguistics*. Cambridge University Press.

Prior, M. T. (2019). Elephants in the room: An "affective turn," or just feeling our way? *The Modern Language Journal*, *103*(2), 516–527. https://doi.org/10.1111/modl.12573

Révész, A., Michel, M., & Gilabert, R. (2016). Measuring cognitive task demands using dual-task methodology, subjective self-ratings, and expert judgments: A validation study. *Studies in Second Language Acquisition*, *38*(4), 703–737. https://doi.org/10.1017/S0272263115000339

Robinson, P. (2001). Task complexity, task difficulty, and task production: Exploring interactions in a componential framework. *Applied Linguistics*, 22, 27–57. https://doi.org/10.1093/applin/22.1.27.

Rothman, J., & Slabakova, R. (2018). The generative approach to SLA and its place in modern second language studies. *Studies in Second Language Acquisition*, *40*(2), 417–442. https://doi.org/10.1017/S0272263117000134

Schoonen, R. (2015). Structural equation modeling in L2 Research. In L. Plonsky (Ed.), *Advancing quantitative methods in second language research* (pp. 213–242). Routledge.

Serafini, E. (2023, this volume). From differential to dynamic: The role of working memory in second language (L2) learning. In K. Kersten, & A. Winsler (Eds.), *Understanding variability in second language acquisition, bilingualism, and cognition – A multi-layered perspective*. Routledge.

Skehan, P. (1998). *A cognitive approach to language learning*. Oxford University Press.

Teltemann, J., et al. (2023, this volume). Immigrant achievement and language use across countries – The role of family background and education systems. In K. Kersten & A. Winsler (Eds.), *Understanding variability in second language acquisition, bilingualism, and cognition – A multi-layered perspective*. Routledge.

Winsler, A. (2023, this volume). Becoming bilingual in Miami, USA: Predictors and outcomes of speed of English acquisition for low-income, dual-language learners. In K. Kersten & A. Winsler (Eds.), *Understanding variability in second language acquisition, bilingualism, and cognition – A multi-layered perspective*. Routledge.

12 Commentary

Toward a developmental science of language acquisition

Werner Greve

Introduction

Explaining an individual's development of language is, at first sight, just one special case of explaining the phenomena of human ontogenesis. Humans come into the world very unfinished. They bring only a few vital basic skills with them (breathing, swallowing, sucking, digesting, crying) – everything else has to develop in the further course of individual ontogenesis. Many human abilities do not develop in a culturally relative way. The development of eye–hand coordination, walking, and puberty takes place universally in very narrow temporal corridors and are relatively robust to contextual variations unless serious deviation in internal and/or external developmental conditions are present. Other developments depend entirely on the sociocultural context. Riding a horse, swimming, blacksmithing, cabinet carpentry, or dancing a waltz are learned by people only when taught. Only the ability to learn them is universal.

The development of language, as an individual ability, is situated between these two poles. Not only is it a basic universal ability to learn to speak, it is also universal that people speak, i.e., that they communicate by means of language. At the same time, however, language is profoundly cultural. Not only the structure (vocabulary, grammar, etc.) but also the cultural connotations of communication, the sociocultural relevance and meaning of the concepts underlying language reflect the culture in which it is embedded in countless ways. This has the consequence, significant for empirical research, that language, as a social phenomenon, has a normative side. It is possible to use a language incorrectly. "Deviant" developments in motor skills, on the other hand, such as a unique way that someone walks, might be statistically rare, but they are not "incorrect". This, in turn, also means that language is highly structured, which is useful for testing. Not only grammatically, but also semantically, language is interconnected by numerous implicative relations that first constitute meaning. These meanings often refer to cultural practices, customs, or shared understandings – as soon as language goes

DOI: 10.4324/9781003155683-15

beyond the mere designation of things ("tree"), cultural knowledge is not only a prerequisite but literally part of language understanding and thus a condition for language acquisition. This, in turn, means that language acquisition is, to a large extent, socialization, and thus not a separate segment of development or merely a prototypical example of development, but also (especially in education) an indispensable means of individual and social development.

At the same time, it is clear that (individual) language development is not only dependent on many necessary preconditions but is influenced by numerous other conditions, which obviously affect not only individual competence configurations but also sociocultural preconditions and factors (precisely because language is a social phenomenon). It follows that explaining language development requires a complex model that must integrate different forms and levels of influence, including multiple and dynamic interactions (Kersten, 2023, this volume). This is further complicated by the fact that the developmental dimension of "language acquisition" combines a highly complex variety of phenomena. Single languages or language variants or several (more or less closely related) languages can be acquired and maintained in varying time intervals in extremely different ways (as differentiated by Winsler, 2023, this volume). Moreover, there are several developmental paths toward language acquisition that are equally effective (Serafini, 2023, this volume). In short, to look for one explanation for language acquisition would be an impossible and actually pointless demand.

Is there any hope to find rules or laws behind this plethora of phenomena or influences or moderators of these influences (Festman et al., 2023, this volume) or layers (Kersten, 2023, this volume)? I would think so with regard to two aspects. First, we can and are supposed to look for "strong" predictors. It would be scientifically wrong to call them "strong(er) causal influences," as there is no such thing as "strength" or "ranking" in causal relationships (Mackie, 1974). But given the actual distribution of conditions in a certain local or global constellation of variables, the predictive strength as stated in an analysis of variance (which, of course, just reflects an actual distribution of variances) might be helpful in practice (e.g., for questions concerning aspects that I can change). I will come back to this point in the conclusion.

Second, the search for necessary conditions for language development is certainly not hopeless, nor is the search for viable explanatory models. In fact, explanatory models for many facets of language acquisition (e.g., early or later second language acquisition, the cognitive consequences of multilingualism; cf. Festman et al., 2023, this volume) have been developed and tested in the past decades on the basis of rich and increasingly methodologically sophisticated and differentiated empirical research. In doing so, however, the conceptual and empirical internal relations of the variables taken into account in each case, and in particular the conceptual level at which these variables can be classified in each case, have not always been considered with sufficient precision (Kersten & Greve, 2023, this volume).

It is primarily to this latter task that the present volume is devoted. For this reason alone, it is most welcome, but not only for this reason. The inter- and transdisciplinary approach expressed and implemented in the contributions gathered here is at least equally valuable. It is obvious that, in addition to linguistic theories and methods, (developmental) psychological, sociological, biological, but also mathematical and cultural studies (to name only a few of the more important disciplines) are essential for explaining language development at different levels. The thematic breadth of the contributions, but especially their predominantly cross-disciplinary co-authorships, reflects this in rare and impressive diversity. The volume goes far beyond an additive combination of disciplinary methods or concepts. Several contributions that at first glance seem to belong only to one discipline integrate theoretical, methodological, and empirical arguments from several disciplines (e.g., Dewaele, 2023; Kersten, 2023; Teltemann et al., 2023; Winsler, 2023; all from this volume). About 30 years ago, some authors called for a "developmental science" (Bornstein & Lamb, 2005; Cairns et al., 1996) with an integrative view of developmental processes. They strongly argued for the need to expand the boundaries of perspectives beyond disciplinary and subject-specific research. However, this approach was rarely followed and put into practice, with only some individual exceptions (Petermann et al., 2004). The present volume, however, is a notable example of the application of developmental science to a highly socially relevant developmental phenomenon.

Admittedly, just calling for an interdisciplinary perspective does not solve the task of explaining language development and acquisition, nor does it render it any easier. However, this should not be discouraging. Not least because of the intrepidness with which the contributions collected here present and discuss explanatory perspectives and empirical findings that they are intended to illustrate or test, this volume is highly welcome.

Broadening the perspective – the benefits of disciplinary pluralism

It stands to reason that the ability to speak, and in particular the ability to speak several languages, can be classified in two explanatory contexts. On the one hand, obviously, a number of individual cognitive preconditions have to be fulfilled in order to succeed. A sufficiently extensive vocabulary and complex linguistic structures have to be represented cognitively and made reliably available. In concrete speech acts, these (and other) internal pieces of information have to be compared with numerous external pieces of information (some of which have also to be inhibited). There can be no doubt that language comprehension and production is first and foremost a cognitive process. Second, since language is a profoundly social phenomenon, its acquisition is also linked to social context. These are thus two dimensions of necessary conditions without which explanation cannot succeed, i.e., internal and external developmental conditions. Consistently, various contributions in this volume focus on cognitive (Festman et al., 2023) or social (Teltemann et al., 2023) aspects of language acquisition or, in particular, on their interaction (Bruhn et al., 2023; Dewaele, 2023; Kersten, 2023; Winsler, 2023; all this volume).

As plausible and undoubtedly significant as this is, it is easy to underestimate other facets of this multilayered connection. Thus, it is particularly welcome that emotional (Dewaele, 2023, this volume) and motivational (Winsler, 2023; Teltemann et al., 2023, this volume) aspects are explicitly examined as well, which are also relevant especially in pedagogical contexts. Dewaele is one of the authors who pointed out the importance of emotions relatively early on. One does not have to follow his assessment that especially the impact of so-called positive psychology on SLA research has given the necessary tailwind to the attention emotions deserve, to see that the discussion has changed in the past decade. Edited volumes, journals, and conferences show an increasing interest in the topic (Dewaele, 2023, this volume). The theoretical and empirical arguments of these contributions make it very clear that without taking emotional and motivational dimensions and conditions into account, an explanation of development will not succeed. Admittedly, the processes that actually take effect here have not yet been clarified (for example, different explanations can be thought of for the role that attachment could play in language development: Winsler, 2023, this volume). But the empirically demonstrated relevance of interindividual differences with respect to motivational (Teltemann et al., 2023, Winsler, 2023) and emotional (Dewaele, 2023, all this volume) aspects of the person (here: dispositions) broadens the view in a simultaneously liberating and inspiring way.

Further academic discussion and research, thus initiated and inspired, can only benefit from the systematic transdisciplinarity so convincingly demonstrated in this volume. A case in point is, for instance, the learners' attitudes towards language, which have been addressed several times (Dewaele, 2023, this volume). Here it would be important to clarify the concept of attitude more carefully. Apart from the discussion to what extent self-reports can be more reliable than implicit measures, basic conceptual questions are still unresolved: e.g., to what extent emotional or motivational aspects are components, conditions. or consequences of attitudes (Albarrazín et al., 2005).

At the same time, the problem of traits as predictors becomes apparent again in several contributions, with trait emotional intelligence as a prototypical example (Dewaele, 2023; Winsler, 2023, this volume). In the theoretical argumentation, Dewaele, for example, focuses quite convincingly on emotional processes, but empirically, this is typically operationalized with questionnaire data (similar to motivational processes; Winsler, 2023; Teltemann et al., 2023, both this volume). Strictly speaking, with self-reports, the influence of self-concepts is being tested. And even if these self-concepts were valid estimators of traits, they test for the influence of "traits," not of "processes." Second, since traits are defined by the frequency of behavior, i.e., by what they purportedly explain, explanations of behavior that refer to traits are in danger of circularity (Greve & Kappes, 2017). Even more important, however, is the objection that referring to traits is not really the theoretically intended level of explanation, because interindividual differences are used for *prediction* instead of *testing* for processes.

"A multilayered perspective" – challenges of transgressing and integrating conceptual levels

Actually, theories of language development are often in danger of being purely predictive models (see Kersten & Greve, 2023, this volume). In order to achieve a differentiated explanation, it is certainly insufficient to insert variables that have empirically been shown to be statistical predictors into models without clarifying in detail how the causal mechanisms are assumed to work. Sometimes plausible ideas are formulated or implicitly suggested for this purpose, but the concrete mechanism remains unclear even there (for example, it is rarely examined whether there could be a more parsimonious explanation, i.e., whether the variable that is explicitly named in each case could be omitted for the explanation). This applies to container variables in particular. Macro variables such as age, gender, or socioeconomic status (SES), which have no causal explanatory value, are prototypical of this (Kersten, 2023; Kersten & Greve, 2023, this volume). Even if plausible stories can be told about the effectiveness of a variable (SES of family of origin with resources and competencies of parents as a condition of children's language acquisition, for instance; Teltemann et al., 2023, this volume), these aspects are rarely tested and especially not attempted to be refuted in many studies in the field. Actually, such variables will often not be necessary conditions even in the given configuration, and, moreover, there will be several sufficient configurations leading to identical levels of competence. In this respect, primary and secondary effects (Teltemann et al., 2023, this volume) may also only be appropriately classified in relation to the chosen focus. Actually, the competence of parents, which is part of SES, is secondary to the concrete interaction between them and their children (Kersten, 2023, this volume), which, in turn, could represent a secondary condition for the memorization of a word or rule or pronunciation, etc.

This leads to another challenge to which this volume pays specific attention. Almost all contributions consider conditions (predictors) of language acquisition that are located at several theoretical levels: subpersonal (e.g., working memory: Bruhn et al., 2023; Kersten, 2023; Serafini,

2023) and personal (anxiety: Dewaele, 2023; self-control: Winsler, 2023; motivation: Teltemann et al., 2023; prior language acquisition: Nguyen & Winsler, 2023) individual conditions as well as micro- and macrosocial ones (SES of parents: Kersten, 2023; Bruhn et al., 2023; migration: Telteman et al., 2023, all this volume). It is noteworthy that almost all of them also discuss the theoretical interactions between variables and thus between the respective conceptual levels (Kersten, 2023; Kersten & Greve, 2023, both this volume). This fundamental distinction of theoretical conceptual levels (micro, macro level) is so important because the question of whether a variable is a macro or micro variable depends first of all on the degree of "resolution" or decomposition of the research focus. "Memory," for example, is a micro variable in relation to "person" and to "intelligence," but it is a macro variable in relation to "sensory memory" or "phonological loop." This does not create a problem in principle (as the contributions by Kersten, 2023, and Bruhn et al., 2023, both this volume, make clear), but sometimes it makes transfer of explanations between the different conceptual levels difficult. In this respect, too, the discussion in this volume is exemplary.

However, this cross-level argument also has theoretical challenges. For example, the theoretical framework that Teltemann et al. (2023, this volume) outline represents in many respects a psychological theory because of its highly focused actional perspective. It is concerned with explaining individual actions. This makes the special potential of the approach pursued in this edition very clear. For future work, it now seems natural to rigorously integrate the theoretical and empirical action-theoretical arguments, for example, on motives guiding actions, from other disciplines.

Kersten's contribution (2023, this volume) is perhaps the most explicit (and in this respect empirically particularly testable) with respect to relations between layers. It consistently implements the argument that more complex variables can only act as mediated via proximal variables. Indeed, a mediated relationship is shown to be highly plausible in the examples it examines (for example, social status is partially mediated via interaction between parents and children). This is instructive both theoretically and practically. Practically, it provides concrete starting points (parenting) for correlations that are shown elsewhere only in the abstract (social class predicts language competence: Bruhn et al., 2023, this volume). Theoretically, it helps to decompose container variables, as the goal of scientific work in these contexts is to stop using such variables in theoretical explanatory models. For clearly determined practical purposes, such as political argumentations or educational application, such variables may remain important and useful.

Presumably, the "proximity of stimulation hypothesis" underlying Kersten's analyses, which assumes that the effect of distal variables must be mediated by proximal ones and can only (or at least "best") be explained by them, is perhaps not unlimitedly applicable. Of course, in some respects, it is true by definition, because distal is meaningfully defined by the fact that the relation to the dependent variable must be mediated by a proximal variable (because the pure temporal or spatial "distance" to the effect cannot be critical for the classification of a condition as "distal"). But there will be mediated effects that cannot be completely reduced to the effect of the mediator. For example, the effect of a slap I receive will have to be mediated by the wrist or elbow (otherwise it will not occur). But given the same joint strength, a difference in effect will have to be accounted for by other factors, such as the body force and shoulder input. It is true that even then, the distal effect will only be mediated by the proximal effect (without the joint, the slap would not reach the opponent's face), but that does not mean that in all contexts, the causal explanation can be reduced to the wrist. (Analogously, a "distal" evolutionary explanation of the phylogeny of language (Fitch, 2010) has not, after all, been rendered irrelevant by the (relatively more) "proximal" explanations of individual language acquisition via contextual and individual variables addressed in this volume). There is also the difficult question of whether emergent causes cannot achieve effects beyond their (proximal, constitutive) components that these components cannot achieve individually (Kersten & Greve, 2023, this volume). The consciousness that governs individual actions is not reducible to the neurons that compose it or to the efferent neural pathways that control the hand that eventually delivers the slap. Sometimes distal conditions are simply aggregates. Intelligence is no more "distant" from performance in a test task than is working memory but merely comprises several components, including working memory.

Notwithstanding such complex details, the way to predict the effect of aggregate or container variables via the more immediately effective aspects in each case (parent interaction instead of SES) is highly welcome. Statistical prediction of macro variables (of whatever kind) can only be translated into effective and concrete recommendations for action if we understand the respective concrete mechanisms in more detail.

A closer look – understanding causal processes requires detailed investigations and theoretical rigor

This leads to the task of investigating concrete causal mechanisms in detail. This task is complex because the empirical findings are influenced by many different factors that not only concern technical aspects of the respective study (operationalizations, study design) but are often also influenced by (moderating) effects of further variables. A highly instructive example of this is the question of whether the early acquisition of a second or further languages helps or hinders this person's cognitive competencies. The original concern that the particular demands of acquiring and situationally "managing" multiple languages would draw on numerous resources to their detriment was countered more than 50 years ago by the conjecture that this stimulation might just enhance those resources (cognitive advantage hypothesis; CA). The intensive discussion that has produced a wealth of empirical studies since then (Festman et al., 2023; see also Winsler, 2023, both this volume) cannot be regarded as concluded despite (or because) of increasingly differentiated methods and designs and because of very heterogeneous results. Festman et al. show in their careful and very detailed overview that numerous conditions from methodological (e.g., recording) to causal (situational and individual conditions of influence) to conceptual (variants and configurations of multilingualism) differentiate the relation in question.

Beyond the empirical issues, there is also a fundamental aspect to this discussion that is instructive. The perspective that identifying moderator variables represents progress in explaining the dependent variable is largely common sense. Qualifying a main statistical effect by a specified variable (interaction) makes the prediction better, which thus becomes a better candidate for explanation. The perspective that Festman et al. discuss here adds an important complementary perspective to this fundamentally correct idea, which is, therefore, extremely relevant because it is (far too) rarely raised at all, let alone discussed in detail. This perspective points out that a context that needs to be infinitely qualified is actually no longer one. At the very least, then, everything suggests that the original model (on which the main effect had been based) can hardly be sustained anymore. It has to be presumed that it was a statistical, not a causal, effect, e.g., because it mapped the predictive value of a container variable. In fact, determining the dependent variable (the difficulties of which Festman et al. point out) is not even the biggest problem. It would not be dangerous but rather theoretically and practically important for the relationship between the variables if there were different facets of a CA of multilingualism which would profit in different ways. More difficult indeed is an (increasingly) large number of moderators. As the impressive synopsis by Festman et al. clearly shows, a CA of bilingualism depends on so many conditions like language, age, input quality, etc., and also on personal variables, that it hardly makes sense anymore to speak of "the" CA in contexts of theoretically sound explanations. In practical terms, however, this may be different – a statistical main effect may, for example, be politically relevant and helpful, e.g., as a response to critical positions that fear a damaging effect of multilingual developmental conditions. I will come back to this in the conclusion.

Serafini's (2023, this volume) contribution is instructive in this respect. It is a technical overview contribution that also specifically addresses the micro level. What role does working memory (WM), which could possibly benefit from CA, play in language acquisition and, more specifically, in explaining individual differences in performance? Again, there are not only methodological and empirical challenges, but also theoretical ones for this question. Her contribution discusses the numerous arguments and positions of cognitive and developmental psychology on what WM is in the first place and how "its" interaction with the phenomenon (here language skills) could be explained. If, as Baddeley assumes, there are subsystems to WM, this interaction also extends to these subsystems. As Serafini's contribution plausibly shows, it is not enough to use reliable measurement (operationalization) for the explanation (here of WM), but a theoretical model is required. Accordingly, the point of her chapter is not to consider WM as a static interindividual varying variable but rather to take into account the intraindividual dynamics of this system. Not least for this, dynamic systems are of particular theoretical importance.

This is excellently followed by the contribution of Bruhn et al. (2023, this volume). Its subject is the question of whether interventions can mitigate or reduce the relation between SES and cognitive conditions for language acquisition (phonological awareness, nonverbal intelligence, working memory). This also corresponds to the intention of the contributions of Teltemann et al. and Winsler, but also particularly with respect to the analysis of Kersten, who finds a mediation effect with different data, not the moderation effect studied here. However, the two studies presented by Bruhn et al. find a buffering effect neither of specific training programs (phonological awareness) nor of bilingual instruction on the relationship between SES and cognitive skills. It is extremely rewarding to finally read a detailed account of the fact that predicted (and possibly hoped for) effects cannot be empirically shown. It is clear that in a first step, methodological problems have to be discussed, but it is also clear that theoretical implications (if the findings can be replicated) have to be considered. This is precisely what this contribution does, which is why it is, in some respects, the most empirically original contribution in the volume. At the same time, it is instructive – after all, it is about gaining knowledge. The theoretical discussion initiated by the contribution of Bruhn et al. could perhaps be gainfully pursued from here. The relationship between SES and cognitive ability needs to be described theoretically, precisely because SES is a container variable, while the predictive aspects and the practical and political significance of the relationship that Bruhn et al. find remain unaffected.

It would be important for future studies to increasingly continue along the lines pursued in these chapters, i.e., to consider container variables such as SES or gender as starting points rather than outcomes of well-designed studies. One can certainly call such variables predictors. However, they can only be considered "resources" in a broader, metaphorical sense, because an actual causal relationship cannot be reconstructed even in terms of a mediation. Statistical mediation in the case of container variables (Kersten, 2023, this volume) can, after all, empirically illustrate what the container contains. It could actually go back to a completely different necessary condition, which either correlates with the container or is implied (or contained) in it or is causally influenced by it (if it were an emergent phenomenon). Which of these three variants applies in each case has to be discussed theoretically and then, if necessary, to be investigated empirically (Kersten & Greve, 2023, this volume). This is, of course, not an objection against the studies presented in this volume, as they explicitly concede the aspect that SES is a container variable (Kersten, 2023; Bruhn et al., 2023, both this volume), but a general theoretical challenge in the social sciences.

This line of thought does not only concern the cognitive mechanisms mentioned here. For example, the data presented by Dewaele and numerous colleagues, although not completely consistent in detail, very convergently and convincingly demonstrate a connection between individual emotions (social anxiety, joy) on the one hand and language acquisition (more precisely, language competence) on the other. Here, too, future studies can go into more detail. For instance, it is clear that not only longitudinal data but especially very carefully selected (e.g., matched) samples (with different languages, social background conditions, teaching conditions, but also controlled individual competencies) will be needed to test causal assumptions in a robust way. Dewaele does not deny this. For this, too, the present volume could lead the way. It will not always be possible to isolate small empirical aspects (as in the context of the CA hypothesis; Festman et al., 2023; Winsler, 2023, both this volume) in such a way that experimental studies become feasible, but it is clear that more careful attention to designs and methods is needed.

One aspect that is less in the foreground in the contributions presented here (with the important exception of Festman et al.) is the assessment or operationalization of the respective variables under consideration. This has nothing to do with the question of conceptual levels (even a complex variable such as SES can be operationalized in a relatively straightforward and simple manner). Several times, the authors of the contributions emphasize, for example, the necessity of not thinking of linguistic competence in a one-dimensional way. Nguyen and Winsler (2023, this volume), for example, explicitly stress the importance of carefully differentiating and empirically accounting for the numerous variations in which language is acquired and how intensively (see also the differentiated overview by Festman et al., 2023, but also the remarks by Winsler, 2023, both this volume). It is very clear that all rough divisions such as monolinguals versus bilinguals can only be a very first, often misleading indicator. In fact, the concepts of "bilingual" or "multilingual" are almost something like container variables, addressing very heterogeneous groups. The internal variance of a group of bilinguals is likely to be considerably larger than the differences of the average of this group to the monolingual group (which may well have heterogeneous life experiences and thus developmental stimuli and so is not homogeneous in itself). In such cases, the mean will be a poor estimator of what characterizes individual members of the group so designated in each case.

This does not mean that data collection must always and necessarily be complex and demanding. Operationalizations that consist of only a single or a few items need not always be inadequate (one can hardly capture height more validly than with a single item, and gender is also often estimated well with a few items), but whenever complex variables (migration background, SES) are involved, the concern increases that relevant variance will be lost. For example, social desirability may be an important factor for, say, the question of educational aspirations, especially since it is likely to be confounded with migration destination, country of origin, and especially culture of origin. This is not only a question of more precise recording (with respect to SES, see also Kersten, 2023, this volume) but, above all, a theoretical question. For instance, what Festman et al. call the "task-related" problem that different indicators of EF produce different effects is only partly a methodological problem (e.g., in that different tasks have different reliabilities); above all, it needs to be theoretically clarified which concrete performance is an indicator or criterion for the (presumed) underlying competence and for what reason. Again, the critical distance of Festman et al.'s contribution to the heterogeneity of the research landscape is to be supported. The CA debate would certainly benefit from theoretical and empirical rigor.

Another promising question that is possibly still somewhat underemphasized in some contributions is that of the conceptual as well as empirical interrelation of cognitive, emotional, and motivational factors – in particular the investigation of the question to what extent emotional and cognitive processes are actually categorically different. The perspectives on this question, which have been intensively discussed for half a century (at least since the debate between Lazarus and Zajonc; an introduction is provided by Reisenzein et al., 2003), cannot be comprehensively unfolded here. But the question particularly important to this discussion here is to what extent emotional processes, which are at least partially based on cognitive ones, influence language acquisition. One possible candidate are emotion-regulatory processes, which, similar to coping processes (Greve et al., in press), partially rest on cognitive resources (e.g., EFs), which in turn are related to language (acquisition) processes (even if, as Festman et al. argue, the interaction processes here are not yet conclusively clarified).

From static factors to dynamic processes – toward a dynamic perspective on language development

Nguyen and Winsler's (2023, this volume) contribution stimulatingly shifts the perspective predominantly taken in the contributions discussed earlier. This is also an engaging part of the overall picture generated in this volume. The question of the consequences of multilingualism is (apart from the CA hypothesis; Festman et al., 2023, this volume) less often addressed. While the social advantage of multilingualism is in some ways evident, the specific finding reported here goes beyond that. Nguyen and Winsler's (2023, this volume) data show that language competence can trigger a self-reinforcing dynamic ("snowball effect") – the more languages one learns and the earlier one learns them, the more likely and the better one is to learn even more languages later.

Again, first of all, in terms of practical news, it is important that the advantage provided by multilingualism can be self-reinforcing. It will, ceteris paribus, grow over time. Above all, it is interesting that the dynamical systems discussed by Lenzing et al. (2023, this volume; see also Serafini, 2023, this volume) may find an interesting and, so far, apparently mathematically unexploited field of application. The autoregressive dynamical effects implied here (e.g., in Nguyen & Winsler, 2023, this volume) may be more accurately modeled in dynamical systems (even if this does not yet clarify the causal processes). This is all the more true since the analyses in several contributions (see in particular Kersten, 2023, this volume) show that cognitive abilities, in turn, make a predictive contribution to later further language acquisition, which could itself benefit from multilingualism. Even if the contribution of Lenzing et al. (2023, this volume) at first sight comprises a relatively abstract discussion of complex interaction dynamics and their modelability, it is perhaps the most forward-looking contribution of this volume and, in this respect, a particularly valuable chapter. The consideration of static factors, apart from all the related challenges, does not really capture the dynamic hierarchically interactive events that we call "development" (see in particular the instructive contribution by Serafini, 2023, this volume).

This leads back to the general idea mentioned in connection with the more detailed examination of individual contexts (here using the example of CA). The present collection of chapters, precisely because the contributions argue in such an exemplary differentiated way, taking such an extraordinarily large number of facets into account, shows the theoretical task of the field all the more clearly. A good theory cannot be based on listing a multitude of variables, each of which (under the given variance conditions) makes a particular contribution or shows an interaction effect. The collection will always have to remain unfinished, especially since behind the more complex (macro) variables, there must always be an uncountable number of "relative" micro variables.

The more productive research direction, it can be assumed, is perhaps rather a change of perspective from a variable-oriented to a process perspective. It is fitting that developmental psychology, after a long phase of phase-oriented description of developmental trajectories (almost all classical theories did this), experienced a "processual turn," as it were, in the 1990s (Greve & Kappes, in press). Sequential descriptions are increasingly being replaced by processual explanations of developmental phenomena. Perhaps it is actually more rewarding to look for basal processes. For example, Festman et al. discuss findings by D'Souza et al. (2020) that suggest that "infants exposed to two languages were faster at disengaging attention to a known stimulus and shifting to a new one." In a slightly different context, they cite findings by Tsimpli et al. (2020) that children living in more sociolinguistically diverse cultures have higher

CA (beyond only a multilingual advantage). Such findings point to more basal effects of stimulation (see also Kersten, 2023, this volume, on this idea), and it would be worth considering whether this stimulation needs to be linguistic in nature or just sufficiently relevant to the individual. In fact, many of the findings that Festman et al. discuss suggest that acquiring and using a language demands capacities – and, hence, trains – cognitive control functions. One may assume, and the field of language development makes this clear, that the future of developmental science will essentially lie in complex dynamic modeling. To do so, however, it will be necessary to leave behind the metaphorical use of this term and aim for more precise mathematical modeling (Lenzing et al., 2023, this volume).

Dimensions of relevance – divergence and convergence of scientific and practical reasoning

To compensate for potential disadvantages of people with a migration background or precarious social status (Teltemann et al., 2023, this volume) are partly practical and partly moral concerns. This includes to improve the promotion of multilingualism because it will effectively help those young people who are to shape our future, because it compensates for the disadvantages of migration or poverty or both (Kersten, 2023; Bruhn et al., 2023, both this volume) and because it might make humans more cognitively flexible (in case the CA applies, but see Festman et al., 2023, this volume). It is clear, and many of the contributions emphasize this explicitly, that explaining processes of language acquisition is significant and consequential in practical terms. For example, the finding of self-reinforcing effects of early language support reported by Nguyen and Winsler (2023, this volume) is highly inspiring in practical terms. When compared with the findings in Teltemann et al. (2023), Bruhn et al. (2023), and Kersten (2023, all this volume), according to which SES and education are correlated anyway, and a central element of education is (or entails) language competence, then this suggests the political conclusion that investing in language education as early as possible (in preschool) can help to slow down the social/educational gap (Teltemann et al., 2023, this volume). Perhaps the study and modeling of this point will at the same time be exemplary for similarly polarizing social dynamics in other fields as well, from financial and educational resources to social and cultural competencies, which are linked to linguistic ones in a variety of ways.

In a global world, in a world in which millions of people change their homes, or at least leave them, communicative competence is a key condition. Precisely for this reason, the temptation is not small to take a morally or politically, in any case practically motivated, but perhaps selective view also in scientific discussions ("high motivation and deprivation") (Teltemann et al., 2023, this volume). Migration is often motivated by stressful, precarious, dangerous, or otherwise disadvantaged conditions (Teltemann et al., 2023, this volume). Practically, this is unquestionably relevant, but scientifically, it easily obscures the fact that it is not migration or culture change in itself that is the problem. A soccer player from Eastern Europe or Sub-Saharan Africa, a programmer from the Far East, a financial banker from the Anglo-American-speaking world are also immigrants (Teltemann et al., 2023, this volume, explicitly point out that immigrants are a heterogeneous group but perhaps have such examples less in mind). For them, however, the disadvantages and obstacles to integration do not work even if they have only an imperfect command of the national language even after a long time in the country of immigration.

The point, of course, is not an objection against a sociological (or, in general, against a macro) perspective, but it does point to a perhaps underestimated problem. A theoretical explanation can be refuted by a single counterexample of little practical relevance. This may be an exceptional case, which is why the relevance (e.g., representativeness) of the counterexample in practical terms may well be questioned. And, of course, the flip side of an explanation ("theory") relativized by any counterexample is a rapid loss of empirical content (Festman et al., 2023, this volume). This shows that migration is by no means the causally relevant factor here, but factors confounded with it are, although it will be an extremely significant predictor in practice. This is precisely why the consideration of individual motivational factors (Teltemann et al., 2023, this volume) is so important, as addressed. It is this aspect that makes the multilayered approach taken throughout here so compelling.

From the theoretical viewpoint, it is a question of how development works, what controls it, what drives it, and for the reasons given in the introduction, language development is a particular example of this. Practical and theoretical questions need not be mutually exclusive, of course, but do not naturally converge, e.g., because the basic science question does not, cannot, and thus should not care about moral concerns or because practical concerns are satisfied with "good enough," with "statistically strongest effects," even if a study that is good enough for practical purposes (perhaps has produced an effect that suggests a plan of action) explains nothing (is perhaps methodologically vulnerable in some respects), or there are principled objections to looking for the "strength" of an effect (i.e., x contributes more to z than y).

This volume certainly does not have to decide alternatively whether it wants to make a practical or a theoretical contribution. Kurt Lewin's oft-quoted bon mot that nothing is more practical than a good theory has long since made it into common sense. Admittedly, false theories can also be extremely practical. The discipline of personality psychology, which has shown many times over the past century that people's behavior can be predicted from basal "traits," is a good example of this. Traits can never provide an explanation, but they can certainly provide an accurate and useful prediction (Greve & Kappes, 2017).

Sometimes even the questions are different. For example, it is of course practically informative to what extent a different intensity or quality of second language acquisition can predict cognitive differences, but the causal process is by no means described and explained by this. This is even more true for even more distal variables (e.g., social prestige of the languages learned).

Conversely, small-scale scientific objections are often virtually irrelevant. The studies Winsler reports (2023, this volume) are an impressive example of this, and not only in terms of sample size (which makes significance testing almost unnecessary). The question (one of several) of which factors predict the speed and success of language acquisition is particularly relevant from a practical point of view. This is without regard to the scientific difficulties of comparing factors, especially those of different conceptual decomposition (such as when discussing the predictive role of gender), but this is not an objection to the significance of the findings summarized here, as long as they are not interpreted as testing theories. Thus, the evidence that the vast majority of dual-language learners, when they begin language acquisition at preschool age 4, learn the second language at least as well as monolingual children learn their first language, is not only encouraging but also leads to the recommendation that when this is not the case, early intervention with targeted support should be provided.

This is also true for more principled points of discussion. For example, the epistemological danger of inductive research is perhaps more noteworthy for theoretical substantive explanations than for practical intentions. To start a research path (e.g., emotional or motivational influences on language development), it is certainly useful to first acquire connoisseurship with respect to a field; this will hardly succeed other than inductively. Thus, it can be heuristically fruitful to search for sufficiently potent predictors (for foreign language acquisition, but perhaps also for individual aspects presumed to be important, such as accompanying emotions). Challenging, then, is the shift to a deductive test.

For the claim of theory-guided research envisaged here, it is not sufficient to cite a theory that asserts something and then to test the corresponding assumption, and it is even less theory guided to refer to a larger number of previous empirical research studies that have also investigated (and found or not found) the respective focused context. This is professional research, without question, serious, and widely used. But this way, theoretical progress and especially theoretical integration will hardly succeed. Rather, it is necessary to discuss different competing, similar, or contrasting theoretical models, which claim to explain a certain phenomenon common to all, in a first step with respect to their content. This would also require identifying points of intersection between these models in terms of content, which is sometimes obscured by linguistic difference, and also disentangling conceptual levels (proximal vs. distal, micro vs. macro conditions) and conceptual gaps (e.g., container variables).

Then one can formulate a coherent theory and then specifically search for the most substantial (i.e., most prone to failure) assumption and try to refute it.

Reading the book as a whole, one could say that, in sum, it implements exactly such a program. The framework that influencing factors at different levels have to be taken into account and empirically tested and substantiated forms the framework for all contributions (albeit in a somewhat different and not always explicitly formulated manner in each case). Teltemann et al. focus on the macro perspective (here causal mechanisms would have to be discussed in more detail). Festman et al. and Serafini focus on a special but (especially in Kersten's explicated configuration) causal micro aspect. Nguyen and Winsler add another independent variable of particular dynamical relevance that Lenzing et al. and Serafini could integrate into a dynamical framework. Kersten as well as Bruhn et al. discuss the relation of different levels. Winsler and Dewaele broaden the view for other influencing factors on the intraindividual level (the heuristic function of research). All of this work taken together forms a starting point that is as rich as it is differentiated, as inspiring as it is focused, for the path that can now be followed. Read in this way, the book is also a manifesto for a research program in a developmental science of language acquisition. Nothing could be more welcome.

References

Albarrazín, D., Johnson, B. T., & Zanna, M. P. (Eds.). (2005). *The handbook of attitudes*. Psychology Press.

Bornstein, M. H., & Lamb, M. E. (Eds.). (2005). *Developmental science* (5th ed.). Erlbaum.

Bruhn, A.-C., Miller, L., Mähler, C., Ponto, K., & Kersten, K. (2023, this volume). Can type of schooling compensate for low SES? Investigating effects of instruction and SES on cognitive skills. In K. Kersten & A. Winsler (Eds.), *Understanding variability in second language acquisition, bilingualism, and cognition: A multi-layered perspective*. Routledge.

Cairns, B. B., Elder, G. H., & Costello, E. J. (Eds.). (1996). *Developmental science*. Cambridge University Press.

D'Souza, D., Brady D., Haensel, J. X., & D'Souza, H. (2020). Is mere exposure enough? The effects of bilingual environments on infant cognitive development. *Royal Society Open Science*, 7180191. https://doi.org/10.1098/rsos.180191

Dewaele, J.-M. (2023, this volume). The interplay between learner-internal variables and levels of anxiety and enjoyment among Spanish EFL learners. In K. Kersten & A. Winsler (Eds.), *Understanding variability in second language acquisition, bilingualism, and cognition: A multi-layered perspective*. Routledge.

Festman, J., Czapka, S., & Winsler, A. (2023, this volume). How many moderators does is take till we know . . . that too many bilingual advantage effects have died? In K. Kersten & A. Winsler (Eds.), *Understanding variability in second language acquisition, bilingualism, and cognition – A multi-layered perspective*. Routledge.

Fitch, W. T. (2010). *The evolution of language*. Cambridge University Press.

Greve, W., & Kappes, C. (2017). Emergent personality development – The interplay of adaptation and history. *European Journal of Personality, 31*, 545–546. doi:10.1002/per.2128

Greve, W., & Kappes, C. (in press). The development of accommodative coping: Conditions and consequences from a lifespan perspective. In M. Zimmer-Gembeck & M. Skinner (Eds.), *Handbook on the development of coping*. Cambridge University Press.

Greve, W., Koch, M., Rasche, V., & Kersten, K. (2021). Extending the scope of the 'cognitive advantage' hypothesis: Multilingual individuals show higher flexibility of goal adjustment. *Journal of Multilingual and Multicultural Development*. doi:10.1080/01434632.2021.1922420.

Kersten, K. (2023, this volume). The proximity of stimulation hypothesis: Investigating the interplay of social and instructional variables with the cognitive-linguistic skills of young L2 learners. In K. Kersten, & A. Winsler (Eds.), *Understanding variability in second language acquisition, bilingualism, and cognition – A multi-layered perspective*. Routledge.

Kersten, K., & Greve, W. (2023, this volume). Investigating cognitive-linguistic development in SLA: Theoretical and methodological challenges for empirical research. In K. Kersten & A. Winsler (Eds.), *Understanding variability in second language acquisition, bilingualism, and cognition – A multi-layered perspective*. Routledge.

Lenzing, A., Pienemann, M., & Nicholas, H. (2023, this volume). Lost in translation? On some key features of dynamical systems theorizing invoked in SLA research. In K. Kersten & A. Winsler (Eds.), *Understanding variability in second language acquisition, bilingualism, and cognition – A multi-layered perspective*. Routledge.

Mackie, J. L. (1974). *The cement of the universe: A study of causation*. Clarendon Press.

Nguyen, M. V. H., & Winsler, A. (2023, this volume). Early bilingualism increases the likelihood of taking (and mastering) foreign language courses later in secondary school. In K. Kersten & A. Winsler (Eds.), *Understanding variability in second language acquisition, bilingualism, and cognition – A multi-layered perspective*. Routledge.

Petermann, F., Niebank, K., & Scheinthauer, H. (2004). *Entwicklungwissenschaft* [*Developmental science*]. Springer.

Reisenzein, R., Meyer, W.-U., & Schützwohl, A. (2003). *Einführung in die Emotionspsychologie (Bd. 3: Kognitive Emotionstheorien)* [*Introduction to psychology of emotions (Vol. 3: Cognitive theories of emotion)*]. Huber.

Serafini, E. (2023, this volume). From differential to dynamic: The role of working memory in second language (L2) learning. In K. Kersten & A. Winsler (Eds.), *Understanding variability in second language acquisition, bilingualism, and cognition – A multi-layered perspective*. Routledge.

Teltemann, J. (2023, this volume). Immigrant achievement and language use across countries – The role of family background and education systems. In K. Kersten & A. Winsler (Eds.), *Understanding variability in second language acquisition, bilingualism, and cognition – A multi-layered perspective*. Routledge.

Tsimpli, I. M., Vogelzang, M., Balasubramanian, A., Marinis, T., Alladi, S., Reddy, A., & Panda, M. (2020). linguistic diversity, multilingualism, and cognitive skills: A study of disadvantaged children in India. *Languages*, *5*(1), 10. https://doi.org/10.3390/languages5010010

Winsler, A. (2023, this volume). Becoming bilingual in Miami, USA: Predictors and outcomes of speed of English acquisition for low-income, dual-language learners. In K. Kersten & A. Winsler (Eds.), *Understanding variability in second language acquisition, bilingualism, and cognition – A multi-layered perspective*. Routledge.

Index

Note: Page numbers in *italics* refers to figures and page numbers in **bold** refers to tables on the corresponding page.

academic achievement xv, 163, 166, 169, 174, 191, 245–246, 248, 253, 292–293, 295–296, 325
additive bilingualism 161–162
age: of acquisition 94–95, 104, 241, 244; of arrival 196; of exposure 145, 164; of language learning 100
aspirations 187, 193–195, 203–205, 207, 347
attitude(s): toward English 226–229, **228**, 229, 231, 233; toward foreign language 218, 220–223, 231–234; toward teacher xv, 221–223, 226–227, 229, 232–233
attractor(s) 25–27, 43, 45, 51, 59, 60–62, 64–67, 72, 278, 330

behavior problems 172
bidialectism 90–91, 108
bifurcation(s) 55, 60–62, *61*, **62**, 64–66, 72
bilingual advantage(s) xv, 80–83, 85–87, 90–91, 93, 95–96, 98, 100, 101–111, 149–150, 163, 243–244, **274**, 279, 298–299, 310
bilingual education xv, 161, 169, 173, 175–178, 297, 307–308, 310–312
bilingual first language acquisition 83, 85, 160, 298, 306
bilingual program(s) 88, 146–147, 152, 170, 176–177, 178n1, 297, 299, 306, **307**, 310
biliteracy 87–89, 92–93, 108
butterfly effect 25–26, 43, 45, 58

causal effect(s) 4, 15, 21–22, 33, 136, 150, 344
causality 6, 32, 35n2, 207, 225, 231, 233
chaos 40, 41, 48–49, 53–54, 58–59, 60–64
chaotic system 27, 55, 58, 59, 60, 62–63
cognitive ability(ies) 88, 98, 148–150, 241, 243–244, 246, 252–254, 257, 259, **274**, 275–276, 279, 298, 301, 307, 310, 312, 345, 348
cognitive advantage(s) 83, 86, 88–89, 91, 93, 102, 152, 165, 344
cognitive stimulation 295, 297
Complex Dynamic Systems Theory (CDST) 132, 136, 269, 277–279, 280, 330
conceptual (in)dependence of variables 13–14
conceptual layers of variables (lower-level, higher-level) 4, 7, 34, 218
confounder variable(s) 81–82, *82*, 108, *110*, 208
container variable(s) xv, 7, 15, *16*, 17–19, *21*, 20–23, 30–31, 35n7, 132, 136–140, *138*, 142, 145, 148, 151, 294, 311, 341–346, 351

degree of: bilingualism xv, 85, 87, 94, 149–150, **274**, 298, 310; multilingualism 132, *142*, 145, 148, 152, 226, 228, 231

deterministic xv, 27, 46, 48–50, 53, 58–59, 61–62, 66, 74n4; determinism 47
Developmental Conceptual View of Human Development 135
developmental science xvi, 337, 339, 349, 352
discrimination 194, 242
distal variable(s) *see* variable(s)
Douglas Fir Group xiv, 132, 135, 139, *140*, 151, 328
Dual Language Learners (DLLs) xv, 94, 96, 98, 160–163, 166, 167–169, 171–177, 240–241, 245–246, **251**, 253–255, **255**, 257, 351
dynamic: approach(es) xv, 25, 39, 40, 41–46, 49, 64, 66–69, 72, 74n4, 219; system(s) xv, 5, 25, 26, 29, 34, 39, 40, 42–43, 66, 69, 131–132, 136, 269, 277, 279, 345; Systems Theory (DST) 40, 46, 69, 132, 136, 269, 277

Early Second Language Acquisition (ESLA) 160–161, 170, 173, 177, 241
educational achievement(s) 186, 190–192, 194, 195, 201, 205
emergence 15, 20, 21–22, *21*, 35n8, 40–41, 44, 47, 64, 71, 88, 138, 163, 278
emotion(s) 16, 23, 165, 168, 217–220, 223–225, 232–233, 324, 340, 346–347, 351
English for Speakers of Other Languages (ESOL) programs 165–166, 168–177, 178n1, 247
English proficiency 162–163, 165, 167–168, 170–172, 174, 177–178, 225, 240, 247, 276
epistemological 32, 35n2, 323, 330, 351
executive function(s)(ing) (EF) 15, 18, *82*, 82, 85–91, 93–111, *110*, 164, 172, 177, 243–244, 271–278, **274**, 295, 299, 302, 309, 347
experience-dependent 241
external variable(s) *see* variable(s)

first generation 185, 187, 196, 206–207
fixed point(s) 50–51, *52*, 53, 55, 60, 62, 66
focus on form 297, 324, 328
foreign language classroom anxiety (FLCA) xv, 218–233, **228**, *229–230*, 333
foreign language enjoyment (FLE) xv, 218, 220–233, **228**, *229–230*

general linear model(s)(ing) 5, 25, 132, 139, 170, 198, *200–201*, *203–204*
generative grammar 324

heritage language(s) 91, 93, **104**, 108, 253, 257
higher-order trait complexes 280
Highest International Socio-Economic Index of occupational Status (HISEI) 143, 295, 301, 306, 309
home environment 295
human capital 187

immersion xv, 88–89, 93, 95, 108, 143, 146–147, 149, 150, **161**, 164, 169, 170, 175, 223, 240, 242
immigration 103, 104, 109, 185, 187, 189, 205, 350
individual differences (IDs) xv, 27, 68, 71, 80–81, 98, 165, 171, 217, 243–244, 268, 269, 270, 273, 276–280, 292, 296
inequality(ies) 173, 186, 190, 192, 195, 206, 208
initial condition(s) 26, 40, 48–51, **51**, *53–55*, *56*, 57–60, *57*, 62–63, *63*, 66, 74n6, 278
input quality 92, 132, 141–142, 144, 146–148, 151–152, 153n7, 297–298, 344
instability 51, 66
institution 189, 226, 228, 230, 234n2, 292, 301
integration 131, 185–188, 190, 199, 207–208, 220, 326, 328, 350–351
intelligence xvi, 3, 6, 8–9, *12*, 14, *16*, 17–18, 20–21, 27, 30, 47, 80, 88–90, 93, 96–99, 104, 106, 109, *140*, 293, 295, 301, **304**, 306, **307**, 307–309, 311–312, 340, 342–343, 345
interconnected xiv, 45, 134–135, 280, 337; interconnectedness 43, 45–46, 278–279
interdisciplinary xiv, xvi, 131, 330–331, 339; interdisciplinarity 326, 331

interference 85–87, 90–91, 95–96, 101–102, 106, 108, 244, 271
internal variable(s) *see* variable(s)
International Socio-Economic Index of occupational status (ISEI) 294, 301
INUS conditions 6, 32

L2 grammar *142*, 145, 148, 149–152, 273
L2 lexicon *142*, 145, 148, 152
L2 proficiency *14*, *16*, 95, 172, 243–244, 245, 269, 272, 275–278
L3 acquisition 240, 242, 254
language balance 85–86
language proximity 91, 108
language status 168, 171, 246, 247, 249, **251**, 253, 254–255, *256*, 257, *258*
latent variable(s) *see* variable(s)
learning context(s) 147, 259, 269, 277, 279
linearity 26, 42–43

macro level variable(s) *see* variable(s)
manifest variable(s) *see* variable(s)
mediation 13, 138–139, 146–147, 153n4, 225, 345
meso level variable(s) *see* variable(s)
Miami School Readiness Project (MSRP) 165–170, 175, 177, 246, 252
micro level variable(s) *see* variable(s)
minority home language 240, 242, 245–246, 259
Model of Cognitive Growth and Language 133, *140*
moderation 249, 254, **255**, *256*, *258*, 310–311, 345
moderator variable(s) *see* variable(s)
Modular Cognition Framework (MDF) 132–134, *134*, *140*, 141, 147
motivation 3, 8–12, 14, 18, 20–21, 23–24, 33, 35n5, 88, 147, 161, 165, 186–187, 197, 203, 217, 220, 223, 225, 253, 269, 278, 292, 342, 349
multilingualism xv, 81, *82*, 93, 107–108, *110*, 132, 141, 145, 148, 152, 154n10, 222–223, 226, 228, 231, 244, 325, 333, 338, 344, 347–349
multiple language exposure xv, 241, 254, 259
music xvi, 99–100

nano level variable(s) *see* variable(s)
neuroemergentist 244
non-chaotic system *see* chaotic system
nonlinear(ity) 5, 25–27, 29, 40, 42–43, 45, 74n4, 244–245, 278
nonverbal intelligence 89, *140*, 293, 301, **304**, 306, **307**, 311–312, 345

One Person-One Language 92, 297, 301
open science 111, 199, 328
orbit(s) 48, *50–51*, **51**, *52*, *55*, *56*, *57–58*, *57*, 63, *63*, 66

parent-child interaction(s) xv, 3, 102, 132, 138, 141–145, 148, 151, 191, 311
performance measure(s) 81, 105, 107, 108, 111
periodic behavior 55, 58, 63
phonological awareness xvi, 9, 132, 141, *142*, 145–147, 149, 151–152, 243, 279, 293, 296, 300, 302–303, **304–305**, 306–309, 311–312, 345
Phonological Working Memory (PWM) 271–278
physical activity 99
preschool(s) xvi, 86, 97, 100, 104, 148, 160–161, 168, 170, *172*, 172, 173–175, 177, 190–191, 206, 248, 292, 293, 296–297, 299, 300–303, 306–307, **307**, 309–313, 349, 351
proximal variable(s) variable(s) *see* variable(s)
Proximity of Stimulation Hypothesis xv, 131–132, 139, 141, 148, 150, 342

reading 90, *138*, 145, 169, 171, 174, 176, 192–193, 195, 197, **199**, 200–202, *201*, 204–205, *204*, 208n1, 248, **251**, 252, 254, 270, 272–273, **274**, 276–277, 296–297, 311, 352
replication xvi, 81, 329, 332
resources: external 131, 133, 292; internal 133, 134

school composition 194
school readiness 166, 167, 170–171, 174, 177, 246–247, 249, **251**, 252, 259
second generation 186, 187, 192, 195–196, **198–199**, 198, *200*, 200–201, *201*, 203–204, *203–204*, 206
sequential bilingual(ism) 85, 160, 170, 242, 257
simultaneous bilingual(ism) 83, 85, 101, 160, 242, 257
snowball effect 244–245, 253, 259, 347
social skills 165, 167–168, 171–173, 176–177, **251**, 252
societal language 92, 160–161, 177, 196, 240–241, 245
socioeconomic status (SES) 7, 11, 17, 80, 88, 102–103, 132, 136, *138*, *140*, 143, 162, 189, 192–195, 197, 201, 202, 204, 293–294, 299, 301, **304**, **307**, 308, 311–312, 324–325, 333, 341
sociology 131, 185, 325–326, 330
Spanish 84, 85, 87, 89–90, 93–95, 101, 107, 161–162, 166–171, 173, 177–178, 217–218, 225–226, 230, 233, 234n2, 241, 245–246, 248–249, **250**, 253–255, **255**, *256*, 257, 275–278
speed of L2 acquisition 165, 166, 168, 171–172, 174, 176–177
stability 26, 51, 53–54, 60, 62–63, 65, 222, 278
standardization xvi, 190, 206, 332
stratification 206
structural equation modes(ling) (SEM) xv, 4, *16*, 31, 34, 132, 139, 141, *142*, 143, 145–146, 150–151, 328
subtractive bilingualism 161–162
teacher input 144–145, 149
Teacher Input Observation Scheme (TIOS) 144, 147, 151–152, 153n8
tracking 206–207, 324
two-way immersion programs (TWI) 88, 169–170, 175–176, 198, 242

uncertainty principle 41

variability 26–27, 29, 65, 67–71, 85, 160–161, 164, 177, 268, 275, 279, 280, 323
variable(s): distal 132, 136–139, *138*, 141, 146, 151–152, 342, 351; external 102, 109, 136, 139, 140, 143, 152, 224, 279, 311; internal xiv, 132, 136, 140, 142, 145, 217–218, 221, 231; latent 31, 108; macro level 135–136, 139, *140*, 222, 333, 342; manifest 31; meso level 132, 135–136, *138*, 139, 141–143, *142*, 151, 333; micro level 7, 132, 135, *138*, 139, 142–143, *142*, 151, 218, 232, 279–280, 333, 344; moderator 23–24, *24*, 35n5, 81–83, *82*, 85, 87, 89, 91, 93, 96, 98, 100, 102, 108–110, *110*, 139, **305**, **307**, 309, 344; nano level 4, 7, 132, 140–141, *142*, 145, 151, 218, 231, 233; proximal 137–139, *138*, 141–142, 146, 148, 150–152, 311, 328, 342–343

Working Memory (WM) xv, xvi, 3, 7, 8–9, *12*, 12–15, *16*, 18–20, 23, 89, 91, 93, 97–101, 105–106, 132, *140*, 141, *142*, 144–146, 149–152, 243–244, 268–280, **274**, 293, 295, 298–299, 301–303, 308, 324, 333, 341, 343–345